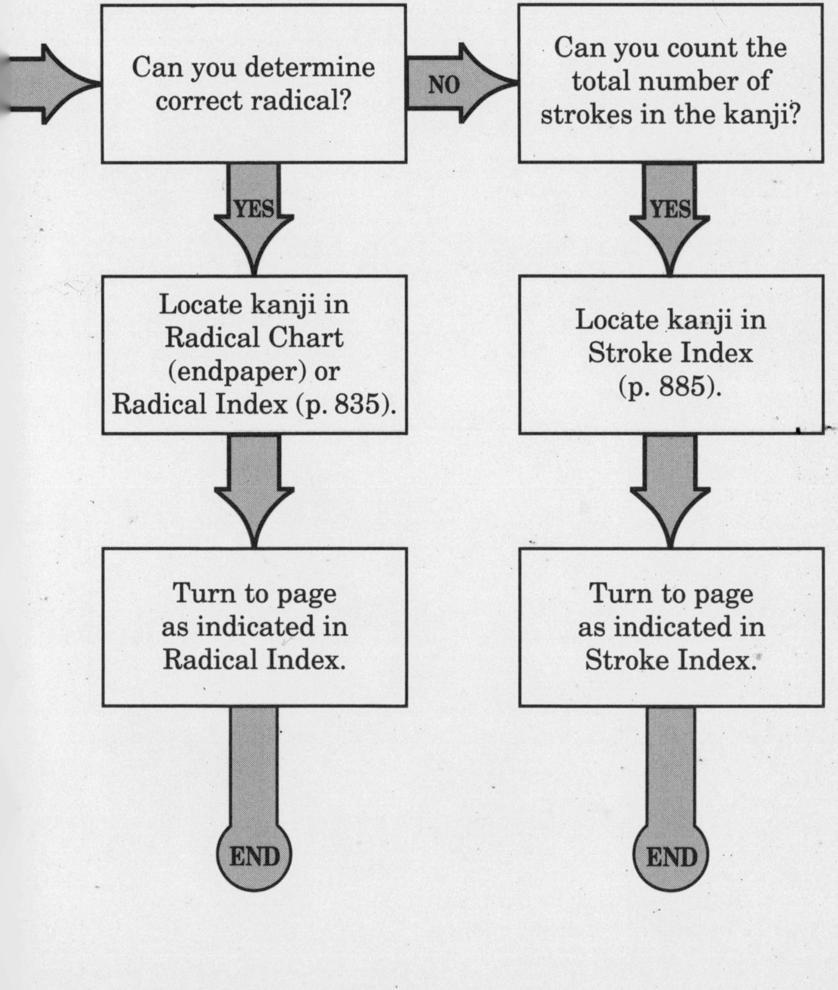

Can you determine correct radical?

NO

Can you count the total number of strokes in the kanji?

YES

Locate kanji in Radical Chart (endpaper) or Radical Index (p. 835).

YES

Locate kanji in Stroke Index (p. 885).

Turn to page as indicated in Radical Index.

Turn to page as indicated in Stroke Index.

END

END

KODANSHA'S COMPACT KANJI GUIDE

KODANSHA'S COMPACT KANJI GUIDE

A new character dictionary for students and professionals

KODANSHA INTERNATIONAL
Tokyo • New York • London

Distributed in the United States by Kodansha America, Inc, 114 Fifth Avenue, New York, 10011, and in the United Kingdom and continental Europe by Kodansha Europe Ltd., Gillingham House, 38-34 Gillingham Street, London SW1V 1HU. Published by Kodansha International Ltd., 17-14, Otowa 1-chome, Bunkyo-ku, Tokyo 112 and Kodansha America, Inc.

Printed in Japan.
First edition, 1991

91 92 93 10 9 8 7 6 5 4 3 2 1

ISBN 4-7700-1553-4

Library of Congress Cataloging-in-Publication Data

Kodansha's compact Kanji guide
p. cm.
ISBN 4-7700-1553-4
1. Japanese language—Dictionaries—English.
2. Chinese characters—Dictionaries. I. Kodansha.
PL679.K567 1992
495.6' 11—dc20 91-34851
CIP

CONTENTS

CONTENTS

KODANSHA'S COMPACT KANJI GUIDE

PUBLISHER'S NOTE

Kodansha's Compact Kanji Guide is an up-to-date dictionary of Jōyō Kanji, the 1,945 most commonly used characters in modern Japanese writing. It aims to be as comprehensive as possible within self-imposed limits, but at the same time, and most importantly, to be portable and handy. Moreover, maximum priority has been given to ease of access: first, by listing the characters according to their most familiar, traditional radicals; second, by providing three types of indices to facilitate the often time-consuming task of locating the desired character. Definitions of individual characters and kanji compounds are given in clear, straightforward English. Distinctions are made between noun and verb forms of character compounds for utmost precision.

In the realm of kanji compounds, particular attention has been paid to combinations that appear frequently in contemporary newspapers, magazines, and other forms of mass media, but which are sometimes neglected in Japanese-English dictionaries. Thus, the *Guide* does not confine itself to the standard selection of compounds. It chooses, rather, to include any kanji combination that is likely to be a problem for the student of modern Japanese.

The *Guide* devotes considerable space to the language of the business world—financial terms, business jargon, special business senses of ordinary words, and many standard business abbreviations. Some 2,000 kanji compounds of immediate use to the businessperson studying Japanese are set off for ready reference. It is hoped that this sampling will provide a foundation for further study and the eventual mastery of this sphere of written Japanese.

The *Guide*'s convenient, handy format has been achieved by focusing on a judicious selection of general and specialized kanji compounds, to the exclusion of rarer and more archaic words and meanings. The result is a compact, portable dictionary designed to serve the needs of the increasing number of people throughout the world who are learning to read and write Japanese.

In the compilation of the dictionary, numerous domestic Japanese and Japanese-English character dictionaries were consulted, the most important of which are listed below. Meanings given for characters and compounds follow modern domestic and Japanese-English practice.

Nelson, Andrew Nathaniel. *The Modern Reader's Japanese-English Character Dictionary*. Second revised edition. Tokyo: Charles E. Tuttle Company, 1974.

Nishio Minoru et al. *Iwanami Kokugo Jiten*. Tokyo: Iwanami Shoten, 1986.

Onoue Kanehide et al. *Ōbunsha Shōgaku Kanji Saishin Jiten*. Tokyo: Obunsha, 1990.

Ōmura Hama et al. *Sanseidō Shōgaku Kanwa Jiten*. Tokyo: Sanseido, 1989.

Masuda, Koh, et al. *Kenkyusha's New Japanese-English Dictionary*. Fourth edition. Tokyo: Kenkyusha, 1974.

Spann, M., and W. Hadamitzky. *Japanese Character Dictionary: With Compound Lookup via any Kanji*. Tokyo: Nichigai Associates, 1989.

Suzuki Shūji et al. *Kadokawa Saishin Kanwa Jiten*. Tokyo: Kadokawa Shoten, 1990.

Umesao Tadao et al. *Nihongo Daijiten*. Tokyo: Kodansha, 1989.

Yamaguchi Akiho et al. *Iwanami Kango Jiten*. Tokyo: Iwanami Shoten, 1987.

Global Management Group. *Shin Bijinesu Eigo Daijiten*. Tokyo: PMC, 1990.

As with most undertakings of this scope, the preparation of *Kodansha's Compact Kanji Guide* was a collaborative effort. Of the many people who took part in the project, the publisher wishes in particular to thank Yvette Flower, whose invaluable advice and energetic, dependable work were a great factor in bringing the book into being. Special thanks are also owed to Kaoru Ichikawa of AJALT, who rigorously reviewed the choice of entries for relevance and accuracy. The publisher is likewise heavily indebted to Stefan Kaiser of the School of Oriental and African Studies, University of London, who kindly undertook the task of writing the introduction to the Japanese writing system. A heartfelt thank-you is due Yukie Seki, Yoshie Hamano, and Megumi Shimonoto, whose efforts were indispensable to the completion of the book. Appreciation is also extended to Laura Holland for her timely assistance. The publisher is grateful to the Toppan Printing Company for developing the computer program that expedited the typesetting of the dictionary.

INTRODUCTION TO THE JAPANESE WRITING SYSTEM

Stefan Kaiser

1. A Mixed Writing System

Japanese is written with a combination of kanji (Chinese characters) and two sets of phonetic syllabaries or *kana*, known as *hiragana* and *katakana*. Apart from a few exceptions, such as children's books (written in *hiragana*), Japanese Braille (*hiragana* based), and telegrams (traditionally written in *katakana*), these components are rarely used independently in running text.

Kanji, *hiragana*, and *katakana* are therefore not three separate writing systems but rather three different but complementary scripts used in conjunction within the Japanese writing system. They can be broadly defined as follows: (1) Kanji. Used for elements that carry meaning (or content), such as proper and common nouns, and the stem part of verbs and adjectives. (2) *Katakana* (the angular *kana* script). Used in a similar way to that of italics in English: namely, for foreign words and names (other than those that have been rendered into kanji), certain scientific and technical terms (such as names of species), and for emphasis of a particular word or phrase in a sentence. (3) *Hiragana* (the cursive *kana* script). Used for functional elements expressing grammatical relations (case particles, conjunctions, etc.) and inflectional endings.

In sum, kanji and *katakana* can be grouped together as expressing content units (often compared to building blocks), whereas *hiragana* is used to hold units (blocks) together within sentences like mortar.

この自動車はデザインがたいへん優れている。
"The design of this car is quite outstanding.

Here, the noun *jidōsha* "car" and the stem of the verb *sugure-ru* "be outstanding" are written in kanji; the foreign word *dezain* "design" is written in *katakana*; and grammatical elements such as the determiner *kono* "this," the adverb of degree *taihen* "quite," the topic and subject particles *wa* and *ga*, and the inflectional ending *-te iru* are written in *hiragana*. (For an explanation of *hiragana* usage for the penultimate syllable *re* in vowel-stem verbs, see section 4, below.)

2. The Function of Kanji in Running Japanese Text

As Japanese does not mark word boundaries in text, the use of visually distinct kanji (and *katakana*) within the basic *hiragana* script itself functions as an indicator of a word boundary. As kanji are used for content words, a typical unit of meaning begins with a kanji and ends with *hiragana* (particles or inflectional endings etc.).

3. Readings

As the term "Chinese characters" implies, kanji were originally imported from China, along with Buddhism (in its Chinese form) and Chinese culture, accompanied by a large number of Chinese loanwords pertaining to these areas. A kanji therefore entered Japan accompanied by its Chinese pronunciation, in a form adapted to the Japanese sound system; this is called its ON (音) reading. Later, Japanese readings developed for many kanji by using them to express a Japanese word of equivalent or related meaning. This is called the KUN (訓) reading. Thus, the Chinese word for "child" acquired the KUN reading こ ("child" in native Japanese) in addition to its ON reading シ. Sometimes several Japanese words became attached to one kanji, as in the following example which has a total of two ON and eight KUN readings:

上
ジョウ・ショウ
うえ・うわ・かみ・あ(げる)・あ(がる)・の(ぼる)・の(ぼせる)・の(ぼす)

There are some kanji that have more than one ON reading. This is because readings entered Japan from China in three major waves, at different times and from different areas in China, or in other cases, such as 楽, because the kanji had more than one meaning attached to it in the original Chinese. 楽 has two ON readings: pronounced ガク, it means "music"; pronounced ラク, "easy, happy."

Kanji with multiple readings, however, are infrequent: of the 1,945 Jōyō Kanji, about two-thirds have either only a single ON reading or one ON and one KUN reading.

4. The Use of *Okurigana*

Most verbs and adjectives have their (unchanging) stems written in kanji, and their (changing) inflectional endings written in *hiragana*.

VERBS
consonant-stem: 読む・読んだ・読めば
vowel-stem: 起きる・起きた・起きれば
食べる・食べた・食べれば

ADJECTIVES
-i: 早い・早かった・早ければ
-shii: 新しい・新しかった・新しければ

This use of *hiragana* is referred to as *okurigana*, which literally means "*kana* suffix." There are a number of conventions to be observed when using *okurigana*, whose main function, as alluded to above, is to show the inflectional ending of a verb or adjective. The following points should also be noted: *okurigana* does not always show the inflectional ending clearly (*yom-u*, for example, would be a better analysis of a consonant-stem verb than *yo-mu*). Likewise, vowel-stem verbs and *-shii* adjectives follow a stylistic convention whereby the penultimate syllable, though not being strictly a part of the inflectional ending, is written as *okurigana*. Further examples of adjectives whose penultimate syllables conventionally appear in the *kana* script are 大きい and 小さい.

5. Readings: Single Elements and Compounds (熟語 *Jukugo*)

• ON or KUN?

Kanji are used to write either Chinese loanwords (漢語 *kango*) or native Japanese words (和語 *wago*). There is a marked difference between their usage in that, while *kango* are usually found as compounds comprising two or more single elements, *wago* most commonly consist of a single kanji.

When used in *kango*, therefore, kanji typically represent what we may call "the building blocks of word formation," whereas *wago* free-words are commonly expressed by one kanji (although it is not uncommon to find *wago* compounds in written Japanese). To illustrate this point with an example given earlier, the kanji for "child" can only be used alone in its *wago* form, as in the following sentence:

この子は大きい子だ。
"This child is a big child."

Used in *kango*, however, it can only be used in compounds.

子孫 シソン "descendant"
子宮 シキュウ "uterus"
子音 シオン "vowel"
母子 ボシ "mother and child"
分子 ブンシ "element; molecule"

This use of kanji proved invaluable during the introduction of Western technology in the nineteenth century, when in both China and Japan a great many new terms had to be coined in order to convey new ideas and technology. Take, for instance, the element 圧 アツ "pressing down; pressure."

圧縮 アッシュク "compression"
圧搾 アッサク "constriction"
圧力 アツリョク "pressure"
気圧 キアツ "atmospheric pressure"
血圧 ケツアツ "blood pressure"
高圧 コウアツ "high pressure"
水圧 スイアツ "water/hydraulic pressure"

電圧 デンアツ "voltage"

Thus, given the fact that a compound can be either a *kango* or *wago* combination, the learner of Japanese often has trouble deciding the correct reading of a kanji in running text (is it ON or is it KUN?). Unfortunately, there is no foolproof way to determine the right reading, but some statistical tendencies do help in forming a number of ground rules.

Ground Rule 1

Groups of kanji do not generally mix in their readings; i.e., they are read as either ON or KUN.

ON: 教育学概論 キョウイクガクガイロン　制度化 セイドカ
KUN: 安値 やすね　閏年 うるうどし

Ground Rule 2

A kanji that is part of a compound is almost always read in its ON reading.

音楽 オンガク　政治改革 セイジカイカク

Ground Rule 3

If a compound contains *okurigana*, it normally has a KUN reading.

乗り換える のりかえる　引き渡す ひきわたす

Ground Rule 4

A kanji that stands alone is normally read in its KUN reading.

この子は大きい子だ。

Although there are exceptions to these rules, they can nevertheless serve as useful guidelines to the beginner while he or she learns to determine how a kanji is read from experience.

• *Ateji*

One area of kanji usage whose unpredictable nature makes it particularly difficult for the learner is *ateji*. *Ateji* are kanji that are used to represent Japanese sounds regardless of their meaning or, conversely, meanings regardless of their sounds.

乙女 オトめ "maiden," where the first part of the Japanese word is similar in sound to the kanji's ON reading (オツ).
意気地なし イくジなし "spineless," where the first and third syllables represent ON readings, and the second, an approximation of the kanji's KUN reading.

Sometimes kanji with auspicious meanings are chosen for *ateji*; this is particularly common in the case of personal names.

美千代 Michiyo ("beauty" + "one thousand" + "generations")

Ateji include cases where a compound made from two kanji elements is equated with a Japanese word of equal or similar meaning.

悪戯 いたずら "mischief"
悪阻 つわり "morning sickness"

6. How Many Kanji Does One Need?

The Japan Industrial Standard (JIS) kanji codes of 1978 (rev. 1983) list well over 6,000 kanji, a number that may be regarded as the upper level of kanji usage in Japan. In newspapers and magazines, the total number used has been counted at approximately 3,300 or so. In contrast, the Jōyō Kanji number only 1,945. How useful is this number for reading Japanese?

Because the more frequent kanji are encountered over and over again, one can in fact achieve a great deal with a limited number of kanji; thus, the most frequent 500 cover about eighty percent of newspaper kanji; that figure increases to ninety-four percent if you know the top 1,000 kanji.

7. Kanji Composition

The majority (about two-thirds) of Jōyō Kanji are "phonetic compounds"; these are made up from a "radical" indicating the field of meaning to which the kanji belongs, and a "phonetic," which gives an indication of the ON reading. These two elements are arranged in a variety of combinations (the shaded section is the radical; examples are at right).

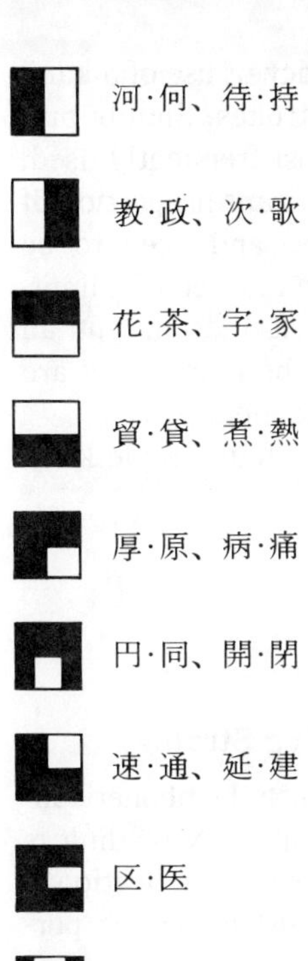

The remainder can be divided into simple kanji and non-phonetic compounds. Simple kanji are typically stylized drawings of objects.

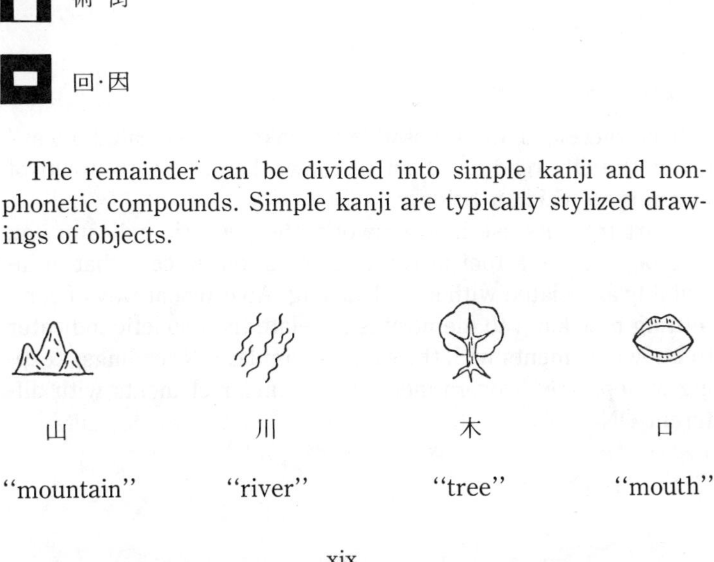

There is a correlation between the frequency of use of a kanji and its complexity in terms of number of strokes. Simply put, the kanji with the fewest strokes are the most frequently used. The implications of this fact are that a significant proportion of simple kanji (which give no phonetic clues and need to be memorized on the basis of their shape) are composed of a limited number of strokes and do not, for that reason, put an undue strain on the learner's memory. Furthermore, they are encountered so often that they are easily retained.

Non-phonetic compounds consist of two or four simple kanji put together to indicate a new idea.

roof + pig = house 家
tree + tree = woods 林
tree + tree + tree = forest 森

8. Phonetic Compounds and Kanji Learning Strategy

The proportion of phonetic compounds in which the phonetic indicator gives a perfect indication of the kanji's ON reading is almost fifty-eight percent (a), while a partly reliable indication is achieved in nearly thirty-three percent (b); just under ten percent of cases provide no useful indication (c).

a) 寺 ジ　持 ジ
b) 古 コ　苦 ク
c) 十 ジュウ　針 シン

It is, therefore, quite possible to make an "educated guess" about the ON reading of an unknown kanji (and the field of meaning to which it belongs).

Apart from its use in guesswork, the phonetic indicator can also be used as a tool in the memorization process that is inevitably associated with kanji learning. An efficient way of committing new kanji to memory is to relate the phonetic indicator to known elements with the same or similar ON readings, keeping in separate drawers identical or similar elements with different ON.

9. Kanji Made in Japan: *Kokuji*

A number of kanji have been made up by the Japanese on the Chinese model. The composition of these kanji is mostly of the non-phonetic compound variety, such as 畑 はたけ (burning + field = dry field), and 峠 とうげ (mountain + high/low = mountain pass), and therefore tend not to have an ON reading. However, some have both ON and KUN, like 働 ドウ はたら·く, and some even have ON readings only, such as 塀 ヘイ and 錠 ジョウ. Although not part of the Jōyō Kanji list, there are many more such characters, of which a good number are names of indigenous fish and vegetation.

10. Kanji and Writing Styles

Finally, a word should be said about the stylistic dimension of kanji in general and Jōyō Kanji in particular. The use of kanji in a text can be regarded as a broad indicator of technical content, as they typically express Sino-Japanese vocabulary. This explains why kanji are used liberally in scientific articles etc. but only sparingly in poetry.

Insofar as the Jōyō Kanji are concerned, the media and even many academic periodicals tend, by and large, to abide by the official list. Literature, on the other hand, is quite a different story, making good use of *ateji* and other kanji not officially recognized. Some authors even go out of their way to dot their texts with rare and abstruse kanji, employing their multifunctional nature (variant readings etc.) as stylistic devices.

USER'S MANUAL

This section offers you a few tips on how to use *Kodansha's Compact Kanji Guide*—how to get the information you need as efficiently as possible. It is organized into the following sections: (1) keywords, (2) the organization of the book, (3) how to look up the characters, (4) how to look up the compounds, (5) sample entries with explanatory notes, and (6) abbreviations.

1. Keywords

This section sets out to explain the meaning of the following keywords and how they are used throughout this dictionary: kanji, radical, stroke number, stroke order, ON reading, KUN reading, *jukugo*, and *gojūon-jun*.

Kanji 漢字

"Kanji" (literally "Han letters") is the term used by the Japanese for the ideographs borrowed from China. They are ideographs in the sense that each character symbolizes a single idea and, by extension, represents the sound associated with that idea. Characters are used alongside the native phonetic syllabaries, *hiragana* and *katakana*, to express meaning as opposed to indicating the grammatical form of a word or phrase.

Radical 部首

A "radical" (*bushu*) is that part of a character that indicates the field of meaning to which the kanji belongs. It may appear at the left- or right-hand side of a kanji, at the top or bottom, or it may be an enclosure. Alternatively, as in the case of simple kanji, the character itself may be a radical. Chinese characters have been classified according to their radicals for nearly three centuries, and like most domestic character dictionaries for Japanese consumption, *Kodansha's Compact Kanji Guide* orders kanji by radical. It is therefore quite important for the student of written

Japanese to be able to identify a radical both promptly and correctly.

Some radicals have variants. A variant is an abbreviated form of a radical, usually with a lower stroke count. A complete list of the radicals and their variants, arranged strictly by stroke count, has been collected together in the Radical Chart printed inside the back cover of the book. In contrast to the Radical Chart, both the Radical Index and the running column of radicals in the margin of the body of the book list variants according to the number of strokes of their parent radical, not the abbreviated number of strokes of the variant itself. For example, the variant 扌, which has three strokes, is listed under its parent radical 手, which has four.

Stroke Number 画数

"Stroke number" (*kakusū*) is the term that refers to the total number of strokes that make up a single character. The kanji listed in *Kodansha's Compact Kanji Guide* contain between 1 and 23 strokes. Over two-thirds of these have a stroke number of between 9 and 12 strokes. As kanji are often listed according to their stroke number, we have appended an index that classifies the Jōyō Kanji by the total number of strokes. In addition, within each radical section all characters have been put in stroke-number order.

Stroke Order 書き順

The strokes of a Chinese character are written in a set sequence, known as "stroke order" (*kakijun*). It is essential to learn the correct stroke order if you wish to write kanji. The stroke order for all 1,945 Jōyō Kanji is shown at the head of each entry.

ON Reading 音読み

Nearly all kanji entered Japan accompanied by a Chinese pronunciation in a form adapted to the Japanese sound system; this is called an ON reading (*on-yomi*). All ON readings are shown in *katakana*.

KUN Reading 訓読み

Kanji acquired further readings used to express native Japanese words of equivalent or related meaning, often called KUN readings (*kun-yomi*). In order to distinguish between ON and KUN readings, all KUN readings are given here in *hiragana*.

Jukugo 熟語

Two or more kanji can be combined in the form of a compound to make new words. These compounds are known as *jukugo*. Here the term *jukugo* refers to those compounds where all the kanji are read with their ON reading.

Gojūon-jun 五十音順

Gojūon-jun refers to the standard order of the two Japanese phonetic syllabaries. Literally it means the "order of the fifty sounds" and is reproduced below for both *hiragana* and *katakana*. Japanese words appearing in *Kodansha's Compact Kanji Guide* are generally listed according to the *gojūon-jun* standard.

Hiragana

あ	か	さ	た	な	は	ま	や	ら	わ	ん
い	き	し	ち	に	ひ	み		り		
う	く	す	つ	ぬ	ふ	む	ゆ	る		
え	け	せ	て	ね	へ	め		れ		
お	こ	そ	と	の	ほ	も	よ	ろ	を	

Katakana

ア	カ	サ	タ	ナ	ハ	マ	ヤ	ラ	ワ	ン
イ	キ	シ	チ	ニ	ヒ	ミ		リ		
ウ	ク	ス	ツ	ヌ	フ	ム	ユ	ル		
エ	ケ	セ	テ	ネ	ヘ	メ		レ		
オ	コ	ソ	ト	ノ	ホ	モ	ヨ	ロ	ヲ	

Note: The tables are read from top to bottom, left to right: i.e., *a, i, u, e, o, ka, ki, ku,* etc.

2. About the Organization of the Book

This section deals with the structure and organization of *Kodansha's Compact Kanji Guide*.

Jōyō Kanji

In 1946 the Japanese Ministry of Education issued a list of 1,945 "Common Use Characters" (Jōyō Kanji) in an attempt to simplify the written language, with the recommendation that publishers and writers confine themselves to these characters. Today nearly all newspapers and major periodicals have adopted this official list, making the Jōyō Kanji the single most relevant list of characters for the student of written Japanese. Accordingly, each of the 1,945 Jōyō Kanji is explained in a separate entry in this dictionary.

Arrangement of Characters

As mentioned above, it is most convenient to arrange kanji according to their radicals, and in fact most character dictionaries, both for native Japanese speakers and foreign learners as well, are structured in this way. All entry characters in *Kodansha's Compact Kanji Guide* are listed by their traditionally attributed radical. Thus the 1,945 Jōyō Kanji are divided into 218 radical sections. The radical sections themselves are arranged by stroke number, the first radical being of a single stroke and the final radical containing fourteen strokes. Within each radical section, the kanji are also arranged by their stroke number, a character of a lower stroke number coming before one of a higher stroke number.

Compounds

It is possible in most cases to combine two or more characters together and make a compound. *Kodansha's Compact Kanji Guide* lists a generous selection of commonly used compounds for each entry character where compounds exist. However, such compounds are listed only when the entry character is the first kanji in the compound. Within each entry there are three categories of compounds.

a) *Jukugo* Group, where the entry character is read in its ON reading

b) KUN Group, where the entry character is read in its KUN reading

c) Business Group, where the compound is a business word

Compounds within each category are arranged in *gojūon-jun* order.

3. How to Look Up the Characters

There are three ways to look up characters in *Kodansha's Compact Kanji Guide*: by radical, by ON/KUN reading, and by stroke number.

Radical

Perhaps the quickest way to find a kanji is by using the Radical Chart printed inside the back cover. The Radical Chart is a table showing the radicals and their variants in stroke-number order and indicating the page on which each radical section begins. Looking up a character in this way depends on your skill at being able to identify a radical correctly (see "Kanji Composition," p. xviii). The procedure for looking up a character in this way is as follows: (a) determine the radical; (b) count the number of strokes contained in the radical; (c) locate the radical in the Radical Chart; (d) go to the page number as indicated in the chart; (e) and, last of all, find the character within its radical section.

There will be occasions when you will waste a lot of time looking for a character in the wrong radical section. This sometimes happens because the character in question has two or more possible radicals. In such cases, use of the Radical Index is recommended. This is a very useful index. Not only does it show all the characters that belong to a particular radical section, but it also lists those characters whose radicals are easily mistaken. Take the character 頭 "head," for instance. It contains two possible radicals: the radical 豆 "bean" and the radical 頁 "page." Unless you know that the correct radical for 頭 is 豆, then you will not be able to find the character by using just the Radical Chart. However, 頭 is listed under both radicals in the Radical Index. Consequently, unless you are absolutely sure of a kanji's correct radical, you should first check in the Radical Index.

ON/KUN Reading
If you know either the ON or KUN reading of a Chinese character, then it may be quicker to go to the ON/KUN Index. Here the regular ON/KUN readings, as established by the Japanese Ministry of Education, are listed in *gojūon-jun* order, together with the kanji number. As elsewhere in the book, ON readings are shown in *katakana* and KUN readings in *hiragana*.

Stroke Number
When you have problems determining the correct radical and don't know the ON or KUN reading of a kanji, you should refer to the Stroke Index. Here the characters are classified according to their stroke number. You simply count the number of strokes contained in the character, and then look it up in the corresponding list in the Stroke Index.

The various ways of looking up characters are summarized in the diagram printed inside the front cover.

4. How to Look Up the Compounds
Once you have learned how to look up characters, finding a compound is a relatively easy task. The first thing to remember is that all compounds in *Kodansha's Compact Kanji Guide* are listed under the character that is the initial kanji in the compound. For example, the compound 洗濯 "washing; laundry" is listed under the character 洗, not the character 濯. The second thing to have in mind is that, where applicable, there are three separate compound groups:

a) *Jukugo* Group (clue: first kanji is read with its ON reading)
b) KUN Group (clue: first kanji is read with its KUN reading)
c) Business Group (clue: compound is a business word or word used in a business context)

Take, for example, the compound 断言 ダンゲン "assertion; affirmation; declaration." This compound will be found under the entry for the character 断. When you go to this entry you will find that there are two compound groups—the *jukugo* and KUN groups. In this case, however, the first kanji is used with its ON reading and will therefore be located in the *jukugo* group, marked by the symbol 熟.

Again, take the compound 旅人 たびびと "traveler; wayfarer; pilgrim," which is listed under the entry for 旅. Here, the first kanji is read in KUN and so it can be found in the KUN group, marked with the symbol 訓.

Finally, how about 普通銀行 フツウギンコウ "ordinary bank," which is listed under the entry for the first character of the compound 普. As the word is obviously a business word, it is located in the Business Group with the symbol ¥.

5. Sample Entries with Explanatory Notes

This section deals with the typography used throughout *Kodansha's Compact Kanji Guide.*

Radical Section Header

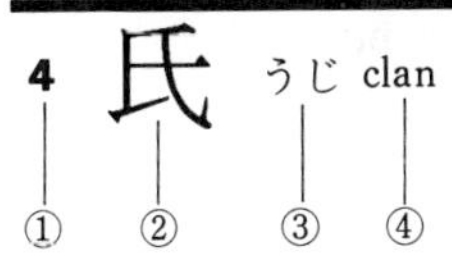

① This digit represents the radical or variant's stroke number.
② Radical or variant.
③ Traditional Japanese name of radical or variant.
④ Given English name of radical or variant.

Character Entry

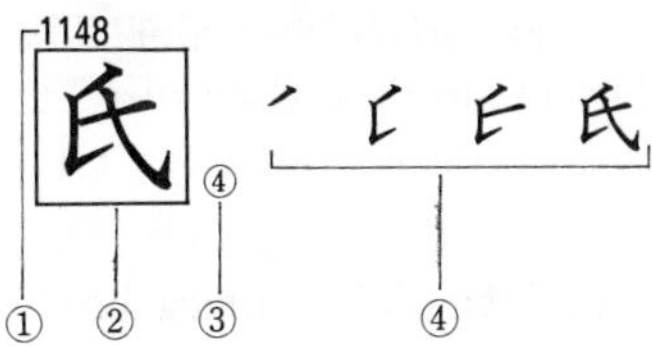

① Kanji number. This is the number that is used to identify

the character in each of the indices that have been appended at the back of the book.

② Kanji box. An enlarged example of the entry character in a box.

③ Stroke number. The total number of strokes contained in the entry character.

④ Stroke order. The order of strokes when writing the entry character.

ON Reading

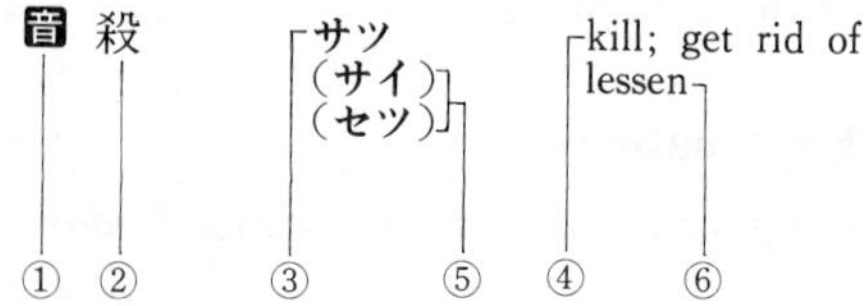

① ON reading symbol—the character for ON 音 in a black box.

② Entry character illustrated in standard type.

③ Regular ON reading.

④ Meaning attached to the regular ON reading.

⑤ Irregular ON reading.

⑥ Meaning attached to the irregular ON reading.

Compounds (*Jukugo*)

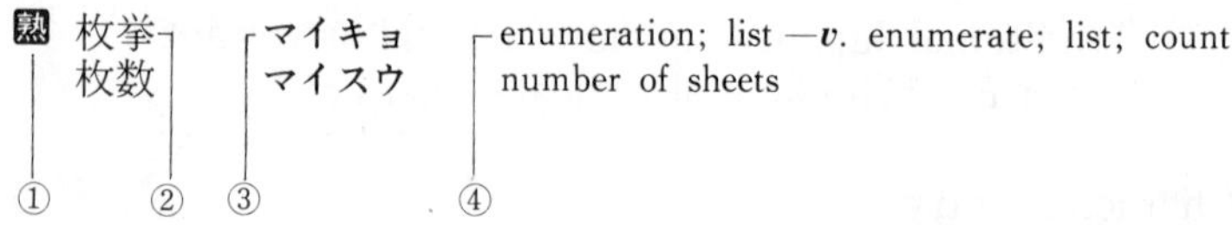

Compounds are listed as shown above in *gojūon-jun* order. The compound can be made into a verb by adding the verb *suru* "to do" when a verb form (indicated by the abbreviations *v* or *vt*) is included in the definition.

① *Jukugo* symbol—the character for *juku* 熟 in a black box.

② Compound.

③ Regular reading of compound.

④ Definition/explanation of the meaning and usage of the compound.

KUN Reading and KUN Compounds

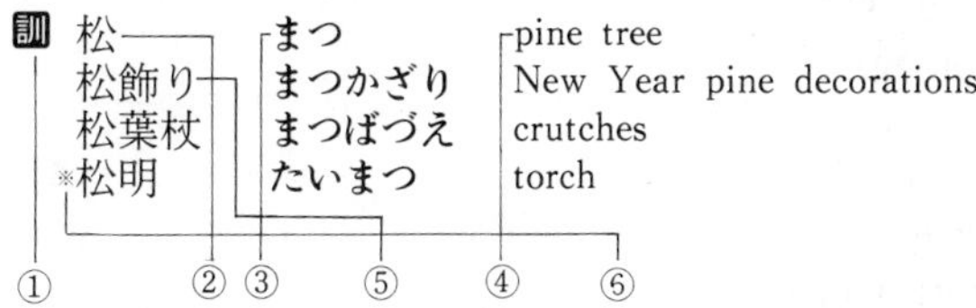

① KUN reading symbol—the character for KUN 訓 in a black box.
② Entry character.
③ Regular KUN reading.
④ Meaning attached to this KUN reading.
⑤ Regular KUN compound.
⑥ Symbol to indicate irregular reading.

Business Words

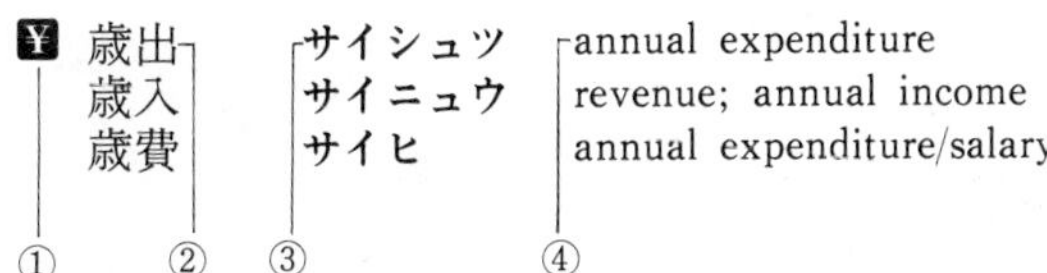

A brief selection of commonly used business words appears at the end of many entries in this dictionary.

① Business word symbol—the yen sign in a black box.
② Business compounds.
③ Regular readings.
④ Definitions/explanations of meaning and usage.

6. Abbreviations

adj.	adjective
bas.	baseball
bio.	biology
Bud.	Buddhist
chem.	chemistry
clas.	classical
col.	colloquial
derog.	derogatory
fig.	figurative(ly)
hist.	historical
hon.	honorific
hum.	humble
med.	medicine
n.	noun
phy.	physics
v.	verb
vi.	intransitive verb
vt.	transitive verb

THE JŌYŌ KANJI

1 一 いち one

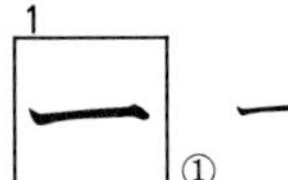

音	一	イチ	one; equal; the first; whole
		イツ	one; entirely
熟	一因	イチイン	one cause among many; a single factor
	一員	イチイン	a member of a group; one member
	一円	イチエン	the whole area; all over; one yen
	一応	イチオウ	tentatively; provisionally; anyhow; once; in outline; for the time being
	一月	イチガツ	January
	一丸	イチガン	one lump
	一群	イチグン	one group
	一芸	イチゲイ	one art; one of the arts
	一合目	イチゴウめ	arbitrary tenth of the height of a mountain; beginning of a mountain climb
	一言	イチゴン	(one) word/phrase; utterance
	一次	イチジ	the first ***math***. linear
	一時	イチジ	for a time; (at) one time; once; one o'clock
	一日	イチジツ	one/some day; first day of the month
	一日千秋	イチジツセンシュウ	feel as if a day were so many years; waiting impatiently
	一巡	イチジュン	once around —***vi***. go once around; go round the block
	一助	イチジョ	aid; some help
	一条	イチジョウ	one line; one of a series of articles in a document; an event
	一場	イチジョウ	one scene/place
	一族	イチゾク	one's whole family; one's kinsmen
	一存	イチゾン	one's own will/opinion
	一代	イチダイ	one life/dynasty; one/first generation
	一大事	イチダイジ	serious matter/affair
	一団	イチダン	body; group; crowd of people
	一段落	イチダンラク	pause; one pause for the present —***vi***. pause; suspend
	一同	イチドウ	all present; all persons concerned; everybody
	一読	イチドク	a reading —***v***. read over; read through once
	一日	イチニチ	some day; all day; one day
	一任	イチニン	delegation; trust —***v***. leave a matter to a person; entrust

一人前	イチニンまえ	grown-up; adult; one adult portion (of food)
一年	イチネン	one year
一念	イチネン	zeal; enthusiasm; concentration
一部	イチブ	one part/section/book
一部始終	イチブシジュウ	the whole story from beginning to end; all the details
一望	イチボウ	one view —***v***. look out; take in the view
一望千里	イチボウセンリ	a fine view of a boundless plain; a clear view in the distance
一味	イチミ	the same group/party; a single flavor
一名	イチメイ	one person; another name; alias
一命	イチメイ	(one) life
一面	イチメン	one side
一網打尽	イチモウダジン	catching a lot of fish in the same net
一文	イチモン	old Japanese coin; one tenth of a sen; tiny sum of money
一門	イチモン	whole family; one clan
一問一答	イチモンイットウ	question and answer —***vi***. give an immediate answer to each question
一夜	イチヤ	one night; some night; single night
一躍	イチヤク	at a bound —***vi***. raise (to the top) in one go
一様	イチヨウ	even; equality
一覧	イチラン	a look; a glance —***v***. look over; take a look; glance through
一理	イチリ	some truth; a truth
一利一害	イチリイチガイ	advantages and disadvantages
一律	イチリツ	equality; monotony; uniformity
一流	イチリュウ	first or highest in a group; unique; first class
一両日	イチリョウジツ	a day or two
一輪	イチリン	one flower/wheel; the next full moon
一例	イチレイ	an example
一連	イチレン	series; ream
一路	イチロ	road; straight
一割	イチワリ	ten percent
一家	イッカ	family; master; an authority
一画	イッカク	a stroke in writing; building lot
一括	イッカツ	summary —***v***. do all at once; complete at one time
一貫	イッカン	consistency —***v***. run through
一喜一憂	イッキイチユウ	joy and sorrow —***vi***. swing from joy to sorrow
一級	イッキュウ	first/top class; first rate
一挙一動	イッキョイチドウ	one's every action
一挙両得	イッキョリョウトク	kill two birds with one stone

一計	イッケイ	plan; idea
一見	イッケン	(one) glance —*v*. have a look; glance; take a quick look
一件	イッケン	affair; matter; item
一考	イッコウ	consideration —*v*. consider
一行	イッコウ	one event; party; group
一刻	イッコク	moment; instant
一切	イッサイ	all; entire; whole
一策	イッサク	plan; idea
一式	イッシキ	complete set
一首	イッシュ	one poem
一種	イッシュ	one kind/type
一周	イッシュウ	a round; one lap —*v*. go round
一蹴	イッシュウ	refusal —*v*. refuse
一瞬	イッシュン	instant; moment
一緒	イッショ	all in one; together; with; at the same time; in the lump; same
一笑	イッショウ	laugh —*v*. laugh at
一生	イッショウ	one's (whole) life
一生懸命 (一所懸命)	イッショウケンメイ (イッショケンメイ)	with all one's might; the hardest one can try
一身	イッシン	oneself; one's whole body
一身上	イッシンジョウ	personal; private
一新	イッシン	renewal —*v*. renew; change completely
一進一退	イッシンイッタイ	advance and retreat; ebb and flow
一心不乱	イッシンフラン	heart and soul; concentration
一睡	イッスイ	wink of sleep; nap
一世	イッセ	one existence (past, present, or future)
一世	イッセイ	a life; era; the first monarch in line of succession; first generation of immigrants
一席	イッセキ	meeting; sitting; first place
一石二鳥	イッセキニチョウ	kill two birds with one stone
一節	イッセツ	one paragraph/phrase
一説	イッセツ	another opinion/view; one opinion; one way of looking at things
一線	イッセン	a line; the front line
一掃	イッソウ	a clean sweep —*v*. dispel; eradicate
一体	イッタイ	one body; a style; a form; (who/what) on earth?
一帯	イッタイ	tract of land; whole area
一隊	イッタイ	company of soldiers
一旦	イッタン	once

1

●一 丨 丶 丿 乙 乚 亅

	一端	イッタン	one end; a part; outline
	一致	イッチ	agreement; unity; accord —***vi***. be in agreement; be united
	一致団結	イッチダンケツ	cooperation —***v***. unite (in doing); cooperate
	一朝一夕	イッチョウ イッセキ	brief space of time
	一長一短	イッチョウ イッタン	merits and demerits
	一対	イッツイ	pair
	一手	イッテ	move in go or shogi; monopoly
	一定	イッテイ	fixed; definite; certain —***v***. fix; set; settle; define
	一滴	イッテキ	drop of liquid
	一転	イッテン	change; complete change —***vi***. make a complete change
	一等	イットウ	first place/prize/class
	一時	イットキ	short time
	一派	イッパ	school of thought
	一般	イッパン	ordinary; general
	一般的	イッパンテキ	general; ordinary
	一筆	イッピツ	one uninterrupted stroke of a pen; brief note
	一服	イップク	dose of medicine; puff of a cigarette; rest —***v***. have/take a rest
	一幅	イップク	scroll
	一片	イッペン	piece; fragment of a thin object
	一辺	イッペン	one side
	一辺倒	イッペントウ	loyal support; unquestioning devotion
	一変	イッペン	(complete) change —***v***. change (completely)
	一歩	イッポ	step; footstep
	一方	イッポウ	one side/part; on one hand
	一方的	イッポウテキ	one-sided; unilateral
	一本気	イッポンギ	single-minded
	一本調子	イッポンチョウシ	a monotone; monotony
訓	一つ	ひとつ	one
	一	ひと	(prefix) one; single
	一雨	ひとあめ	shower; rainfall
	一息	ひといき	breath; rest; breather
	一重	ひとえ	single; onefold
	一癖	ひとくせ	peculiarity; idiosyncrasy
	一粒種	ひとつぶだね	one's only child
	一昔	ひとむかし	decade
	一休み	ひとやすみ	brief rest; breather; break —***vi***. take a rest; take a breather
	※一日	ついたち	first day (of the month); 1st

¥	一任業務	イチニンギョウム	descretionary business
	一般会計	イッパンカイケイ	General Account
	一般事業債	イッパンジギョウサイ	general corporate bonds

2

七 ② 一 七

音	七	シチ	seven
熟	七月	シチガツ	July
	七五三	シチゴサン	(celebration of) a child's third, fifth, and seventh years
	七五調	シチゴチョウ	the seven-and-five-syllable meter in Japanese poetry
	七転八倒	シチテンバットウ	writhing in agony/pain —***vi***. writhe in agony/pain
	七福神	シチフクジン	Seven Gods of Good Fortune
	七面鳥	シチメンチョウ	turkey
訓	七	なな	seven
	七つ	ななつ	seven
	七日	なのか	seventh day (of the month); 7th
	※七夕	たなばた	the seventh day of the seventh month of the lunar calendar
	※七夕祭	たなばたまつり	Star Festival; Tanabata Matsuri

3

丁 ② 一 丁

音	丁	チョウ	leaf; page; block; even number
		テイ	youth; servant; the fourth of the ten calendar signs; polite
熟	丁度	チョウド	exactly; just; right;quite
	丁場	チョウば	the distance between stages
	丁半	チョウハン	odd and even numbers
	丁字	テイジ	T
	丁字形	テイジケイ	T-shaped
	丁字路	テイジロ	T junction
	丁重	テイチョウ	polite; courteous; civil; respectful; reverent
	丁寧	テイネイ	polite; courteous; careful; scrupulous; thorough
	丁寧語	テイネイゴ	polite respect language
訓	※丁	ひのと	*hinoto* (fourth sign of the lunar calendar)

1

4

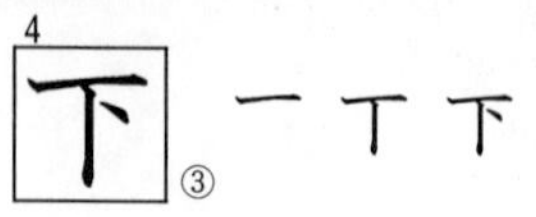

一 丨 丶 丿 乙 乚 亅

音	下	カ	under; lower part; descend; below; lower; go down; fall
		ゲ	below; lower part; be inferior; lower
熟	下位	カイ	lower rank; subordinate position
	下院	カイン	Lower House
	下記	カキ	the following; undermentioned; below
	下級	カキュウ	lower class/grade
	下弦	カゲン	waning moon; last phase of the moon
	下降	カコウ	descent; fall; drop —***vi***. descend; fall; drop; decline
	下層	カソウ	lower classes
	下等	カトウ	low grade; meanness; inferiority
	下半身	カハンシン	lower half of the body
	下部	カブ	lower part
	下流	カリュウ	lower part of a river; downstream
	下界	ゲカイ	the earth; here below
	下戸	ゲコ	teetotaler; nondrinker
	下校	ゲコウ	leaving school for the day; coming home from school —***vi***. leave school for the day; come home from school
	下剤	ゲザイ	***med***. laxative; purgative
	下山	ゲザン	descent of a mountain —***vi***. climb down a mountain
	下車	ゲシャ	alighting —***vi***. alight from a train, car, bus
	下宿	ゲシュク	lodgings; boarding house —***vi***. lodge; board; take up lodgings
	下旬	ゲジュン	the last ten days of a month; the last third of a month
	下水	ゲスイ	sewage; sewer; drainage
	下船	ゲセン	disembarkation; going ashore —***vi***. leave a ship; go ashore
	下足	ゲソク	footwear
	下駄	ゲタ	*geta* (wooden clogs)
	下段	ゲダン	lowest step; lower berth
	下馬評	ゲバヒョウ	common talk; gossip; rumor
	下品	ゲヒン	coarse; rude; vulgar
	下落	ゲラク	fall; decline; drop; deterioration —***v***. fall; decline; drop; deteriorate
	下痢	ゲリ	diarrhea; loose bowels —***vi***. suffer from diarrhea; pass fluid stools
	下劣	ゲレツ	meanness; baseness; vulgarity

訓	下	した	low; inferior to; below; under; young
	下絵	したえ	rough sketch; undersketch; design
	下書き	したがき	rough draft
	下着	したぎ	underwear; undergarments
	下心	したごころ	ulterior motive
	下地	したヂ	groundwork; preparations; first coat (of paint/lacquer); aptitude
	下調べ	したしらべ	preliminary inquiry; preparations
	下積み	したづみ	goods at the bottom of a pile; lowest social classes; the lowest
	下手	したて(したで)	inferiority; downwards
	下火	したび	fire that has burnt out; decline
	下町	したまち	*shitamachi* (traditional working-class neighborhood)
	下見	したみ	preliminary examination; clapboard; narrow board thicker at one edge than the other used for sliding
	下役	したヤク	petty official; underling
	下りる	おりる	***vi.*** come down; get off/down/out
	下ろす	おろす	***vt.*** take down; grate; put down
	下す	くだす	***vt.*** let down; subdue; give; issue; pass; have loose bowels
	下る	くだる	***vi.*** descend; go down; pass
	下り	くだり	descent; going down; away from the center of town
	下さる	くださる	***vt. hon.*** give; receive; oblige; favor with
	下がる	さがる	***vi.*** come down; leave; hang down; fall
	下げる	さげる	***vt.*** take down; lower; hang
	下	しも	low; lower part; the governed; lower classes; lower half of the body
	下座	しもザ	lower seat
	下々	しもじも	the masses; lower classes
	下手	しもて	downwards; right side of a stage; actor's right
	下	もと	under; base
	※下手	へた	unskillful; poor at
¥	下げ足	さげあし	downward trend
	下げ屋	さげや	lower (in a quotation)
	下請け	したうけ	subcontract; subcontracting
	下支え	したざさえ	support
	下値	したね	lower price
	下放れ	したばなれ	down gap

5

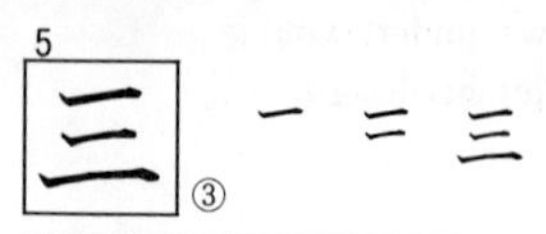

音	三	サン	three
熟	三角	サンカク	triangle
	三角関係	サンカクカンケイ	eternal triangle; love triangle
	三角形	サンカクケイ	triangle
	三角州	サンカクス	delta
	三月	サンガツ	March
	三脚	サンキャク	tripod
	三権	サンケン	three branches of government
	三原色	サンゲンショク	three primary colors
	三次元	サンジゲン	three-dimensional (3-D)
	三段跳び	サンダンとび	triple jump; hop, step, and jump
	三拍子	サンビョウシ	triple time; three-part time
	三方	サンポウ	three directions/sides; small wooden stand
	三面記事	サンメンキジ	city news; police news
	※三味線	シャミセン	*shamisen* (three-string Japanese mandolin)
訓	三つ	みっつ	three
	三	み	three
	三日	みっか	third day (of the month); 3rd
	三日月	みかづき	new/crescent moon
	三つ	みつ	three

6

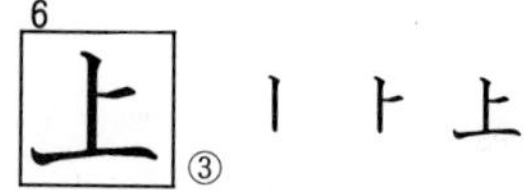

音	上	ジョウ (ショウ)	upper part; good; first; rise; get on
熟	上位	ジョウイ	superior/higher rank
	上映	ジョウエイ	movie screening/showing —***v***. screen; show/put on a movie
	上演	ジョウエン	performance; presentation —***v***. perform; present
	上官	ジョウカン	senior officer; superior
	上記	ジョウキ	the above; the above-mentioned
	上気	ジョウキ	blushing; rush of blood to the cheeks —***vi***. have a rush of blood to the head; blush; go red in the cheeks
	上機嫌	ジョウキゲン	good humor/mood
	上級	ジョウキュウ	upper grade; upper; higher; senior

上京	ジョウキョウ	going to Tokyo —*vi*. come up to Tokyo
上下	ジョウゲ	vertical; up and down; top and bottom; fluctuation; social standing —*v*. go up and down; rise and fall; fluctuate
上下関係	ジョウゲカンケイ	social standing
上下動	ジョウゲドウ	up-and-down movement; vertical earthquake
上限	ジョウゲン	upper limit; maximum
上弦	ジョウゲン	moon in its first quarter
上戸	ジョウゴ	heavy drinker
上司	ジョウシ	one's superior/boss
上質	ジョウシツ	fine/choice quality
上述	ジョウジュツ	the above; the above-mentioned
上旬	ジョウジュン	first ten days of the month; beginning/first part of the month
上昇	ジョウショウ	rise; ascension —*vi*. rise; go up; ascend
上々	ジョウジョウ	excellent; the very best
上申	ジョウシン	report —*v*. report to one's superiors
上申書	ジョウシンショ	written report
上水	ジョウスイ	water supply; tap/city water
上水道	ジョウスイドウ	water works
上訴	ジョウソ	appeal —*v*. appeal to a higher court
上奏	ジョウソウ	report —*v*. report to the emperor
上層	ジョウソウ	upper class/layer/stratum/air
上体	ジョウタイ	upper part of the body
上代	ジョウダイ	in old/ancient times
上達	ジョウタツ	advancement; progress; improvement —*vi*. make progress; advance; improve; become proficient
上段	ジョウダン	upper section/deck/berth
上程	ジョウテイ	lay before/introduce/present to the Diet
上出来	ジョウでき	good work; well-made; well-done
上等	ジョウトウ	fine/top quality; excellent
上人	ショウニン	saint; holy priest
上半身	ジョウハンシン	upper half of the body
上品	ジョウヒン	elegant; refined; in good taste
上部	ジョウブ	upper part; top
上物	ジョウもの	choice/high quality goods
上陸	ジョウリク	landing; disembarkation —*vi*. land; make a landing; go on shore
上流	ジョウリュウ	upper reaches of a river; upstream; upper classes
訓 上がり	あがり	rise; income; returns; proceeds
上がる	あがる	***vi***. rise; go up; come in; enter; be promoted; (rain) stops ***hon***. eat

1

一 丨 丶 丿 乙 乚 亅

上げる	あげる	***v.*** raise; lift; invite; send; give; be promoted; vomit
上	うえ	top; upper part; above; over; on; upon; older; senior; better
上	うわ	(prefix) upper; up-
上書き	うわがき	address
上着	うわぎ	coat; jacket
上手	うわて	upper part/course
上の空	うわのそら	absentmindedly
上辺	うわべ	surface; outward; seeming
上回る	うわまわる	***vi.*** exceed; be better; surpass
上向き	うわむき	upward; looking up
上目使い	うわめづかい	upturned eyes/glance
上役	うわヤク	one's superior
上	かみ	up a river; upstream
上方	かみがた	Kyoto and vicinity; the Kyoto-Osaka area
上座	かみザ	front seat; seat of honor; top of the class
上手	かみて	upper part/course; right hand side of the stage
上せる	のぼせる	***vt.*** put in; put on record ***vi.*** feel dizzy; get upset
上り	のぼり	ascent; going up; toward the center of town
上る	のぼる	***vi.*** climb; go up; reach; amount to
※上手	じょうず	skillful; clever; good; expert
¥ 上ザヤ	うわザヤ	higher in quotation
上値	うわね	higher price
上乗せ	うわのせ	rise in prise
上放れ	うわばなれ	up gap
上屋	うわや	shed
上寄る	うわよる	open higher
上院	ジョウイン	Upper House
上場	ジョウジョウ	listed —***v.*** list; be listed at a stock market
上場株	ジョウジョウかぶ	listed stock
上場企業	ジョウジョウキギョウ	listed company
上場基準	ジョウジョウキジュン	initial listing requirement
上場銘柄	ジョウジョウメイがら	listed issue
上伸	ジョウシン	(share prices) jump; rise; upward turn

7
丈 ③ 一 ナ 丈

音	丈	ジョウ	length
熟	丈夫	ジョウブ	strong; robust; solid; durable; health
訓	丈	たけ	height; length; size

8
万 ③ 一 丂 万

音	万	バン	countless; myriad; all
		マン	ten thousand; myriad
熟	万感	バンカン	flood of emotions; various emotions
	万古	バンコ	perpetuity; eternity
	万国	バンコク	all nations
	万歳	バンザイ	Hurrah!
	万策	バンサク	every means; all possible ways
	万事	バンジ	everything; all
	万障	バンショウ	all obstacles; various problems/business
	万全	バンゼン	perfect; sure
	万難	バンナン	innumerable difficulties; all obstacles
	万人	バンニン	all people; everybody
	万能	バンノウ	almighty; omnipotent; all-around; all-purpose
	万般	バンパン	all; everything
	万物	バンブツ	all things; all creation
	万民	バンミン	all the people; nation
	万有	バンユウ	all things; all creation; universal
	万有引力	バンユウインリョク	universal gravitation
	万一	マンイチ	by any chance; should happen to
	万華鏡	マンゲキョウ	kaleidoscope
	万年	マンネン	eternity; perpetuity; ten thousand years
	万年筆	マンネンヒツ	fountain-pen
	万引き	マンびき	shoplifting; shoplifter
	万病	マンビョウ	all kinds of diseases; all diseases
	万力	マンリキ	vise
訓	※万	よろず	ten thousand; all sorts of; everything

9

与 ③

一 与 与

音	与	ヨ	give; join
訓	与える	あたえる	*vt.* give; bestow; cause
	※与する	くみする	*vi.* take part in; side with
¥	与信業務	ヨシンギョウム	credit business
	与党	ヨトウ	the Government; the Administration; party in power
	与野党	ヨヤトウ	governing and opposition parties

10

不 ④

一 ア 不 不

音	不	フ ブ	not
熟	不安	フアン	uneasy; uncertain; insecure; suspenseful; fearful; nervous
	不安定	フアンテイ	instability; lack of stability
	不案内	フアンナイ	ignorance; unfamiliarity
	不意	フイ	suddenly; unexpectedly
	不運	フウン	misfortune
	不穏	フオン	disorder; disquiet; unrest
	不可	フカ	bad; wrong; improper; impossible
	不可解	フカカイ	mysterious; beyond comprehension; inscrutable
	不可欠	フカケツ	indispensable; essential; vital
	不可抗力	フカコウリョク	beyond human control; unpreventable
	不可思議	フカシギ	strange; mysterious
	不可侵	フカシン	inviolable; sacred; nonaggressive
	不可分	フカブン	inseparable; indivisible; undetachable
	不快	フカイ	unpleasant; rotten; disagreeable; offensive; sickness
	不快指数	フカイシスウ	discomfort index
	不覚	フカク	negligent; improvident; unprepared; unexpected
	不恰好	ブカッコウ	unshapely; ill-fitting; awkward
	不規則	フキソク	irregular; unsystematic
	不吉	フキツ	unlucky; inauspicious; ominous
	不気味	ブキミ	weird; eerie; ominous; uncanny
	不朽	フキュウ	immortal; eternal; undying
	不急	フキュウ	nonurgent; not pressing

不興	フキョウ	displeasure; ill humor; disgrace
不義理	フギリ	ingratitude; dishonesty; injustice
不器量	ブキリョウ	plain; ugly; homely
不謹慎	フキンシン	imprudent; indiscreet; immodest; rash
不具	フグ	***derog.*** deformed; malformed; crippled
不遇	フグウ	underestimated; unrecognized (talent/ability); misfortune; bad luck; ill fate
不屈	フクツ	inflexible; invincible; inexhaustible; indomitable
不景気	フケイキ	depression (esp. economic)
不経済	フケイザイ	uneconomical; wasteful; extravagant; expensive
不潔	フケツ	dirty; smutty; unclean; impure
不言実行	フゲンジッコウ	work before talk; action before words
不孝	フコウ	undutiful; disobedient; impious; thankless; ungrateful
不幸	フコウ	unhappy; unfortunate; unlucky; death of a close relative
不合格	フゴウカク	failure; disqualification
不合理	フゴウリ	irrational; illogical; unreasonable; preposterous
不心得	フこころえ	indiscreet; imprudent; unwise
不在	フザイ	absence; being away
不在投票	フザイトウヒョウ	absentee voting
不作	フサク	poor crop; bad harvest
不作法	ブサホウ	bad manners/form; rudeness
不治	フジ	incurable; malignant (disease)
不時	フジ	emergency; unexpectedness; sudden
不思議	フシギ	mysterious; wonderful; marvelous; strange; uncanny
不自然	フシゼン	unnatural; artificial
不時着	フジチャク	forced/emergency landing
不実	フジツ	unfaithful; insincere; cold-hearted; untruth; falsehood
不始末	フシマツ	mismanagement; misconduct; malpractise; improvidence
不死身	フジみ	immortal; invincible; indomitable
不自由	フジユウ	inconvenient; uncomfortable —***vi.*** be troubled by
不純	フジュン	impure; foul; mixed
不順	フジュン	changeable; unsettled; unfavorable; irregular
不詳	フショウ	unknown; unidentified
不浄	フジョウ	uncleaniness; dirtiness; impurity; menstruation; feces; urine
不祥事	フショウジ	scandal
不承不承	フショウブショウ	unwillingly; reluctantly; grudgingly
不信	フシン	distrust; mistrust; disbelief; insincerity; fidelity

不信任	フシンニン	lack of confidence
不振	フシン	dull; inactive; slack; stagnate; depressed
不審	フシン	suspicion; doubt; distrust
不随	フズイ	paralysis; palsy
不正	フセイ	injustice; unfairness; wrong; illegality
不世出	フセイシュツ	rare
不成績	フセイセキ	poor results; bad record; underachievement
不摂生	フセッセイ	neglect of health; unwholesome living
不全	フゼン	imperfect; incomplete
不戦勝	フセンショウ	unearned win; win by default
不相応	フソウオウ	unsuitable; unfit; inappropriate; unbecoming
不足	フソク	lack; insufficiency; shortage; need; want; discontent; dissatisfaction —***vi***. lack; be short of; be discontented
不測	フソク	unforeseen; unexpected
不断	フダン	ceaseless; incessant; continual; usually; habitually
不調	フチョウ	bad condition; rupture; failure; fiasco
不通	フツウ	interruption; suspension (of traffic); unreliable; hard to understand; unclear
不都合	フツゴウ	inconvenient; inexpedient
不定	フテイ	indefinite; uncertain; unsettled; unfixed
不定期	フテイキ	irregular (time period)
不体裁	フテイサイ	unseemly; unsightly; indecent; improper
不敵	フテキ	brave; daring; intrepid; fearless
不出来	フデき	poor work; failure; bungle
不適合	フテキゴウ	incongruent
不手際	フてぎわ	clumsy; awkward; inept
不徹底	フテッテイ	inconclusive; inconsistent; weak
不当	フトウ	injustice; wrongfulness; impropriety; unreasonableness
不同	フドウ	unequal; uneven; irregular; dissimilar
不動	フドウ	immovability; immobility; firmness; stability
不統一	フトウイツ	disorganized; disunited; divided; chaotic
不徳	フトク	vice; immorality; delinquency
不慣れ	フなれ	inexperience
不人情	フニンジョウ	unkind; unfeeling; inhuman; cold-hearted
不燃	フネン	incombustible; fireproof
不能	フノウ	inability; impotence
不敗	フハイ	invincible; undefeated; unbeatable
不発	フハツ	misfire; backfire
不備	フビ	deficiency; imperfection; inadequacy; lack; defect
不評	フヒョウ	unpopular; disreputable

不平等	フビョウドウ	unequal; unfair
不服	フフク	dissatisfaction; discontentment; disagreement; objection; protest
不平	フヘイ	complaint; grievance; discontent; displeasure
不変	フヘン	unchangeable; invariable; constant
不便	フベン	inconvenient
不法	フホウ	unlawful; illegal; unjust
不本意	フホンイ	reluctant; unwilling
不満	フマン	discontent; dissatifaction; displeasure
不眠	フミン	insomnia; loss of sleep
不眠不休	フミンフキュウ	without resting/sleeping; devotedly
不向き	フむき	unsuitable; unfit; ill-fitting
不明	フメイ	unknown; obscure; unclear; vague; ambiguous
不名誉	フメイヨ	dishonor; disgrace; discredit; infamy; shame
不滅	フメツ	immortality
不毛	フモウ	unproductive; sterile; infertile; barren (land, projects, etc.)
不問	フモン	ignore; disregard
不夜城	フヤジョウ	nightless quarter; city that never sleeps
不要	フヨウ	unnecessary; useless; needless
不用	フヨウ	useless; unnecessary
不用意	フヨウイ	unprepared; not organized
不用心	ブヨウジン	careless; imprudent; insecure; unsafe
不養生	フヨウジョウ	neglect of one's health
不利	フリ	disadvantage
不慮	フリョ	unexpected; unforeseen
不良	フリョウ	badness; inferiority; deliquency
不漁	フリョウ	poor catch (of fish)
不労不死	フロウフシ	eternal youth; immortality
不和	フワ	discord; trouble; differences; disharmony
¥ 不況	フキョウ	depression; slump; recession
不均衡	フキンコウ	imbalance; unbalance
不動産	フドウサン	real estate; realty
不良債権	フリョウサイケン	bad debts
不渡り手形	フわたりてがた	dishonored notes (bill)

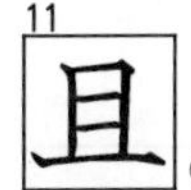

11 且 ⑤ 丨 冂 日 日 且

音 且	(ショ)	moreover; besides
訓 且つ	かつ	also; moreover; besides

12

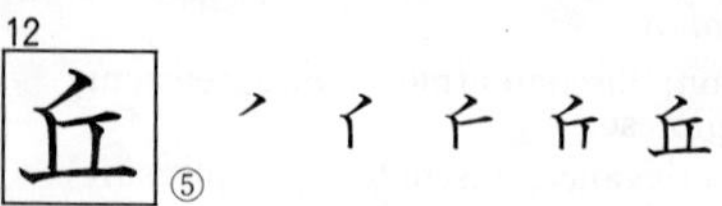

音	丘	キュウ	hill; mound
熟	丘陵	キュウリョウ	hill; hillock
訓	丘	おか	hill

13

世 ⑤

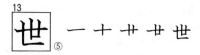

音	世	セ セイ	world; life
熟	世紀	セイキ	century
	世界	セカイ	world; earth; circle; sphere
	世界的	セカイテキ	worldwide; international
	世間	セケン	the world; people; the public; circle of acquaintances
	世間体	セケンテイ	decency; appearances
	世間話	セケンばなし	chat; small talk
	世襲	セシュウ	hereditary; descent —***v.*** inherit
	世情	セジョウ	worldly matters; the ways of the world
	世相	セソウ	social conditions/aspects
	世俗	セゾク	worldly things
	世帯	セタイ	household
	世代	セダイ	generation
	世論	セロン（よロン）	public opinion; consensus of opinion
	世話	セワ	aid; help; assistance; service; care; trouble; everyday life —***v.*** help; assist; serve; care
	お世辞	おセジ	compliment
訓	世	よ	society; times; life
	世の中	よのなか	in the world/society; at large

14

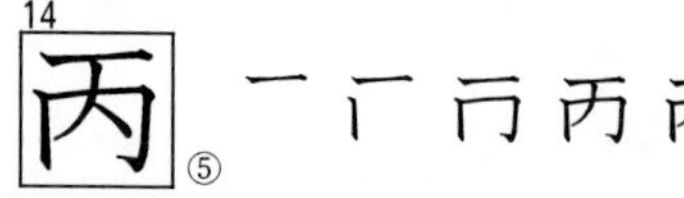

音	丙	ヘイ	third in a series; C
訓	※丙	ひのえ	*hinoe* (third sign of lunar calendar)

15

両 ⑥

一 丆 丙 丙 両 両

音	両	リョウ	both; two; *ryō* (old Japanese coin); (counter for cars, carriages, rolling stock)
熟	両院	リョウイン	both houses (of parliament/congress); upper and lower houses
	両替	リョウがえ	money exchange —*v*. exchange money
	両極	リョウキョク	the two poles; both extremities
	両軍	リョウグン	two armies
	両日	リョウジツ	both/two days
	両者	リョウシャ	both people
	両親	リョウシン	parents
	両性	リョウセイ	both sexes; male and female
	両生類	リョウセイルイ	amphibia (animal)
	両端	リョウタン	both ends/edges; sitting on the fence
	両断	リョウダン	divided into two —*v*. cut in two
	両刀	リョウトウ	two swords
	両人	リョウニン	two/both people
	両刃	リョウば	double-edged
	両方	リョウホウ	both
	両面	リョウメン	both faces/sides
	両雄	リョウユウ	two great men
	両用	リョウヨウ	serving a double purpose
	両様	リョウヨウ	two/both ways
	両翼	リョウヨク	both wings/flanks
	両立	リョウリツ	coexistence; compatibility —*vi*. coexist; be compatible
	両輪	リョウリン	two wheels

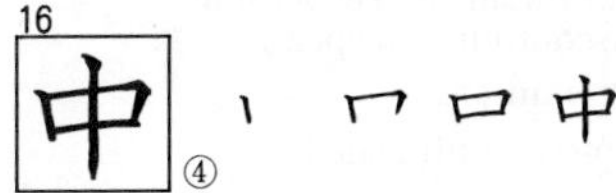

1 丨 ぼう rod; stick; line

16

中 ④

丨 ㄇ 口 中

音	中	チュウ	center; middle; medium; mediocrity; average
熟	中央	チュウオウ	center; middle; heart

1

一 •丨 丶 丿 乙 乚 亅

中華	チュウカ	China; Chinese (food, etc.)
中核	チュウカク	core; kernel; nucleus
中学生	チュウガクセイ	junior high school student
中学校	チュウガッコウ	junior high/middle school
中型	チュウがた	medium-size
中間	チュウカン	middle; midway
中期	チュウキ	middle period
中級	チュウキュウ	medium grade
中近東	チュウキントウ	The Near and Middle East
中位	チュウくらい	medium size; middling; moderate; passable
中継	チュウケイ	relay; broadcast —***v***. relay; broadcast
中堅	チュウケン	backbone; nucleus; main body; center; people forming the backbone
中古	チュウコ	the middle ages; second hand; old
中古車	チュウコシャ	used/second hand car
中国	チュウゴク	China
中腰	チュウごし	half-sitting posture
中座	チュウザ	leaving in the middle of a meeting —***vi***. leave before the meeting is over
中産階級	チュウサンカイキュウ	the middle class
中止	チュウシ	discontinuance; interruption; suspension; stoppage —***v***. discontinue; interrupt; suspend; stop
中旬	チュウジュン	middle ten days of a month
中傷	チュウショウ	slander; libel; malicious gossip —***v***. slander; libel
中心	チュウシン	center; middle; heart; balance
中枢	チュウスウ	pivot; hub; nucleus
中世	チュウセイ	Middle Ages
中性	チュウセイ	neuter
中性子	チュウセイシ	***phy***. neutron
中絶	チュウゼツ	abortion; interruption; suspension; intermission; stoppage —***v***. interrupt; suspend; stop; abort
中退	チュウタイ	dropping out of school
中段	チュウダン	middle of the stairs; middle berth
中断	チュウダン	interruption; discontinuance; suspension —***v***. interrupt; discontinue; suspend
中途	チュウト	halfway; midway; mid-course
中途半端	チュウトハンパ	undone; not complete; unfinished
中東	チュウトウ	Middle East
中道	チュウドウ	halfway; middle of the road
中毒	チュウドク	poisoning; toxication; intoxication —***v***. be poisoned
中二階	チュウニカイ	mezzanine floor

	中肉中背	チュウニク チュウぜい	medium height and build; middle-sized person
	中日	チュウニチ	equinox; China and Japan
	中年	チュウネン	middle age; middle-aged person
	中盤	チュウバン	middle stage/phase
	中腹	チュウフク	heart of the mountain
	中米	チュウベイ	Central America
	中庸	チュウヨウ	moderation; mean; middle
	中立	チュウリツ	neutrality; neutral; independent —***vi***. be neutral/independent
	中立国	チュウリツコク	neutral power/country
	中流	チュウリュウ	midstream; middle class
	中和	チュウワ	neutralization; counteraction —***v***. neutralize; counteract
	お中元	おチュウゲン	*ochūgen* (midyear gift)
訓	中	なか	interior; middle; inside; contents; among; mean
	中入り	なかいり	recess; intermission; interval
	中頃	なかごろ	middle
	中身	なかみ	interior; contents; substance
	中休み	なかやすみ	rest; recess; break
	中指	なかゆび	middle finger
¥	中央銀行	チュウオウ ギンコウ	central bank
	中央集権	チュウオウ シュウケン	centralization of government
	中間決済	チュウカン ケッサイ	semi-annual settlement
	中間配当	チュウカン ハイトウ	interim dividend
	中堅株	チュウケン かぶ	middle-priced stock
	中堅企業	チュウケン キギョウ	medium-sized enterprize
	中小企業	チョウショウ キギョウ	small and medium-sized enterprises

1 丶 てん dot; point

17

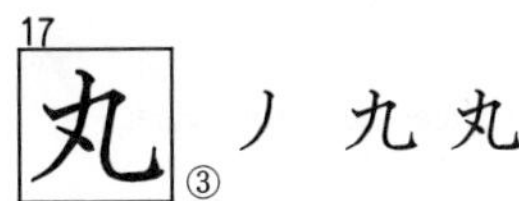

音	丸	ガン	ball; round

熟	丸薬	ガンヤク	pill
訓	丸	まる	ball; circle; whole; castle tower
	丸い	まるい	round; globular; spherical
	丸暗記	まるアンキ	memorize everything just as it is
	丸木舟	まるきぶね	canoe
	丸損	まるゾン	complete loss
	丸太	まるタ	log
	丸出し	まるだし	exposed; uncovered
	丸裸	まるはだか	stark naked
	丸々	まるまる	completely; entirely; wholly
	丸見え	まるみえ	fully exposed to view; in plain sight
	丸め込む	まるめこむ	***vt***. cajole; coax; wheedle
	丸める	まるめる	***vt***. round; shave; make round; make a circle

18

丹 ④ ノ 冂 月 丹

音	丹	タン	red; red lead; cinnabar
熟	丹精	タンセイ	exertion; efforts; labor; work; sincerity —***vi***. exert oneself; apply oneself; work sincerely
	丹前	タンゼン	padded kimono
	丹念	タンネン	elaborate; diligent; careful; laborious

19

主 ⑤ 丶 亠 亍 丰 主

音	主	シュ	master; lord; the Lord; first concern; chief; main; principle
		（ス）	master
熟	主位	シュイ	position of leadership; central position
	主因	シュイン	primary/main cause; main factor
	主演	シュエン	star of a movie or a play
	主客	シュカク（シュキャク）	host and guest; primary and subordinate
	主観	シュカン	subjectivity
	主観的	シュカンテキ	subjective
	主管	シュカン	supervision; superintendence —***v***. supervise; have charge of
	主眼	シュガン	main point; principal objective
	主義	シュギ	principle; doctrine; belief

主君 シュクン one's lord/master
主計 シュケイ accountant; accounting
主権 シュケン sovereignty
主権在民 シュケンザイミン sovereignty rests with the people
主権者 シュケンシャ sovereign; supreme ruler
主語 シュゴ ***gram***. subject
主査 シュサ chief examiner/investigator
主宰 シュサイ superintendence; presidency —***v***. supervise; preside over
主宰者 シュサイシャ leader; chairman
主催 シュサイ sponsorship; promotion —***v***. sponsor; be promoted
主旨 シュシ purport; main point
主事 シュジ director; superintendent
主治医 シュジイ family doctor; attending physician
主従 シュジュウ master and servant; employer and employee
主将 シュショウ captain; supreme commander; commander-in-chief
主唱 シュショウ advocacy —***v***. advocate
主食 シュショク staple/principal food
主審 シュシン chief umpire; referee
主人 シュジン one's husband; head of the family; owner; proprietor
主人公 シュジンコウ hero; heroine; protagonist
主席 シュセキ the Chairman (as used in China-Chairman Mao, etc.)
主体 シュタイ main constituent; subject
主題 シュダイ theme; subject
主張 シュチョウ assertion; insistence; emphasis; advocacy —***v***. assert; insist; emphasize; advocate; lay stress on
主導 シュドウ leadership
主任 シュニン chief; head; manager
主犯 シュハン principal offender; ring leader
主筆 シュヒツ editor-in-chief; chief editor
主賓 シュヒン guest of honor
主婦 シュフ housewife
主部 シュブ main part; subject
主役 シュヤク leading part; starring role; star
主要 シュヨウ principal; chief; main
主流 シュリュウ main current/stream
主力 シュリョク main force

訓 主 おも chief; principal; leading
主 ぬし master; owner

1 丿 の at the top; *no* (katakana)

20 久 ③ ノ ク 久

音 久 キュウ (ク) long; long-standing

熟 久遠 クオン eternity

訓 久しい ひさしい long; long-continued; long time

久し振り ひさしぶり for the first time in a long while; long time no see

21 及 ③ ノ 乃 及

音 及 キュウ catch up with; come level with; reach; attain; amount to; expand; reach; range; extend; spread; diffuse; in addition; together with; including; and

熟 及第 キュウダイ examination pass —***vi***. pass an examination; make the grade

及落 キュウラク examination result; passing and failing

訓 及び および and; as well as

及ぶ およぶ ***vi***. reach; attain to; amount to; come up to (standard); match; equal; be a match for

及ぼす およぼす ***vt***. exercise (influence upon); cause (harm)

22 屯 ④ 一 ㇗ 㐅 屯

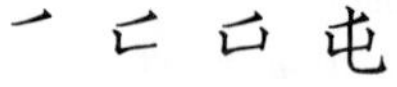

音 屯 トン station

熟 屯田兵 トンデンヘイ colonial troops; colonial soldier

23 乏 ④ ノ ㇒ 乏 乏

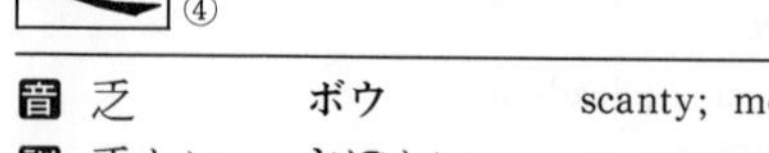

音 乏 ボウ scanty; meager; scarce

訓 乏しい とぼしい scanty; meager; scarce

24

乗 ⑨

音	乗	ジョウ	get on; ride; multiply
熟	乗じる	ジョウじる	*v*. take advantage of (weakness, darkness, etc.); multiply
	乗員	ジョウイン	crew; crew member
	乗客	ジョウキャク	passenger
	乗降	ジョウコウ	getting on and off —***vi***. get on and off
	乗車	ジョウシャ	taking a train/taxi —***vi***. take a train/taxi
	乗車賃	ジョウシャチン	fare; busfare; trainfare
	乗除	ジョウジョ	multiplication and division —***v***. multiply and divide
	乗数	ジョウスウ	***math***. multiplier
	乗船	ジョウセン	boarding ship; embarkation —***vi***. get on; board; embark
	乗馬	ジョウバ	riding; horseback riding —***vi***. ride/mount a horse
	乗法	ジョウホウ	***math***. multiplication
	乗務員	ジョウムイン	train crew; crew member
訓	乗る	のる	***vi***. get/step onto; take; board; mount; ride
	乗せる	のせる	***vt***. help a person get on; give a person a lift; take someone in
	乗り合い	のりあい	riding together; fellow passanger partnership
	乗り換える	のりかえる	***vi***. transfer/change/switch (trains, buses, etc.)
	乗り気	のりキ	interest; enthusiasm
	乗り切る	のりきる	***vi***. ride out; weather; survive
	乗組員	のりくみイン	crew
	乗り越える	のりこえる	***vt***. climb over; overcome
	乗り越す	のりこす	***vt***. go past one's destination
	乗り手	のりて	rider; passenger
	乗り場	のりば	stop; place to get on
	乗り物	のりもの	vehicle; vessel; aircraft; ride (at an amusement park)
¥	乗っ取り	のっとり	buyout; takeover
	乗換え	のりかえ	carrying-over; continuation; refunding
	乗換取引	のりかえとりひき	swap; changeover

1 乙 おつ second

25

乙 ① 乙

音	乙	オツ	grade B; the second in a series
熟	※乙女	おとめ	maiden; girl; virgin

26

九 ② ノ 九

音	九	キュウ	nine
		ク	nine
熟	九官鳥	キュウカンチョウ	myna bird; hill myna
	九死	キュウシ	narrowly escape death
	九月	クガツ	September
	九九	クク	***math***. multiplication table
訓	九つ	ここのつ	nine
	九日	ここのか	ninth day (of the month); 9th

27

乾 ⑪ 一 十 𠂇 古 吉 吉 直 卓 𠦝 𠦝 乾

音	乾	カン	dry
熟	乾性	カンセイ	dryness
	乾燥	カンソウ	dryness; aridity —***v***. dry; dehydrate; become dry/parched
	乾電池	カンデンチ	dry cell/battery
	乾杯	カンパイ	toast; cheers —***vi***. drink a toast
	乾物	カンブツ	dried goods/foods
	乾布摩擦	カンプマサツ	having a rubdown with a dry towel
訓	乾く	かわく	***vi***. dry up; run dry; be parched
	乾かす	かわかす	***vt***. dry; dessicate; weather
	※乾す	ほす	***vt***. dry; dry up; drink up

1 乚 つりばり fishhook

28

乱 ⑦

音	乱	ラン	disorder; riot; rebellion
熟	乱交	ランコウ	orgy
	乱雑	ランザツ	disorder; confusion
	乱視	ランシ	astigmatism
	乱射	ランシャ	random shooting —***vi***. fire/shoot at random
	乱心	ランシン	derangement; insanity —***vi***. become mentally deranged/insane
	乱世	ランセ	tumultuous times
	乱戦	ランセン	confused/free-for-all fight
	乱造	ランゾウ	overproduction; careless manufacture —***v***. overproduce
	乱丁	ランチョウ	mixed-up collation
	乱闘	ラントウ	free-for-all fight —***vi***. have a free-for-all fight
	乱読	ランドク	indiscriminate reading —***v***. read indiscriminately
	乱入	ランニュウ	intrusion; trespassing (in large numbers) —***vi***. intrude/trespass (in large numbers)
	乱売	ランバイ	dumping/selling at a loss —***v***. dump/sell at a loss
	乱筆	ランピツ	hasty writing; scrawl
	乱暴	ランボウ	violence; rough; reckless —***vi***. be violent/rough/reckless
	乱脈	ランミャク	confusion; chaos
	乱用	ランヨウ	abuse; misuse; misappropriation —***v***. abuse; misuse; missappropriate
	乱立	ランリツ	profusion —***vi***. profuse; flood
訓	乱れる	みだれる	***vi***. be in disorder; be confused/disorganized
	乱す	みだす	***vt***. put in disorder
¥	乱高下	ランコウゲ	violent fluctuations; jumps and slumps —***v***. fluctuate violently

29

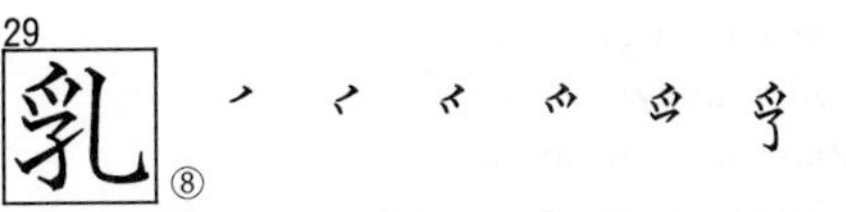

乳 ⑧

音	乳	ニュウ	milk
熟	乳牛	ニュウギュウ	cow in milk; dairy cow

	乳剤	ニュウザイ	emulsion
	乳酸	ニュウサン	lactic acid
	乳酸菌	ニュウサンキン	lactic acid bacilli
	乳歯	ニュウシ	milk tooth
	乳児	ニュウジ	baby; infant; suckling
	乳製品	ニュウセイヒン	dairy product
	乳頭	ニュウトウ	nipple; teat
	乳幼児	ニュウヨウジ	infants
訓	乳	ちち	mother's milk; breast
	乳	ち	milk
	乳首	ちくび	nipple; teat
	乳飲み子	ちのみご	unweaned baby; suckling child
	乳房	ちぶさ	breasts; udder
	※乳母	うば	nurse; wet nurse; nanny

---

1 亅 はねぼう feathered stick; hook; barb

30

⑧ 一 〒 〒 亖 亖 亖 亖 事

音	事	ジ (ズ)	matter; work
熟	事業	ジギョウ	work; undertaking; business; enterprise
	事件	ジケン	event; happening; incident; matter; affair
	事故	ジコ	accident; mishap; hitch; incident
	事後	ジゴ	after the event/fact
	事後承諾	ジゴショウダク	*ex post facto* approval
	事項	ジコウ	matters; facts; data
	事実	ジジツ	fact; the truth; actually; really; as a matter of fact
	事実無根	ジジツムコン	groundless; false; unfounded
	事情	ジジョウ	reasons; circumstances; the situation; the case; conditions
	事前	ジゼン	beforehand; in advance
	事前調査	ジゼンチョウサ	feasibility study
	事態	ジタイ	situation; state of affairs
	事大主義	ジダイシュギ	submission to power; toadyism
	事典	ジテン	encyclopedia
	事物	ジブツ	things

	事変	ジヘン	incident; disturbance
	事務	ジム	office/clerical work; business
	事務員	ジムイン	clerk
	事務所	ジムショ	office
	事務的	ジムテキ	clerical; businesslike
	事由	ジユウ	reason; cause
訓	事	こと	thing; matter; incident; circumstances; work
	事柄	ことがら	matter; affair; circumstances
	事毎	ことごと	everything; always
¥	事業家	ジギョウカ	entrepreneur; businessman
	事業債	ジギョウサイ	industrial bond
	事業税	ジギョウゼイ	business tax
	事業年度	ジギョウネンド	business year
	事業費	ジギョウヒ	business expenses

2 二 に two

31

二 ② 一 二

音	二	ニ	two; twice; again; next; (prefix) bi-
熟	二回	ニカイ	twice; two times; again
	二階	ニカイ	second floor; upstairs
	二月	ニガツ	February
	二級	ニキュウ	second-class
	二元	ニゲン	duality
	二号	ニゴウ	number two; concubine; mistress
	二言	ニゴン	duplicity; double-dealing; say something twice
	二次	ニジ	second (time)
	二次試験	ニジシケン	secondary examination
	二次的	ニジテキ	secondary
	二重	ニジュウ	duplicated; double
	二重人格	ニジュウジンカク	dual personality
	二乗	ニジョウ	***math***. square of a number —***v***. square (a number)
	二世	ニセイ	second generation; second generation of Japanese immigrants
	二足	ニソク	two legs/feet/pairs
	二束三文	ニソクサンモン	dirt-cheap
	二兎	ニト	two hares/rabbits
	二度	ニド	twice; two times
	二等	ニトウ	second-class/rate
	二等分	ニトウブン	bisection —***v***. bisect
	二の次	ニのつぎ	secondary importance
	二の舞	ニのまい	same mistake
	二倍	ニバイ	double; twice; two-fold; as much again
	二番	ニバン	second; number two; runner-up
	二百十日	ニヒャクとうか	210th day; first day of spring
	二部	ニブ	two parts/copies
	二分	ニブン	division into two parts; bisection —***v***. divide into two parts; halve; bisect
	二枚	ニマイ	two leaves/sheets
	二枚舌	ニマイじた	double-tongued; duplicity; equivocation
	二毛作	ニモウサク	two crops a year; double cropping
	二流	ニリュウ	second-rate

	二輪	ニリン	two wheels/flowers
	二輪車	ニリンシャ	two-wheeled vehicle; bicycle
訓	二つ	ふたつ	two
	二	ふた	(prefix) two; bi-; double
	二重	ふたえ	fold; two-layered; double
	二心	ふたごころ	duplicity; double-dealing; treachery
	二葉	ふたば	seed leaf; bud; sprout
	二股	ふたまた	fork; branch; parting
	※二十	はたち	twenty years old
	※二十歳	はたち	twenty years old
	※二十日	はつか	twentieth day (of the month); 20th
	※二人	ふたり	two people; couple; we two; you two
	※二日	ふつか	second day (of the month); 2nd

32

五 ④ 一 丆 万 五

音	五	ゴ	five
熟	五月	ゴガツ	May
	五感	ゴカン	the five senses
	五色	ゴシキ	the five colors (blue, red, yellow, white, and black)
	五十音図	ゴジュウオンズ	***gram.*** systematic table of the fifty sounds of the Japanese language
	五体満足	ゴタイマンゾク	person who is without any physical defect
	五分	ゴブ	five percent; half
	五分五分	ゴブゴブ	fifty-fifty
	五輪大会	ゴリンタイカイ	Olympic games
訓	五つ	いつつ	five
	五	いつ	five
	※五月晴れ	さつきばれ	clearing up/clear sky (in May); lull in the early summer rain
	※五月雨	さみだれ	early summer rain

33

互 ④ 一 工 互 互

音	互	ゴ	each other; mutual
熟	互角	ゴカク	equality; equal; balanced
	互助	ゴジョ	mutual aid/help —***vi.*** aid/help mutually

	互選	ゴセン	election by mutual vote —*v*. elect by mutual vote
訓	互い	たがい	each other; mutual
	互い違い	たがいちがい	alternately

34

井 ④

音	井	セイ （ショウ）	well
訓	井	い	well
	井戸	いど	well

35

亜 ⑦

音	亜	ア	（prefix） sub-; Asia
熟	亜鉛	アエン	zinc
	亜種	アシュ	subspecies
	亜熱帯	アネッタイ	subtropical zones
	亜流	アリュウ	follower; adherent; epigone

36

来 ⑦

音	来	ライ	come; next; since
熟	来意	ライイ	purpose of one's visit
	来客	ライキャク	visitor; caller
	来月	ライゲツ	next month
	来校	ライコウ	coming to school —*vi*. come to school
	来航	ライコウ	arrival of ships/by ships —*vi*. arrive by ship
	来襲	ライシュウ	attack; invasion; raid —*vi*. attack; invade; raid
	来週	ライシュウ	next week
	来春	ライシュン	next spring
	来場	ライジョウ	attendance —*vi*. attend; be in attendance
	来信	ライシン	received letter
	来診	ライシン	doctor's visit; house call —*vi*. make a house call
	来世	ライセ	afterlife; next world

	来朝	ライチョウ	***clas.*** visit/arrival in Japan —***v.*** visit/arrive in Japan
	来店	ライテン	visit to a store/shop —***vi.*** visit a store/shop
	来日	ライニチ	coming to Japan —***vi.*** come to Japan
	来年	ライネン	next year
	来賓	ライヒン	guest; visitor
	来訪	ライホウ	visit; call —***vi.*** come visiting/calling
訓	来る	くる	come
	来る	きたる	***vi.*** come; be forth coming
	来す	きたす	***vt.*** cause/bring about (unpleasant circumstamces)

---

2 亠 なべぶた kettle lid

37

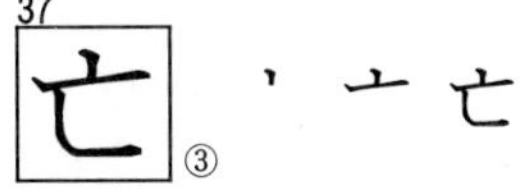

③

音	亡	ボウ (モウ)	dead
熟	亡君	ボウクン	one's deceased lord
	亡兄	ボウケイ	one's late elder brother
	亡国	ボウコク	ruined country; destruction/ruination (of a country)
	亡妻	ボウサイ	one's late wife
	亡失	ボウシツ	loss —***v.*** lose; be lost
	亡夫	ボウフ	one's late husband
	亡父	ボウフ	one's late father
	亡母	ボウボ	one's late mother
	亡命	ボウメイ	escaping one's native country for political reasons; defecting —***vi.*** flee one's country; defect
	亡命者	ボウメイシャ	exile; émigré; refugee; defector
	亡霊	ボウレイ	ghost; soul of a dead person
	亡者	モウジャ	ghost; the dead
訓	亡びる	ほろびる	***vi.*** perish; come to ruin
	亡ぼす	ほろぼす	***vt.*** destroy; bring to ruin
	亡い	ない	the late/deceased
	亡き	なき	the late/deceased
	亡骸	なきがら	corpse; dead body
	亡くなる	なくなる	***vi.*** die; pass away

38

交 ⑥ 丶 亠 亠 六 交 交

音	交	コウ	intercourse; exchange; cross; mix
熟	交易	コウエキ	trade; commerce; barter —*v*. trade; exchange; barter
	交換	コウカン	exchange; interchange; give and take; substitution —*v*. exchange; reciprocate; substitute
	交互	コウゴ	alternation; interaction
	交差	コウサ	crossing; point of intersection —*v*. cross; intersect
	交差点	コウサテン	crossing; intersection; junction
	交際	コウサイ	intercourse; association; society; company; fellowship —***vi***. associate/fraternize with; keep company with
	交錯	コウサク	mixture; blending; complexity; intricacy —***vi***. mingle with; be complicated/intricate
	交渉	コウショウ	negotiation; bargaining; relationship —***vi***. negotiate; bargain; discuss; have a relationship
	交戦	コウセン	war; hostilities; combat; action —***vi***. fight; engage in hostilities/combat
	交替	コウタイ	relief; change; shift —***vi***. take turns; alternate; rotate; relieve
	交通	コウツウ	traffic; communication; transportation; navigation
	交通機関	コウツウキカン	transit system
	交通費	コウツウヒ	traveling expenses; fare
	交配	コウハイ	crossbreeding; hybridization; crossfertilization —*v*. hybridize; cross; crossbreed; interbreed
	交番	コウバン	police box
	交付	コウフ	delivery; grant; transfer; service —*v*. deliver; grant; transfer; service
	交友	コウユウ	friend; aquaintance
	交遊	コウユウ	companionship; friendship —***vi***. associate with; keep company with
	交流	コウリュウ	alternating current (AC); interchange
訓	交わす	かわす	***vt***. exchange; cross; intersect
	交う	かう	(suffix) cross; intersect
	交ざる	まざる	***vi***. mix; mingle; blend
	交える	まじえる	***vt***. mix; cross; exchange
	交じる	まじる	***vi***. be mixed/mingled/blended; mix; mingle; join

交わる	まじわる	***vi***. associate with; keep company with; cross; intersect; join
交ぜる	まぜる	***vt***. blend; mix; include

39
京 ⑧

音	京	キョウ	capital; metropolis; Kyoto; Tokyo; ten quadrillion
		ケイ	
熟	京風	キョウフウ	Kyoto-style (food)
訓	京	みやこ	capital; metropolis

40
享 ⑧

音	享	キョウ	receive; accept; possess; enjoy
熟	享受	キョウジュ	enjoyment of artistic beauty —***v***. enjoy; have; be given
	享年	キョウネン	age when one dies; length of one's life
	享楽	キョウラク	enjoyment —***v***. enjoy
	享楽主義	キョウラクシュギ	epicurism; hedonism

41
亭 ⑨

音	亭	テイ	inn; restaurant; arbor
熟	亭主	テイシュ	master; host; landlord; innkeeper; one's husband

2 人 ひと man

42
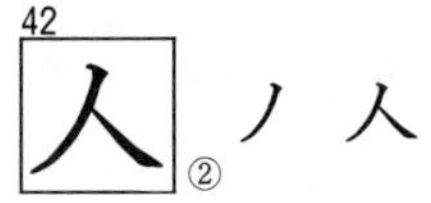

人 ②

音	人	ジン	man
		ニン	man; character

熟

人為	ジンイ	act of man
人為的	ジンイテキ	artificial
人員	ジンイン	number of persons; staff; personnel
人家	ジンカ	house; dwelling
人格	ジンカク	personality; character
人格化	ジンカクカ	personification —*v*. personify
人絹	ジンケン	rayon; artificial silk
人権	ジンケン	human rights
人権宣言	ジンケンセンゲン	Declaration of Human Rights
人件費	ジンケンヒ	personnel expenses
人後	ジンゴ	next person
人工	ジンコウ	artificial; man-made
人工衛星	ジンコウエイセイ	artificial satelite
人工栄養	ジンコウエイヨウ	bottle feeding
人工呼吸	ジンコウコキュウ	artificial respiration; mouth-to-mouth resuscitation —***vi***. give mouth-to-mouth resuscitation
人工受精	ジンコウジュセイ	artificial insemination —***vi***. be artificially inseminated
人工知能	ジンコウチノウ	artificial intelligence
人工的	ジンコウテキ	artificial; man-made
人口	ジンコウ	population
人口密度	ジンコウミツド	population density
人災	ジンサイ	disaster caused by human error
人材	ジンザイ	talent; ability
人士	ジンシ	man of good breeding; gentleman
人事	ジンジ	personnel affairs
人事不省	ジンジフセイ	unconscious; fainting; coma
人種	ジンシュ	race; ethnic group
人種差別	ジンシュサベツ	racial discrimination —***vi***. discriminate on the basis of race
人種的偏見	ジンシュテキヘンケン	racial prejudice
人心	ジンシン	the people's mind; public feeling
人生	ジンセイ	life
人生観	ジンセイカン	view of life; outlook on life
人跡	ジンセキ	human traces
人跡未踏	ジンセキミトウ	unexplored; untrodden
人選	ジンセン	selection of a suitable person —***vi***. select a suitable person
人造	ジンゾウ	artificial; manmade; imitation; synthetic
人造繊維	ジンゾウセンイ	synthetic fiber
人造人間	ジンゾウニンゲン	robot
人造皮革	ジンゾウヒカク	artificial leather

	人体	ジンタイ	human body
	人知	ジンチ	human intelligence/knowledge/understanding
	人畜	ジンチク	man and beast; human or animal
	人的	ジンテキ	human
	人道	ジンドウ	humanity
	人道主義	ジンドウシュギ	humanitarianism
	人道的	ジンドウテキ	humane
	人頭税	ジントウゼイ	poll tax
	人徳	ジントク	natural virtue
	人品	ジンピン	character; personality; appearance
	人物	ジンブツ	character; person; figure
	人物画	ジンブツガ	portrait
	人物画家	ジンブツガカ	portrait painter
	人望	ジンボウ	popularity
	人民	ジンミン	the people/citizens
	人名	ジンメイ	person's name
	人命	ジンメイ	human life; people's lives
	人力車	ジンリキシャ	rickshaw
	人力	ジンリョク	human power/strength
	人類	ジンルイ	human race; mankind; humanity
	人類学	ジンルイガク	anthropology
	人気	ニンキ	popularity
	人気歌手	ニンキカシュ	pop singer/idol
	人気作家	ニンキサッカ	popular writer
	人魚	ニンギョ	mermaid
	人形	ニンギョウ	doll; puppet
	人間	ニンゲン	man; human being; mankind
	人間衛星	ニンゲンエイセイ	manned satellite
	人間関係	ニンゲンカンケイ	human relations
	人間国宝	ニンゲンコクホウ	living national treasure
	人間性	ニンゲンセイ	humanity
	人間味	ニンゲンミ	warm-hearted
	人情	ニンジョウ	humaneness; human feelings
	人参	ニンジン	carrot
	人数	ニンズウ	number of persons
	人相	ニンソウ	looks; physiognomy
	人足	ニンソク	***derog***. laborer; navvy [derogatory]
	人夫	ニンプ	***derog***. laborer; navvy [derogatory]
訓	人	ひと	man; person; people
	人影	ひとかげ	figure; form; shadow
	人柄	ひとがら	person; character; type/kind/sort (of person)

	人気	ひとけ	sign/presense of people
	人事	ひとごと	other people's affairs
	人殺し	ひとごろし	murder —*v.* murder
	人里	ひとざと	village; human dwellings
	人質	ひとジチ	hostage
	人手	ひとで	help; hand
	人出	ひとで	crowds; crowded
	人並み	ひとなみ	ordinary; commonplace; average
	人波	ひとなみ	surging crowd
	人々	ひとびと	people; each person
	人前	ひとまえ	in public; in the prescence of others
	人任せ	ひとまかせ	leaving (work) to someone else
	人見知り	ひとみしり	bashful/shy (in front of strangers)
	人目	ひとめ	notice; attention
¥	人為相場	ジンイソウバ	artificial price; manipulated quotation
	人員整理	ジンインセイリ	personnel cut/reduction
	人件費	ジンケンヒ	personnel expenses; labor cost
	人材銀行	ジンザイギンコウ	talent bank
	人気株	ニンキかぶ	active stock

43

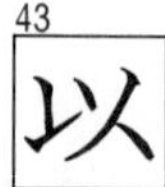

⑤ 丶 𠄌 𠄌丶 𠂎 以

音	以	イ	by; since; with
熟	以遠	イエン	beyond; farther
	以下	イカ	less than; below; not more than
	以外	イガイ	except; outside of; excluding; besides
	以後	イゴ	after this; from now on; hereafter; henceforth; since
	以降	イコウ	from that time; from now on
	以上	イジョウ	not less than; or more; and over; more than
	以心伝心	イシンデンシン	communion of mind with mind; telepathy; empathy
	以前	イゼン	formerly; before
	以内	イナイ	within; less than; not more than
	以来	イライ	since then; from that time on; ever since
訓	以て	もって	by means of
	以ての外	もってのほか	outrageous; preposterous; scandalous

2 𠆢 やね roof

44

介 ④ ノ 𠆢 介 介

音	介	**カイ**	mediate; interpose
熟	介する	**カイする**	***vt***. help; support; aid
	介在	**カイザイ**	interposition —***vi***. interpose; lie between
	介入	**カイニュウ**	intervention —***vi***. intervene
	介抱	**カイホウ**	nursing; care —***v***. nurse/care for

45

今 ④ ノ 入 𠆢 今

音	今	**キン**	present
		コン	now; this time
熟	今回	**コンカイ**	lately; this time
	今月	**コンゲツ**	this month
	今後	**コンゴ**	after this; henceforth; hereafter
	今昔	**コンジャク**	past and present
	今週	**コンシュウ**	this week
	今度	**コンド**	this/next time
	今日	**コンニチ**	today
	今晩	**コンバン**	this evening
訓	今	いま	now
	※今日	きょう	today
	※今朝	けさ	this morning
	※今年	ことし	this year

46

令 ⑤ ノ 入 𠆢 今 令

音	令	**レイ**	rule; order; command (honorific prefix)
熟	令室	**レイシツ**	***hon***. your wife
	令状	**レイジョウ**	warrant; writ
	令嬢	**レイジョウ**	***hon***. your daughter
	令息	**レイソク**	***hon***. your son

	令夫人	レイフジン	***hon***. Mrs.; Lady; Madam; your wife

47

会 ⑥ ノ 人 亼 亼 会 会

音	会	エ	meet; memorial service
		カイ	meet; meeting; society
熟	会釈	エシャク	bow; greeting —***vi***. bow; greet
	会得	エトク	comprehension; understanding —***v***. comprehend; understand
	会員	カイイン	member; membership
	会館	カイカン	hall; assembly hall
	会議	カイギ	conference; meeting —***vi***. have a conference/meeting
	会合	カイゴウ	meeting; gathering; assembly —***vi***. meet; gather; assemble
	会社	カイシャ	company; corporation
	会食	カイショク	dining together —***vi***. dine together
	会則	カイソク	rules of an association
	会談	カイダン	talk; conference; conversation —***vi***. talk together; have a conference
	会報	カイホウ	bulletin; report
	会話	カイワ	conversation; talk —***vi***. converse; talk
訓	会う	あう	***vi***. meet
¥	会期	カイキ	session/period (of a meeting)
	会計	カイケイ	accounts; finance; bill; accounting —***v***. settle accounts; pay bills
	会計監査	カイケイカンサ	accounting audit
	会計帳簿	カイケイチョウボ	book of accounts
	会計年度	カイケイネンド	fiscal year
	会社法	カイシャホウ	company law
	会頭	カイトウ	president (of a society, etc.)

48

企 ⑥ ノ 人 个 仐 企 企

音	企	キ	plan; plot
熟	企画	キカク	plan; planning —***v***. plan
	企図	キト	plan; project; design; attempt —***v***. plan; design; attempt
訓	企て	くわだて	plan; scheme; project

企てる　くわだてる　*vt*. plan; scheme; design; attempt; try; undertake

¥ 企業　キギョウ　enterprise

49
全 ⑥
ノ 𠆢 亼 仐 仝 全

音 全　ゼン　all; complete

熟 全域　ゼンイキ　the whole area

全員　ゼンイン　all the members; the whole staff/crew

全快　ゼンカイ　full recovery —***vi***. recover fully

全壊　ゼンカイ　complete destruction —***vi***. be completely destroyed

全額　ゼンガク　sum total

全権　ゼンケン　full authority

全校　ゼンコウ　whole school; all the schools

全国　ゼンコク　the whole country; nationwide; national

全集　ゼンシュウ　complete/collected works

全書　ゼンショ　complete book; compendium

全焼　ゼンショウ　total destruction by fire —***vi***. be totally destroyed by fire

全勝　ゼンショウ　complete victory —***vi***. win a complete victory

全身　ゼンシン　the whole body

全盛　ゼンセイ　prime; height of prosperity

全盛期　ゼンセイキ　one's prime period

全然　ゼンゼン　utterly; entirely; not at all

全速力　ゼンソクリョク　full speed; top speed

全体　ゼンタイ　the whole; in all

全治　ゼンチ　complete cure —***vi***. fully recover; heal completely

全長　ゼンチョウ　overall length

全土　ゼンド　the whole country

全敗　ゼンパイ　complete defeat —***vi***. be/defeated completely

全廃　ゼンパイ　total abolition —***v***. be totally abolished

全般　ゼンパン　whole; general; overall

全部　ゼンブ　all; whole; entirely

全文　ゼンブン　full text; whole sentence

全貌　ゼンボウ　the whole thing

全滅　ゼンメツ　annihilation; extermination; destruction —***v***. annihilate; exterminate; destroy

全面的　ゼンメンテキ　full; general

	全訳	ゼンヤク	complete/unabridged translation —*v*. make a complete and unabridged translation
	全容	ゼンヨウ	full story/picture
	全力	ゼンリョク	all one's power; one's every effort; full capacity
訓	全うする	まっとうする	***vt***. accomplish; fulfil
	全く	まったく	entirely; completely; truly; indeed

50

余 ⑦ ノ 𠆢 亼 今 쇠 余 余

音	余	ヨ	remainder; the rest; other; more than; myself; I
熟	余韻	ヨイン	trailing note; reverberation; aftertaste
	余暇	ヨカ	leisure; spare time
	余技	ヨギ	hobby; avocation
	余儀なく	ヨギなく	unavoidable; obliged to
	余興	ヨキョウ	entertainment; side show
	余計	ヨケイ	unnecessary; more than enough; extra; uncalled for
	余罪	ヨザイ	other crimes
	余剰	ヨジョウ	surplus
	余震	ヨシン	aftershock (of an earthquake)
	余人	ヨジン	other people; others
	余生	ヨセイ	the rest of one's life
	余勢	ヨセイ	surplus energy
	余談	ヨダン	digression
	余地	ヨチ	room; place; margin; scope
	余熱	ヨネツ	lingering summer heat
	余念	ヨネン	thinking of other matters
	余波	ヨハ	after/secondary effects; consequences
	余白	ヨハク	blank; space; margin
	余病	ヨビョウ	complications; secondary disease
	余分	ヨブン	extra; excess
	余程	ヨほど	very; much; to a great degree
	余命	ヨメイ	the rest of one's life
	余裕	ヨユウ	surplus; leeway; room; margin
	余力	ヨリョク	remaining strength; surplus energy
訓	余る	あまる	***vi***. remain; be more than enough; exceed
	余り	あまり	remainder; surplus; more than; very; as a result of

	余す	あます	*vt.* leave; save
¥	余財	ヨザイ	spare cash; surplus assets

51

舎 ⑧

音	舎	シャ	inn; building
熟	舎監	シャカン	dormitory superintendent
	舎利	シャリ	***Bud.*** one's remains/ashes; rice (in sushi bar)

52

倉 ⑩

音	倉	ソウ	warehouse; storehouse
熟	倉庫	ソウコ	warehouse
訓	倉	くら	warehouse; storehouse
	倉敷	くらしき	storage place
	倉主	くらぬし	warehouse owner

53

傘 ⑫

音	傘	サン	umbrella
熟	傘下	サンカ	under the umbrella; affiliated; subsidary
訓	傘	かさ	umbrella

54

舗 ⑮

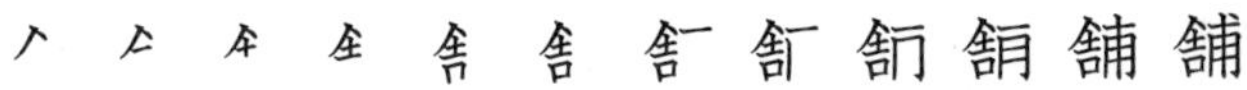

音	舗	ホ	shop; store
熟	舗装	ホソウ	pavement; paving —*v.* pave (a road, street, etc.)
	舗道	ホドウ	pavement; paved street

2 亻 にんべん man to the left

55

化 ノ イ イ' 化 ④

音	化	カ	transform; change
		ケ	die; civilize; change
熟	化学	カガク	chemistry
	化合	カゴウ	***chem***. chemical combination; compound —***vi***. combine to make a compound out of two or more elements
	化石	カセキ	fossil
	化繊	カセン	synthetic fiber
	化膿	カノウ	***med***. festering; suppuration; discharge of pus —***vi***. fester; suppurate; generate pus
	化粧	ケショウ	cosmetic makeup; toiletries (make up; put on make up)
	化粧室	ケショウシツ	toilet; lavatory
	化粧品	ケショウヒン	makeup; cosmetics
	化身	ケシン	incarnation/manifestation of a god or buddha; reincarnation
訓	化ける	ばける	***vi***. transform; disguise oneself
	化かす	ばかす	***vt***. bewitch; enchant; deceive
	化けの皮	ばけのかわ	disguise
	化け物	ばけもの	apparition; goblin; monster

56

仁 ノ イ 仁 仁 ④

音	仁	ジン	compassion
		(ニ)	
熟	仁愛	ジンアイ	benevolence
	仁義	ジンギ	humanity and justice; duty; respect
	仁術	ジンジュツ	benevolent act; caring profession; art of healing
	仁徳	ジントク	benevolence
	仁王	ニオウ	the two Deva kings

57

仏 ④

ノ イ 仏 仏

音	仏	フツ	France; French
		ブツ	Buddha; Buddhism
熟	仏閣	ブッカク	Buddhist temple
	仏教	ブッキョウ	Buddhism
	仏具	ブツグ	Buddhist altar articles
	仏寺	ブツジ	Buddhist temple
	仏事	ブツジ	Buddhist memorial service
	仏式	ブッシキ	Buddhist rite
	仏舎利	ブッシャリ	Buddha's ashes
	仏心	ブッシン	Buddha's heart/character
	仏前	ブツゼン	before/in front of Buddha/the tablet of the deceased; Buddhist altar offerings
	仏像	ブツゾウ	Buddhist image
	仏陀	ブツダ	Buddha
	仏壇	ブツダン	household Buddhist altar
	仏頂面	ブッチョウづら	sour face; pout; scowl
	仏典	ブッテン	Buddist scripture/literature
	仏殿	ブツデン	Buddhist temple
	仏道	ブツドウ	Buddhism
	仏法	ブッポウ	Buddhism
	仏法僧	ブッポウソウ	Buddha, doctrine, and priesthood; broad-billed roller; Japanese scops owl
	仏間	ブツマ	Buddhist altar room
	仏滅	ブツメツ	Buddha's death ***fig***. unlucky day (on the Japanese calendar)
	仏門	ブツモン	Buddhism; Buddhist priesthood
	※仏蘭西	フランス	France
訓	仏	ほとけ	Buddha; Buddhist image; the dead
	仏心	ほとけごころ	merciful; kindhearted (like Buddha)
	仏様	ほとけさま	Buddha; dead person

58

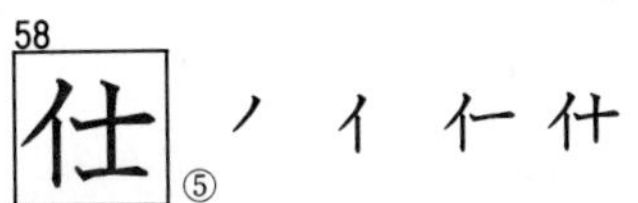

音	仕	シ	serve; work; to do
		ジ	
熟	仕上げる	シあげる	***vt***. finish; complete

	仕打ち	シうち	treatment; behavior; action; conduct
	仕送り	シおくり	allowance; remittance —*v*. send/remit money; make an al lowance
	仕返し	シかえし	revenge; retaliation —*vi*. avenge oneself; retaliate
	仕掛ける	シかける	*vt*. start; begin; set up; prepare; challenge
	仕官	シカン	government service —*vi*. enter government service
	仕切り	シきり	dividing line; boundary; partition
	仕草	シぐさ	behavior; acting; gestures
	仕事	シごと	occupation; work; job; business
	仕込む	シこむ	*vt*. train; teach; stock up
	仕立て	シたて	tailoring
	仕立てる	シたてる	*vt*. sew; tailor; prepare; train
	仕舞う	シまう	*vt*. put away; put back; close; close down; finish
訓	仕える	つかえる	*vi*. serve; work under; be clogged/blocked
¥	仕入れ	シいれ	purchase; stocking
	仕掛かり品	シかかりヒン	work in process
	仕切り	シきり	transaction on dealer's basis
	仕組み	シくみ	set up; structure; mechanism
	仕手	シて	speculator
	仕手株	シてかぶ	speculative leaders

59

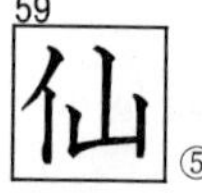

ノ 亻 亻 仙 仙

音	仙	セン	hermit; wizard
熟	仙人	センニン	hermit; wizard

60

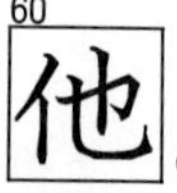

ノ 亻 仁 他 他

音	他	タ	other; another; outside; different
熟	他意	タイ	another intention; ulterior motive; secret purpose
	他界	タカイ	death; demise; the other world; another world —*vi*. die; pass away
	他国	タコク	strange land; foreign country; another province
	他言	タゴン	disclosure —*v*. divulge; reveal; let out; disclose
	他殺	タサツ	murder; homicide; manslaughter

	他薦	タセン	recommendation by another person —*v*. be recommended by another person
	他人	タニン	another person; others; unrelated person; outsider; third party; stranger
	他方	タホウ	the other hand/side; another side/place
	他面	タメン	the other/another side
	他力本願	タリキホンガン	salvation through faith in the Amida Buddha
訓	他	ほか	other; another
¥	他人資本	タニンシホン	borrowed capital

61

代 ⑤ ノ イ 仁 代 代

音	代	タイ	
		ダイ	substitution; proxy; reign; era
熟	代案	ダイアン	alternative plan
	代議員	ダイギイン	representative; delegate
	代議士	ダイギシ	congressman; dietman; member of Parliament
	代償	ダイショウ	compensation; indemnification —*v*. compensate; indemnify
	代数	ダイスウ	***math***. algebra
	代打	ダイダ	***bas***. pinch hitter —***vi***. pinch hit
	代々	ダイダイ	from generation to generation
	代読	ダイドク	reading by proxy —*v*. read by proxy; read on behalf of someone else
	代筆	ダイヒツ	writing by proxy —*v*. write on behalf of someone else
	代表	ダイヒョウ	representative; delegation; deputation —*v*. represent; be representative of; stand/act for
	代表的	ダイヒョウテキ	representative; typical
	代弁	ダイベン	speaking by proxy; agency; commission; payment by proxy —*v*. speak/pay by proxy
	代名詞	ダイメイシ	***gram***. pronoun
	代役	ダイヤク	substitution; substitute; understudy
	代用	ダイヨウ	substitution —*v*. substitute
	代理	ダイリ	representation; agency; proxy —*v*. act for; represent; deputy
訓	代える	かえる	***vt***. change; alter; convert; renew; reform
	代わる	かわる	***vi***. take the place of; replace; be substituted
	代わり	かわり	substitute; deputy; alternative; compensation
	代	よ	the world; society; age; era; rule; reign
¥	代価	ダイカ	price; cost

代金	ダイキン	price; cost; charge; bill; fee
代行	ダイコウ	proxy —*v*. carry out as proxy; act for another
代表者	ダイヒョウシャ	representative; delegate
代表団	ダイヒョウダン	delegation
代理店	ダイリテン	agency; agent

62

付 ⑤ ノ イ 仁 付 付

音	付	フ	attach
熟	付する	フする	***vt***. add; attach; wear; apply; use; refer to
	付加	フカ	addition; annexation; supplement; appendix —*v*. add; annex; supplement; append
	付記	フキ	written addition; additional/supplementary (written) remark —*v*. add in writing; append
	付近	フキン	neighborhood; vicinity; environs
	付随	フズイ	annex; accompanied —***vi***. be annexed; accompany; go with; follow; attend
	付箋	フセン	memo tag; slip
	付属	フゾク	belonging to; adjunctive; incidental; subsidiary; branch school —***vi***. be attached/belong to
	付着	フチャク	adherence; sticking; adhesion; cohesion —***vi***. adhere to; stick; attach
	付与	フヨ	grant; bestowal; allowance —*v*. give; grant; allow; bestow
	付録	フロク	supplement in a book/magazine; appendix
	付和雷同	フワライドウ	blind following —***vi***. follow blindly/suit
訓	付く	つく	***vi***. stick; adhere; touch; reach; come; set; be dyed/colored; be decided
	付き合う	つきあう	***vi***. accompany; socialize; go out together
	付き添う	つきそう	***vi***. accompany; be with
	付ける	つける	***vt***. add; attach; append; fix; put on; wear; apply; use; add; join; attend to; name; light a fire; load
¥	付随業務	フズイギョウム	appended business

63

仮 ⑥ ノ イ 亻 仃 仮 仮

音	仮	カ	temporary; provisional; forgive
		(ケ)	false; feigned

熟	仮死	カシ	***med***. suspended animation; asphyxia; temporary suspension of the vital functions
	仮借	カシャク	pardoning; leniency; forgiveness; borrowing —***v***. pardon; be lenient; borrow; forgive
	仮称	カショウ	tentative/provisional name —***v***. give (something) a provisional name
	仮性	カセイ	(prefix) false; psuedo-
	仮設	カセツ	temporary construction —***v***. put up a temporary construction; construct temporarily
	仮説	カセツ	hypothesis
	仮装	カソウ	disguise; fancy clothes —***vi***. disguise oneself; wear fancy clothes
	仮定	カテイ	supposition; assumption; presumption —***v***. suppose; assume; presume
	仮名	カな	*kana* (Japanese syllabary)
	仮眠	カミン	doze; nap —***vi***. take a nap; have forty winks
	仮名	カメイ	pseudonym; assumed name; alias
	仮面	カメン	mask
	仮病	ケビョウ	feigned illness
訓	仮	かり	temporary
¥	仮受金	かりうけキン	suspense receipt
	仮需要	かりジュヨウ	credit/loan demand; emergency/speculative demand
	仮払金	かりばらいキン	temporary payment

64

休 ⑥ ノ イ 仁 什 休 休

音	休	キュウ	resting; taking a break; giving up; quitting
熟	休暇	キュウカ	holiday; holidays; vacation
	休会	キュウカイ	adjournment; recess —***vi***. adjourn
	休学	キュウガク	temporary absence from school —***vi***. be absent from school for a time
	休火山	キュウカザン	dormant volcano
	休刊	キュウカン	suspension/discontinuation of publication —***vi***. suspend publication
	休憩	キュウケイ	rest; break; time off —***vi***. rest; have a break
	休校	キュウコウ	closing down of school —***vi***. close; be closed
	休止	キュウシ	pause; standstill; suspension; stoppage —***v***. cease; pause; suspend; stop
	休日	キュウジツ	holiday; day off
	休診	キュウシン	No Surgery Today —***vi***. close a doctor's surgery (for the day)

	休戦	キュウセン	armistice; truce; ceasefire —***vi***. conclude an armistice; cease firing
	休息	キュウソク	rest; repose; relaxation; respite —***vi***. rest; take a rest; relax
	休養	キュウヨウ	rest; relaxation; recuperation —***vi***. rest; take a rest; recuperate
訓	休み	やすみ	rest; respite; break; repose; holiday
	休む	やすむ	***vi***. rest from; stop; suspend; be absent
¥	休業	キュウギョウ	shutdown; closure of business operation —***vi***. close a business
	休職	キュウショク	temporary retirement —***vi***. retire from work for a short time

65

仰 ⑥

ノ イ … 仰

音	仰	ギョウ (コウ)	look up; respect; revere
熟	仰角	ギョウカク	elevation ***math***. angle of elevation
	仰天	ギョウテン	astonishment —***vi***. be astounded
訓	仰ぐ	あおぐ	***v***. look up; respect; ask for; depend on; drink
	仰向け	あおむけ	turning to face upward
	仰せ	おおせ	***hon***. what you say

66

件 ⑥

ノ イ … 件

音	件	ケン	matter; case (counter for cases)
熟	件数	ケンスウ	number of cases
訓	※件	くだり	clause; paragraph
	※件の	くだんの	the same; the said; in question

67

仲 ⑥

ノ イ … 仲

音	仲	チュウ	relations; relationships; terms
熟	仲介	チュウカイ	intermediation; mediation; agency —***v***. mediate; intercede
	仲裁	チュウサイ	arbitration; mediation; intervention; intercession —***v***. arbitrate; mediate; intervene; interceed

訓	仲	なか	relations; relationship; terms
	仲居	なかい	parlormaid; waitress
	仲買	なかがい	broking; brokerage
	仲買人	なかがいニン	broker; middleman; agent
	仲違い	なかたがい	quarrel; discord; dissension —***vi***. quarrel; get into a dispute
	仲立ち	なかだち	mediation; matchmaking —***v***. mediate; matchmake
	仲直り	なかなおり	reconciliation; peacemaking; restoration of friendship —***vi***. reconcile; make up; make the peace
	仲間	なかま	company; party; set; circle; friends
	仲良し	なかよし	intimacy; familiar terms; intimate friend
	※仲人	なこうど	go-between; marriage broker; matchmaker

68

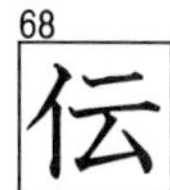
⑥ ノ イ 亻 仁 伝 伝

音	伝	デン	convey; transmit; communicate; legend; tradition; life; biography
熟	伝記	デンキ	biography; life
	伝言	デンゴン	message —***v***. leave word; give/send a message
	伝言板	デンゴンバン	message board
	伝授	デンジュ	initiation; instruction —***v***. initiate; instruct
	伝承	デンショウ	oral tradition; transmission; handing down —***v***. hand down; transmit by word of mouth
	伝説	デンセツ	legend; tradition
	伝染	デンセン	contagion; infection; communication of disease —***vi***. be contagious/infectious/infective
	伝染病	デンセンビョウ	contagious disease
	伝送	デンソウ	transmission —***v***. transmit
	伝達	デンタツ	transmission; conveyance; communication; propagation —***v***. transmit; convey; communicate; deliver; notify
	伝統	デントウ	tradition; conversion
	伝統的	デントウテキ	traditional; conventional
	伝道	デンドウ	missionary work; evangelism —***vi***. evangelize; engage in missionary work
	伝導	デンドウ	conduction; transmission —***v***. conduct; transmit
	伝播	デンパ	dissemination; circulation; propagation; diffusion —***vi***. be propagated/disseminated/circulated
	伝票	デンピョウ	chit; slip; ticket
	伝聞	デンブン	rumor; hearsay; report —***v***. hear from others; be informed; learn by hearsay

	伝来	デンライ	introduction; transmission —*vi*. be transmitted/handed down/introduced
	伝令	デンレイ	message
訓	伝える	つたえる	***vt***. convey; report; deliver; communicate; transmit; teach
	伝わる	つたわる	***vi***. be handed down/transmitted/conveyed/introduced
	伝う	つたう	***vi***. go along
	伝え	つたえ	legend
	伝わり	つたわり	propagation
	伝	つて	intermediary; introducer; medium

69

任 ⑥ ノ イ 亻 仁 仟 任

音	任	ニン	trust, duty
熟	任じる	ニンじる	appoint; nominate; assume; profess; pose
	任意	ニンイ	option; pleasure; discretion
	任官	ニンカン	appointment; installation; commission —***vi***. be appointed/installed/commissioned
	任期	ニンキ	term/period of office
	任地	ニンチ	place of one's appointment; one's post
	任務	ニンム	duty; office; task; function; mission
	任命	ニンメイ	appointment; nomination; designation; commission —***v***. appoint; nominate; designate; commission
	任免	ニンメン	appointment and dismissal; hiring and firing —***v***. appoint and dismiss
	任用	ニンヨウ	employment; appointment —***v***. employ; appoint
訓	任せる	まかせる	***vt***. entrust; delegate; commission
	任す	まかす	***vt***. entrust; delegate; commission
¥	任意積立金	ニンイつみたてキン	voluntary reserve

70

伐 ⑥ ノ イ 亻 代 伐 伐

音	伐	バツ	subjugate; cut
熟	伐採	バッサイ	lumbering; felling —***v***. lumber; fell

71
伏 ⑥ ノ イ 仁 什 伕 伏

音	伏	フク	bend down
熟	伏線	フクセン	foreshadowing; precautionary measures
	伏兵	フクヘイ	ambush
訓	伏す	ふす	bend down; prostrate oneself be bed-ridden; lie down; hide
	伏せる	ふせる	turn downward; cover; lay; conceal
	伏して	ふして	bowing down; respectfully

72
位 ⑦ ノ イ 亻' 亻亠 亻立 位 位

音	位	イ	rank; position; grade
熟	位置	イチ	position; situation; location —***vi***. be positioned/situated/located
	位牌	イハイ	Buddhist mortuary tablet
訓	位	くらい	grade; rank; dignity; the throne; about; approximately
	位する	くらいする	***vi***. rank; be ranked/located/placed

73
何 ⑦ ノ イ 仁 仃 何 何 何

音	何	カ	what
訓	何	なに	what; anything else
		(なん)	what
	何事	なにごと	what; everything; whatever
	何者	なにもの	who; what
	何十	なんジュウ	(how) many; tens of
	何度	なんド	how many degrees; how many times; how often
	何人	なんニン	how many (people)

74

佐 ⑦

音	佐	サ	assist; help aid; colonel
熟	佐官	サカン	field officer; captain; commander

75

作 ⑦

音	作	サ	working
		サク	make; work; harvest
熟	作業	サギョウ	work; operations —***vi***. work; operate
	作業員	サギョウイン	worker
	作業時間	サギョウジカン	working hours
	作為	サクイ	deliberate; intentional; contrived
	作意	サクイ	intentional; deliberate
	作柄	サクがら	crops
	作詞	サクシ	lyrical writing —***v***. write lyrics
	作詩	サクシ	poetry composition —***vi***. write poetry/verse
	作者	サクシャ	author; writer; poet
	作図	サクズ	drawing figures; construction of diagrams —***v***. draw a diagram; construct a shape
	作製	サクセイ	manufacture; production —***v***. manufacture; production
	作成	サクセイ	preparation; drawing up —***v***. make; prepare; draw up
	作戦	サクセン	tactics; operations; action; strategy
	作品	サクヒン	work (of art, literature, etc.)
	作風	サクフウ	literary style; style
	作文	サクブン	composition; essay
	作物	サクモツ	crops; farm produce
	作家	サッカ	novelist; write; author
	作曲	サッキョク	musical composition —***v***. compose/write music
	作曲家	サッキョクカ	composer
	作法	サホウ	manners; etiquette
	作用	サヨウ	action; effect —***vi***. act on
訓	作る	つくる	***vt***. make; manufacture; grow; till; form; establish; cook
	作り	つくり	composition; workmanship
	作り出す	つくりだす	***vt***. make; manufacture

76

伺 ⑦

音	伺	シ	visit
熟	伺候	**シコウ**	waiting upon a person; presenting oneself to a superior —*vi*. wait upon a person; present oneself to a superior
訓	伺う	うかがう	***vt. hon.*** ask; visit

77

似 ⑦

音	似	ジ	resemble
訓	似合う	にあう	***vi.*** go well with; look good with
	似顔絵	にがおえ	portrait
	似る	にる	***vi.*** resemble; look like

78

住 ⑦

音	住	ジュウ	live
熟	住居	ジュウキョ	residence; house; home
	住所	ジュウショ	address
	住職	ジュウショク	chief priest (of a Buddhist temple)
	住宅	ジュウタク	house; residence
	住人	ジュウニン	inhabitant; resident
	住民	ジュウミン	inhabitant; resident
訓	住む	すむ	***vi.*** live; dwell; be resident
	住まい	すまい	house; residence; home
	住まう	すまう	***vi.*** live; dwell; be resident

79

伸 ⑦

音	伸	シン	extend; stretch; grow
熟	伸縮	シンシュク	expansion and contraction; elasticity —*v*. be elastic

	伸縮自在	シンシュクジザイ	elastic
	伸長	シンチョウ	elongation; lengthing —*v*. elongate; lengthen
	伸張	シンチョウ	extension; expansion —*v*. extend; expand
訓	伸びる	のびる	***vi***. grow; get long; slacken; improve; increase
	伸び	のび	increase; growth
	伸び伸び	のびのび	free and easy; carefree —***vi***. be free and easy; be carefree
	伸び率	のびリツ	rate of growth/increase
	伸ばす	のばす	***vt***. make long; grow; extend; straight; stretch; develop; expand

80

体 ⑦ ノ 亻 仁 什 什 休 体

音	体	タイ	body; style; form; substance; center
		テイ	appearance
熟	体位	タイイ	physique; posture; body position
	体育	タイイク	physical education/training
	体温	タイオン	temperature; body temperature/heat
	体温計	タイオンケイ	thermometer
	体格	タイカク	physique; constitution; frame
	体形	タイケイ	form; figure
	体系	タイケイ	system; organization; scheme
	体験	タイケン	experience; personal experience —*v*. have an experience; experience; undergo
	体質	タイシツ	one's physical constitution
	体臭	タイシュウ	body odor
	体重	タイジュウ	(body) weight
	体制	タイセイ	structure; system; organization; order; the Establishment
	体勢	タイセイ	posture; stance
	体積	タイセキ	volume; capacity
	体操	タイソウ	gymnastics; physical exercises; calisthenics —***vi***. practice gymnastics/calisthenics
	体得	タイトク	realization; experience; comprehension; mastering —*v*. realize; learn; comprehend; master
	体内	タイナイ	inside the body
	体罰	タイバツ	corporal punishment
	体面	タイメン	honor; dignity; prestige; reputation; appearances
	体力	タイリョク	physical strength; stamina
	体裁	テイサイ	appearance; decency; form; style

訓 体　からだ　body

81

但 ⑦

ノ 亻 亻 们 伯 但 但

音 但　タン　however

訓 但し　ただし　but; however; on condition that; provided that

但し書　ただしがき　proviso; provisory clause

82

低 ⑦

ノ 亻 亻 仁 仾 低 低

音 低　テイ　low

熟 低圧　テイアツ　low pressure/tension/voltage

低位　テイイ　low position/rank/degree

低音　テイオン　low voice; bass; low pitched sound

低温　テイオン　low temperature

低下　テイカ　lowering; fall; decline; drop; dip; depreciation; deterioration —***v***. fall; drop; dip; decline; lower; depreciate; dteriorate

低額　テイガク　small amount

低気圧　テイキアツ　low atmospheric pressure

低級　テイキュウ　low grade/class

低空　テイクウ　low altitude

低血圧　テイケツアツ　***med***. low blood pressure

低減　テイゲン　fall; depreciation; reduction; decrease

低質　テイシツ　low quality

低速　テイソク　low speed

低俗　テイゾク　vulgar

低地　テイチ　low-lying land; lowlands; flats

低調　テイチョウ　dull; weak; inactive; bearish

低能　テイノウ　weak intellect; low intelligence; feeble mindedness

低木　テイボク　shrub

低迷　テイメイ　overhanging; threatening; floundering —***v***. overhang; threaten; flounder

低落　テイラク　fall; depreciation; slump —***v***. fall; depreciate; decline; go down

低率　テイリツ　low rate/ratio

訓 低い　ひくい　low; short; humble; mean

低まる　ひくまる　***vi***. sink; become lower

	低める	ひくめる	***vt***. lower; make low; bring down
¥	低位株	テイイかぶ	low-priced stock
	低額	テイガク	small amount
	低価法	テイカホウ	valuation on lowest of original cost or current market principle
	低賃金	テイチンギン	low wages
	低利	テイリ	low rate of interest

83

伯 ⑦

ノ … 伯

音	伯	ハク	uncle and aunt; count; earl
熟	伯爵	ハクシャク	count; earl
	伯仲	ハクチュウ	equal; matching; even; on par —***vi***. be equal; match; be even/on par
訓	※伯父	おじ	one's uncle
	※伯母	おば	one's aunt

84

伴 ⑦

ノ … 伴

音	伴	ハン バン	company
熟	伴奏	バンソウ	musical accompaniment —***vi***. play an accompaniment; accompany a person
	伴侶	ハンリョ	partner; companion; associate
訓	伴う	ともなう	***v***. accompany; go/take/be with; involve; entail

85

依 ⑧

ノ … 依

音	依	イ （エ）	rely on; as before
熟	依然	イゼン	as before; still; as ever
	依存	イゾン	dependence; reliance —***vi***. depend; rely on; trust
	依託	イタク	trust; reliance —***v***. entrust; rely on
	依頼	イライ	request; solicitation —***v***. request; solicit; entrust; depend; rely on

	依頼状	**イライジョウ**	letter of request; written request
	依怙地	**エコジ**	obstinacy; stubbornness; spitefulness; selfishness
	依怙ひいき	**エコ**ひいき	partial; unfair —*v*. be partial to; show favoritism to
訓	依る	よる	***vi***. depend/rely on

86

価 ⑧ ノ 亻 仁 仃 佰 価 価 価

音	価	**カ**	price; value
熟	価値	**カチ**	value; worth
訓	価	あたい	price; value —***vi***. price; put a price on; value; praise
¥	価格	**カカク**	price; value; cost

87

佳 ⑧ ノ 亻 仁 仕 佳 佳 佳 佳

音	佳	**カ**	excellence; beautiful
熟	佳境	**カキョウ**	most interesting part; climax
	佳作	**カサク**	fine piece of work
	佳人	**カジン**	beautiful woman
訓	※佳い	よい	fine; beautiful; excellent

88

供 ⑧ ノ 亻 仁 什 供 供 供 供

音	供	**キョウ** (**ク**)	offer; submit; serve (a meal); supply
熟	供する	**キョウ**する	***vt***. offer; submit; serve (a meal); supply
	供給	**キョウキュウ**	supply; service —***v***. supply; provide; furnish; serve
	供述	**キョウジュツ**	testimony; statement; deposition; confession —***v***. testify; state; confess (to a fact)
	供物	**クモツ**	offering (to ancestors)
	供養	**クヨウ**	memorial service —***v***. hold a memorial service
訓	供える	そなえる	***vt***. offer (to a god); make an offering
	供	とも	attendant; servant retinue

89

使 ⑧ ノ イ 亻 仁 佢 佢 使 使

音	使	シ	use; messenger
熟	使者	シシャ	messenger; envoy
	使節	シセツ	envoy; delegate; delegation; mission (to a foreign country)
	使徒	シト	apostle; disciple
	使命	シメイ	mission
	使用	シヨウ	use —*v.* use; make use of; employ
	使用人	シヨウニン	person who works under his/her master; employee; servant
訓	使う	つかう	***vt.*** use; handle; employ
	使い	つかい	errand; messenger
	使い方	つかいかた	usage; how to use
	使い込む	つかいこむ	***vt.*** embezzle; defalcate; appropriate (money) for one's own use
	使い捨て	つかいすて	disposable
	使い手	つかいて	user; consumer
	使い道	つかいみち	way of using

90

侍 ⑧ ノ イ 亻 仕 仹 侍 侍 侍

音	侍	ジ	wait on
熟	侍する	ジする	***vi.*** attend on (the lord); wait on (a lady)
	侍者	ジシャ	servant to a lord
	侍従	ジジュウ	chamberlain; lord-in-waiting
	侍女	ジジョ	lady's maid; lady-in-waiting
訓	侍	さむらい	samurai; warrior
	※侍る	はべる	***vi.*** attend; wait on; serve ***clas.*** be

91

侮 ⑧ ノ イ 亻 仁 佐 佐 侮 侮

音	侮	ブ	despise
熟	侮辱	ブジョク	insult; affront —*v.* insult
	侮蔑	ブベツ	contempt; scorn —*v.* contempt; scorn; slight

訓	侮る	あなどる	despise; look down on

92
併 ⑧
ノ 亻 亻 亻 亻 亻 併 併

音	併	ヘイ	put together
熟	併合	ヘイゴウ	annexation; amalgamation; merge —*v.* annexe; amalgamate; merge
	併殺	ヘイサツ	***bas.*** double play —*v.* ***bas.*** make a double play
	併置	ヘイチ	putting two things in the same place —*v.* put two or more things in the same place; construct two or more things simultaneously
	併発	ヘイハツ	concurrence —*v.* occur simultaneously
	併有	ヘイユウ	combining/owning two or more things together —*v.* combine/own two or more things together
	併用	ヘイヨウ	joint-use; combined-use —*v.* use together/in combination
訓	併せる	あわせる	put together; combine; merge

93
例 ⑧
ノ 亻 亻 亻 亻 伢 例 例

音	例	レイ	example; precedent; practice
熟	例会	レイカイ	regular meeting
	例外	レイガイ	exception
	例証	レイショウ	example; illustration —*v.* show by example; illustrate
	例題	レイダイ	exercise; example
	例年	レイネン	every year; normal/average year
	例文	レイブン	example sentence (in a dictionary, etc.)
訓	例えば	たとえば	for example
	例話	たとえばなし	verbal example
	例える	たとえる	***vt.*** show by example; illustrate
	※例	ためし	instance; example; precedent

94
係 ⑨
ノ 亻 亻 亻 亻 亻 俘 係 係

音	係	ケイ	connection; involve; concern; affect

熟 係争 ケイソウ dispute; conflict; conflaguration; litigation —*vi*. dispute; be in conflict

訓 係 かかり the person in charge/responsible
係る かかる *vi*. affect; engender; modify
係わり かかわり involvement; connection
係わる かかわる *vi*. have to do with; be involved with

95

侯 ⑨

ノ 亻 亻 亻 亻 伊 伻 侯 侯

音 侯 コウ feudal lord; marquis

熟 侯爵 コウシャク marquis; marquess

96

俊 ⑨

ノ 亻 亻 亻 亻 亻 亻 俊 俊

音 俊 シュン excel

熟 俊英 シュンエイ distinguished person
俊才 シュンサイ man of talent; genius
俊足 シュンソク swift-footed; fast
俊敏 シュンビン alert and agile

97

信 ⑨

ノ 亻 亻 亻 亻 信 信 信 信

音 信 シン fidelity; trust; letter

熟 信じる シンじる *vt*. believe; trust; have faith in
信義 シンギ faith; loyalty; honor
信教 シンキョウ religious belief; religion
信仰 シンコウ faith; belief —*v*. have faith in; believe in
信号 シンゴウ signal; traffic lights
信実 シンジツ sincerity
信者 シンジャ believer in a religion
信書 シンショ correspondence; letter
信条 シンジョウ belief; creed; principle
信賞必罰 シンショウヒツバツ certain penalty and certain reward
信心 シンジン faith; belief; piety —*v*. believe; worship
信託 シンタク trust

	信徒	シント	adherent; believer
	信任	シンニン	confidence; trust —*v*. place confidence in; trust
	信念	シンネン	belief; faith; conviction
	信服	シンプク	self-conviction —*vi*. convince oneself; be convinced
	信望	シンボウ	confidence; popularity
	信奉	シンポウ	belief; faith —*v*. believe; have faith in; espouse
	信奉者	シンポウシャ	devotee; follower; adherent
	信用	シンヨウ	confidence; trust; faith; reliance; reputation —*v*. believe; trust; have faith in; have confidence in; be reliable/reputable
	信頼	シンライ	reliance; confidence; trust —*v*. trust; rely on; depend on
¥	信託銀行	シンタクギンコウ	trust bank
	信販 (信用販売)	シンパン (シンヨウハンバイ)	sale on credit
	信用金庫	シンヨウキンコ	credit association; cooperative bank
	信用組合	シンヨウくみあい	credit association
	信用状	シンヨウジョウ	letter of credit
	信用創造	シンヨウソウゾウ	credit creation
	信用取引	シンヨウとりひき	margin transaction

98

侵 ⑨ ノ イ 亻 亻 亻 亻 亻 侵 侵

音	侵	シン	invade
熟	侵害	シンガイ	infringement; invasion —*v*. infringe; encroach; invade; violate
	侵攻	シンコウ	invasion —*v*. invade
	侵入	シンニュウ	invasion; incursion; raid; intrusion —*vi*. invade; incur; raid; intrude; trespass; march into
	侵入軍	シンニュウグン	invading army
	侵入者	シンニュウシャ	invader; trespasser; intruder
	侵犯	シンパン	invasion; violation; infringement —*v*. invade; violate; infringe
	侵略	シンリャク	aggression; invasion —*v*. invade; act aggressively
	侵略国	シンリャクコク	aggressor nation
	侵略者	シンリャクシャ	invader
	侵略的	シンリャクテキ	aggressive
訓	侵す	おかす	*vt*. invade; violate; infringe; encroach

99

促 ⑨

音	促	ソク	urge; promote; prompt
熟	促音	ソクオン	assimilated sound
	促進	ソクシン	promotion; encouragement —*v*. promote; encourage
	促成	ソクセイ	growth promotion —*v*. prompt growth
訓	促す	うながす	***vt***. urge; promote; prompt

100

俗 ⑨

音	俗	ゾク	custom; manners; worldliness; laymen; vulgarity
熟	俗悪	ゾクアク	vulgar; coarse
	俗語	ゾクゴ	slang; colloquial language
	俗字	ゾクジ	popular form of a Chinese character
	俗事	ゾクジ	worldly affairs
	俗称	ゾクショウ	common/popular name
	俗人	ゾクジン	layman; worldly minded person
	俗世間	ゾクセケン	this world; secular society
	俗説	ゾクセツ	common saying; folklore
	俗評	ゾクヒョウ	popular opinion
	俗物	ゾクブツ	worldly-minded person; person of vulgar tastes
	俗名	ゾクミョウ	secular name
	俗名	ゾクメイ	popular/common name
	俗話	ゾクワ	gossip
	俗化	ゾッカ	vulgarization; popularization —*v*. vulgarize; popularize

101

便 ⑨

音	便	ビン	mail; transport; flight; opportunity
		ベン	convenience; facilities; excrement; feces
熟	便乗	ビンジョウ	getting in a car or on a boat (with someone); taking advantate of —***vi***. get in a car (with someone); take advantage of

便箋	ビンセン	letter paper
便意	ベンイ	urge to go to the toilet; call of nature
便益	ベンエキ	convenience; benefit; advantage
便器	ベンキ	toilet; urinal
便宜	ベンギ	convenience; expedience
便宜上	ベンギジョウ	for convenience
便宜的	ベンギテキ	convenient; expendient
便所	ベンジョ	toilet; lavatory
便通	ベンツウ	bowel movement
便秘	ベンピ	constipation
便法	ベンポウ	convenient/easy way
便覧	ベンラン (ビンラン)	handbook; manual
便利	ベンリ	convenient; handy
便利屋	ベンリヤ	handyman
訓 便り	たより	news; tidings

102

保 ⑨ ノ イ 亻 亻 亻 伻 伻 保 保

音 保	ホ	keep; preserve; maintain
熟 保安	ホアン	maintenance of public peace and security
保育	ホイク	childcare; —*v*. bring up/raise a child
保育園	ホイクエン	nursery (school)
保育所	ホイクジョ	nursery (school)
保温	ホオン	keeping warm; heat maintenance —*vi*. keep warm
保管	ホカン	custody; deposit; storage —*v*. keep in custody; store
保菌者	ホキンシャ	carrier (of a disease)
保険	ホケン	insurance; assurance
保健	ホケン	health preservation; hygiene
保健所	ホケンジョ	health center
保護	ホゴ	protection; shelter —*v*. protect; shelter
保護国	ホゴコク	protectorate
保護者	ホゴシャ	guardian; protector
保護色	ホゴショク	protective coloration
保持	ホジ	maintenance; preservation —*v*. maintain; preserve; keep (a memory, etc.)
保持者	ホジシャ	(record) holder
保釈	ホシャク	bail —*v*. bail
保守	ホシュ	conservation —*v*. conserve; preserve; maintain

	保守的	ホシュテキ	conservative
	保守党	ホシュトウ	conservative party
	保証	ホショウ	guarantee —*v*. guarantee; promise
	保障	ホショウ	guarantee; security —*v*. guarantee; assure
	保身	ホシン	self-protection
	保全	ホゼン	preservation —*v*. preserve; conserve
	保存	ホゾン	preservation —*v*. preserve; conserve
	保母	ホボ	kindergarten teacher
	保有	ホユウ	possession; ownership —*v*. possess; own; hold; maintain
	保有者	ホユウシャ	owner; holder
	保養	ホヨウ	recreation; recuperation; health preservation —*vi*. recreate; recuperate
	保養所	ホヨウジョ	sanatorium; rest home
	保養地	ホヨウチ	health resort
	保留	ホリュウ	reservation; putting on hold —*v*. reserve; defer
訓	保つ	たもつ	*vt*. keep; preserve; maintain
¥	保険会社	ホケンガイシャ	insurance company
	保険金	ホケンキン	insurance money
	保険つなぎ	ホケンつなぎ	short sale against the box
	保険料	ホケンリョウ	insurance premium
	保護預かり	ホゴあずかり	safety deposit
	保護主義	ホゴシュギ	protectionism
	保護貿易	ホゴボウエキ	protectionistic trade
	保証金	ホショウキン	security deposit; key money
	保証人	ホショウニン	guarantor

103

倹 ⑩

ノ イ 仆 仒 佱 佮 倹

音	倹	ケン	economize; be thrift; frugal
熟	倹約	ケンヤク	economy; thrift; fruguality —*v*. economize; be thrifty/frugal

104

個 10 4

ノ イ 亻 们 侗 個

音	個	コ	piece (counter for small objects)
熟	個々	ココ	separately; individually

	個人	コジン	individual
	個人差	コジンサ	difference among individuals
	個人主義	コジンシュギ	individualism
	個人的	コジンテキ	individually; personally; privately
	個数	コスウ	number of items
	個性	コセイ	personality; individuality; originality
	個展	コテン	personal exhibition; one-man show
	個別	コベツ	individually; separately; one by one
¥	個人株主	コジンかぶぬし	individual stockholder

105
候 ⑩
ノ 亻 … 候

音	候	コウ	attend; season
熟	候補	コウホ	candidacy
	候補者	コウホシャ	candidate; applicant
訓	候	そうろう	***vi. clas.*** be; exist

106
借 ⑩
ノ 亻 … 借

音	借	シャク	borrow
訓	借りる	かりる	***vt.*** borrow; have a loan; get into debt
	借り	かり	debt; loan
	借り倒す	かりたおす	***vt.*** fail to pay a debt; bilk
	借り主	かりぬし	borrower
¥	借り入れ金	かりいれキン	loan (of money); borrowed money; debt
	借方勘定	カリカタカンジョウ	debtor account
	借地	シャクチ	leased/rented land
	借家	シャクヤ	rented house
	借家人	シャクヤニン	tenant
	借用	シャクヨウ	borrowing —***v.*** borrow
	借用証書	シャクヨウショウショ	loan bond; certificate of loan
	借款	シャッカン	loan (an overseas loan)
	借金	シャッキン	debt —***vi.*** borrow money; get into debt

107
修 ⑩

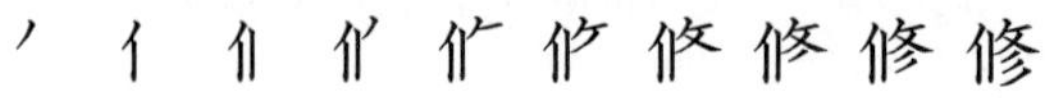

音	修	シュウ （シュ）	learn; repair
熟	修業	シュウギョウ	studying; learning —*v*. study; learn
	修士	シュウシ	master's degree
	修飾	シュウショク	decoration; ornamentation ***gram***. modification —*v*. decorate; ornament ***gram***. modify
	修繕	シュウゼン	repair —*v*. repair; mend; fix
	修築	シュウチク	building repairs —*v*. make repairs to a building
	修道院	シュウドウイン	monastery; abbey; religious house
	修道士	シュウドウシ	monk; friar
	修得	シュウトク	acquisition of skills —*v*. acquire; learn; master
	修理	シュウリ	repair; mending —*v*. repair; mend; fix
	修了	シュウリョウ	completion of a course —*v*. complete; finish
	修練	シュウレン	training; practice —*v*. train; practice; rehearse
	修行	シュギョウ	training; religious training —*v*. practice asceticism
訓	修まる	おさまる	***vi***. conduct oneself well
	修める	おさめる	***vt***. study; master; behave oneself
¥	修正	シュウセイ	amendment; revision; correcting —*v*. amend; revise; correct
	修復	シュウフク	restoration —*v*. restore; repair

108
値 ⑩

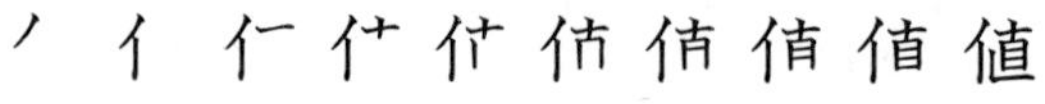

音	値	チ	value; price; cost
訓	値する	あたいする	***vi***. be worth; be worthy; deserve; merit
	値	あたい	price; cost; value; worth; merit
	値	ね	price; cost; figure; value
	値打ち	ねうち	price; value
	値段	ねダン	price; cost
¥	値上がり	ねあがり	rise in price; rising prices
	値上げ	ねあげ	rise in price —*v*. raise prices
	値動き	ねうごき	price fluctuation
	値を崩す	ねをくずす	lower prices
	値がさ株	ねがさかぶ	high-priced stocks

値切る	ねぎる	***vt***. beat down the price; haggle
値崩れ	ねくずれ	(sudden/sharp) drop in price (caused by oversupply)
値頃	ねごろ	reasonable/moderate price
値下げ	ねさげ	reduction in price; price decrease —***v***. lower prices
値ざや	ねざや	margin; spread
値幅制限	ねはばセイゲン	restriction of price range
値引き	ねびき	discount; price reduction —***v***. reduce prices

109

倒 ⑩

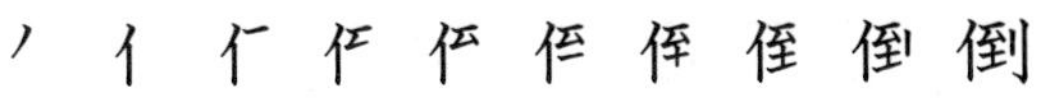

音	倒	トウ	fall down; upside down
熟	倒壊	トウカイ	collapse; destruction —***vi***. collapse; be destroyed
	倒置	トウチ	turning upside down —***v***. turn upside down
	倒置法	トウチホウ	***gram***. inversion
	倒立	トウリツ	handstand —***vi***. do a handstand
訓	倒す	たおす	***vt***. bring/throw down; beat; defeat
	倒れる	たおれる	***vi***. fall; collapse; topple; break down; be ruined; go to ruin
¥	倒産	トウサン	bankruptcy; insolvency —***vi***. become bankrupt/insolvent

110

俳 ⑩

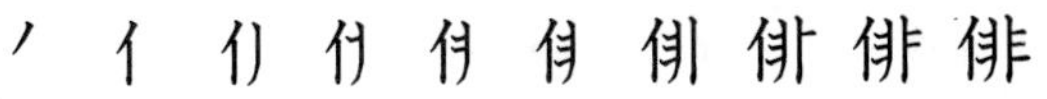

音	俳	ハイ	performer; haiku poetry
熟	俳諧	ハイカイ	comic linked verse
	俳句	ハイク	haiku poem
	俳号	ハイゴウ	haiku poet's pen name
	俳人	ハイジン	haiku poet
	俳壇	ハイダン	the haiku world/poets
	俳優	ハイユウ	actor; actress

111

倍 ⑩

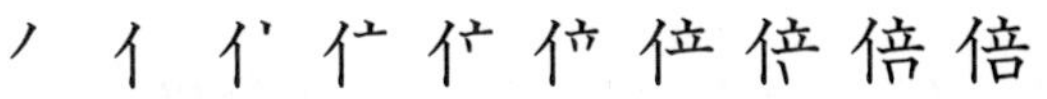

音	倍	バイ	times

熟	倍加	バイカ	doubling; great/marked increase —*v.* double; increase twofold; add much to
	倍額	バイガク	double the price
	倍数	バイスウ	***math.*** multiple
	倍増	バイゾウ	redoubling; double —*v.* redouble; double
	倍率	バイリツ	magnification

112

俵 ⑩

ノ 亻 仁 仕 仹 佳 佬 侼 俵 俵

音	俵	ヒョウ	straw bag (counter for sacks)
訓	俵	たわら	straw bag

113

倣 ⑩

ノ 亻 亻 仿 仿 仿 仿 傚 倣 倣

音	倣	ホウ	imitate; follow; emulate
訓	倣う	ならう	***vt.*** imitate; follow; emulate

114

俸 ⑩

ノ 亻 仁 仨 仨 伕 俟 俸 俸 俸

音	俸	ホウ	pay; salary
熟	俸給	ホウキュウ	salary; pay; wages
	俸禄	ホウロク	stipend; pay; salary

115

倫 ⑩

ノ 亻 亻 仒 仒 伶 倫 倫 倫 倫

音	倫	リン	ethics; sequence
熟	倫理	リンリ	ethics; morals

116

偽 ⑪

ノ 亻 亻 仯 伪 伪 偽 偽 偽 偽 偽

音	偽	ギ	falsify; deceive

熟	偽証	ギショウ	false evidence; perjury —*v*. bear false witness; commit perjury
	偽善	ギゼン	hypocrisy
	偽善的	ギゼンテキ	hypocritical
	偽造	ギゾウ	forgery; fabrication —*v*. forge; fabricate
	偽名	ギメイ	false name
訓	偽る	いつわる	***vt***. lie; deceive; feign; pretend
	偽	にせ	imitation; counterfeit; phony
	偽物	にせもの	imitation; counterfeit

117

偶 ⑪

ノ 亻 亻 伄 伒 佀 佀 偶 偶 偶 偶

音	偶	グウ	surprise; unexpected
熟	偶数	グウスウ	***math***. even number
	偶然	グウゼン	by chance; accidentally
	偶像	グウゾウ	image; statue
	偶発	グウハツ	accidental occurrence —***vi***. occur accidently
¥	偶発債務	グウハツサイム	contingent/accidental liability

118

健 ⑪

ノ 亻 亻 亻 亻 亻 亻 律 倢 倢 健

音	健	ケン	health
熟	健脚	ケンキャク	good walker
	健康	ケンコウ	health
	健康的	ケンコウテキ	healthy
	健康保健	ケンコウホケン	health insurance
	健在	ケンザイ	in good health ; alive and well
	健全	ケンゼン	healthy; normal; sound; wholesome
	健闘	ケントウ	good fight —*v*. put up a good fight
	健忘症	ケンボウショウ	forgetfulness; amnesia
訓	健やか	すこやか	healthy; fit; well

119

側 ⑪

ノ 亻 亻 们 们 们 伹 伹 俱 側 側

音	側	ソク	side

2 二亠人𠆢亻儿入八冂冖冫几凵刀刂力勹匕匚十卜卩㔾厂厶又了⺈マ

熟	側線	ソクセン	siding; sidetrack; side lines
	側面	ソクメン	side; flank
	側近	ソッキン	close associate
訓	側	がわ	side

120

停 ⑪

音	停	テイ	stop
熟	停学	テイガク	suspension from school
	停止	テイシ	suspension; stoppage; stay; prohibition; temporary ban; standstill; stop; halt; deadlock; stalemate; interruption; cessation —*v*. suspend; stop; prohibit; cease; come to an end
	停戦	テイセン	truce; ceasefire; armistice —*v*. cease fire; stop fighting
	停車	テイシャ	stop; stoppage —***vi***. stop; come to a halt
	停滞	テイタイ	stagnation; retention; congestion; falling into arrears —*v*. be stagnant; stagnate; congest; be sluggish; fall into arrears
	停電	テイデン	power failure/cut —*v*. have a power cut
	停泊	テイハク	anchorage; anchoring; mooring —*v*. anchor; lie; berth; moor
	停留	テイリュウ	stoppage; stop —*v*. stop; halt
	停留所	テイリュウジョ	stop; stand; station; depot
訓	停まる	とまる	***vi***. stop; cease; be stopped/suspended
	停める	とめる	***vt***. stop; suspend
¥	停職	テイショク	suspension from office

121

偵 ⑪

音	偵	テイ	spy
熟	偵察	テイサツ	reconnaissance; scouting —*v*. scout; patrol

122

偏 ⑪

音	偏	ヘン	lean toward; be biased; left-hand side of a *kanji*

熟	偏する	ヘンする	*vi*. lean toward; be biased
	偏愛	ヘンアイ	partiality; favoritism —*v*. favor
	偏狭	ヘンキョウ	narrow-minded; intolerant
	偏屈	ヘンクツ	obstinate; bigoted; narrow-minded
	偏見	ヘンケン	prejudice; biased view
	偏向	ヘンコウ	bias; leanings; deviations; tendency
	偏差	ヘンサ	bias/deviation (in statistics, etc)
	偏差値	ヘンサチ	deviation (value)
	偏在	ヘンザイ	uneven distribution —*vi*. be unevenly distributed
	偏執	ヘンシュウ	bigotry; obstinacy
	偏食	ヘンショク	unbalanced diet —*vi*. have an unbalanced diet
	偏人	ヘンジン	eccentric person
	偏頭痛	ヘンズツウ	migraine headache
	偏重	ヘンチョウ	overemphasis —*v*. overemphasize
	偏平	ヘンペイ	flat; level; even
	偏平足	ヘンペイソク	flat feet
	偏流	ヘンリュウ	drift; drifting
訓	偏る	かたよる	*vi*. lean toward; be biased
	偏り	かたより	inclination; deviation; polarization
	※偏に	ひとえに	earnestly; humbly; solely

123

偉 ⑫

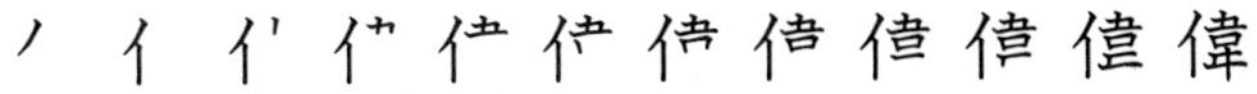

音	偉	イ	great; grand; famous; eminent; lofty; distinguished
熟	偉業	イギョウ	great work/achievement/feat
	偉丈夫	イジョウブ	prodigy; hero; great man
	偉人	イジン	great man/mind; hero
	偉大	イダイ	greatness; grandeur; might; eminence; distinction
訓	偉い	えらい	great; grand; mighty; celebrated; heroic; serious

124

備 ⑫

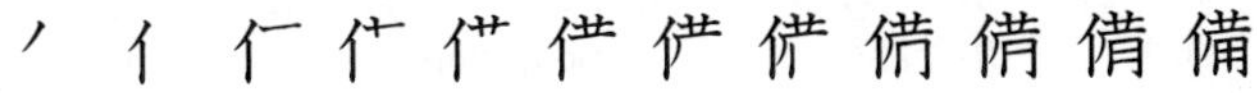

音	備	ビ	provide; furnish; preparation
熟	備考	ビコウ	note; remarks
	備品	ビヒン	fixture; equipment; kit

	備忘録	ビボウロク	memorandum; notebook
訓	備える	そなえる	***vt***. provide; possess; equip
	備え	そなえ	provision; preparations; preparedness; equipment
	備え付ける	そなえつける	***vt***. provide; furnish; equip; fit; outfit
	備わる	そなわる	***vi***. be furnished/provided/equipped

125

傍 ⑫

音	傍	ボウ	side
熟	傍観	ボウカン	looking on; spectating —***v***. look on; spectate
	傍系	ボウケイ	collateral family line; affiliated; subsidiary
	傍若無人	ボウジャクブジン	impudent; arrogant; insolent
	傍受	ボウジュ	intercepting/monitoring/tapping (radio signals, etc.) —***v***. intercept/monitor/tap (radio signals, etc.)
	傍線	ボウセン	sideline; underline (for emphasis, etc.)
	傍聴	ボウチョウ	attendance at the proceeding (at a court, meeting, etc.) —***v***. attend the proceedings (at a court, meeting, etc.)
	傍聴席	ボウチョウセキ	visitors' gallery (in a court)
訓	傍ら	かたわら	side

126

傾 ⑬

音	傾	ケイ	incline; slope; slant; tend; devote; concentrate
熟	傾向	ケイコウ	tendency; trend; propensity; inclination
	傾斜	ケイシャ	inclination; slope —***v***. incline; slope; slant
	傾聴	ケイチョウ	listening closely/intently —***v***. listen closely/intently
	傾倒	ケイトウ	devotion; concentration —***vi***. devote oneself to; concentrate on
訓	傾く	かたむく	***vi***. tilt; lean; lurch; tip; slop; slant; decline
	傾ける	かたむける	***vt***. tilt; lean; be ruined; devote; concentrate
	傾き	かたむき	inclination; slope; slant; tendency; trend

127

傑 ⑬

音	傑	ケツ	great
熟	傑作	ケッサク	masterpiece
	傑出	ケッシュツ	excellence; prominence —***vi***. excel at; be prominent in; stand out; shine

128

催 ⑬

音	催	サイ	urge; encourage; hold
熟	催促	サイソク	demand; urge; request —***v***. demand; press; urge; request
	催眠	サイミン	hypnosis
	催眠剤	サイミンザイ	sleeping pill
	催眠術	サイミンジュツ	hypnotism
	催涙	サイルイ	***med***. lachrymal
訓	催し	もよおし	meeting; function; is sponsored by; under the auspices of
	催す	もよおす	***v***. hold (a party); feel (sleepy, chilly, etc.)

129

債 ⑬

音	債	サイ	debt; duty; obligation
¥	債権	サイケン	credit; claim; obligatory right
	債権国	サイケンコク	creditor nation
	債権者	サイケンシャ	creditor
	債権所有者	サイケン ショユウシャ	bond holder
	債権取引所	サイケン とりひきジョ	bond market
	債権発行	サイケンハッコウ	loan issue; flotation; issuance
	債券	サイケン	(loan) bond; debenture
	債務	サイム	debt; liabilities; obligation
	債務国	サイムコク	debtor nation
	債務者	サイムシャ	debtor

130

傷 ⑬

ノ イ 亻 亻 亻 亻 亻 亻 亻 亻 傷 傷

音	傷	ショウ	wound; injure; damage
熟	傷害	ショウガイ	injury
	傷害保険	ショウガイホケン	accident insurance
	傷心	ショウシン	broken heart; heartbreak; grief; sorrow
訓	傷む	いたむ	*v.* be damaged/hurt/bruised/spoilt
	傷める	いためる	*vt.* damage; hurt; spoil
	傷	きず	injury; wound; cut; flaw; defect
	傷跡	きずあと	scar
	傷口	きずぐち	wound; sore
	傷付く	きずつく	*vi.* be hurt/injured/damaged
	傷付ける	きずつける	*vt.* wound; injure; bruise; scratch; crack
	傷物	きずもの	defective article

131

僧 ⑬

ノ イ 亻 亻 亻 亻 亻 亻 亻 亻 亻 僧

音	僧	ソウ	priest; monk
熟	僧庵	ソウアン	monk's cell; hermitage
	僧院	ソウイン	monastery; temple
	僧正	ソウジョウ	high priest; bishop
	僧俗	ソウゾク	clergy and laity
	僧尼	ソウニ	monks and nuns
	僧兵	ソウヘイ	monk soldier
	僧侶	ソウリョ	priest; monk; bonze

132

働 ⑬

ノ イ 亻 亻 亻 亻 亻 亻 亻 亻 亻 働

音	働	ドウ	work
訓	働く	はたらく	*vi.* work
	働き	はたらき	work; labor; achievements; function; effect; workings
	働き口	はたらきぐち	job; position
	働き者	はたらきもの	hard worker

133

像 ⑭

音 像 ゾウ image

134

僕 ⑭

音 僕 ボク manservant; I; me (male)
僕婢 ボクヒ male and female servants

訓 ※僕 しもべ manservant

135

僚 ⑭

音 僚 リョウ colleague; official

熟 僚友 リョウユウ colleague; co-worker

136

億 ⑮

音 億 オク one-hundred million; 100,000,000

熟 億万長者 オクマンチョウジャ billionaire; multimillionaire
億劫 オックウ bothersome; troublesome

137

儀 ⑮

音 儀 ギ rule; ceremony

熟 儀式 ギシキ ceremony; function
儀礼 ギレイ etiquette; courtesy
儀礼的 ギレイテキ formal

138

儒 ⑯

音	儒	ジュ	Confucianism
熟	儒学	ジュガク	Confucianism
	儒教	ジュキョウ	Confucianism

139

償 ⑰

音	償	ショウ	compensate
訓	償う	つぐなう	***vt***. compensate; recompense; make up for; atone
¥	償還	ショウカン	repayment; refund; redemption —***v***. repay; refund; pay back
	償却	ショウキャク	repayment; refund; depreciation; redemption; amortization —***v***. repay; refund; depreciate; redeem

140

優 ⑰

音	優	ユウ	superior; gentle; actor
熟	優位	ユウイ	high position
	優越	ユウエツ	superiority; supremacy —***vi***. be superior to
	優越感	ユウエツカン	superiority complex
	優雅	ユウガ	elegance; grace; refinement
	優遇	ユウグウ	kind treatment; hospitality —***v***. treat someone well
	優秀	ユウシュウ	excellent; superior
	優柔不断	ユウジュウフダン	irresolute; indecisive
	優勝	ユウショウ	championship; victory —***v***. win
	優勢	ユウセイ	predominance; superiority
	優先	ユウセン	preference; superiority —***vi***. be prior to; have preference to
	優先的	ユウセンテキ	preferential
	優待	ユウタイ	generous/preferential treatment —***v***. treat generously; receive hospitality
	優等	ユウトウ	excellent; superior
	優美	ユウビ	graceful; elegant

	優良	ユウリョウ	excellent; superior
	優劣	ユウレツ	superiority and inferiority; relative merits
訓	優れる	すぐれる	*vi*. excel; surpass
	優しい	やさしい	graceful; gentle; kind
	※優る	まさる	*vi*. excel; surpass
¥	優先株	ユウセンかぶ	preferred stock
	優良株	ユウリョウかぶ	blue chip

2 儿 ひとあし legs

141

元 ④ 一 二 テ 元

音	元	ガン	
		ゲン	the origin; background; cause
熟	元日	ガンジツ	New Year's Day
	元祖	ガンソ	originator; founder; ancestor; forerunner
	元旦	ガンタン	New Year's Day
	元年	ガンネン	first year of an imperial era
	元来	ガンライ	originally; essentially; by nature
	元気	ゲンキ	healthy; happy; jolly; cheerful
	元首	ゲンシュ	head of state
	元帥	ゲンスイ	general of the army; field marshal
	元素	ゲンソ	***chem***. element
	元服	ゲンプク	coming of age day for boys —*v*. celebrate one's coming of age
	元老	ゲンロウ	elder statesman
訓	元	もと	origin; originally; background; cause; former; ex-
	元帳	もとチョウ	ledger
	元通り	もとどおり	former; as it used to be
	元々	もともと	originally; from the outset; by nature
¥	元金	ガンキン	principal; capital
	元本	ガンポン	capital; principal
	元利	ガンリ	principal and interest
	元手	もとで	capital; funds; assets
	元値	もとね	the cost; cost price

142

兄 ⑤

音	兄	ケイ	elder brother; elder brother of one's spouse
		(キョウ)	elder brother
熟	兄弟	キョウダイ	brother(s); brothers and sisters
	兄弟姉妹	ケイテイシマイ	brothers and sisters
訓	兄	あに	one's elder brother
	兄弟子	あにでし	senior fellow disciple/pupil
	兄嫁	あによめ	wife of one's elder brother
	※お兄さん	おにいさん	your elder brother; another person's elder brother

143

光 ⑥

音	光	コウ	light; shine; brilliance; time
熟	光陰	コウイン	time; Father Time
	光栄	コウエイ	honor; glory; privilege
	光化学	コウカガク	photochemistry
	光学	コウガク	optics; optical science
	光学器械	コウガクキカイ	optical instrument
	光輝	コウキ	brilliance
	光景	コウケイ	scene; sight; spectacle; scenery; view
	光合成	コウゴウセイ	photosynthesis
	光線	コウセン	light; ray/beam of light
	光沢	コウタク	gloss; luster; brilliance; glaze; polish
	光度	コウド	***phy***. luminous intensity; light intensity; brightness; luminosity
	光年	コウネン	light-year
	光明	コウミョウ	hope; light; bright future
訓	光	ひかり	light; ray; beam; lumisary; influence; power
	光る	ひかる	***vi***. shine; be bright/brilliant; illuminate; glitter
¥	光熱費	コウネツヒ	light and fuel costs; utilities
	光ディスク	ひかりディスク	optical disc
	光ファイバー	ひかりファイバー	optical fiber
	光メモリー	ひかりメモリー	optoelectronic memory

144

充 ⑥

丶 亠 𠫓 𠫔 𠫕 充

音 充 ジュウ allot; overflow; be full

熟 充血 ジュウケツ ***med***. congestion —***vi***. congest; be congested with blood

充実 ジュウジツ full; substantial —***vi***. live a full life; live life to the full

充実感 ジュウジツカン sense of fulfillment

充足 ジュウソク contentment —***v***. satisfy; be contented; make content

充電 ジュウデン battery charging; electricity storage —***v***. charge a battery; store electricity

充当 ジュウトウ appropriation —***v***. allot

充分 ジュウブン plenty of; enough; entirely; really

充満 ジュウマン fullness; completeness —***vi***. be full of; be filled

訓 充てる あてる ***vt***. assign; use; allot

145

先 ⑥

丿 𠂉 𠂒 生 𠧢 先

音 先 セン future; priority; precedence

熟 先覚者 センカクシャ pioneer (in a particular field)

先客 センキャク previous visitor/customer

先駆者 センクシャ forerunner/pioneer (in a particular field)

先月 センゲツ last month

先見 センケン foresight

先賢 センケン wise men of old; ancient sage

先刻 センコク while ago; already

先史時代 センシジダイ prehistoric times

先日 センジツ the other day

先週 センシュウ last week

先人 センジン ancestor; predecessor

先陣 センジン vanguard; advanced guard

先進国 センシンコク advanced/developed nation

先生 センセイ teacher; master; doctor

先祖 センゾ ancestor

先代 センダイ predecessor; previous age/generation

先達 センダツ pioneer (in a field); leader; guide

先端 センタン tip; point; end; the latest; advanced

	先着	センチャク	first arrival
	先手	センて	first move; initiative
	先天的	センテンテキ	inborn; congenital; hereditary
	先頭	セントウ	head; lead
	先導	センドウ	guidance; leadership —*v*. guide; lead
	先入観	センニュウカン	prejudice; preconception; preoccupation
	先年	センネン	former years; a few years ago
	先輩	センパイ	superior; senior; older graduate
	先発	センパツ	starting in advance —*vi*. start in advance; go ahead
	先般	センパン	some time ago; the other day
	先方	センポウ	the other part; the other member/partner
	先例	センレイ	precedent
訓	先	さき	tip; point; end; lead; the future; recent
	先立つ	さきだつ	*vi*. coming forward; precede; die before (someone)
	先回り	さきまわり	*vi*. beat (a person) to it
	※先ず	まず	first; nearly; anyway; well
¥	先入れ先出し法	さきいれさきだしホウ	first-in-first-out method
	先高	さきだか	higher quotations for future months
	先物	さきもの	futures
	先物買い	さきものがい	purchase of futures; forward buying
	先物取引	さきものとりひき	futures transaction
	先安	さきやす	lower quotations for future months
	先駆株	センクかぶ	forerunner
	先行投資	センコウトウシ	prior investment

146

兆 ⑥ 丿 ⺁ 𠃊 兆 兆 兆

音	兆	チョウ	sign; indication; sympton; omen; trillion; 1,000,000,000
熟	兆候	チョウコウ	sign; indication; omen; symptom
訓	兆し	きざし	signs; symptoms; indication; sprouting; germination
	兆す	きざす	*vi*. show signs of; indicate; show symptons; sprout; germinate

147

克 ⑦

一 十 𠂇 古 古 声 克

音	克	コク	overcome; conquer
熟	克服	コクフク	conquest; subjugation; overcoming —*v*. conquer; subjugate; overcome
	克明	コクメイ	fidelity; diligence; conscientiousness
	克己	コッキ	self-denial; self-control; self-restraint

148

児 ⑦

丨 丨丨 丨冂 丨日 旧 旧 児

音	児	ジ	infant; child
		(ニ)	infant
熟	児童	ジドウ	child; elementary school pupil
	児童憲章	ジドウケンショウ	The Children's Charter
	児童文学	ジドウブンガク	children's literature

149

免 ⑧

ノ ク 冖 ⺈ 尓 免 免 免

音	免	メン	exemption; permission; dismissal
熟	免疫	メンエキ	***med***. immunity (from disease, etc.)
	免許	メンキョ	license; permission
	免除	メンジョ	exemption; immunity —*v*. be exempt
	免状	メンジョウ	license; diploma
	免職	メンショク	discharge/dismissal (from a job) —*v*. discharge; dismiss; fire
	免責	メンセキ	exemption from responsibility —*v*. exempt (somebody) from responsibility
訓	免れる	まぬがれる (まぬかれる)	***vt***. escape; be saved; avoid; evade
¥	免許証	メンキョショウ	license; certificate; permit
	免許制	メンキョセイ	licensing system
	免税	メンゼイ	tax exemption —*v*. make (a product, etc.) exempt from tax
	免責	メンセキ	insurance deductible

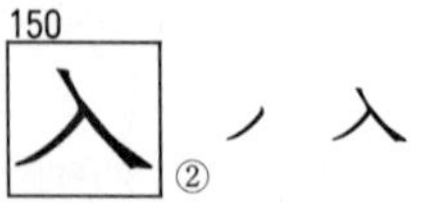

2 入 いる enter

150

入 ノ 入 ②

音	入	ニュウ	enter
熟	入院	ニュウイン	hospitalization; admittance into a hospital —*vi*. be hospitalized; go into hospital
	入営	ニュウエイ	enrollment/enlistment (in the army) —*vi*. enlist/enroll/volunteer (for the army)
	入会	ニュウカイ	admission/entrance/enrollment (into a club) —*vi*. register/join a club; become a club member)
	入閣	ニュウカク	entry into the Cabinet —*vi*. enter the Cabinet
	入学	ニュウガク	entrance into a school; matriculation —*vi*. enter/be admitted into a school; matriculate
	入居	ニュウキョ	occupancy —*vi*. move (into a flat, house, etc.)
	入居者	ニュウキョシャ	tenant
	入金	ニュウキン	receipt of money —*vi*. receive money; make a part payment
	入港	ニュウコウ	arrival in port —*vi*. enter/make port
	入国	ニュウコク	entry into a country; immigration —*vi*. gain entry into a country
	入社	ニュウシャ	joining a company —*vi*. join a company; become a member of a company
	入手	ニュウシュ	receipt; aquisition; procurement —*v*. procure; obtain; come by
	入所	ニュウショ	entrance; admission (to a training school, laboratory, prison, etc.) —*vi*. enter; be admitted; be put into prison
	入賞	ニュウショウ	winning a prize —*vi*. win a prize
	入場	ニュウジョウ	entrance; admission; admittance; —*vi*. enter; get in; be admitted
	入植	ニュウショク	immigration; settlement —*vi*. immigrate; settle
	入信	ニュウシン	religious conversion —*vi*. be converted; come to believe
	入籍	ニュウセキ	entry into the family register —*v*. have one's name put into the family register
	入選	ニュウセン	winning —*vi*. be accepted/selected
	入隊	ニュウタイ	joining the army; enlistment; enrollment —*vi*. join; enlist
	入団	ニュウダン	joining an organization; enlistment —*vi*. join an organization; enlist
	入湯	ニュウトウ	taking a hot bath —*vi*. take/have a bath

入念　ニュウネン　careful
入梅　ニュウバイ　beginning of the rainy season
入費　ニュウヒ　expenditure; expenses
入部　ニュウブ　admission into a club —*vi*. enter/be admitted into a club
入門　ニュウモン　becoming a disciple; learner's book —*vi*. become a pupil
入門書　ニュウモンショ　guide; primer; manual; introduction
入用　ニュウヨウ　need; want; demand; necessity
入浴　ニュウヨク　bath; bathing —*vi*. take a bath; bathe
入力　ニュウリョク　input —*v*. input

訓 入れる　いれる　*vt*. put in; insert; employ; make tea
入れ替える　いれかえる　*vt*. replace; substitute
入れ知恵　いれぢえ　idea put into one's head
入れ歯　いれば　false tooth/teeth
入れ物　いれもの　receptable; container
入る　いる　*v*. go/come in; set; sink; begin; attain; crack
入口　いりぐち　entrance
入る　はいる　*vi*. enter; come in; break in; join; begin

¥ 入荷　ニュウカ　receipt of goods —*v*. receive (goods)
入札　ニュウサツ　tender; bid; bidding —*vi*. tender; offer tender; make a bid
入超　ニュウチョウ　excess of imports; adverse balance of trade

2 八 は eight

151

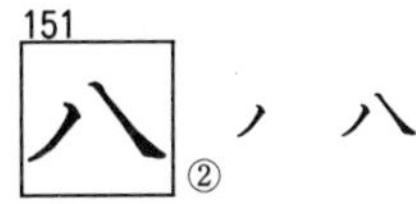

音 八　ハチ　eight

熟 八月　ハチガツ　August
八十八夜　ハチジュウハチヤ　eighty-eighth day from the beginning of spring
八幡　ハチマン　Hachiman (the god of war)
八頭身　ハットウシン　well-proportioned figure
八方　ハッポウ　every side; all around
八方美人　ハッポウビジン　everybody's friend

訓 八　や　eight
八重　やえ　eightfold
八重歯　やえば　double/extra tooth

八つ	やつ	eight
八つ	やっつ	eight
※八日	ようか	eighth day (of the month); 8th
※八百屋	やおや	greengrocer

152

公 ④ ノ 八 公 公

音	公	コウ (ク)	the public; duke
熟	公卿	クギョウ	court noble
	公家	クゲ	court noble
	公安	コウアン	public peace
	公園	コウエン	park
	公演	コウエン	public performance —***vi***. perform in public
	公開	コウカイ	open to the public —***v***. be open to the public
	公害	コウガイ	pollution
	公休日	コウキュウび	legal/public holiday
	公共	コウキョウ	the public
	公告	コウコク	public notice —***v***. give notice to the public
	公算	コウサン	probability
	公私	コウシ	public and private matters
	公使	コウシ	vice-ambassador
	公式	コウシキ	***math***. formula
	公衆	コウシュウ	the public
	公衆衛生	コウシュウエイセイ	public health
	公称	コウショウ	nominal; public/official name —***vi***. name publicly/officially
	公職	コウショク	public office
	公正	コウセイ	justice
	公選	コウセン	election by popular vote —***v***. elect by popular vote
	公然	コウゼン	open; public; not secret
	公聴会	コウチョウカイ	public hearing
	公道	コウドウ	public road
	公認	コウニン	official recognition; authorized —***v***. recognize officially
	公判	コウハン	public/open trial
	公費	コウヒ	public expenses
	公表	コウヒョウ	public announcement —***v***. announce publicly

	公布	コウフ	promulgation; proclaimation —*v.* promulgate; proclaim
	公平	コウヘイ	fairness
	公報	コウホウ	official gazette —*v.* keep an official gazette
	公民	コウミン	citizen
	公民館	コウミンカン	community center
	公務	コウム	public duties
	公務員	コウムイン	civil servant
	公明正大	コウメイセイダイ	fairness; fair and square; just and right
	公用	コウヨウ	official business
	公立	コウリツ	public foundation/institution
訓	公	おおやけ	the public
¥	公営	コウエイ	public management
	公益	コウエキ	public interest
	公開価格	コウカイカカク	price of introduced stock
	公開株	コウカイかぶ	introduced stock
	公開市場	コウカイシジョウ	open market
	公共団体	コウキョウダンタイ	public body
	公共料金	コウキョウリョウキン	public utilities charge
	公庫	コウコ	People's Finance Corporation; finance/loan corporation
	公債	コウサイ	public loan/bond
	公社	コウシャ	public corporation
	公社債	コウシャサイ	public corporate bonds and debentures
	公団	コウダン	public corporation
	公定価格	コウテイカカク	official price
	公定歩合	コウテイブアイ	official discount rate
	公認会計士	コウニンカイケイシ	certified public accountant
	公募	コウボ	public subscription/offer/placement —*v.* offer (shares) for public subscription
	公募債	コウボサイ	public issue
	公明党	コウメイトウ	Komeito (the *clean and fair* government party)

153

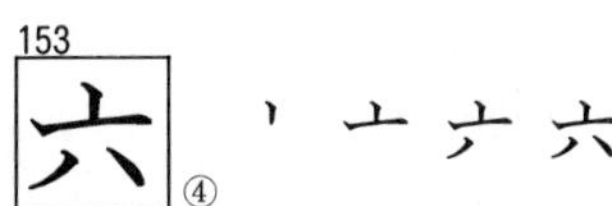

音	六	ロク (リク)	six
熟	六合	リクゴウ	universe; cosmos

六書　リクショ　the six styles of Chinese characters
六月　ロクガツ　June
六三制　ロクサンセイ　6-3 educational system (six years of elementary school and three years of junior high school)
六角形　ロッカクケイ　***math***. hexagon
六法全書　ロッポウゼンショ　Compendium of Laws; the statute books

訓　六つ　むっつ　six
六　む　six
六つ　むつ　six
※六日　むいカ　the sixth day (of a month); 6th

154

共 ⑥

一 十 卄 廿 共 共

音　共　キョウ　together; common; joint; (prefix) co-

熟　共栄　キョウエイ　mutual prosperity —***vi***. prosper
共演　キョウエン　costar —***vi***. costar
共学　キョウガク　coeducation
共感　キョウカン　sympathy —***vi***. feel sympathy
共催　キョウサイ　joint sponsorship —***v***. sponsor jointly
共済組合　キョウサイくみあい　benefit society
共産主義　キョウサンシュギ　Communism
共存　キョウゾン　coexistence —***vi***. coexist
共通　キョウツウ　common —***vi***. commune; be common
共通語　キョウツウゴ　common language
共同　キョウドウ　cooperation; union —***vi***. cooperate; collaborate
共同募金　キョウドウボキン　community chest
共犯　キョウハン　complicity
共謀　キョウボウ　collusion; conspiracy —***v***. collude; conspire
共鳴　キョウメイ　resonance; agreement; sympathy —***vi***. agree; sympathize
共有　キョウユウ　common ownership —***v***. own communally
共用　キョウヨウ　common use —***v***. use communally
共和国　キョウワコク　republic

訓　共　とも　together; common; joint; co-

¥　共産党　キョウサントウ　Communist Party
共通農業政策　キョウツウノウギョウセイサク　Common Agricultural Policy (C.A.P.)
共同請負　キョウドウうけおい　joint venture

共同経営	キョウドウ ケイエイ	cooperative management
共同資本	キョウドウシホン	joint capital
共同出資者	キョウドウ シュッシシャ	partner
共有資産	キョウユウシサン	common property
共和党	キョウワトウ	Republican Party (US)

155

兵 ⑦

ノ 亻 𠂉 斤 丘 乒 兵

音	兵	ヘイ ヒョウ	soldier; weapon; warfare
熟	兵糧	ヒョウロウ	provisions for troops
	兵員	ヘイイン	military strength; numerical strength of an army
	兵営	ヘイエイ	barracks
	兵役	ヘイエキ	military service
	兵器	ヘイキ	arms; weapon
	兵士	ヘイシ	soldier
	兵舎	ヘイシャ	barracks
	兵隊	ヘイタイ	troops; soldier
	兵法	ヘイホウ (ヒョウホウ)	military tactics; strategy
	兵力	ヘイリョク	military force; troop strength

156

具 ⑧

丨 冂 冃 月 目 旦 具 具

音	具	グ	equipment; tool; utensil; detail
熟	具合	グアイ	condition; circumstances
	具体案	グタイアン	definite/concrete plan
	具体化	グタイカ	embodiment; materialization —*v.* embody; manifest
	具体的	グタイテキ	concrete; definite; tangible

157

典 ⑧

丶 冂 巾 冊 冊 曲 典 典

音	典	テン	book; model; ceremony; celebration; code

2 二亠人𠆢亻儿入八● 冂冖冫几凵刀刂力勹匕匚十卜卩㔾厂厶又了⺈マ

熟	典雅	テンガ	refinement; elegance
	典拠	テンキョ	authority
	典型	テンケイ	model; type; pattern
	典型的	テンケイテキ	typical; representative; model; ideal
	典礼	テンレイ	ceremony

158

興 ⑯

音	興	キョウ	interest
		コウ	spring up
熟	興じる	キョウじる	*vi*. amuse oneself; have fun; make merry
	興醒める	キョウざめる	*vi*. spoil the fun; damper (a person's) enthusiasm
	興味	キョウミ	interest
	興行	コウギョウ	public entertainment; entertainment industry; performance —*v*. give a performance; produce; show; exhibit
	興廃	コウハイ	rise and fall; fate; destiny
	興奮	コウフン	excitement; stimulation —*vi*. be excited/aroused/stimulated
	興亡	コウボウ	rise and fall; ups and downs; existence; destiny
	興隆	コウリュウ	rise; prosperity —*vi*. rise; flourish; prosper; thrive; grow
訓	興す	おこす	*vt*. revive; resuscitate
	興る	おこる	*vi*. rise; flourish; be prosperous
¥	興業	コウギョウ	industrial enterprise; promotion of industry
	興業銀行	コウギョウギンコウ	industrial bank

2 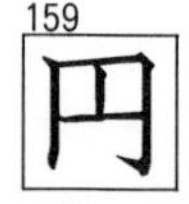 どうがまえ upside-down box

159

円 ④

丨 冂 冂 円

音	円	エン	round; circle; yen (unit of currency)
熟	円滑	エンカツ	even and uninterrupted; smooth
	円形	エンケイ	circular; round
	円周	エンシュウ	circumference

	円周率	エンシュウリツ	***math***. pi; π
	円熟	エンジュク	maturity; mellowness —***vi***. be matured/well-rounded
	円陣	エンジン	circle of people
	円柱	エンチュウ	column; pillar
	円筒	エントウ	cylinder
	円盤	エンバン	disk; discus; flying saucer
	円舞曲	エンブキョク	waltz (music)
	円満	エンマン	harmony; peaceful; perfect; well-roundedness
訓	円い	まるい	round; circular; spherical; globular
¥	円相場	エンソウバ	exchange rate of the yen
	円高	エンだか	appreciation of the yen
	円建て	エンだて	yen-based
	円建て外債	エンだてガイサイ	yen-denominated foreign bond
	円安	エンやす	depreciation of the yen

160

内 ④ 丨 冂 内 内

音	内	ナイ (ダイ)	inside
熟	内裏	ダイリ	imperial palace
	内意	ナイイ	secret intention; private opinion
	内縁	ナイエン	common-law marriage
	内科	ナイカ	internal medicine
	内海	ナイカイ	inland sea
	内外	ナイガイ	inside and outside; interior and exterior; some; about
	内角	ナイカク	***math***. interior angle
	内閣	ナイカク	Cabinet; administration
	内規	ナイキ	bylaw; customary rules
	内勤	ナイキン	office duty; indoor service; desk work —***vi***. work in an office
	内外科	ナイゲカ	internal medicine and surgery
	内向	ナイコウ	introversion
	内向的	ナイコウテキ	introverted; unsociable
	内妻	ナイサイ	common-law wife
	内在	ナイザイ	immanence; indwelling; inherence —***vi***. be immanent; indwell; inhere
	内在的	ナイザイテキ	immanent; indwelling; inherent; intrinsic
	内耳	ナイジ	***med***. internal ear; labyrinth
	内実	ナイジツ	facts; truth

内出血	ナイシュッケツ	***med***. internal bleeding; internal hemorrhage —***vi***. ***med***. bleed internally
内緒	ナイショ	secret; private; confidential
内助	ナイジョ	wife's help; internal assistance —***v***. help one's husband; get inside help
内情	ナイジョウ	internal conditions; inside affairs
内職	ナイショク	side job —***vi***. do another job on the side; moonlight
内心	ナイシン	one's heart/real intention; inner center
内申	ナイシン	unofficial report —***v***. make an unofficial report
内診	ナイシン	***med***. internal examination —***v***. ***med***. examine internally; make an internal examination
内申書	ナイシンショ	report on a pupil; secret school report
内政	ナイセイ	internal/domestic affairs
内省	ナイセイ	reflection; introspection; inward-looking; self-examination —***v***. introspect; reflect on oneself
内省的	ナイセイテキ	introspective; reflective; indrawn
内戦	ナイセン	civil war
内線	ナイセン	interior wiring; (telephone) extension
内蔵	ナイゾウ	built-in; containing —***v***. contain; have built-in
内臓	ナイゾウ	internal organs
内諾	ナイダク	informal consent —***v***. give informal consent
内談	ナイダン	private talk; personal conversation —***vi***. have a private talk/word
内地	ナイチ	inland; the interior; back country
内通	ナイツウ	secret communication/understanding; treachery; betrayal —***vi***. collude; conspire; betray
内定	ナイテイ	informal/tentative decision —***v***. decide tentatively; make an informal decision
内偵	ナイテイ	scouting; reconnaisance —***v***. scout; make private inquiries
内的	ナイテキ	inner; internal; intrinsic
内々	ナイナイ	private; secret; confidential
内燃機関	ナイネンキカン	internal-combustion engine
内部	ナイブ	interior; inner part; inside
内服	ナイフク	***med***. internal use (of medicine) —***v***. take (medicine) internally
内服薬	ナイフクヤク	internal medicine; medicine for internal use
内紛	ナイフン	internal trouble; srtife; storm in a teacup
内分	ナイブン	***math***. interior division —***v***. ***math***. divide internally
内聞	ナイブン	secret; secrecy; privacy
内分泌	ナイブンピツ	***med***. incretion; internal secretion
内包	ナイホウ	connotation; comprehension —***v***. connote; contain; involve

	内密	ナイミツ	secret; private; confidential; backdoor; under-the-table
	内務	ナイム	home/domestic affairs
	内面	ナイメン	inside; interior
	内約	ナイヤク	private contract; tacit agreement —***v***. make a private agreement; have a tacit understanding
	内憂	ナイユウ	domestic/internal troubles
	内容	ナイヨウ	contents; substance; details; depth
	内乱	ナイラン	civil war; insurrection; rebellion
	内覧	ナイラン	preview; preliminary inspection —***v***. preview; give a preliminary inspection
	内陸	ナイリク	inland
訓	内	うち	inside; interior; house; within
	内気	うちキ	reserved; shy; timid
	内金	うちキン	money paid on account; deposit; down payment
	内幕	うちマク	inside; inner workings
	内輪	うちわ	inside; family circle; moderate; conservative
	内訳	うちわけ	items; details; breakdown; classification
¥	内閣官房長官	ナイカクカンボウチョウカン	chief cabinet secretary
	内需	ナイジュ	domestic demand (requirements)
	内政	ナイセイ	domestic (internal) affairs (politics)
	内務省	ナイムショウ	Ministry of Home Affairs

161

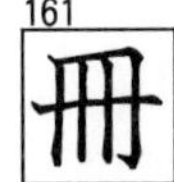

⑤ 丨 冂 冂 冊 冊

音	冊	サク	
		サツ	book; volume (counter for books)
熟	冊子	サッシ	book; booklet; pamphlet

162

⑥ 一 丆 冂 币 再 再

音	再	サイ (サ)	again; repeat; second; (prefix) re-
熟	再演	サイエン	repeat/second performance —***v***. perform again; give a second performance
	再会	サイカイ	reunion; meeting again —***vi***. meet again

2

二亠人𠆢亻儿入八●冂冖冫几凵刀刂力勹匕匚十卜卩㔾厂厶又了ㄅマ

再開	サイカイ	reopening; resumption —*v*. reopen; resume
再刊	サイカン	republication; reissue —*v*. republish; reissue
再起	サイキ	comeback; recovery —*vi*. make a comeback; recover; resume
再建	サイケン	reconstruction; rebuilding —*v*. reconstruct; rebuild
再現	サイゲン	reappearance; reproduction; reincarnation —*v*. reappear; reproduce; reincarnate
再検討	サイケントウ	reexamination; reconsideration; review; reppraisal —*v*. reexamine; reconsider; review; reppraise
再考	サイコウ	reconsideration; second thought; reflection —*v*. reconsider; reflect; think over again
再婚	サイコン	second marriage; remarriage —*vi*. remarry
再々	サイサイ	often; repeatedly; over and over
再三再四	サイサンサイシ	repeatedly; time and time again
再審	サイシン	retrial; review —*v*. retry; review
再生	サイセイ	regeneration; restoration; recycle —*v*. come to life again; recycle; regenerate; playback a recording
再生産	サイセイサン	reproduction —*v*. reproduce
再製	サイセイ	recycling —*v*. remanufacture; remake; recycle
再選	サイセン	reelection —*v*. reelect
再度	サイド	second time; twice; again
再読	サイドク	second reading —*v*. reread; read a book again
再入国	サイニュウコク	reentery (into a country) —*vi*. reenter (a country)
再入国許可	サイニュウコクキョカ	reentry permit
再任	サイニン	reappointment; reinstatement —*vi*. reappoint; reinstate
再認識	サイニンシキ	recognizing anew —*v*. recognize anew; realize
再燃	サイネン	recurrence; revival —*vi*. recur; revive; be revived
再発	サイハツ	recurrence; relapse —*vi*. recur; come back
再版	サイハン	reprint; second impression —*v*. reprint; print a second edition
再放送	サイホウソウ	repeat of a program; rebroadcast; rerun —*v*. repeat; show a rerun
再来	サイライ	second coming —*vi*. come again
訓 再び	ふたたび	again; once more
¥ 再販価格	サイハンカカク	resale price
再販制度	サイハンセイド	resale system

2 冖 わかんむり wa crown; *wa* (katakana)

163
冗 ④

冖 冗

音	冗	ジョウ	waste
熟	冗談	ジョウダン	joke
	冗長	ジョウチョウ	wordiness; verbosity; long-winded
	冗費	ジョウヒ	unnecessary expenses; wasteful spending; squandering

164
写 ⑤

冖 写 写

音	写	シャ	copy; film; photograph
熟	写実	シャジツ	realism
	写実的	シャジツテキ	realistic
	写植	シャショク	photocomposition; phototypesetting
	写真	シャシン	photograph; photo
	写真家	シャシンカ	photographer; cameraman
	写生	シャセイ	sketch; sketching
	写本	シャホン	written copy; manuscript
訓	写す	うつす	***vt***. copy; reproduce; take a photo
	写る	うつる	***vi***. be taken (a photo); come out; appear; be projected on a screen

165
冠 ⑨

冖 冗 冠 冠

音	冠	カン	crown; coronet
熟	冠婚葬祭	カンコンソウサイ	coming of age, marriage, funeral, and ancestor worship; ceremonial occasions
	冠水	カンスイ	submergence; flooding —***vi***. be covered with water; be flooded
訓	冠	かんむり	crown; top part of a Chinese character

2 冫 にすい ice

166

冷 ⑦

丶 冫 冫 冫 冷 冷 冷

音	冷	レイ	cold
熟	冷害	レイガイ	cold-weather damage
	冷気	レイキ	cold; chill; cold weather
	冷却	レイキャク	cooling —*v*. cool off/down; cool
	冷遇	レイグウ	cold reception/treatment —*v*. treat/receive coldly
	冷血	レイケツ	coldhearted; cold-blooded
	冷血動物	レイケツドウブツ	cold-blooded animal
	冷酷	レイコク	cruel; callous
	冷笑	レイショウ	sneer; scornful laugh —*v*. sneer; laugh scornfully
	冷水	レイスイ	cold/ice water
	冷静	レイセイ	calm; cool
	冷戦	レイセン	cold war
	冷蔵	レイゾウ	cold storage; refrigeration —*v*. keep in cold storage; refrigerate
	冷蔵庫	レイゾウコ	refrigerator
	冷淡	レイタン	cold; coldhearted; indifferent; apathetic
	冷凍	レイトウ	refrigeration; freezing; frozen —*v*. refrigerate; freeze
	冷凍機	レイトウキ	freezer
	冷房	レイボウ	air conditioning
訓	冷たい	つめたい	cold
	冷える	ひえる	***vi***. get cold
	冷	ひや	cold water/saké/rice
	冷やかす	ひやかす	***vt***. tease; banter
	冷やす	ひやす	***vt***. cool; refrigerate
	冷や奴	ひややっこ	chilled tofu
	冷ます	さます	***vt***. let cool
	冷める	さめる	***vi***. get cold; cool down

167

准 ⑩

丶 冫 冫 冫 冫 冫 冫 准 准 准

音	准	ジュン	apply correspondingly

熟 准将 ジュンショウ brigadier-general

168

凍 ⑩ 丶 冫 … 凍

音	凍	**トウ**	freeze
熟	凍結	**トウケツ**	freezing —*v*. freeze; freeze up; be frozen
	凍死	**トウシ**	death from cold —*vi*. freeze to death
	凍傷	**トウショウ**	frostbite
訓	凍る	**こおる**	*v*. freeze; be frozen
	凍える	**こごえる**	*vi*. be frozen/chilled/numbed
¥	凍結株	**トウケツかぶ**	frozen stock

169

凝 ⑯ 冫 … 凝

音	凝	**ギョウ**	grow stiff; congelation; clot; concentrate
熟	凝結	**ギョウケツ**	congelation; solidification; freezing —*vi*. congeal; solidify; freeze
	凝固	**ギョウコ**	congelation; solidification; freezing —*vi*. congeal; solidify; freeze
	凝視	**ギョウシ**	steady gaze; stare; fixation —*v*. gaze; stare
	凝縮	**ギョウシュク**	condensation —*v*. condense
訓	凝らす	**こらす**	*vt*. concentrate
	凝る	**こる**	*vi*. grow stiff; clot; refine; devote oneself to

2 几 つくえ table

170

凡 ③ 丿 几 凡

音	凡	**ボン** (ハン)	common; ordinary; mediocre
熟	凡例	**ハンレイ**	introductory notes
	凡才	**ボンサイ**	mediocre talent
	凡作	**ボンサク**	mediocre work (novel, etc.)
	凡人	**ボンジン**	ordinary person

	凡俗	ボンゾク	mediocre; common; vulgar; ordinary person
	凡庸	ボンヨウ	mediocre; commonplace; banal
訓	※凡そ	およそ	approximately; generally
	※凡て	すべて	all

171

風 ⑨

丿 几 凡 凡 凧 凬 凬 風 風

音	風	フウ	wind; air; look; appearance; fashion; style; type
		(フ)	
熟	風圧	フウアツ	wind pressure
	風雨	フウウ	wind and rain; rainstorm
	風雲	フウウン	winds and clouds; times of change
	風雲児	フウウンジ	adventurer; soldier of fortune
	風化	フウカ	weathering —***vi***. weather
	風雅	フウガ	elegant; refined; tasteful
	風害	フウガイ	storm damage; gale damage
	風格	フウカク	personality; character; style
	風変わり	フウがわり	eccentric; peculiar
	風紀	フウキ	public morals
	風景	フウケイ	scenery; landscape; view
	風月	フウゲツ	wind and moon; the beauty of nature
	風光	フウコウ	scenery; natural beauty
	風采	フウサイ	appearance; bearing
	風刺	フウシ	satire —***v***. satirize
	風車	フウシャ	windmill
	風習	フウシュウ	customs; manners; ways
	風疹	フウシン	***med***. German measles; rubella
	風水害	フウスイガイ	storm and flood damage
	風雪	フウセツ	blizzard; snow storm
	風説	フウセツ	rumor
	風船	フウセン	balloon
	風速	フウソク	wind velocity
	風速計	フウソクケイ	anemometer
	風俗	フウゾク	customs; manners; morals
	風俗営業	フウゾクエイギョウ	disreputable businesses (hostess clubs, massage parlors, etc.)
	風潮	フウチョウ	tide; trend of the times; social climate
	風体	フウテイ	appearance; looks; attitude
	風土	フウド	climate; topography; natural features

	風土病	フウドビョウ	endemic disease
	風波	フウハ	wind and waves; storm; rough seas; fight; disagreement
	風評	フウヒョウ	rumor
	風物	フウブツ	scenery; nature; natural objects; seasonal scenery
	風物詩	フウブツシ	nature poem; poem about a season
	風聞	フウブン	rumor; report
	風貌	フウボウ	looks; features
	風味	フウミ	taste; flavor
	風来坊	フウライボウ	wanderer; vagabond
	風流	フウリュウ	elegant; refined
	風力	フウリョク	wind force
	風鈴	フウリン	wind chime
	風情	フゼイ	taste; appearance; air
	風呂	フロ	bath
	風呂桶	フロオケ	bathtub
	風呂敷	フロしき	wrapping cloth
	風呂場	フロば	bathroom
訓	風	(かざ)	(prefix) wind
	風足	かざあし	wind velocity
	風上	かざかみ	windward
	風下	かざしも	leeward
	風見	かざみ	weathercock; weather vane
	風向き	かざむき	wind direction ***fig***. situation; condition; (bad) temper
	風	かぜ	wind
	風当たり	かぜあたり	force of the wind; criticism; opposition
	※風邪	かぜ	a cold

2 凵 うけばこ open box

172

④ ノ メ 凶 凶

音	凶	キョウ	ill fortune; poor workmanship; violence; injury
熟	凶悪	キョウアク	terrible; evil
	凶器	キョウキ	murder weapon

	凶行	キョウコウ	terrible happening (murder or assault)
	凶作	キョウサク	poor harvest
	凶報	キョウホウ	bad news; sad tidings
	凶暴	キョウボウ	violence

173

凹 ⑤

音	凹	オウ	hollow; concave
熟	凹凸	オウトツ	unevenness; ruggedness; irregularity
訓	凹み	へこみ	hollow; dent
	凹む	へこむ	***vi***. sink; collapse; hollow out; cave in

174

出 ⑤

音	出	シュツ (スイ)	go/put out; exit
熟	出演	シュツエン	stage/TV appearance —***vi***. appear on the stage/TV
	出火	シュッカ	outbreak of fire; fire —***vi***. break out in flames; catch fire
	出荷	シュッカ	shipment; shipping —***v***. ship; forward
	出願	シュツガン	application —***v***. apply
	出金	シュッキン	contribution; expenses; investment —***vi***. pay; contribute; invest
	出家	シュッケ	Buddhist priest —***vi***. become a priest; renounce the world
	出血	シュッケツ	bleeding —***vi***. bleed
	出欠	シュッケツ	attendance
	出現	シュツゲン	appearance; emergence —***vi***. appear; emerge; come into existence
	出航	シュッコウ	departure —***vi***. sail; leave; fly; take off
	出港	シュッコウ	departure from a port —***vi***. leave from a port
	出国	シュッコク	leaving a country —***vi***. leave/get out of a country
	出札	シュッサツ	ticket issue —***vi***. issue a ticket
	出産	シュッサン	childbirth —***v***. give birth to
	出所	シュッショ	source; release from prison —***vi***. be released from prison
	出生	シュッセイ (シュッショウ)	birth —***vi***. give birth

	出生地	シュッセイチ	birthplace
	出生率	シュッセイリツ	birth rate
	出場	シュツジョウ	participation —***vi***. participate; take part
	出色	シュッショク	eminent; outstanding; remarkable; excellent
	出身	シュッシン	one's hometown
	出陣	シュツジン	going to battle/the front —***vi***. go to battle/the front
	出世	シュッセ	success in life; promotion —***vi***. rise; be promoted
	出席	シュッセキ	presence; attendance —***vi***. be present; attend
	出張	シュッチョウ	business trip —***vi***. take a business trip
	出廷	シュッテイ	court appearance —***vi***. appear in court
	出典	シュッテン	source (of a quote, etc.)
	出頭	シュットウ	appearance; presentation —***vi***. appear; present oneself
	出動	シュツドウ	dispatch —***vi***. dispatch; call in; alert
	出馬	シュツバ	in person —***vi***. run for; go in person
	出発	シュッパツ	start; departure —***vi***. depart; leave
	出帆	シュッパン	sailing for —***vi***. sail for
	出版	シュッパン	publication; publishing —***v***. publish
	出品	シュッピン	exhibition; exhibit —***v***. exhibit; enter; be on display
	出没	シュツボツ	appearance and disappearance; coming and going —***vi***. frequent; be haunted by
	出漁	シュツリョウ	fishing (on a boat) —***vi***. go out fishing (on a boat)
	出力	シュツリョク	output
訓	出す	だす	***vt***. let out; show; hold out
	出る	でる	***vi***. go out; start; leave; rise; appear; protrude
	出会う	であう	***vi***. meet; run into; encounter
	出掛ける	でかける	***vi***. go out; leave
	出来事	できごと	happening; affair; incident; event
	出来物	できもの	swelling; tumor
	出来る	できる	***vi***. be finished/ready/made from; come into being; can; be possible
¥	出資	シュッシ	investment —***vi***. invest; provide capital
	出超	シュッチョウ	excess of exports
	出費	シュッピ	expenses; expenditure
	出納	スイトウ	receipts and disbursements
	出来高	できだか	volume
	出来値	できね	actual price

175

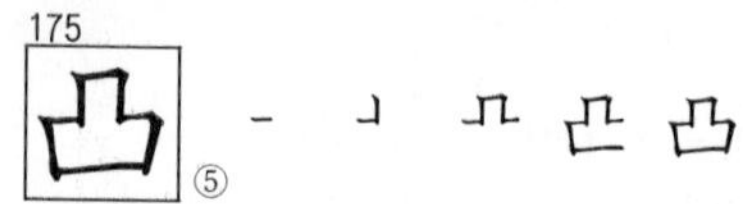

音	凸	トツ	convex
熟	凸版	トッパン	relief printing; letter press
	凸レンズ	トツレンズ	convex lens

176

画 ⑧

音	画	ガ	picture; painting
		カク	stroke in calligraphy; division; plan
熟	画家	ガカ	painter; artist
	画一的	カクイツテキ	uniform; uniformized
	画策	カクサク	plan; scheme —*v.* plan; scheme
	画数	カクスウ	number of strokes (in a Chinese character)
	画然	カクゼン	distinct; clear cut
	画材	ガザイ	painting materials
	画商	ガショウ	picture/art dealer
	画像	ガゾウ	portrait
	画題	ガダイ	title/subject of a painting
	画期的	カッキテキ	epoch-making
	画伯	ガハク	great/master painter
	画風	ガフウ	style of painting
	画面	ガメン	picture; (television) screen
	画用紙	ガヨウシ	drawing paper
	画廊	ガロウ	art gallery
訓	画	え	picture; painting

2 刀 かたな knife; sword

177

刀 ② フ 刀

音	刀	トウ	sword
熟	刀剣	トウケン	swords

	刀工	トウコウ	swordmaker; swordsmith
	刀匠	トウショウ	swordsmith
	刀身	トウシン	sword blade
	刀自	トジ	Madame; lady; matron; mistress
訓	刀	かたな	sword; blade; knife

178

刃 ③ フ 刀 刃

音	刃	ジン （ニン）	edge
熟	刃傷	ニンジョウ	bloodshed
訓	刃	は	blade
	刃物	はもの	cutlery; knives and forks
	刃渡り	はわたり	length of a blade; walking on swords

179

切 ④ 一 七 切 切

音	切	セツ （サイ）	cut all
熟	切開	セッカイ	incision ***med***. section; operation —***v***. make an incision; carry out a surgical operation
	切実	セツジツ	pressing; acute; keen; urgent; earnest
	切除	セツジョ	cutting off; removal ***med***. excision —***v***. cut off; remove ***med***. excise
	切々	セツセツ	ardent; earnest; sincere
	切断	セツダン	cutting; section; amputation —***v***. cut; sever; amputate
	切ない	セツない	melancholic
	切に	セツに	desperately; very much
	切迫	セッパク	imminence —***vi***. draw near; impend; be imminent; become acute
	切腹	セップク	hara-kiri; suicide by disembowelment —***vi***. commit hara-kiri; disembowel oneself
	切望	セツボウ	earnest desire; yearning —***v***. desire earnestly; yearn for
訓	切る	きる	***v***. cut; give up; finish
	切れる	きれる	***vi***. break; cut well; be sharp
	切り上げる	きりあげる	***vt***. stop doing something

切り替える　きりかえる　*vt*. change
切手　きって　postage stamp
切符　きっぷ　ticket

¥ 切り上げ　きりあげ　revolution; upward valuation
切り替える　きりかえる　*vt*. convert; review
切り詰める　きりつめる　*vt*. cut down; economize

180

分　ノ 八 分 分 ④

音 分　ブ　rate; percentage; one percent; thickness; *bu* (unit of length, approx. 3.03 cm)
フン　minute (of time or arc); *fun* (unit of weight, approx. 375 mg)
ブン　dividing; portion

熟 分化　ブンカ　specialization; differentiation —***vi***. specialize; differentiate
分解　ブンカイ　resolution; decomposition; dissection —***v***. be resolved; decompose; dissect; fall apart; take apart
分割　ブンカツ　division; partition —***v***. divide; partition
分岐　ブンキ　divergence —***vi***. diverge; branch off
分岐点　ブンキテン　turning point; junction; crossroads
分業　ブンギョウ　division of labor —***v***. divide an operation into separate tasks
分極化　ブンキョクカ　polarization —***vi***. polarize
分家　ブンケ　branch family —***vi***. move out and set up a branch family
分権　ブンケン　decentralization of power/authority
分光　ブンコウ　***phy***. spectrum —***v***. separate a ray of light into a spectrum
分校　ブンコウ　branch school
分際　ブンザイ　one's status/position
分冊　ブンサツ　division of a book into separate volumes; volume —***v***. divide into separate volumes
分散　ブンサン　dispersion —***vi***. disperse; be dispersed; break up
分詞　ブンシ　***gram***. participle
分子　ブンシ　***chem***. molecule ***math***. numerator ***n***. elements; function
分室　ブンシツ　branch office; partitioned room
分宿　ブンシュク　separate hotels, etc. —***vi***. stay at separate hotels, etc.
分掌　ブンショウ　division of a job into separate tasks —***v***. divide a job into separate tasks

分乗	ブンジョウ	separate cars/buses —***vi***. ride in separate cars /buses
分身	ブンシン	child; branch(of a family/organization)
分水	ブンスイ	diversion/shedding of water; diverted water —***vi***. divert/shed water
分水界	ブンスイカイ	watershed; (continental) divide
分水嶺	ブンスイレイ	watershed; (continental) divide
分数	ブンスウ	***math***. fraction
分析	ブンセキ	analysis —***v***. analyse; assay
分節	ブンセツ	decomposition; division; articulation —***v***. break something down into its constituent parts; divide a sentence into clauses; articulate (each syllable)
分隊	ブンタイ	squad; division; detachment
分担	ブンタン	division; share; assignment —***v***. divide; share; assign; allot
分団	ブンダン	branch; chapter; group
分銅	ブンドウ	balance weight
分度器	ブンドキ	protractor
分納	ブンノウ	installment —***v***. pay in installments
分派	ブンパ	branch; faction; sect; denomination; separation; division —***vi***. branch out into factions/sects; separate; divide
分売	ブンバイ	separate sales —***v***. sell separately; break up and sell
分配	ブンパイ	distribution; division; share —***v***. distribute; divide; share
分泌	ブンピ(ツ)	***med***. secretion —***v***. secrete
分筆	ブンピツ	subdivision (of a lot) —***vi***. subdivide land
分布	ブンプ	distribution —***v***. distribute
分別	フンベツ	discretion; good sense —***v***. be discrete
分別	ブンベツ	classification —***v***. classify; sort; separate
分娩	ブンベン	childbirth —***v***. give birth to
分母	ブンボ	***math***. denominator
分野	ブンヤ	field; sphere; realm
分与	ブンヨ	distribution; allocation; apportionment —***v***. distribute; allocate; apportion
分離	ブンリ	separation; segregation; selectivity —***v***. separate; segregate; select
分立	ブンリツ	separation; independence —***v***. separate; make independent; act separately/independently
分流	ブンリュウ	tributary; branch
分留	ブンリュウ	fractional distillation —***v***. carry out fractional distillation
分量	ブンリョウ	quantity; amount; dose
分類	ブンルイ	classification —***v***. classify; sort; break down

	分裂	ブンレツ	division; split; schism; segmentation —*vi*. split; break up; segment
訓	分ける	わける	*vi*. divide into; separate; classify; share
	分け合う	わけあう	*vt*. share
	分け前	わけまえ	one's share; cut
	分け目	わけめ	part; parting
	分かる	わかる	*vi*. understand; see; appreciate; know; find out; recognize
	分らず屋	わからずや	obstinate person; blockhead
	分かれる	わかれる	*vi*. branch off; separate; be divided; disperse; break up
	分かれ道	わかれみち	branch/forked road
	分かれ目	わかれめ	turning point; dividing line
	分かつ	わかつ	*vt*. share; know; divide; separate
¥	分割払い	ブンカツばらい	installment; easy payment; hire purchase
	分散投資	ブンサントウシ	diversified investment
	分譲	ブンジョウ	sale (of land) in lots/parcels —*v*. sell off (land) in lots/parcels

181

⑦ 、 ラ ネ ネ ネ 初 初

音	初	ショ	beginning
熟	初夏	ショカ	early summer; beginning of summer
	初回	ショカイ	the first time; the beginning
	初刊	ショカン	first publication
	初期	ショキ	early days; first stages
	初級	ショキュウ	beginner's class
	初産	ショサン (ういザン)	first birth
	初志	ショシ	original intention/purpose
	初秋	ショシュウ	early fall/autumn
	初春	ショシュン	early spring; beginning of spring
	初旬	ショジュン	first ten days of a month
	初心	ショシン	original intention; immaturity; inexperience
	初心者	ショシンシャ	beginner; novice
	初診	ショシン	first medical examination
	初代	ショダイ	first generation; the first
	初対面	ショタイメン	first meeting
	初潮	ショチョウ	***med***. one's first menstruation
	初冬	ショトウ	early winter; beginning of winter
	初等	ショトウ	elementary

	初七日	ショなのか	seventh day from a person's death
	初日	ショニチ	first day; the start
	初版	ショハン	first edition
	初犯	ショハン	first offense
	初歩	ショホ	the first step; rudiments; elements
	初夜	ショヤ	wedding night
	初老	ショロウ	middle-aged; elderly
訓	初め	はじめ	beginning; outset
	初めて	はじめて	for the first time
	初	はつ	first
	初恋	はつこい	first love
	初荷	はつに	first cargo of the New Year
	初耳	はつみみ	news heard for the first time
	初詣	はつもうで	first shrine visit of the year
	初物	はつもの	first product of the season
	初雪	はつゆき	first snowfall of the year
	初夢	はつゆめ	one's dream on the second day of the New Year
	初める	そめる	***vt***. start; begin
	※初々しい	ういういしい	innocent; naive
	※初子	ういご	one's first child
	※初陣	ういじん	one's first military campaign; first competition

182

⑧ 丶 丷 䒑 兰 乒 关 券 券

音	券	ケン	ticket

2 刂 りっとう standing sword

183

音	刈	ガイ	mow; cut
訓	刈る	かる	mow; cut
	刈り入れる	かりいれる	***vt***. harvest; collect; reap
	刈り込む	かりこむ	***vt***. cut; clip; trim; crop

184

刊 ⑤ 一 二 干 刊 刊

音	刊	カン	publish
熟	刊行	カンコウ	publication —*vt.* publish; issue; bring out
訓	刊む	きざむ	*vt.* engrave; chisel; carve

185

刑 ⑥ 一 二 于 开 刑 刑

音	刑	ケイ	punishment; penal; penalty
熟	刑期	ケイキ	prison term/sentence
	刑死	ケイシ	death penalty; execution —*vi.* be executed
	刑事	ケイジ	police detective
	刑事裁判所	ケイジサイバンショ	criminal court
	刑事犯	ケイジハン	criminal offense
	刑罰	ケイバツ	penalty; punishment
	刑法	ケイホウ	criminal law; the penal code
	刑務所	ケイムショ	jail; prison

186

列 ⑥ 一 ア 万 歹 列 列

音	列	レツ	line; row; queue
熟	列する	レッする	*v.* line up; queue
	列記	レッキ	written list; enumeration —*v.* list; enumerate
	列挙	レッキョ	list; enumeration —*v.* list; enumerate
	列強	レッキョウ	treaty/world powers
	列国	レッコク	nations; the powers
	列車	レッシャ	train
	列席	レッセキ	attendance; presence —*vi.* attend; be present
	列伝	レツデン	biographies
	列島	レットウ	chain of islands; archipelago
訓	列なる	つらなる	*vi.* lie in a row
	列ねる	つらねる	*vt.* put/lie in a row

187

判 ⑦

丶 丷 䒑 兰 半 判 判

音	判	ハン バン	judge; decide; seal; stamp; format
熟	判決	ハンケツ	judgment; judicial decision —***v***. judge; pass judgement
	判例	ハンレイ	precedent; leading case
	判事	ハンジ	judge; justice
	判然	ハンゼン	clear; evident
	判断	ハンダン	judgment; decision; conclusion; divination —***v***. judge; make judgment; decide; conclude
	判定	ハンテイ	judgment; decision; adjudication —***v***. judge; decide; adjudicate
	判読	ハンドク	interpretation; reading; decipherment (of unclear writing) —***v***. interpret; read; decipher (unclear writing)
	判別	ハンベツ	discrimination; distinction —***v***. distinguish; discriminate
	判明	ハンメイ	clear; confirmed —***vi***. become clear; be ascertained/confirmed
訓	※判る	わかる	***vi***. understand; become clear/evident

188

別 ⑦

丨 口 口 另 另 別 別

音	別	ベツ	different; separate; another; special; parting; farewell
熟	別格	ベッカク	special; exceptional
	別館	ベッカン	annex; separate building
	別記	ベッキ	stated elsewhere —***v***. be stated elsewhere
	別居	ベッキョ	(legal) separation (of a married couple); living apart —***vi***. live separately; be separated
	別口	ベツくち	different kind/item
	別個	ベッコ	separate; different
	別冊	ベッサツ	separate volume; supplement
	別紙	ベッシ	attached sheet; enclosure
	別辞	ベツジ	parting words; farewell speech
	別室	ベッシツ	separate/special room
	別種	ベッシュ	another/different kind
	別称	ベッショウ	another name; alias; pseudonym
	別状	ベツジョウ	something unusual/different

	別人	ベツジン	another/different person
	別世界	ベッセカイ	another world
	別席	ベッセキ	different/special seat; different/special room
	別送	ベッソウ	by separate mail; under separate cover —*v*. send by separate mail
	別荘	ベッソウ	villa; country residence
	別宅	ベッタク	second home/residence
	別段	ベツダン	special; particular
	別邸	ベッテイ	villa; separate residence
	別天地	ベッテンチ	another world
	別途	ベット	different method; separatedly
	別納	ベツノウ	payment made at different time or in a different way —*v*. pay at a different time; pay in a different way
	別嬪	ベッピン	***col***. beautiful woman
	別便	ベツビン	by separate mail
	別封	ベップウ	by separate cover —*v*. send by separate cover
	別々	ベツベツ	separate; individual
	別法	ベッポウ	different way/method
	別棟	ベツむね	separate/different building; annex
	別名	ベツメイ	another name (used in biology when referring to the different names used for the same animal or plant)
	別物	ベツもの	something else; exception; special case
	別離	ベツリ	parting; separation
訓	別ける	わける	***vt***. divide; separate; distinguish
	別れ道	わかれみち	forked road; crossroads
	別れ目	わかれめ	turning point; junction
	別れる	わかれる	***vi***. part company with; leave; separate; get divorced; diverge
	別け隔て	わけへだて	making distinctions; discriminating
	別つ	わかつ	***vt***. divide; separate; distinguish

189

利 ⑦

丿 二 千 禾 禾 利 利

音	利	リ	profit; advantage; interest
熟	利する	リする	*v*. profit; benefit; do (a person) good
	利害	リガイ	advantages and disadvantages; interests
	利器	リキ	sharp-edged/useful tool; convenience
	利権	リケン	rights; interests; concession
	利己	リコ	egoism; self-interest

	利己主義	リコシュギ	egoism; selfishness
	利口	リコウ	smart; clever; bright
	利点	リテン	advantage; point in favor
	利得	リトク	profit; benefit; gain
	利尿	リニョウ	urination
	利発	リハツ	cleverness; intelligence
	利用	リヨウ	utilization; application —*v*. utilize; apply; make use of
訓	利く	きく	***vi***. take effect; work
	利かす	きかす	***vt***. make effective; use; exercise
	利腕	ききうで	one hand more skillful than other
	効き目	ききめ	effect; efficacy
¥	利上げ	りあげ	increase in the interest rate
	利益	リエキ	profit; gain; returns
	利益準備金	リエキジュンビキン	legal retained earnings
	利益準備金積立額	リエキジュンビキンつみたてガク	provision of legal retained surplus
	利食い	りぐい	profit taking (cashing); realizing; reselling at a profit
	利ざや	りざや	margin of profit
	利子	リシ	interest
	利潤	リジュン	profit
	利殖	リショク	moneymaking —***v***. make money
	利息	リソク	interest (on a loan)
	利払い	りばらい	interest payment
	利用者	リヨウシャ	user
	利率	リリツ	rate of interest

190

⑧

音	刻	コク	carve
熟	刻一刻	コクイッコク	gradually; moment by moment
	刻印	コクイン	carved seal —***v***. impress a seal
	刻限	コクゲン	fixed/appointed time
	刻々	コクコク	every moment; moment by moment; gradually
	刻苦	コック	hard work; arduous labor —***vi***. work hard; be arduous
訓	刻む	きざむ	***vt***. carve; engrave; sculpt

191

刷 ⑧

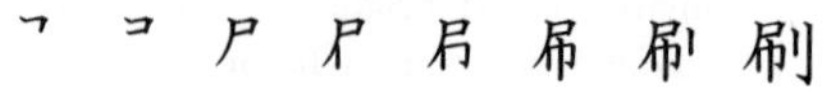

音	刷	サツ	print; reform
熟	刷新	サッシン	reform —*v*. reform
訓	刷る	する	***vt***. print

192

刺 ⑧

音	刺	シ	stab; pierce; stick
熟	刺客	シカク	assassin
	刺激	シゲキ	stimulus; stimulation; incentive —*v*. stimulate; irritate; spur
	刺殺	シサツ	death by stabbing —*v*. stab to death; put out; ***bas***. put out
	刺繡	シシュウ	embroidery —*v*. embroider
	刺青	シセイ	tattoo —*v*. tattoo
訓	刺す	さす	***vt***. pierce; stab; prick; bite; sting; sew; stick
	刺さる	ささる	***vi***. stick; get stuck
	刺し身	さしみ	*sashimi* (Japanese dish of thinly-sliced raw fish)

193

制 ⑧

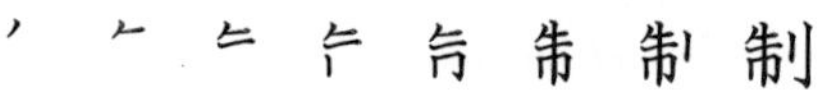

音	制	セイ	regulation; control
熟	制する	セイする	***vt***. control; command; dominate
	制圧	セイアツ	control —*v*. gain control; suppress
	制癌剤	セイガンザイ	anticancer drug
	制御	セイギョ	control —*v*. control
	制御装置	セイギョソウチ	control system/device
	制空権	セイクウケン	air superiority
	制限	セイゲン	limit; restriction; limitation —*v*. limit; restrict; control
	制裁	セイサイ	punishment; sanction; penalty —*v*. punish; sanction; penalize
	制裁金	セイサイキン	penalty; fine
	制作	セイサク	work; production —*v*. produce; make

制作者	セイサクシャ	producer
制止	セイシ	check; control; restrain —*v*. control; restrain; hold back; check
制定	セイテイ	enactment; establishment —*v*. enact; establish; create
制度	セイド	system; institution; organization
制度化	セイドカ	systematization; organization —*v*. systematize; organize
制動	セイドウ	brake; braking —*v*. brake
制動機	セイドウキ	brake
制覇	セイハ	supremacy; championship; conquest —*vi*. conquer; dominate; win
制服	セイフク	uniform
制帽	セイボウ	regulation/school cap
制約	セイヤク	restriction; limitation; condition —*v*. restrict; limit
制令	セイレイ	regulations

194

到 ⑧

一 𠫔 五 조 至 至 到 到

音	到	トウ	reach
熟	到達	トウタツ	arrival; attainment —*vi*. arrive; reach; attain; touch
	到着	トウチャク	arrival —*vi*. arrive at; reach
	到底（〜ない）	トウテイ（〜ない）	not possibly; not at all; by no means; hardly
	到来	トウライ	arrival; advent; influx —*vi*. come; arrive; occur

195

削 ⑨

丨 丷 㐅 𭕄 肖 肖 肖 肖 削

音	削	サク	shave; sharpen; delete; erase
熟	削減	サクゲン	reduction; cut; cutback; curtailment —*v*. reduce; cut; curtail
	削除	サクジョ	elimination; deletion —*v*. eliminate; delete; cross out
訓	削る	けずる	*vt*. shave; scrape; sharpen; remove; delete; erase; cut

196

前 ⑨

丶 丷 䒑 … 前

音	前	ゼン	before; fornt
熟	前衛	ゼンエイ	vanguard; advance guard; avant-guarde
	前回	ゼンカイ	last time
	前科者	ゼンカもの	person's criminal record
	前記	ゼンキ	above-mentioned
	前期	ゼンキ	first term; preceeding period
	前言	ゼンゲン	one's previous remarks
	前後	ゼンゴ	about; approximately; order; sequence; front and back —*vi*. reverse order
	前座	ゼンザ	minor performer; opening performance
	前菜	ゼンサイ	hors d'oeuvres
	前史	ゼンシ	prehistory
	前日	ゼンジツ	previous day; day before
	前者	ゼンシャ	the former
	前述	ゼンジュツ	the above-mentioned —*vi*. mention above
	前身	ゼンシン	one's form in a previous existence; previous form; former position
	前進	ゼンシン	advance; drive; progress —*vi*. advance; drive forward; progress
	前世	ゼンセ	previous existence
	前線	ゼンセン	front lines; the front; front (meteorology)
	前奏	ゼンソウ	prelude (in music)
	前奏曲	ゼンソウキョク	prelude; overture
	前代	ゼンダイ	previous generation; former ages
	前代未聞	ゼンダイミモン	news heard for the first time
	前兆	ゼンチョウ	omen; portent; sign
	前提	ゼンテイ	premise; prerequiste
	前途	ゼント	one's future prospects; the road ahead
	前任	ゼンニン	former official; previous job
	前年	ゼンネン	preceeding year; last year
	前半	ゼンハン	first half
	前文	ゼンブン	preamble; the above statement
	前面	ゼンメン	front
	前夜	ゼンヤ	last night; previous night
	前夜祭	ゼンヤサイ	celebration held on the eve of an anniversary or event
	前略	ゼンリャク	first part omitted (salutation in letter)
	前例	ゼンレイ	precedent

	前歴	ゼンレキ	one's past record
訓	前	まえ	before; front
	前売り	まえうり	advance sale —*vi*. sell in advance
	前置き	まえおき	introductory remark; preliminary —*vi*. make introductory remarks
	前払い	まえばらい	advance payment —*v*. pay in advance
¥	前期繰越利益金	ゼンキくりこしリエキキン	retained earnings brought forward
	前期損益修正	ゼンキソンエキシュウセイ	prior period adjustments
	前渡金	ゼントキン	advance payments
	前年同期	ゼンネンドウキ	corresponding period the previous year
	前場	ゼンば	morning session
	前受金	まえうけキン	advances received
	前受収益	まえうけシュウエキ	deferred income
	前払費用	まえばらいヒヨウ	prepaid expenses
	前引け	まえびけ	closing of the morning session

197

⑨

音	則	ソク	rule

198

剣 ⑩

音	剣	ケン	sword
熟	剣士	ケンシ	fencer; swordsman
	剣術	ケンジュツ	fencing; swordmanship
	剣道	ケンドウ	kendo (Japanese fencing)
	剣法	ケンポウ	art of fencing; swordmanship
訓	剣	つるぎ	sword

199

剛 ⑩

音	剛	ゴウ	firm; hard; solid; brave; strong
熟	剛健	ゴウケン	sturdiness; fortitude; robustness

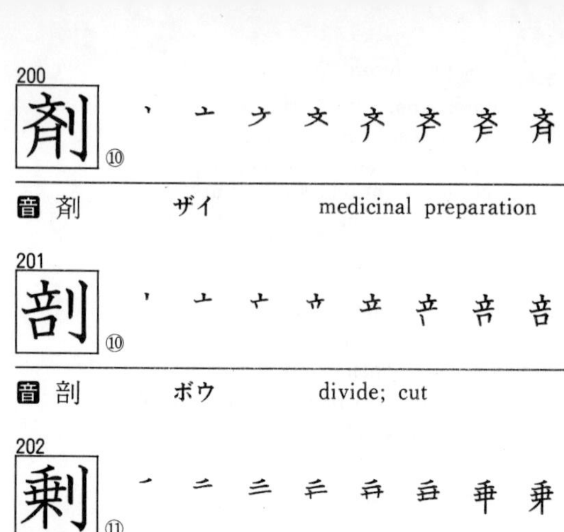

200 剤 ⑩

音	剤	ザイ	medicinal preparation

201 剖 ⑩

音	剖	ボウ	divide; cut

202 剰 ⑪

音	剰	ジョウ	extra; surplus
熟	剰余	ジョウヨ	surplus; remainder; balance; residue
¥	剰余金	ジョウヨキン	retained earnings

203 副 ⑪

音	副	フク	accompany; vice-; deputy; assistant
熟	副官	フクカン	adjutant; aide
	副業	フクギョウ	side job
	副作用	フクサヨウ	***med***. ill/side effect
	副産物	フクサンブツ	byproduct
	副詞	フクシ	***gram***. adverb
	副次的	フクジテキ	secondary
	副収入	フクシュウニュウ	additional/side income
	副賞	フクショウ	extra/supplementary prize
	副将	フクショウ	second-in-command; vice-captain
	副食	フクショク	side dish (to be eaten with rice)
	副葬品	フクソウヒン	articles buried with the dead
	副題	フクダイ	subtitle; subheading
	副読本	フクドクホン	supplementary reader
	副本	フクホン	duplicate; copy (of a written work)
訓	※副う	そう	***vi***. accompany

¥	副会長	フクカイチョウ	vice-chairman
	副社長	フクシャチョウ	(company) vice-president

204

割 ⑫

音	割	カツ	divide; cut
熟	割愛	カツアイ	omission —*v*. omit; part with
	割拠	カッキョ	holding one's own ground —***vi***. hold one's own ground
	割腹	カップク	*hara-kiri* (self-disembowelment) —***vi***. disembowel oneself
	割礼	カツレイ	circumcision
訓	割る	わる	***vt***. break; divide; split; water; allot
	割	わり	rate; one tenth; ten percent; division
	割り当てる	わりあてる	***vt***. assign; allot; distribute
	割り切る	わりきる	***vt***. divide; leave no doubt; give a clear-cut solution (for a problem)
	割れる	われる	***vi***. break; be divisible; crack; be torn
	割く	さく	***vt***. tear; sever; estrange; spare
¥	割賦	カップ	installment
	割合	わりあい	ratio; proportion
	割り当て	わりあて	allotment; allocation
	割高	わりだか	comparatively high price
	割引き	わりびき	discount
	割引債	わりびきサイ	discount bond
	割引手形	わりびきてがた	discounted notes
	割引料	わりびきりょう	discount charge
	割り引く	わりびく	***vt***. discount; give a discount; reduce
	割安	わりやす	comparatively low price
	～割れ	～われ	(suffix) below the level

205

創 ⑫

音	創	ソウ	create; originate; make; wound; injury
熟	創案	ソウアン	original idea —*v*. come up with an original idea
	創意	ソウイ	originality; inventiveness
	創痍	ソウイ	wound

創刊	ソウカン	first edition —*v.* start/launch a magazine
創業	ソウギョウ	inauguration; establishment —*v.* found; establish
創建	ソウケン	foundation; establishment —*v.* found; establish
創作	ソウサク	creation; work —*v.* create; write a novel/story
創始	ソウシ	origination; creation —*v.* originate; create; found
創世	ソウセイ	creation of the world
創世記	ソウセイキ	Genesis
創設	ソウセツ	foundation; establishment —*v.* found; establish
創造	ソウゾウ	creation —*v.* create
創立	ソウリツ	foundation; establishment

206

劇 ⑮

音	劇	ゲキ	play; drama; the theater; acute; sharp
熟	劇化	ゲキカ	dramatization —*vi.* dramatize
	劇画	ゲキガ	comics with a realistic narrative
	劇作家	ゲキサッカ	dramatist
	劇場	ゲキジョウ	theater; play house
	劇団	ゲキダン	troupe; theatrical company
	劇中劇	ゲキチュウゲキ	play within a play
	劇的	ゲキテキ	dramatic; dramatically
	劇毒	ゲキドク	deadly poison
	劇薬	ゲキヤク	powerful drug

2 力 ちから strength; power

207

力 ② フ 力

音	力	リキ	strength; force; power
		リョク	strength; force; power
熟	力演	リキエン	superb performance —*vi.* give a superb performance
	力学	リキガク	dynamics; mechanics
	力作	リキサク	great work; masterpiece
	力士	リキシ	sumo wrestler

	力説	リキセツ	emphasis; stress —*v*. emphasize; stress
	力走	リキソウ	sprinting; fast running —*vi*. run as fast as one can; sprint
	力点	リキテン	fulcrum; emphasis
	力む	リキむ	*vi*. exert one's strength; strain; bear down
	力量	リキリョウ	ability; capacity; physical strength
訓	力	ちから	force; power; strength
	力一杯	ちからイッパイ	with full force; with all one's might
	力仕事	ちからシごと	physical labor
	力添え	ちからぞえ	aid; help; assistance —*vi*. aid; help; assist
	力試し	ちからだめし	trial of one's strength; test of one's ability
	力づける	ちからづける	*vt*. encourage; cheer up
	力持ち	ちからもち	man of great (physical) strength

208

加 ⑤ フ カ カ 加 加

音	加	カ	add; increase; join; participate; Canada; California
熟	加害	カガイ	assault; violence
	加害者	カガイシャ	assailant
	加減	カゲン	addition and subtraction; degree; extent; adjustment —*v*. allow for; make allowances for; adjust; moderate
	加護	カゴ	divine protection —*v*. receive divine protection
	加算	カサン	***math***. addition —*v*. add; include
	加勢	カセイ	help; aid; support; assistance —*vi*. help; aid; support; assist
	加速	カソク	acceleration —*v*. accelerate
	加速度	カソクド	acceleration rate
	加担	カタン	support; help; assistance; participation —*v*. support; help; assist; participate
	加入	カニュウ	joining; admission; entry; affiliation —*vi*. join; enter; affiliate
	加入者	カニュウシャ	member; subscriber
	加熱	カネツ	heating —*v*. heat up
	加筆	カヒツ	correction; revision (of an essay, a painting, etc.) —*v*. correct; revise
	加法	カホウ	***math***. addition
	加味	カミ	flavoring; seasoning —*v*. flavor; season
	加盟	カメイ	affiliation; participation —*vi*. join; affiliate; participate

訓	加える	くわえる	***vt.*** add; increase; include
	加わる	くわわる	***vi.*** join; participate; take part
¥	加工	カコウ	industrial process; processing; manufacturing; treatment —***v.*** process; work; treat
	加工品	カコウヒン	finished article; processed goods
	加重平均	カジュウヘイキン	weighted average/mean
	加重平均利回り	カジュウヘイキンりまわり	compound yield based a weighted average

209 功 ⑤

音	功	コウ（ク）	exploit; achievement; merit
熟	功徳	クドク	act of charity; blessings
	功罪	コウザイ	merits and demerits; pros and cons
	功績	コウセキ	meritorious deed; services; merits; achievement
	功名	コウミョウ	great exploit; distinguished services
	功名心	コウミョウシン	ambition; aspiration; love of fame
	功利的	コウリテキ	utilitarian; matter of fact
	功労	コウロウ	merits; service; exploit
	功労者	コウロウシャ	person of distinguished service

210 劣 ⑥

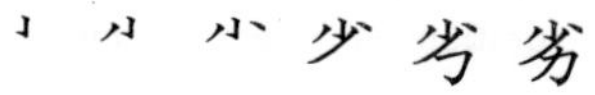

音	劣	レツ	inferior
熟	劣悪	レツアク	poor; inferior; coarse
	劣勢	レッセイ	numerical inferiority
	劣性	レッセイ	(racial, sexual, etc.) inferiority
	劣等	レットウ	inferiority
	劣等感	レットウカン	inferiority complex
訓	劣る	おとる	***vi.*** be inferior to

211 助 ⑦

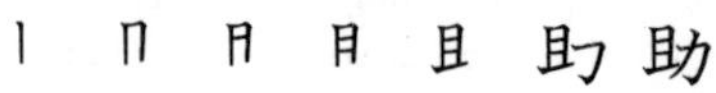

音	助	ジョ	help

熟	助演	ジョエン	supporting performance/role —*v*. play a supporting role
	助教授	ジョキョウジュ	assistant professor
	助言	ジョゲン	advice; counsel —*vi*. advise; counsel
	助詞	ジョシ	***gram***. particle
	助手	ジョシュ	helper; assistant
	助成	ジョセイ	aid; help with research or an enterprise —*v*. help; aid; assist
	助走	ジョソウ	run-up; approach run —*vi*. run up; make an approach run
	助長	ジョチョウ	promotion; encouragement —*v*. promote; encourage
	助動詞	ジョドウシ	***gram***. auxiliary verb
	助命	ジョメイ	sparing a person's life —*v*. spare a person's life
	助役	ジョヤク	assistant stationmaster; deputy mayor
	助力	ジョリョク	aid; help assistance; cooperation; support
訓	助	すけ	help; aid; assistance
	助太刀	すけだち	help; assistance; support
	助っ人	すけっと	helper; assistant
	助平	すけべイ	lechery; lewdness
	助かる	たすかる	***vi***. be helped/saved/rescued
	助ける	たすける	***vt***. help; assist; rescue; save

212

努 ⑦

音	努	ド	effort; endeavor
熟	努力	ドリョク	effort; endeavor; exertion; labor; strain; industry —*vi*. endeavor; do one's best; strive; make efforts
訓	努める	つとめる	***vt***. endeavor; make efforts; strive; apply oneself; try hard

213

励 ⑦

音	励	レイ	encouragement; diligence
熟	励行	レイコウ	strict enforcement —*v*. enforce strictly
訓	励ます	はげます	***vt***. encourage; urge
	励む	はげむ	***vi***. be diligent

214

⑦

音	労	ロウ	work; labor; toil
熟	労役	ロウエキ	labor; work; toil
	労苦	ロウク	labor; pains; toil
	労作	ロウサク	laborious work; toil; labor
	労働	ロウドウ	labor; work; toil —*vi*. labor; work; toil
	労働者	ロウドウシャ	laborer; worker
	労働力	ロウドウリョク	labor; manpower; workforce
	労務者	ロウムシャ	worker; laborer
	労力	ロウリョク	labor; effort; trouble
訓	労る	いたわる	*vt*. sympathize with; be kind to; treat well; *vi*. get sick/ill
¥	労使	ロウシ	labor and management
	労資	ロウシ	capital and labor
	労働組合	ロウドウくみあい	labor union
	労働集約的農業	ロウドウシュウヤクテキノウギョウ	labor-intensive industry
	労働省	ロウドウショウ	Ministry of Labor
	労働人口	ロウドウジンコウ	working population
	労働大臣	ロウドウダイジン	minister of labor
	労働費	ロウドウヒ	labor cost

215
劾
⑧

音	劾	ガイ	impeach; investigate

216
効
⑧

音	効	コウ	effect; efficacy; efficiency
熟	効果	コウカ	effect; effectiveness; efficiency
	効果的	コウカテキ	effective; effectual; successful
	効能	コウノウ	efficacy; effect; virtue; benefit; effectiveness
	効用	コウヨウ	effect; use; usefulness; utility; benefit

	効率	コウリツ	utility factor; efficiency
	効力	コウリョク	effect; efficacy; value; validity; force
訓	効き目	ききめ	effect; virtue; efficacy
	効く	きく	*vi*. be effective; work; act

217
勅 ⑨

音	勅	チョク	imperial edict
熟	勅語	チョクゴ	imperial rescript
	勅使	チョクシ	imperial envoy
	勅旨	チョクシ	imperial mandate
	勅令	チョクレイ	imperial decree

218
勇 ⑨

音	勇	ユウ	courage; bravery; heroism
熟	勇敢	ユウカン	heroism; gallantry; bravery
	勇気	ユウキ	courage; bravery; valor; nerve; audacity
	勇士	ユウシ	brave man; hero
	勇姿	ユウシ	brave/gallant figure
	勇者	ユウシャ	brave man; hero; man of valor
	勇将	ユウショウ	brave general; great soldier
	勇壮	ユウソウ	bravery; heroism
	勇退	ユウタイ	voluntary retirement —*v*. retire voluntarily; bow out
	勇断	ユウダン	resolute decision
	勇猛	ユウモウ	valor; daring; bravery
	勇躍	ユウヤク	high spirits —*vi*. be in high spirits; take heart
訓	勇ましい	いさましい	courageous; valiant
	勇む	いさむ	*vi*. cheer up; be in high spirits

219
勉 ⑩

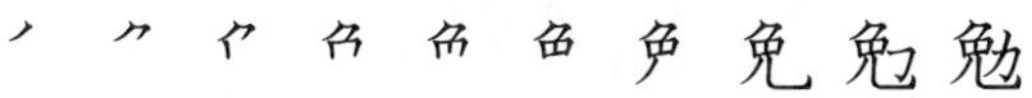

音	勉	ベン	diligence
熟	勉学	ベンガク	diligent study —*v*. study hard

二 亠 人 𠆢 亻 儿 入 八 冂 冖 冫 几 凵 刀 刂 • 力 勹 匕 匚 十 卜 卩 㔾 厂 厶 又 了 𠂊 マ

	勉強	ベンキョウ	studying; diligence ***col***. selling cheap —***v***. study; be diligent ***col***. sell cheaply
	勉励	ベンレイ	diligence; industriousness —***vi***. be diligent/industrious; work hard
訓	※勉める	つとめる	make efforts; work hard; be diligent

220

勘 ⑪

音	勘	カン	think; intuition; ponder
熟	勘定	カンジョウ	counting; computation; accounts; payment of bills —***v***. count; reckon; calculate; compute
	勘違い	カンちがい	misunderstanding —***vi***. misunderstand; mistake; guess wrong
	勘当	カンドウ	disowning; disinheritance; renunciation —***v***. disown; disinherit; renounce
	勘弁	カンベン	pardon; forgiveness; permission; excuse —***v***. pardon; forgive; permit; excuse

221

動 ⑪

音	動	ドウ	movement; motion
熟	動じる	ドウじる	***vi***. be upset/perturbed/confused
	動員	ドウイン	mobilization —***v***. mobilize; set in motion
	動悸	ドウキ	palpitation (of the heart)
	動機	ドウキ	motive; inducement; incentive
	動議	ドウギ	motion (of a meeting)
	動向	ドウコウ	trend; tendency; movement
	動作	ドウサ	movement; motion; action
	動詞	ドウシ	***gram***. verb
	動静	ドウセイ	movements; state of things; conditions
	動的	ドウテキ	dynamic; kinetic
	動転	ドウテン	fright —***vi***. be frightened
	動物	ドウブツ	animal; beast
	動物園	ドウブツエン	zoo; zoological gardens
	動脈	ドウミャク	artery
	動揺	ドウヨウ	shaking; trembling; restlessness; unrest —***vi***. shake; tremble; be restless/disturbed
	動乱	ドウラン	disturbance; upheaval; agitation; commotion; riot
	動力	ドウリョク	power; dynamic force; moment

訓	動かす	うごかす	*vt*. move; stir; put in motion; inspire; touch; impress
	動く	うごく	*vi*. move; stir; budge; shake; work; operate; be moved/touched

222

務 ⑪

フ マ ヌ 予 矛 矛 矛 矜 務 務 務

音	務	ム	serve; work
訓	務め	つとめ	work; responsibility
	務める	つとめる	*vt*. work; serve

223

勤 ⑫

一 十 廾 廾 芇 苩 茾 革 堇 堇 勤 勤

音	勤	キン	work; hold a post; exert oneself; endeavor; be diligent; try hard
		ゴン	
熟	勤勉	キンベン	diligence; industry; hard work
	勤労	キンロウ	labor; work; service; industry
訓	勤まる	つとまる	*vi*. be fit for; be equal to
	勤める	つとめる	*vt*. serve; work; hold a position; be diligent
	勤め先	つとめさき	one's place of work; the office
¥	勤続	キンゾク	continuance in office
	勤務	キンム	service; duty —*vi*. serve; work
	勤務先	キンムサキ	one's workplace
	勤務時間	キンムジカン	working/office hours
	勤労者	キンロウシャ	worker; laborer

224

勝 ⑫

丿 刀 月 月 月 月' 月' 胖 胖 胅 勝 勝

音	勝	ショウ	win; excel
熟	勝因	ショウイン	the cause of victory
	勝運	ショウウン	one's winning luck
	勝機	ショウキ	winning opportunity/chance
	勝算	ショウサン	chance of success; prospects; odds; chances
	勝者	ショウシャ	winner; victor

	勝敗	ショウハイ	victory or defeat; win or lose; the outcome
	勝負	ショウブ	match; game; contest —***vi***. play; have a game; have a match
	勝利	ショウリ	victory; triumph
訓	勝つ	かつ	***vi***. win; beat; defeat
	勝ち気	かちき	unyielding spirit
	勝ち抜く	かちぬく	***vi***. win; advance to the next round
	勝ち目	かちめ	chances of winning
	勝る	まさる	***vi***. excel; be superior to

225

募 ⑫

音	募	ボ	appeal; invite; raise; grow intense
熟	募金	ボキン	fund raising —***vi***. raise money
	募集	ボシュウ	recruitment; solicitation —***v***. recruit; solicit
訓	募る	つのる	***v***. appeal; invite (donations); raise (funds); grow intense; deteriorate (illness, etc.)
¥	募集（債権）	ボシュウ（サイケン）	flotation; subscription

226

勧 ⑬

音	勧	カン	advise; urge; encourage
熟	勧業	カンギョウ	encouragement of industry
	勧告	カンコク	advice; counsel; recommendation —***v***. advise; consel; recommend
	勧誘	カンユウ	solicitation; persuasion; inducement —***v***. solicit; canvass; persuade; induce
訓	勧める	すすめる	***vt***. advise; encourage; urge

227

勢 ⑬

音	勢	セイ	power; force; energy; vigor
熟	勢揃い	セイぞろい	array; full line up
	勢力	セイリョク	influence; force
訓	勢い	いきおい	force; energy; vigor

2 勹 つつみがまえ wrapping

228
勺 ③ ノ 勺 勺

音	勺	シャク	*shaku* (unit of capacity, approx. 818 ml)

229
匁 ④ ノ 勹 勿 匁

訓	匁	もんめ	*monme* (unit of weight, approx. 3.75g)

230
包 ⑤ ノ 勹 勹 匀 包

音	包	ホウ	wrap; cover; envelop; conceal
熟	包囲	ホウイ	siege; surrounding (the enemy) —***v***. besiege; surround (the enemy)
	包括	ホウカツ	included —***v***. include
	包括的	ホウカツテキ	inclusive; comprehensive
	包含	ホウガン	including —***v***. include; contain; imply
	包茎	ホウケイ	foreskin; uncircumsized penis
	包装	ホウソウ	packing; packaging; wrapping —***v***. pack; package; wrap
	包帯	ホウタイ	bandage; dressing
	包丁	ホウチョウ	kitchen knife; cooking knife
	包皮	ホウヒ	outer skin; foreskin
	包容	ホウヨウ	tolerance; implication; comprehension —***v***. tolerate; comprehend imply
	包容力	ホウヨウリョク	capacity; tolerance; broad-mindedness
訓	包み紙	つつみがみ	wrapping paper
	包み込む	つつみこむ	***vt***. wrap up
	包む	つつむ	***vt***. wrap; cover; envelop; conceal

2 匕 ひ spoon; *hi* (katakana)

231
北 ⑤

音	北	ホク	north
熟	北緯	ホクイ	north latitude
	北欧	ホクオウ	Northern Europe
	北上	ホクジョウ	going north —*vi.* go north
	北端	ホクタン	northern extremity/tip
	北斗七星	ホクトシチセイ	Big Dipper
	北部	ホクブ	north; northern part
	北米	ホクベイ	North America
	北洋	ホクヨウ	northern sea
	北海道	ホッカイドウ	Hokkaido
	北極	ホッキョク	North Pole
	北極熊	ホッキョクぐま	polar bear
	北極圏	ホッキョクケン	Arctic Circle
	北極星	ホッキョクセイ	North Star; Polaris
	北氷洋	ホッピョウヨウ	Arctic Ocean
	北方	ホッポウ	north; northward; northern
訓	北	きた	north
	北回帰線	きたカイキセン	Tropic of Cancer
	北風	きたかぜ	north wind
	北大西洋	きたタイセイヨウ	North Atlantic
	北朝鮮	きたチョウセン	North Korea
	北半球	きたハンキュウ	Northern Hemisphere
	北向き	きたむき	facing north

232
旨 ⑥

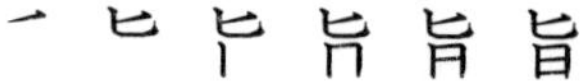

音	旨	シ	effect; principle
訓	旨	むね	effect; principle; meaning; gist; main points
	※旨い	うまい	delicious; tasty; good

2 匚 はこがまえ box on side

233
区 ④ 一 フ ヌ 区

音	区	ク	divide; punctuate; partition; borough; ward; diverse
熟	区域	クイキ	the limits; boundary; domain
	区画	クカク	division; demarcation —*v*. divide; demarcate
	区間	クカン	section between two points; territory
	区分	クブン	division; demarcation —*v*. divide; demarcate
	区別	クベツ	distinguishing; discrimination —*v*. distinguish; discriminate
	区民	クミン	ward/borough citizens
	区役所	クヤクショ	ward office
	区立	クリツ	funded/run and organized by the ward/borough

234
匹 ④ 一 ア 兀 匹

音	匹	ヒツ	same kind; comparable; man of low birth
熟	匹敵	ヒッテキ	match; equal; rival —*vi*. match; equal; rival; compare with
訓	匹	ひき	(counter for birds, animals, fish, insects); *hiki* (unit of length for measuring cloth, approx. 21.8 m)

235
巨 ② 丨 厂 戶 巨 巨

音	巨	キョ	huge; enormous; immense
熟	巨額	キョガク	very large sum of money; fortune
	巨視的	キョシテキ	macroscopic
	巨匠	キョショウ	person renowned for his craft; master craftsman
	巨人	キョジン	giant; Titan; Goliath; person who is particularly big; person with special powers
	巨体	キョタイ	very large body; gigantic figure
	巨大	キョダイ	huge; gigantic; enormous; mega-
	巨頭	キョトウ	leading figure; bigwig; big shot

	巨費	キョヒ	large outlay; great cost
	巨万	キョマン	millions; extremely numerous
¥	巨大企業	キョダイキギョウ	big business; business giant
	巨大国	キョダイコク	superpower

236

匠 ⑥ 一 ア ア 斤 斤 匠

音	匠	ショウ	craftsman
訓	※匠	たくみ	skillful; clever

237

医 ⑦ 一 ア ㄷ 三 医 医 医

音	医	イ	heal; cure; doctor; medicine
熟	医院	イイン	physician's office; doctor's surgery
	医学	イガク	medical science; medicine
	医師	イシ	doctor; physician
	医務	イム	medical affairs
	医薬品	イヤクヒン	medicine; drugs
	医療	イリョウ	medical treatment/care

238

匿 ⑩ 一 二 ⺾ 艹 芀 若 若 若 若 匿

音	匿	トク	hide
熟	匿名	トクメイ	anonymity; alias

2 十 じゅう ten; cross

239

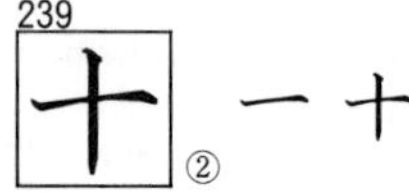

十 ② 一 十

音	十	ジュウ	ten
熟	十一月	ジュウイチガツ	November

	十月	ジュウガツ	October
	十五夜	ジュウゴヤ	full-moon night
	十字	ジュウジ	cross
	十字架	ジュウジカ	cross; Holy Cross
	十字軍	ジュウジグン	Crusaders
	十字路	ジュウジロ	crossroads
	十二月	ジュウニガツ	December
	十二支	ジュウニシ	twelve signs of the Chinese/Japanese zodiac
	十二分	ジュウニブン	more than enough
	十人十色	ジュウニンといろ	everyone to his own taste; to each his own
	十人並	ジュウニンなみ	average; ordinary
	十年一日	ジュウネンイチジツ	without any change over a long period
	十八番	ジュウハチバン	what one is best at
	十分	ジュウブン	enough; plenty
	十中八九	ジュッチュウハック	almost
訓	十	と	ten
	十	とお	ten
	十日	とおか	tenth day (of the month); 10th
	※十八番	おはこ	what one is best at

240

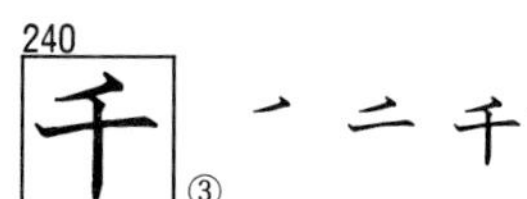

音	千	セン	thousand
熟	千金	センキン	lot of money
	千差万別	センサバンベツ	infinite variety; various kinds
	千秋楽	センシュウラク	the last day of a play, sumo, etc.
	千里眼	センリガン	clairvoyance
訓	千	ち	one thousand

241

午 ④ ノ ⺈ 𠂉 午

音	午	ゴ	noon
熟	午後	ゴゴ	afternoon; p.m.
	午睡	ゴスイ	nap —***vi***. take a nap
	午前	ゴゼン	morning; a.m.
訓	※午	うま	the horse (seventh sign of the Chinese zodiac)

242

升 ④ ノ 𠂇 チ 升

音	升	ショウ	*shō* (unit of capacity, approx. 1.8ℓ)
訓	升	ます	measure; box

243

半 ⑤ 丶 丷 䒑 兰 半

音	半	ハン	half
熟	半永久的	ハンエイキュウテキ	semipermanent
	半円	ハンエン	semicircle; half-circle
	半音	ハンオン	semitone; halftone
	半開	ハンカイ	half open; partly open; semi-civilized
	半額	ハンガク	half the sum; half price
	半期	ハンキ	half year; half term
	半旗	ハンキ	flag at half-mast
	半休	ハンキュウ	half-holiday
	半球	ハンキュウ	hemisphere
	半径	ハンケイ	***math***. radius
	半月	ハンゲツ	half moon; half-month
	半減	ハンゲン	reduction by half —***v***. reduce by half; halve; take off half
	半紙	ハンシ	common Japanese paper
	半信半疑	ハンシハンギ	incredulous; half in doubt; dubious
	半死半生	ハンシハンショウ	more dead than alive; all but dead; half dead
	半周	ハンシュウ	semicircle —***vi***. go half way around a circuit, etc.
	半熟	ハンジュク	half-boiled; half-done; half-ripe
	半身	ハンシン	half the body
	半身不随	ハンシンフズイ	***med***. paralysis of one lateral half of the body
	半数	ハンスウ	half the number (of objects)
	半生	ハンセイ	half one's life; half a lifetime
	半世紀	ハンセイキ	half a century
	半袖	ハンそで	half-length sleeves; short sleeves
	半田	ハンだ	solder; pewter
	半濁音	ハンダクオン	semi-voiced sound
	半濁点	ハンダクテン	semi-voiced sound sign
	半月	ハンつき	half a month; half-month

	半纏	ハンテン	*hanten* (half-length Japanese style coat)
	半島	ハントウ	peninsula
	半時	ハンとき	about an hour; short time; short while; half an hour
	半年	ハンとし	half a year; half year
	半日	ハンニチ	half a day; half day
	半値	ハンね	half price
	半端	ハンパ	odd thing; fragment
	半々	ハンハン	half and half; fifty-fifty
	半分	ハンブン	half
	半面	ハンメン	one side; half; profile
訓	半ば	なかば	half; semi-; middle; center; in part; partially
¥	半導体	ハンドウタイ	semiconductor

244

協 ⑧

一 十 ￼ 忄 协 協 協 協

音	協	キョウ	co-operation; group; organization
熟	協会	キョウカイ	association; league; society
	協議	キョウギ	conference; council; consultation —*v*. confer; consult; deliberate
	協賛	キョウサン	support; cooperation —*v*. support; cooperate
	協奏曲	キョウソウキョク	concerto
	協調	キョウチョウ	cooperation; harmony; conciliation —*v*. cooperate; act in union/harmony/concert
	協定	キョウテイ	agreement; convention; pact —*v*. agree upon; arrange; make an agreement
	協同	キョウドウ	cooperation; collaboration; union —*v*. cooperate with; collaborate; work together
	協約	キョウヤク	agreement; convention; pact —***vi***. translate (a book) jointly (with)
	協力	キョウリョク	cooperation; collaboration; working together —***vi***. cooperate; work together; collaborate
¥	協業化	キョウギョウカ	grouping into a cooperative
	協調融資	キョウチョウユウシ	joint financing; participation loan
	協調融資国	キョウチョウユウシコク	syndication group
	協同組合	キョウドウくみあい	cooperative association

245

⑧

音	卒	ソツ	soldier; private; sudden; come to an end; die; graduate
熟	卒業	ソツギョウ	graduation —*v*. graduate
	卒中	ソッチュウ	***med***. apoplexy; cerebral stroke
	卒倒	ソットウ	swooning —*v*. swoon

246

卓 ⑧

音	卓	タク	desk; table; excellence; eminence
熟	卓越	タクエツ	excellence; superiority; eminence —***vi***. excel; surpass; be distinguished; transcend
	卓上	タクジョウ	desk top; on top of a desk
	卓球	タッキュウ	table tennis; ping-pong
	卓見	タッケン	farsightedness

247

⑨

音	南	ナン	south
熟	南緯	ナンイ	south latitude
	南下	ナンカ	going south —***vi***. go down south
	南極	ナンキョク	South Pole
	南極圏	ナンキョクケン	Antarctic Circle
	南船北馬	ナンセンホクバ	constant traveling; being on the move
	南端	ナンタン	southern extremity/tip
	南中	ナンチュウ	southing; culmination —***vi***. go south; cross the meridian; culminate
	南蛮	ナンバン	southern barbarians; cayenne pepper
	南米	ナンベイ	South America
	南洋	ナンヨウ	South Seas
訓	南	みなみ	south
	南半球	みなみハンキュウ	Southern Hemisphere

248

卑 ⑨

ノ ｨ 㐅 冂 冃 甶 由 甴 卑

音	卑	ヒ	humble; base; ignoble; vulgar
熟	卑怯	ヒキョウ	cowardice; meanness; unfairness
	卑怯者	ヒキョウもの	coward
	卑近	ヒキン	common; ordinary
	卑屈	ヒクツ	mean; inferior; poor
	卑下	ヒゲ	humble; humility; self-abasement —*v.* humble oneself
	卑語	ヒゴ	vulgar word/expression
	卑俗	ヒゾク	vulgar; coarse
	卑劣	ヒレツ	mean; unfair; contemptible; sneaky
	卑猥	ヒワイ	indecency; obscenity; coarseness
訓	卑しい	いやしい	mean; humble
	卑しむ	いやしむ	***vt.*** despise; condemn; disdain; scorn; look down on
	卑しめる	いやしめる	***vt.*** despise; condemn; disdain; scorn; look down on

249

⑫

一 十 十 忄 忄 忄 忄 扌 扌 扌 博 博

音	博	ハク	broad; doctor; professor
		(バク)	gambling
熟	博する	ハクする	***vt.*** gain/win (reputation); win/enjoy (credit/confidence)
	博愛	ハクアイ	philantropy; charity; benevelonce; humanity
	博学	ハクガク	erudition; extensive learning; wide knowledge
	博士	ハクシ(ハカセ)	doctor; professor
	博士号	ハクシゴウ (ハカセゴウ)	doctorate
	博識	ハクシキ	wide knowledge; erudition
	博徒	バクト	professional gambler
	博物館	ハクブツカン	museum
	博覧	ハクラン	wide reading; extensive knowledge —***vi.*** be widely read;have extensive knowledge
	博覧会	ハクランカイ	fair; exhibition; exposition
	※博打	バクチ	gambling; gaming; speculation; venture

二 亠 人 𠆢 亻 儿 入 八 冂 冖 冫 几 凵 刀 刂 力 勹 匕 匚 十 • 卜 • 卩 㔾 厂 厶 又 了 𠂊 マ

2 卜 ぼく divination; *to* (katakana)

250
占 ⑤
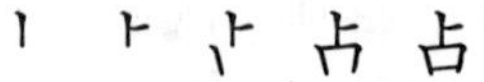

音	占	**セン**	occupy; hold
熟	占拠	**センキョ**	occupation —***v***. occupy
	占星術	**センセイジュツ**	astrology
	占有	**センユウ**	occupancy; exclusive possession —***v***. occupy/possess exclusively
	占領	**センリョウ**	occupation; capture —***v***. occupy; capture
訓	占う	うらなう	***vt***. divine; tell fortunes
	占師	うらないシ	fortune teller
	占める	しめる	***vt***. occupy

2 卩 わりふ／ふしづくり joint; seal

251
印 ⑥
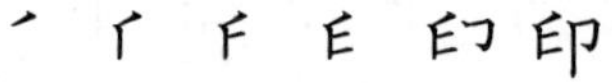

音	印	**イン**	stamp; printing; seal
	印鑑	**インカン**	official personal seal
	印刷	**インサツ**	printing —***v***. print
	印紙	**インシ**	revenue stamp
	印字	**インジ**	printing —***v***. print
	印象	**インショウ**	impression
	印象的	**インショウテキ**	impressive; memorable
	印税	**インゼイ**	royalty (on a book)
訓	印	しるし	sign; proof; signal
	印す	しるす	***vt***. mark; inscribe

252
却 ⑦
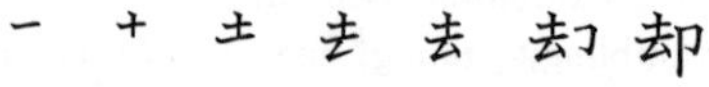

音	却	**キャク**	retreat; recede; repulse; repel; avoid

熟	却下	キャッカ	rejection; dismissal; turndown —*v*. reject; dismiss; turn down

253

即 ⑦

音	即	ソク	at once; immediate; as is; on the spot
熟	即位	ソクイ	accession to the throne; coronation —*v*. ascend/accede to the throne
	即応	ソクオウ	conformity —*v*. conform; adapt; meet
	即座	ソクザ	prompt; on the spot
	即死	ソクシ	instantaneous death —*v*. die instantly
	即時	ソクジ	instantly; immediately; on the spot
	即日	ソクジツ	on the same day
	即席	ソクセキ	impromptu; instant; extemporaneous
	即断	ソクダン	prompt decision —*v*. make a prompt decision
	即答	ソクトウ	ready answer —*v*. give a ready answer
	即決	ソッケツ	prompt decision —*v*. make a prompt decision
	即刻	ソッコク	instantly; immediately; at once
訓	※即ち	すなわち	namely; i.e.
	※即く	つく	***vi***. ascend; succeed to
¥	即売	ソクバイ	spot sale —*v*. make a spot sale
	即金	ソッキン	payment in cash

254

卵 ⑦

音	卵	ラン	egg
熟	卵黄	ランオウ	yolk
	卵殻	ランカク	eggshell
	卵管	ランカン	***med***. fallopian tube
	卵子	ランシ	***med***. ovum; egg cell
	卵生	ランセイ	***med***. oviparity
	卵巣	ランソウ	***med***. ovary
	卵白	ランパク	white of an egg; albumin
訓	卵	たまご	spawn; egg

255

卸 ⑨

ノ ⺈ 𠂉 午 午 缶 金 釦 卸

訓	卸	おろし	wholesale
	卸す	おろす	wholesale; sell by wholesale
¥	卸売	おろしうり	wholesale
	卸値	おろしね	wholesale price

2 㔾 わりふ／ふしづくり crooked seal

256

危 ⑥

ノ ク ⺈ 产 厃 危

音	危	キ	dangerous; hurt
熟	危害	キガイ	harm; injury
	危機	キキ	crisis; emergency
	危機一髪	キキイッパツ	imminent danger; close shave
	危惧	キグ	fear; misgivings; apprehensions —*v*. feel misgivings; be apprehensive
	危険	キケン	danger; hazard; risk
	危篤	キトク	critical condition
訓	危ない	あぶない	dangerous; doubtful; risky
	危うい	あやうい	dangerous; critical; hazardous; risky
	危ぶむ	あやぶむ	***vi***. fear; be apprehensive/afraid

2 厂 がんだれ cliff

257

厄 ④

一 厂 𠂆 厄

音	厄	ヤク	misfortune; disaster
熟	厄年	ヤクどし	unlucky/bad year
	厄払い	ヤクばらい	exorcism —***vi***. exorcize; drive away evil
	厄日	ヤクび	unlucky/evil day
	厄介	ヤッカイ	troublesome; burdensome; help; care

258 厚 ⑨

音	厚	コウ	thick; kind; tender
熟	厚意	コウイ	favor; kind intentions; kindness
	厚顔	コウガン	impudence; shamelessness
	厚情	コウジョウ	kindness
訓	厚い	あつい	thick; heavy; bulky; kind; cordial; tender; warm; deep
	厚着	あつぎ	thick/warm clothes —***vi***. be thick/warmly dressed
	厚化粧	あつゲショウ	heavy/thick makeup
	厚手	あつで	thick; bulky
¥	厚相 (厚生大臣)	コウショウ (コウセイダイジン)	minister of health and welfare
	厚生	コウセイ	public welfare
	厚生省	コウセイショウ	Ministry of Welfare

259 厘 ⑨

音	厘	リン	*rin* (former unit of currency, 1/1000 yen); *rin* (unit of lengh, approx. 0.3 mm; unit of weight, approx. 375 mg)
熟	厘毛	リンモウ	insignificant amount of money; a little

260 原 ⑩

音	原	ゲン	plain; field; source; origin; crude
熟	原案	ゲンアン	original bill/plan
	原因	ゲンイン	cause; factor; factor
	原画	ゲンガ	original picture
	原形	ゲンケイ	original form
	原型	ゲンケイ	model; prototype; archetype
	原語	ゲンゴ	original language; the original
	原稿	ゲンコウ	manuscript; draft; notes
	原稿用紙	ゲンコウヨウシ	manuscript paper; Japanese writing pad

	原告	ゲンコク	prosecutor; plaintiff; complainant
	原材料	ゲンザイリョウ	raw materials
	原作	ゲンサク	original story; the original; the book
	原産	ゲンサン	country of origin; native
	原始	ゲンシ	genesis; primitive; primeval
	原子	ゲンシ	atom
	原子核	ゲンシカク	atomic nucleus
	原子爆弾	ゲンシバクダン	atomic/nuclear bomb
	原子力	ゲンシリョク	atomic energy; nuclear power
	原子力発電所	ゲンシリョクハツデンショ	nuclear power plant
	原子炉	ゲンシロ	nuclear reactor
	原紙	ゲンシ	stencil paper; stencil
	原始時代	ゲンシジダイ	primitive age
	原始人	ゲンシジン	primitive man
	原始的	ゲンシテキ	primitive; primeval
	原住民	ゲンジュウミン	natives; aborigines
	原書	ゲンショ	original book; the original; in the original
	原色	ゲンショク	primary color
	原図	ゲンズ	original drawing/plan/map
	原寸	ゲンスン	actual size; life-size; full-size
	原則	ゲンソク	general/fundamental rule; principle
	原典	ゲンテン	original text
	原動力	ゲンドウリョク	motivating power; driving force
	原爆	ゲンバク	A-bomb; atomic bomb
	原文	ゲンブン	original text; the original
	原簿	ゲンボ	ledger
	原木	ゲンボク	raw lumber
	原野	ゲンヤ	wilderness; field; plain
	原油	ゲンユ	crude oil; petroleum
	原理	ゲンリ	principle
	原料	ゲンリョウ	raw materials
訓	原	はら	plain; field
¥	原価	ゲンカ	cost; cost price; cost of production; prime cost
	原価計算	ゲンカケイサン	cost accounting; costing
	原価主義	ゲンカシュギ	cost principle
	原価償却	ゲンカショウキャク	depreciation —*v.* depreciate

2 ム む *mu* (katakana)

261

去 ⑤ 一 十 土 去 去

音	去	キョ コ	depart; go away; leave; the past; remove; clear away
熟	去就	キョシュウ	one's course of action
	去年	キョネン	last year
	去来	キョライ	coming and going; recurrence —***vi***. recur
訓	去る	さる	***vi***. take off; remove; eliminate; take away; get rid of; divorce; leave; depart from; pass; elapse; be over

262

弁 ⑤ ム ム 厶 弁 弁

音	弁	ベン	speech; dialect; valve; petal; distinguish between; braid; bind
熟	弁じる	ベンじる	***vi***. speak; talk; debate; discriminate; pledge; vow; solve; finish; arrange
	弁解	ベンカイ	explanation; justification; defense; excuse; apology —***v***. explain; justify; excuse; apologize
	弁護	ベンゴ	defense; pleading for —***v***. defend; plead for
	弁護士	ベンゴシ	lawyer; attorney
	弁護団	ベンゴダン	the defense counsel (composed of several attorneys-at-law)
	弁護人	ベンゴニン	counsel; defender; lawyer
	弁才	ベンサイ	oratorical talents; eloquence
	弁済	ベンサイ	compensation; settlement; return of a borrowed item —***vi***. compensate; settle; return
	弁士	ベンシ	speaker; orator; silent movie narrator
	弁償	ベンショウ	compensation; indemnification —***v***. compensate; indemnify
	弁証法	ベンショウホウ	logical argumentation; dialectic
	弁舌	ベンゼツ	speech; eloquence
	弁天	ベンテン	Sarasvati (Indian goddess of music, eloquence, wisdom, and wealth)
	弁当	ベントウ	(box) lunch; packed lunch

弁別	ベンベツ	discrimination; distinction —*v*. discriminate; distinguish
弁膜	ベンマク	***med***. valve (in internal organs)
弁務官	ベンムカン	commissioner (in colony/commonwealth country)
弁明	ベンメイ	explanation; justification —***vi***. explain; justify
弁理	ベンリ	management; dealing
弁理士	ベンリシ	patent attorney (lawyer, agent)
弁論	ベンロン	argument; debate —***vi***. argue; debate

263

⑧

音	参	サン	visit; go; worship join; assemble
熟	参じる	サンじる	***vi***. go; visit
	参加	サンカ	participation —***vi***. participate in; take part enter
	参賀	サンガ	congratulatory visit to the imperial palace —***vi***. visit the imperial palace to express congratulations
	参会	サンカイ	attendance at a meeting —***vi***. attend a meeting
	参観	サンカン	visit; observation —*v*. visit; observe
	参議院	サンギイン	House of Councilors; Upper House
	参詣	サンケイ	visit to a temple or a shrine —***vi***. visit a temple or a shrine
	参考	サンコウ	reference; consultation
	参考書	サンコウショ	reference book
	参考人	サンコウニン	witness
	参集	サンシュウ	gathering; collecting —***vi***. gather; collect
	参照	サンショウ	reference; consultation; comparison —*v*. refer; consult; compare
	参上	サンジョウ	***hum***. visit —***vi***. ***hum***. visit; go to see
	参政権	サンセイケン	suffrage; right to vote; franchise
	参戦	サンセン	participation in a war —***vi***. enter a war
	参道	サンドウ	approach/path leading to a shrine
	参拝	サンパイ	worship at a shrine or temple —***vi***. go and worship at a shrine or temple
	参謀	サンボウ	staff officer
	参謀本部	サンボウホンブ	General Staff Office
	参列者	サンレツシャ	attendant; one of those present
訓	参る	まいる	***hum***. ***vi***. come; go; visit; worship

2 又 また again

264

又 ②

フ 又

音	又	（ユウ）	another; again
訓	又	また	again; also; moreover
	又貸し	またがし	subletting; subleasing —*v.* sublet; sublease
	又聞き	またぎき	indirect information; hearsay —*v.* hear secondhand; learn by hearsay

265

収 ④

丨 丩 収 収

音	収	シュウ	receive payment; harvest; store; keep
熟	収穫	シュウカク	harvest; crop —*v.* harvest; reap
	収拾	シュウシュウ	control; reinstating order —*v.* put under control; settle
	収集	シュウシュウ	collection; collecting —*v.* collect; gather; amass
	収縮	シュウシュク	shrinkage; contraction —*v.* shrink; contract
	収束	シュウソク	conclusion; convergence —*v.* gather and bundle; conclude; converge
	収納	シュウノウ	receipt of payment/goods —*v.* receive payment/goods
	収納家具	シュウノウカグ	cabinet
	収納庫	シュウノウコ	shed; closet
	収容	シュウヨウ	accommodation of people/things in a place —*v.* accommodate; send
	収容所	シュウヨウジョ	concentration camp
	収録	シュウロク	record; recording —*v.* record music/pictures (on magnetic tape, etc.)
	収賄	シュウワイ	accepting/taking of bribes (accept/take bribes)
訓	収まる	おさまる	***vi.*** hold; contain; settle down
	収める	おさめる	***vt.*** put away/back; include; obtain; pay a bill
¥	収益	シュウエキ	earnings; profit; proceeds
	収益金	シュウエキキン	earnings; profit; proceeds
	収益力	シュウエキリョク	earning power
	収支	シュウシ	income and expenditure; earnings and expenses
	収支一覧表	シュウシイチランヒョウ	balance sheet

二 亠 人 𠆢 亻 儿 入 八 冂 冖 冫 几 凵 刀 刂 力 勹 匕 匸 十 卜 卩 㔾 厂 厶 ● 又 了 𠂊 マ

	収支決算	シュウシケッサン	settlement of accounts
	収税	シュウゼイ	tax collection; taxation —***v***. collect taxes
	収入	シュウニュウ	income; earnings; means; revenue; proceeds
	収入印紙	シュウニュウインシ	revenue stamp; fiscal stamp
	収納伝票	シュウノウデンピョウ	receipt

266

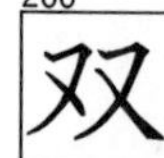

④ フ ヌ 刄 双

音	双	ソウ	pair; both
熟	双眼鏡	ソウガンキョウ	binoculars
	双肩	ソウケン	one's shoulders
	双書	ソウショ	series (of books, etc.)
	双生児	ソウセイジ	twins
	双方	ソウホウ	both parties/sides
訓	双	ふた	pair; both
	双子	ふたご	twins; twin

267

反 ④ 一 厂 万 反

音	反	ハン	return; disobey
		(タン)	dry goods; drapery
		(ホン)	
熟	反する	ハンする	***vi***. be opposed/contrary to; go against
	反物	タンもの	dry goods; drapery
	反意語	ハンイゴ	***gram***. antonym
	反映	ハンエイ	reflection; influence —***v***. reflect; be reflected; influence
	反感	ハンカン	ill feeling; antipathy; adverse sentiment
	反旗	ハンキ	standard of revolt; banner of rebellion
	反逆	ハンギャク	treason; treachery; insurrection; rebellion; mutiny —***vi***. turn traitor; rebel; revolt
	反共	ハンキョウ	anti-communist
	反響	ハンキョウ	echo; reverberation; repurcussions; influence —***vi***. echo; resound; reverberate
	反撃	ハンゲキ	counterattack; counteroffensive —***vi***. make a counteroffensive; counterattack; strike back

	反語	ハンゴ	rhetorical question; irony
	反抗	ハンコウ	resistance; insubordination; opposition; disobedience —*vi*. oppose; resist; offer resitance to; disobey
	反抗的	ハンコウテキ	rebellious; defiant; antagonistic; hostile
	反作用	ハンサヨウ	*phy*. reaction; counterreaction
	反射	ハンシャ	reflection; reflex —*v*. reflect
	反証	ハンショウ	counterevidence; proof to the contrary; disproof —*v*. disprove; prove to the contrary
	反省	ハンセイ	reflection; self-examination; introspection; reconsideration —*v*. examine oneself; reflect; introspect; reconsider
	反戦	ハンセン	antiwar
	反則	ハンソク	foul; irregularity; violation of rules
	反対	ハンタイ	opposition; resistance; contrast; reverse; inverse —*vi*. oppose; resist; contrast
	反転	ハンテン	turning over; reversal —*v*. turn around; be reversed
	反動	ハンドウ	reaction; counteraction
	反応	ハンノウ	reaction; response; effect —*vi*. react/respond to; act upon
	反発	ハンパツ	repulsion; opposition; resistance; rebellion —*v*. repel; repulse; oppose; resist; rebel
	反比例	ハンピレイ	inverse proportion —*vi*. be inversely proportionate
	反復	ハンプク	repitition —*v*. repeat; do over again
	反面	ハンメン	other side; reverse
	反目	ハンモク	antagonism; variance; hostility; enmity; feud —*vi*. be at odds; feud with
	反乱	ハンラン	rebellion; revolt; insurrection —*vi*. rebel; revolt; rise up
	反論	ハンロン	refutation; counterargument —*v*. refute
訓	反らす	そらす	*vt*. bend; warp; curve
	反る	そる	*vi*. warp; be warped/curved
¥	反対売買	ハンタイバイバイ	cross trade
	反騰	ハントウ	sharp rally
	反発	ハンパツ	rally; rebound
	反落	ハンラク	reactionary fall (in stock price)

268

友 ④ 一ナ方友

音	友	ユウ	friend
熟	友愛	ユウアイ	friendship; brotherly love

2

二亠人𠆢亻儿入八冂冖冫几凵刀刂力勹匕匚十卜卩㔾厂厶●又了𠂉マ

	友軍	ユウグン	friendly troops; allied army
	友好	ユウコウ	friendship; amity
	友情	ユウジョウ	friendship; fellowship
	友人	ユウジン	friend
訓	友	とも	friend
	友達	ともだち	friend

269

取 ⑧

一 丅 F 下 E 耳 取 取

音	取	シュ	take
熟	取材	シュザイ	data collection; gathering material —***vi***. collect data; gather material
	取材記者	シュザイキシャ	reporter
	取捨	シュシャ	choice; selection
	取得	シュトク	acquisition —***v***. acquire
訓	取る	とる	***vt***. take; remove; gather; get
	取り敢えず	とりあえず	first of all; in the meantime; for the time being
	取り上げる	とりあげる	***vt***. pick up; take up; adopt; take away; deliver a baby
	取り扱う	とりあつかう	***vt***. handle; treat; deal
	取り入る	とりいる	***vi***. ingratiate oneself; curry favor; flatter
	取り入れる	とりいれる	***vt***. take in; harvest; introduce; accept; adopt
	取り替える	とりかえる	***vt***. exchange; change; renew; replace
	取り組む	とりくむ	***vi***. wrestle; tackle
	取り消す	とりけす	***vt***. cancel; withdraw; retract
	取り込む	とりこむ	***vt***. take in; pocket; embezzle; be busy
	取り下げる	とりさげる	***vt***. withdraw
	取り締まる	とりしまる	***vt***. control; regulate; supervise
	取り付ける	とりつける	***vt***. install; fit; be equipped
	取り外す	とりはずす	***vt***. take down; remove; detach; dismantle
¥	取り扱い	とりあつかい	handling; treatment; transaction
	取り崩し	とりくずし	disposition; liquidation
	取り組み	とりくみ	drawing of bill; technical position; open interest
	取締役	とりしまりヤク	director
	取締役会	とりしまりヤクカイ	board of directors
	取引	とりひき	business; dealings
	取引所	とりひきジョ	exchange; stock exchange
	取引先	とりひきさき	customer; client; business connection

取り止め　とりやめ　cancellation

270

受 ⑧

音	受	ジュ	accept
熟	受刑	ジュケイ	under sentence —*vi*. serve a prison sentence
	受刑者	ジュケイシャ	convict
	受験	ジュケン	examination —*v*. sit an examination
	受講	ジュコウ	lecture attendance —*v*. attend a lecture
	受賞	ジュショウ	receiving a prize; prize winning —*v*. receive a prize; win a prize; be awarded a prize
	受賞作品	ジュショウサクヒン	prize-winning novel or work
	受信	ジュシン	reception of telecommunications —*v*. receive
	受信人	ジュシンニン	addressee
	受像	ジュゾウ	on T.V. —*v*. receive a picture/image
	受諾	ジュダク	acceptance; consent —*v*. accept; agree to
	受注	ジュチュウ	acceptance of an order —*v*. accept/receive an order
	受動的	ジュドウテキ	passive
	受難	ジュナン	sufferings; ordeals; Passion of Christ
	受粉	ジュフン	pollination —*vi*. pollinate
	受理	ジュリ	acceptance of forms, papers, etc. —*v*. accept; receive
	受話器	ジュワキ	telephone receiver
訓	受かる	うかる	*vi*. pass an examination
	受け入れる	うけいれる	*vt*. receive; accept
	受け売り	うけうり	retailing; borrowing; parrot learning
	受け継ぐ	うけつぐ	*vt*. inherit; succeed to (one's father's business); take over (a task)
	受付	うけつけ	information; reception
	受け付ける	うけつける	*vt*. accept; receive
	受け取る	うけとる	receive
	受身	うけみ	defensive fall; break-fall; negative; passive; ***gram***. passive voice
	受け持つ	うけもつ	*vt*. take charge of; be in charge of
	受ける	うける	*vt*. be given; receive; get; obtain; suffer; accept
¥	受け取り	うけとり	receipt
	受取手形	うけとりてがた	bill receivable
	受取配当金	うけとりハイトウキン	dividends earned

受取利息	うけとりりそく	interest received
受取利息割引料	うけとりリソクわりびきりょう	interest and discounts earned
受け渡し	うけわたし	delivery
受益者	ジュエキシャ	beneficiary
受領証	ジュリョウショウ	receipt; proof of payment
受託銀行	ジュタクギンコウ	trustee bank
受納	ジュノウ	acceptance of money or goods —*v.* accept
受領	ジュリョウ	receipt; acceptance —*v.* receive; accept

271

叔 ⑧

音 叔	シュク	uncle
訓 ※叔父	おじ	one's uncle
※叔母	おば	one's aunt

272

叙 ⑨

音 叙	ジョ	preface; state
熟 叙する	ジョする	***vt.*** confer (a rank on a person); describe; narrate
叙勲	ジョクン	decoration; medal —*v.* decorate; confer a decoration
叙景	ジョケイ	descriptions of scenery
叙事詩	ジョジシ	epic poem
叙述	ジョジュツ	description; narration —*v.* describe; narrate
叙情	ジョジョウ	lyricism
叙情詩	ジョジョウシ	lyric poetry

---

2 了 りょう finish; end

273

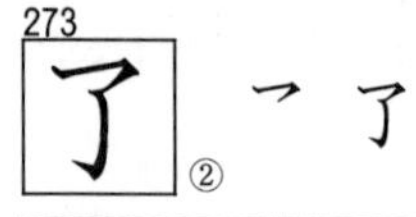

了 ②

音 了	リョウ	complete; finish; understand

熟	了解	リョウカイ	Roger!; understanding; comprehension —*v*. understand; comprehend
	了見	リョウケン	idea; forgiveness; intention; discretion —*vi*. forgive; intend; be discreet
	了承	リョウショウ	acknowledgment; understanding —*v*. acknowledge; understand

---

2 ⺈ く *ku* (katakana)

274

争 ⑥

ノ ⺈ 𠂊 刍 刍 争

音	争	ソウ	conflict; dispute; argue
熟	争議	ソウギ	dispute; strife; conflict
	争奪	ソウダツ	scrambling/contending for —*v*. scramble/contend for
	争乱	ソウラン	rioting; disturbance
訓	争う	あらそう	*vt*. compete; dispute; argue

---

2 マ ま *ma* (katakana)

275

予 ④

フ マ 乊 予

音	予	ヨ	previously; beforehand myself; I
熟	予覚	ヨカク	premonition; hunch —*v*. have a hunch
	予感	ヨカン	premonition; hunch —*v*. have a premonition/hunch
	予期	ヨキ	anticipation; expectation —*v*. anticipate; expect
	予見	ヨケン	forecast; foreknowledge —*v*. foresee; foreknow
	予言	ヨゲン	prediction —*v*. predict
	予行	ヨコウ	rehearsal —*v*. rehearse
	予告	ヨコク	advance notice; preview —*v*. notify beforehand
	予習	ヨシュウ	lesson preparation —*v*. prepare lessons
	予選	ヨセン	preliminary selection/screening; championship
	予想	ヨソウ	expectation; anticipation; conjecture —*v*. expect; anticipate; conjecture; imagine; guess

	予測	ヨソク	forecast; estimate; prediction —*v.* forecast; estimate; predict
	予断	ヨダン	prediction; guess —*v.* predict; guess
	予知	ヨチ	foreknowledge —*v.* foresee; foretell; predict
	予定	ヨテイ	plan; prearrangement; expectation —*v.* make a plan; prearrange
	予備	ヨビ	in reserve; spare; preliminary; preparatory
	予備校	ヨビコウ	preparatory school
	予備知識	ヨビチシキ	preliminary/background knowledge
	予報	ヨホウ	forecast; prediction —*v.* forecast; predict
	予防	ヨボウ	prevention; protection —*v.* prevent; protect
	予防接種	ヨボウセッシュ	***med.*** inoculation
	予約	ヨヤク	reservations; booking; advance order; subscription; appointment —*v.* make a reservation; book previously
訓	※予め	あらかじめ	previously; in advance
	※予て	かねて	previously; already
¥	予算	ヨサン	budget; estimate
	予算案	ヨサンアン	draft budget; bill of budget
	予備会議	ヨビカイギ	preliminary negotiation

3 口 くち／くちへん mouth

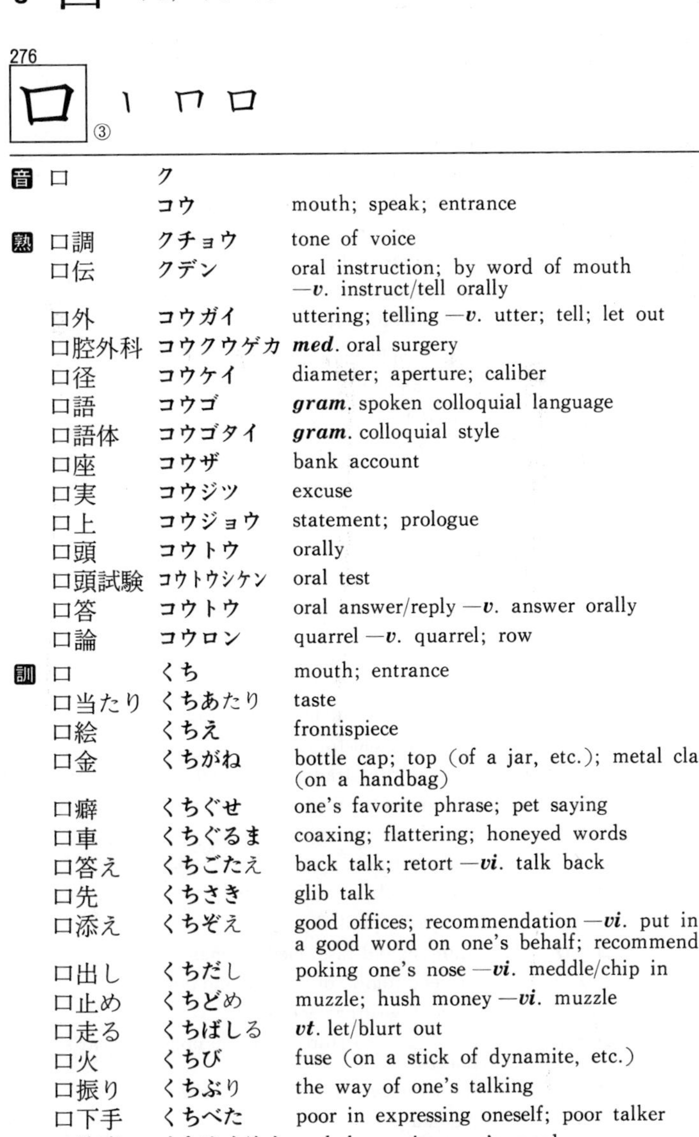

276

口 ③

丨 ロ 口

音	口	ク	
		コウ	mouth; speak; entrance
熟	口調	クチョウ	tone of voice
	口伝	クデン	oral instruction; by word of mouth —*v*. instruct/tell orally
	口外	コウガイ	uttering; telling —*v*. utter; tell; let out
	口腔外科	コウクウゲカ	***med***. oral surgery
	口径	コウケイ	diameter; aperture; caliber
	口語	コウゴ	***gram***. spoken colloquial language
	口語体	コウゴタイ	***gram***. colloquial style
	口座	コウザ	bank account
	口実	コウジツ	excuse
	口上	コウジョウ	statement; prologue
	口頭	コウトウ	orally
	口頭試験	コウトウシケン	oral test
	口答	コウトウ	oral answer/reply —*v*. answer orally
	口論	コウロン	quarrel —*v*. quarrel; row
訓	口	くち	mouth; entrance
	口当たり	くちあたり	taste
	口絵	くちえ	frontispiece
	口金	くちがね	bottle cap; top (of a jar, etc.); metal clasp (on a handbag)
	口癖	くちぐせ	one's favorite phrase; pet saying
	口車	くちぐるま	coaxing; flattering; honeyed words
	口答え	くちごたえ	back talk; retort —***vi***. talk back
	口先	くちさき	glib talk
	口添え	くちぞえ	good offices; recommendation —***vi***. put in a good word on one's behalf; recommend
	口出し	くちだし	poking one's nose —***vi***. meddle/chip in
	口止め	くちどめ	muzzle; hush money —***vi***. muzzle
	口走る	くちばしる	***vt***. let/blurt out
	口火	くちび	fuse (on a stick of dynamite, etc.)
	口振り	くちぶり	the way of one's talking
	口下手	くちべた	poor in expressing oneself; poor talker
	口約束	くちやくそく	verbal promise; one's word

277

右 ⑤ ノ ナ 才 右 右

音	右	ウ	
		ユウ	right; right hand
熟	右往左往	ウオウサオウ	in all directions —*vi*. go right and left; go this way and that way
	右折	ウセツ	turn right —*vi*. make a right turn
	右党	ウトウ	right-wing party
	右派	ウハ	the right; rightists
	右方	ウホウ	the right; the right side
	右翼	ウヨク	right-wing; right field/flank
訓	右	みぎ	right; right-hand
	右利き	みぎきき	right-handed
	右巻き	みぎまき	clockwise
	右回り	みぎまわり	clockwise

278

古 ⑤ 一 十 𠂇 古 古

音	古	コ	old; ancient; antique; classic
熟	古稀	コキ	seventy years old
	古語	コゴ	archaic word
	古今	ココン	ancient and modern times; all ages
	古参	コサン	seniority; old-timer
	古式	コシキ	ancient rite; traditional ritual
	古人	コジン	the ancients; men of old
	古跡	コセキ	historic remains/place
	古代	コダイ	ancient times; antiquity
	古典	コテン	classics; classical literature
	古都	コト	ancient capital/city
	古風	コフウ	antique; old-fashioned; archaic; classic
	古墳	コフン	ancient tomb; old burial mound
	古文	コブン	ancient writings; classics
	古米	コマイ	old rice; rice stored from a previous year's harvest
	古来	コライ	from ancient times; time-honored
	古老	コロウ	old man; elderly person
訓	古い	ふるい	old

古傷	ふるきず	old wound; (a person's) misdeeds/scandals
古臭い	ふるくさい	antiquated; old-fashioned; hackneyed
古す	ふるす	(suffix) used; worn out
古巣	ふるす	old nest
古めかしい	ふるめかしい	old; old-fashioned
※古	いにしえ	ancient times; old days

279

⑤ ㇇ 刀 刀 召 召

音	召	ショウ	summon
熟	召喚	ショウカン	summons; subpoena —*v*. summon; serve a summons
	召還	ショウカン	recall —*v*. recall
	召集	ショウシュウ	summons; call; call-up; conscription; the draft —*v*. summon; call; call-up; conscript; draft
	召集令状	ショウシュウレイジョウ	call-up/draft papers
訓	召す	めす	***vt***. call; summon
	召し上がる	めしあがる	***vt***. ***hon***. eat; drink; partake
	召使	めしつかい	servant; maid

280

台

⑤ ㇜ ム 𠫓 台 台

音	台	タイ	
		ダイ	stately mansion; stand; basis; (counter for vehicles, machines, etc.)
熟	台紙	ダイシ	pasteboard
	台地	ダイチ	plateau
	台帳	ダイチョウ	ledger; register; script
	台所	ダイどころ	kitchen
	台無し	ダイなし	ruined; spoiled; coming to nothing
	台風	タイフウ	typhoon
	台本	ダイホン	script; scenario; screenplay
訓	※台詞	せりふ	script; lines

281

各 ⑥ ノ ク 夂 冬 各 各

音	各	カク	each; every
熟	各位	カクイ	every one; all the members concerned
	各自	カクジ	each person; everyone
	各人各様	カクジンカクヨウ	in all their respective ways
訓	各（各々）	おのおの	each; every one

282

吉 ⑥ 一 十 士 吉 吉 吉

音	吉	キチ	good; fortunate; lucky; auspicious
		キツ	lucky; good luck
熟	吉日	キチニチ（キチジツ）（キツジツ）	lucky/auspicious day
	吉凶	キッキョウ	good or ill luck; fortune
	吉報	キッポウ	good news/tidings
訓	※吉い	よい	good; fortunate; auspicious

283

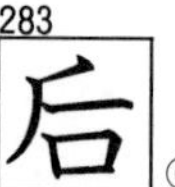

⑥ 一 厂 斤 斤 后 后

音	后	コウ	empress; emperor's wife
熟	后妃	コウヒ	queen consort; empress; queen
訓	※后	きさき	empress; queen; consort

284

⑥ ノ 人 亼 今 合 合

音	合	ガッ	
		ゴウ	combine; join; union; fit; match
		（カッ）	
熟	合作	ガッサク	joint work/production; collaboration —*v.* collaborate; produce jointly
	合衆国	ガッシュウコク	United States

	合宿	ガッシュク	communal lodgings —***vi***. lodge together; be billeted together
	合唱	ガッショウ	chorus; ensemble —***v***. sing together/in chorus
	合掌	ガッショウ	prayer —***vi***. join one's hands in prayer
	合奏	ガッソウ	concert; ensemble —***v***. play in concert
	合致	ガッチ	agreement; coincidence; concurrence —***vi***. correspond to; be in agreement; concur
	合点	ガッテン (ガテン)	understanding; comprehension —***vi***. understand; comprehend; grasp the meaning
	合羽	カッパ	raincoat; mackintosh
	合併	ガッペイ	combination; union; amalgamation; merger; coalition —***v***. combine; unite; amalgamate; merge
	合意	ゴウイ	mutual consent/agreement; concurrence —***vi***. come to mutual agreement; concur
	合一	ゴウイツ	unity; union; oneness —***v***. unite; be united; act as one
	合格	ゴウカク	success in an examination; passing an examination —***vi***. pass an examination
	合議	ゴウギ	conference; consultation; counsel —***v***. confer; consult; hold a conference
	合金	ゴウキン	alloy; compound metal
	合計	ゴウケイ	total; aggregate —***v***. add up; total
	合成	ゴウセイ	composition; synthesis —***v***. compose; compound; synthesize
	合同	ゴウドウ	union; combination; amalgamation; merger; fusion —***v***. combine; unite; amalgamate; incorporate; merge
	合板	ゴウバン	plywood; veneer board
	合理化	ゴウリカ	rationalization —***v***. rationalize
	合理的	ゴウリテキ	rational; logical; reasonable
	合流	ゴウリュウ	confluence; conflux; linking; union —***vi***. join; link; unite
訓	合鍵	あいかぎ	duplicate key; master key; passkey
	合う	あう	***vi***. fit; suit; agree; be agreeable; be right; be correct
	合図	あいズ	signal; sign; alarm
	合わす	あわす	***vt***. expose/subject to
	合わせる	あわせる	***vt***. expose/subject to

285

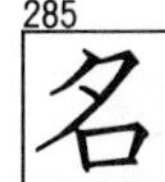
⑥ ノ ク タ タ 名 名

音	名	ミョウ	
		メイ	name; fame; reputation

熟

名字	ミョウジ	surname
名代	ミョウダイ	proxy; deputy; representative
名案	メイアン	good idea
名医	メイイ	famous doctor; skilled physician
名園	メイエン	famous garden
名家	メイカ	distinguished family; celebrity
名菓	メイカ	famous cake
名歌	メイカ	famous/excellent poem or song
名画	メイガ	famous picture; masterpiece
名義	メイギ	official name; moral duty
名曲	メイキョク	famous music
名句	メイク	famous haiku; well-put phrase
名月	メイゲツ	harvest moon
名言	メイゲン	wise saying; apt remark
名工	メイコウ	master craftsman
名作	メイサク	literary masterpiece
名産	メイサン	noted product/speciality of a particular area
名山	メイザン	famous mountain
名士	メイシ	prominent figure; celebrity
名刺	メイシ	calling/business card
名詞	メイシ	***gram***. noun
名実	メイジツ	in name and fact
名手	メイシュ	expert
名所	メイショ	place of interest
名将	メイショウ	famous general/military commander
名称	メイショウ	name
名勝	メイショウ	scenic spot
名人	メイジン	master; expert; virtuoso
名声	メイセイ	fame; reputation
名僧	メイソウ	eminent priest
名著	メイチョ	famous work; great book
名店街	メイテンガイ	street of famous shops
名刀	メイトウ	fine sword; famed blade
名馬	メイバ	fine horse
名物	メイブツ	noted product of a particular area; standout
名文	メイブン	excellent composition; fine prose
名分	メイブン	moral duty; justice
名目	メイモク	name; pretext; nominal; ostensible
名門	メイモン	famous family; prestigious school
名訳	メイヤク	excellent/famous translation

	名優	メイユウ	famous actor; star
	名誉	メイヨ	honor; glory; fame; prestige
訓	名	な	name; fame; reputation
	名残	なごり	traces; remains; vestiges
	名指す	なざす	***vt***. name; call by a name
	名代	なだい	fame
	名高い	なだかい	famous; renowned
	名付ける	なづける	***vt***. name; call; entitle
	名無し	ななし	nameless; anonymous; unknown
	名主	なぬし	***hist***. village headman (Edo period)
	名札	なふだ	name plate/tag
	名前	なまえ	name
¥	名義書き換え	メイギかきかえ	stock transfer
	名目賃金	メイモクチンギン	nominal wages

286

⑦ ノ 八 𠆢 今 今 含 含

音	含	ガン	hold; include
熟	含蓄	ガンチク	implication; significance; suggestiveness
	含有	ガンユウ	containment; holding —***v***. contain; have; hold
訓	含む	ふくむ	***vt***. contain; keep in one's mouth
	含める	ふくめる	***vt***. include
¥	含み益	ふくみえき	hidden/off-record profit
	含み資産	ふくみシサン	hidden/off-record assets
	含み損	ふくみゾン	hidden/off-record loss

287

君

⑦ フ ヨ ヨ 尹 尹 君 君

音	君	クン	you; lord; splendid person; (suffix) attached to the names of young men
熟	君子	クンシ	gentleman; man of virture
	君主	クンシュ	monarch
	君主国	クンシュコク	monarchy
	君臨	クンリン	reigning —***vi***. reign
訓	君	きみ	you (used among friends, by teachers to students, by seniors to juniors, etc.)

288 告 ⑦

音	告	コク	tell; announce; inform
熟	告示	コクジ	notification; notice; bulletin —*v*. notify; proclaim; announce
	告訴	コクソ	complaint; accusation; legal action —*v*. accuse; charge; complain
	告知	コクチ	notice; announcement —*v*. notify; announce
	告白	コクハク	confession; avowal; admission —*v*. confess; admit; declare
	告発	コクハツ	prosecution; indictment; accusation —*v*. prosecute; indict; accuse; charge
	告別	コクベツ	leave-taking; parting —*vi*. take leave of; bid farewell
訓	告げる	つげる	*vt*. notice; inform; proclaim
	告げ口	つげぐち	telling tales —*vi*. tell tales; rat on
	お告げ	おつげ	announcement

289 否 ⑦

音	否	ヒ	no; negative; refuse; decline
熟	否決	ヒケツ	rejection; voting against —*v*. reject; vote against
	否定	ヒテイ	denial; negation —*v*. deny; negate
	否定的	ヒテイテキ	negative; contradictory
	否認	ヒニン	denial; repudiation —*v*. deny; repudiate
訓	否	いな	no
	否や	いなや	as soon as; no sooner than; yes or no; objection; if; whether
	否	いや	no; nay; yes; well
	否々	いやいや	grudgingly; by no means
	否応なし	いやオウなし	whether one likes it or not

290 唇 ⑩

音	唇	シン	lip
訓	唇	くちびる	lip

291

哲 ⑩

一 寸 才 扌' 扩 扩 折 折 哲 哲

音	哲	テツ	sage; philosophy
熟	哲学	テツガク	philosophy
	哲人	テツジン	philosopher
訓	※哲い	さとい	clever; intelligent

292

唐 ⑩

丶 亠 广 户 庐 序 庚 庚 唐 唐

音	唐	トウ	China
熟	唐突	トウトツ	abruptly; in an abrupt way
訓	唐	から	(former name) China; Cathay
	唐紙	からかみ	sliding screen
	唐草模様	からくさモヨウ	arabesque pattern

293

啓 ⑪

一 ㇇ ㇇ 戸 戸 户' 所 改 啟 啓 啓

音	啓	ケイ	enlighten; state; say
熟	啓示	ケイジ	revelation —*v.* reveal
	啓上	ケイジョウ	Dear Sir/Madam (opening phrase of a letter)
	啓発	ケイハツ	enlightenment —*v.* enlighten; illuminate; educate
	啓蒙	ケイモウ	enlightenment —*v.* enlighten; illuminate; educate

294

喜 ⑫

一 十 士 吉 吉 吉 吉 吉 壴 喜 喜 喜

音	喜	キ	gladness; joy; happiness
熟	喜劇	キゲキ	comedy
	喜寿	キジュ	one's seventy-seventh birthday
	喜色	キショク	countenance; mood; humor; feelings; happy expression

	喜怒哀楽	キドアイラク	joy and anger; emotion; feelings
訓	喜び	よろこび	joy; happiness
	喜ぶ	よろこぶ	***vi***. rejoice; be glad/happy

295

善 ⑫

音	善	ゼン	good
熟	善悪	ゼンアク	good and evil
	善意	ゼンイ	good faith; well-intentioned; good will
	善行	ゼンコウ	good conduct/deed
	善後策	ゼンゴサク	remedial measures
	善処	ゼンショ	appropriate action —***vi***. take appropriate action
	善戦	ゼンセン	good fight —***vi***. put up a good fight
	善男善女	ゼンナンゼンニョ	devout men and women
	善人	ゼンニン	good man/people
	善良	ゼンリョウ	good; good-natured; virtuous
訓	善い	よい	right; fine; good

296

吸 ⑥

音	吸	キュウ	inhale; suck; smoke
熟	吸引	キュウイン	absorbtion; suction —***v***. absorb; suck
	吸気	キュウキ	air supply; ventilation
	吸血鬼	キュウケツキ	vampire
	吸湿性	キュウシツセイ	***chem***. hygroscopicity
	吸収	キュウシュウ	absorption; imbibition —***v***. absorb; imbibe
	吸着	キュウチャク	absorption —***vi***. absorb
	吸入	キュウニュウ	inhalation —***v***. breathe in; inhale
	吸盤	キュウバン	sucker; cupule
訓	吸う	すう	***vt***. breathe in; inhale; imbibe; smoke
	吸い上げる	すいあげる	***vt***. suck/pump up
	吸い殻	すいがら	cigarette end; butt
	吸い込む	すいこむ	***vt***. inhale; breathe in; imbibe
	吸い出す	すいだす	***vt***. suck out; aspirate
	吸い付く	すいつく	***vi***. stick/cling to; adhere
	吸い物	すいもの	*suimono* (Japanese clear soup)

297

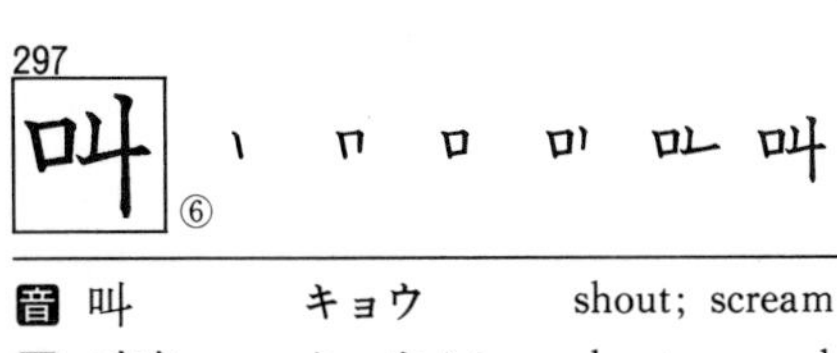

音	叫	キョウ	shout; scream
熟	叫喚	キョウカン	shout; cry; shriek; scream
訓	叫ぶ	さけぶ	***vi***. shout; scream; call out
	叫び声	さけびごえ	shout; cry; exclamation; yell; clamor; shriek; scream; wail

298

吐 ⑥

音	吐	ト	vomit; spit out; emit; express
熟	吐息	トイキ	sigh; gasp: sharp intake of breath
	吐血	トケツ	vomiting of blood ***med***. hemoptysis; stomach hemorrhage —***vi***. vomit/cough up blood; suffer a stomach hemorrhage
訓	吐く	はく	***vt***. vomit; spew; spit out; throw up; belch; emit; express; confess

299

吟 ⑦

音	吟	ギン	reciting/writing poetry
熟	吟じる	ギンじる	***vt***. recite/write poetry
	吟詠	ギンエイ	singing; recital —***v***. sing; give a recital
	吟味	ギンミ	close examination; inquiring; scrutiny —***v***. examine; inquire; scrutinize

300

吹 ⑦

音	吹	スイ	blow
熟	吹奏楽	スイソウガク	wind music
訓	吹く	ふく	***v***. blow; breathe; play a musical instrument
	吹聴	ふいチョウ	spreading; publicizing; boasting; advertising —***v***. spread; make public/known; boast; advertize
	※吹雪	ふぶき	snowstorm

301

呼 ⑧

丶 ㇆ 口 口' 口ˊ 吖 吀 呼

音	呼	コ	call; expire; exhale; breathe out
熟	呼応	コオウ	shouting; agreement; correlation —*v*. shout to each other; agree; go together; correlate; act in concert
	呼気	コキ	expiration; exhalation
	呼吸	コキュウ	breathing; respiration —*v*. breathe
	呼吸器	コキュウキ	***med***. respiratory organs
	呼称	コショウ	given name —*v*. call/give somebody a name
訓	呼ぶ	よぶ	***vt***. call; ring for; invite; name
	呼び声	よびごえ	call; cries
	呼び捨て	よびすて	calling a person by name without any honorific title
	呼び出す	よびだす	***vt***. ask to come; call up; summon
	呼鈴	よびリン	bell; doorbell

302

味 ⑧

丶 ㇆ 口 口一 口二 吽 味 味

音	味	ミ	taste; flavor
熟	味覚	ミカク	taste; sense of taste
	味方	ミかた	friend; ally; supporter
	味噌汁	ミソしる	miso soup
	味読	ミドク	read with appreciation
訓	味	あじ	taste; flavor
	味気ない	あじケない	dull; wearisome; dreary; wretched
	味付け	あじつけ	seasoning; salting —*v*. season; salt
	味わう	あじわう	***vt***. taste; experience; relish; appreciate

303

咲 ⑨

丶 ㇆ 口 口' 口'' 口⺌ 口⺌ 咲 咲

訓	咲く	さく	***vi***. bloom; blossom
	咲き乱れる	さきみだれる	***vi***. be in full bloom

304 **唆** ⑩

音	唆	サ	suggest; coax; incite
熟	唆す	そそのかす	*vt*. tempt; incite; coax; suggest

305 **喝** ⑪

音	喝	カツ	cheers; shout
熟	喝采	カッサイ	applause; cheers —*v*. applaud; cheer

306 **唱** ⑪

音	唱	ショウ	recite; sing; advocate
熟	唱歌	ショウカ	singing; songs
	唱和	ショウワ	chorus —*vi*. sing in chorus/unison
訓	唱える	となえる	*vt*. recite; chant; advocate; urge; preach

307 **唯** ⑪

音	唯	ユイ (イ)	only; soley; merely
熟	唯一	ユイイツ	only; sole
	唯我独尊	ユイガドクソン	self-conceit; vain glory
	唯心論	ユイシンロン	idealism; spiritualism
	唯美主義	ユイビシュギ	estheticism
	唯物論	ユイブツロン	materialism
	唯名論	ユイメイロン	nominalism
訓	※唯	ただ	solely; only; merely
	※唯今	ただいま	right now; just now; I'm back (said by person returning home)

308 喚 ⑫

音	喚	カン	cry; scream
熟	喚起	カンキ	awakening —***v***. awaken; arouse; evoke
	喚声	カンセイ	loud cry
	喚問	カンモン	summons —***v***. summon
訓	※喚ぶ	よぶ	***vt***. call; summon

309 喫 ⑫

音	喫	キツ	eat; drink; smoke
熟	喫煙	キツエン	smoking —***vi***. smoke; have a smoke
	喫茶店	キッサテン	coffee house/shop; café

310 嘆 ⑬

音	嘆	タン	grieve; lament; deplore; sigh
熟	嘆願	タンガン	entreaty; appeal; petition; suit —***v***. entreat; appeal; petition; sue
	嘆声	タンセイ	sigh; lamentation
	嘆息	タンソク	sigh; lamentation; grief; deploration —***vi***. sigh; lament; grieve
訓	嘆く	なげく	***v***. sigh; grieve; lament; deplore
	嘆き	なげき	grief; sorrow; lamentation
	嘆かわしい	なげかわしい	sad; wretched; lamentable; regretable; deplorable

311 嘱 ⑮

音	嘱	ショク	request; expect
熟	嘱託	ショクタク	entrust; commission; contract —***v***. entrust; employ temporarily
	嘱望	ショクボウ	promising; hopeful —***v***. pin one's hopes on; be promising

312

⑮

音	噴	フン	emit; spout; spew forth
熟	噴煙	フンエン	thick smoke (from a volcano, etc.)
	噴火	フンカ	(volcanic) eruption —*vi.* erupt
	噴火口	フンカコウ	crater (of a volcano)
	噴火山	フンカザン	active volcano
	噴射	フンシャ	jet; spray; injection —*v.* shoot out/spray (water)
	噴出	フンシュツ	eruption; gushing; spouting —*v.* spew/gush/spurt out
	噴水	フンスイ	fountain; jet of water
	噴霧器	フンムキ	sprayer; vaporizer
訓	噴く	ふく	gush; emit; spew forth

313

嚇 ⑰

音	嚇	カク	threaten; intimidate
熟	嚇努	カクド	fury; rage —*vi.* become furious; get angry

314

可 ⑤

音	可	カ	possible; can; permit; good
熟	可動	カドウ	movable; mobile
	可燃性	カネンセイ	inflammability; combustibility
	可燃物	カネンブツ	inflammable/combustible substance
	可能	カノウ	possible
	可能性	カノウセイ	possibility
	可否	カヒ	right or wrong; pro and con; for and against
	可憐	カレン	pretty; cute; coy
	可愛い	カワイい	cute; pretty; dear; darling; charming
	可哀相	カワイソウ	poor; pitiable; pathetic; pitiful
訓	※可い	よい	good; fine; nice

¥	可決	カケツ	passage (of a bill); approval; adoption (of a recommendation) —*v.* pass a bill; carry a motion
	可処分所得	カショブンショトク	disposable income; dispensible earnings

315

句 ⑤

ノ 勹 勺 句 句

音	句	ク	phrase; part of a sentence; haiku poem
熟	句会	クカイ	haiku gathering; meeting for the purpose of reading haiku
	句集	クシュウ	haiku anthology
	句点	クテン	period; full stop
	句読点	クトウテン	punctuation marks

316

号 ⑤

丶 ㄇ 口 旦 号

音	号	ゴウ	shout; cry; name; sign; title; order; command
熟	号外	ゴウガイ	extra/special edition (of a newspaper, magazine, periodical, etc.)
	号泣	ゴウキュウ	wailing; lamentation; moaning; weeping —***vi***. wail; lament; moan; weep bitterly
	号数	ゴウスウ	number (of editions)
	号砲	ゴウホウ	signal/watch gun
	号令	ゴウレイ	order; command —***vi***. order; command; give an order

317

史 ⑤

丶 ㄇ 口 史 史

音	史	シ	history
熟	史学	シガク	history; historical studies
	史実	シジツ	historical fact
	史上	シジョウ	in history; historical
	史跡	シセキ	historic place/site
	史料	シリョウ	historical records

318

司 ⑤ 𠃌 ㇕ 𠮟 司 司

音	司	シ	official; officer; control; manage
熟	司会	シカイ	presiding; taking the chair —*v*. preside; take the chair
	司会者	シカイシャ	master of ceremonies (MC); chairman
	司祭	シサイ	Roman Catholic priest
	司書	シショ	librarian
	司法	シホウ	the judiciary
	司法官	シホウカン	judicial officer; judges and prosecutors
	司法行政	シホウギョウセイ	judicial administration; the judiciary
	司法権	シホウケン	right to justice
	司令	シレイ	command; commander —*v*. command
	司令部	シレイブ	military headquarters
訓	※司る	つかさどる	***vt***. manage; look after; control; take charge

319

向 ⑥ ノ 丿 门 向 向 向

音	向	コウ	face; front; opposite; the other side
熟	向学心	コウガクシン	love of learning; desire to learn
	向上	コウジョウ	improvement; elevation; rise —***vi***. rise; be elevated; become higher; improve; advance
訓	向かう	むかう	***vi***. face; front; look at; be opposite; meet; confront; approach
	向き	むき	direction; quarter; exposure; aspect
	向く	むく	***vi***. turn; look to; face; point; tend; suit
	向ける	むける	***vt***. turn; face; direct; point; aim; send; address; refer
	向こう	むこう	the other side; beyond; one's destination; the other party

320

同 ⑥

音	同	ドウ	same; similar
熟	同意	ドウイ	same meaning/opinion; agreement; consent —***vi***. agree with; consent to; approve
	同意語	ドウイゴ	***gram***. synonym

同一	ドウイツ	identity; sameness; oneness; equality; indiscrimination
同一視	ドウイツシ	***vt***. regard A in the same light as B; look at things indiscriminately
同音語	ドウオンゴ	***gram***. homophone
同化	ドウカ	adaptation; assimilation —***v***. adapt; assimilate
同格	ドウカク	same rank; equal footing; equality
同額	ドウガク	equal sum/amount (of money)
同感	ドウカン	same sentiment; sympathy; empathy; agreement; concurrence
同期	ドウキ	same period/class; synchronism
同義	ドウギ	synonymy; same meaning
同義語	ドウギゴ	***gram***. synonym
同居	ドウキョ	living together —***vi***. live together
同郷	ドウキョウ	same province/village
同業	ドウギョウ	same trade/business
同権	ドウケン	equal rights
同行	ドウコウ	going/traveling together —***vi***. go/travel together
同好	ドウコウ	same tastes; liking the same thing
同士	ドウシ	fellow; companion
同志	ドウシ	same mind; congenial spirit; like-minded person
同乗	ドウジョウ	riding together; sharing a carriage —***vi***. ride together; share a carriage
同乗者	ドウジョウシャ	fellow passenger
同情	ドウジョウ	sympathy; compassion; fellow feeling —***vi***. sympathize; be sympathetic; have compassion
同人	ドウジン	same person; coterie; clique; fraternity; club
同姓	ドウセイ	of the same surname
同性	ドウセイ	same sex
同性愛	ドウセイアイ	homosexuality
同席	ドウセキ	sitting with/together —***vi***. sit with
同然	ドウゼン	same
同窓	ドウソウ	alumnus
同調	ドウチョウ	alignment; conformity —***vi***. align oneself; conform; follow suit; fall into line
同等	ドウトウ	equality; parity
同伴	ドウハン	company; companion —***v***. accompany; go with
同封	ドウフウ	enclosure (in a letter) —***v***. enclose (in a letter)
同胞	ドウホウ	brethren; brothers and sisters; citizens of a country
同盟	ドウメイ	alliance; league; union; confederation —***v***. ally with; form an alliance/union
同様	ドウヨウ	same; similar; identical
同僚	ドウリョウ	colleague

	同類	ドウルイ	same kind/class
訓	同じ	おなじ	same

321

吏 ⑥ 一 𠀋 … 吏

音	吏	リ	official
熟	吏員	リイン	official

322

呉 ⑦

音	呉	ゴ	Wu dynasty; be given
熟	呉音	ゴオン	Wu pronunciation of Chinese characters
	呉服	ゴフク	kimono fabrics; drapery and haberdashery
	呉服屋	ゴフクや	shop selling kimono fabrics
訓	呉れる	くれる	***vt***. give

323

呈 ⑦

音	呈	テイ	present
熟	呈示	テイジ	presentation —***v***. present; idicate; bring up; suggest; come up with
	呈上	テイジョウ	presentation —***v***. present

324

周 ⑧ 丿 冂 月 円 用 周 周 周

音	周	シュウ	round; surround; Zhou/Chou dynasty
熟	周囲	シュウイ	circumference; girth; periphery; surroundings; the environment
	周回	シュウカイ	lap; going around —***v***. go around
	周忌	シュウキ	anniversary of a person's death
	周期	シュウキ	period; cycle
	周航	シュウコウ	sailing around; circumnavigation —***vi***. sail around; circumnavigate
	周旋	シュウセン	agency; brokerage —***v***. act as an agent; broker

	周知	シュウチ	well-known; widely-known
	周到	シュウトウ	careful; scrupulous; meticulous
	周年	シュウネン	(suffix) whole year; anniversary
	周波	シュウハ	cycle; frequency
	周波数	シュウハスウ	frequency
	周辺	シュウヘン	outskirts; around; environs
	周遊	シュウユウ	tour; excursion
訓	周り	まわり	surroundings; neighborhood; environment; those around one
¥	周旋業	シュウセンギョウ	brokerage
	周旋業者	シュウセンギョウシャ	broker; agency

325

命 ⑧

音	命	ミョウ	
		メイ	life; destiny; fate order; command
熟	命じる	メイじる	order; command
	命運	メイウン	fate
	命数	メイスウ	one's natural life span; destiny
	命題	メイダイ	proposition
	命中	メイチュウ	hit —***vi***. hit (the target)
	命日	メイニチ	anniversary of a death
	命脈	メイミャク	life
	命名	メイメイ	naming; christening; calling —***vi***. name; christen; call
	命令	メイレイ	order; command —***v***. order; command
訓	命	いのち	life
	命懸け	いのちがけ	desperate; risking one's life
	命知らず	いのちしらず	recklessness; daredevil
	命取り	いのちとり	fatal
	命拾い	いのちびろい	narrow escape from death
	※命	みこと	lord; prince

326

和 ⑧

ノ 二 千 禾 禾 禾 和 和

音	和	ワ	peace; harmony; Japan
		(オ)	

熟	和尚	オショウ	chief priest of a Buddhist temple
	和英	ワエイ	Japanese and English languages; Japan and England
	和音	ワオン	chord (in music)
	和歌	ワカ	*tanka* (31-syllable poem)
	和解	ワカイ	amicable settlement; compromise; reconciliation —***vi***. be reconciled; settle one's differences
	和菓子	ワガシ	Japanese cakes
	和気	ワキ	harmony; peacefulness; calm (sea, wind, etc.)
	和合	ワゴウ	harmony; concord; concord of husband and wife —***vi***. be in harmony/concord
	和裁	ワサイ	Japanese dress-making; sewing kimono
	和紙	ワシ	*washi* (Japanese paper)
	和室	ワシツ	Japanese-style room
	和食	ワショク	Japanese cuisine
	和声	ワセイ	harmony (in music)
	和製	ワセイ	made in Japan
	和装	ワソウ	Japanese dress
	和風	ワフウ	Japanese style
	和服	ワフク	kimono; Japanese clothes
	和文	ワブン	something written in Japanese; Japanese writing (especially *kana*)
	和平	ワヘイ	peace
	和睦	ワボク	reconciliation; rapport; peace —***vi***. be reconciled; make peace
	和訳	ワヤク	translation into Japanese —***v***. translate into Japanese
	和洋	ワヨウ	Japanese and Western
	和様	ワヨウ	Japanese style
訓	和む	なごむ	***v***. become calm; calm down ***vt***. calm down; moderate
	和やか	なごやか	peaceful; calm
	和らぐ	やわらぐ	***vi***. soften; become soft/gentle/peaceful ***vt***. soften; moderate
	和らげる	やわらげる	***vt***. soften; lessen; relieve; pacify; moderate; modify
	※和える	あえる	***vt***. dress food (with mayonnaise, etc.)

327

⑨ 丶 亠 六 亡 古 亨 亨 哀 哀

音	哀	アイ	pity; pathos; regret; sadness; sorrow

口 囗 土 士 夂 夕 大 女 子 宀 寸 小 ⺌ ⺍ 尢 尸 山 川 工 己 巾 干 幺 广 廴 廾 弋 弓 彐 彡 彳 艹 辶 阝 阝 亠 忄 扌 犭 氵

熟	哀願	アイガン	earnest request; entreaty; appeal; petition —*v*. make an earnest request; entreat; implore; appeal; petition
	哀愁	アイシュウ	sadness; sorrow; grief; pathos
	哀調	アイチョウ	mournful melody
	哀悼	アイトウ	mourning; grief; lamentation —*v*. mourn; grieve; lament
訓	哀れ	あわれ	pity; pathos; sorrow; misery
	哀れむ	あわれむ	***vt***. pity; feel compassion/sympathy
	哀しい	かなしい	sad; sorrowful; pathetic; pitiful

328

品 ⑨

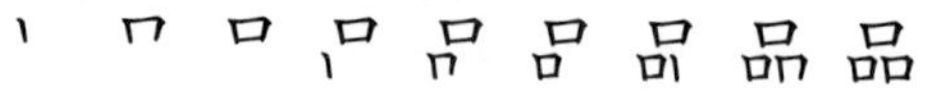

音	品	ヒン	article; refinement
熟	品	ヒン	elegance; grace; refinement; dignity; article; piece; item; course
	品位	ヒンイ	dignity; nobility; grade; carat
	品格	ヒンカク	dignity; nobility
	品行	ヒンコウ	conduct; behavior; actions
	品行方正	ヒンコウホウセイ	well-mannered; exemplary conduct
	品詞	ヒンシ	***gram***. part of speech
	品質	ヒンシツ	quality
	品種	ヒンシュ	kind; variety; type; grade; breed
	品性	ヒンセイ	character
	品評会	ヒンピョウカイ	competitive show/exhibition; fair
	品目	ヒンモク	item; list of articles
訓	品	しな	article; goods; wares; quality; personality
	品書き	しながき	catalog; menu
	品切れ	しなぎれ	out of stock; sold out
	品物	しなもの	article; thing; goods; wares; stuff; stock
¥	品薄	しなうす	shortage of goods/stock/supply
	品薄株	しなうすかぶ	rare stock; narrow market securities
	品揃え	しなぞろえ	assembling; assortment
	品質管理	ヒンシツカンリ	quality control

329

員 ⑩

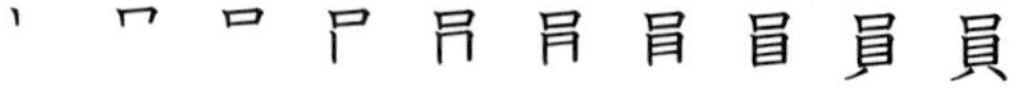

音	員	イン	member; staff

熟 員数 インズウ the number of persons or things

330

商 ⑪

丶 亠 ㇖ 产 产 产 产 产 产 产 商

音	商	ショウ	trade; merchant; business; commerce
熟	商科	ショウカ	commercial department; department of business and commerce
	商魂	ショウコン	commercial spirit
	商船	ショウセン	merchant ship/marine
	商店	ショウテン	store; shop
	商店街	ショウテンガイ	shopping center/mall
	商人	ショウニン	merchant; tradesman; dealer
訓	商う	あきなう	***vt***. sell; deal; trade
¥	商い	あきない	trade; business
	商会	ショウカイ	company; firm
	商況	ショウキョウ	business trends; market situation
	商業	ショウギョウ	commerce; trade; business
	商業化	ショウギョウカ	commercialization —***v***. commercialize
	商業界	ショウギョウカイ	business circles; commercial world
	商業銀行	ショウギョウギンコウ	commercial bank
	商業手形	ショウギョウてがた	commercial paper (CP)
	商号	ショウゴウ	trade/shop name
	商工会議所	ショウコウカイギショ	Chamber of Commerce and Industry
	商工組合中央金庫	ショウコウくみあいチュウオウキンコ	Central Cooperative Bank for Commerce and Industry
	商事	ショウジ	business affairs
	商社	ショウシャ	trading company
	商戦	ショウセン	sales battle; selling competition
	商談	ショウダン	business discussion/negotiations —***vi***. talk business
	商売	ショウバイ	trade; business; commerce; occupation —***v***. trade; do business
	商標	ショウヒョウ	trademark; brand
	商品	ショウヒン	commodity; merchandise; goods
	商法	ショウホウ	commercial law
	商用	ショウヨウ	business; business call/use

331
問 ⑪

音	問	モン	question; problem
熟	問罪	モンザイ	accusation; indictment —***vi***. accuse; indict
	問責	モンセキ	censure; reprimand —***v***. censure; reprimand
	問題	モンダイ	question; problem; issue
	問答	モンドウ	questions and answers —***v***. question and answer
訓	問う	とう	***vt***. inquire; ask; care about; accuse
	問い	とい	question; inquiry
	問い合わせる	といあわせる	***vt***. inquire; ask about
	※問屋	とんや	wholesale dealer

332
喪 ⑫

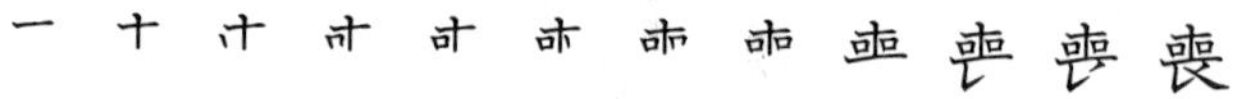

音	喪	ソウ	mourning; loss
熟	喪失	ソウシツ	loss —***v***. lose
訓	喪	も	mourning; loss
	喪章	もショウ	mourning badge/band
	喪中	もチュウ	period of mourning
	喪服	もフク	mourning clothes

333
嗣 ⑬

音	嗣	シ	heir
熟	嗣子	シシ	heir

334
器 ⑮

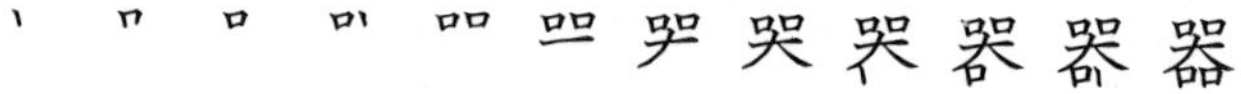

音	器	キ	receptacle; vessel; organ
熟	器械	キカイ	instrument; appliance
	器械体操	キカイタイソウ	gymnastics
	器楽	キガク	instrumental music

器官	キカン	***med.*** body organ
器具	キグ	implement; appliance; apparatus
器材	キザイ	materials; tools and materials
器物	キブツ	utensil; vessel; container
器用	キヨウ	skillfulness; dexterity
器量	キリョウ	countenance; talent; ability
訓 器	うつわ	vessel; container; utensil; capacity

3 囗 くにがまえ box

335

四 ⑤

丨 冂 门 四 四

音 四	シ	four
熟 四角	シカク	square
四角四面	シカクシメン	stiff; serious; stuffy; prim
四月	シガツ	April
四季	シキ	the four seasons
四苦八苦	シクハック	struggling —***vi.*** struggle; sweat blood
四散	シサン	dispersion; scatter —***vi.*** disperse; scatter
四捨五入	シシャゴニュウ	***math.*** rounding off —***v.*** round off
四方	シホウ	in all directions
四六時中	シロクジチュウ	day and night; twenty-four hours a day ***fig.*** always; often
訓 四	よん	four
四	よ	four
四つ	よつ	four
四日	よっか	fourth day (of the month); 4th
四っつ	よっつ	four
四隅	よすみ	four corners

336

囚 ⑤

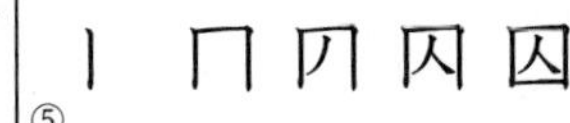

音 囚	シュウ	capture; prisoner
熟 囚人	シュウジン	prisoner; convict

337
因 ⑥

音	因	イン	cause
熟	因果	インガ	cause and effect; retribution; karma; fate
	因果応報	インガオウホウ	reward in accordance with deed; law of cause and effect
	因襲	インシュウ	conventions
	因縁	インネン	fate; origin; karma; pretext
訓	因る	よる	***vi.*** be caused by; be due to
	※因む	ちなむ	***vi.*** be related/connected
	※因みに	ちなみに	by the way

338
回 ⑥

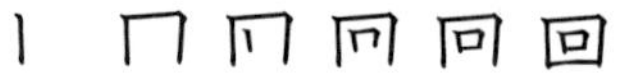

音	回	カイ	pass; turn; go round; circumference
		(エ)	turn round; service
熟	回帰線	カイキセン	the tropics
	回教	カイキョウ	Islam
	回顧	カイコ	recollection; retrospection —***v.*** look back on; recollect; retrospect
	回収	カイシュウ	withdrawal; collection; recovery —***v.*** withdraw from circulation; recover; collect
	回診	カイシン	doctor's round of visits —***vi.*** make house calls; visit one's patients
	回数	カイスウ	frequency; common occurence
	回数券	カイスウケン	coupon (commutation) ticket
	回送	カイソウ	forwarding; transportation —***v.*** forward; send on; transport
	回想	カイソウ	retrospection; reminiscence; recollection —***v.*** retrospect; recollect
	回虫	カイチュウ	***med.*** roundworm; intestinal worm
	回転	カイテン	rotation —***vi.*** revolve; rotate; turn around
	回答	カイトウ	reply; answer; response —***vi.*** reply; answer; respond
	回避	カイヒ	evasion; avoidance —***v.*** evade; dodge; avoid
	回復	カイフク	restoration; recovery —***v.*** restore; recover
	回復期	カイフクキ	convalescence
	回覧	カイラン	circulation —***v.*** circulate; send around
	回路	カイロ	electric circuit

訓	回る	まわる	***vi***. go around; pass; spread
	回す	まわす	***vt***. turn; pass; revolve
	回り	まわり	circumference; surroundings; by way of
	回り道	まわりみち	making a detour

339

団 ⑥

音	団	ダン (トン)	body; group; corps; organization; association
熟	団員	ダンイン	group member
	団結	ダンケツ	unity; union; solidarity; combination —***vi***. unite; be united; stand together; combine
	団子	ダンゴ	dumpling
	団体	ダンタイ	party; company; group; body; organization; association
	団地	ダンチ	housing development; public housing complex
	団長	ダンチョウ	leader; head of a group
	団欒	ダンラン	happy circle/family; sitting in a circle —***vi***. sit in a circle

340

囲 ⑦

音	囲	イ	surround; enclose
熟	囲碁	イゴ	game of go
	囲炉裏	イロリ	Japanese-style open hearth
訓	囲む	かこむ	***vt***. enclose; surround; encircle
	囲う	かこう	***vt***. enclose; fence
	囲い	かこい	enclosure; fence
	囲み	かこみ	surrounding the enemy; enclosure

341

困 ⑦

音	困	コン	suffer; distress
熟	困窮	コンキュウ	poverty; need; want; destitution —***vi***. be poor; be destitute
	困苦	コンク	hardships; adversity; trials; suffering
	困難	コンナン	difficulty; hurdle; trouble; distress

訓	困る	こまる	*vi.* suffer; be in trouble; have a problem

342

図 ⑦

音	図	ズ	drawing; picture; plan; figure
		ト	plan
熟	図案	ズアン	design; device; sketch; plan
	図画	ズガ	drawing; sketching
	図解	ズカイ	illustration; explanatory diagram —*v.* illustrate; explain with diagrams
	図鑑	ズカン	picture book
	図形	ズケイ	figure; device; diagram
	図示	ズシ	illustration; graphic representation —*v.* illustrate; represent graphically
	図式	ズシキ	diagram; graph; chart; figure
	図版	ズハン	figure; illustration; plate
	図板	ズバン	drafting/drawing board
	図表	ズヒョウ	diagram; chart; graph
	図譜	ズフ	picture book
	図法	ズホウ	drawing; draftmanship
	図面	ズメン	drawing; sketch; map
	図書	トショ	books
	図書館	トショカン	library
訓	図る	はかる	*vt.* plan; devise; contrive; design; plot

343

⑧

音	固	コ	hard; solid; obstinate
熟	固形	コケイ	solid body; solid
	固持	コジ	persistence —*v.* be persistent; hold to; stand by; stick to
	固辞	コジ	categorical refusal —*v.* categorically refuse; refuse flatly
	固執	コシツ	persistence; insistence —*v.* persist; stick/cling to; insist on
	固守	コシュ	adherence; persistence; insistence —*v.* adhere to; persist in; insist on
	固体	コタイ	solid; solid matter
	固定	コテイ	fixed; settled —*v.* fix; settle

	固有	コユウ	peculiar; characteristic; indigenous; particular
	固有名詞	コユウメイシ	***gram***. proper noun
訓	固い	かたい	hard; tough; tight; firm; strict; obstinate; rigid
	固まる	かたまる	***vi***. harden; become stiff; congeal; coagulate; thicken
	固める	かためる	***vt***. make hard; strengthen; fortify; solidify
¥	固定金利	コテイキンリ	fixed rate of interest
	固定資産	コテイシサン	fixed assets
	固定資産売却益	コテイシサンバイキャクエキ	profits on disposal of fixed assets
	固定資産売却損	コテイシサンバイキャクソン	losses on disposal of fixed assets
	固定負債	コテイフサイ	fixed liabilities

344

⑧

音	国	コク	state; country; nation; province
熟	国営	コクエイ	state/government management
	国学	コクガク	study of classical Japanese literature, history, and thought (late Edo period)
	国技	コクギ	national sport
	国語	コクゴ	one's mother tongue; the Japanese language
	国際	コクサイ	international
	国際化	コクサイカ	internationalization —***v***. internationalize
	国際的	コクサイテキ	international; universal; cosmopolitan
	国際連合	コクサイレンゴウ	United Nations
	国策	コクサク	national policy
	国産	コクサン	domestic production
	国字	コクジ	Japanese script; *kanji* invented in Japan
	国事	コクジ	affairs of state; national affairs
	国情	コクジョウ	conditions of a country; state of affairs
	国政	コクセイ	national administration; government
	国勢	コクセイ	state of a country
	国勢調査	コクセイチョウサ	census
	国籍	コクセキ	nationality; citizenship
	国葬	コクソウ	state funeral
	国体	コクタイ	polity; national structure
	国土	コクド	country; territory; realm; domain
	国道	コクドウ	national road/highway
	国内	コクナイ	internal; domestic

	国費	コクヒ	national expenditure
	国賓	コクヒン	state/national guest
	国文学	コクブンガク	Japanese literature
	国宝	コクホウ	national treasure
	国防	コクボウ	national defense
	国民	コクミン	nation; people; nationality
	国民性	コクミンセイ	national character
	国務	コクム	affairs of state; state affairs
	国立	コクリツ	national
	国力	コクリョク	national power/resourses
	国家	コッカ	state; nation; country
	国家主義	コッカシュギ	nationalism
	国家的	コッカテキ	national; state
	国歌	コッカ	national anthem
	国花	コッカ	national flower
	国会	コッカイ	Diet; national assembly; congress; parliament
	国旗	コッキ	national flag
	国境	コッキョウ	border; frontier
	国交	コッコウ	diplomatic relations
訓	国	くに	state; nation; country; province
	国柄	くにがら	national character
¥	国営化	コクエイカ	nationalization —*v*. nationalize
	国債	コクサイ	government/national bond
	国際収支	コクサイシュウシ	balance of international payments
	国際通貨基金	コクサイツウカキキン	International Monetary Fund (IMF)
	国税	コクゼイ	national/direct taxes
	国民総生産	コクミンソウセイサン	gross national product (GNP)
	国務大臣	コクムダイジン	minister of state
	国有	コクユウ	state ownership —*v*. be owned by the state

345

⑫

音	圏	ケン	circle; sphere; range; zone
熟	圏外	ケンガイ	out of the sphere/range
	圏内	ケンナイ	within the sphere/range

346

⑬ 丨 冂 冖 冂 円 冃 冋 冐 冑 冑 園 園 園

音	園	エン	garden; park
熟	園芸	エンゲイ	gardening; horticulture; floriculture
	園児	エンジ	kindergarten pupils
	園長	エンチョウ	head zookeeper; head of a kindergarten
	園遊会	エンユウカイ	garden party
訓	園	その	garden

3 土 つち／つちへん earth

347

土

③ 一 十 土

音	土	ト	
		ド	soil; earth; dirt
熟	土方	ドかた	construction worker; navvy
	土管	ドカン	earthen pipe
	土器	ドキ	earthenware; crockery
	土下座	ドゲザ	prostrating oneself; paying obeisance —*vi*. prostrate oneself; apologize; show respect; pay obeisance
	土建	ドケン	civil engineering and construction
	土工	ドコウ	construction worker; navvy
	土左衛門	ドザエモン	drowned person
	土質	ドシツ	soil quality
	土砂	ドシャ	earth and sand
	土砂降り	ドシャぶり	pouring/heavy rain
	土壌	ドジョウ	soil; earth
	土人	ドジン	native; aboriginal
	土製	ドセイ	earthen; made of clay
	土星	ドセイ	the planet Saturn
	土葬	ドソウ	interment; burial
	土蔵	ドゾウ	warehouse; storehouse
	土足	ドソク	with one's shoes on
	土台	ドダイ	foundation; groundwork; base; basis; cornerstone

	土壇場	ドタンバ	place of execution; scaffold; last moment of life
	土地	トチ	earth; land
	土着	ドチャク	native; aboriginal; indigenous
	土手	ドて	embankment; dike
	土鍋	ドなべ	earthenware pot; casserole
	土俵	ドヒョウ	sandbag; ring for sumo wrestling
	土木	ドボク	engineering/public works
	土間	ドマ	unfloored part of the house; earthen floored room; pit in a theater
	土民	ドミン	natives; aborigines
	土用	ドヨウ	dog days; midsummer; hottest period of summer
	土曜日	ドヨウび	Saturday
訓	土	つち	Mother Earth; earth; soil; ground; clay
	土煙	つちけむり	cloud of dust
	土踏まず	つちふまず	arch of the foot
	土埃	つちぼこり	dust
	※土産	みやげ	souvenir

348

圧 ⑤

一 厂 圧

音	圧	アツ	pressure; press down
熟	圧する	アッする	***vt***. press; press down; oppress
	圧搾	アッサク	compression; pressure; pressing —***v***. reduce in size or volume as if by squeezing; compress; press hard
	圧死	アッシ	death from crushing —***v***. be crushed to death; be suffocated
	圧縮	アッシュク	compression; constriction; condensation —***v***. compress; constrict; make compact; condense
	圧勝	アッショウ	landslide win; sweeping victory —***vi***. defeat decisively; win a landslide victory
	圧倒	アットウ	overpowering; overcoming —***v***. overwhelm; overpower; overcome
	圧倒的	アットウテキ	overwhelming; overpowering
	圧迫	アッパク	unjust exercize of power; oppression; suppression —***v***. oppress; be oppressive; suppress
	圧力	アツリョク	pressure; stress
¥	圧縮記帳	アッシュクキチョウ	reduced-value entry (of acquired property)
	圧力団体	アツリョクダンタイ	pressure group

349

在 ⑥

音	在	ザイ	be
熟	在外	ザイガイ	being abroad/overseas
	在学	ザイガク	enrolled —*vi*. be in school; be a student at; be enrolled at
	在勤	ザイキン	while working —*vi*. be working; be at work
	在庫	ザイコ	stock; inventory
	在住	ザイジュウ	living; in residence —*vi*. live; be in residence at
	在住者	ザイジュウシャ	resident
	在職	ザイショク	in the office; at work —*vi*. be in office
	在籍	ザイセキ	registered; enrolled; on the roll —*vi*. be registered; be enrolled; be on the roll
	在宅	ザイタク	at home —*vi*. be at home
	在来	ザイライ	usual; common; conventionally
	在留	ザイリュウ	in residence —*vi*. reside; live
	在留邦人	ザイリュウホウジン	Japanese residents abroad
訓	在る	ある	*vi*. be; exist; live; be situated; be located
¥	在外資産	ザイガイシサン	overseas assets
	在外投資	ザイガイトウシ	overseas investments
	在庫一掃	ザイコイッソウ	stock clearance
	在庫過剰	ザイコカジョウ	overstocking
	在庫管理	ザイコカンリ	stock control; inventory management
	在庫表	ザイコヒョウ	stock list; inventory

350

 ⑧

音	垂	スイ	droop; hang down
熟	垂訓	スイクン	teaching; instruction
	垂線	スイセン	perpendicular (line)
	垂涎	スイゼン	envy; covetness —*vi*. envy; covet
	垂直	スイチョク	perpendicular; vertical; plumb; sheer; at right angles
	垂範	スイハン	example —*vi*. set an example
訓	垂らす	たらす	*vt*. hang down; suspend; slouch
	垂れる	たれる	*v*. hang down; droop; drop; drip

	垂氷	たるひ	icicle
	垂水	たるみ	waterfall

351

執 ⑪

音	執	シツ	execute; perform; carry out; do
		シュウ	stick to; attachment; tenacity
熟	執権	シッケン	regent; regency
	執行	シッコウ	execution (of a deed, etc.) —*v*. execute; carry out
	執行委員	シッコウイイン	executive committee
	執行人	シッコウニン	executor; executioner
	執行猶予	シッコウユウヨ	suspended sentence; probation
	執事	シツジ	butler; steward; majordomo
	執政	シッセイ	administration; governing; government
	執刀	シットウ	operation —*vi*. operate; perform an operation
	執筆	シッピツ	writing —*v*. write
	執務	シツム	work —*vi*. attend to one's business
	執拗	シツヨウ	obstinacy; persistence; tenacity
	執心	シュウシン	attachment; infatuation —*vi*. be attached; be infatuated
	執着	シュウチャク	deep attachment; tenacity —*vi*. be attached; stick to; insist
	執念	シュウネン	devotion; tenacity; persistence
訓	執る	とる	*vt*. do; handle; execute; write; command; defend

352

報 ⑫

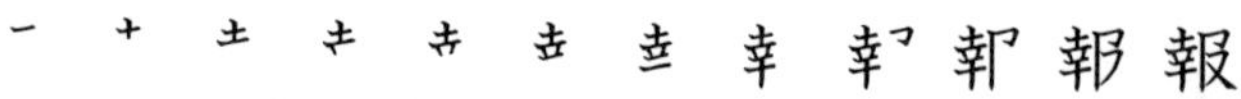

音	報	ホウ	news; report; reward
熟	報じる	ホウじる	*v*. repay; requite; report; inform
	報恩	ホウオン	showing gratitude; repaying a kindness
	報国	ホウコク	service to one's country
	報告	ホウコク	report —*v*. report; make a report
	報告書	ホウコクショ	(written) report/statement
	報酬	ホウシュウ	pay; remuneration; salary
	報奨	ホウショウ	compensation; bonus; reward —*v*. compensate; reward; remunerate

	報償	ホウショウ	compensation; reward; remuneration —***vi***. be compensated/rewarded/remunerated
	報知	ホウチ	information; news; intelligence —***v***. inform; make known; announce
	報道	ホウドウ	reporting; news coverage —***v***. report; inform; make known
	報道陣	ホウドウジン	press corps
	報徳	ホウトク	showing gratitude; repaying a kindness
	報復	ホウフク	revenge; vengence —***vi***. take revenge; revenge oneself
訓	報いる	むくいる	***vt***. reward; repay; retaliate; avenge oneself

353

型 ⑨

一 二 チ 开 开 刑 刑 型 型

音	型	ケイ	pattern; model; shape; form
訓	型	かた	model; pattern; mold; shape; form
	型紙	かたがみ	paper pattern
	型通り	かたどおり	in due/correct form; formal; formulaic (speech)
	型破り	かたやぶり	unconventional; unusual; break with tradition
	型	がた	(suffix) -type; -model

354

基 ⑪

一 十 卄 廿 甘 甘 其 其 其 基 基

音	基	キ	foundation; radical
熟	基金	キキン	fund; endowment
	基準	キジュン	standard; criterion
	基数	キスウ	***math***. cardinal numbers
	基礎	キソ	foundation; basics
	基地	キチ	(military) base
	基点	キテン	***math***. cardinal/reference point
	基盤	キバン	base; basis
	基本	キホン	basis; foundation
	基本的	キホンテキ	basically; fundamentally
訓	基	もと	basis; base
	基	もとい	basis; foundation
	基づく	もとづく	***vi***. be based on; originate; be due to

355
堂 ⑪

音	堂	ドウ	palace; temple
熟	堂々	ドウドウ	stately; imposing; dignified
	堂々巡り	ドウドウめぐり	going round and round in circles

356

⑫

音	堅	ケン	hard; solid; robust; strong; firm
熟	堅固	ケンゴ	firm; strong
	堅持	ケンジ	perseverance; maintenence —*v*. hold fast; stick to; maintain
	堅実	ケンジツ	steady; sound; reliable; stable; steady
訓	堅い	かたい	hard; tough; stiff; firm; strict; strong
	堅苦しい	かたくるしい	unrelaxed; formal

357

⑫

音	堕	ダ	fall; idle
熟	堕胎	ダタイ	abortion —***vi***. have an abortion; be aborted
	堕落	ダラク	depravity; corruption; degradation; delinquency; decadence —***vi***. become depraved; degenerate; fall into decadence

358

⑫

音	塁	ルイ	fort; base (in baseball)
熟	塁手	ルイシュ	***bas***. baseman
	塁審	ルイシン	***bas***. base umpire
	塁打	ルイダ	***bas***. base hit; single

359

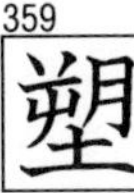

⑬

音	塑	ソ	molding; plastic
熟	塑像	ソゾウ	plastic image; clay figure
	塑造	ソゾウ	modeling; molding

360

⑬

音	塗	ト	paint
熟	塗装	トソウ	coating; painting —*v*. coat with paint
	塗布	トフ	application (of paint, etc.) —*v*. apply (paint, etc.)
	塗料	トリョウ	paints; paints and varnish; coating
訓	塗る	ぬる	***vt***. paint; gild
	塗り立て	ぬりたて	freshly painted

361

⑬

音	墓	ボ	tomb; grave
熟	墓穴	ボケツ	grave
	墓参	ボサン	visiting a grave —***vi***. visit a grave
	墓所	ボショ	graveyard; cemetery
	墓前	ボゼン	before the grave; in front of a grave
	墓地	ボチ	graveyard; cemetery
	墓碑	ボヒ	tombstone; grave stone; headstone
	墓碑銘	ボヒメイ	epitaph (on a headstone)
	墓標	ボヒョウ	grave post
訓	墓	はか	tomb; grave
	墓石	はかいし	gravestone; headstone
	墓場	はかば	graveyard; cemetery
	墓守	はかもり	gravekeeper
	お墓参り	おはかまいり	visiting a grave —***vi***. visit a grave

362 **塾** ⑭

音	塾	ジュク	private/cram school
熟	塾生	ジュクセイ	student of a private school; person studying at a cram school

363 **墨** ⑭

音	墨	ボク	India ink; ink stick; Mexico; Sumida River
熟	墨画	ボクガ	*sumie* (India ink drawing)
	墨守	ボクシュ	strict adherence (to tradition, etc.) —***v***. show strict adherence (to tradition, etc.)
	墨汁	ボクジュウ	India ink
訓	墨	すみ	*sumi* (India ink; ink stick)
	墨色	すみいろ	shade of India ink
	墨絵	すみえ	*sumie* (India ink drawing)
	お墨付き	おすみつき	recommendation from a superior/famous person

364 **墜** ⑮

音	墜	ツイ	fall
熟	墜死	ツイシ	death by falling —***vi***. fall to death
	墜落	ツイラク	(plane) crash; fall —***vi***. fall; drop; crash

365 **墾** ⑯

音	墾	コン	clear land

366 **壁** ⑯

音	壁	ヘキ	wall

熟	壁画	ヘキガ	fresco; mural
訓	壁	かべ	wall
	壁掛け	かべかけ	tapestry; wall hanging
	壁紙	かべがみ	wallpaper
	壁際	かべぎわ	by/near the wall
	壁新聞	かべシンブン	wall newspaper/poster

367

地 ⑥

一 十 土 圠 坩 地

音	地	ジ	earth; ground; soil; land; spot; place; district; region
		チ	
熟	地金	ジがね	metal; ore; one's true character/colors
	地声	ジごえ	one's natural voice
	地獄	ジゴク	hell
	地所	ジショ	land; ground; piece of land
	地震	ジシン	earthquake
	地震帯	ジシンタイ	earthquake zone/belt
	地蔵	ジゾウ	Jizō (Buddhist guardian deity of children)
	地鎮祭	ジチンサイ	Shintō ceremony of purifying a building site
	地主	ジぬし	landlord; landowner
	地盤	ジバン	ground; base; foundation; sphere of influence; constituency
	地味	ジミ	plain; simple; quiet; sober; conservative
	地道	ジみち	the honest way; beaten track
	地面	ジメン	ground; earth's surface
	地元	ジもと	local
	地元民	ジもとミン	local people; people of the district
	地位	チイ	position; status; standing; place
	地域	チイキ	area; region; zone
	地下	チカ	underground
	地階	チカイ	basement; cellar
	地殻	チカク	earth's crust
	地下資源	チカシゲン	underground resources
	地下水	チカスイ	ground water
	地下鉄	チカテツ	subway; the underground
	地下道	チカドウ	underpass
	地球	チキュウ	earth; globe
	地球儀	チキュウギ	globe (model of the earth)
	地区	チク	area; disrict; region; zone

	地形	チケイ	topography
	地軸	チジク	earth's axis
	地質	チシツ	geology; geological features
	地上	チジョウ	on the ground; on earth
	地図	チズ	map; atlas; chart; plan
	地勢	チセイ	topography; geographical features; physical aspect
	地層	チソウ	layer; stratum
	地帯	チタイ	zone; area; region; belt
	地点	チテン	spot; point; place; position
	地熱	チネツ	terrestrial heat
	地表	チヒョウ	earth's surface
	地平線	チヘイセン	horizon; skyline
	地方	チホウ	district; region; area; locality
	地方化	チホウカ	localization —*v*. localize
	地方自治	チホウジチ	local autonomy; self-government; home rule
	地方色	チホウショク	local color
	地方新聞	チホウシンブン	local newspaper
	地方分権	チホウブンケン	decentralization of power
	地理	チリ	geography; geographical features; topography
訓	地	つち	earth; soil; dirt; ground
¥	地価	チカ	land price/value
	地方銀行	チホウギンコウ	regional/local bank
	地方公共団体	チホウコウキョウダンタイ	local (prefectural, etc.) government
	地方債	チホウサイ	municipal/local bonds
	地方自治体	チホウジチタイ	local (prefectural, etc.) government
	地方取引	チホウトリヒキ	regional stock exchange

368

⑦ 一 十 土 圴 圴 均 均

音	均	キン	equal; identical; the same
熟	均一	キンイツ	uniformity; equality
	均衡	キンコウ	equilibrium; balance
	均質	キンシツ	homogeneity
	均整	キンセイ	symmetry
	均斉	キンセイ	symmetry
	均等	キントウ	equality; uniformity; evenness —*v*. be equal/uniform/even
	均分	キンブン	equal division —*v*. divide equally

¥	均一料金	キンイツリョウキン	flat rate
	均衡予算	キンコウヨサン	balanced budget

369

坑 ⑦

一 十 土 圹 圹 坑 坑

音	坑	コウ	pit; mine
熟	坑道	コウドウ	level; gallery; shaft; pit; tunnel
	坑夫	コウフ	miner; pit worker

370

坂 ⑦

一 十 土 圹 圹 坜 坂

音	坂	ハン	slope
訓	坂	さか	slope
	坂道	さかみち	sloping road; slope

371

坊 ⑦

一 十 土 圹 圹 坊 坊

音	坊	ボウ (ボッ)	priest's residence; Buddhist priest
熟	坊主	ボウズ	Buddhist priest; bonze; shaven head; boy; rascal
	坊や	ボウや	little boy
	坊ちゃん	ボッちゃん	(your) boy/son; young master

372

坪 ⑧

一 十 土 圹 圹 圹 坪 坪

音	坪	(ヘイ)	*hei* (unit of area, approx. 3.3㎡)
訓	坪	つぼ	*tsubo* (unit of area, approx. 3.3㎡)

373

垣 ⑨

音	垣	(エン)	fence
訓	垣	かき	fence
	垣根	かきね	fence; hedge

374

城 ⑨

音	城	ジョウ	castle
	城下町	ジョウカまち	castle town
	城主	ジョウシュ	feudal lord; lord of a castle
	城跡	ジョウセキ (しろあと)	castle ruins
訓	城	しろ	castle; fort

375

埋 ⑩

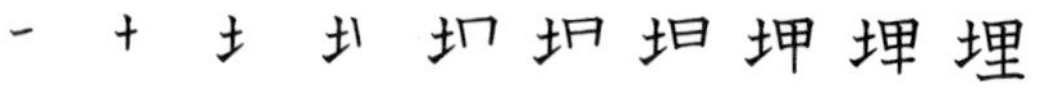

音	埋	マイ	bury; fill up
熟	埋設	マイセツ	installing; laying —*v*. install; lay
	埋葬	マイソウ	burial; interment —*v*. bury; inter
	埋蔵	マイゾウ	buried stores; underground reserve —*v*. store underground
	埋没	マイボツ	buried; obscure —*vi*. lie buried; be buried; fall into obscurity
訓	埋まる	うまる	*vi*. be buried/filled up
	埋める	うめる	*vt*. bury; fill up
	埋め合わせる	うめあわせる	*vt*. make up with; compensate
	埋め立てる	うめたてる	*vt*. reclaim (land from the sea); fill in/up
	埋もれる	うもれる	*vi*. be buried

376

域 ⑪

音	域	イキ	district; region; boundary; scope

熟 域外 イキガイ outside the region/scope
域内 イキナイ within the region/scope

377
培 ⑪ 一 十 土 圵 圹 圻 坮 垃 垆 培 培

音 培 バイ cultivate
熟 培養 バイヨウ cultivation; nurture; culture of bacteria —*v*. cultivate; nurture; culture; breed; raise;
訓 培う つちかう *vt*. cultivate; nurture; breed; raise; grow

378
堀 ⑪ 一 十 土 圷 圸 坧 坼 堀 堀 堀 堀

訓 堀 ほり moat; ditch; canal

379
堪 ⑫ 一 十 土 圹 坩 坩 坩 堪 堪 堪 堪 堪

音 堪 カン endure; bear
(タン)
熟 堪忍 カンニン patience; forbearance —*vi*. be patient; have patience; put up with
堪忍袋 カンニンぶくろ controling one's anger
堪能 タンノウ skill; proficiency; satisfaction —*vi*. be satisfied; be fed up with; have enough of
訓 堪える たえる *vi*. endure; bear; put up with; be up to; be able to

380
場 ⑫ 一 十 土 圵 圹 坦 坦 坦 埸 場 場 場

音 場 ジョウ place; scene
熟 場外 ジョウガイ outside of the grounds/premises
場内 ジョウナイ in the hall/grounds
訓 場 ば place; spot; room; space; scene; field
場合 ばあい situation; circumstances; conditions; case; occasion
場数 ばかず experience

	場所	ばショ	place; spot; site; location; room; space
	場末	ばすえ	the suburbs/outskirts; off the beaten track
	場違い	ばちがい	not the place; out of place
	場面	ばメン	scene; sight
¥	場外株式	ジョウガイかぶシキ	unlisted/over-the-counter stock
	場外市場	ジョウガイシジョウ	over-the-counter market
	場外取り引き	ジョウガイとりひき	over-the-counter transaction
	場立ち	ばだち	floor representative

381

塚 ⑫

音	塚	(チョウ)	mound
訓	塚	つか	mound; hillock; tumulus

382

堤 ⑫

音	堤	テイ	bank
熟	堤防	テイボウ	bank; embankment
訓	堤	つつみ	bank; embankment; dike

383

塔 ⑫

音	塔	トウ	tower
熟	塔婆	トウバ	pagoda; stupa

384

塀 ⑫

音	塀	ヘイ	wall; fence

385

塩 ⑬

音	塩	エン	salt
熟	塩化	エンカ	***chem***. chloridation; saltification —***vi***. ***chem***. chloridate; saltify
	塩酸	エンサン	***chem***. hydrochloric acid
	塩水	エンスイ (しおみず)	salt water; brine
	塩素	エンソ	***chem***. chlorine
	塩田	エンデン	salt field/farm
	塩分	エンブン	saltiness; amount of salt; salt content
訓	塩	しお	salt
	塩辛い	しおからい	salty; briny

386

塊 ⑬

音	塊	カイ	clod; lump
熟	塊状	カイジョウ	massive
訓	塊	かたまり	lump; group

387

境 ⑭

音	境	キョウ (ケイ)	barrier; border; place; fortune; chance; fate; circumstances
熟	境界	キョウカイ	boundary; border; frontier
	境遇	キョウグウ	one's lot; circumstances; station in life
	境地	キョウチ	state; stage
	境内	ケイダイ	precincts; grounds; compound
訓	境	さかい	border; boundary; frontier

388

増 ⑭

音	増	ゾウ	increase

熟	増員	ゾウイン	personnel increase —*v*. increase the staff
	増加	ゾウカ	increase; addition; rise; growth —*v*. increase; add; rise; grow
	増額	ゾウガク	increase —*v*. increase; raise
	増刊	ゾウカン	special edition; extra number —*v*. publish a special edition
	増強	ゾウキョウ	reinforcement —*v*. reinforce; augment; beef up
	増結	ゾウケツ	additional cars/carriages —*v*. add cars/carriages (to a train)
	増減	ゾウゲン	increase and decrease —*v*. increase of decrease; vary (in quantity)
	増刷	ゾウサツ	reprinting; additional printing —*v*. reprint; print additional copies
	増殖	ゾウショク	increase; multiplication; propagation —*v*. increase; multiply; propagate
	増進	ゾウシン	improvement; increase —*v*. improve; increase; further
	増水	ゾウスイ	rising/swelling (of a river); flooding —*v*. swell; rise; flood
	増設	ゾウセツ	extension —*v*. build on; extend; establish; install more
	増大	ゾウダイ	increase; enlargement —*v*. increase; enlarge
	増築	ゾウチク	extension —*v*. build on; extend; enlarge
	増長	ゾウチョウ	*v*. grow presumptuous/impudent
	増発	ゾウハツ	extra train; extra issue (of bonds) —*v*. put on an extra train; issue extra (bonds)
	増兵	ゾウヘイ	reinforcements —*v*. reinforce
	増補	ゾウホ	enlargement; supplement —*v*. enlarge; supplement
訓	増える	ふえる	***vi***. increase; rise; raise
	増やす	ふやす	***vi***. increase; rise; raise
	増す	ます	***vi***. increase; rise; raise
¥	増益	ゾウエキ	profit increase
	増産	ゾウサン	expansion/increase in production —*v*. expand/increase production
	増資	ゾウシ	increase of capital stock —*v*. increase capital stock
	増収	ゾウシュウ	increased revenue/income/yield —*v*. increase revenue/income/yield
	増税	ゾウゼイ	tax increase —*v*. increase/raise taxes

389

⑮

音	墳	フン	(burial) mound; tomb
熟	墳墓	フンボ	grave; tomb

390

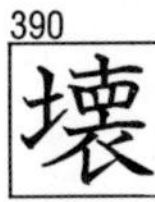

⑯ 壊

音	壊	カイ	destroy; crumble; break
熟	壊血病	カイケツビョウ	***med***. scurvy
	壊滅	カイメツ	destruction; annihilation; demolition —***v***. destroy; annihilate; demolish; waste
訓	壊す	こわす	***vt***. break; destroy; demolish; tear down
	壊れる	こわれる	***vi***. break; be broken
	※壊る	やぶる	***vt***. tear; rip; break; beat

391

壌 ⑯

音	壌	ジョウ	soil
熟	壌土	ジョウド	fertile soil
訓	※壌	つち	soil; earth; ground

392

⑯ 壇

音	壇	ダン (タン)	platform; raised floor; stage

3 士 さむらい samurai; gentleman

393

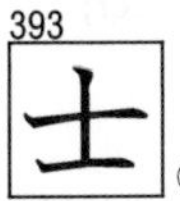

③ 一 十 士

音	士	シ	samurai; warrior; man; gentleman
熟	士官	シカン	military officer
	士気	シキ	morale
	士族	シゾク	samurai family; descendant of a samurai
	士農工商	シノウコウショウ	***hist***. the military, agricultural, industrial and mercantile classes of feudal Japan (Edo period)

394

壮 ⑥

丨 丬 丬 丬 壮 壮

音	壮	ソウ	manhood; strength; prosperity
熟	壮快	ソウカイ	stirring; exhilarating; thrilling
	壮観	ソウカン	grand sight; awe-inspiring view
	壮健	ソウケン	healthy
	壮者	ソウシャ	man in his prime
	壮絶	ソウゼツ	sublime; magnificent
	壮大	ソウダイ	grand; magnificent; splendid
	壮年	ソウネン	prime of manhood
	壮麗	ソウレイ	splendor; glory
	壮烈	ソウレツ	heroic; brave

395

壱 ⑦

一 十 士 士 声 壱 壱

音	壱	イチ	one (used on Japanese currency and official documents)
熟	壱万円	イチマンエン	ten thousand yen

396

声 ⑦

一 十 士 士 吉 吉 声

音	声	セイ (ショウ)	voice; reputation
熟	声域	セイイキ	voice range; register
	声援	セイエン	cheering; encouragement; support —*v.* cheer; encourage; support
	声楽	セイガク	vocal music; singing
	声楽家	セイガクカ	vocalist
	声帯	セイタイ	vocal chords
	声望	セイボウ	popularity; fame; reputation
	声明	セイメイ	declaration; proclamation —*v.* declare; proclaim
	声明書	セイメイショ	statement; public/official statement
	声優	セイユウ	actor/actress specializing in dubbing films
	声量	セイリョウ	volume
訓	声	こえ	voice

声	こわ	(prefix) voice; vocal
声高	こわだか	loud voice
声音	こわね	tone of voice

397
売 ⑦ 一 十 士 声 声 売 売

音	売	バイ	sell
熟	売却	バイキャク	sale; disposal by sale —*v*. sell; sell off
	売国奴	バイコクド	traitor
	売春	バイシュン	prostitution; harloty; streetwalking —*vi*. prostitute; walk the streets; sell oneself for money
	売春婦	バイシュンフ	prostitute; street girl
	売店	バイテン	stand; stall; booth
	売買	バイバイ	buying and selling; trade; dealing; transaction —*v*. buy and sell; trade/deal in; market; handle
	売名	バイメイ	self-advertisement
	売約	バイヤク	sales contract
訓	売る	うる	***vt***. sell; deal offer; deceive
	売り	うり	sale; selling;
	売り切れ	うりきれ	being sold out; exhausted supplies; sold out
	売り込む	うりこむ	***vt***. sell; find a new market and sell; advertise oneself
	売り出す	うりだす	***vt***. offer for sale; become popular
	売り主	うりぬし	seller; vendor
	売り場	うりば	counter; shop; store
	売れる	うれる	***vi***. sell; be in demand; be well know/popular
	売れ口	うれくち	market; outlet; one's place of employment
	売れっ子	うれっこ	popular singer/actor
	売れ行き	うれゆき	market; sale; demand
¥	売上げ	うりあげ	proceeds; takings
	売上原価	うりあげゲンカ	cost of sales/goods sold
	売上総利益	うりあげソウリエキ	gross profit
	売上高	うりあげだか	sales
	売掛金	うりかけキン	accounts receivable
	売気配	うりケハイ	asked quotation
	売越し	うりこし	selling a balance
	売出し	うりだし	secondary offering
	売叩き	うりたたき	bear raid; gunning for a stock

売りつなぎ	うりつなぎ	hedge-selling; short selling (against the box)
売り場	うりば	counter; best time to sell
売価	バイカ	selling/labeled price

---

3 夂 ふゆがしら／なつあし winter

398

処 ⑤ ノ ク 夂 夂 処

音	処	ショ	place; deal with
熟	処する	ショする	***vi***. face; conduct; deal with; manage
	処刑	ショケイ	execution —***v***. execute
	処女	ショジョ	virgin
	処女作	ショジョサク	maiden work
	処世訓	ショセイクン	the secret of getting along in the world
	処置	ショチ	treatment; disposal; measures —***v***. dispose; deal with; take measures; treat
	処罰	ショバツ	punishment; penalty —***v***. punish; penalize
	処分	ショブン	disposal; punishment; measure —***v***. dispose of; deal with; punish
	処方	ショホウ	***med***. prescription —***v***. prescribe
	処理	ショリ	management —***v***. deal with; handle

399

冬 ⑤ ノ ク 夂 冬 冬

音	冬	トウ	winter
熟	冬季	トウキ	winter
	冬期	トウキ	wintertime
	冬至	トウジ	winter solstice
	冬眠	トウミン	hibernation —***vi***. hibernate
訓	冬	ふゆ	winter
	冬ごもり	ふゆごもり	winter confinement; wintering —***vi***. stay indoors for the winter
	冬物	ふゆもの	winter clothing/wear
	冬休み	ふゆやすみ	winter vacation

400

麦 ⑦ 一 十 キ 主 丰 麦 麦

音	麦	バク	barley; wheat
熟	麦芽	バクガ	malt; germ wheat; barley
訓	麦	むぎ	wheat; barley; oats; rye

401

変 ⑨ ' 亠 ナ 亣 亦 亦 亦 変 変

音	変	ヘン	change; strange; mishap; accident; flat (in music)
熟	変じる	ヘンじる	*v*. change; alter; renew
	変圧器	ヘンアツキ	transformer (voltage)
	変移	ヘンイ	change; alteration —*v*. change; alter
	変異	ヘンイ	change; fluctuation; variation; mishap —***vi***. change; fluctuation; be different
	変化	ヘンカ	change; transformation —***vi***. change; transform
	変革	ヘンカク	reformation; change; revolution —*v*. reform; change; be revolutionized
	変換	ヘンカン	change; conversion ***math***. transformation —*v*. change; convert
	変化	ヘンゲ	goblin; apparition; god that has taken on human form
	変形	ヘンケイ	transformation; modification; deformation —*v*. transform; modify; deform
	変幻自在	ヘンゲンジザイ	ever-changing; changeable; unexpected; free
	変更	ヘンコウ	change; alteration; ammendment —*v*. change; alter; ammend
	変死	ヘンシ	unnatural death (by accident, murder, suicide, etc.) —***vi***. die an unnatural death
	変質	ヘンシツ	deterioration; degeneration —***vi***. be degenerate
	変質者	ヘンシツシャ	pervert; deviant
	変種	ヘンシュ	variety; strain
	変色	ヘンショク	discoloration; change of color —*v*. change the color; discolor
	変身	ヘンシン	metamorphosis; transformation —***vi***. metamorphose; transform
	変心	ヘンシン	change of mind/heart; fickleness —***vi***. change one's mind; be fickle
	変人	ヘンジン	odd person; eccentric
	変数	ヘンスウ	***math***. variable

	変成	ヘンセイ	metamorphosis; change of shape/form —*v*. change shape/form
	変遷	ヘンセン	changes; vicissitudes —***vi***. change unpredictably
	変装	ヘンソウ	disguise —***vi***. be disguised
	変速	ヘンソク	changing speed/gears
	変則	ヘンソク	irregular; abnormal
	変態	ヘンタイ	metamorphosis; abnormal; perverted
	変調	ヘンチョウ	change of tone/key; irregular; abnormal
	変哲もない	ヘンテツもない	commonplace; ordinary
	変転	ヘンテン	great changes; vicissitudes —***vi***. change unpredictably
	変動	ヘンドウ	change; fluctuation —***vi***. change; fluctuate
	変貌	ヘンボウ	transfiguration; transformation —***vi***. be transformed; change one's appearance
	変名	ヘンメイ (ヘンミョウ)	assumed name; name change —***vi***. change one's name; assume an alias
	変容	ヘンヨウ	changed appearance —*v*. change appearance
訓	変える	かえる	***vt***. change; alter; move
	変わる	かわる	***vi***. change; be different/strange
	変わり種	かわりだね	exceptional case; different from the rest
	変わり果てる	かわりはてる	***vi***. change completely
	変わり目	かわりめ	change; turning point; transition
	変わり者	かわりもの	odd person; eccentric
¥	変動所得	ヘンドウショトク	transitory income
	変動相場	ヘンドウソウバ	floating exchange rate
	変動費	ヘンドウヒ	variable costs

402

⑩

音	夏	カ	summer
		(ゲ)	summer
熟	夏季	カキ	summer season
	夏期	カキ	summer period
	夏至	ゲシ	summer solstice
訓	夏	なつ	summer
	夏場	なつば	summertime; summer resort
	夏休み	なつやすみ	summer holiday/vacation

403

夕 ノ ク 夕 ③

音	夕	**セキ**	evening
訓	夕	**ゆう**	evening
	夕方	**ゆうがた**	evening
	夕刊	**ゆうカン**	evening paper/edition
	夕暮れ	**ゆうぐれ**	evening
	夕食	**ゆうショク**	dinner; evening meal
	夕立	**ゆうだち**	sudden shower in the evening or late afternoon
	夕飯	**ゆうハン**	dinner; evening meal
	夕日	**ゆうひ**	setting sun
	夕焼け	**ゆうやけ**	sunset

404

外 ノ ク 夕 外 外 ⑤

音	外	**ガイ**	appearance; outside; unfasten
		ゲ	outside
熟	外苑	**ガイエン**	outer garden (of a palace, etc.)
	外界	**ガイカイ**	external world; outside; physical world
	外海	**ガイカイ (そとうみ)**	open sea
	外角	**ガイカク**	***bas.*** outcorner; external angle
	外患	**ガイカン**	external/foreign troubles
	外観	**ガイカン**	external appearance
	外気	**ガイキ**	open air
	外勤	**ガイキン**	outside duty; canvassing
	外見	**ガイケン**	outward appearance; faces
	外交	**ガイコウ**	diplomacy
	外交官	**ガイコウカン**	diplomat
	外耳	**ガイジ**	***med.*** external ear; concha
	外出	**ガイシュツ**	going out; outing; airing —***vi.*** go out
	外傷	**ガイショウ**	external wound
	外食	**ガイショク**	eating/dining out —***vi.*** dine/eat out
	外人	**ガイジン**	foreigner

	外地	ガイチ	foreign area; overseas land
	外電	ガイデン	foreign telegram; dispatch from overseas
	外泊	ガイハク	sleeping/stopping/staying out (overnight) —***vi***. sleep over; stop out overnight
	外部	ガイブ	outside; outer; external
	外米	ガイマイ	imported/foreign rice
	外面	ガイメン	outward appearance; the outside; exterior
	外遊	ガイユウ	foreign travel —***vi***. take a trip abroad
	外洋	ガイヨウ	ocean
	外用薬	ガイヨウヤク	external remedy; medicine for external use
	外来	ガイライ	from abroad; outpatients
	外来語	ガイライゴ	***gram***. adopted word; loanword
	外科	ゲカ	surgery; department of surgery in a hospital
訓	外	そと	outside
	外す	はずす	***vt***. remove; miss; avoid
	外れる	はずれる	***vi***. be off; be contrary to; miss
	外	ほか	other; another
	※外様	とざま	***hist***. *Tozama*-daimyo (non-Tokugawa daimyo, Edo period)
¥	外貨	ガイカ	foreign currency/goods
	外貨準備	ガイカジュンビ	foreign exchange reserves
	外国為替（外為）	ガイコクかわせ（ガイタメ）	foreign exchange
	外国銀行（外銀）	ガイコクギンコウ（ガイギン）	foreign bank
	外国債権（外債）	ガイコクサイケン（ガイサイ）	foreign bond/loan
	外国資本（外資）	ガイコクシホン（ガイシ）	foreign capital
	外国需要（外需）	ガイコクジュヨウ（ガイジュ）	foreign demand; demand from abroad
	外国通貨（外貨）	ガイコクツウカ（ガイカ）	foreign currency
	外債	ガイサイ	foreign bond; foreign debt; foreign loan
	外資	ガイシ	foreign capital; foreign investiment
	外資系企業	ガイシケイキギョウ	foreign-affiliate; enterprise with foreign capital
	外資導入	ガイシドウニュウ	introduction of foreign capital
	外部資本	ガイブシホン	outside capital; borrowed capital
	外務省	ガイムショウ	Ministry of Foreign Affairs
	外務大臣（外相）	ガイムダイジン（ガイショウ）	minister of foreign affairs

405

多 ⑥

ノ ク タ タ 多 多

音	多	タ	many; much; multiple
熟	多額	タガク	large sum/amount
	多角的	タカクテキ	many sided; versatile; diversified; multilateral
	多角形	タカッケイ	polygon
	多感	タカン	sensibility; susceptibility; sentimentality
	多義	タギ	polysemy; diverse meanings
	多芸	タゲイ	versatility; well versed in the arts
	多才	タサイ	versatility; versatile talents
	多彩	タサイ	colorful
	多事	タジ	eventfulness; pressure of business
	多種	タシュ	various kinds
	多種多様	タシュタヨウ	variety; diversity
	多少	タショウ	more or less; approximately; some; a few
	多情	タジョウ	wanton; fickle; inconstant; licentious
	多数	タスウ	large number; multitude; majority; predominance
	多数決	タスウケツ	majority rule
	多勢	タゼイ	great numbers; numerical superiority
	多大	タダイ	great quantity; large amount
	多読	タドク	wide/extensive reading —*v*. be widely read; read extensively
	多難	タナン	full of difficulties
	多人数	タニンズウ	great number of people
	多年	タネン	many years; number of years
	多分	タブン	plenty; much; many; a great deal; probably; perhaps; maybe
	多忙	タボウ	pressure of work; busy
	多方面	タホウメン	many quarters/directions
	多面	タメン	many faces/sides
	多量	タリョウ	large quantities; abundance; a great deal
訓	多い	おおい	many; much; a lot of
¥	多角化	タカクカ	diversification —*v*. diversify
	多国籍企業	タコクセキキギョウ	multinational enterprise

406

夜 ⑧

音	夜	ヤ	night
熟	夜陰	ヤイン	darkness of night
	夜会	ヤカイ	evening party; ball
	夜学	ヤガク	night school; evening classes
	夜間	ヤカン	night; night time
	夜気	ヤキ	night air; stillness of the night
	夜曲	ヤキョク	nocturne
	夜勤	ヤキン	night duty/shift —***vi***. do night duty; work at night
	夜具	ヤグ	bedding
	夜景	ヤケイ	night view
	夜警	ヤケイ	night watch
	夜行	ヤコウ	night train/travel
	夜光虫	ヤコウチュウ	night-glowing insect
	夜叉	ヤシャ	Yasha (female demon in Buddhist mythology)
	夜襲	ヤシュウ	night attack —***v***. make a night attack; attack in darkness
	夜半	ヤハン	midnight; dead of night
	夜分	ヤブン	night; evening
	夜盲症	ヤモウショウ	***med***. night blindness
	夜来	ヤライ	since last night; overnight
訓	夜	よ	night
	夜明かし	よあかし	staying up all night —***vi***. stay up overnight
	夜明け	よあけ	dawn; daybreak
	夜霧	よぎり	night fog
	夜通し	よどおし	overnight
	夜中	よなか	midnight; dead of night
	夜這	よばい	creep in to see a woman at night
	夜目	よめ	watching in the dark
	夜	よる	night

407

⑬

音	夢	ム	dream
熟	夢幻	ムゲン	dreams and fantasies

	夢想	ムソウ	dream; vision; fantasy —*v*. dream; fantasize; have a vision
	夢中	ムチュウ	rapture; absorption; intentness; frantic
	夢遊病	ムユウビョウ	sleepwalking
訓	夢	ゆめ	dream
	夢心地	ゆめごこち	trance; ecstasy
	夢路	ゆめじ	dream; dreaming

3 大 だい big

408

大 ③ 一 ナ 大

音	大	タイ	large; many; importance; whole
		ダイ	big; excellent; dimension; prosperity
熟	大安	タイアン (ダイアン)	luck/auspicious day (on the Japanese calendar)
	大意	タイイ	gist; purport; substance; ration; holocaust
	大英帝国	ダイエイテイコク	British Empire
	大家	タイカ	mansion; illustrious family; master; authority
	大火	タイカ	great fire; conflagration
	大会	タイカイ	mass meeting; tournament; convention
	大学	ダイガク	university; college
	大学院	ダイガクイン	graduate school
	大学生	ダイガクセイ	university/college student
	大観	タイカン	general/philosophical/comprehensive view —*v*. take a general view; make a general survey; have a broad outlook
	大寒	ダイカン	the coldest season (the latter part of January); very cold weather
	大気	タイキ	atmosphere; air
	大気圏	タイキケン	atmosphere
	大器	タイキ	great talent; large vessel
	大儀	タイギ	irksome; laborious; tedious
	大規模	ダイキボ	large-scale; mass
	大挙	タイキョ	in great force —***vi***. come in great force
	大局	タイキョク	the whole situation; main issue
	大工	ダイク	carpenter
	大軍	タイグン	large army
	大群	タイグン	large crowd

大言壮語 タイゲンソウゴ big talk; boasting; bragging —*vi*. talk big; boast; brag

大綱 タイコウ general rules; fundamental principles; outline

大国 タイコク large/great country

大差 タイサ great difference; striking contrast

大罪 ダイザイ great crime; felony; mortal sin

大作 タイサク major work; masterpiece

大志 タイシ ambition; aspiration

大使 タイシ ambassador

大使館 タイシカン embassy

大師 ダイシ great teacher of Buddhism; Kobo Daishi

大事 ダイジ important; grave; serious; valuable

大衆 タイシュウ masses; crowd of people

大将 タイショウ general; admiral

大勝 タイショウ great/landslide victory —*vi*. win by a landslide

大小 ダイショウ large and small size

大乗 ダイジョウ Great Vehicle; Mahayana Buddhism

大丈夫 ダイジョウブ safe; certain; sure; OK

大静脈 ダイジョウミャク ***med***. main vein

大食 タイショク gluttony; heavy eating —*vi*. eat heavily; eat like a horse

大臣 ダイジン minister of state

大成 タイセイ completion; accomplishment —*v*. complete; accomplish; attain; mature

大勢 タイセイ general trend/tendency/situation

大政奉還 タイセイホウカン ***hist***. restoration of imperial rule (14 October 1867)

大切 タイセツ important; valuable

大体 ダイタイ outline; summary; generally; essentially

大々的 ダイダイテキ on a large scale; great; grand; gigantic; immense

大多数 ダイタスウ majority

大胆 ダイタン boldness; daring

大地 ダイチ earth; ground

大抵 タイテイ usually; mostly; generally; almost

大敵 タイテキ powerful enemy

大同小異 ダイドウショウイ general similarity

大動脈 ダイドウミャク ***med***. main artery

大統領 ダイトウリョウ president (of a republic)

大任 タイニン important charge/position

大破 タイハ ruin; dilapidation; havoc —*v*. be crippled/wrecked/in ruins

大敗 タイハイ terrible defeat —*vi*. sustain a terrible defeat

大半 タイハン greater part; majority; bulk

	大病	タイビョウ	serious/major illness
	大分	ダイブ	very; much
	大仏	ダイブツ	great Buddha (statue)
	大部分	ダイブブン	the majority (of); mostly; for the most part
	大別	タイベツ	broad classification —***v***. make a general classification; divide into main classes
	大変	タイヘン	very; greatly; awfully
	大便	ダイベン	feces; stool
	大枚	タイマイ	large sum of money
	大名	ダイミョウ	*daimyo* (feudal lords of the Edo period)
	大役	タイヤク	important task; heavy duty
	大洋	タイヨウ	ocean
	大陸	タイリク	continent
	大量	タイリョウ	large quantity; magnanimity; generosity; liberality
	大量生産	タイリョウセイサン	mass production —***v***. mass produce
	大漁	タイリョウ	large catch of fish
	大輪	タイリン	large flower/wheel
	大老	タイロウ	***hist***. Shogun's chief minister (Edo period)
訓	大	おお	big; large; great
	大きい	おおきい	big; large; great; grand
	大きさ	おおきさ	size; dimensions; magnitude
	大型	おおがた	large size
	大柄	おおがら	large pattern/build/frame
	大筋	おおすじ	outline
	大詰め	おおづめ	final; end; conclusion
	大手	おおて	front gate of a castle; major company
	大道具	おおドウグ	stage setting
	大判	おおバン	large sheet of paper; *ōban* (coinage used during the Edo period)
	大水	おおみず	flood; overflow
	大物	おおもの	big figure; important person
	大家	おおや	landlord; landlady
	大いに	おおいに	very; much; far; greatly
	※大晦日	おおみそか	New Year's Eve
¥	大口	おおぐち	large lot (amount, size)
	大蔵省	おおくらショウ	Ministry of Finance
	大蔵大臣	おおくらダイジン	minister of finance
	大底	おおそこ	major bottom (stock price trend, etc.)
	大台乗せ	おおだいのせ	reaching/hitting a mark
	大台割れ	おおだいわれ	dropping below a mark
	大手(企業)	おおて(キギョウ)	leading enterprise (company)

大幅	おおはば	full width
大引け	おおびけ	close; closing
大衆相場	タイシュウソウバ	public market
大納会	ダイノウカイ	final session of the year (stock market, etc.)
大発会	ダイハッカイ	first session of the year (stock market, etc.)

409

太 ④ 一 ナ 大 太

音	太	タ	big; fat; thick
		タイ	big; fat; thick; deep; beginning
熟	太古	タイコ	remote ages; ancient times; prehistoric days
	太鼓	タイコ	drum
	太子	タイシ	crown prince; prince
	太平洋	タイヘイヨウ	Pacific Ocean
	太陽	タイヨウ	sun
	太陽熱	タイヨウネツ	solar heat; heat of the sun's rays
	太刀	タチ	long sword
訓	太い	ふとい	big; large; fat; thick
	太さ	ふとさ	thickness
	太る	ふとる	***vi.*** grow fat; put on weight

410

天 ④ 一 ニ チ 天

音	天	テン	sky; air; the heavens; heaven; nature; fate; destiny
熟	天王星	テンオウセイ	the planet Jupiter
	天下	テンカ	whole country; land; realm
	天下一品	テンカイッピン	beyond comparison; unrivalled
	天涯	テンガイ	horizon; skyline; far-off country
	天蓋	テンガイ	canopy/sunshade (for Buddhist statues or priests)
	天気	テンキ	the weather/elements; atmospheric conditions
	天気予報	テンキヨホウ	weather forecast
	天球	テンキュウ	celestial sphere
	天狗	テング	*tengu* (long-nosed goblin)
	天空	テンクウ	the sky/air/firmament
	天恵	テンケイ	heaven's blessing; gift of nature
	天候	テンコウ	weather; elements

天国	テンゴク	heaven
天才	テンサイ	genius
天災	テンサイ	natural disaster/calamity; act of God
天子	テンシ	son of heaven; emperor
天使	テンシ	angel
天竺	テンジク	***clas***. India
天寿	テンジュ	natural span of life
天守閣	テンシュカク	castle tower; donjon; keep
天上	テンジョウ	the heavens
天井	テンジョウ	ceiling; roof; top
天井桟敷	テンジョウさじき	upper gallery of a theater
天職	テンショク	mission; vocation
天神	テンジン	heavenly gods
天真爛漫	テンシンランマン	innocence; naivety
天性	テンセイ	nature; by nature; naturally
天体	テンタイ	heavenly body
天地	テンチ	heaven and earth; top and bottom
天頂	テンチョウ	zenith
天童	テンドウ	Buddhist angel
天女	テンニョ	celestial nymph
天人	テンニン	angel; heavenly being
天然	テンネン	nature; spontaneity
天然記念物	テンネンキネンブツ	natural monument
天然資源	テンネンシゲン	natural resources
天然色	テンネンショク	natural color
天然痘	テンネントウ	***med***. smallpox
天皇	テンノウ	emperor (Japanese only)
天罰	テンバツ	divine wrath
天火	テンぴ	oven
天引き	テンびき	deduction; deduction in advance —***v***. deduct; knock off
天秤	テンビン	balance; scales
天秤座	テンビンザ	Libra, seventh sign of the zodiac
天賦	テンプ	nature; given by nature
天分	テンブン	one's nature; natural gifts
天変地異	テンペンチイ	natural disasters
天幕	テンマク	tent; pavilion; marquee; awning
天窓	テンまど	skylight
天命	テンメイ	will of the gods; fate; destiny; life
天文	テンモン	astromony; astrology
天文学	テンモンガク	astronomy

	天文台	テンモンダイ	astronomical observatory
	天与	テンヨ	gift of heaven; godsend
	天理教	テンリキョウ	Tenriism (new religion)
訓	天	あま	the heavens; heaven
	天下り	あまくだり	descent from heaven ***fig***. appointment of a former official to an important post in a private company (through influence from above)
	天照大神	あまてらすおおみかみ	Sun Goddess (in Japanese mythology)
	天の河	あまのがわ	Milky Way
	天	あめ	heaven; the sky; the heavens

411
夫 ④ 一 二 チ 夫

音	夫	フ (フウ)	husband
熟	夫婦	フウフ	man and wife; husband and wife; married couple
	夫妻	フサイ	husband and wife
	夫人	フジン	woman; lady; female
訓	夫	おっと	husband; man
	※夫婦	めおと	man and wife; husband and wife; married couple

412
央 ⑤ 丨 冂 口 央 央

音	央	オウ	center; middle

413
失 ⑤ ノ 𠂉 二 生 失

音	失	シツ	lose; error; failure
熟	失する	シッする	***vt***. miss; forget
	失意	シツイ	disappointment
	失火	シッカ	accidental fire —***vi***. catch on fire accidentally
	失格	シッカク	disqualification; elimination —***vi***. disqualify; eliminate

	失脚	シッキャク	fall; downfall —*vi*. lose; bring about one's downfall
	失禁	シッキン	incontinence —*vi*. be incontinent
	失敬	シッケイ	rudeness; theft —*vi*. steal; take; help oneself to
	失言	シツゲン	slip of the tongue —*vi*. make a slip of the tongue
	失効	シッコウ	invalidation —*vi*. lapse; lose validity; expire; run out
	失策	シッサク	error; mistake —*vi*. err; blunder
	失笑	シッショウ	spontaneous laughter —*vi*. burst out laughing
	失職	シッショク	unemployment —*vi*. lose one's job; become unemployed
	失神	シッシン	faint —*vi*. faint; lose consciousness
	失政	シッセイ	misgovernment; misrule
	失踪	シッソウ	disappearance —*vi*. disappear; vanish; go missing
	失速	シッソク	stall —*vi*. stall
	失態	シッタイ	blunder
	失墜	シッツイ	loss; fall —*v*. lose; fall
	失敗	シッパイ	failure; mistake; blunder —*vi*. fail; blunder be unsuccessful
	失望	シツボウ	disappointment; despair —*vi*. be disappointed
	失明	シツメイ	loss of sight; blindness —*vi*. lose one's eyesight; become blind
	失礼	シツレイ	impoliteness; rudeness; bad manners —*vi*. be impolite/rude; have bad manners
	失恋	シツレン	unrequited love —*vi*. be unlucky in love; have a broken heart
訓	失う	うしなう	*vt*. lose; miss
¥	失業	シツギョウ	unemployment —*vi*. lose one's job; be out of work
	失業者	シツギョウシャ	the unemployed; unemployed person
	失業率	シツギョウリツ	unemployment rate

414

⑧ 一 ナ 大 厺 夻 奋 奇 奇

音	奇	キ	strange; novel
熟	奇異	キイ	strange; queer; singular; odd
	奇禍	キカ	accident; disaster; mishap
	奇怪	キカイ	mysterious; weird; strange; outrageous; uncanny
	奇遇	キグウ	chance meeting
	奇形	キケイ	deformation; malformation
	奇習	キシュウ	strange custom

奇襲	キシュウ	surprise attack —***v***. make a surprise attack
奇術	キジュツ	jugglery; conjuring tricks; sleight of hand; magic
奇人	キジン	eccentric person; crank
奇数	キスウ	***math***. odd number
奇跡	キセキ	miracle
奇想天外	キソウテンガイ	original idea; unexpected
奇抜	キバツ	novel; original; uncoventional
奇妙	キミョウ	strange; curious; weird; queer
奇麗	キレイ	beautiful; pretty

415

奉 ⑧

一 二 三 夫 夫 夫 夫 奉

音	奉	ホウ	offer
		(ブ)	offer
熟	奉じる	ほうじる	***vt***. present; dedicate; obey; follow; believe in; serve
	奉迎	ホウゲイ	welcoming/meeting (a person of high social standing) —***v***. welcome/meet (a person of high social standing)
	奉献	ホウケン	dedication; offering; consecration —***v***. dedicate; offer; consecrate
	奉公	ホウコウ	public duty; service —***vi***. be of service; carry out one's duties; serve one's master
	奉仕	ホウシ	service (to country, society, elders, etc.) —***vi***. serve (one's country, society, elders, etc.)
	奉書	ホウショ	thick, high-quality paper ***hist***. edict from daimyo to lower classes (Edo period)
	奉職	ホウショク	public service —***vi***. be in the service of; hold a post
	奉納	ホウノウ	dedication/offering (to Buddhas, gods) —***v***. dedicate/offer (to Buddhas, gods)
訓	奉る	たてまつる	offer; present; revere

416

奔 ⑧

一 ナ 大 太 本 奔 奔 奔

音	奔	ホン	run
熟	奔走	ホンソウ	running about to achieve a purpose; busily making arrangements —***vi***. run about for a purpose; be busy arranging something
	奔放	ホンポウ	wild; extravagant; uninhibited

奔流	ホンリュウ	rapids; torrent; rushing current

417

契 ⑨

一 十 キ 丰 丰㇇ 丰刀 㓞 契 契

音	契	ケイ	promise; pledge; oath
熟	契機	ケイキ	opportunity; chance
訓	契り	ちぎり	pledge; vow; plight
	契る	ちぎる	***vt***. pledge; vow; promise; plight one's troth; promise to marry
¥	契約	ケイヤク	contract; agreement —***v***. enter into/sign a contract
	契約書	ケイヤクショ	written contract

418

奏 ⑨

一 二 三 丰 夫 夫 奏 奏 奏

音	奏	ソウ	play; present; report; take effect
熟	奏する	ソウする	***vt***. play a musical instrument; report to the emperor
	奏楽	ソウガク	instrumental music
	奏功	ソウコウ	achieving one's aim —***vi***. succeed in achieving the aim
	奏効	ソウコウ	effectiveness —***vi***. be effective
	奏上	ソウジョウ	reporting to the emperor —***v***. report to the emperor
訓	奏でる	かなでる	***vt***. play (a musical instrument)

419

奥 ⑫

丿 丨 冂 冂 冂 冂 冂 冂 冂 奥 奥 奥

音	奥	オウ	deep; profound; recesses; interior
熟	奥義	オウギ(おくギ)	secret principles; esoteric mysteries
訓	奥	おく	inner part; innermost part; interior
	奥まる	おくまる	***vi***. extend far back; lie deep within
	奥書	おくがき	postscript; endorsement
	奥様	おくさま	***hon***. (your) wife; married woman
	奥さん	おくさん	***hon***. (your) wife; married woman
	奥底	おくそこ	the depth; the bottom

口 囗 土 士 夊 夕 •大 女 子 宀 寸 小 ⺌ ⺍ 尢 尸 山 川 工 己 巾 干 幺 广 廴 廾 弋 弓 ヨ 彡 彳 艹 辶 阝 阝 ⺍ 忄 扌 犭 氵

奥地	おくチ	the interior; hinterland
奥手	おくて	slow to mature; late to develop
奥の手	おくのて	the last resort; one's best card
奥の間	おくのま	the inner room
奥歯	おくば	***med.*** molar
奥床しい	おくゆかしい	graceful; elegant; refined
奥行き	おくゆき	depth; length

420

奨 ⑬

音	奨	ショウ	recommend
熟	奨学金	ショウガクキン	scholarship; fellowship
	奨励	ショウレイ	encouragement; incentive —***v.*** encourage

421

奪 ⑭

音	奪	ダツ	plunder; take; seize; wrest; snatch
熟	奪回	ダッカイ	recapture; recovery; retaking —***v.*** recapture; recover; retake
	奪還	ダッカン	recapture; recovery; retaking —***v.*** recapture; recover; retake
	奪取	ダッシュ	capture; seizure; wrestling —***v.*** capture; carry; wrest; seize; snatch
訓	奪う	うばう	***vt.*** take by force; seize; wrest; plunder; usurp

422

奮 ⑯

音	奮	フン	be enlivened/invigorated
熟	奮起	フンキ	inspiration —***vi.*** rouse oneself; be inspired
	奮戦	フンセン	hard fighting —***vi.*** fight hard/furiously
	奮然	フンゼン	vigorously; courageously; resolutely
	奮闘	フントウ	struggle; striving —***vi.*** struggle/strive for
	奮発	フンパツ	exertion; strenuous efforts; extravagance with money —***vi.*** exert oneself; splurge
訓	奮う	ふるう	screw up courage; be inspired; wield; flourish
	奮って	ふるって	voluntarily; willingly; heartily

3 女 おんな／おんなへん woman

423

女 ③ く 女 女

音	女	ジョ	woman; girl; female
		ニョ	woman; girl
		（ニョウ）	
熟	女医	ジョイ	woman doctor
	女王	ジョオウ	queen
	女子	ジョシ	girl; woman
	女子学生	ジョシガクセイ	female student
	女史	ジョシ	Mrs.; Ms.; Miss
	女児	ジョジ	girl
	女性	ジョセイ	woman; female
	女性的	ジョセイテキ	feminine; womanish; effeminate
	女装	ジョソウ	women's clothing —*vi*. dress up like a woman; put on women's clothing
	女中	ジョチュウ	maid
	女難	ジョナン	woman trouble
	女優	ジョユウ	actress
	女流	ジョリュウ	women; female
	女流作家	ジョリュウサッカ	woman writer
	女房	ニョウボウ	court lady; one's wife
	女人	ニョニン	woman
訓	女	おんな	woman; female
	女盛り	おんなざかり	peak of womanhood
	女手	おんなで	woman's handwriting
	女	め	woman
	女神	めがみ	goddess

424

妄 ⑥ ・ 亠 亡 妄 妄 妄

音	妄	ボウ	
		モウ	incoherent; reckless; false

熟	妄信	モウシン	blind acceptance —*v*. accept blindly
	妄想	モウソウ	wild fantasy; delusion —*v*. be deluded
	妄念	モウネン	irrelevant/incoherent thoughts

425

妥 ⑦

音	妥	ダ	moderate; stable; calm
熟	妥協	ダキョウ	compromise; agreement; understanding —***vi***. compromise; make a compromise; reach an agreement
	妥結	ダケツ	compromise settlement; agreement —***vi***. compromise; reach an agreement
	妥当	ダトウ	proper; appropriate; valid —***vi***. apply; hold good
	妥当性	ダトウセイ	propriety; appropriateness; adequacy; pertinence

426

委 ⑧

音	委	イ	leave to; entrust; minute; detailed
熟	委細	イサイ	details; particulars; circumstances
	委嘱	イショク	committing with trust and confidence; commission; entrusting; nomination; appointment —*v*. entrust; commission; request; nominate; appoint
	委託	イタク	consignment; trust; charge; commission —*v*. consign; entrust; charge; deposit; put a matter to a person
	委任	イニン	proxy; trust; charge; commission; delegation —*v*. entrust; commission; charge; delegate
訓	委せる	まかせる	***vt***. entrust; leave to; delegate
	委ねる	ゆだねる	***vt***. commit; entrust; delegate
	※委しい	くわしい	details; particulars; circumstances
¥	委員	イイン	member of the committee; commissioner
	委員会	イインカイ	committee; commission
	委託売買	イタクバイバイ	brokerage; agency; transaction

427

妻 ⑧

音	妻	サイ	wife
熟	妻子	サイシ	one's wife and children
	妻帯	サイタイ	married; connubial; matrimonial —*vi*. get married; marry
	妻帯者	サイタイシャ	married man
訓	妻	つま	wife

428

威 ⑨

音	威	イ	power; authority; threat
熟	威圧	イアツ	coercion; overpowering; high-handedness —*v*. restrain or dominate by force; coerce; overpower; overawe
	威圧的	イアツテキ	coercive; overbearing; domineering
	威嚇	イカク	menace; intimidation; threat —*v*. menace; intimidate; threaten
	威厳	イゲン	dignity; majesty; stateliness
	威光	イコウ	influence; authority; power
	威勢	イセイ	vigor; influence; high spirits
	威張る	イばる	*vi*. be proud/haughty; put on airs
	威力	イリョク	power; might; authority; influence
訓	威かす	おどかす	*vt*. threaten; menace; intimidate
	威す	おどす	*vt*. threaten; menace; intimidate

429

⑨

音	姿	シ	figure
熟	姿勢	シセイ	posture; attitude; profile
	姿態	シタイ	figure; pose
訓	姿	すがた	figure; image; appearance; looks
	姿見	すがたみ	full-length mirror

430
婆 ⑪

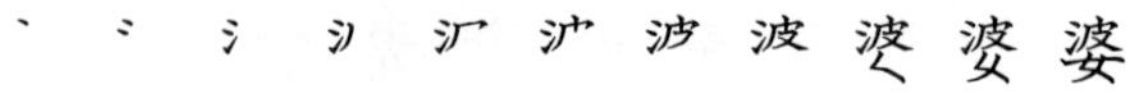

音	婆	バ	old woman
訓	※婆	ばば	old woman
	※お婆さん	おばあさん	one's grandmother; old woman

431
奴 ⑤

音	奴	ド ヌ	servant
熟	奴隷	ドレイ	slave
	奴婢	ヌヒ	servant; slave
訓	※奴	やつ	***col.*** fellow; chap; guy; he; she
	※奴	やっこ	servant; valet; footman; clown

432
好 ⑥

音	好	コウ	good; favorable; prefer; like; love
熟	好意	コウイ	goodwill; good wishes; regard; kindness; favor; friendliness
	好感	コウカン	favorable/good impression; good feeling/will
	好機	コウキ	good opportunity/time
	好奇心	コウキシン	curiosity; inquisitiveness
	好色	コウショク	sensuality; amorousness; lust; eroticism
	好人物	コウジンブツ	good-natured person; good fellow; nice chap
	好調	コウチョウ	good condition; favorable; satisfactory; promising
	好都合	コウツゴウ	favorable; convenient; fortunate; prosperous
	好適	コウテキ	suitable; ideal; good best
	好敵手	コウテキシュ	good match; worthy opponent
	好転	コウテン	favorable turn; change for the better; improvement ―***vi***. take a favorable turn; change for the better; improve
	好評	コウヒョウ	favorable criticism/comment; public favor
	好物	コウブツ	favorite; delight; favorite food

訓	好む	このむ	***vt.*** like; fancy; be fond of; love; care for; prefer
	好ましい	このましい	desirable; welcome; nice; good
	好み	このみ	taste; liking; choice; preference
	好き	すき	like; favorite; preference
	好く	すく	***vt.*** like; love; be fond of; care for
	※好い	いい（よい）	good; favorable; desirable
¥	好況	コウキョウ	good business conditions; prosperity; boom; brisk market
	好景気	コウケイキ	prosperity; good times; boom
	好材料	コウザイリョウ	good news; favorable factor

433

如 ⑥

く 女 女 如 如 如

音	如	ジョ	the same
		ニョ	like
熟	如才無い	ジョサイない	cautious; clever; adroit; considerate
	如実	ニョジツ	realistically; vividly; graphic
	如来	ニョライ	Buddha
訓	※如何	いかが	how; what

434

妃 ⑥

く 女 女 妃 妃 妃

音	妃	ヒ	queen; (married) princess
熟	妃殿下	ヒデンカ	Her Highness

435

妊 ⑦

く 女 女 妊 妊 妊 妊

音	妊	ニン	conceive
熟	妊産婦	ニンサンプ	pregnant and nursing mothers
	妊娠	ニンシン	conception; pregnancy; gestation —***vi.*** conceive; become pregnant
	妊娠中絶	ニンシンチュウゼツ	***med.*** abortion; termination of pregnancy
	妊婦	ニンプ	pregnant woman; woman with child
訓	妊む	はらむ	***v.*** conceive; become pregnant

436
妨 ⑦

く 女 女 女' 女亠 女方 妨

音	妨	ボウ	prevent; obstruct; hinder
熟	妨害	ボウガイ	obstruction; disturbance; interference —*v*. obstruct; disturb; interfer
	妨害物	ボウガイブツ	obstacle
訓	妨げる	さまたげる	***vt***. hinder; prevent; obstruct

437
妙 ⑦

く 女 女 女丨 女刂 女小 妙

音	妙	ミョウ	strange; odd; mystery
熟	妙案	ミョウアン	good idea; ingenious plan
	妙技	ミョウギ	extraordinary skill
	妙手	ミョウシュ	master; expert; virtuoso
	妙味	ミョウミ	delicious taste; charm; exquisite beauty
	妙薬	ミョウヤク	wonder drug
訓	※妙なる	たえなる	exquisite; superb; delicate; charming

438
姉 ⑧

く 女 女 女' 女亠 女亣 女市 姉

音	姉	シ	elder sister; lady
熟	姉妹	シマイ	sisters
	姉妹都市	シマイトシ	sister city; twin town
訓	姉	あね	one's elder sister
	姉御	あねゴ	one's elder sister; the boss's wife; proprietress; woman boss
	姉さん女房	あねさん ニョウボウ	wife who is older than her husband
	※お姉さん	おねえさん	elder sister; (term of address for a girl older than oneself)

439
始 ⑧

く 女 女 女厶 女厶 女台 始 始

音	始	シ	beginning; start; origin

熟 始球式 シキュウシキ ***bas***. opening ceremony of a baseball game in which an honorary guest throws the first ball
始業 シギョウ beginning of work or class —***vi***. start work or class
始業式 シギョウシキ opening ceremony for school or work
始終 シジュウ whole story; from beginning to end; always; constantly; frequently; the beginning and the end
始祖 シソ founder; ancestor
始動 シドウ starting an engine —***v***. start up an engine
始発 シハツ station of origin; first train of the day
始発駅 シハツエキ station of origin; first station on a line
始末 シマツ ordering; taking care of —***v***. put in order; take care of; come to pass
始末書 シマツショ written explanation/apology (for an accident, etc.)

訓 始まり はじまり opening; beginning; start
始まる はじまる ***vi***. begin; start; date from
始める はじめる ***vt***. begin; start; commence
始め はじめ beginning; founding; origin

440
姓 ⑧

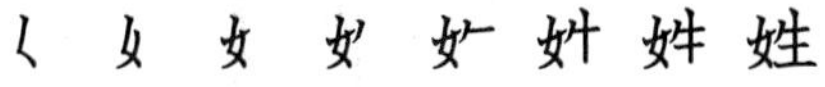

音 姓 ショウ birth
セイ surname
熟 姓名 セイメイ full name

441
妹 ⑧

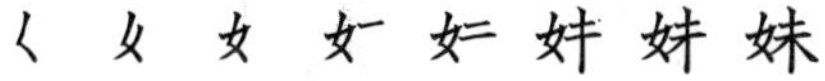

音 妹 マイ younger sister
訓 妹 いもうと younger sister

442
姻 ⑨

音 姻 イン marriage; relative
熟 姻戚 インセキ relative by marriage

443

娯 ⑩

音	娯	ゴ	amuse oneself
熟	娯楽	ゴラク	amusement; recreation

444

娠 ⑩

音	娠	シン	pregnant

445

姫 ⑩

音	姫	キ	princess
訓	姫	ひめ	princess
	姫君	ひめぎみ	princess

446

娘 ⑩

音	娘	ジョウ	daughter; girl; young woman
訓	娘	むすめ	daughter; girl; young woman
	娘心	むすめごころ	girlish innocence
	娘盛り	むすめざかり	the prime of young womanhood
	娘婿	むすめむこ	son-in-law

447

婚 ⑪

音	婚	コン	marriage; matrimony; wedlock
熟	婚姻	コンイン	marriage; matrimony; wedlock —***vi***. marry; be married
	婚期	コンキ	marriageable age
	婚約	コンヤク	engagement —***vi***. get engaged
	婚礼	コンレイ	wedding ceremony

448

婦 ⑪

音	婦	フ	woman; wife
熟	婦警	フケイ	policewoman
	婦女	フジョ	woman
	婦人	フジン	woman; lady
	婦人用	フジンヨウ	for ladies; women's
	婦長	フチョウ	head nurse

449

婿 ⑫

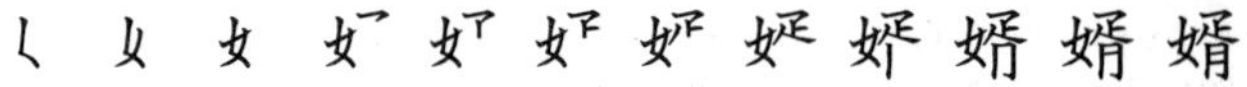

音	婿	セイ	son-in-law
訓	婿	むこ	son-in-law; bridegroom
	婿養子	むこヨウシ	son-in-law taken into the family; adopted son-in-law

450

媒 ⑫

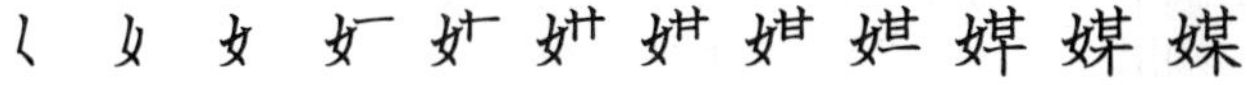

音	媒	バイ	intermediation
熟	媒介	バイカイ	agency; intervention; intermediation; matchmaking —*v*. mediate; intervene; act as an agent; matchmake
	媒酌	バイシャク	matchmaking —*v*. arrange a marriage; act as a go-between
	媒酌人	バイシャクニン	matchmaker; go-between
	媒体	バイタイ	medium

451

嫁 ⑬

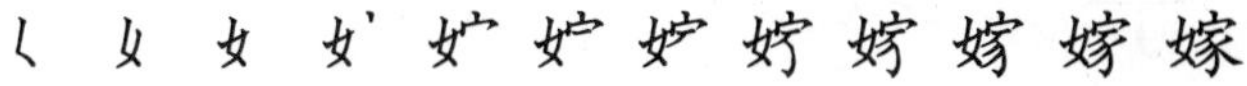

音	嫁	カ	marry
訓	嫁ぐ	とつぐ	***vi***. marry; be married
	嫁	よめ	bride; daughter-in-law
	嫁入り	よめいり	wedding; matrimony —***vi***. get married; marry into (women only)

3
口囗土士夂夕大女子宀寸小⺌⺍尢尸山川工己巾干幺广廴廾弋弓彐彡彳艹辶阝阝⺍忄扌犭氵

452

嫌 ⑬

音	嫌	ケン	hate; dislike; detest
		ゲン	temper; disposition
熟	嫌悪	ケンオ	hated —*v*. hate; loathe; detest
	嫌疑	ケンギ	suspicion of a crime
訓	嫌	いや	disagreeable; unpleasant; distasteful
	嫌がる	いやがる	***vt***. dislike; be unwilling to do
	嫌気	いやケ	disgust; bearish sentiment
	嫌味	いやミ	sarcasm; catty remarks
	嫌い	きらい	hateful; unpleasant; disagreeable
	嫌う	きらう	***vt***. dislike; hate; detest; loathe

453

嫡 ⑭

音	嫡	チャク	legitimate child; descendant
熟	嫡子	チャクシ	heir; legitimate son
	嫡出	チャクシュツ	legitimacy
	嫡男	チャクナン	eldest son; heir

454

嬢 ⑯

音	嬢	ジョウ	girl
訓	※嬢	むすめ	girl; one's daughter

3 子 こ／こへん child

455

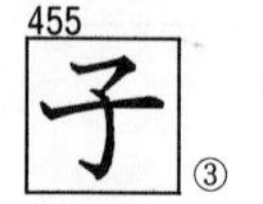

③

音	子	シ	child; son; man; Confucius
熟	子宮	シキュウ	***med***. womb; uterus

	子細	シサイ	details; particulars; reasons; circumstances; meaning
	子爵	シシャク	viscount
	子息	シソク	son
	子孫	シソン	posterity; descendant
	子弟	シテイ	boys; children; younger people
訓	子	こ	child
	子供	こども	child; children
	子分	こブン	follower; henchman
	子煩悩	こボンノウ	fond; doting
	子持ち	こもち	parent
	子守	こもり	baby-sitting
	子役	こヤク	child actor
	※子	ね	the rat (first sign of the Chinese zodiac)
¥	子会社	こガイシャ	subsidiary; affiliated company

456

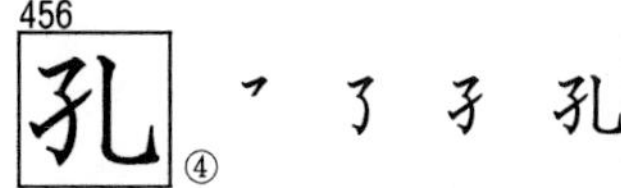

音	孔	コウ	hole; Confucius
熟	孔子	コウシ	Confucius
	※孔雀	クジャク	peacock; peahen
訓	※孔	あな	hole

457

字 ⑥

音	字	ジ	letter; character
熟	字音	ジオン	the Japanized pronunciation of a Chinese character
	字義	ジギ	meaning of a Chinese character
	字句	ジク	words; phrases; wording; expression; letters and phrases
	字書	ジショ	dictionary
	字体	ジタイ	form of a character; typeface
	字典	ジテン	dictionary
	字引	ジびき	dictionary
	字幕	ジマク	movie subtitle
訓	字	あざ	section of a village

458

存 ⑥

音	存	ソン	be; exist
		ゾン	be; exist
熟	存外	ゾンガイ	unexpectedly; beyond expectations; contrary to expectations
	存在	ソンザイ	existence —*v.* exist
	存続	ソンゾク	continued existence; duration —*v.* continue (to exist); endure; last
	存念	ゾンネン	idea; thought; concept
	存分	ゾンブン	to one's heart's content; as much as one wants; without reserve
	存命	ゾンメイ	living —*v.* be alive
	存立	ソンリツ	existence; substistence —*v.* exist; subsist

459

 ⑦

音	孝	コウ	filial piety; obedience to one's parents
熟	孝行	コウコウ	filial piety; obedience to one's parents —*vi.* be dutiful to one's parents; be a good son/daughter

460

学 ⑧

音	学	ガク	study; science
熟	学位	ガクイ	academic degree
	学園	ガクエン	school; educational institution
	学業	ガクギョウ	studies; schoolwork
	学芸	ガクゲイ	art and science
	学士	ガクシ	bachelor's degree
	学資	ガクシ	educational fund
	学識	ガクシキ	scholarship; learning
	学者	ガクシャ	scholar; learned person
	学習	ガクシュウ	study; learning —*v.* study; learn
	学術	ガクジュツ	science; learning
	学生	ガクセイ	student
	学制	ガクセイ	educational system

	学説	ガクセツ	theory; doctrine
	学徒	ガクト	students and pupils
	学童	ガクドウ	schoolchild; pupil
	学年	ガクネン	school year; grade
	学費	ガクヒ	school expenses; tuition fees
	学名	ガクメイ	scientific name
	学問	ガクモン	learning and research —***vi***. pursue learning
	学友	ガクユウ	schoolmate
	学用品	ガクヨウヒン	school supplies
	学歴	ガクレキ	school career; educational background
	学割	ガクわり	student discounts
	学科	ガッカ	school subject; branch of learning
	学会	ガッカイ	learned society; academia; meeting of scholars
	学界	ガッカイ	academic world; academia
	学期	ガッキ	school term
	学区	ガック	school precincts
訓	学ぶ	まなぶ	***vt***. learn; study

461

⑧

音	季	キ	season
熟	季刊	キカン	quarterly publication
	季節	キセツ	season
	季節風	キセツフウ	monsoon

462

孤 ⑨

音	孤	コ	orphan; alone; isolated
熟	孤軍奮闘	コグンフントウ	single-handed struggle —***v***. fight alone against all odds; struggle single-handedly
	孤児	コジ	orphan
	孤児院	コジイン	orphanage
	孤島	コトウ	solitary island
	孤独	コドク	solitude; loneliness; isolation
	孤立	コリツ	isolation —***v***. stand alone; be in isolation

463

孫 ⑩

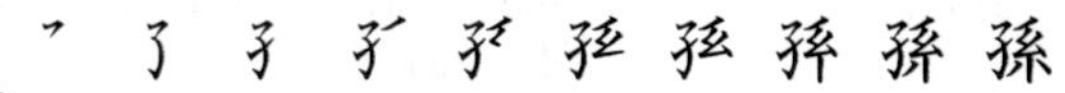

音 孫 ソン descendants
訓 孫 まご grandchild
孫子 まごこ children and grandchildren; descendants

---

3 宀 うかんむり *u* (katakana)

464

安 ⑥

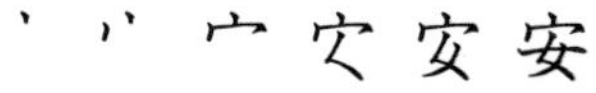

音	安	アン	safe; stable; easy; peaceful; inexpensive
熟	安易	アンイ	easy; simple; straightforward; easygoing; carefree
	安価	アンカ	cheapness; low price
	安産	アンザン	easy birth/delivery —***v***. have an easy birth; give birth easily
	安住	アンジュウ	peaceful living —***vi***. live in peace
	安心	アンシン	peace of mind; relief; safety —***vi***. feel at rest/relieved/assured
	安静	アンセイ	free from activity or labor; rest; quiet; repose
	安全	アンゼン	free from harm or risk; safety; security
	安全第一	アンゼンダイイチ	safety first
	安全地帯	アンゼンチタイ	safety zone
	安息	アンソク	repose; rest —***vi***. rest; take a break
	安泰	アンタイ	peace; tranquillty; safety; security
	安置	アンチ	installation —***v***. install; enshrine
	安直	アンチョク	inexpensive
	安定	アンテイ	stability; stabilization; steadiness —***vi***. be stable/steady/balanced/settled
	安定性	アンテイセイ	stability
	安否	アンピ	safety; welfare
	安眠	アンミン	quiet/restful sleep —***vi***. sleep well; have a good sleep
	安楽死	アンラクシ	painless death; mercy killing; euthanasia
訓	安い	やすい	cheap; easy; calm
	安上がり	やすあがり	doing something cheaply
	安らか	やすらか	peaceful; tranquil; calm

安らぎ　やすらぎ　peace of mind; serenity; calmness
安んじる　やすんじる　*v.* be reassured; have peace of mind; be contented

¥ 安全保障（安保）　アンゼンホショウ（アンポ）　security
安定市況　アンテイシキョウ　stable market
安値　やすね　low price/rate; low level

465
宇 ⑥
丶 丷 宀 宀 宀 宇

音 宇　ウ　expanse; universe; cosmos; space;eaves; roof

熟 宇宙　ウチュウ　the universe; outer space
宇宙船　ウチュウセン　spaceship; spacecraft
宇宙飛行士　ウチュウヒコウシ　astronaut; spaceman

466
守 ⑥
丶 丷 宀 宀 守 守

音 守　シュ　defend
（ス）　protect

熟 守衛　シュエイ　guard; doorman; doorkeeper
守護　シュゴ　protection —*v.* protect; guard
守護神　シュゴシン　guardian diety
守勢　シュセイ　defensive
守備　シュビ　defense —*v.* defend; guard

訓 守る　まもる　*vt.* defend; protect; keep one's word; abide by
守り　まもり　defense; protection; safeguard
守　もり　nursemaid

467
宅 ⑥
丶 丷 宀 宀 宀 宅

音 宅　タク　home; house; residence; our home; my husband

熟 宅地　タクチ　building lot; land for housing; residential land

3
口 囗 土 士 夂 夕 大 女 子 宀 寸 小 ⺌ ⺍ 尢 尸 山 川 工 己 巾 干 幺 广 廴 廾 弋 弓 彐 彡 彳 艹 辶 阝 阝 ⺌ 忄 扌 犭 氵

468

完 ⑦

音	完	カン	complete; perfect
熟	完結	カンケツ	completion; conclusion; termination —***v***. complete; conclude; finish; end
	完勝	カンショウ	complete victory —***vi***. defeat decisively; win a landslide victory
	完遂	カンスイ	successful execution; accomplishment —***v***. complete; carry through
	完成	カンセイ	completion; accomplishment; perfection —***v***. complete; conclude; finish; accomplish
	完全	カンゼン	perfection; completeness
	完投	カントウ	***bas***. pitching a whole game —***vi***. pitch a whole game
	完納	カンノウ	full payment —***v***. pay in full
	完敗	カンパイ	complete defeat —***vi***. suffer a complete defeat
	完備	カンビ	perfection; completion —***v***. be perfect/complete
	完封	カンプウ	complete blockade —***v***. blockade
	完璧	カンペキ	perfection
	完了	カンリョウ	completion; conclusion —***v***. complete; conclude
訓	※完うする	まっとうする	***vt***. accomplish; fulfill; complete

469

 ⑧

音	官	カン	official; government; senses
熟	官軍	カングン	government forces; Imperial Army
	官公庁	カンコウチョウ	government and municipal offices
	官舎	カンシャ	official residence
	官職	カンショク	government/official post
	官製	カンセイ	government manufacture
	官庁	カンチョウ	government office
	官邸	カンテイ	residence of a high official or Cabinet minister
	官能	カンノウ	senses; sensual
	官能的	カンノウテキ	sensual
	官報	カンポウ	official gazette
	官吏	カンリ	government official; civil servant
	官僚	カンリョウ	bureaucracy

470

⑧

音	実	ジツ	substance; sincerity; truth; reality; actual
熟	実印	ジツイン	registered seal
	実益	ジツエキ	practical use; usefulness; actual profit
	実演	ジツエン	stage show; demonstration
	実家	ジッカ	one's parents' home
	実害	ジツガイ	actual harm
	実学	ジツガク	practical science; studies of use in everyday life
	実感	ジッカン	actual feeling; atmosphere —*v*. realize
	実技	ジツギ	actual technique; practical skills; technical skill
	実況	ジッキョウ	real/actual condition
	実況放送	ジッキョウホウソウ	live broadcasting
	実兄	ジッケイ	one's real brother
	実刑	ジッケイ	prison sentence
	実権	ジッケン	real power; actual control
	実験	ジッケン	experimentation; experiment; test —*v*. experiment
	実験室	ジッケンシツ	laboratory
	実験的	ジッケンテキ	experimental
	実現	ジツゲン	realization; materialization —*v*. be realized; materialize
	実行	ジッコウ	practice; action; execution —*v*. carry out; put into practice; execute
	実行可能	ジッコウカノウ	practical; feasible
	実際	ジッサイ	in practice; fact; truth; reality; actuality; really; indeed
	実在	ジツザイ	real/actual existence —*vi*. exist
	実在論	ジツザイロン	realism
	実子	ジッシ	one's real/own child
	実施	ジッシ	execution; enforcement —*v*. put into effect/operation/force
	実質	ジッシツ	substance; essence
	実写	ジッシャ	photograph or movie of actual scenery or people —*v*. photograph or film actual scenery or people
	実社会	ジッシャカイ	the real world
	実習	ジッシュウ	practical training —*v*. practice; have training
	実証	ジッショウ	proof —*v*. prove; demonstrate
	実情	ジツジョウ	actual conditions
	実数	ジッスウ	***math***. real/actual number

	実績	ジッセキ	actual results; achievements
	実践	ジッセン	practice —***v***. practice
	実戦	ジッセン	actual fighting/service; combat
	実測	ジッソク	actual survey/measurement —***v***. measure; survey
	実存	ジツゾン	existence —***vi***. exist
	実存主義	ジツゾンシュギ	existentialism
	実体	ジッタイ	substance; solid
	実態	ジッタイ	actual condition
	実弾	ジツダン	live cartridge/ammunition
	実地	ジッチ	in actual practice; the scene (of a crime)
	実直	ジッチョク	honest; steady; conscientious
	実費	ジッピ	actual expenses
	実否	ジッピ	true or not
	実父	ジップ	one's real/own father
	実物	ジツブツ	the real thing; the genuine article; real life
	実物大	ジツブツダイ	actual/life/full size
	実母	ジツボ	one's real/own mother
	実名	ジツメイ	one's real name
	実用	ジツヨウ	practical use
	実用化	ジツヨウカ	practicality —***v***. put a thing to practical use
	実用主義	ジツヨウシュギ	pragmatism
	実用的	ジツヨウテキ	practical
	実用品	ジツヨウヒン	daily necessities; domestic articles
	実利	ジツリ	utility; actual benefit
	実利的	ジツリテキ	utilitarian
	実力	ジツリョク	real ability; force; arms
	実力行使	ジツリョクコウシ	use of force
	実力者	ジツリョクシャ	influential person; powerful figure
	実例	ジツレイ	instance; example
	実録	ジツロク	true record
	実話	ジツワ	true story; story taken from real life
訓	実	み	seed; berry; fruit; nut; ingredients; content; substance
	実る	みのる	***vi***. bear fruit; bear fruitful results
	実り	みのり	ripening; fruitful; productive
¥	実株	ジツかぶ	spot stocks/shares; real stock
	実業家	ジツギョウカ	business man
	実業界	ジツギョウカイ	business world/circles/community
	実行委員	ジッコウイイン	executive committee
	実行予算	ジッコウヨサン	working budget
	実質所得	ジッシツショトク	real income
	実質賃金	ジッシツチンギン	real wages

実収	ジッシュウ	net income/profit
実地訓練	ジッチクンレン	on-the-job training
実働時間	ジツドウジカン	actual working hours
実物取引	ジツブツとりひき	spot/cash transaction
実務	ジツム	practical business affairs
実力主義	ジツリョクシュギ	merit system

471
宗 ⑧

音	宗	シュウ	sect; religion; denomination
		ソウ	founder; head; leader
熟	宗教	シュウキョウ	religion
	宗教家	シュウキョウカ	man of religion
	宗旨	シュウシ	tenets; doctrine; sect; religion
	宗祖	シュウソ	founder of a sect
	宗徒	シュウト	believer; adherent
	宗派	シュウハ	sect; denomination
	宗家	ソウケ	head family; originator
	宗匠	ソウショウ	master; teacher

472
宙 ⑧

音	宙	チュウ	sky; air; space
熟	宙返り	チュウがえり	somersault; looping the loop —***vi***. turn a somersault; turn loops

473
定 ⑧

音	定	テイ	fixed; constant; regular
		ジョウ	
熟	定規	ジョウギ	ruler; scale
	定圧	テイアツ	constant pressure
	定員	テイイン	capacity; seating/passenger capacity; regular staff
	定期	テイキ	fixed period
	定期券	テイキケン	pass; season ticket

	定期船	テイキセン	liner
	定義	テイギ	definition —***v***. define
	定休日	テイキュウび	regular holiday
	定形	テイケイ	fixed form; regular shape
	定型	テイケイ	type; definate form
	定型的	テイケイテキ	typical; stereotyped
	定見	テイケン	definite view; firm conviction
	定限	テイゲン	fixed limit; limits; limitation; restriction —***v***. limit; restrict; confine
	定刻	テイコク	appointed hour; scheduled time
	定時	テイジ	regular/fixed time
	定住	テイジュウ	settlement; domicile —***v***. settle down; reside
	定住者	テイジュウシャ	permanent resident; settler
	定食	テイショク	set meal
	定数	テイスウ	fixed number; constant; invariable; fate
	定説	テイセツ	established theory
	定着	テイチャク	fixing; fastening; fixation; anchoring —***v***. fix; fasten; anchor; take root
	定点	テイテン	fixed point
	定年	テイネン	age limit; retirement age
	定評	テイヒョウ	established reputation; fixed opinion
	定本	テイホン	standard/authentic text
	定理	テイリ	theorem
	定率	テイリツ	fixed rate
	定量	テイリョウ	fixed quantity; measurement; dose —***v***. measure
	定例	テイレイ	established usage; precedent
訓	定まる	さだまる	***vi***. be decided/determined/fixed/settled
	定める	さだめる	***vt***. decide; determine; appoint; set; lay down; prescribe
	定か	さだか	certain; fixed
¥	定価	テイカ	fixed/marked/labled/list price
	定額	テイガク	fixed/required amount; flat sum
	定額貯金	テイガクチョキン	fixed amount; savings; fixed deposit
	定款	テイカン	articles of association
	定期預金	テイキヨキン	fixed term deposit; time deposit
	定職	テイショク	regular occupation; fixed employment
	定率法	テイリツホウ	fixed rate method

474

宝 ⑧

丶 丷 宀 宀 宁 宇 宝 宝

音	宝	ホウ	treasure
熟	宝玉	ホウギョク	jewel; gem; precious stone
	宝庫	ホウコ	treasure house
	宝石	ホウセキ	jewel; gem; precious stone
	宝典	ホウテン	valued/useful book; book of Buddhist sutras
	宝刀	ホウトウ	treasured sword
	宝物	ホウブツ	treasure
訓	宝	たから	treasure
	宝籤	たからくじ	lottery; raffle
	宝島	たからじま	treasure island
	宝物	たからもの	treasure

475

宣 ⑨

丶 丷 宀 宀 宀 宁 宣 宣 宣

音	宣	セン	declare; edict; announce
熟	宣教師	センキョウシ	missionary
	宣言	センゲン	declaration; statement —*v*. declare; state
	宣告	センコク	pronouncement; sentence; verdict —*v*. pronounce; sentence; give a verdict
	宣誓	センセイ	oath; vow; pledge —*v*. make an oath; vow; pledge
	宣戦	センセン	declaration of war —***vi***. declare war
	宣伝	センデン	propaganda; advertising; publicity —*v*. propagate; advertize; publicize
訓	※宣べる	のべる	***vt***. state; declare

476

客 ⑨

丶 丷 宀 宀 宀 安 客 客 客

音	客	キャク (カク)	guest; visitor; visiting; traveler; customer; client; the past
熟	客死	カクシ (キャクシ)	dying away from home; dying in a foreign country —***vi***. die away from home; die overseas
	客員教授	キャクイン キョウジュ	visiting/guest professor
	客室	キャクシツ	guest room

	客車	キャクシャ	passenger vehicle; coach; carriage
	客船	キャクセン	passenger vessel/liner
	客間	キャクま	drawing room; parlor; guest room
	客観	キャッカン	object (in philosophy)
	客観的	キャッカンテキ	objective
¥	客注	キャクチュウ	customer order

477

室 ⑨

音	室	シツ	room; wife; concubine
熟	室温	シツオン	room temperature
	室外	シツガイ	outside the room
	室内	シツナイ	inside the room
	室内楽	シツナイガク	chamber music
訓	室	むろ	cellar; hot house; drying room
	室町	むろまち	***hist***. Muromachi period/culture (1338-1573)

478

宜 ⑧

音	宜	ギ	right; good; suitable
訓	※宜しい	よろしい	good; suitable; right
	※宜しく	よろしく	well; suitably; properly; send one's best regards

479

宴 ⑩

音	宴	エン	banquet
熟	宴会	エンカイ	feast; banquet; social party
	宴席	エンセキ	dinner party; banquet
訓	※宴	うたげ	party; banquet; feast

480

⑩

音	家	カ	house; family
		ケ	house; family
熟	家屋	カオク	house
	家業	カギョウ	one's trade or business
	家具	カグ	furniture
	家系	カケイ	family line; lineage
	家計	カケイ	household economy; housekeeping expenses
	家財	カザイ	household goods
	家事	カジ	housework
	家臣	カシン	***hist***. retainer/vassal (Edo period)
	家政	カセイ	housekeeping
	家政婦	カセイフ	housekeeper
	家族	カゾク	family
	家畜	カチク	domestic animals
	家庭	カテイ	home; household; family
	家伝	カデン	handed down from father to son; hereditary
	家内	カナイ	family; one's wife
	家風	カフウ	family custom
	家宝	カホウ	heirloom
	家名	カメイ	family name
	家老	カロウ	***hist***. chief/principal retainer (Edo period)
	家来	ケライ	subordinates loyal to a lord; vassal; retinue
訓	家	いえ	house; home; ancestry
	家柄	いえがら	birth; status
	家主	いえぬし（やぬし）	landlady; landlord; houseowner
	家元	いえもと	***hist***. the head of a school (of a traditional art)
	家屋敷	いえやしき	***hist***. estate; mansion
	家	や	house
	家賃	やチン	rent for a house, apartment, etc.

481

⑩

音	害	ガイ	harm; damage
熟	害する	ガイする	***vt***. injure; harm; hurt; impair

害悪	ガイアク	evil; vice
害虫	ガイチュウ	harmful/noxious insect
害毒	ガイドク	evil influence; evil; harm

482
宮 ⑩

音	宮	キュウ	palace; imperial dwelling; shrine
		グウ	
		(ク)	
熟	宮城	キュウジョウ	imperial palace
	宮廷	キュウテイ	court; palace
	宮殿	キュウデン	palace
	宮内庁	クナイチョウ	Imperial Household Agency
訓	宮	みや	(Shinto) shrine; imperial prince

483
宰 ⑩

音	宰	サイ	govern; minister; control; supervise
熟	宰相	サイショウ	prime minister
	宰領	サイリョウ	supervision; superintendence; supervisor; superintendent —*v.* supervise; oversee; organize

484
宵 ⑩

音	宵	ショウ	evening
訓	宵	よい	early evening
	宵の口	よいのくち	early evening
	宵闇	よいやみ	dusk; twilight

485
容 ⑩

音	容	ヨウ	form; appearance; content
熟	容易	ヨウイ	easy; simple
	容器	ヨウキ	vessel; container

	容疑	ヨウギ	suspicion (of a crime)
	容疑者	ヨウギシャ	suspect
	容姿	ヨウシ	face and figure; looks; appearances
	容赦	ヨウシャ	pardon; mercy; forgiveness —*v*. pardon; forgive
	容色	ヨウショク	features; looks; personal appearance
	容積	ヨウセキ	capacity; volume
	容体	ヨウダイ	condition (of an illness)
	容認	ヨウニン	admission; approval; acceptance —*v*. admit; approve; accept
	容貌	ヨウボウ	looks; personal appearance
	容量	ヨウリョウ	capacity; volume
訓	※容れる	いれる	***vt***. put/let in; admit; accept

486

寄 ⑪

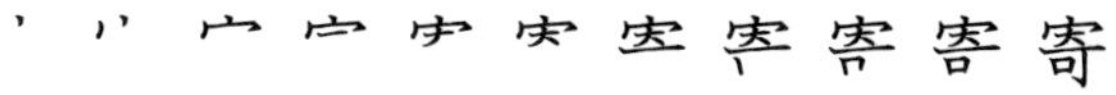

音	寄	キ	call at; depend on; approach; contribute; donation
熟	寄港	キコウ	port call —***vi***. call at port
	寄稿	キコウ	newspaper/magazine contributor —***vi***. contribute to a newspaper; write for a magazine
	寄宿舎	キシュクシャ	dormitory
	寄生	キセイ	parasitism —***vi***. be parasitic; be a parasite
	寄贈	キゾウ	presentation; donation; gift —*v*. present; donate; make a gift
	寄付	キフ	contribution; donation —*v*. contribute; donate
	寄与	キヨ	contribution; services —*v*. contribute; render services
	寄留	キリュウ	sojourn; temporary residence —***vi***. sojourn; reside temporarily
訓	寄る	よる	***vi***. draw near; drop in; come together; stop at a place
	寄せる	よせる	***v***. allow (a person); put (a thing) aside; send (a letter); be dependent on (a person); contribute an article (to a magazine)
	寄り合い	よりあい	meeting; assembly; gathering
	寄り道	よりみち	dropping in on the way —***vi***. drop in on the way
	※寄席	よせ	variety entertainment/show
¥	寄りつき	よりつき	open; opening price; opening of the session/market

3 口 囗 土 士 夂 夕 大 女 子 宀 寸 小 ⺌ ⺍ 尢 尸 山 川 工 己 巾 干 幺 广 廴 廾 弋 弓 ⺕ 彡 彳 ⺾ 辶 阝 阝 ⺍ 忄 扌 犭 氵

487

寂 ⑪

丶 丷 宀 宀 宇 宇 宇 宇 宇 宋 寂 寂

音	寂	ジャク (セキ)	lonely
熟	寂然	セキゼン (ジャクネン)	loneliness; desolation; seclusion
	寂寞	セキバク	solitude; loneliness; desolation
	寂寥	セキリョウ	loneliness; desolation
訓	寂しい	さびしい	lonely; sad; deserted; empty
	寂れる	さびれる	***vi.*** decline; be deserted; become desolate
	寂	さび	mellow; seasoned; grace; aged beauty

488

宿 ⑪

丶 丷 宀 宀 宀 宀 宀 宀 宿 宿 宿

音	宿	シュク	inn; stay
熟	宿縁	シュクエン	destiny; fate
	宿願	シュクガン	long-cherished desire; dream
	宿舎	シュクシャ	dormitory; housing; lodgings; accomodations
	宿題	シュクダイ	homework; assignment
	宿直	シュクチョク	night duty
	宿敵	シュクテキ	old foe; archenemy
	宿泊	シュクハク	lodging —***vi.*** lodge
	宿命	シュクメイ	fate; destiny
	宿命論	シュクメイロン	fatalism
訓	宿	やど	inn; hotel; lodgings; shelter
	宿る	やどる	***vi.*** dwell; live; stay; lodge; harbor
	宿す	やどす	***vt.*** be pregnant; harbor; give lodgings to
	宿帳	やどチョウ	hotel register
	宿賃	やどチン	hotel bill
	宿無し	やどなし	homeless person; vagabond; tramp
	宿屋	やどや	inn; hotel

489

密 ⑪

丶 丷 宀 宀 宓 宓 宓 宓 宓 密 密

音	密	ミツ	close; dense; crowded; minute; fine; secret

口 囗 土 士 夂 夕 大 女 子 宀 寸 小 ⺌ ⺍ 尢 尸 山 川 工 己 巾 干 幺 广 廴 廾 弋 弓 彐 彡 彳 艹 辶 阝 阝 ⺍ 忄 扌 犭 氵

熟	密画	ミツガ	detailed drawing
	密会	ミッカイ	clandestine meeting —*vi*. meet secretly; have a secret rendezvous
	密議	ミツギ	secret conference/consultation
	密航	ミッコウ	stow away; secret passage on a ship —*vi*. stowaway
	密行	ミッコウ	prowling —*v*. prowl about; go secretly
	密告	ミッコク	secret information —*v*. provide secret information
	密告者	ミッコクシャ	informer; betrayer
	密旨	ミッシ	secret orders
	密事	ミツジ	secret
	密室	ミッシツ	secret/locked room
	密集	ミッシュウ	crowd —*vi*. mass together
	密書	ミッショ	secret written message
	密生	ミッセイ	thick/luxurious growth —*vi*. grow thick/luxuriantly
	密接	ミッセツ	close; intimate —*vi*. be close/intimate
	密造	ミツゾウ	illegal manufacture —*v*. manufacture illegally
	密談	ミツダン	secret talk —*vi*. take part in secret conversations
	密着	ミッチャク	sticking; adherence —*vi*. stick/adhere to
	密通	ミッツウ	adultery; secret relationship —*vi*. commit adultery; have an affair
	密偵	ミッテイ	spy; undercover agent
	密度	ミツド	density
	密入国	ミツニュウコク	illegal immigration —*vi*. enter a country illegally
	密売	ミツバイ	illicit sale; smuggling; bootlegging —*v*. smuggle; bootleg
	密封	ミップウ	sealed up/tight —*v*. seal up/tight
	密閉	ミッペイ	shut tight —*v*. seal airtight
	密約	ミツヤク	secret agreement —*vi*. make a secret agreement
	密輸	ミツユ	smuggling; contraband —*v*. smuggle
	密猟	ミツリョウ	poaching —*v*. poach
	密漁	ミツリョウ	fish poaching —*v*. poach fish
	密林	ミツリン	jungle; dense forest

490

⑫

音	寒	カン	cold; poor
熟	寒気	カンキ	cold weather

	寒暑	カンショ	heat and cold; temperature
	寒村	カンソン	remote/lonely village
	寒帯	カンタイ	frigid zone; arctic regions
	寒暖	カンダン	hot and cold; temperature
	寒暖計	カンダンケイ	thermometer
	寒中	カンチュウ	midwinter; depth of winter
	寒波	カンパ	cold wave
	寒流	カンリュウ	cold current
	寒冷	カンレイ	coldness; chill
訓	寒い	さむい	cold; chilly
	寒気	さむケ	chill; cold fit; rigor
	寒さ	さむさ	coldness; the cold

491

⑫

音	富	フ (フウ)	wealth; rich; affluent; ample
熟	富貴	フウキ	wealth and rank
	富強	フキョウ	rich and powerful (country)
	富豪	フゴウ	rich man; millionaire
	富国	フコク	rich country
	富裕	フユウ	rich; wealthy; affluent
	富有	フユウ	wealthy; affluent; rich
	富力	フリョク	wealth; resources
訓	富	とみ	wealth; resources; assets
	富む	とむ	***vi***. be rich; abound in

492

⑬

音	寛	カン	tolerant; broad-minded; lenient
熟	寛大	カンダイ	generosity; broad-mindedness; liberality; leniency
	寛容	カンヨウ	magnanimity; tolerance; forbearance
訓	※寛ぐ	くつろぐ	***vi***. be at ease; relax
	※寛い	ひろい	generous; broad-minded; magnanimous

493

⑬

音	寝	シン	sleep
熟	寝具	シング	bedclothes; bedding
	寝室	シンシツ	bedroom
	寝食	シンショク	eating and sleeping
	寝台	シンダイ	bed; sleeping berth
	寝台車	シンダイシャ	sleeping car; sleeper
訓	寝る	ねる	***vi***. lie down; sleep
	寝返り	ねがえり	tossing and turning (in one's sleep); betrayal
	寝かす	ねかす	***vt***. put to bed; lay down
	寝言	ねごと	talking in one's sleep
	寝床	ねどこ	bed
	寝冷え	ねびえ	catching cold (in one's sleep) —***vi***. catch cold (in one's sleep)
	寝坊	ねボウ	oversleeping; late riser —***vi***. oversleep; get up late
	寝間着	ねまき	nightclothes; nightgown; nightdress; pajamas

494

寡 ⑭

音	寡	カ	few; widow
熟	寡婦	カフ	widow
	寡聞	カブン	ill-informed; little knowledge
	寡黙	カモク	speaking few words; taciturn
訓	寡	やもめ	widow
	※寡ない	すくない	not many; a few

495

⑭

音	察	サツ	investigate; guess
熟	察する	サッする	***vt***. investigate; guess
	察知	サッチ	perception; sense —***v***. perceive; sense; gather; infer

496

寧 ⑭

音	寧	ネイ	peaceful; calm

497

審 ⑮

音	審	シン	judge
熟	審議	シンギ	deliberation; discussion —***v***. deliberate; discuss
	審査	シンサ	judgment; examination; inspection —***v***. examine; inspect; screen; judge
	審判	シンパン	referee; judgment —***v***. referee; umpire; judge

498

寮 ⑮

音	寮	リョウ	dormitory; hotel
熟	寮生	リョウセイ	dormitory student; boarder
	寮長	リョウチョウ	dormitory director

3 寸 すん inch

499

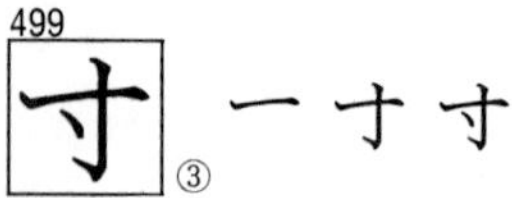

音	寸	スン	*sun* (unit of length, approx. 3.03 cm); small; tiny
熟	寸暇	スンカ	moment's leisure; spare moment
	寸劇	スンゲキ	short play; sketch; skit
	寸志	スンシ	small present (small amount of money)
	寸前	スンゼン	just/right/immediately before
	寸断	スンダン	***vt***. tear/cut to pieces
	寸評	スンピョウ	short review; brief comment
	寸分	スンブン	bit; little
	寸法	スンポウ	measure; measurements; dimensions; plan

500

寺 ⑥

一 十 土 圭 寺 寺

音	寺	ジ	temple
熟	寺院	ジイン	temple
	寺社	ジシャ	shrines and temples
訓	寺	てら	Buddhist temple

501

寿 ⑦

一 二 三 丰 声 寿 寿

音	寿	ジュ	age; congratulations
熟	寿命	ジュミョウ	life; life-span; life expectancy
	※寿司	スシ	*sushi* (vinegared rice and raw fish)
訓	寿	ことぶき	congratulations; happiness; long life

502

対 ⑦

丶 亠 ナ 文 文一 対 対

音	対	タイ ツイ	set; couple; response; oppose; face
熟	対する	タイする	***vi***. be against; oppose; face
	対応	タイオウ	correspondence; equivalence; counterpart —***vi***. correspond to; be equivalent to; tackle; deal with; cope
	対角線	タイカクセン	diagonal (line)
	対決	タイケツ	confrontation; face-to-face meeting —***vi***. confront; have a showdown; stand face-to-face
	対向	タイコウ	opposite
	対抗	タイコウ	opposition; confrontation; antagonism —***vi***. oppose; confront; antagonize
	対策	タイサク	countermeasure; counterplan; countermove
	対処	タイショ	coping; dealing; tackling —***vi***. cope/deal with; tackle
	対称	タイショウ	symmetry ***gram***. the second person
	対象	タイショウ	object; subject; target
	対照	タイショウ	contrast; comparison —***v***. contrast; compare
	対戦	タイセン	competition —***vi***. compete; oppose

	対談	タイダン	talk; conversation; dialog; interview —*vi*. talk/converse with; have an interview with
	対等	タイトウ	equality; equal footing; equal terms; parity
	対比	タイヒ	contrast; comparison; opposition; analogy —*v*. contrast; compare; oppose; analogize
	対面	タイメン	interview; meeting —*vi*. interview; meet; see; have an interview
	対立	タイリツ	opposition; confrontation; contrast —*vi*. be opposed/confronted with
	対話	タイワ	dialog; conversation —*vi*. have a dialog/conversation with
	対句	ツイク	antithesis; parallelism
	対語	ツイゴ	***gram***. antonym

503

⑨

音	専	セン	solely; exclusive
熟	専科	センカ	special course (of study)
	専業	センギョウ	profession; main occupation
	専攻	センコウ	one's major (at university, etc.) —*v*. major in (biochemistry, etc.)
	専心	センシン	devotion; concentration; undivided attention —*vi*. be devoted; concentrate; give one's undivided attention
	専制政治	センセイセイジ	absolute/despotic government
	専任	センニン	full-time
	専念	センネン	close/undivided attention —*vi*. give one's close/undivided attention
	専売	センバイ	monopoly —*v*. monopolize
	専務	センム	managing director
	専門	センモン	specialty
	専門家	センモンカ	person specialized in certain fields
	専門店	センモンテン	specialty store
	専有	センユウ	exclusive possession; monopoly —*v*. possess exclusively; monopolize
	専用	センヨウ	exclusive use; private/personal use —*v*. have exclusive use of
訓	専ら	もっぱら	exclusively
¥	専売特許	センバイトッキョ	patent

504

封 ⑨

一 十 土 圭 圭 圭 圭 封 封

音	封	フウ	seal
		ホウ	fief
熟	封じる	フウじる	***vt.*** seal; blockade; silence
	封印	フウイン	seal —***v.*** seal (a letter)
	封緘	フウカン	seal an envelope
	封切り	フウきり	(film/movie) release; opening a letter
	封鎖	フウサ	blockade; freezing —***v.*** blockade; block; freeze
	封書	フウショ	sealed letter
	封筒	フウトウ	envelope
	封入	フウニュウ	enclosure (in a letter) —***v.*** enclose (in a letter)
	封建	ホウケン	feudalism
	封建時代	ホウケンジダイ	feudal age
	封建社会	ホウケンシャカイ	feudal society
	封建制度	ホウケンセイド	feudalism
	封建的	ホウケンテキ	feudal

505

射 ⑩

丿 亻 亻 介 自 自 身 身 射 射

音	射	シャ	archery; fire
熟	射撃	シャゲキ	shooting —***v.*** shoot; fire
	射幸	シャコウ	speculation
	射幸心	シャコウシン	speculative spirit
	射幸的	シャコウテキ	speculative
	射殺	シャサツ	death by shooting —***v.*** shoot to death
	射手	シャシュ	marksman; archer
	射出	シャシュツ	ejection; radiation; discharge —***v.*** fire; eject; spout; radiate
	射精	シャセイ	ejaculation; seminal emission —***vi.*** ejaculate
	射程	シャテイ	shooting/firing range
	射的	シャテキ	target practice
	射利心	シャリシン	mercenary spirit
訓	射る	いる	***vt.*** shoot; fire

506

将 ⑩

音	将	ショウ	commander; general
熟	将棋	ショウギ	*shōgi* (Japanese chess)
	将軍	ショウグン	shogun; military dictator; general
	将来	ショウライ	the future

507

尉 ⑪

音	尉	イ	military company officer
熟	尉官	イカン	military company officer

508

尋 ⑫

音	尋	ジン	ask
熟	尋常	ジンジョウ	ordinary; mediocre
	尋問	ジンモン	questioning —*v*. question; examine
訓	尋ねる	たずねる	***vt***. search for; ask; inquire

509

⑫

音	尊	ソン	esteem; value; respect
熟	尊敬	ソンケイ	respect; esteem; honor —*v*. respect; hold in esteem; honor
	尊厳	ソンゲン	dignity
	尊大	ソンダイ	haughty; arrogant; self-important
	尊重	ソンチョウ	respect; esteem —*v*. respect; hold in esteem
	尊王	ソンノウ	reverence for the emperor; advocacy of imperial rule
	尊父	ソンプ	***hon***. your father
訓	尊い	たっとい	exalted; valuable; precious; noble
	尊ぶ	たっとぶ	***vt***. respect; esteem; value
	尊い	とうとい	noble; precious; exalted valulable

尊ぶ	とうとぶ	***vt***. respect; value; esteem

510
導 ⑮ 丷 䒑 艹 ⺌ 首 首 首 首 道 道 道 導

音	導	ドウ	guide; transmit; conduct
熟	導火線	ドウカセン	fuse; cause; agency; impetus; incentive
	導線	ドウセン	leading wire
	導体	ドウタイ	conductor (of electricity, heat, etc.)
	導入	ドウニュウ	introduction; induction; invitation —***v***. introduce; induce; invite
訓	導き	みちびき	guidance; showing the way; instruction
	導く	みちびく	***vt***. guide; lead; conduct; show; introduce; instruct

3 小 しょう small

511
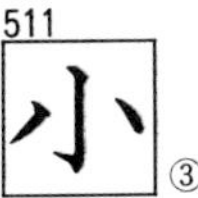
③ 亅 小 小

音	小	ショウ	small; little; younger; (prefix) sub-
熟	小異	ショウイ	minor differences
	小学生	ショウガクセイ	elementary school pupil
	小学校	ショウガッコウ	elementary/primary school
	小休止	ショウキュウシ	break; breather —***v***. take a break/breather
	小計	ショウケイ	subtotal
	小康	ショウコウ	lull; letup; remission
	小国	ショウコク	little country; minor power
	小差	ショウサ	narrow margin
	小冊子	ショウサッシ	pamphlet; booklet
	小市民	ショウシミン	petty bourgeois
	小食	ショウショク	light eating
	小心	ショウシン	timidity; cowardice
	小心者	ショウシンもの	coward; timid person
	小数	ショウスウ	***math***. decimal
	小数点	ショウスウテン	***math***. decimal point
	小生	ショウセイ	***hum***. I; me
	小節	ショウセツ	bar of music; measure

	小説	ショウセツ	novel; fiction
	小説家	ショウセツカ	novelist
	小児	ショウニ	small child; infant
	小児科	ショウニカ	***med***. pediatrics
	小便	ショウベン	urine; piss; pee —***vi***. pass urine; piss; pee
訓	小さい	ちいさい	small; little; tiny; young
	小	お	(prefix) small; little; sub-
	小	こ	(prefix) small; little; sub-
	小型	こがた	small size; small; compact
	小型化	こがたカ	miniature; small; compact —***v***. miniaturize; compact
	小柄	こがら	small build/size/stature
	小言	こごと	scolding; rebuke; preaching; lecture; grumbling
	小細工	こザイク	cheap/petty tricks
	小雨	こさめ	light/fine rain; drizzle
	小銭	こぜに	small change
	小僧	こゾウ	priestling; novice; shop boy; errand boy; urchin; brat
	小遣い	こづかい	spending/pocket money
	小包	こづつみ	parcel; package
	小手先	こてさき	cheap/petty tricks
	小話	こばなし	short tale; anecdote
	小人	こびと	dwarf; pygmy
	小間使い	こまづかい	maid
	小間物屋	こまものや	notions dealer; haberdasher
	小麦	こむぎ	wheat
	小麦粉	こむぎこ	flour
	小屋	こや	hut; shed; shack; cabin
¥	小売店	こうりテン	kiosk (selling magazines, newspapers, sweets, etc.)
	小売り	こうり	retail
	小切手	こぎって	check
	小切手帳	こぎってチョウ	checkbook
	小口	こぐち	small lots

512

④ 亅 小 小 少

音	少	ショウ	few; young
熟	少額	ショウガク	small sum/amount of money
	少女	ショウジョ	girl

	少々	ショウショウ	just a little; few
	少食	ショウショク	light eating; small appetite
	少数	ショウスウ	small number
	少年	ショウネン	boy; juvenile
	少量	ショウリョウ	small quantity; morsel
訓	少ない	すくない	few; not many; little
	少し	すこし	little; not much

---

3 ⺌ さかさしょう small on top

513

当 ⑥

丨 丷 ⺌ 当 当 当

音	当	トウ	right; justice; fairness; this; the present; the current; right now
熟	当局	トウキョク	authorities; the powers that be
	当座	トウザ	the time being; the present
	当時	トウジ	at the present time; then; in those days
	当事者	トウジシャ	party concerned; interested party
	当日	トウジツ	that/the day; the appointed day
	当初	トウショ	at first; at the beginning
	当世	トウセイ	present day; the day/age/era
	当選	トウセン	winning; return to office; election —***vi***. be elected/returned to office; win an election
	当然	トウゼン	naturally; justly; properly; as a matter of course
	当地	トウチ	this place/area here
	当直	トウチョク	being on duty/watch —***vi***. be on duty; keep watch
	当人	トウニン	the said person; the person in question; the man himself
	当年	トウネン	this year; that year; those days
	当番	トウバン	being on duty/watch/guard
	当否	トウヒ	right or wrong; justice; propriety; fitness; suitability
	当分	トウブン	for the time being
	当方	トウホウ	our part; I; we
	当面	トウメン	present; urgent; pressing; immediate —***vi***. face; confront
	当落	トウラク	result of an election

	当惑	トウワク	perplexity; embarrassment; discomfiture; dilemma; confusion —*vi*. be perplexed/bewildered
訓	当たる	あたる	hit; strike; touch; be touched; be equal; match; ***col***. -have food poisoning
	当たり	あたり	hit; success; strike
	当たり前	あたりまえ	proper; right; just; fair; common; normal; usual
	当てる	あてる	apply; lay; hold; hit; strike; guess; succeed; expose
¥	～当たり	～あたり	(suffix) per-
	当期未処分利益	トウキミショブンリエキ	unappropriated retained earnings
	当期利益	トウキリエキ	net income
	当局	トウキョク	the authorities concerned
	当座貸越	トウザかしこし	overdraft; overdrawn
	当座資産	トウザシサン	liquid assets
	当座預金	トウザヨキン	current account; deposit
	当日取引	トウニチとりひき	cash delivery

514
尚 ⑧

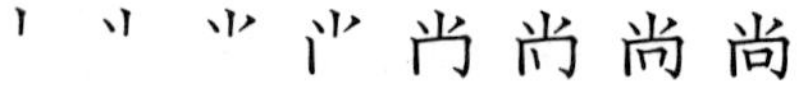

音	尚	ショウ	respect
熟	尚早	ショウソウ	too early/soon
訓	※尚	なお	moreover; furthermore

515
党 ⑩

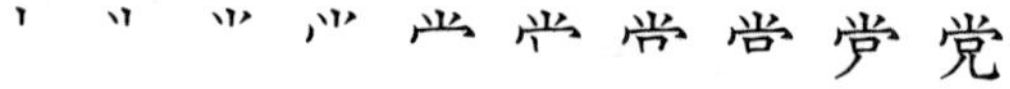

音	党	トウ	company; (political) party
熟	党員	トウイン	party member
	党議	トウギ	party policy; platform; party decision
	党首	トウシュ	party leader
	党籍	トウセキ	party register
	党派	トウハ	party/action/school of thought
	党利	トウリ	party interests

516
単 ⑨

音	単	タン	single; simple
熟	単位	タンイ	unit
	単元	タンゲン	unit
	単語	タンゴ	word
	単行本	タンコウボン	separate volume; one volume (not a series, etc.); hardcover book
	単純	タンジュン	simplicity
	単身	タンシン	alone; by oneself; unaccompanied
	単数	タンスウ	singular number
	単線	タンセン	single track
	単調	タンチョウ	monotony; dullness; humdrum
	単刀直入	タントウチョクニュウ	straightforward; direct; frank; to the point
	単独	タンドク	singleness; independence; separateness
	単文	タンブン	simple sentence
¥	単価	タンカ	unit cost/price
	単式	タンシキ	single entry bookkeeping; simple system
	単利	タンリ	simple interest

517

⑪

音	巣	ソウ	nest; web; hive
熟	巣窟	ソウクツ	den; hangout
訓	巣	す	nest; shelter; web; hive
	巣くう	すくう	***vi.*** build a nest
	巣立つ	すだつ	***vi.*** leave the nest; graduate; start out in life

518

⑫

音	営	エイ	run; manage; administer

訓	営み	いとなみ	business; trade
	営む	いとなむ	***vt.*** run a business; engage in commercial activities
¥	営業	エイギョウ	business; trade; commerce —***v.*** conduct business; trade
	営業外収益	エイギョウガイシュウエキ	non-operating income or revenue; other income
	営業外費用	エイギョウガイヒヨウ	non-operating expenses
	営業外利益	エイギョウガイリエキ	non-operating profit
	営業収益	エイギョウシュウエキ	operating profit
	営業実績	エイギョウジッセキ	business result
	営業費用	エイギョウヒヨウ	operating expenses
	営業不振	エイギョウフシン	slump in business
	営業妨害	エイギョウボウガイ	obstruction of business
	営業報告書	エイギョウホウコクショ	business report
	営業利益	エイギョウリエキ	operating profit
	営団	エイダン	management corporation
	営利	エイリ	gain; profit-making
	営林	エイリン	forest management; forestry

519

⑰

音	厳	ゲン (ゴン)	strict; severe; stern; solemn
熟	厳戒	ゲンカイ	strict guard/alert —***v.*** keep strict guard; be on strict alert
	厳格	ゲンカク	strict; severe; stern; rigid
	厳禁	ゲンキン	strict prohibition —***v.*** be strictly prohibited
	厳守	ゲンシュ	strict observance —***v.*** keep strictly to; adhere rigidly; obey
	厳重	ゲンジュウ	stern; severe; strict; tight; close
	厳粛	ゲンシュク	solemn; grave; awesome
	厳正	ゲンセイ	strict; rigid; fair; impartial
	厳選	ゲンセン	careful selection —***v.*** select carefully; hand pick
	厳然	ゲンゼン	grim; grave; solemn
	厳冬	ゲントウ	severe/hard winter
	厳罰	ゲンバツ	severe/heavy punishment
	厳父	ゲンプ	strict father; (another person's) father
	厳密	ゲンミツ	strict; close; clear cut;

	厳命	ゲンメイ	strict command —*v*. give a strict command
訓	厳か	おごそか	solemn; stately
	厳しい	きびしい	severe; strict; stern

3 尢 だいのまげあし crooked leg

520
就 ⑫

丶 亠 亠 亡 古 亨 亨 京 京 就 就 就

音	就	シュウ (ジュ)	get a job; install; study with; set out
熟	就学	シュウガク	entering/starting school —***vi***. enter/start school
	就学率	シュウガクリツ	percentage of pupils attending school
	就寝	シュウシン	going to bed —***vi***. go to bed
	就任	シュウニン	inauguration/installation in a new position —***vi***. take up a position
	就任式	シュウニンシキ	inauguration; inaugural ceremony
訓	就く	つく	***vi***. get a job; become; study under
	就ける	つける	***vt***. seat; appoint a person; install
¥	就業	シュウギョウ	arriving at work; starting work —***vi***. start/begin work
	就業時間	シュウギョウジカン	working hours
	就業人口	シュウギョウジンコウ	work force
	就職	シュウショク	finding employment; job hunting —***vi***. find work; get a job
	就職活動	シュウショクカツドウ	job hunting
	就職口	シュウショクグチ	position; situation; opening
	就職先	シュウショクサキ	place of employment
	就職試験	シュウショクシケン	examination for employment
	就職難	シュウショクナン	job shortage
	就職率	シュウショクリツ	rate of employment
	就労	シュウロウ	starting work; being employed —***vi***. get to work; start working; be employed

3 尸 しかばね corpse; flag

521
尺 ④

音	尺	シャク	*shaku* (unit of measurement, approx. 30.3 cm)
熟	尺度	シャクド	measure; standard; criterion
	尺八	シャクハチ	*shakuhachi* (bamboo flute)
	尺貫法	シャッカンホウ	the *shaku-kan* system of weights and measures

522
尼 ⑤

音	尼	ニ	nun
熟	尼僧	ニソウ	nun; sister; priestess
訓	尼	あま	nun; sister
	尼寺	あまでら	nunnery; convent

523
尽 ⑥

音	尽	ジン	serve; run out
熟	尽力	ジンリョク	exertion; effort; endeavor —***vi***. exert; make an effort/endeavor
訓	尽かす	つかす	***vt***. run out of; use up
	尽きる	つきる	***vi***. run out; be spent/exhausted
	尽くす	つくす	***vt***. make an effort; exhaust; try hard

524
局 ⑦

音	局	キョク	part; bureau; chamber
熟	局所	キョクショ	local; part of the body (normally sexual organs)
	局地	キョクチ	locality
	局部	キョクブ	limited part; section
	局面	キョクメン	position; situation; phase

525

尿 ⑦

音	尿	ニョウ	urine
熟	尿意	ニョウイ	desire to pass water
	尿道	ニョウドウ	***med***. urethra

526

尾 ⑦

音	尾	ビ	tail
熟	尾行	ビコウ	follow —***vi***. follow; shadow; tail
	尾骨	ビコツ	***med***. coccyx
	尾灯	ビトウ	taillight
	尾翼	ビヨク	tail (of a plane)
	尾篭	ビロウ	indecent; indelicate
訓	尾	お	tail
	尾根	おね	mountain ridge

527

居 ⑧

音	居	キョ	be; live; sit
熟	居住	キョジュウ	residence; abode; dwelling —***vi***. reside; dwell
	居所	キョショ	one's abode; one's place of residence
	居留地	キョリュウチ	settlement; concession
訓	居心地	いごこチ	comfortable; at ease; cosy; smug
	居酒屋	いざかや	tavern; bar
	居間	いま	living room
	居る	いる	***vi***. be; exist; live; sit
	居留守	いルス	pretend to be out

528

屈 ⑧

音	屈	クツ	stoop; bow; lean over; be broken/crushed/sprained

熟	屈する	クッする	*v*. bend; yield; submit; give in
	屈強	クッキョウ	strong; sturdy; stalwart
	屈曲	クッキョク	bend; flex —*vi*. bend; curve; turn
	屈指	クッシ	leading; foremost; prominent
	屈辱	クツジョク	humiliation; indignity
	屈伸	クッシン	expansion and contraction; bending and stretching —*vi*. expand and contract; bend and stretch
	屈折	クッセツ	bend; turn —*vi*. bend; curve; turn
	屈服	クップク	submission; surrender —*vi*. submit; surrender

529

届 ⑧

音	届	（カイ）	send; report
訓	届く	とどく	*vi*. reach; attain
	届ける	とどける	*vt*. report; notify; send; forward
	届け	とどけ	report; notice; forwarding; delivery
	届け出で	とどけいで	notification; entry
	届け先	とどけさき	destination; receiver's address; consignee
	届け出る	とどけでる	*vt*. submit/give notice

530

屋 ⑨

音	屋	オク	house; roof
熟	屋外	オクガイ	the outdoors/open air
	屋上	オクジョウ	rooftop; roof
	屋内	オクナイ	indoors
訓	屋	や	house; roof; store name; seller
	屋号	やゴウ	store name
	屋敷	やしき	mansion; residence
	屋台	やタイ	pushcart/mobile stall
	屋根	やね	roof

531

展 ⑩

音	展	テン	display; spread

熟	展開	テンカイ	unfolding; development; evolution; discovery; deployment —*v*. unfold; develop; evolve; deploy
	展示	テンジ	display; exhibition —*v*. exhibit; display; have on view
	展望	テンボウ	view; prospect; outlook; review —*v*. have a view of; look over; survey; review; pass
	展望鏡	テンボウキョウ	telescope
	展望台	テンボウダイ	observatory; observation post
	展覧	テンラン	exhibition; show —*v*. exhibit; display; show
	展覧会	テンランカイ	exhibition; exhibit; show

532

属 ⑫

音	属	ショク	
		ゾク	belong to; be attached to; genus
熟	属目	ショクモク	attention; observation
	属性	ゾクセイ	attribute
	属地	ゾクチ	territory; possession
	属領	ゾクリョウ	territory; possession; dependency
	属国	ゾッコク	dependency; vassal state

533

層 ⑭

音	層	ソウ	layer; class; stratum
熟	層雲	ソウウン	stratus

534

履 ⑮

音	履	リ	footwear; do
熟	履行	リコウ	implementation; execution —*v*. perform; fulfill; implement; carry out
	履歴	リレキ	personal history; background; career
	履歴書	リレキショ	one's personal/life history; résumé
訓	履く	はく	put on (footwear, socks, trousers, a skirt)
	履物	はきもの	footwear

3 山 やま mountain

535

山 ③ 丨 山 山

音	山	サン	mountain
熟	山河	サンガ	mountains and rivers
	山岳	サンガク	mountains
	山間	サンカン	in the mountains
	山菜	サンサイ	edible wild plants
	山水画	サンスイガ	landscape (painting)
	山積	サンセキ	pile; accumulation —*vi*. pile up; accumulate
	山荘	サンソウ	mountain cottage/villa
	山村	サンソン	mountain village
	山頂	サンチョウ	mountaintop; summit; peak
	山腹	サンプク	hillside; mountainside
	山脈	サンミャク	mountain range
	山門	サンモン	temple gate; main gate of a Buddhist temple
	山野	サンヤ	hills and fields; countryside
	山林	サンリン	forest in the mountains; mountains and forest
	山麓	サンロク	foot of a mountain
訓	山	やま	mountain; hill; mine; heap; pile; climax; peak; crisis (of an illness)
	山男	やまおとこ	woodsman; mountain laborer
	山崩れ	やまくずれ	landslide
	山小屋	やまごや	mountain hut/lodge
	山里	やまざと	mountain hamlet/village
	山師	やまシ	prospecter; miner; speculator; imposter; swindler
	山津波	やまつなみ	landslide
	山積み	やまづみ	heap; huge amount
	山の手	やまのて	uptown; residential
	山登り	やまのぼり	mountain-climbing —*vi*. climb mountains

536

⑦ 丨 山 山 山一 山十 峙 岐

音	岐	キ	branch; fork
熟	岐路	キロ	forked road

537

 ⑧

音	岳	ガク	high mountain
熟	岳父	ガクフ	one's wife's father/father-in-law
訓	岳	たけ	mountain peak

538

岩 ⑧

音	岩	ガン	rock
熟	岩塩	ガンエン	rock salt
	岩窟	ガンクツ	cavern; cave; grotto
	岩礁	ガンショウ	reef; rocks covered by the water
	岩石	ガンセキ	rock; crag; stones and rocks
	岩頭	ガントウ	top of a rock; rock head
	岩壁	ガンペキ	rock wall/face
訓	岩	いわ	rock; crag; reef
	岩陰	いわかげ	shade of a rock

539

岸 ⑧

音	岸	ガン	shore
熟	岸壁	ガンペキ	quay; rock; sea wall
訓	岸	きし	seashore; cliff

540

岬 ⑧

音	岬	(コウ)	cape
訓	岬	みさき	cape; point; headland; promontory

541

峡 ⑨

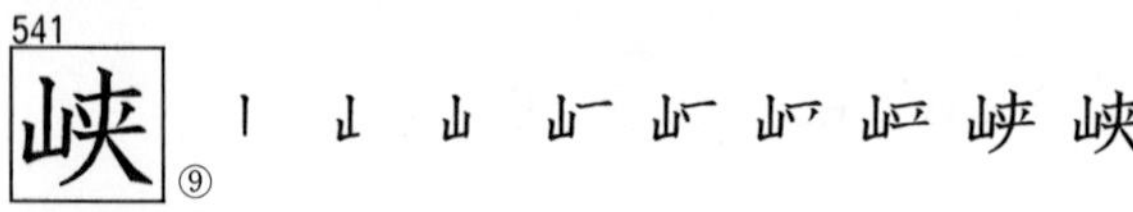

音	峡	キョウ	ravine; gorge; narrow valley
熟	峡谷	キョウコク	gorge; ravine; glen
	峡路	キョウロ	defile; narrow (pass)

542

峠 ⑨

訓	峠	とうげ	ridge; pass; crisis

543

島 ⑩

音	島	トウ	island
熟	島民	トウミン	islanders; natives of an island
訓	島	しま	island
	島国	しまぐに	island nation
	島国根性	しまぐに コンジョウ	insular spirit; insularism
	島流し	しまながし	exile; banishment

544

峰 ⑩

音	峰	ホウ	peak; summit; back (of a sword)
訓	峰	みね	peak; summit; back (of a sword)
	峰打ち	みねうち	***vt.*** strike (a person) with the back of one's sword

545

崎 ⑪

訓	崎	さき	cape; headland

546
崇 ⑪

丶 ⺌ 山 屮 屵 岀 岂 岜 崇 崇 崇

音	崇	**スウ**	noble; worship
熟	崇敬	**スウケイ**	reverence; veneration —*v.* venerate; revere; pay respect; hold in esteem
	崇高	**スウコウ**	sublime; lofty; grand; noble
	崇拝	**スウハイ**	worship; adoration; admiration; cult —*v.* worship; venerate; adore; admire; idolize
	崇拝者	**スウハイシャ**	worshipper; admirer
訓	※崇める	**あがめる**	***vt.*** worship; revere; venerate

547
崩 ⑪

丶 ⺌ 山 屵 岃 岉 岉 峅 崩 崩 崩

音	崩	**ホウ**	crumble; fall to pieces; collapse
熟	崩じる	**ホウじる**	***vi.*** die; pass away (use of the emperor)
	崩壊	**ホウカイ**	collapse; disintegration —***vi.*** collapse; disintergrate
	崩御	**ホウギョ**	demise/death of the emperor —***vi.*** (the emperor) passes away
訓	崩す	**くずす**	***vt.*** demolish; change/break (a large bill); simplify (the way of writing a *kanji*)
	崩れる	**くずれる**	***vi.*** crumble; fall to pieces; collapse; break

3 川 かわ river

548
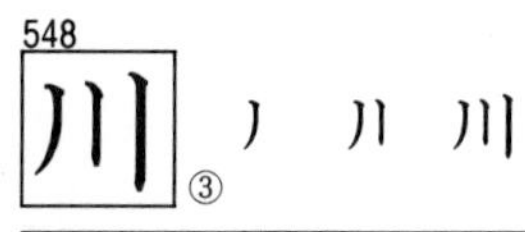

音	川	**セン**	river
熟	川柳	**センリュウ**	*senryū* (satirical haiku)
訓	川	**かわ**	river
	川上	**かわかみ**	upper stream
	川下	**かわしも**	lower stream
	川瀬	**かわせ**	shallows; rapids
	川床	**かわどこ**	riverbed

川面	かわも	surface of a river
※川原	かわら	dry riverbed

549

州 ⑥ 丶 丿 丬 川 州 州

音	州	シュウ	province; state; continent
訓	州	す	sand bank

3 工 え *e* (katakana)

550

工 ③ 一 丅 工

音	工	コウ (ク)	artisan; work; craft; construction
熟	工夫	クフウ	device; idea
	工面	クメン	contrivance; management —*v.* contrive; manage
	工員	コウイン	factory worker
	工学	コウガク	engineering
	工業	コウギョウ	industry; manufacturing
	工具	コウグ	tool; implement
	工芸	コウゲイ	industrial arts
	工作	コウサク	handicraft; handiwork; construction —*v.* make; construct
	工事	コウジ	construction work
	工場	コウジョウ (コウば)	factory
	工賃	コウチン	pay; wages
	工程	コウテイ	process
¥	工業化	コウギョウカ	industrialization —*v.* industrialize
	工費	コウヒ	construction costs

551

巧 ⑤ 一 丅 工 工 巧

音	巧	コウ	skill

熟	巧者	コウシャ	clever; skillful; dexterous
	巧妙	コウミョウ	skill; dexterity; ingenuity
訓	巧み	たくみ	skill; dexterity; cunning

552

左 ⑤

一 ナ 𠂇 𠂇 左

音	左	サ	left
熟	左官	サカン	plasterer
	左記	サキ	the following; the above
	左折	サセツ	left turn —***vi***. make a left turn; turn to the left
	左折禁止	サセツキンシ	No Left Turn (road marking)
	左遷	サセン	relegation; demotion —***v***. relegate; demote
	左派	サハ	left-wing party; the left
	左右	サユウ	right and left; both ways; opposite directions —***v***. control; influence
	左翼	サヨク	the left wing; leftist
訓	左	ひだり	left
	左手	ひだりて	left hand
	左前	ひだりまえ	wrong way; adversity; downward course

553

差 ⑩

丶 丷 䒑 𢆉 𦍌 羊 差 差 差 差

音	差	サ	point; indicate; difference; distinguish
熟	差異(差違)	サイ	difference
	差額	サガク	balance; margin; difference
	差別	サベツ	discrimination; prejudice —***v***. discriminate (against)
	差別待遇	サベツタイグウ	discrimination among people; treating people differently
	差別用語	サベツヨウゴ	discriminatory language; derogatory term
訓	差す	さす	***v***. pour; fill; add; apply; offer; point at -***vi***. shine
	差し上げる	さしあげる	***vi***. give; present; offer
	差し入れる	さしいれる	***vt***. insert; put into
	差し押さえる	さしおさえる	***vt***. seize; attach; distrain
	差し金	さしがね	instigation; suggestion
	差し込む	さしこむ	insert; plug in

	差出人	さしだしニン	sender
	差し支える	さしつかえる	***vi***. interfere
	差止め	さしどめ	prohibition; ban; suspension
	差し引く	さしひく	***vt***. deduct
	差向い	さしむかい	face to face
	差し戻し	さしもどし	returning; sending back; referring (a case) back (to the original court)
¥	差益	サエキ	profit margin
	差額税	サガクゼイ	differential tarriff
	差金決済	サキンケッサイ	making up differences
	差損	サソン	loss from the difference of quotations
	差別関税	サベツカンゼイ	selective taxes

3 己 おのれ self; snake

554

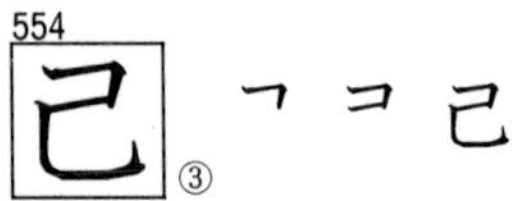

③

音	己	キ	myself
		コ	self
訓	己	おのれ	oneself ***col***. you bastard (term of abuse)

555

巻 ⑨ 丶 丷 䒑 兰 龹 关 券 巻 巻

音	巻	カン	volume; scroll
熟	巻頭	カントウ	beginning of a book
	巻末	カンマツ	end of a book
訓	巻き	まき	roll; volume; tome; book
	巻き貝	まきがい	snail; conch
	巻き尺	まきジャク	tape measure
	巻き添え	まきぞえ	involvement; entanglement; embroilment
	巻物	まきもの	scroll
	巻く	まく	***v***. roll; coil

3 巾 はば／はばへん width; cloth

556
市 ⑤
丶 亠 亣 冂 市

音	市	シ	market; city; municipality; urban; municipal
熟	市営	シエイ	municipal management
	市街	シガイ	the streets; the city
	市外	シガイ	outskirts of a town; out of town
	市議会	シギカイ	city assembly/council
	市制	シセイ	municipal organization
	市政	シセイ	municipal government/administration
	市長	シチョウ	mayor
	市民	シミン	citizen
	市民権	シミンケン	citizenship
	市役所	シヤクショ	city hall; municipal office
	市立	シリツ (いちリツ)	municipal
訓	市	いち	market; fair
	市場	いちば	market
	市松模様	いちまつモヨウ	checked pattern
¥	市価	シカ	market price
	市況	シキョウ	market condition
	市場	シジョウ	market; exchange; marketplace
	市場価格	シジョウカカク	market price/value
	市場性	シジョウセイ	marketability
	市場占有率	シジョウセンユウリツ	market share
	市場相場	シジョウソウば	market prices
	市場調査	シジョウチョウサ	market survey/research —*v.* carry out market research
	市販	シハン	marketing; offering for sale —*v.* market; put on the market

557
布 ⑤
ノ ナ 才 右 布

音	布	フ	cloth; spread
熟	布教	フキョウ	propagation of religion; missionary work —*v.* propagate religion

	布巾	フキン	dishcloth
	布告	フコク	declaration; proclamation; notification —*v*. declare; proclaim; announce; decree
	布陣	フジン	the line-up/lines —*vi*. take up one's position (for a battle, contest, etc.)
	布施	フセ	offering; alms; charity
	布石	フセキ	initial stage in a go match; arrangements; preparations
	布団	フトン	futon; quilt; mattress
訓	布	ぬの	cloth; material
	布地	ぬのジ	cloth; material

558

帆 ⑥

丨 口 巾 巾丿 帆 帆

音	帆	ハン	sail
熟	帆船	ハンセン	sailing ship
	帆走	ハンソウ	sailing —*vi*. sail; go by ship
訓	帆	ほ	sail
	帆柱	ほばしら	mast

559

希 ⑦

丿 乄 㐅 产 肴 肴 希

音	希	キ	rare; wish
熟	希少	キショウ	scarce; rare
	希少価値	キショウカチ	scarcity value
	希代	キダイ	rarity; uniqueness
	希薄	キハク	thinness; rarefaction
	希望	キボウ	hope; wish; desire; ambition —*v*. hope; wish; desire; aspire to
	※希有	ケウ	rarity; unusual; uncommon
訓	※希	まれ	rare; uncommon; unusual

560

帥 ⑨

丿 亻 𠂤 𠂤 自 自 帥 帥 帥

音	帥	スイ	command; leader

561
帝 ⑨

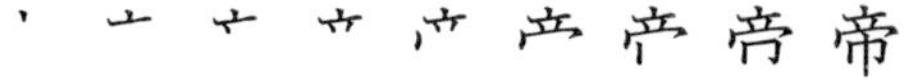

音	帝	テイ	emperor
熟	帝王	テイオウ	sovereign; monarch; emperor
	帝国	テイコク	empire
	帝政	テイセイ	imperial government/rule; imperialism
	帝都	テイト	imperial capital/metropolis
訓	※帝	みかど	emperor

562
帰 ⑩

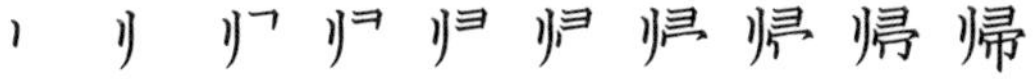

音	帰	キ	return
熟	帰依	キエ	***Bud***. becoming a believer —***vi***. become a believer
	帰化	キカ	naturalization —***vi***. become naturalized
	帰還	キカン	return; repatriation —***vi***. return; be repatriated
	帰京	キキョウ	returning to Tokyo —***vi***. return to Tokyo
	帰郷	キキョウ	going home; returning to one's home town —***vi***. return to one's home town
	帰結	キケツ	conclusion; end; result; consequence —***vi***. be concluded; end
	帰国	キコク	return to one's country —***vi***. return/come back to one's country; go/come home
	帰省	キセイ	coming home; homecoming —***vi***. go/come/return home; visit one's native place
	帰着	キチャク	return; coming back; conclusion —***vi***. return; come back; conclude; bring to a conclusion
	帰途	キト	on one's way back
	帰路	キロ	homeward journey
訓	帰す	かえす	***vt***. dismiss; release
	帰る	かえる	***vi***. return; go home; leave

563
師 ⑩

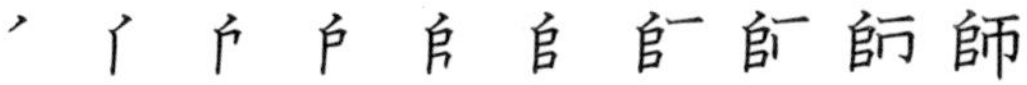

音	師	シ	army; teacher; missionary
熟	師事	シジ	studying under a person —***vi***. study under a person; become a person's student

	師匠	シショウ	teacher; master
	師団	シダン	division of soldiers
	師弟	シテイ	master and pupil; teacher and student
	師範	シハン	instructor
訓	※師走	しわす（しはす）	the twelfth month of the lunar calendar; December

564

席 ⑩

音	席	セキ	seat; place
熟	席次	セキジ	ranking; precedance; seating order
	席上	セキジョウ	at the meeting; on the occasion
	席巻	セッケン	sweeping; conquest

565

帯 ⑩

音	帯	タイ	belt; band; wear; zone
熟	帯出	タイシュツ	borrowing —*v*. carry out; take out; borrow
訓	帯	おび	*obi* (sash used to tie around a kimono); belt; sash; girdle
	帯状	おびジョウ	long, narrow strip
	帯封	おびフウ	wrapper around a posted newspaper, magazine, etc.
	帯びる	おびる	***vt***. wear; put on; bear; carry; be entrusted/vested with

566

常 ⑪

音	常	ジョウ	ordinary; common; normal
熟	常温	ジョウオン	normal/room/average/uniform temperature
	常軌	ジョウキ	normal/proper/common course
	常客	ジョウキャク	regular customers; a regular
	常勤	ジョウキン	full-time/regular employment —***vi***. be in full-time/regular employment
	常時	ジョウジ	always; habitually
	常識	ジョウシキ	common sense/decency/practice; reasonable; sensible

	常習	ジョウシュウ	bad habit —*v.* be in the habit of
	常習者	ジョウシュウシャ	addict
	常習犯	ジョウシュウハン	habitual offender; confirmed criminal
	常食	ジョウショク	diet; staple food —*v.* eat everyday; live on a diet of
	常人	ジョウジン	ordinary man
	常数	ジョウスウ	***math.*** constant
	常設	ジョウセツ	permanent; standing —*v.* establish permanently
	常態	ジョウタイ	normal condition
	常道	ジョウドウ	regular/usual way; proper behavior/conduct
	常任	ジョウニン	permanent; regular; standing
	常備	ジョウビ	standing; reserve —*v.* have always ready; be provided with
	常用	ジョウヨウ	common/everyday use —*v.* use commonly/regularly; have everyday use of
	常用漢字	ジョウヨウカンジ	*jōyō kanji* (the 1,945 Chinese characters in common use)
	常緑樹	ジョウリョクジュ	evergreen tree
	常連	ジョウレン	regular customer; frequenters
訓	常	つね	common; everyday; ordinary; normal; always; constantly
	常々	つねづね	always; at all times
	常	とこ	(prefix) everlasting; permanent
	常夏	とこなつ	everlasting/permanent summer
¥	常任理事国	ジョウニン リジコク	permanent member (of the U.N. Security Council)

567

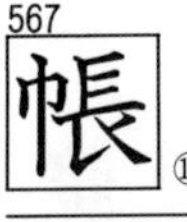

⑪

音	帳	チョウ	curtain; book; register; album
熟	帳尻	チョウジリ	balance of accounts
	帳場	チョウば	counter; counting house; office; front desk
	帳簿	チョウボ	account book; ledger; register
	帳面	チョウメン	notebook; register; account book
訓	※帳	とばり	curtain; hangings

568

幅 ⑫

音	幅	フク	width; (counter for hanging scrolls)

熟	幅員	フクイン	width; breadth; extent
訓	幅	はば	width; breadth; range; influence
	幅跳び	はばとび	long jump
	幅広い	はばひろい	broad; extensive

569
帽 ⑫

音	帽	ボウ	hat; cap
熟	帽子	ボウシ	hat
	帽章	ボウショウ	badge on a cap

570
幕 ⑬

音	幕	バク	Japanese feudal government
		マク	curtain; act
熟	幕府	バクフ	shogunate; military government
	幕末	バクマツ	***hist.*** last years of the Tokugawa shogunate
	幕僚	バクリョウ	staff of an important project; staff officers
	幕内	マクうち	senior-grade sumo wrestler
	幕切れ	マクぎれ	end
	幕下	マクした	junior-grade sumo wrestler

571
幣 ⑮

音	幣	ヘイ	offering to the gods/emperor/guest; money; currency
熟	幣制	ヘイセイ	monetary system
	幣束	ヘイソク	Shinto offerings of cloth, rope, or cut paper
	幣帛	ヘイハク	Shinto offerings of cloth, rope, or cut paper
	幣物	ヘイモツ (ヘイブツ)	Shinto offerings of cloth, rope, or cut paper; offering; gift
訓	※幣	ぬさ	Shinto offerings of cloth, rope, or cut paper

3 口 囗 土 士 夂 夕 大 女 子 宀 寸 小 ⺌ ⺍ 尢 尸 山 川 工 己 巾 干● 幺 广 廴 廾 弋 弓 彐 彡 彳 ⺾ 辶 阝 阝 ⺍ 忄 扌 犭 氵

572

干 ③

一 二 干

音	干	カン	dry; concern; perpetrate; ebb
熟	干害	カンガイ	drought disaster/damage
	干渉	カンショウ	interference; meddling; intervention —*v*. interfere; meddle; intervene
	干拓	カンタク	land reclamation by drainage —*v*. reclaim land by drainage; drain off
	干潮	カンチョウ	ebb/low tide
	干満	カンマン	ebb and flow; tide
訓	干潟	ひがた	dry beach
	干物	ひもの	dried fish
	干る	ひる	***vi***. dry; parch; recede; fall; ebb
	干す	ほす	***vt***. dry; drain; drink up

573

平 ⑤

一 ㇐ ㇇ 㐅 平

音	平	ヘイ	flat; level; even; calm; ordinary; common; peaceful
		ビョウ	
熟	平等	ビョウドウ	equality; impartiality
	平安	ヘイアン	peace; safety and security ***hist***. Heian period/court (794-1185)
	平易	ヘイイ	easy; simple; straightforward
	平温	ヘイオン	usual temperature
	平穏	ヘイオン	calm; peaceful
	平気	ヘイキ	calm; unconcerned; nonchalant
	平均	ヘイキン	average; mean
	平原	ヘイゲン	plain; prairie
	平行	ヘイコウ	parallel —***vi***. be parallel
	平行線	ヘイコウセン	parallel line
	平日	ヘイジツ	weekdays; every day apart from Sundays and National Holidays
	平常	ヘイジョウ	usual; common; everyday
	平身低頭	ヘイシンテイトウ	bowing; prostration —***vi***. bow to the ground; prostrate oneself

	平静	ヘイセイ	tranquillity; calmness; peacefulness
	平生	ヘイゼイ	usual; everyday; ordinary
	平然	ヘイゼン	calmness; nonchalance
	平素	ヘイソ	usual; commonplace; ordinary
	平坦	ヘイタン	even surface; flat; regular
	平地	ヘイチ	level/flat land; even surface
	平熱	ヘイねつ	normal body temperature
	平年	ヘイネン	normal year; not a leap year
	平服	ヘイフク	plain/everyday clothes
	平方	ヘイホウ	***math***. square of a number; square (meter, etc.) —***v***. square a number
	平方根	ヘイホウコン	***math***. square root
	平凡	ヘイボン	common; ordinary; mediocre
	平民	ヘイミン	common people
	平野	ヘイヤ	plain; open field
	平和	ヘイワ	peace
訓	平ら	たいら	flat; level
	平	ひら	common; ordinary; average
	平謝り	ひらあやまり	humble apology
	平泳ぎ	ひらおよぎ	breast stroke
	平仮名	ひらがな	*hiragana* (the cursive syllabary)
	平たい	ひらたい	flat; level
	平屋	ひらや	one-story house

574

⑥

音	年	ネン	year; age
熟	年賀	ネンガ	New Year's greetings
	年賀状	ネンガジョウ	New Year's greeting card
	年月日	ネンガッぴ	date; year, month, and date
	年刊	ネンカン	yearly publication; annual
	年間	ネンカン	period of a year
	年鑑	ネンカン	yearbook
	年忌	ネンキ	anniversary service for a dead person
	年季	ネンキ	apprenticeship; experience; training
	年期	ネンキ	period of years; length of time (in years)
	年貢	ネング	land tax; ground rent
	年月	ネンゲツ	a long period of time
	年限	ネンゲン	period of years; length of time (in years)
	年功	ネンコウ	long experience/service

	年号	ネンゴウ	name of an era
	年始	ネンシ	beginning of the year
	年次	ネンジ	annual; yearly
	年収	ネンシュウ	yearly income; annual salary
	年中	ネンジュウ	whole year; always; perpetually
	年中行事	ネンチュウギョウジ	annual functions; regular events
	年少	ネンショウ	youth
	年代	ネンダイ	era; age; epoch; period
	年長	ネンチョウ	seniority
	年度	ネンド	year; term; fiscal/financial year
	年頭	ネントウ	beginning of the year
	年内	ネンナイ	within the year; before the year is out
	年輩	ネンパイ	elderly age; age; years
	年表	ネンピョウ	chronological table
	年譜	ネンプ	chronological record; chronology
	年別	ネンベツ	annual variation; classification by year
	年俸	ネンポウ	annual salary; yearly stipend
	年報	ネンポウ	annual report
	年末	ネンマツ	year-end; end of the year
	年齢	ネンレイ	age; years
訓	年	とし	year; age; years
	年上	としうえ	older
	年子	としご	children born in consecutive years
	年下	としした	younger
¥	年額	ネンガク	annual sum; yearly amount
	年給	ネンキュウ	annual salary
	年金	ネンキン	pension; annuity
	年産	ネンサン	yearly output; annual production
	年度	ネンド	fiscal year
	年利	ネンリ	annual interest

575

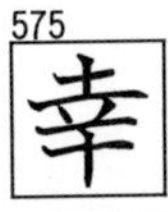
⑧ 一 十 土 キ 圭 幸 幸 幸

音	幸	コウ	happiness; good luck; felicity
熟	幸運	コウウン	good fortune/luck; happiness
	幸福	コウフク	happiness; felicity; well-being; bliss
訓	幸い	さいわい	happiness; felicity; bliss; good luck/fortune
	幸	さち	happiness; fortune; luck

	幸せ	しあわせ	happiness; felicity; bliss

576 **幹** ⑬

音	幹	カン	tree trunk; body; ability
熟	幹事	カンジ	manager; secretary; person in charge of a party
	幹線	カンセン	trunk/main line
訓	幹	みき	tree trunk; important part
¥	幹事長	カンジチョウ	chief secretary; secretary-general
	幹部	カンブ	leading members; managing staff; executives; party organizers

3 幺 いとがしら short thread

577 **幻** ⑤

音	幻	ゲン	phantom; illusion; fantasy
熟	幻影	ゲンエイ	illusion; vision; dream
	幻覚	ゲンカク	hallucination
	幻想	ゲンソウ	fantasy; illusion; dream —*v.* fantasize; hallucinate; dream
	幻想的	ゲンソウテキ	fantastic; illusory; dreamy
	幻灯	ゲントウ	slide
	幻滅	ゲンメツ	disillusionment —*vi.* be disillusioned
	幻惑	ゲンワク	dazzling; bewitching —*v.* dazzle; bewitch
訓	幻	まぼろし	phantom; illusion; hallucination

578 **幼** ⑤

音	幼	ヨウ	infant; small child
熟	幼魚	ヨウギョ	young fish
	幼児	ヨウジ	infant; toddler; baby
	幼時	ヨウジ	childhood; infancy
	幼少	ヨウショウ	childhood; infancy

	幼稚	ヨウチ	childish; infantile; puerile
	幼稚園	ヨウチエン	kindergarten
	幼虫	ヨウチュウ	larva
	幼年	ヨウネン	childhood; infancy; child
	幼名	ヨウメイ	one's infant name
訓	幼い	おさない	young; infantile; childish
	幼な顔	おさながお	how one looked as a baby
	幼子	おさなご	little child; baby
	幼心	おさなごころ	child's mind/heart
	※幼ない	いとけない	young; infant

579

⑨

音	幽	ユウ	confine to a room; faint; dim; weak; indistinct
熟	幽界	ユウカイ	Hades; realm of the dead
	幽玄	ユウゲン	mystery; the occult
	幽谷	ユウコク	deep valley; ravine; glen
	幽閉	ユウヘイ	confinement; house arrest; imprisonment —*v.* confine; shut up
	幽霊	ユウレイ	ghost; apparition; spirit
訓	※幽かな	かすかな	faint; dim; weak; indistinct; hazy; poor; wretched

580

幾 ⑫

音	幾	キ	nearly; almost
熟	幾何学	キカガク	geometry
訓	幾	いく	how much/many
	幾重	いくえ	how many folds/ply; repeatedly; earnestly
	幾多	いくタ	many
	幾つ	いくつ	how much/many
	幾日	いくニチ	how many days

3 广 まだれ dotted cliff

581

広 ⑤ 丶 亠 广 広 広

音	広	コウ	wide; broad; spacious; spread
熟	広義	コウギ	broad sense
	広言	コウゲン	big talk; brag; boast; boasting —***vi***. talk big; brag; boast
	広原	コウゲン	vast plain; open country
	広告	コウコク	advertisement; notice; announcement —***v***. advertise; announce; give publicity to
	広大	コウダイ	vast; extensive; immense; huge
	広報	コウホウ	public information; publicity; public relations
訓	広い	ひろい	wide; broad; spacious; large
	広場	ひろば	open space; square; plaza
	広々	ひろびろ	wide; open; vast
	広間	ひろま	hall; saloon
	広がる	ひろがる	***vi***. spread out; expand; extend; stretch
	広げる	ひろげる	***vt***. extend; expand; enlarge; widen; unfold; open; lay out
	広さ	ひろさ	area; extent; dimensions
	広まる	ひろまる	***vi***. spread; be diffused/propagated
	広める	ひろめる	***vt***. extend; widen; broaden; spread; diffuse; propagate

582

庁 ⑤ 丶 亠 广 庁 庁

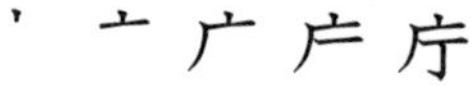

音	庁	チョウ	agency; office; board
熟	庁舎	チョウシャ	government building

583

序 ⑦ 丶 亠 广 序 序 序 序

音	序	ジョ	introduction
熟	序曲	ジョキョク	overture
	序文	ジョブン	preface; foreword; introduction

	序幕	ジョマク	opening/first act
	序列	ジョレツ	order; rank; ranking
	序論	ジョロン	introduction

584
床 ⑦

丶 亠 广 户 庁 庄 床

音	床	ショウ	bed; seat; the ground
訓	床	とこ	bed
	床の間	とこのま	*tokonoma* (alcove in a traditional Japanese home)
	床屋	とこや	barbershop; barber
	床	ゆか	floor
	床板	ゆかいた	floorboard
	床上	ゆかうえ	above the floor
	床下	ゆかした	under the floor

585
底 ⑧

丶 亠 广 户 庀 庀 底 底

音	底	テイ	bottom; base; kind; sort
熟	底止	テイシ	cessation —*v*. cease; stop; end
	底辺	テイヘン	***math***. base (of a triangle) ***fig***. bottom/lower levels (of society)
	底本	テイホン	original text; source book
	底流	テイリュウ	undercurrent; underflow
訓	底	そこ	base; bottom; lower part
	底力	そこぢから	latent energy; hidden power
¥	底値	そこね	rock-bottom/bedrock price

586
店 ⑧

丶 亠 广 广 庁 庁 店 店

音	店	テン	shop
熟	店員	テンイン	clerk; shop assistant; salesman; saleswoman
	店主	テンシュ	shopkeeper; storekeeper; store owner
	店頭	テントウ	shop front; counter; shop; store
	店屋物	テンやもの	dishes from a caterer; dishes prepared at a store

訓	店	みせ	stall; shop; office; place of business
	店先	みせさき	storefront
	店仕舞い	みせジまい	closing down of a business —*v*. close down a business
	店番	みせバン	tending a store; store tender; salesman
	店開き	みせびらき	opening of business —*v*. open business
	※店	たな	shop; store; house to let
¥	店頭株	テントウかぶ	over-the-counter stock; counter share
	店頭販売	テントウハンバイ	over-the-counter transaction
	店舗	テンポ	store; shop; outlet
	※店卸し	たなおろし	stocktaking; inventory; faultfinding; disparagement —*v*. take stock; take an inventory
	※店晒し	たなざらし	shop-soiled goods

587

府 ⑧

丶 亠 广 广 庁 庁 府 府

音	府	フ	capital; prefecture (used only for Osaka and Kyoto)
熟	府庁	フチョウ	prefectural office
	府立	フリツ	prefectural

588

度 ⑨

丶 亠 广 广 庐 庐 庐 庹 度

音	度	ド (タク) (ト)	degree; frequency; extent; measure; time
熟	度合い	ドあい	degree; extent; rate
	度外視	ドガイシ	neglect; disregard —*v*. neglect; disregard; overlook; ignore
	度胸	ドキョウ	courage; pluck; mettle; guts; nerve
	度数	ドスウ	number of times; frequency; incidence; degree
	度量	ドリョウ	generosity; liberality; magnamity; length and volume
	度量衡	ドリョウコウ	weights and measures
訓	度	たび	time; occasion; every time
	度重なる	たびかさなる	***vi***. be repeated/repetitive
	度々	たびたび	often; repeatedly; over and over

589
庫 ⑩

音	庫	コ （ク）	warehouse; store
訓	※庫	くら	warehouse; store; emporium

590

座 ⑩

音	座	ザ	sitting; gathering; theater
熟	座興	ザキョウ	joke; entertainment; fun
	座高	ザコウ	one's height when sitting
	座敷	ザシキ	Japanese-style room; guest room
	座礁	ザショウ	running aground; stranding —***vi***. run aground; be stranded
	座席	ザセキ	seat
	座禅	ザゼン	*zazen* (Zen meditation)
	座像	ザゾウ	seated statue; seated figure
	座談	ザダン	conversation; discussion —***vi***. converse; discuss
	座長	ザチョウ	chairman; chairperson
	座蒲団	ザブトン	cushion
	座右	ザユウ	at one's side; within arm's reach
訓	座る	すわる	***vi***. sit down; be seated

591

庭 ⑩

音	庭	テイ	garden
熟	庭園	テイエン	garden; park
	庭球	テイキュウ	tennis
訓	庭	にわ	garden
	庭石	にわいし	garden stone
	庭先	にわさき	in the garden
	庭師	にわシ	landscape gardener; garden designer

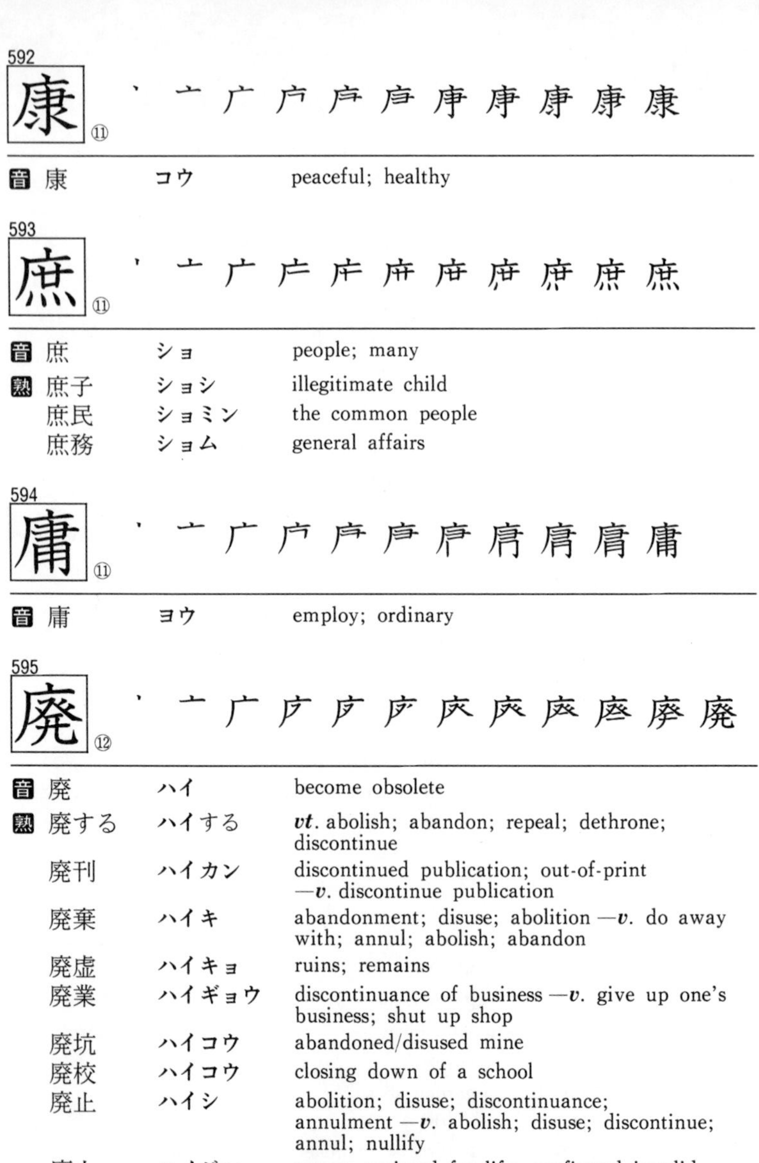

592

康 ⑪

音	康	コウ	peaceful; healthy

593

庶 ⑪

音	庶	ショ	people; many
熟	庶子	ショシ	illegitimate child
	庶民	ショミン	the common people
	庶務	ショム	general affairs

594

庸 ⑪

音	庸	ヨウ	employ; ordinary

595

廃 ⑫

音	廃	ハイ	become obsolete
熟	廃する	ハイする	***vt***. abolish; abandon; repeal; dethrone; discontinue
	廃刊	ハイカン	discontinued publication; out-of-print —***v***. discontinue publication
	廃棄	ハイキ	abandonment; disuse; abolition —***v***. do away with; annul; abolish; abandon
	廃虚	ハイキョ	ruins; remains
	廃業	ハイギョウ	discontinuance of business —***v***. give up one's business; shut up shop
	廃坑	ハイコウ	abandoned/disused mine
	廃校	ハイコウ	closing down of a school
	廃止	ハイシ	abolition; disuse; discontinuance; annulment —***v***. abolish; disuse; discontinue; annul; nullify
	廃人	ハイジン	person maimed for life; confirmed invalid
	廃絶	ハイゼツ	extinction —***v***. become extinct; be discontinued
	廃藩置県	ハイハンチケン	***hist***. abolition of clans and establishment of prefectures (Meiji period)

	廃品	ハイヒン	scrap; junk; waste
	廃品回収	ハイヒンカイシュウ	scrap collection
	廃物	ハイブツ	scrap; useless thing; waste; trash
訓	廃る	すたる	*vi.* go out of use; fall into disuse; become obsolete; die out
	廃れる	すたれる	*vi.* go out of use; fall into disuse; become obselete; die out

596

廊 ⑫ 丶 亠 广 广 庐 庐 庐 盾 盾 廊 廊 廊

音	廊	ロウ	corridor; hall
熟	廊下	ロウカ	corridor; hall

597

廉 ⑬ 丶 广 广 庐 产 庐 庐 庐 庐 廉 廉 廉 廉

音	廉	レン	purity; honest; low price
熟	廉価	レンカ	low price
	廉潔	レンケツ	honest; upright
	廉直	レンチョク	honesty; integrity
	廉売	レンバイ	bargain sale —*v.* sell cheaply

3 廴 えんにょう stretching

598

廷 ⑦ 一 二 千 壬 廷 廷 廷

音	廷	テイ	court
熟	廷臣	テイシン	court official; courtier
	廷吏	テイリ	sergeant

599

延 ⑧ 一 丆 下 正 正 延 延 延

音	延	エン	extend; lengthen; postpone

熟	延引	エンイン	delay; postponement; procrastination —*vi*. be delayed/postponed/put off
	延期	エンキ	delay; postponement; procrastination —*v*. delay; postpone; procrastinate; put off
	延焼	エンショウ	spread of a fire —*vi*. spread; catch fire
	延着	エンチャク	delayed/late arrival —*vi*. arrive late; be delayed
	延長	エンチョウ	extension; continuation —*v*. lengthen in time, scope, or range; extend; continue; prolong
訓	延ばす	のばす	*vt*. lengthen; stretch; extend; postpone; put off
	延びる	のびる	*vi*. lengthen; stretch; extend; be put off; be delayed
	延び	のび	postponement; putting off; stretching; growth; extension
	延び延び	のびのび	long delay
	延べる	のべる	*vt*. spread; extend; postpone; put off
	延べ	のべ	total; aggregate
¥	延滞	エンタイ	delay (in payment) —*vi*. be behind (with payments); be in arrears
	延べ払い	のべばらい	deferred payment

600

⑨

音	建	ケン (コン)	build
熟	建国	ケンコク	foundation of a state
	建設	ケンセツ	construction; building; establishment —*v*. construct; build; establish
	建造	ケンゾウ	building; construction —*v*. build; construct
	建造物	ケンゾウブツ	structure
	建築	ケンチク	building; construction; architecture —*v*. build; construct
	建築家	ケンチクカ	architecture
	建立	コンリュウ	erection/construction (of a shrine or a temple) —*v*. erect/construct (a shrine or temple)
訓	建つ	たつ	*vi*. be built/set up/erected
	建てる	たてる	*vt*. build; construct; erect
	建具	たてグ	door; sliding door; window frames; fittings; fixtures
	建具屋	たてグや	joiner
	建坪	たてつぼ	floor space
	建て前	たてまえ	*tatemae* (principle); roof-raising ceremony
	建物	たてもの	building
¥	建設省	ケンセツショウ	Ministry of Construction

建て玉　たてだま　commitment; outstanding loan
建て値　たてね　market price

3 廾 こまぬき twenty legs

601
弊 ⑮ 丶 丷 丷 尚 尚 尚 尚 敝 敝 敝 敝 弊

音	弊	ヘイ	abuse; evil; get old/shabby/tired (humble)
熟	弊害	ヘイガイ	evil; ill effects
	弊社	ヘイシャ	***hum***. our company; we
	弊習	ヘイシュウ	bad habit/manners
	弊村	ヘイソン	impoverished village; ***hum***. our village
	弊風	ヘイフウ	bad habit/manners

3 弋 しきたすき／しきがまえ ceremony

602
式 ⑥ 一 二 テ 王 式 式

音	式	シキ	ceremony; formula; system; equation; expression
熟	式辞	シキジ	address (at a ceremony)
	式場	シキジョウ	ceremonial hall
	式台	シキダイ	step in a Japanese entryway
	式典	シキテン	ceremony
	式服	シキフク	formal/ceremonial dress

603
弐 ⑥ 一 二 二 三 弐 弐

音	弐	ニ	two (used on official documents)
熟	弐万円	ニマンエン	twenty thousand yen

3 弓 ゆみ／ゆみへん bow

604
弓
ㇷ コ 弓 ③

音	弓	キュウ	bow; bow-shaped
熟	弓術	キュウジュツ	archery; bowmanship
	弓状	キュウジョウ	bow-shaped; arched
	弓道	キュウドウ	*kyūdō* (Japanese archery)
訓	弓	ゆみ	bow
	弓矢	ゆみや	bow and arrow

605
引
ㇷ コ 弓 引 ④

音	引	イン	pull; attract; guide; lead
熟	引火	インカ	ignition; combustion —***vi***. ignite; set fire to; combust
	引責	インセキ	assumption of responsibility —***vi***. assume responsibility
	引率	インソツ	leadership; command —***v***. lead; head; command
	引退	インタイ	retirement —***vi***. retire; withdraw from public life
	引用	インヨウ	quotation; citation —***v***. quote; cite
	引力	インリョク	gravitation
	引例	インレイ	quotation; citation
訓	引く	ひく	***vt***. pull; draw; reduce; retire; drag; lay on; refer to
	引き受ける	ひきうける	***vt***. accept an offer; assume; take over; guarantee
	引き換える	ひきかえる	***vt***. change; exchange; convert
	引き算	ひきザン	***math***. subtraction
	引き出し	ひきだし	drawer
	引き立てる	ひきたてる	***vt***. make (someone/something) stand out
	引き取る	ひきとる	***vt***. take over
	引き抜く	ひきぬく	***vt***. pull out
	引き分ける	ひきわける	***v***. draw; tie
	引け目	ひけめ	inferiority complex
	引っ越す	ひっこす	***vi***. move house

	引っ張る	ひっぱる	***vt***. pull
¥	引き合い	ひきあい	inquiry; deal
	引き上げ	ひきあげ	pulling up; raise; increase
	引当金	ひきあてキン	allowance; revenues
	引き受け	ひきうけ	underwriting
	引受会社	ひきうけガイシャ	accepting corporation; underwriter
	引け	ひけ	closing; close

606

弔 ④

音	弔	チョウ	mourn
熟	弔意	チョウイ	condolence; mourning; sympathy
	弔辞	チョウジ	memorial address
	弔電	チョウデン	condolatory telegram
	弔文	チョウブン	funeral address
	弔問	チョウモン	sympathy call —***v***. make a sympathy call
訓	弔い	とむらい	funeral; burial; mass for the dead; condolence
	弔う	とむらう	***vt***. mourn; condole; perform a Buddhist memorial service

607

弟 ⑦

音	弟	テイ (ダイ) (デ)	younger brother
熟	弟妹	テイマイ	younger brothers and sisters
	弟子	デシ	disciple
訓	弟	おとうと	younger brother

608

弦 ⑧

音	弦	ゲン	bowstring; string
熟	弦楽	ゲンガク	music of stringed instruments
	弦楽器	ゲンガッキ	stringed instrument
訓	弦	つる	string (on an instrument)

609

弧 ⑨

音	弧	コ	arc
熟	弧状	コジョウ	arch

610

弱 ⑩

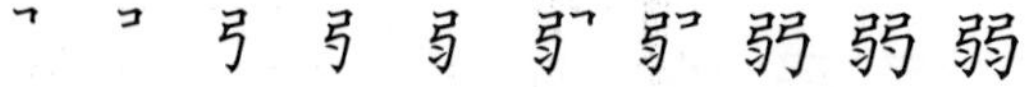

音	弱	ジャク	weak
熟	弱酸	ジャクサン	weak acid
	弱視	ジャクシ	weak sight; amblyopia
	弱小	ジャクショウ	small and weak; young
	弱震	ジャクシン	minor earthquake; tremor
	弱体	ジャクタイ	weak body/system
	弱点	ジャクテン	weakness; weak point; shortcoming; defect
	弱電機	ジャクデンキ	light electric appliance
	弱肉強食	ジャクニク キョウショク	survival of the fittest; law of the jungle
	弱年	ジャクネン	youth
	弱輩	ジャクハイ	young fellow; kid
	弱化	ジャッカ	weakening —*v.* weaken
	弱冠	ジャッカン	youth
訓	弱い	よわい	weak; frail; feeble; poor; bad
	弱気	よわキ	timid; fainthearted
	弱腰	よわごし	weak attitude
	弱音	よわね	complaint
	弱火	よわび	slow flame; low heat
	弱虫	よわむし	coward; weakling
	弱々しい	よわよわしい	feeble; faint; frail; delicate; fragile
	弱さ	よわさ	weakness; feebleness; frailty
	弱まる	よわまる	***vi***. get weak; abate; drop; calm down
	弱み	よわみ	weak position; vulnerability; weak point
	弱める	よわめる	***vt***. weaken; impair; decrease; turn down; lower; dilute
	弱る	よわる	***vi***. grow weak; weaken; be at a loss what to do; be in a fix
	弱り果てる	よわりはてる	***vi***. be weak with exhaustion; be annoyed; be fed up

611

強 ⑪

フ コ 弓 弓' 弓' 弘 弘 弘 弹 強 強

音	強	キョウ	strong; strengthen; force
		ゴウ	strong
熟	強化	キョウカ	strengthening; intensification; reinforcement —*v*. strengthen; solidify; build up; intensify
	強健	キョウケン	robust health; strong constitution
	強固	キョウコ	firmness; stability; solidity; security; strength
	強行	キョウコウ	enforcement; force —*v*. enforce; force
	強硬	キョウコウ	tough elements; hard-liners
	強豪	キョウゴウ	veteran; strong player
	強震	キョウシン	strong earthquake
	強勢	キョウセイ	emphasis; stress
	強制	キョウセイ	compulsion; coercion; duress —*v*. compel; force; coerce
	強壮	キョウソウ	robustness
	強大	キョウダイ	mighty; powerful; strong
	強調	キョウチョウ	emphasis —*v*. emphasize
	強度	キョウド	intensity; strength
	強要	キョウヨウ	persistent demand; extortion —*v*. exact; compel; force; coerce
	強力	キョウリョク	power; might
	強烈	キョウレツ	intense; strong; severe
	強引	ゴウイン	force
	強情	ゴウジョウ	obstinacy; stubbornness
	強奪	ゴウダツ	seizure; extortion; robbery —*v*. seize; rob with violence
	強盗	ゴウトウ	burglar; robber; housebreaker
	強欲	ゴウヨク	avarice; greed; greediness
訓	強い	つよい	strong
	強まる	つよまる	*vi*. become strong; be intensified; increase; be emphasized
	強める	つよめる	*vt*. strengthen; intensify; increase; emphasize
	強いる	しいる	*vt*. force; compel; press
¥	強行採決	キョウコウサイケツ	forcing a vote —*v*. force a vote (in the House of Representatives)
	強制的	キョウセイテキ	mandatory; compulsory
	強制破産	キョウセイハサン	forced liquidation
	強気筋	つよキすじ	bull (long) account (interest)
	強含み	つよふくみ	strengthening; strong feeling (market)

612

張 ⑪

音	張	チョウ	stretch
熟	張本人	チョウホンニン	ringleader
	張力	チョウリョク	tension; tensile force
訓	張る	はる	*v*. stretch; spread; extend; strain; tighten
	張り合う	はりあう	***vi***. rival; emulate; compete
	張り切る	はりきる	***vi***. be in high spirits
	張り子	はりこ	papier-mâché
	張り込む	はりこむ	***vi***. keep watch/lookout; be eager; invest

613

弾 ⑫

音	弾	ダン	bullet; projectile; missile; bounce; spring; rebound
熟	弾圧	ダンアツ	oppression; suppression; pressure; coercion —***v***. oppress; surpress; repress; crush
	弾劾	ダンガイ	impeachment; denunciation; accusation; censure —***v***. impeach; denounce; accuse
	弾丸	ダンガン	bullet; projectile; cannonball
	弾性	ダンセイ	elasticity
	弾道	ダンドウ	trajectory; line of fire
	弾薬	ダンヤク	ammunition; munitions
	弾力	ダンリョク	elasticity; elastic force; resilience; spring
訓	弾む	はずむ	***v***. spring; bound; rebound; be stimulated/encouraged
	弾く	ひく	***vt***. play (a musical instrument)
	弾	たま	bullet

3  けいがしら pig's head

614

粛 ⑪

音	粛	シュク	be discreet

熟	粛正	シュクセイ	enforcement; cleanup —*v.* enforce; clean up
	粛清	シュクセイ	political purge —*v.* purge
	粛然	シュクゼン	silently; quietly; solemnly

3 彡 さんづくり short hair

615

形 ⑦

一 二 于 开 开 开 形

音	形	ケイ	shape; form; appearance
		ギョウ	form; figure; model
熟	形相	ギョウソウ	looks; figure; face
	形骸化	ケイガイカ	becoming a mere name; taking the teeth out —*vi.* become a mere name; take the teeth out
	形式	ケイシキ	formation
	形式的	ケイシキテキ	formally; perfunctory
	形而上	ケイジジョウ	metaphysical
	形状	ケイジョウ	shape; state
	形勢	ケイセイ	situation; state of affairs
	形成	ケイセイ	formation —*v.* form; build/make up
	形成外科	ケイセイゲカ	plastic/cosmetic surgery
	形跡	ケイセキ	traces; evidence
	形態	ケイタイ	form; shape
	形容	ケイヨウ	description; qualification; modification —*v.* describe; modify; qualify
	形容詞	ケイヨウシ	***gram.*** adjective
	形容動詞	ケイヨウドウシ	***gram.*** adjectival verb (verb used to qualify/modify a noun)
訓	形	かた	shape; form; model; pattern
	形	かたち	shape; form
	形見	かたみ	keepsake; memento

616

彩 ⑪

一 〻 〻 爫 乎 乎 采 采 采 彩 彩

音	彩	サイ	color
熟	彩色	サイショク (サイシキ)	coloring —*v.* color

訓	彩る	いろどる	*vt*. color; be bright
	彩り	いろどり	coloring; color scheme

617

彫 ⑪

丿 冂 月 冃 用 冉 周 周 周´ 周﹅ 彫

音	彫	チョウ	engrave
熟	彫金	チョウキン	metal carving; chasing
	彫刻	チョウコク	sculpture; carving; engraving —*v*. sculpture; carve; engrave
	彫刻家	チョウコクカ	sculptor; engraver; carver
	彫塑	チョウソ	carving and modeling; clay model
	彫像	チョウゾウ	statue
訓	彫る	ほる	*vt*. carve; engrave; sculpture; tattoo

618

彰 ⑭

丶 亠 亣 立 产 音 音 章 章 章 彰

音	彰	ショウ	manifest

619

影 ⑮

丨 口 日 旦 早 昌 景 景 景 景 影

音	影	エイ	shadow; shape
熟	影響	エイキョウ	influence; effect —*vi*. influence; affect
訓	影	かげ	shadow; image; ghost
	影絵	かげえ	shadow picture
	影法師	かげボウシ	shadow; silhouette
	影武者	かげムシャ	dummy general

---

3 彳 ぎょうにんべん going man

620

役 ⑦

丿 ク 彳 彳 彴 役 役

音	役	エキ	war; battle; service

	役	ヤク	post; role; duty; charge
熟	役者	ヤクシャ	actor
	役所	ヤクショ	government office
	役立つ	ヤクだつ	***vi***. be useful; serve a purpose
	役立てる	ヤクだてる	***vt***. put to use; make use of
	役人	ヤクニン	officer
	役場	ヤクば	town office
	役割	ヤクわり	part; role
¥	役員	ヤクイン	director on the board; corporate executive
	役員賞与	ヤクインショウヨ	bonus for directors and auditors

621 往 ⑧

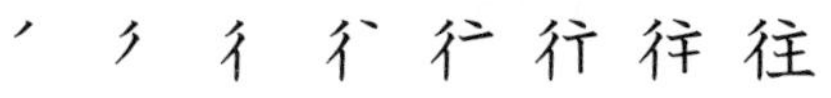

音	往	オウ	go; former; past
熟	往々	オウオウ	sometimes; occasionally; now and then
	往時	オウジ	the past; things past
	往生	オウジョウ	death; submission —***vi***. die; pass away; submit
	往信	オウシン	outgoing letter; letter sent
	往診	オウシン	physician's house call —***vi***. make a house call
	往年	オウネン	former years; formerly; the past
	往復	オウフク	round/return trip —***v***. go and come back; make a round trip
	往来	オウライ	coming and going; street traffic —***vi***. come and go
	往路	オウロ	outward trip/journey
訓	往く	ゆく	***vi***. go

622 径 ⑧

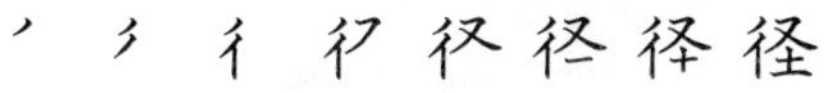

音	径	ケイ	lane; small road; path; diameter
熟	径路	ケイロ	course; route; process

623 征 ⑧

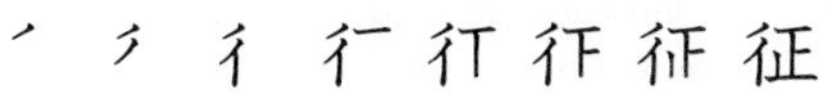

音	征	セイ	attack

3 口口土士夂夕大女子宀寸小⺌⺍尢尸山川工己巾干幺广廴廾弋弓彐彡彳艹辶阝阝⺍忄扌犭氵

熟	征伐	セイバツ	subjugation; conquest —*v.* conquer; subjugate
	征服	セイフク	conquest —*v.* conquer; overcome; subdue
	征服者	セイフクシャ	conqueror

624
彼 ⑧
ノ ㇀ 彳 彳 彳 彳 彼 彼

音	彼	ヒ	he; that
熟	彼我	ヒガ	oneself and others; each other
	彼岸	ヒガン	equinoctial week; the other shore; that
訓	彼	かれ	he; boyfriend; lover
	彼氏	かれシ	he; boyfriend; lover
	彼等	かれら	they
	彼	かの	that
	彼女	かのジョ	she; girlfriend; lover
	※彼方	かなた	there; yonder; the other side

625
後 ⑨
ノ ㇀ 彳 彳 彳 彳 彳 後 後

音	後	ゴ （コウ）	after; post; later
熟	後遺症	コウイショウ	***med.*** prognostic symptoms; aftereffect
	後援	コウエン	support; backing —*v.* support; give support to; back up
	後悔	コウカイ	repentance; regret; remorse —*v.* repent; regret; show remorse
	後学	コウガク	future scholars; future reference
	後記	コウキ	postscript
	後期	コウキ	latter period
	後継者	コウケイシャ	successor; heir; heiress
	後見人	コウケンニン	guardian
	後者	コウシャ	latter
	後進	コウシン	reversing —*v.* reverse; back up; go backwards
	後進国	コウシンコク	developing country
	後世	コウセイ	future generations; ages to come
	後続	コウゾク	following; succeeding; next
	後退	コウタイ	retreat; recession; retrogression; step back —***vi.*** retreat; retrogress; go backwards; step back
	後天的	コウテンテキ	acquired; postnatal

	後任	**コウニン**	successor
	後年	**コウネン**	future years; in years to come; later; afterwards
	後輩	**コウハイ**	one's junior; underclassmen
	後半	**コウハン**	latter/second half
	後家	**ゴケ**	widow
	後光	**ゴコウ**	halo
	後妻	**ゴサイ**	second wife
	後日	**ゴジツ**	later date; later on; in the future
	後手	**ゴて**	one step behind; too late; second player (in go or shōgi)
訓	後	**あと**	later; after; next; the rest
	後押し	**あとおし**	push; support; backup —***v***. push; support; back up
	後始末	**あとシマツ**	settlement
	後ずさり	**あとずさり**	stepping back —***vi***. step back
	後回し	**あとまわし**	postponement; putting off
	後ろ	**うしろ**	back; behind
	後ろめたい	**うしろめたい**	feel uneasy/guilty; have a bad conscience
	後ろ指	**うしろゆび**	suspicion
	後れる	**おくれる**	***vi***. be late; be backward
	後	**のち**	later; afterwards; in the future
¥	後入れ先出し法	**あといれさきだしホウ**	last-in first-out method
	後配株	**コウハイかぶ**	deferred stock
	後場	**ゴば**	afternoon session

626

待 ⑨

丿 彳 彳 彳一 彳十 彳土 彳圭 待 待

音	待	**タイ**	wait; treat
熟	待機	**タイキ**	waiting for a chance —***vi***. watch and wait; wait and see
	待遇	**タイグウ**	treatment; reception; service; pay; salary —***v***. treat; receive; entertain
	待避	**タイヒ**	sheltering —***v***. take shelter
	待望	**タイボウ**	eager waiting —***v***. wait eagerly
訓	待つ	**まつ**	***vt***. wait
	待合室	**まちあいシツ**	waiting room

口囗土士夂夕大女子宀寸小⺌⺍尢尸山川工己巾干幺广廴廾弋弓ヨ彡•彳艹辶阝阝亠忄扌犭氵

627

律 ⑨

ノ ク 彳 彳 行 行 律 律 律

音	律	リツ (リチ)	law; regulation; rhythm
熟	律する	リッする	*vt.* judge; measure
	律儀	リチギ	honesty; integrity; loyalty
	律動	リツドウ	rhythm —*vi.* have rhythm; be rhythmic
	律法	リッポウ	law; rule
	律令	リツリョウ	code of laws; laws and orders

628

従 ⑩

ノ ク 彳 彳 彳 彳 彳 彳 従 従

音	従	ジュウ (ジュ) (ショウ)	obey; follow; engage in junior grade
熟	従業員	ジュウギョウイン	employee
	従軍	ジュウグン	going to the front with the army —*vi.* go to the front with the army
	従事	ジュウジ	engagement; involvement —*vi.* engage in; be involved in
	従順	ジュウジュン	obedience; submission
	従属	ジュウゾク	subordination —*vi.* be subordinate to
	従来	ジュウライ	hitherto; as in the past; as usual
訓	従う	したがう	*vi.* follow; accompany; obey; conform; comply
	従える	したがえる	*vt.* be attended/followed by
	従って	したがって	accordingly; consequently; therefore; in obedience to; as; in proportion to

629

徐 ⑩

ノ ク 彳 彳 彳 徐 徐 徐 徐 徐

音	徐	ジョ	slow
熟	徐行	ジョコウ	slow speed; slowly —*vi.* go slowly; go at slow speed
	徐々に	ジョジョに	gradually; little by little; slowly

630 徒 ⑩

音	徒	ト	on foot; empty; vain; companions; disciple; punishment
熟	徒競争	トキョウソウ	footrace; race on foot
	徒弟	トテイ	apprentice; disciple
	徒党	トトウ	faction; conspirators; league
	徒歩	トホ	walking; going on foot
	徒労	トロウ	futile effort; vain attempt; fruitless labor
訓	※徒	あだ	empty; vain

631 得 ⑪

音	得	トク	obtain; acquire; ability
熟	得する	トクする	***vi***. obtain; acquire; get
	得意	トクイ	pride; triumph; forte; strong point; customer; patron
	得策	トクサク	good policy; best plan
	得失	トクシツ	relative merits; advantages and disadvantages; profit and loss
	得心	トクシン	conviction; consent; compliance —***vi***. consent to; comply with; be convinced of
	得点	トクテン	score; marks obtained —***vi***. score; gain marks
	得票	トクヒョウ	polling score —***vi***. poll; gain/win votes
	得票数	トクヒョウスウ	number of votes polled
訓	得る	うる	***vt***. obtain; acquire; get; can; be able to
	得る	える	***vt***. get; have; obtain; acquire; can; be able to
	得手	えて	strong point; forte

632 御 ⑫

音	御	ギョ	skilled driving; control; manage
		ゴ	(honorific prefix)
熟	御する	ギョする	***vt***. control; manage
	御者	ギョシャ	coach driver; carriage handler
	御所	ゴショ	imperial palace

	御破算	ゴハサン	calculating anew; calling the whole thing off; making a fresh start
	御用	ゴヨウ	business; order; government service
	御来光	ゴライコウ	view of the rising sun from a mountain top
	御陵	ゴリョウ	imperial tomb
訓	御	おん	(honorific prefix)
	御中	おんチュウ	Messrs

633

循 ⑫

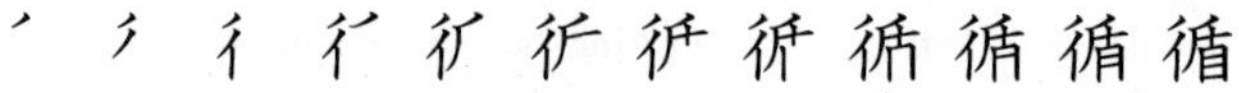

音	循	ジュン	follow; circulate
熟	循環	ジュンカン	circulation; cycle —*vi*. circulate; go in circles
	循環器	ジュンカンキ	***med***. /circulatory organ

634

復 ⑫

音	復	フク	return; repeat; be restored
熟	復する	フクする	*v*. return; be restored; reply; take revenge
	復位	フクイ	restoration; reinstatement —*vi*. be restored/reinstated
	復員	フクイン	demobilization —*v*. be demobilized and sent home
	復縁	フクエン	reconciliation (with one's husband/wife) —*vi*. be reconciled (with one's husband/wife)
	復元	フクゲン	restoration (to the original state) —*v*. restore; reconstruct
	復習	フクシュウ	review; revision —*v*. review; revise
	復讐	フクシュウ	revenge —*vi*. revenge oneself; avenge
	復唱	フクショウ	repeat —*v*. repeat an order aloud
	復職	フクショク	reinstatement; reappointment —*vi*. be reinstated/reappointed in one's job
	復命	フクメイ	report —*v*. report (to one's superior)
	復路	フクロ	return trip
	復活	フッカツ	rebirth; revival —*v*. be reborn/brought back to life
	復活祭	フッカツサイ	Easter
	復刊	フッカン	republication; reissue —*v*. republish; reissue
	復帰	フッキ	return; reinstatement —*vi*. return; reinstate; come back
	復旧	フッキュウ	restoration; recovery —*v*. restore; be restored

復古	フッコ	restoration (of the old regime/situation) —*v*. restore; be restored
復古調	フッコチョウ	reactionary mood
復興	フッコウ	reconstruction; revival —*v*. reconstruct; revive
復刻	フッコク	republication; reissue —*v*. republish; reissue
訓 ※復	また	again

635

微 ⑬

音 微	ビ (ミ)	minute; slight
熟 微温	ビオン	lukewarm; tepid
微行	ビコウ	traveling incognito —***vi***. travel incognito
微光	ビコウ	faint light; glimmering
微細	ビサイ	minute; tiny
微視的	ビシテキ	microscopic
微弱	ビジャク	faint; feeble
微小	ビショウ	microscopic; minute; tiny
微少	ビショウ	minute quantity
微笑	ビショウ	smile
微震	ビシン	slight earthquake/tremor
微生物	ビセイブツ	***bio***. microorganism; microbe
微動	ビドウ	tremor; quiver; slight shock
微熱	ビネツ	***med***. slight fever
微風	ビフウ	gentle breeze
微分	ビブン	***math***. differential calculus
微妙	ビミョウ	delicate; subtle
微粒子	ビリュウシ	tiny particle; fine-grained
微量	ビリョウ	minute amount
微力	ビリョク	***hum***. my (poor) ability
微々たる	ビビたる	slight; meager; trifling
微塵	ミジン	particle; bit; iota
訓 ※微か	かすか	faint; dim

636

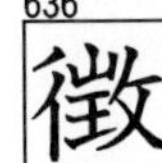

⑭

音 徴	チョウ	sign; symbol; indication; omen; demand; call

熟	徴候	チョウコウ	sign; indication; omen
	徴収	チョウシュウ	collection; levy; imposition —*v*. collect; levy; impose
	徴集	チョウシュウ	levy; enlistment; enrollment; recruitment —*v*. levy; enlist; conscript; recruit; call up
	徴税	チョウゼイ	tax collection —*v*. collect/raise/levy taxes
	徴発	チョウハツ	requisition; commandeering —*v*. requisition; commandeer
	徴兵	チョウヘイ	conscription; enlistment; the draft —*vi*. conscript; enlist; draft
	徴兵制度	チョウヘイセイド	conscription system
	徴募	チョウボ	recruitment —*vt*. recruit
	徴用	チョウヨウ	commandeering; drafting; requisition —*v*. commandeer; draft; requisition; levy

637

徳 ⑭

音	徳	トク	virtue; goodness; grace; character
熟	徳育	トクイク	moral education/training
	徳政	トクセイ	benevolent administration
	徳性	トクセイ	morality
	徳望	トクボウ	moral influence
	徳目	トクモク	individual article of ethics
	徳用	トクヨウ	economical
	徳行	トッコウ	virtuous conduct; virtue; goodness

638

徹 ⑮

音	徹	テツ	penetrate
熟	徹する	テッする	*vi*. penetrate; go right through; be thorough/complete
	徹底	テッテイ	thoroughness; completeness —*vi*. be thorough/complete/exhaustive
	徹底的	テッテイテキ	thorough; complete; perfect
	徹頭徹尾	テットウテツビ	throughout; thoroughly; from beginning to end
	徹夜	テツヤ	all-night vigil/sitting —*vi*. sit/stay up all night; keep vigil

639
芋 ⑥ 一 十 艹 芏 芏 芋

訓	芋	いも	potato

640
芝 ⑥ 一 十 艹 艹 芝 芝

訓	芝	しば	lawn; turf
	芝居	しばい	play; drama; theater
	※芝生	しばふ	lawn; turf

641
花 ⑦ 一 十 艹 艹 芢 芢 花

音	花	カ	flower; gaudy
熟	花壇	カダン	flower bed
	花鳥風月	カチョウフウゲツ	beauties of nature; elegant pursuits
	花瓶	カビン	vase
	花粉	カフン	pollen
	花弁	カベン	petal
訓	花	はな	flower; cherry blossoms; gratuity; flower arrangement
	花形	はながた	floral pattern; celebrity; popular star
	花束	はなたば	bouquet; bunch of flowers
	花火	はなび	fireworks
	花見	はなみ	cherry-blossom viewing
	花婿	はなむこ	bridegroom
	花嫁	はなよめ	bride

642
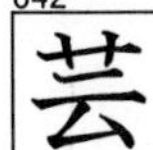
⑦ 一 十 艹 艹 芸 芸 芸

音	芸	ゲイ	learning; art; entertainment

熟	芸者	ゲイシャ	geisha
	芸術	ゲイジュツ	art; the arts
	芸当	ゲイトウ	feat; trick; stunt; performance
	芸道	ゲイドウ	art; accomplishments
	芸人	ゲイニン	artist; entertainer; public performer
	芸能	ゲイノウ	public entertainment; performing arts
	芸名	ゲイメイ	stage name

643

芳 ⑦

一 十 艹 艹 芏 芎 芳

音	芳	ホウ	fragrance; (honorific prefix)
熟	芳香	ホウコウ	fragrance; perfume; aroma
	芳志	ホウシ	***hon***. your good wishes/kindness
	芳醇	ホウジュン	mellow/rich (saké)
	芳書	ホウショ	***hon***. your kind letter
	芳情	ホウジョウ	***hon***. your kindness
	芳心	ホウシン	***hon***. your good wishes/kindness
	芳墨	ホウボク	scented ink ***hon***. your kind letter
	芳名	ホウメイ	***hon***. your name; good name/reputation
	芳名録	ホウメイロク	visitor's book; name list
	芳烈	ホウレツ	perfume; fragrance; aroma
訓	芳しい	かんばしい	fragrant; aromatic; excellent; superior
	※芳ばしい	こうばしい	fragrant; aromatic

644

英 ⑧

一 十 艹 艹 苎 苎 英 英

音	英	エイ	brilliant; eminent; England; English
熟	英気	エイキ	virility; energy; vigor
	英語	エイゴ	the English language
	英国	エイコク	England; Britain
	英才	エイサイ	genius; talent
	英断	エイダン	decisive judgment
	英知	エイチ	wisdom; intelligence
	英文	エイブン	English writing
	英文学	エイブンガク	English literature
	英文法	エイブンポウ	English grammar
	英米	エイベイ	England and America; English and American

英訳	エイヤク	English translation —*v*. translate into English
英雄	エイユウ	hero
英霊	エイレイ	the spirits of the war dead; the souls of those killed in battle

645

芽 ⑧

一 十 艹 艹 芒 芏 芽 芽

音	芽	ガ	bud
訓	芽	め	bud; good luck
	芽生え	めばえ	sprout; bud
	芽生える	めばえる	***vi***. spring up; sprout

646

苦 ⑧

一 十 艹 艹 芏 芐 苦 苦

音	苦	ク	bitter; pain; hard work
熟	苦学	クガク	self-support through university —***vi***. pay one's way/work through university
	苦境	クキョウ	distressed circumstances; dire straits
	苦行	クギョウ	penance; aseticism —***vi***. do penance; practice aseticism
	苦言	クゲン	outspoken advice; bitter counsel
	苦汁(をなめる)	クジュウ(をなめる)	experience the bitterness of life
	苦笑	クショウ	wry smile; strained laugh —***vi***. smile wryly
	苦情	クジョウ	complaint; grievance; objection
	苦心	クシン	pains; effort; labor; trouble; hard work —***vi***. make painstaking efforts
	苦戦	クセン	hard fight; desperate battle —***vi***. fight hard; battle desperately
	苦痛	クツウ	pain; anguish
	苦闘	クトウ	bitter struggle; hard fight —***vi***. put up a bitter struggle/hard fight
	苦難	クナン	distress; suffering; affliction
	苦肉の策	クニクのサク	last resort; desperate/clumsy measure taken under the pressure of necessity
	苦悩	クノウ	suffering; distress; affliction —***vi***. suffer; be distressed/afflicted
	苦杯	クハイ	bitter cup/experience
	苦楽	クラク	joys and sorrows
	苦慮	クリョ	anxiety; worry; concern —***vi***. be anxious; worry; feel concern

	苦労	クロウ	trouble; hardship; suffering —*vi*. be troubled; suffer hardship
訓	苦しい	くるしい	painful; hard; difficult; embarrassing
	苦しむ	くるしむ	*vi*. suffer from; groan; agonize; be troubled with; worry oneself; be at a loss
	苦しめる	くるしめる	*vt*. torment; torture; distress; trouble; inflict pain
	苦い	にがい	bitter; hard; trying
	苦手	にがて	weak point; be bad (at)
	苦り切る	にがりきる	*vi*. pull a sour face

647

茎 ⑧

一 十 艹 艾 芆 苳 茎 茎

音	茎	ケイ	stalk; stem; stalk shaped
訓	茎	くき	stalk; stem

648

若 ⑧

一 十 艹 艹 产 若 若 若

音	若	ジャク (ニャク)	young
熟	若年	ジャクネン	youth
	若輩	ジャクハイ	young fellow
	若干	ジャッカン	some; a few
訓	若い	わかい	young; immature; green
	若草	わかくさ	green/young grass
	若気	わかゲ	youthful impatience
	若様	わかさま	prince
	若衆	わかシュウ	young person
	若造	わかゾウ	stripling
	若旦那	わかダンナ	young master
	若作り	わかづくり	making oneself up to look young; mutton dressed up as lamb
	若手	わかて	young person
	若向き	わかむき	suitable for younger people
	若者	わかもの	young man/people; youth
	若し	もし	if; in case of; suppose
	若しくは	もしくは	or; either
	※若人	わこうど	young person/people

649

苗 ⑧

一 十 艹 艹 艹 芇 苗 苗

音	苗	ビョウ	seedling; sapling; shoot
熟	※苗字	ミョウジ	surname; family name
訓	苗	なえ	young plant; (rice) seedling
	苗木	なえぎ	sapling; young tree
	苗床	なえどこ	seedbed

650

茂 ⑧

一 十 艹 艹 芦 芪 茂 茂

音	茂	モ	grow thickly/luxuriantly
訓	茂る	しげる	***vi***. grow thickly/luxuriantly

651

荒 ⑨

一 十 艹 艹 艹 芒 芦 芹 荒

音	荒	コウ	barren; wild; rough; savage
熟	荒天	コウテン	stormy weather
	荒土	コウド	barren land; wasteland; waste
	荒廃	コウハイ	devastation; desolation; waste; ruin —***vi***. be devastated; go to ruin
	荒涼	コウリョウ	desolate; dreary; bleak; deserted; inhospitable
訓	荒い	あらい	rude; wild; rough; savage; violent
	荒らす	あらす	***vt***. devastate; lay waste; damage; harm
	荒物	あらもの	kitchenware; kitchen utensils; sundry goods used for daily life
	荒れる	あれる	***vi***. become rough; rage; be wild; ran waste; be devasted

652

草 ⑨

一 十 艹 艹 艹 苩 苜 苴 草

音	草	ソウ	grass; small plants; original; draft; cursive handwriting
熟	草案	ソウアン	(rough) draft; rough copy
	草原	ソウゲン	grassy plain; grass land

	草稿	ソウコウ	draft; notes; manuscript
	草書	ソウショ	cursive form of a Chinese character
	草食	ソウショク	herbivorous
	草々	ソウソウ	In haste (closing words of a letter)
	草創	ソウソウ	inauguration; inception; beginning of construction of a temple or shrine
	草木	ソウモク	plants and trees; vegetation
	※草履	ゾウリ	*zōri* (sandals)
訓	草	くさ	grass; small plants
	草分け	くさわけ	early settler; pioneer

653

荘 ⑨

一 ⺈ 艹 ⺾ 荘 荘 荘 荘 荘

音	荘	ショウ	manor
		ソウ	solemn; villa; inn; village
熟	荘園	ショウエン	***hist***. manor (of Heian period nobles)
	荘厳	ソウゴン	sublime; grand; majestic
	荘重	ソウチョウ	solemn; sublime; impressive

654

茶 ⑨

一 ⺈ 艹 艾 艾 苓 茶 茶 茶

音	茶	チャ	tea plant; tea; light brown
		サ	tea
熟	茶道	サドウ	tea ceremony
	茶飯事	サハンジ	everyday affair
	茶話会	サワカイ	tea party
	茶色	チャいろ	brown
	茶菓子	チャガシ	tea cake
	茶釜	チャがま	tea kettle
	茶室	チャシツ	tea arbor; tea ceremony room
	茶所	チャどころ	tea-growing disrict; tea-producing center
	茶の間	チャのま	living/sitting room
	茶番	チャバン	tea maker; farce
	茶目	チャめ	playful
	茶碗	チャワン	(rice) bowl; teacup

655

荷 ⑩

一 十 艹 艹 芢 茌 茌 荷 荷 荷

音	荷	カ	load; burden; cargo
熟	荷担	カタン	help; assistance; support; aid —*vi*. help; assist; support; aid
訓	荷	に	load; burden
	荷札	にふだ	luggage tag
	荷物	にモツ	load; burden; luggage; baggage
¥	荷受人	にうけニン	consignee
	荷送人	におくりニン	shipper
	荷為替手形	にがわせてがた	(documentary) bill of exchange

656

 ⑩

一 十 艹 艹 芏 芏 芔 苷 莛 華

音	華	カ	floweriness; flower; gaudy
		(ケ)	flower
熟	華道	カドウ	art of flower arrangement
	華美	カビ	gaudiness; splendor
	華麗	カレイ	gorgeousness; magnificence
訓	華	はな	flower; cherry blossoms
	華々しい	はなばなしい	splendid; brilliant; glorious
	華やか	はなやか	showy; gaudy; colorful

657

菓 ⑪

一 十 艹 艹 芇 苜 苜 荁 草 菓 菓

音	菓	カ	cake; candy; fruit
熟	菓子	カシ	cake; candy

658

菊 ⑪

一 十 艹 艹 芍 芍 芍 芍 菊 菊 菊

音	菊	キク	chrysanthemum
熟	菊花	キクカ (キッカ)	chrysanthemum

659

菌 ⑪

一 十 廾 广 芦 芦 芦 菌 菌 菌 菌

音	菌	キン	mushroom; toadstool; bacteria
熟	菌糸	キンシ	spawn; hypha
	菌類	キンルイ	fungi

660

菜 ⑪

一 十 廾 廾 芯 芯 芯 苎 苹 菜 菜

音	菜	サイ	vegetables; greens
熟	菜園	サイエン	vegetable/kitchen garden
	菜食	サイショク	vegetable diet; vegetarian meal —*vi*. live on vegetables; follow a vegetarian diet
	菜食主義者	サイショクシュギシャ	vegetarian
訓	菜	な	vegetables; greens
	菜種	なたね	rapeseed
	菜の花	なのはな	rape blossoms

661

著 ⑪

一 十 廾 廾 芏 芏 芛 茅 著 著 著

音	著	チョ	work; written by; author; remarkable
熟	著作	チョサク	literary work; writing; authorship —*v*. write (a novel, etc.)
	著作権	チョサクケン	copyright; literary property
	著作者	チョサクシャ	author; writer
	著者	チョシャ	author; writer
	著述	チョジュツ	writing books; book; literary work —*v*. write a book
	著書	チョショ	literary work; book
	著名	チョメイ	prominence; eminence; distinction; celebrity
訓	著す	あらわす	*vt*. write; publish
	著しい	いちじるしい	remarkable; distinguished; striking

662

葬 ⑫

一 十 艹 艹 芦 茢 茢 茢 菀 葬 葬 葬

音 葬 ソウ bury; inter

熟 葬儀 ソウギ funeral

葬儀屋 ソウギや undertaker

葬式 ソウシキ funeral

葬礼 ソウレイ funeral

訓 葬る ほうむる ***vt***. bury; inter

663

葉 ⑫

一 十 艹 廾 芏 芒 苷 苹 莅 葉 葉 葉

音 葉 ヨウ leaf; (counter for flat, thin objects)

熟 葉柄 ヨウヘイ leaf stem

葉脈 ヨウミャク vein (of a leaf)

葉緑素 ヨウリョクソ chlorophyl

訓 葉 は leaf

葉書 はがき postcard

葉末 はずえ leaf tip

葉月 はづき eighth lunar month

葉巻 はまき cigar

664

落 ⑫

一 十 艹 艹 艹 汁 汁 莎 莈 落 落 落

音 落 ラク fall; fail; be defeated

熟 落書き ラクがき graffiti —***v***. scribble; scrawl; doodle

落伍 ラクゴ falling/dropping behind; falling out of —***vi***. fall behind; drop/fall out of line; drop to the rear

落語 ラクゴ *rakugo* (comic story telling)

落差 ラクサ water head/level; difference in height

落日 ラクジツ setting sun

落城 ラクジョウ fall of a castle —***vi***. fall; surender

落成 ラクセイ completion of construction —***vi***. be completed/finished/ready for occupancy

落成式 ラクセイシキ building-completion ceremony

	落選	ラクセン	defeat in an election; failure to get elected —*vi*. be defeated/unsuccessful in an election
	落第	ラクダイ	failure in an examination —*vi*. fail to pass an examination
	落胆	ラクタン	discouragement; disheartenment —*v*. be discouraged/disheartened
	落着	ラクチャク	settlement —*vi*. come to a settlement; be settled
	落丁	ラクチョウ	missing pages (in a book)
	落馬	ラクバ	fall from one's horse —*vi*. fall/be thrown off one's horse
	落盤	ラクバン	cave-in —*vi*. cave in
	落命	ラクメイ	death —*vi*. die; pass away; be killed
	落葉	ラクヨウ	fallen leaves —*vi*. shed/cast leaves
	落葉樹	ラクヨウジュ	deciduous tree
	落陽	ラクヨウ	setting sun
	落雷	ラクライ	falling of a thunderbolt —*vi*. be struck by lightning
	落下	ラッカ	fall; descend; drop —*vi*. fall; descend; drop
	落下傘	ラッカサン	parachute
	落花生	ラッカセイ	peanuts
訓	落ちる	おちる	*vi*. fall; fail
	落ち着く	おちつく	calm/settle down
	落ち目	おちめ	decline of fortune; adversity
	落とす	おとす	*vt*. drop; let fall; lose
	落とし穴	おとしあな	pitfall; pit; trap; tricky
	落とし子	おとしご	illegitimate child
	落とし物	おとしもの	lost article; article accidentally dropped
¥	落札	ラクサツ	successful bid

665

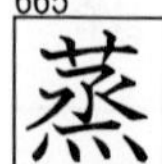
⑬

音	蒸	ジョウ	vapor
熟	蒸気	ジョウキ	steam; vapor
	蒸気機関	ジョウキキカン	steam engine
	蒸発	ジョウハツ	evaporation; vaporization —*vi*. evaporate; vaporize
	蒸留	ジョウリュウ	distillation —*v*. distill
	蒸留酒	ジョウリュウシュ	distilled/hard liquor
訓	蒸す	むす	*v*. steam; be sultry; be hot and humid
	蒸し暑い	むしあつい	muggy; sultry; hot and humid
	蒸し焼き	むしやき	baking; roasting

	蒸らす	むらす	***vt***. steam
	蒸れる	むれる	***vi***. be steamed/stuffy; get sticky

666

蓄 ⑬

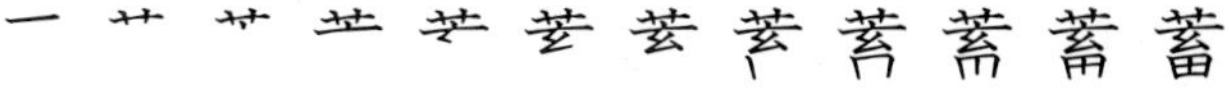

音	蓄	チク	store; stock; accumulate
熟	蓄音機	チクオンキ	phonograph; record player
	蓄財	チクザイ	accumulation of wealth —***vi***. accumulate wealth; make/amass money
	蓄積	チクセキ	accumulation; stockpiling —***v***. accumulate; amass; hoard
訓	蓄える	たくわえる	***vt***. store; stock; stay up; lay up

667

蔵 ⑮

音	蔵	ゾウ	warehouse; storehouse; repository
熟	蔵書	ゾウショ	private library; book collection
訓	蔵	くら	warehouse
¥	蔵相（大蔵大臣）	ゾウショウ（おおくらダイジン）	Finance Minister

668

薫 ⑯

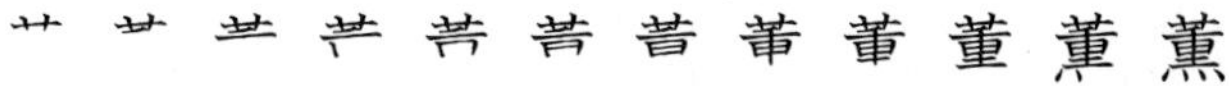

音	薫	クン	fragrance
熟	薫陶	クントウ	discipline; training; education —***v***. discipline; train; educate
	薫風	クンプウ	light balmy/summer breeze
訓	薫る	かおる	***vi***. smell sweet; be fragrant

669

薪 ⑯

音	薪	シン	firewood
熟	薪炭	シンタン	firewood and charcoal; winter fuel

訓	薪	たきぎ	firewood

670

薦 ⑯

音	薦	セン	recommend
訓	薦める	すすめる	***vt***. recommend

671

⑯

音	薄	ハク	thin
熟	薄謝	ハクシャ	***hum***. token of gratitude
	薄弱	ハクジャク	weakness; feebleness; flimsiness; infirmity
	薄情	ハクジョウ	heartless; unfeeling; coldhearted
	薄氷	ハクヒョウ	thin ice; thin coat of ice
	薄命	ハクメイ	unhappiness; misfortune; short life
	薄利	ハクリ	small profits; narrow profit margin
	薄給	ハッキュウ	small salary; low wages; pittance
	薄幸	ハッコウ	ill fated; unfortunate; unlucky; hapless
訓	薄い	うすい	thin; weak; scanty; sparse
	薄明かり	うすあかり	twilight; dim light; glimmer
	薄まる	うすまる	***v***. become thin/weak
	薄める	うすめる	***vt***. make thin; weaken; dilute
	薄らぐ	うすらぐ	***vi***. thin; wear thin; fade; grow pale
	薄れる	うすれる	***vi***. thin; wear thin; fade; grow pale
	薄着	うすぎ	light dress; scanty clothing —***vi***. be lightly dressed
	薄暗い	うすぐらい	gloomy; somber; dusky
	薄化粧	うすゲショウ	light make-up
	薄手	うすで	slight cut; minor injury; thin article (material, china, etc.)
	薄目	うすめ	comparative lightness; half-closed eyes
	薄笑い	うすわらい	half-smile

672

薬 ⑯

音	薬	ヤク	medicine; chemical

熟	薬学	ヤクガク	pharmacology
	薬剤	ヤクザイ	medicine; drugs
	薬剤師	ヤクザイシ	pharmacist
	薬師如来	ヤクシニョライ	Buddha who can cure any ailment
	薬草	ヤクソウ	medicinal herbs
	薬品	ヤクヒン	drugs; chemicals
	薬方	ヤクホウ	prescription
	薬味	ヤクミ	spices; seasoning
	薬用	ヤクヨウ	medicinal
	薬局	ヤッキョク	pharmacy; chemist's shop
	薬効	ヤッコウ	effect of medicine
訓	薬	くすり	medicine; drugs; chemicals
	薬屋	くすりや	drugstore; chemist's shop
	薬指	くすりゆび	ring/fourth finger

673

藩 ⑱

音	藩	ハン	feudal clan; fief; feudal domain
熟	藩士	ハンシ	clansman; retainer of a daimyo
	藩主	ハンシュ	feudal lord

674

藻 ⑲

音	藻	ソウ	duckweed
訓	藻	も	waterweed

3 辶 しんにょう road

675

⑤

訓	込む	こむ	***vi.*** be crowded; be congested; be packed
	込み合う	こみあう	***vi.*** crowded
	込み入る	こみいる	***vi.*** complicated
	込める	こめる	***vt.*** load; include; put into; concentrate

676

辺 ⑤

フ 力 刀 刃 辺

音	辺	ヘン	edge; boundary; border; vicinity; neighborhood; surrounding area
熟	辺境	ヘンキョウ	remote frontier; border country
	辺地	ヘンチ	remote place; out-of-the-way location
	辺土	ヘンド	place long way away from the city; remote region
	辺鄙	ヘンピ	remote; out-of-the-way; rural
	辺幅	ヘンプク	outward appearance
訓	辺り	あたり	neighborhood; surrounding area; vicinity
	辺	べ	neighborhood; surrounding area; vicinity
	※辺	ほとり	neighborhood; surrounding area; vicinity

677

⑥

く 巛 巛 巛 巡 巡

音	巡	ジュン	make a round; tour
熟	巡回	ジュンカイ	patrol; round —***vi***. go around; make one's round; patrol
	巡業	ジュンギョウ	tour; touring —***vi***. make a provincial tour
	巡航	ジュンコウ	cruise; cruising —***vi***. cruise
	巡査	ジュンサ	policeman
	巡視	ジュンシ	patrol; round of inspection —***v***. patrol; make an inspection
	巡礼	ジュンレイ	***Bud***. pilgrimage; pilgrim —***vi***. make a pilgrimage
訓	巡る	めぐる	***vi***. travel around; circle; circulate
	巡り合わせ	めぐりあわせ	fortune; good/bad luck
	※お巡りさん	おまわりさん	policeman

678

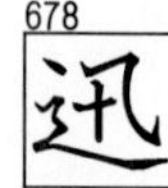

⑥

乁 刁 刊 汛 汛 迅

音	迅	ジン	swift
熟	迅速	ジンソク	prompt; quick; swift; rapid

679

近 ⑦

音	近	キン	near; approach; recent; close
熟	近影	キンエイ	recent photograph; new portrait
	近刊	キンカン	recent publication/issue
	近眼	キンガン	nearsightedness; myopia
	近況	キンキョウ	recent condition; present situation
	近々	キンキン	shortly; before long
	近郊	キンコウ	suburbs; outskirts
	近視	キンシ	nearsightedness; myopia
	近日	キンジツ	soon; shortly; in a few days
	近所	キンジョ	neighborhood; vicinity
	近親	キンシン	close relation
	近世	キンセイ	modern/recent times
	近接	キンセツ	approach; contiguity —***vi***. approach; be contiguous
	近代	キンダイ	the modern age
	近代化	キンダイカ	modernization
	近代的	キンダイテキ	modern
	近年	キンネン	recent years
	近辺	キンペン	neighborhood; vicinity
	近隣	キンリン	neighborhood; vicinity
訓	近い	ちかい	close; nearby
	近頃	ちかごろ	recently; nowadays
	近々	ちかぢか	before long
	近づく	ちかづく	***vi***. come/go near; approach
	近道	ちかみち	short cut

680

⑦

音	迎	ゲイ	welcome
熟	迎合	ゲイゴウ	getting along easily with other —***vi***. accommodate oneself; cater; get along easily with others
	迎春	ゲイシュン	New Year greetings
	迎賓館	ゲイヒンカン	reception hall; guest house
訓	迎える	むかえる	***vt***. meet; greet; receive; welcome
	迎え	むかえ	meeting

681

返 ⑦

一 厂 万 反 `反 钣 返

音	返	ヘン	return
熟	返還	ヘンカン	returning (to original owner/place) —*v*. return; give back
	返却	ヘンキャク	returning; repaying; refunding —*v*. return; repay; refund
	返事	ヘンジ	answer; reply; response —*vi*. answer; reply; respond
	返書	ヘンショ	letter of reply
	返上	ヘンジョウ	returning; sending back —*v*. return; send back; give back
	返信	ヘンシン	letter of reply
	返送	ヘンソウ	sending back; returning —*v*. send back; return
	返電	ヘンデン	telegram in reply
	返答	ヘントウ	answer; reply; response —*vi*. answer; reply; respond
	返杯	ヘンパイ	offering back a cup of saké (in return for a previously accepted cup) —*vi*. offer a return cup of saké
	返本	ヘンポン	returning unsold books to the publisher; returns —*v*. return unsold books to the publisher
	返礼	ヘンレイ	return present; giving a present in return for a previously received gift —*vi*. make a gift in return for a previous gift/favor
訓	返す	かえす	*vt*. return; give/send/bring back
	返す返す	かえすがえす	repeat; do over and over again
	返り討ち	かえりうち	die while trying to kill an enemy
	返る	かえる	*vi*. return; be given/sent back; come back
¥	返金	ヘンキン	repayment (of money); refundment —*vi*. pay back; refund
	返済	ヘンサイ	repayment (of a loan); returning (borrowed goods) —*v*. repay; return
	返納	ヘンノウ	returning (to original owner/place)
	返品	ヘンピン	return of unsold goods; returns —*v*. return (unsold goods)

682

⑧

一 十 才 木 朮 `朮 沭 述

音	述	ジュツ	state; mention; say

熟	述懐	ジュッカイ	recollection; expression (of one's thoughts); relation —*v*. express one's thoughts; relate; reminisce
	述語	ジュツゴ	***gram***. predicate
訓	述べる	のべる	***vt***. state; describe; mention

683

迭 ⑧

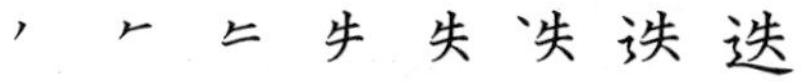

音	迭	テツ	change

684

迫 ⑧

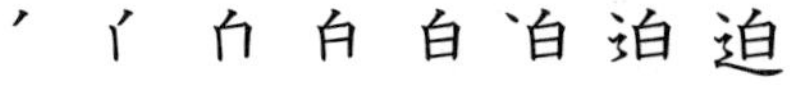

音	迫	ハク	gain upon
熟	迫害	ハクガイ	persecution; oppression; torment —*v*. persecute; oppress; torment
	迫力	ハクリョク	force; power; drive
訓	迫る	せまる	*v*. press; urge; draw near; gain upon

685

逆 ⑨

音	逆	ギャク	opposite; reverse
熟	逆効果	ギャクコウカ (ギャッコウカ)	adverse reaction; boomerang effect
	逆光	ギャクコウ	against the light
	逆算	ギャクサン	inverse operation —*v*. operate inversely
	逆襲	ギャクシュウ	counterattack; retort —*v*. counterattack; retort
	逆上	ギャクジョウ	dizziness; vertigo; frenzy; madness —***vi***. be dizzy; suffer from vertigo; go mad
	逆説	ギャクセツ	paradox
	逆手	ギャクて	dirty trick; backhander; using an opponent's strength against him
	逆転	ギャクテン	reversal; turnabout —*v*. reverse positions; turn about
	逆風	ギャクフウ	headwind; adverse wind
	逆用	ギャクヨウ	reverse use —*v*. use in an opposite way
	逆流	ギャクリュウ	countercurrent; counterflow —***vi***. flow against the current
	逆境	ギャッキョウ	adversity; adverse circumstances

	逆行	ギャッコウ	retrogression; retrogradation —***vi***. retrogress
訓	逆	さか	inverse; upside down
	逆さま	さかさま	inverse; inverted; upside down; topsy-turvy
	逆夢	さかゆめ	dreaming the opposite of reality
	逆らう	さからう	***vi***. oppose; go against; act contrary to
¥	逆指値	ギャクさしね	counterbid
	逆ざや	ギャクざや	negative spread
	逆調	ギャクチョウ	adverse balance of trade; unfavorable trade balance
	逆日歩	ギャクひブ	negative interest per diem
	逆輸入	ギャクユニュウ	reimporting

686
送 ⑨

音	送	ソウ	send
熟	送還	ソウカン	sending back; repatriation —***v***. send back; repatriate
	送球	ソウキュウ	passing/throwing a ball —***vi***. pass/throw a ball
	送金	ソウキン	remittance —***vi***. send a remittance/money
	送迎	ソウゲイ	greeting and farewell —***v***. see someone off and meet them upon return; drop off and pick up
	送検	ソウケン	being sent to the procurator's office —***v***. send to the procurator's office
	送信	ソウシン	(radio/wireless) transmission —***v***. transmit
	送電	ソウデン	power transmission —***v***. transmit power
	送付	ソウフ	sending; forwarding —***v***. send; forward; remit
	送別	ソウベツ	farewell; send off —***v***. see someone off; say farewell
	送料	ソウリョウ	postage; shipping charges
	送話器	ソウワキ	transmitter (of sound)
訓	送る	おくる	***vt***. send
	送り仮名	おくりがな	inflectional *kana* ending

687

⑨

音	退	タイ	retreat; recede; withdraw; expel; drive away; refuse
熟	退位	タイイ	abdication —***vi***. abdicate

	退院	タイイン	leaving hospital; discharge from hospital —***vi***. be discharged from hospital
	退化	タイカ	degeneration; degradation; regression —***vi***. degenerate; degrade; retrograde
	退学	タイガク	leaving school/college; expulsion —***vi***. leave school; withdraw from college; be expelled
	退却	タイキャク	retreat; withdrawal; retirement —***vi***. retreat; withdraw; retire
	退去	タイキョ	leaving; quitting; withdrawl; evacuation —***v***. leave; quit; withdraw; evacuate
	退屈	タイクツ	tedium; boredom —***vi***. be bored
	退校	タイコウ	dismissal/expulsion from school —***vi***. give up school; be expelled
	退散	タイサン	dispersion; melting —***vi***. disperse; break up; melt
	退治	タイジ	subdual; subjugation; elimination; crusade —***v***. subdue; subjugate; suppress; eliminate; crusade
	退社	タイシャ	retirement from a company; leaving the office —***vi***. retire; leave the office
	退出	タイシュツ	leaving; withdrawal —***vi***. leave; withdraw
	退場	タイジョウ	exit; leaving; walk out —***vi***. leave; go away; make one's exit; walk out
	退陣	タイジン	decampment; retirement —***vi***. decamp; withdraw; retire; step down
	退席	タイセキ	leaving one's seat; retirement; withdrawal —***vi***. leave one's seat; retire; withdraw
	退任	タイニン	retirement —***v***. retire
	退避	タイヒ	evacuation —***vi***. evacuate; escape; flee
訓	退く	しりぞく	***vi***. retreat; recede; withdraw; retire
	退ける	しりぞける	***vt***. drive; send away; repel; expel; retire; refuse
¥	退職	タイショク	retirement —***v***. retire from work
	退職金	タイショクキン	retirement allowance

688

⑨ ノ 亻 ｲ' 户 白 自 `自 追 追

音	追	ツイ	run/hunt after
熟	追憶	ツイオク	remembrance; recollection; retrospection; review —***v***. remember; recollect; retrospect; review
	追加	ツイカ	addition; addendum; appendix; supplement —***v***. add; append; supplement
	追及	ツイキュウ	overtaking; catching up —***v***. overtake; catch up with; gain on

	追求	ツイキュウ	pursuit; chase; search —*v*. pursue; chase; follow
	追究	ツイキュウ	close inquiry; thorough investigation —*v*. inquire into; investigate closely; cross-examine
	追撃	ツイゲキ	chase; pursuit; follow up attack —*v*. chase; pursue
	追従	ツイジュウ	following; servility —*vi*. follow; be servile; kowtow
	追従	ツイショウ	flattery; adulation; sycophancy —*vi*. flatter; adulate
	追随	ツイズイ	following —*vi*. follow
	追跡	ツイセキ	pursuit; chase; tracking; stalking —*v*. pursue; chase; track; stalk
	追想	ツイソウ	remembrance; recollection; retrospection; reminiscence —*v*. remember; recollect; retrospect; reminisce
	追徴	ツイチョウ	additional collection; supplementary charge —*v*. make an additional charge of; impose a penalty of
	追徴金	ツイチョウキン	additional charge; imposition; forfeit
	追悼	ツイトウ	mourning —*v*. mourn for
	追突	ツイトツ	rear-end collision —*vi*. collide from behind
	追認	ツイニン	ratification; confirmation —*v*. ratify; confirm
	追放	ツイホウ	banishment; eviction; exile; deportation; purge —*v*. banish; exile; evict; deport; purge
訓	追う	おう	*vt*. drive away; pursue; chase; follow
	追い返す	おいかえす	*vt*. repel; repulse; beat off; drive back
	追い出す	おいだす	*vt*. expel; turn out; throw out; discharge; dismiss
	追い払う	おいはらう	*vt*. drive/turn/send away; repel
¥	追い証	おいショウ	re-margin; additional cover (margin)
	追加予算	ツイカヨサン	supplementary budget

689

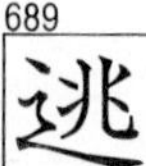
⑨

音	逃	トウ	run away; escape; flee
熟	逃走	トウソウ	flight; desertion; escape; getaway —*vi*. fly; flee; desert; escape; run away
	逃避	トウヒ	escape; evasion; flight —*vi*. escape; evade; fly; take flight
	逃亡	トウボウ	flight; escape; desertion —*vi*. flee; fly; take flight; escape
訓	逃がす	にがす	*vt*. let go; set free; liberate; let loose

逃げ	にげ	escape; getaway; evasion
逃げ道	にげみち	way of escape; way out
逃げる	にげる	***vi***. fly; flee; run away; escape
逃す	のがす	***vt***. let go; set free; liberate; let loose
逃れる	のがれる	***vi***. escape; flee; get away; take flight; evade

690

迷 ⑨

音	迷	メイ	get lost; go astray; be perplexed
熟	迷宮	メイキュウ	labyrinth; maze
	迷彩	メイサイ	camouflage
	迷信	メイシン	superstition
	迷想	メイソウ	illusion; fallacy
	迷妄	メイモウ	illusion; delusion
	迷路	メイロ	labyrinth; maze
	迷惑	メイワク	trouble; annoyance; inconvenience —***vi***. trouble; annoy; be inconvenient
訓	迷う	まよう	***vi***. hesitate; lose one's way
	迷い	まよい	perplexity; doubt; delusion
	迷わせる	まよわせる	***vt***. perplex; lead astray; charm; seduce
	※迷子	まいご	lost child

691

逝 ⑩

音	逝	セイ	die
熟	逝去	セイキョ	death —***vi***. die; pass away
訓	逝く	ゆく	***vi***. die; pass away

692

造 ⑩

音	造	ゾウ	build; make; produce
熟	造営	ゾウエイ	erection; building; construction —***v***. erect; build; construct
	造花	ゾウカ	artificial flowers
	造形	ゾウケイ	molding; modeling —***v***. mold; model
	造詣	ゾウケイ	attainments; scholarship

造作　ゾウサ　trouble; difficulty
造作　ゾウサク　fixtures; facial features
造成　ゾウセイ　construction —*v.* construct; build
造船　ゾウセン　shipbuilding —*v.* build/construct a ship
造幣局　ゾウヘイキョク　the Mint
造林　ゾウリン　forestation

訓 造る　つくる　***vt.*** make; build; produce

693
速 ⑩

音 速　ソク　fast

熟 速成　ソクセイ　intensive training; short course —*v.* train quickly; give intense training
速達　ソクタツ　express/special delivery
速度　ソクド　speed; velocity
速報　ソクホウ　bulletin; news flash —*v.* report promptly; announce quickly
速力　ソクリョク　speed; velocity
速記　ソッキ　shorthand —*v.* write/take down in shorthand
速攻　ソッコウ　swift attack —*v.* launch a swift attack
速効　ソッコウ　quick effect

訓 速い　はやい　fast
速める　はやめる　***vt.*** quicken; accelerate
速やか　すみやか　prompt; speedy

694
逐 ⑩

音 逐　チク　dispel; pursue; drive away

熟 逐一　チクイチ　one by one; minutely; in detail
逐次　チクジ　successively; one after another

訓 逐う　おう　***vt.*** drive away; pursue; chase

695
通 ⑩

音 通　ツウ（ツ）　pass; go to and from; inform; know thoroughly

熟	通じる	ツウじる	*vi*. pass; run; be open to traffic; transmit; be understood
	通じて	ツウじて	through; throughout; all over; in total; together with
	通院	ツウイン	regular hospital visits —*vi*. go to hospital regulary
	通運	ツウウン	transportation; forwarding; express
	通過	ツウカ	passage; passing; pass; transit; carriage —*vi*. pass; pass/go through
	通学	ツウガク	attending school —*vi*. attend school
	通気	ツウキ	ventillation; draft; airing; aeration
	通勤	ツウキン	commuting; going to work —*vi*. commute; go to work
	通行	ツウコウ	traffic; passing; passage; transit —*vi*. pass; go past/through
	通告	ツウコク	notification; notice; announcement; warning —*v*. notify; give notice; announce; warn
	通算	ツウサン	sum total; aggregate; summing-up —*v*. total; include; aggregate; sum up
	通称	ツウショウ	common name; alias
	通常	ツウジョウ	usually; normally; generally
	通信	ツウシン	correspondence; communication; intelligence; dispatch; news —*vi*. correspond; communicate
	通信販売	ツウシンハンバイ	mail order
	通説	ツウセツ	common opinion; popular view
	通俗	ツウゾク	popularity; conventionality
	通達	ツウタツ	notification; communication; circular notice —*v*. notify; communicate
	通知	ツウチ	notice; notification; communication; information; advice —*v*. notify; communicate; inform; advise
	通帳	ツウチョウ	bankbook; passbook
	通読	ツウドク	reading (a book) from cover to cover —*v*. read from cover to cover
	通報	ツウホウ	report; dispatch; advice; bulletin; information —*vi*. report; notify; advise
	通訳	ツウヤク	interpretation; interpreter —*v*. interpret; act as an interpreter
	通用	ツウヨウ	common/popular use; circulation; currency —*vi*. be in common use; circulate; run current
	通例	ツウレイ	usually; commonly; generally; as a rule
	通路	ツウロ	path; passageway
	通話	ツウワ	telephone call/conversation
	通夜	ツヤ	wake; vigil
訓	通う	かよう	*vi*. go to and from; frequent; attend (school, lessons, etc.)
	通る	とおる	*vi*. go along; pass by

	通す	とおす	***vt***. pass through; pierce; admit; let a person pass
	通り	とおり	road; street; passage; understanding; way; manner
	通り掛かる	とおりかかる	***vi***. happen/chance to pass
	通り越す	とおりこす	***vt***. walk/pass by; be more than; exceed
	通り過ぎる	とおりすぎる	***vi***. go past/by
	通り抜ける	とおりぬける	***vi***. pass/walk through; cut across/through
¥	通貨	ツウカ	currency
	通貨供給量	ツウカキョウキュウリョウ	money supply
	通貨単位	ツウカタンイ	currency/monetary unit
	通産省（通商産業省）	ツウサンショウ（ツウショウサンギョウショウ）	Ministry of International Trade and Industry (MITI)
	通産大臣	ツウサンダイジン	Minister of International Trade and Industry
	通常国会	ツウジョウコッカイ	ordinary session of the Diet
	通知預金	ツウチヨキン	deposit at call

696

逓 ⑩

音	逓	テイ	send from stage to stage
熟	逓減	テイゲン	gradual diminution/decrease —***v***. decrease gradually; diminish successively
	逓信	テイシン	communications; transmission
	逓増	テイゾウ	gradual increase —***v***. increase gradually

697

途 ⑩

音	途	ト	way; road
熟	途上	トジョウ	on the way/road; en route
	途絶	トゼツ	interruption; stoppage; cessation; suspension —***vi***. be stopped/cut off/obstructed/interrupted
	途端	トタン	just as; in the act of; the very moment/minute
	途中	トチュウ	on the way; en route; halfway; midway; unfinished; incomplete
	途轍もない	トテツもない	wild; absurd; preposterous
	途方	トホウ	way; means; reason; logic

訓	※途	みち	way; route; road

698
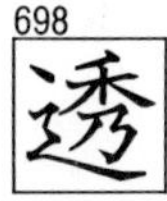
⑩

音	透	トウ	be transparent
熟	透視	トウシ	seeing through; fluoroscopy; radiology —*v.* see through; examine by fluoroscopy
	透写	トウシャ	tracing —*v.* trace out
	透明	トウメイ	transparency; clearness; clarity
	透明人間	トウメイニンゲン	invisible man
訓	透く	すく	***vi.*** be transparent; become sparse
	透ける	すける	***vi.*** be transparent
	透かす	すかす	***vt.*** make transparent; look through; peer into; hold up to the light
	透き通る	すきとおる	***vi.*** be transparent; be seen through
	透き間	すきま	small gap/opening
	透き間風	すきまかぜ	draft

699
連
⑩

音	連	レン	company; relation
熟	連記	レンキ	list —*v.* list up; make a list
	連休	レンキュウ	consecutive holidays
	連係	レンケイ	connection; liaison; contact
	連携	レンケイ	in cooperation/concert with —***vi.*** cooperate with; be in concert
	連結	レンケツ	connection; coupling; consolidated —*v.* connect; couple; consolidate
	連呼	レンコ	repeated calls/shouts —*v.* call/shout repeatedly
	連行	レンコウ	escorting/accompanying (a criminal, etc.) —*v.* escort/accompany (a criminal etc.)
	連合	レンゴウ	union; league; federation —*v.* be in alliance/league with
	連座	レンザ	involvement; accompanying —***vi.*** be involved in; accompany
	連載	レンサイ	(magazine/newspaper) serialization —*v.* serialize (in a magazine/newspaper); run a serial
	連作	レンサク	repeated cultivation of the same crop; linked short stories/*tanka* —*v.* plant (a field) with same crop every year
	連鎖反応	レンサハンノウ	chain reaction

	連山	レンザン	mountain range
	連日	レンジツ	day after day; every day
	連勝	レンショウ	consecutive victories; winning streak —***vi***. keep on winning; be on a winning streak
	連戦	レンセン	series of battles; battle after battle
	連想	レンソウ	association of ideas —***v***. associate (A with B); be reminded of
	連続	レンゾク	continuation; consecutive; in a row —***v***. continue; be consecutive
	連打	レンダ	repeated blows —***v***. hit back; offer repeated blows/strikes
	連帯	レンタイ	solidarity
	連中	レンチュウ	particular group of people; they; crowd
	連動	レンドウ	gears; linkage; drive —***vi***. link; drive
	連破	レンパ	successive wins; winning streak —***v***. win successively; keep on winning; have a winning streak
	連敗	レンパイ	successive defeats; losing streak —***vi***. keep on losing; suffer a losing streak
	連発	レンパツ	rapid machine-gun fire —***v***. fire shots rapidly one after another
	連邦	レンポウ	federation
	連峰	レンポウ	mountain range
	連名	レンメイ	joint signature
	連盟	レンメイ	league; federation; union
	連綿	レンメン	unbroken; consecutive
	連夜	レンヤ	night after night; nightly
	連絡	レンラク	connection; contact; liaison; communicate —***v***. connect; make contact; liaise; communicate
	連絡船	レンラクセン	ferryboat
	連立	レンリツ	alliance; coalition —***v***. make an alliance/coalition
訓	連なる	つらなる	***vi***. stand in a row
	連ねる	つらねる	***vt***. put in a row
	連れる	つれる	***v***. take along; accompany
	連れ	つれ	companion
	連れ子	つれこ	child by a previous marriage
¥	連銀 (連邦銀行)	レンギン (レンポウギンコウ)	Federal/Central Bank (U.S.)
	連結決済	レンケツケッサイ	consolidated statement of accounts
	連結財務諸表	レンケツザイムショヒョウ	consolidated financial statements
	連結指数	レンケツシスウ	chain-index

	連帯責任	レンタイセキニン	solidarity
	連邦準備銀行	レンポウジュンビギンコウ	Federal Reserve Bank (U.S.)

700

逸 ⑪

音	逸	イツ	deviate; flee; miss; lose; leisure; excellent
熟	逸する	イッする	*v*. fail to catch; let go; lose
	逸材	イツザイ	person of talent; able person
	逸脱	イツダツ	departure; deviation; breakaway —*v*. deviate; depart; breakaway
	逸話	イツワ	anecdote
訓	逸らす	そらす	***vt***. let slip; miss; lose; let go
	逸れる	それる	***vi***. deviate from; swerve

701

週 ⑪

音	週	シュウ	week
熟	週間	シュウカン	week
	週刊	シュウカン	weekly publication
	週刊誌	シュウカンシ	weekly magazine
	週休	シュウキュウ	weekly holiday
	週給	シュウキュウ	weekly pay/salary
	週末	シュウマツ	weekend
¥	週休二日制	シュウキュウふつかセイ	five-day work week

702

進 ⑪

音	進	シン	advance
熟	進化	シンカ	evolution —***vi***. evolve; develop
	進学	シンガク	educational progress; development —***vi***. go on to the next stage of one's education
	進学志望者	シンガクシボウシャ	applicants to high school or college
	進学塾	シンガクジュク	cram school

	進学率	シンガクリツ	ratio of students who go on to higher education
	進級	シンキュウ	promotion —*vi*. be promoted
	進軍	シングン	advance; march; marching —*vi*. advance; march on
	進撃	シンゲキ	attack; advance; charge —*vi*. advance; attack; make an attack
	進言	シンゲン	advice; counsel; proposal —*v*. advise; counsel; make a proposal
	進行	シンコウ	advance; progress —*vi*. move forward; advance; make progress
	進攻	シンコウ	attack —*v*. attack; advance
	進取	シンシュ	enterprising; enterprise
	進出	シンシュツ	advance —*vi*. advance; make inroads into; go into
	進退	シンタイ	advance or retreat; movement; behavior
	進駐軍	シンチュウグン	Occupation Forces
	進捗状況	シンチョク ジョウキョウ	progress
	進呈	シンテイ	presentation —*v*. present
	進展	シンテン	development; progress —*vi*. develop; progress
	進度	シンド	progress; degree of progress
	進入	シンニュウ	entry; approach —*vi*. march; make their way; enter; approach
	進歩	シンポ	progress; advance; improvement —*vi*. make progress; advance; improve
	進歩的	シンポテキ	progressive; advanced
	進物	シンモツ	gift
	進路	シンロ	course; route; way
訓	進む	すすむ	*vi*. advance; progress; travel; go forward *vt*. lead; move; go ahead
	進める	すすめる	*vt*. lead; move; advance; proceed; go ahead; be promoted

703

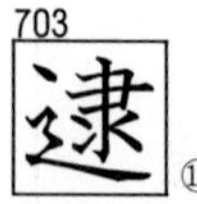

⑪ 　フ ヨ ヨ 쿠 ... 逮

音	逮	タイ	arrest; capture; chase; reach
熟	逮捕	タイホ	arrest; apprehension; capture —*v*. arrest; apprehend; capture; put into custody

704
運 ⑫

音	運	ウン	carry; ship; transport; fate; luck; destiny
熟	運営	ウンエイ	management; operation; administration —*v*. manage; operate; administer
	運河	ウンガ	canal
	運休	ウンキュウ	suspension (of a scheduled train, flight, etc.) —*v*. suspend (a train, flight) etc.
	運行	ウンコウ	revolution; movement; motion —*vi*. revolve; orbit; move around
	運航	ウンコウ	shipping; airline service —*vi*. operate; run; ply
	運勢	ウンセイ	one's stars; fortune; luck
	運送	ウンソウ	transportation; conveyance; shipping; transporting; traffic —*v*. transport; convey; carry; forward; ship
	運賃	ウンチン	freight; shipping charge; tarrif; passenger fare; (goods) rate
	運転	ウンテン	driving; operation —*v*. drive; operate
	運転手	ウンテンシュ	driver
	運転免許	ウンテンメンキョ	driver's license
	運動	ウンドウ	motion; exercise; canvassing; campaign —*vi*. move; exercise; canvass; campaign
	運搬	ウンパン	forwarding; shipping; transporting; carriage —*v*. carry; transport; convey; deliver
	運命	ウンメイ	destiny; fate; luck; fortune; the inevitable
	運輸	ウンユ	transport; traffic
訓	運ぶ	はこぶ	***vt***. carry; ship; progress
¥	運行	ウンコウ	movement; operation; service
	運転資金	ウンテンシキン	operational funds; working capital
	運輸省	ウンユショウ	Ministry of Transport
	運輸大臣	ウンユダイジン	Minister of Transport

705

過 ⑫

音	過	カ	pass; spend; error; excessive
熟	過激	カゲキ	extreme/radical (thought or action)
	過去	カコ	the past; one's past life ***gram***. past tense
	過酷	カコク	severe; harsh; cruel; hard; merciless
	過言	カゴン	saying too much; exaggeration

	過失	カシツ	unintentional mistake; error; negligence
	過日	カジツ	the other day; some days ago
	過重	カジュウ	too great a load; overload
	過小	カショウ	too small
	過少	カショウ	too few/little
	過剰	カジョウ	surplus; excess
	過信	カシン	overconfidence —***v.*** have too much confidence
	過疎	カソ	sparseness; depopulation
	過多	カタ	excess; surplus; too much/many
	過大	カダイ	too big; excessive
	過程	カテイ	process; course
	過度	カド	beyond a reasonable limit; excess
	過渡期	カトキ	transition; transitional period
	過熱	カネツ	overheating —***v.*** overheat
	過半数	カハンスウ	majority
	過敏	カビン	oversensitive
	過不足	カフソク	excess or deficiency
	過分	カブン	generous; excessive; unworthy
	過密	カミツ	overcrowded; overpopulated
	過労	カロウ	overwork; overexertion
訓	過ぎる	すぎる	***vi.*** pass; exceed
	過ごす	すごす	***vt.*** pass/spend (time); live; stay
	過ち	あやまち	mistake; fault; error
	過つ	あやまつ	***vt.*** err; make a mistake
¥	過労死	カロウシ	death from overwork —***vi.*** die from working too hard

706

⑫

音	遇	グウ	unexpected; treatment
熟	遇する	グウする	***vt.*** treat; use; deal with; entertain; receive

707

⑫

音	遂	スイ	carry out
熟	遂行	スイコウ	execution; accomplishment; performance —***v.*** execute; accomplish; perform; carry out
訓	遂げる	とげる	***vt.*** accomplish; achieve; attain; realize; effect

※遂に　ついに　at last; finally

708

達 ⑫

一 十 土 キ 圭 圭 幸 幸 幸 ‵幸 `逹 達

音	達	タツ	lead; deliver; announcement
熟	達する	タッする	*v.* reach; attain; achieve
	達観	タッカン	farsighted-view; philosophic view —*v.* take a farsighted view
	達者	タッシャ	healthy; well; strong; expert; proficient; clever
	達人	タツジン	expert; master
	達成	タッセイ	attainment; achievement; accomplishment —*v.* achieve; attain; accomplish
	達筆	タッピツ	good handwriting/writing style

709

遅 ⑫

フ コ 尸 尸 尸 尸 尸 屋 屖 `屖 遅 遅

音	遅	チ	be late/delayed/slow
熟	遅延	チエン	delay; postponement —*v.* delay; postpone
	遅刻	チコク	lateness; being late —*v.* be/come late
	遅々	チチ	slowly; lagging; tardy
	遅配	チハイ	delay (in delivery, pay, etc.) —*v.* delay (delivery, payment, etc.)
訓	遅らす	おくらす	*vt.* delay; defer; put off
	遅れる	おくれる	*vi.* be late/behind schedule/delayed; fall behind
	遅い	おそい	late; slow

710

道 ⑫

丶 ソ 丷 䒑 䒑 首 首 首 首 `首 道 道

音	道	ドウ (トウ)	road; reason; method; district; way
熟	道義	ドウギ	morality; morals; moral principles
	道具	ドウグ	instrument; appliance; tool; furniture
	道具箱	ドウグばこ	tool box
	道化	ドウケ	buffoonery; tomfoolery
	道化師	ドウケシ	clown
	道場	ドウジョウ	drill hall for martial arts

	道中	ドウチュウ	on a journey; travel on a tour
	道程	ドウテイ	distance; journey
	道徳	ドウトク	morality
	道破	ドウハ	declaration; strong statement —*v*. declare; state strongly
	道標	ドウヒョウ（みちしるべ）	guidepost; signpost
	道楽	ドウラク	hobby; pastime; dissipation; debauchery
	道楽者	ドウラクもの	playboy
	道理	ドウリ	reason; right; justice; truth
	道路	ドウロ	road; way; street
	道路標識	ドウロヒョウシキ	road sign
訓	道	みち	road; way; street; journey; distance; duty; morality
	道案内	みちアンナイ	guidance; guide
	道草を食う	みちくさをくう	***vi***. loiter/tarry on the way —***fig***. lose/waste time
	道順	みちじゅん	route; itinerary

711

⑫

音	遍	ヘン	widely; generally; everywhere; (number) of times
熟	遍在	ヘンザイ	ubiquitous; omnipresent —***vi***. be ubiquitous/omnipresent
	遍歴	ヘンレキ	traveling to various countries; experiencing many things —***vi***. travel abroad; experience
	遍路	ヘンロ	pilgrim; pilgrimage

712

⑫

音	遊	ユウ（ユ）	play; tour; enjoy; oneself; be idle
熟	遊泳	ユウエイ	swimming
	遊園地	ユウエンチ	amusement park; recreation area; playground
	遊学	ユウガク	studying away from home —***v***. study away from home
	遊戯	ユウギ	play; games; sport; entertainment; amusement; pastime
	遊休	ユウキュウ	idle; unused

	遊撃	ユウゲキ	commando attack; shortstop -*bas*. hit and run attack
	遊星	ユウセイ	planet
	遊説	ユウゼイ	canvassing; campaign —*vi*. canvass; campaign
	遊牧民	ユウボクミン	nomads
	遊覧	ユウラン	sightseeing; excursion —*vi*. go sightseeing; go on an excursion
	遊離	ユウリ	isolation; separation —*v*. be isolated/separated
	遊山	ユサン	picnic/outing/excursion to the mountains
訓	遊ぶ	あそぶ	*vi*. play; enjoy oneself; be idle
	遊び	あそび	play; game; sport; amusement; recreation
	遊ばせる	あそばせる	amuse; let play; leave something as it is

713

違 ⑬

丿 ヵ 五 六 ... 韋 違 違

音	違	イ	differ from; unlike; mistake
熟	違憲	イケン	violation of the constitution
	違反	イハン	violation; offense; infringement; breach —*vi*. violate; infringe; disobey; break the law
	違犯	イハン	violation; offense; infringement; breach —*vi*. violate; infringe; disobey; break the law
	違法	イホウ	illegality; lawbreaking; unlawfulness
	違約	イヤク	breach of contract; break a promise; default —*vi*. infringe a contract; break a promise; default
	違和感	イワカン	feeling of being out of place; incongruity
訓	違い	ちがい	difference; mistake
	違う	ちがう	*vi*. differ; be wrong; disagree; oppose
	違える	ちがえる	*vt*. change; alter; vary
	※違う	たがう	*vi*. differ; be different in opinion
	※違える	たがえる	*vt*. change; alter; mistake; confuse
¥	違約金	イヤクキン	penalty; forfeit

714

遠 ⑬

一 十 土 ... 袁 遠 遠

音	遠	エン	distant; far; profound; perspective
		(オン)	far; eternity
熟	遠因	エンイン	remote cause; underlying factor; indirect cause
	遠泳	エンエイ	long-distance swim

	遠海	エンカイ	the open sea; the deep
	遠隔	エンカク	remote; faraway; distant
	遠距離	エンキョリ	long distance
	遠近	エンキン	far and near; distance
	遠景	エンケイ	distant view
	遠視	エンシ	farsightedness; hyperopia
	遠心力	エンシンリョク	centrifugal force
	遠征	エンセイ	military expedition; expedition —***vi***. invade; go on an expedition
	遠足	エンソク	excursion; day-trip; school trip
	遠大	エンダイ	having wide range or effect; far-reaching
	遠望	エンボウ	distant view; perspective —***v***. view from a distance
	遠方	エンポウ	faraway
	遠洋	エンヨウ	the open sea; the deep
	遠来	エンライ	coming from afar
	遠慮	エンリョ	reserve; modesty; forethought; foresight —***v***. be modest; keep a distance; refrain
	遠路	エンロ	long way; roundabout way
訓	遠浅	とおあさ	shallow for a considerable distance; shoal
	遠い	とおい	far; remote; distant
	遠縁	とおエン	distant relative
	遠回し	とおまわし	indirect; roundabout; vague
	遠回り	とおまわり	detour

715

⑬

音	遣	ケン	dispatch; send
熟	遣唐使	ケントウシ	***hist***. Japanese envoys sent to Tang Dynasty China
訓	遣う	つかう	***vt***. spend; consume; waste; worry
	遣わす	つかわす	***vt***. dispatch; send

716

遮 ⑭

音	遮	シャ	interrupt
熟	遮光	シャコウ	preventing light from leaking outside —***v***. shade; shield

遮断	シャダン	interruption; isolation —*v*. cut off; stop; interrupt traffic
遮断器	シャダンキ	railroad crossing gate
遮二無二	シャニムニ	furious; all one's might; like crazy
遮蔽	シャヘイ	shelter; cover —*v*. shelter; shade; cover
訓 遮る	さえぎる	***vt***. interrupt; obstruct; block; intercept
遮り	さえぎり	obstruct; cut off; block; interrupt

717

遭 ⑭

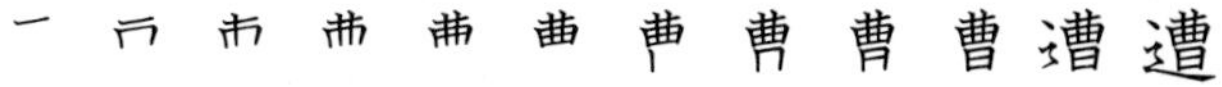

音 遭	ソウ	encounter; meet
熟 遭遇	ソウグウ	encounter; meeting —*v*. encounter; meet
遭難	ソウナン	accident; disaster; mishap —*v*. meet with accident/disaster
訓 遭う	あう	***vi***. meet

718

適 ⑭

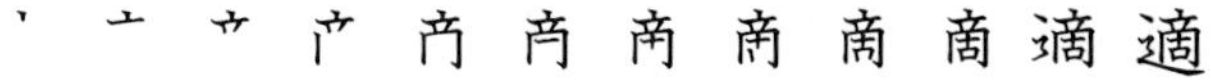

音 適	テキ	suit
熟 適する	テキする	***vi***. fit; suit; agree; be adapted/qualified
適応	テキオウ	adaptation; accommodation; conformity —*v*. be adaptable; be suitable/fitted to
適応性	テキオウセイ	adaptability; flexibility
適格	テキカク	competency
適宜	テキギ	suitable; appropriate; fitting; proper
適合	テキゴウ	conformity; agreement; compatibility —*v*. conform; suit; fit; be compatible
適材適所	テキザイテキショ	right man in the right place
適時	テキジ	timely; opportune
適正	テキセイ	proper; appropriate; right; just
適正化	テキセイカ	rationalization
適性	テキセイ	aptitude
適性検査	テキセイケンサ	aptitude test —*v*. give an aptitude test
適切	テキセツ	pertinent; fit; suitable; adequate; proper; relevent
適中	テキチュウ	hit
適度	テキド	moderation; proper degree; temperance; measure
適当	テキトウ	suitable; fit; proper; adequate

	適任	テキニン	fitness; suitability; competence
	適否	テキヒ	propriety; suitability; fitness; aptitude
	適法	テキホウ	legality; lawfulness
	適役	テキヤク	fit post/role
	適用	テキヨウ	application —*v.* apply
	適量	テキリョウ	proper quantity/dose; dosage
	適例	テキレイ	good example
	適齢	テキレイ	marriageable age
訓	※適う	かなう	***vi.*** suit; fit; be consistent/agreeable

719

⑮

音	遺	イ (ユイ)	leave; abandon
熟	遺憾	イカン	regrettable; lamentable; deplorable
	遺棄	イキ	abandonment; desertion —*v.* abandon; desert; leave unattended
	遺業	イギョウ	work left unfinished by the deceased; unfinished work
	遺骨	イコツ	(one's) ashes; skeletal remains
	遺作	イサク	posthumous work
	遺産	イサン	inheritance; legacy; estate; bequest
	遺志	イシ	one's dying wish; unfulfilled wish of a dying person
	遺児	イジ	child of the deceased; orphaned child
	遺失	イシツ	loss —*v.* lose; leave behind
	遺失物	イシツブツ	lost article/property
	遺書	イショ	note left behind by a dead person; suicide note
	遺跡	イセキ	ruins; relics; remains
	遺族	イゾク	bereaved family; family of the deceased; survivors
	遺体	イタイ	dead body; corpse; remains
	遺伝	イデン	heredity; hereditary transmission; genetic inheritance —***vi.*** be inherited; be transmitted; be handed down
	遺伝子	イデンシ	gene
	遺品	イヒン	article left by the departed
	遺物	イブツ	relic; remains; antiquity; memento
	遺言	ユイゴン	(one's) will; will and testament; one's spoken will and testament —*v.* leave/make a will

720

遵 ⑮

音	遵	ジュン	observe
熟	遵守	ジュンシュ	observance (of the law) —*v*. obey (the law)
	遵法	ジュンポウ	law-abiding

721

選 ⑮

音	選	セン	choose; select
熟	選外	センガイ	left out; not chosen
	選挙	センキョ	election —*v*. elect
	選挙権	センキョケン	right to vote; suffrage
	選考	センコウ	selection; screening —*v*. select; screen
	選者	センジャ	selector; judge
	選手	センシュ	sports player; athlete
	選手権	センシュケン	championship title
	選集	センシュウ	selection; anthology
	選出	センシュツ	election; select —*v*. elect; select; pick out
	選択	センタク	selection; choice —*v*. choose; select
	選定	センテイ	selection; choice —*v*. select; choose
	選抜	センバツ	selection; choice —*v*. select; choose; single out
	選別	センベツ	selection; grading; sorting —*v*. select; grade; sort
	選良	センリョウ	the elite; member of a parliament
訓	選ぶ	えらぶ	***vt***. choose; select
	※選る	える	***vt***. choose; select
	※選る	すぐる	***v***. choose; select
	※選る	よる	***vt***. choose; select
¥	選別買い	センベツがい	selective buying

722

遷 ⑮

音	遷	セン	remove; change
熟	遷都	セント	transfer of the capital city —***vi***. transfer the capital city

3
口 囗 土 士 夂 夕 大 女 子 宀 寸 小 ⺌ ⺍ 尢 尸 山 川 工 己 巾 干 幺 广 廴 廾 弋 弓 彐 彡 彳 艹 ●辶 ●阝 阝 ⺍ 忄 扌 犭 氵

723
還 ⑯

音	還	カン (ゲン)	return
熟	還元	カンゲン	restoration; chemical reduction —*v*. restore; reduce; resolve
	還付	カンプ	return; restoration; restitution —*v*. return; restore; retrocede
	還暦	カンレキ	one's sixty-first birthday
	還俗	ゲンゾク	secularization —*vi*. return to secular life; renounce the cloth
訓	※還る	かえる	*vi*. return; come back
	※還る	めぐる	*vi*. circulate; come around; return

724
避 ⑯

音	避	ヒ	avoid
熟	避暑	ヒショ	summering (in a cool place) —*vi*. spend/pass the summer (in a cool place)
	避暑地	ヒショチ	summer resort
	避難	ヒナン	refuge; shelter; evacuation —*vi*. take/seek refuge/shelter; evacuate
	避難民	ヒナンミン	refugees; evacuees
	避妊	ヒニン	contraception; birth control —*vi*. prevent conception; practice birth control
	避雷針	ヒライシン	lightning rod
訓	避ける	さける	*vt*. avoid; escape
	※避ける	よける	*vt*. avoid; escape

3 阝 こざとへん left village

725
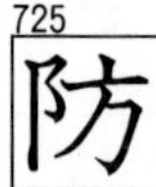
⑦

音	防	ボウ	defend; protect; prevent; (prefix) anti-; -proof; -resistant

熟	防衛	ボウエイ	defense —*v*. defend
	防疫	ボウエキ	prevention against epidemics —*v*. prevent epidemics
	防音	ボウオン	soundproof —*vi*. be soundproof
	防火	ボウカ	fire prevention; fire fighting; fireproof
	防火栓	ボウカセン	fire hydrant
	防火壁	ボウカヘキ	fire wall
	防寒	ボウカン	protection against the cold
	防寒服	ボウカンフク	winter/arctic clothing
	防御	ボウギョ	defense —*v*. defend (against an enemy attack)
	防空	ボウクウ	air defense
	防空壕	ボウクウゴウ	air-raid/bomb shelter
	防護	ボウゴ	protection; custody —*v*. protect (against injury)
	防塞	ボウサイ	roadblock; barricade; fort
	防災	ボウサイ	prevention of disaster
	防止	ボウシ	prevention —*v*. prevent
	防湿	ボウシツ	dampproof
	防臭剤	ボウシュウザイ	deodorant
	防食剤	ボウショクザイ	anti-corrosive
	防塵	ボウジン	dustproof
	防水	ボウスイ	waterproof; watertight —*v*. make waterproof/watertight
	防雪	ボウセツ	snow protection
	防雪林	ボウセツリン	snowbreak (forest)
	防戦	ボウセン	defensive battle/fight —*vi*. fight a defensive battle
	防弾	ボウダン	bulletproof; bombproof
	防虫	ボウチュウ	insect repellent
	防虫剤	ボウチュウザイ	insecticide
	防毒	ボウドク	gasproof
	防波堤	ボウハテイ	breakwater
	防犯	ボウハン	crime prevention
	防備	ボウビ	defensive preparations —*v*. make preparations to defend/protect (against an enemy attack)
	防風	ボウフウ	wind protection/shelter
	防風林	ボウフウリン	windbreak (forest)
	防腐剤	ボウフザイ	preservative
	防壁	ボウヘキ	barrier; bulwark
訓	防ぐ	ふせぐ	*vt*. defend; prevent; protect (from)
¥	防衛庁	ボウエイチョウ	Defense Agency

726

阻 ⑧

フ ３ 阝 阝 阝 阴 阻 阻

音	阻	ソ	obstruct; prevent; impede; block; hamper
熟	阻害	ソガイ	obstruction; hindrance —*v*. obstruct; hinder; impede; check; retard
	阻止	ソシ	deterrence; hinderance; obstruction —*vt*. check; deter; hinder; obstruct
訓	阻む	はばむ	*vt*. impede; obstruct; prevent; block; hamper

727

附 ⑧

フ ３ 阝 阝 阝 阝 附 附

音	附	フ	attach
訓	※附く	つく	*vi*. be attached/affixed/added

728

限 ⑨

フ ３ 阝 阝 阝 阝 阝 阝 限

音	限	ゲン	limit; boundary; restriction
熟	限界	ゲンカイ	limit; boundary; margin
	限定	ゲンテイ	limitation; restriction —*v*. limit; restrict
	限度	ゲンド	limit
訓	限る	かぎる	*vt*. restrict; limit
	限り	かぎり	limits; restriction
¥	限月	ゲンゲツ	delivery month

729

院 ⑩

フ ３ 阝 阝 阝 阝 阝 阝 阝 院

音	院	イン	public place or building (such as hospital or Diet)
熟	院議	インギ	parliamentary/Diet decision
	院長	インチョウ	the director (of a hospital)

730

陥 ⑩

音	陥	カン	fall; fall into
熟	陥没	カンボツ	depression; subsidence; cave-in —*vi.* subside; sink; cave in
	陥落	カンラク	fall; surrender —*vi.* fall; surrender
訓	陥る	おちいる	*vi.* fall into; sink; cave in; subside
	陥れる	おとしいれる	*vt.* entrap; ensnare; capture

731

降 ⑩

音	降	コウ	fall; descend; alight; drop; surrender
熟	降雨	コウウ	rainfall; precipitation
	降下	コウカ	descent; falling; dropping; fall; landing —*vi.* descend; fall; drop; land
	降参	コウサン	surrender; submission; capitulation —*vi.* surrender; submit; capitulate
	降車	コウシャ	alighting; getting off —*vi.* alight; get off/down
	降水量	コウスイリョウ	amount of precipitation/rainfall
	降雪	コウセツ	snowfall; snow
	降誕	コウタン	nativity; birth; advent; incarnation —*vi.* be born; be incarnated; see the light
	降伏	コウフク	surrender; submission; capitulation —*vi.* surrender; submit; capitulate
訓	降りる	おりる	*vi.* come/get down; descend; alight; leave; quit
	降ろす	おろす	*vt.* take down; lower; bring down; drop; have an abortion; grate
	降る	ふる	*vi.* fall; come down; descend; rain; snow

732

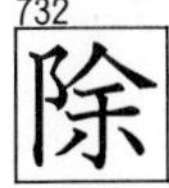

除 ⑩

音	除	ジョ (ジ)	remove; divide
熟	除外	ジョガイ	exception; exclusion —*v.* exclude; leave out
	除去	ジョキョ	removal; riddance —*v.* remove; get rid of
	除籍	ジョセキ	removal from a (family) register —*v.* remove a person's name from a (family) register

	除雪	ジョセツ	snow removal —***vi***. clear away the snow
	除草	ジョソウ	weeding —***vi***. weed
	除幕式	ジョマクシキ	unveiling ceremony
	除名	ジョメイ	expulsion —***v***. expel from (association, political party, etc.)
	除夜	ジョヤ	New Year's Eve
訓	除く	のぞく	***vt***. remove; exclude; expel; leave/take out

733

陣 ⑩

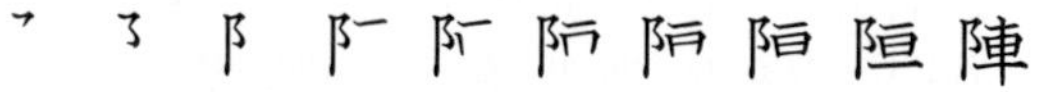

音	陣	ジン	disposition of an army
熟	陣営	ジンエイ	camp
	陣痛	ジンツウ	***med***. labor pains
	陣頭	ジントウ	the front/head
	陣容	ジンヨウ	battle formation

734

陛 ⑩

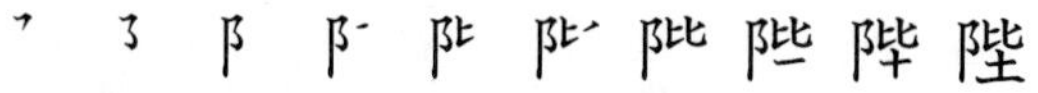

音	陛	ヘイ	stairway in the imperial palace; (honorific word used to describe a monarch)
熟	陛下	ヘイカ	His/Her/Your Majesty

735

陰 ⑪

音	陰	イン	shade; secret; shadow; negative
熟	陰影	インエイ	shadow; shading; gloom
	陰気	インキ	gloominess; gloom; dismalness; melancholy
	陰険	インケン	crafty; treacherous
	陰惨	インサン	disastrous; dismal; weird; gloomy
	陰性	インセイ	negative (of a medical test); dormant
	陰謀	インボウ	plot; intrigue; conspiracy
	陰暦	インレキ	lunar calendar
訓	陰	かげ	shade; behind the scenes
	陰口	かげぐち	backbiting
	陰る	かげる	***vi***. darken; get dark; become cloudy; be obscured

736 険 ⑪

音	険	ケン	steep
熟	険悪	ケンアク	threatening; hostile; cross
訓	険しい	けわしい	steep; stern; sharp

737 陳 ⑪

音	陳	チン	display; state; declare
熟	陳謝	チンシャ	apology; regret —*v*. apologize; express one's regret
	陳述	チンジュツ	statement; declaration; desposition —*v*. state; declare; set forth
	陳情	チンジョウ	appeal; representation; petition —*v*. make an appeal/representation; petition
	陳情書	チンジョウショ	representation; petition
	陳腐	チンプ	commonplace; old-fashioned; antiquated
	陳列	チンレツ	exhibition; show; display —*v*. exhibit; show; display

738 陶 ⑪

音	陶	トウ	earthenware
熟	陶器	トウキ	earthenware; ceramics; pottery
	陶芸	トウゲイ	ceramic art
	陶工	トウコウ	potter; porcelain maker
	陶工術	トウコウジュツ	ceramics; pottery
	陶磁器	トウジキ	china and porcelain; ceramics; pottery
	陶酔	トウスイ	intoxication; fascination; rapture —*vi*. be intoxiated/fascinated/charmed
	陶然	トウゼン	mellow with drink; tipsy
	陶土	トウド	potter's clay; kaolin; china clay
	陶冶	トウヤ	cultivation; training; education —*v*. cultivate; train; educate
訓	※陶	すえ	china; earthenware; ceramics

739 陪 ⑪

音	陪	バイ	accompany a superior
熟	陪審	バイシン	jury
	陪審員	バイシンイン	juror; member of the jury
	陪席	バイセキ	sitting with one's superior —*vi*. sit with one's superior

740 陸 ⑪

音	陸	リク	land
熟	陸運	リクウン	land transport
	陸軍	リクグン	army
	陸上競技	リクジョウキョウギ	field and track events
	陸続	リクゾク	in succession; continuously
	陸地	リクチ	land
	陸路	リクロ	overland route
	陸橋	リッキョウ	overpass; viaduct
訓	※陸	おか	land

741 隆 ⑪

音	隆	リュウ	high; noble; flourishing
熟	隆起	リュウキ	rise; bulge; elevation; protruberance —*vi*. rise; bulge; elevate; protrude
	隆盛	リュウセイ	prosperous; flourishing; thriving
	隆々	リュウリュウ	prosperous; thriving; muscular

742 陵 ⑪

音	陵	リョウ	imperial tomb; insult; outrage; rape; violation
熟	陵辱	リョウジョク	indignity; insult; outrage; rape —*v*. insult; rape; violate; make fun of; embarrass

	陵墓	リョウボ	imperial tomb
訓	陵	みささぎ	imperial tomb

743

階 ⑫

音	階	カイ	stairs; floor; staircase; rank
熟	階下	カイカ	downstairs
	階級	カイキュウ	class
	階上	カイジョウ	upstairs
	階層	カイソウ	class; layer; stratum
	階段	カイダン	stairs

744
隅 ⑫

音	隅	グウ	corner
訓	隅	すみ	corner
	隅田川	すみだがわ	Sumida River (Tokyo)

745

随 ⑫

音	随	ズイ	follow
熟	随意	ズイイ	voluntary; optional
	随一	ズイイチ	foremost; most
	随員	ズイイン	suite; attendant
	随行	ズイコウ	attendance —***vi***. attend; accompany; follow
	随行者	ズイコウシャ	attendant
	随時	ズイジ	any time; all times
	随従	ズイジュウ	following (a lead) —***vi***. follow; play second fiddle
	随従者	ズイジュウシャ	henchman; follower
	随所	ズイショ	everywhere; anywhere
	随想	ズイソウ	occasional/random thoughts
	随筆	ズイヒツ	essay
	随分	ズイブン	fairly; pretty; tolerably

746

隊 ⑫

音	隊	タイ	crew; party
熟	隊員	タイイン	crew member
	隊商	タイショウ	caravan
	隊長	タイチョウ	captain; leader; commanding officer
	隊列	タイレツ	file; rank

747

陽 ⑫

音	陽	ヨウ	the sun; positive; yang
熟	陽気	ヨウキ	weather; cheerful; gay; happy
	陽極	ヨウキョク	positive pole; anode
	陽光	ヨウコウ	sunlight; sunshine
	陽子	ヨウシ	proton
	陽春	ヨウシュン	warm spring; New Year (of the lunar calendar)
	陽性	ヨウセイ	cheerful; positive
	陽転	ヨウテン	positive reaction (to a medical test) —***vi***. react positively (to a medical test)
	陽暦	ヨウレキ	solar calendar
訓	※陽	ひ	sun
	※陽当たり	ひあたり	exposure to the sun

748

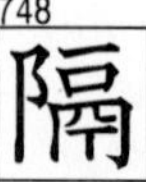

隔 ⑬

音	隔	カク	separate
熟	隔月	カクゲツ	every other month
	隔日	カクジツ	every other day
	隔週	カクシュウ	every other week
	隔世	カクセイ	distant age
	隔絶	カクゼツ	separation; isolation; segregation —***vi***. be separated/isolated/segregated from
	隔年	カクネン	every other year
	隔離	カクリ	isolation; quarantine; segreagation —***v***. isolate; quarantine; segregate

訓	隔たる	へだたる	***vi***. be distant from; be isolated/estranged
	隔てる	へだてる	***vt***. part; separate; segregate; isolate; alienate; estrange
	隔たり	へだたり	distance; interval; difference; estrangement

749

隠 ⑭

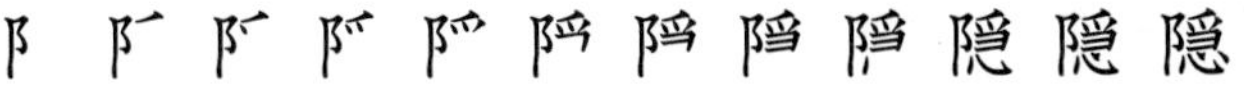

音	隠	イン （オン）	conceal; retire; retirement
熟	隠居	インキョ	retirement; retired person; old gentleman or lady (retire from active life) —***vi***. retire from active life; go into retirement
	隠語	インゴ	secret language; jargon
	隠匿	イントク	concealment; secretion —***v***. hide; conceal; secrete
	隠密	オンミツ	privacy; secrecy; spy
訓	隠れる	かくれる	***vi***. disappear; hide; retire
	隠す	かくす	***vt***. hide

750

際 ⑭

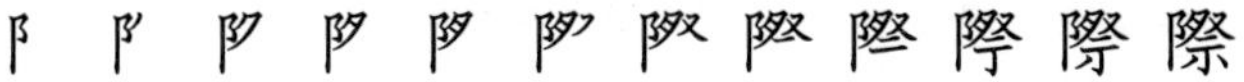

音	際	サイ	case; associate; mix; limit; occasion
熟	際限	サイゲン	limits; bounds
訓	際	きわ	brink; verge
	際立つ	きわだつ	***vi***. stand out; be conspicuous
	際どい	きわどい	risky; close; narrow; indecent
	際物	きわもの	seasonal goods

751

障 ⑭

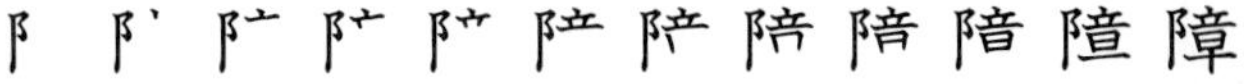

音	障	ショウ	obstacle; hurdle
熟	障害	ショウガイ	obstacle; hindrance; difficulty; handicap; disorder; impediment
	障害者	ショウガイシャ	handicapped person
	障害物	ショウガイブツ	obstacle; hurdle
	障子	ショウジ	*shōji* (paper sliding door)
	障壁	ショウヘキ	barrier; wall

3 口 囗 土 士 夂 夕 大 女 子 宀 寸 小 ⺌ ⺍ 尢 尸 山 川 工 己 巾 干 幺 广 廴 廾 弋 弓 ヨ 彡 彳 艹 辶 阝 阝 ⺍ 忄 扌 犭 氵

訓	障る	さわる	*vi*. interfere; obstruct; be bad for
	障り	さわり	obstacle; obstruction

752

隣 ⑯

音	隣	リン	neighboring; adjacent; adjoin
熟	隣人	リンジン	neighbor
	隣接	リンセツ	adjacent; contiguous; bordering —*vi*. adjoin; be contiguous; border on
訓	隣	となり	next-door; adjoining

---

3 阝 おおざと right village

753

邦 ⑦

音	邦	ホウ	country; our country (Japan)
熟	邦画	ホウガ	Japanese film/picture
	邦楽	ホウガク	Japanese music
	邦人	ホウジン	Japanese person
	邦文	ホウブン	Japanese language
訓	邦	くに	country (Japan)
¥	邦銀	ホウギン	Japanese commercial banks

754

邪 ⑧

音	邪	ジャ	wicked
熟	邪悪	ジャアク	wicked; malicious; viscious
	邪気	ジャキ	malicious; wicked
	邪教	ジャキョウ	heretical religion
	邪険	ジャケン	cruel; harsh; unkind
	邪心	ジャシン	wicked heart
	邪推	ジャスイ	groundless suspicion —*v*. suspect without reason
	邪説	ジャセツ	heresy

邪道	ジャドウ	evil way; misleading
邪念	ジャネン	wicked thought; evil desire
邪魔	ジャマ	obstacle; hindrance; interference; nuisance; bother —*v.* interrupt; disturb; trouble

755
邸 ⑧

音	邸	テイ	mansion
熟	邸宅	テイタク	mansion; residence
訓	※邸	やしき	mansion; residence

756
郊 ⑨

音	郊	コウ	suburbs; the country
熟	郊外	コウガイ	suburbs; outskirts

757
郎 ⑨

音	郎	ロウ	man; husband
熟	郎党	ロウトウ	vassals; retainers

758
郡 ⑩

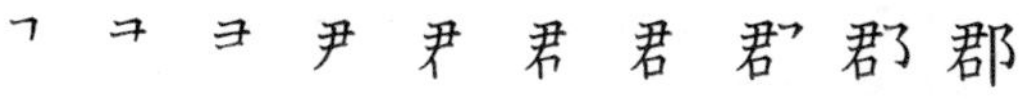

音	郡	グン	territorial division; (suffix) *-gun* (county; district)
熟	郡部	グンブ	rural section; suburban districts; districts classified as *gun*

759
郭 ⑪

音	郭	カク	land enclosure; outline
訓	※郭	くるわ	quarter; district

760

郷 ⑪

音	郷	キョウ ゴウ	town; hometown; country; province
熟	郷愁	キョウシュウ	homesickness
	郷土	キョウド	one's hometown/town of birth
	郷土色	キョウドショク	local color
	郷里	キョウリ	one's hometown

761

都 ⑪

音	都	ト	city; Tokyo
		ツ	all
熟	都合	ツゴウ	arrangements; circumstances
	都度	ツド	every time; each occasion; whenever
	都営	トエイ	metropolitan Tokyo-run (subway)
	都下	トカ	metropolis; capital; Tokyo
	都会	トカイ	city; town
	都市	トシ	city; town; urban area
	都心	トシン	city center
	都内	トナイ	within Tokyo
	都立	トリツ	metropolitan; municipal
訓	都	みやこ	capital; metropolis; seat of government
	都落ち	みやこおち	rustification —***vi***. flee the capital city
¥	都市銀行	トシギンコウ	city bank

762

部 ⑪

音	部	ブ	section; department; club; category; (counter for copies of books, etc.)
熟	部員	ブイン	staff; member of a club
	部下	ブカ	subordinate (worker)
	部首	ブシュ	radicals of Chinese characters
	部署	ブショ	one's post/duty/station
	部数	ブスウ	number of copies; circulation

	部族	ブゾク	tribe
	部隊	ブタイ	(military) unit; corps; detachment
	部長	ブチョウ	department head; head of a club
	部分	ブブン	part
	部落	ブラク	village; community; settlement
	部類	ブルイ	classification; category
	※部屋	へや	room
¥	部品	ブヒン	machine/spare parts
	部門	ブモン	department; field; branch; section; class; division

763

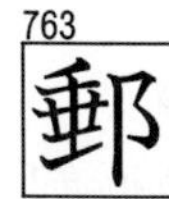

⑪

音	郵	ユウ	mail; post
熟	郵政	ユウセイ	postal system
	郵税	ユウゼイ	postage; rate of postage
	郵送	ユウソウ	mailing —*v*. mail; post
	郵便	ユウビン	mail; post
	郵便局	ユウビンキョク	post office
	郵便箱	ユウビンばこ	mailbox
¥	郵政省	ユウセイショウ	Ministry of Posts and Telecommunications

3 䒑 そいち lining up (artificial radical)

764

⑧

音	並	ヘイ	side-by-side; together; ordinary
熟	並行	ヘイコウ	parallel; side-by-side; together —*vi*. line up in a row; occur simultaneously
	並存	ヘイゾン (ヘイソン)	coexistence —*vi*. coexist
	並立	ヘイリツ	standing side-by-side —*vi*. stand side-by-side
	並列	ヘイレツ	parallel (circuit); arranged in a row —*v*. arrange in a row
訓	並	なみ	ordinary; average; regular
	並木	なみき	row of trees on either side of a street
	並外れる	なみはずれる	*vi*. be out of the ordinary

並幅	なみはば	standard width (about 36 cm)
並ぶ	ならぶ	***vi***. be in a row; rank with; queue up
並べる	ならべる	***vt***. arrange/place in a row; display; lay out; compare
並びに	ならびに	both; and; as well as

765

⑩

音	兼	ケン	concurrent
熟	兼業	ケンギョウ	side job
	兼行	ケンコウ	round the clock; twenty-four hours a day —***v***. work around the clock
	兼任	ケンニン	additional post; side job —***v***. hold an additional post
	兼務	ケンム	additional post; side job —***v***. hold an additional post
	兼用	ケンヨウ	double-use; double purpose —***v***. also serves; can be used both as
訓	兼ねる	かねる	***vt***. be concurrent; combine; serve both as; be both; (suffix) cannot; be hard to; be not in a position to
Y	兼営業務	ケンエイギョウム	multiple businesses —***v***. operate in addition to some other business

3 忄 see ⇨p.370

3 扌 see ⇨p.389

3 犭 see ⇨p.572

3 氵 see ⇨p.516

口 囗 土 士 夂 夕 大 女 子 宀 寸 小 ⺌ ⺍ 尢 尸 山 川 工 己 巾 干 幺 广 廴 廾 弋 弓 ヨ 彡 彳 艹 辶 阝 阝 ⺷ 忄 扌 犭 氵

766

心 ④

音	心	シン	mind; core; heart; soul
熟	心音	シンオン	***med***. heart beat
	心外	シンガイ	regrettable; unexpected; unthinkable
	心眼	シンガン	mind's eye; insight
	心機一転	シンキイッテン	changing one's mind; turning over a new leaf —***v***. changc one's mind; turn over a new leaf
	心境	シンキョウ	state of mind; feelings
	心中	シンジュウ	double/lovers' suicide —***vi***. commit suicide together
	心証	シンショウ	firm belief; conviction; impression
	心象	シンショウ	image; mental picture
	心情	シンジョウ	feelings; emotions
	心身	シンシン	body and mind; mentally and physically
	心身症	シンシンショウ	***med***. psychosomatic disorders
	心酔	シンスイ	ardent admiration —***v***. adore; be an ardent admirer of
	心臓	シンゾウ	***med***. heart
	心臓外科	シンゾウゲカ	open heart surgery
	心中	シンチュウ	at heart; inwardly; feelings
	心痛	シンツウ	worry; concern —***v***. be worried/concerned
	心的	シンテキ	mental; psychological
	心電図	シンデンズ	***med***. electrocardiogram (ECG)
	心配	シンパイ	anxiety; worry; care —***v***. be worried/troubled; worry; care
	心拍	シンパク	heartbeat
	心拍数	シンパクスウ	***med***. pulse rate
	心理	シンリ	mentally; mental state; psychology
	心理学	シンリガク	psychology
	心理的	シンリテキ	psychological; mental
	心霊	シンレイ	spirit; psychic; spiritual
	心霊術	シンレイジュツ	spiritualism
	心労	シンロウ	cares; anxieties; worries
訓	心	こころ	mind; heart; feeling; consideration; attention
	心当たり	こころあたり	in mind; could think of
	心有る	こころある	thoughtful; considerate; sensible; sensitive

心意気	こころイキ	spirit; determination
心得	こころえ	knowledge; understanding; rules; regulations; directions; instructions
心得る	こころえる	***vt.*** know; understand; regard; think; be aware of
心掛け	こころがけ	intention; care; prudence
心配り	こころくばり	consideration; thoughtfulness
心苦しい	こころぐるしい	feeling sorry/bad about
心して	こころして	determinedly; carefully
心強い	こころづよい	reassuring; encouraging
心残り	こころのこり	regret
心細い	こころぼそい	lonely; helpless; hopeless; discouraging
※心地	ここち	feeling; sensation

767

必 ⑤ 丶 ソ 义 义 必

音	必	ヒツ	certain; sure; necessary
熟	必携	ヒッケイ	indispensable; handbook; manual
	必見	ヒッケン	required reading/viewing
	必殺	ヒッサツ	inevitable killing; deadly
	必死	ヒッシ	certain death; desperate; frantic; with all one's might
	必至	ヒッシ	inevitable; desperate; frantic
	必修科目	ヒッシュウカモク	required/obligatory/compulsory subject
	必需品	ヒツジュヒン	necessities; essentials
	必勝	ヒッショウ	sure victory; desperate to win
	必須	ヒッス	indispensable; essential; requisite; compulsory
	必然	ヒツゼン	inevitability; necessity; certainty
	必然性	ヒツゼンセイ	necessity; inevitability
	必然的	ヒツゼンテキ	inevitable; of necessity; as a matter of course
	必着	ヒッチャク	required arrival time
	必中	ヒッチュウ	always hits the target —***vi.*** never fails to hit the target
	必読	ヒツドク	required reading
	必要	ヒツヨウ	necessary; essential
	必要悪	ヒツヨウアク	necessary evil
	必要条件	ヒツヨウジョウケン	necessary condition
訓	必ず	かならず	surely; certainly; without fail; certainly

768

応 ⑦

丶 亠 广 广 応 応 応

音	応	オウ	respond; meet; consent
熟	応じる	オウじる	*vi*. respond to; act in accordance with; consent; be suitable
	応援	オウエン	aid; assistance; support; moral support; cheering —*v*. help; assist; support; give moral support; cheer
	応急	オウキュウ	emergency
	応接	オウセツ	reception —*vi*. receive/see a guest
	応接間	オウセツま	waiting room; reception
	応戦	オウセン	returning fire; fight back —*vi*. return fire; fight back
	応対	オウタイ	reception —*vi*. see one's guests; grant an interview
	応諾	オウダク	consent; assent —*v*. consent/assent to
	応答	オウトウ	reply; response; answer —*vi*. reply; respond; answer
	応分	オウブン	fitting; suitable; appropriate; reasonable
	応募	オウボ	application; enlistment; subscription; enrollment —*vi*. apply for; enlist; subscribe for (to); enroll
	応用	オウヨウ	application; adaptation; improvement —*v*. apply; adapt; put into practice
訓	応える	こたえる	*vi*. respond to; have effect on
¥	応札	オウサツ	tender for
	応募者利回り	オウボシャりまわり	yield/return to subscriber
	応募資金	オウボシキン	subscribed capital (fund)

769

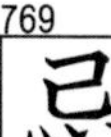

忌 ⑦

ㄱ コ 己 己 忌 忌 忌

音	忌	キ	abominate; mourning
熟	忌中	キチュウ	in mourning
	忌日	キニチ（キジツ）	anniversary of the day someone died
	忌避	キヒ	evasion —*v*. evade; shirk
訓	忌まわしい	いまわしい	abominable; disgusting; offensive
	忌み	いみ	abstinence; taboo
	忌む	いむ	*vt*. hate; loathe; abhor; detest; abstain

770

志 ⑦ 一 十 士 キ 志 志 志

音	志	シ	will; intention; desire; wish
熟	志願	シガン	wish; desire; ambition —*v*. apply; volunteer; wish; want
	志願者	シガンシャ	applicant; candidate
	志願兵	シガンヘイ	volunteer soldier
	志向	シコウ	intention —*v*. intend
	志望	シボウ	wish; desire; ambition —*v*. wish for; desire; aspire
	志望者	シボウシャ	applicant; candidate
訓	志	こころざし	will; resolution; aim; purpose; intention; wish; gift; kindness; consideration
	志す	こころざす	***vi***. intend; aim; aspire; make up one's mind

771

忍 ⑦ フ 刀 刃 刃 忍 忍 忍

音	忍	ニン	bear; endure; conceal; hide; spy
熟	忍苦	ニンク	endurance; stoicism —***vi***. be patient; endure
	忍者	ニンジャ	spy; ninja
	忍従	ニンジュウ	submission; subservience; resignation; passiveness —***vi***. submit; suffer; lie down
	忍術	ニンジュツ	art of invisibility; ninja arts
	忍耐	ニンタイ	perseverance; patience; endurance; fortitude; stoicism —*v*. persevere; be patient; endure
訓	忍ぶ	しのぶ	***vt***. bear; stand; endure; hide oneself; conceal
	忍ばせる	しのばせる	***vt***. conceal; hide; secrete
	忍び	しのび	mystification; spy
	忍び足	しのびあし	stealthy steps
	忍び込む	しのびこむ	***vi***. steal/creep into

772

忘 ⑦ ' 亠 亡 亡 忘 忘 忘

音	忘	ボウ	forget
熟	忘恩	ボウオン	ingratitude
	忘我	ボウガ	self-oblivion; trance; ecstasy

忘却	ボウキャク	oblivion; forgetting —*v*. be oblivious to; forget
忘年会	ボウネンカイ	year-end party
訓 忘れる	わすれる	*v*. forget
忘れ形見	わすれがたみ	memento; keepsake; posthumous child
忘れ物	わすれもの	lost property; item left behind accidentally

773

忠 ⑧

音 忠	チュウ	loyalty; devotion; fidelity; faithfulness
熟 忠義	チュウギ	loyalty; fidelity; devotion
忠孝	チュウコウ	loyalty and filial piety
忠告	チュウコク	advice; warning; caution; admoniton —*v*. advise; warn; caution; admonish
忠実	チュウジツ	honesty; faithfulness; devotion; fidelity; faith
忠臣	チュウシン	loyal retainer
忠誠	チュウセイ	allegiance; loyalty; fidelity; devotion; integrity
忠節	チュウセツ	loyalty; allegiance; fidelity; devotion

774

念 ⑧

音 念	ネン	think
熟 念じる	ネンじる	***vt***. wish; pray
念願	ネンガン	wish; desire; prayer —*v*. wish; desire; pray
念頭	ネントウ	mind
念仏	ネンブツ	Buddhist prayer
念力	ネンリキ	willpower; will; faith

775

急 ⑨

音 急	キュウ	make haste; hasten; acute
熟 急患	キュウカン	emergency case/patient
急激	キュウゲキ	sudden; abrupt; precipitous
急行	キュウコウ	express (train/bus) —***vi***. hasten; go posthaste
急降下	キュウコウカ	nose dive —***vi***. nose-dive
急告	キュウコク	urgent notice

	急死	キュウシ	sudden death —*vi*. die suddenly
	急襲	キュウシュウ	surprise attack/raid —*v*. attack suddenly
	急所	キュウショ	vital part of the body
	急進	キュウシン	rapid progress —*vi*. make rapid progress
	急性	キュウセイ	acute (sickness)
	急逝	キュウセイ	sudden death —*vi*. die suddenly
	急送	キュウソウ	dispatching hurriedly —*v*. send a thing in haste
	急増	キュウゾウ	sudden increase; jump —*vi*. increase rapidly/suddenly
	急速	キュウソク	rapid; swift; prompt
	急停止	キュウテイシ	sudden stop —*vi*. stop suddenly
	急転	キュウテン	sudden change —*vi*. change suddenly; take a sudden turn
	急場	キュウば	emergency; crisis
	急迫	キュウハク	urgency; imminence —*vi*. be imminent/pressing
	急病	キュウビョウ	sudden attack of illness
	急変	キュウヘン	sudden change/transition —*vi*. change suddenly
	急募	キュウボ	urgent recruitment —*v*. recruit in haste
	急報	キュウホウ	urgent message/report —*v*. send an urgent message; report promptly
	急務	キュウム	urgent business; pressing need
	急用	キュウヨウ	urgent business; business demanding immediate attention
	急流	キュウリュウ	rapidly flowing stream
訓	急ぐ	いそぐ	***vi***. hasten; hurry up; go quickly
¥	急騰	キュウトウ	sudden rise; jump
	急落	キュウラク	sudden/sharp drop; fall

776

⑨

音	思	シ	think; thought; idea
熟	思案	シアン	thought; consideration; reflection; worry —*v*. think; consider; reflect; worry
	思考	シコウ	thought; thinking —*v*. think
	思索	シサク	meditation; contemplation —*v*. think; meditate; comtemplate; ponder
	思春期	シシュンキ	puberty; adolescence
	思想	シソウ	thought; idea; thoughts
	思想家	シソウカ	thinker
	思慕	シボ	yearning —*v*. yearn/long for; love
	思慮	シリョ	prudence; consideration; careful thought

訓	思う	おもう	***vt.*** think; consider; suspect; wonder; guess; suppose; imagine; fancy; be in love; wish; desire; recall; remember
	思う存分	おもうゾンブン	as much as one likes
	思い	おもい	thought; feeling; wish; desire; love
	思い浮かべる	おもいうかべる	***vt.*** recall; remember
	思い切って	おもいきって	bravely
	思い出す	おもいだす	***vt.*** recall; remember
	思い出	おもいで	memory; recollections
¥	思惑買い	おもワクがい	speculative buying

777

⑨ 怠

音	怠	タイ	idle; neglect; negligence
熟	怠惰	タイダ	idleness; laziness; indolence; sloth
	怠慢	タイマン	negligence; neglect; procrastination
訓	怠る	おこたる	***vi.*** neglect; be negligent/idle
	怠け者	なまけもの	idler; lazybones
	怠ける	なまける	***v.*** be idle/lazy

778

怒 ⑨

音	怒	ド	anger; indignation; rage; fury
熟	怒気	ドキ	anger; angry mood; fume; indignation; wrath; resentment
	怒号	ドゴウ	roar; outcry; bellow —***vi.*** roar; bellow; howl
	怒声	ドセイ	angry voice
	怒涛	ドトウ	angry waves; high seas; rough waters
訓	怒る	いかる	***vi.*** become angry; get upset
	怒り	いかり	anger; rage; passion; wrath; indignation
	怒る	おこる	***vi.*** become/get angry; lose one's temper

779

恩 ⑩

音	恩	オン	kindness; favor; grace

熟	恩返し	オンがえし	repayment of a favor
	恩義	オンギ	favor; obligation; moral obligation
	恩給	オンキュウ	pension
	恩恵	オンケイ	favor; benefit
	恩師	オンシ	one's former teacher
	恩賜	オンシ	imperial gift
	恩赦	オンシャ	amnesty; general pardon
	恩情	オンジョウ	compassion
	恩知らず	オンしらず	ingratitude; ingrate
	恩人	オンジン	benefactor; patron
	恩寵	オンチョウ	grace; favor
	恩典	オンテン	grace; act of grace

780

恐 ⑩

一 丅 工 玑 巩 巩 巩 恐 恐 恐

音	恐	キョウ	fear; fright
熟	恐喝	キョウカツ	threat; menace; blackmail —*v*. threaten; menace; blackmail
	恐慌	キョウコウ	panic; scare; alarm
	恐縮	キョウシュク	gratitude; appreciation; fear —*vi*. be grateful; appreciate; be frightened
	恐怖	キョウフ	fear; terror; fright
	恐怖症	キョウフショウ	phobia; morbid fear
	恐竜	キョウリュウ	dinosaur
訓	恐れる	おそれる	***vi***. fear; be afraid of; dread
	恐ろしい	おそろしい	terrible; frightening; dreadful
	恐らく	おそらく	perhaps; probably; maybe
	恐れ入る	おそれいる	***vi***. be overwhelmed (with gratitude/shame); be astonished; be sorry to trouble; beg pardon; be defeated; yield; plead quilty
¥	恐慌	キョウコウ	financial panic/crisis

781

恵 ⑩

一 𠂆 丙 冃 亘 亩 声 恵 恵 恵

音	恵	エ	happiness
		ケイ	mercy
熟	恵比寿	エビス	Ebisu (god of wealth)
	恵贈	ケイゾウ	(phrase used to express gratitude after receiving a gift)

訓	恵む	めぐむ	***vt.*** bless; favor
	恵み	めぐみ	blessings; favors

782

⑩

音	息	ソク	breath; son
熟	息災	ソクサイ	healthy; safety; safe and sound
	息女	ソクジョ	daughter
訓	息	いき	breath
	※息子	むすこ	son

783

⑩

音	恥	チ	shyness; bashfulness; shame; disgrace
熟	恥辱	チジョク	disgrace; dishonor; shame; indignity; stigma
訓	恥	はじ	shame; disgrace; dishonor; embarrassment
	恥知らず	はじしらず	shameless; thick-skinned
	恥じらう	はじらう	***vi.*** be shy/coy/bashful
	恥じる	はじる	***vi.*** feel shame; be ashamed of
	恥ずかしい	はずかしい	shy; shameful; disgraceful; embarrassing
	恥ずかしがり屋	はずかしがりや	shy person

784

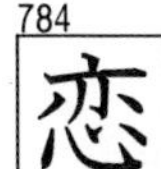
⑩

音	恋	レン	love
熟	恋愛	レンアイ	love —***v.*** love
	恋情	レンジョウ	love; affection
	恋慕	レンボ	falling in love —***vi.*** fall in love with
訓	恋	こい	love
	恋しい	こいしい	dear; beloved
	恋人	こいびと	sweetheart; boyfriend; girlfriend
	恋文	こいぶみ	love letter
	恋う	こう	***vt.*** yearn for

785

悪 ⑪

一 丆 𠀃 亞 ... 悪

音	悪	アク	wrong; incorrect; bad; evil; immoral; ugly; poor quality; inferior; hate
		オ	hate
熟	悪意	アクイ	evil intention; wrongful intent
	悪運	アクウン	the devil's luck
	悪行	アクギョウ	evildoing; wicked act
	悪事	アクジ	evil deed; wrongdoing; wrong; crime
	悪質	アクシツ	full of faults; vicious; corrupt; of poor quality; faulty; defective
	悪臭	アクシュウ	bad smell; stink; stench
	悪習	アクシュウ	bad habit; abuse; vice
	悪循環	アクジュンカン	vicious circle
	悪性	アクセイ	evil nature; malignancy; malevolence
	悪戦苦闘	アクセンクトウ	struggle; desperate fight —*vi*. struggle; fight desperately
	悪態	アクタイ	foul language; curse; slander; abuse
	悪党	アクトウ	bad person; villain; scoundrel; rogue
	悪徳	アクトク	vice; corruption; immorality
	悪人	アクニン	wicked person; wrongdoer
	悪筆	アクヒツ	poor handwriting
	悪評	アクヒョウ	ill repute; bad reputation; notoriety
	悪風	アクフウ	bad custom; vice
	悪文	アクブン	poor writing; writing that is difficult to understand
	悪魔	アクマ	devil; demon; fiend; Satan
	悪夢	アクム	nightmare; bad dream
	悪名	アクメイ	bad reputation; infamy; notoriety
	悪用	アクヨウ	abuse; misuse —*v*. abuse; misuse; put to a bad use
	悪化	アッカ	worsening; deterioration —*vi*. get worse; become impaired; deteriorate
	悪寒	オカン	chill; cold
訓	悪い	わるい	wrong; bad; inferior; ugly
	悪賢い	わるがしこい	cunning; sly; crafty
	悪気	わるギ	malice; spite; ill will; harm
	悪口	わるくち	abuse; slander; foul language
	悪者	わるもの	bad person; rogue; villain
	※悪戯	いたずら	mischief; prank; practical joke
	※悪阻	つわり	morning sickness

786

患 ⑪

音	患	カン	trouble; anxiety
熟	患者	カンジャ	patient
	患部	カンブ	part of the body affected by illness or injury
訓	患う	わずらう	*v.* be ill; feel sick; be worried/tormented
	患い	わずらい	illness; sickness; worry; torment

787

悠 ⑪

音	悠	ユウ	leisure; longtime; distant
熟	悠久	ユウキュウ	eternity; permanence
	悠然	ユウゼン	calm; with perfect composure
	悠長	ユウチョウ	leisurely; slow; easy going
	悠々たる	ユウユウたる	quiet; calm; composed; leisurely

788

悲 78 8

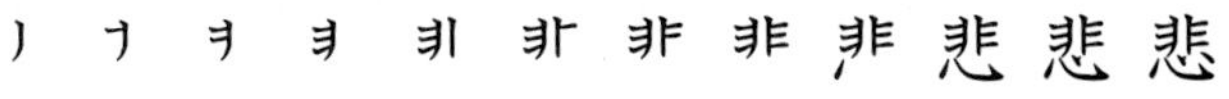

音	悲	ヒ	sad
熟	悲哀	ヒアイ	sorrow; grief; sadness
	悲運	ヒウン	misfortune; bad/ill luck
	悲歌	ヒカ	elegy; sad tune; plaintive melody
	悲観	ヒカン	pessimism; disappointment —***v.*** be pessimistic/disappointed
	悲願	ヒガン	Buddhist prayer for mankind; earnest wish
	悲喜	ヒキ	joy and sorrow
	悲境	ヒキョウ	adversities; unhappy situation; plight
	悲劇	ヒゲキ	tragedy; tragic play
	悲惨	ヒサン	miserable; pathetic; tragic
	悲壮	ヒソウ	tragic but brave; heroic (death)
	悲愴	ヒソウ	pathetic; grievous; mournful
	悲嘆	ヒタン	grief; sorrow; anguish; lamentation —***vi.*** grieve; sorrow; mourn; lament
	悲痛	ヒツウ	bitter; grief; sorrow
	悲報	ヒホウ	sad news

	悲鳴	ヒメイ	scream; shriek
	悲恋	ヒレン	tragic love
	悲話	ヒワ	sad story
訓	悲しい	かなしい	sorrowful; sad
	悲しむ	かなしむ	***vt***. grieve; mourn; sorrow

789

惑 ⑫

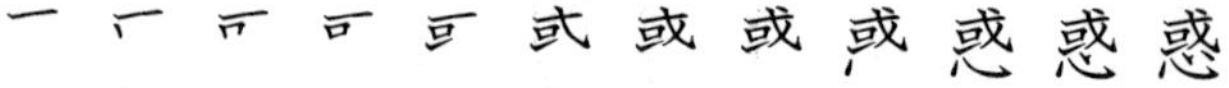

音	惑	ワク	go astray; be misguided/tempted
熟	惑星	ワクセイ	planet
訓	惑う	まどう	***vi***. go astray; be misguided/tempted

790

愛 ⑬

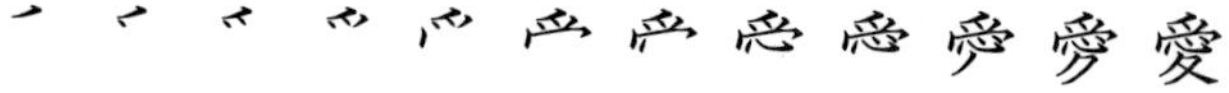

音	愛	アイ	love; affection; attraction; attachment
熟	愛する	アイする	***vt***. love; be attracted to; cherish; hold dear
	愛嬌	アイキョウ	charms; physical grace or attraction
	愛護	アイゴ	protection; preservation; conservation —***v***. protect; preserve; conserve
	愛好	アイコウ	love; liking —***v***. love; like; be a lover of; be fond of
	愛国心	アイコクシン	patriotism; nationalism
	愛妻	アイサイ	one's beloved/darling wife
	愛妻家	アイサイカ	devoted husband; husband who loves and cares for his wife
	愛児	アイジ	beloved/favorite child
	愛称	アイショウ	pet name; nickname
	愛情	アイジョウ	feeling of love; affection; attachment; devotion
	愛人	アイジン	lover; sexual partner
	愛想	アイソ（ウ）	amiablity; sociability; friendliness; congeniality
	愛憎	アイゾウ	love and hatred
	愛着	アイチャク	attachment; affection; love —***v***. become attached to; hold dear
	愛読	アイドク	enjoyable/regular reading —***v***. enjoy reading; read regularly
	愛用	アイヨウ	habitual/regular use —***v***. use habitually; patronize

791

⑬

音	意	イ	mind; feeling; thought; idea; intention; opinion; reason; meaning
熟	意外	イガイ	unexpected; unforeseen; surprising
	意気	イキ	spirits; disposition; temperament; humor
	意気消沈	イキショウチン	depression; dejection —*vi*. be depressed; feel dejected; be dispirited
	意気投合	イキトウゴウ	mutual understanding; sympathy; affinity —*vi*. get on well with; have an affinity for; be like minded
	意気揚々	イキヨウヨウ	triumphant; exultant
	意気地なし	イクジなし	coward; lack of courage or resolution
	意義	イギ	meaning; sense; significance
	意見	イケン	opinion; view; idea; suggestion —*v*. give advice; admonish; reprove
	意向	イコウ	intention; inclination; disposition
	意志	イシ	will; volition
	意思	イシ	intention; intent; purpose
	意地	イジ	temper; obstinacy; pride; nature; dispositon
	意地悪	イジわる	ill-natured; malevolent; spiteful
	意識	イシキ	consciousness; awareness; senses —*v*. be conscious; feel; be aware
	意匠	イショウ	idea; device; design
	意中	イチュウ	one's mind/thoughts/feelings
	意図	イト	intent; intention; aim; idea —*v*. intend; design; aim
	意表	イヒョウ	unexpectedness; surprise
	意味	イミ	meaning; sense; significance; implication —*v*. mean; signify; imply
	意訳	イヤク	free translation —*v*. translate freely
	意欲	イヨク	will; desire; volition

792

⑬

音	感	カン	feel; feeling; inspiration; sensation; sentiment; emotion
熟	感じる	カンじる	*v*. be conscious of; suffer; be impressed; feel
	感化	カンカ	inspiration; influence —*v*. inspire; influence
	感慨	カンガイ	deep emotion

感慨無量	カンガイムリョウ	filled with deep emotion
感覚	カンカク	sense; sensibility; feeling
感激	カンゲキ	deep emotion; impression; enthusiasm —*vi*. be deeply moved/impressed
感光	カンコウ	exposure to light
感謝	カンシャ	thanks; appreciation; gratitude —*v*. thank; be thankful/grateful for
感受性	カンジュセイ	sensibility; receptivity
感傷	カンショウ	sentimentality
感情	カンジョウ	feeling; sentiment; emotion
感触	カンショク	sense of touch
感染	カンセン	infection —*v*. be infected
感想	カンソウ	impressions; thoughts
感嘆	カンタン	great admiration; wonder; amazement —*vi*. admire; marvel; wonder; be amazed
感知	カンチ	perception; awareness —*v*. perceive; become aware of
感づく	カンづく	*vi*. suspect; sense; get wind of
感電	カンデン	electric shock —*vi*. receive an electric shock
感度	カンド	sensitivity; sensibility
感動	カンドウ	impression; emotion; inspiration —*vi*. be impressed/moved/inspired
感服	カンプク	admiration —*vi*. be impressed by
感冒	カンボウ	***med***. cold; catarrh
感銘	カンメイ	deep impression —*vi*. be deeply impressed; make an impression
感涙	カンルイ	tears of gratitude

793

⑬

音	愚	グ	stupid; foolish
熟	愚作	グサク	poor work; trash; rubbish ***hum***. one's own work
	愚痴	グチ	idle complaint; grumble
	愚問	グモン	stupid question ***hum***. one's own question
	愚劣	グレツ	stupidness; foolishness; absurdity
	愚弄	グロウ	mockery; derision; ridicule —*v*. fool; befool; make a fool of; jibe
訓	愚か	おろか	foolish; stupid; witless

794

慈 ⑬ 丶 丷 䒑 䒑 玄 玄 玆 玆 玆 慈 慈 慈

音	慈	ジ	mercy; affection
熟	慈愛	ジアイ	affection; love
	慈雨	ジウ	welcome rain
	慈善	ジゼン	almsgiving; charity
	慈悲	ジヒ	mercy; charity
	慈父	ジフ	affectionate father
	慈母	ジボ	affectionate mother
訓	慈しみ	いつくしみ	love; affection
	慈しむ	いつくしむ	***vt.*** love; be tender

795

愁 ⑬ 一 二 千 禾 禾 禾 禾 秒 秋 秋 愁 愁

音	愁	シュウ	lament; grief; sorrow
熟	愁傷	シュウショウ	grief; deep sorrow
訓	愁い	うれい	grief; sorrow; distress; trouble
	愁える	うれえる	***vt.*** lament; worry; be troubled

796

想 ⑬ 一 十 才 木 木 朷 相 相 相 相 想 想

音	想	ソウ (ソ)	idea; thought
熟	想起	ソウキ	recollection; remembrance
	想像	ソウゾウ	imagination —***v.*** imagine
	想定	ソウテイ	supposition; hypothesis —***v.*** suppose; make a hypothesis
	想念	ソウネン	idea; conception
訓	※想う	おもう	***vt.*** think of; call to mind

797

態 ⑭ 𠂉 厶 台 台 自 自 能 能 能 能 態 態

音	態	タイ	figure; posture; attitude

熟	態勢	タイセイ	attitude; condition
	態度	タイド	attitude; behavior

798

慰 ⑮

音	慰	イ	comfort; console
熟	慰安	イアン	comfort; consolation; solace —*v*. comfort; console; solace
	慰謝料	イシャリョウ	consolation money; compensation; damages
	慰問	イモン	consolation; sympathy —*v*. go to console; show sympathy; inquire after
	慰労	イロウ	recognition of services —*v*. acknowledge a person's services
訓	慰む	なぐさむ	***vt***. be diverted; make fun of; make a plaything of
	慰める	なぐさめる	***vi***. comfort; console; amuse

799

慶 ⑮

音	慶	ケイ	congratulate; celebrate; auspicious
熟	慶賀	ケイガ	congratulations —*v*. congratulate; celebrate
	慶事	ケイジ	happy event
	慶祝	ケイシュク	celebration —*v*. celebrate
	慶弔	ケイチョウ	congratulations and condolences

800

 ⑮

音	憂	ユウ	grieve; be distressed/anxious
熟	憂鬱	ユウウツ	melancholy; dejection; gloom
	憂国	ユウコク	concern about the future of one's country
	憂愁	ユウシュウ	melancholy; grief; gloom
	憂慮	ユウリョ	anxiety; apprehension —*v*. be anxious/apprehensive/concerned; worry
訓	憂い	うい	gloomy; unhappy; sad
	憂い	うれい	grief; anxiety; distress
	憂える	うれえる	***vt***. be distressed/anxious; grieve

801

慮 ⑮

音 慮　リョ　consideration; thought

熟 慮外　リョガイ　unexpected; rude; inconsiderate; thoughtless

訓 ※慮る　おもんぱかる　*vt*. think; consider; be prudent; fear; be apprehensive

802

憩 ⑯

音 憩　ケイ　rest; relaxation

訓 憩い　いこい　rest; relaxation; respite

憩う　いこう　*vi*. rest; take a rest; relax

803

憲 ⑯

音 憲　ケン　constitution

熟 憲章　ケンショウ　charter

憲法　ケンポウ　constitution

訓 憲　のり　law; rule; regulation

804

懇 ⑰

音 懇　コン　kind; polite; courteous; sincere

熟 懇意　コンイ　intimacy; friendship; kindness

懇願　コンガン　entreaty; solicitation; petition —*v*. entreat; implore; beseech; appeal; petition

懇親　コンシン　good fellowship; friendship; intimacy

懇切　コンセツ　kindness; cordiality

懇談　コンダン　familiar talk; chat —*vi*. have a chat; confabulate

訓 懇ろ　ねんごろ　politeness; courtesy; kindness

805

懲 ⑱

音	懲	**チョウ**	punish
熟	懲役	**チョウエキ**	penal servitude
	懲戒	**チョウカイ**	discipline; official reprimand —*v*. reprimand; discipline; reprove
	懲罰	**チョウバツ**	chastisement; discipline; punishment —*v*. chastise; discipline; punish
訓	懲らしめる	こらしめる	***vt***. chastise; chasten; punish; correct; discipline
	懲らす	こらす	***vt***. chastise; chasten; punish; correct; discipline
	懲りる	こりる	***vi***. learn by experience; learn from one's mistakes

806

懸 ⑳

音	懸	**ケン** **ケ**	suspend; hang
熟	懸念	**ケネン**	anxiety; fear; apprehension —*v*. fear; apprehend
	懸案	**ケンアン**	pending problem; undecided matter
	懸賞	**ケンショウ**	prize; reward
	懸垂	**ケンスイ**	hanging; suspending —***vi***. hang; suspend
	懸命	**ケンメイ**	eagerly
訓	懸かる	かかる	***vi***. hang; set about; decide; fall into a trap; rest; be supported
	懸ける	かける	***vt***. hang; suspend; offer; risk

3 忄 りっしんべん heart to the left

807

⑥

音	忙	**ボウ**	busy
熟	忙殺	**ボウサツ**	keeping (someone) very busy; being very busy —*v*. keep (someone) very busy
訓	忙しい	**いそがしい**	busy

※忙しい	せわしい	busy; restless
※忙しない	せわしない	restless; in a hurry

808
快 ⑦ 丶 丶 忄 忄 忄 快 快

音	快	カイ	comfort; pleasure
熟	快活	カイカツ	cheerfulness; liveliness
	快感	カイカン	pleasant sensation; pleasure
	快挙	カイキョ	brilliant achievement; heroic deed
	快勝	カイショウ	easy victory —*vi*. win an easy victory
	快晴	カイセイ	fine weather
	快走	カイソウ	fast running —*vi*. run fast
	快速	カイソク	high/great speed
	快調	カイチョウ	excellent condition; harmony
	快適	カイテキ	comfortable; delightful; agreeable
	快方	カイホウ	convalescence; recovery from illness
	快報	カイホウ	good/welcome news
	快楽	カイラク	pleasure; enjoyment
訓	快い	こころよい	pleasant; comfortable

809
怪 ⑧ 丶 丶 忄 忄 怪 怪 怪 怪

音	怪	カイ （ケ）	strange; suspect; doubtful
熟	怪獣	カイジュウ	monstrous beast; monster
	怪談	カイダン	ghost story
	怪物	カイブツ	monster
	怪力	カイリキ	Herculean strength
	怪我	ケガ	injury
訓	怪しい	あやしい	doubtful; mysterious; dubious
	怪しむ	あやしむ	*vt*. doubt

810
怖 ⑧ 丶 丶 忄 忄 怖 怖 怖 怖

音	怖	フ	fear

訓	怖い	こわい	fearful; frightful; scary; awful
	怖がる	こわがる	***vi***. fear; be afraid/scared

811

性 ⑧

丶 丷 忄 忄 忄 怀 性 性

音	性	セイ	nature; sex; gender
		ショウ	nature
熟	性根	ショウネ	nature; character
	性分	ショウブン	nature; disposition
	性愛	セイアイ	sexual love
	性格	セイカク	character; personality
	性器	セイキ	sexual organs; genitals
	性急	セイキュウ	hasty; impatient
	性教育	セイキョウイク	sex education
	性交	セイコウ	intercourse; sex; coitus —***vi***. have sex; make love
	性向	セイコウ	disposition; nature
	性行	セイコウ	character and conduct
	性行為	セイコウイ	sexual act
	性質	セイシツ	nature; disposition; property
	性的	セイテキ	sexual
	性転換	セイテンカン	sex change —***v***. change one's sex
	性転換者	セイテンカンシャ	transsexual
	性能	セイノウ	performance; efficiency
	性病	セイビョウ	venereal disease
	性病科	セイビョウカ	department for the treatment of venereal diseases
	性癖	セイヘキ	natural tendency; propensity
	性別	セイベツ	distinction of sex; gender
	性本能	セイホンノウ	sex drive/impulse
	性欲	セイヨク	sexual desire; lust

812

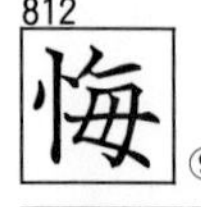

⑨

丶 丷 忄 忄 忄 忄 悔 悔 悔

音	悔	カイ	regret; repent
熟	悔恨	カイコン	remorse; regret —***vi***. feel remorse/regret
訓	悔いる	くいる	***vi***. repent; regret
	悔しい	くやしい	regretful; feel frustrated

悔やむ	くやむ	***vt***. condole; lament

813
恒 ⑨

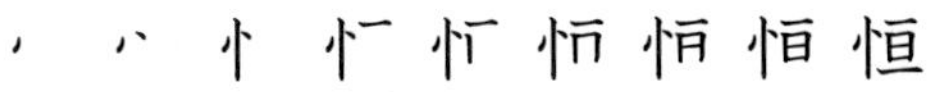

音	恒	**コウ**	constant; fixed; usual
熟	恒久	**コウキュウ**	eternal; everlasting
	恒久性	**コウキュウセイ**	permanency
	恒星	**コウセイ**	fixed star
	恒例	**コウレイ**	usual practice; established custom

814
恨 ⑨

音	恨	**コン**	bear a grudge; regret
訓	恨み	うらみ	grudge; ill feeling; hatred
	恨む	うらむ	***vt***. regret; bear a grudge; show resentment
	恨めしい	うらめしい	reproachful; rueful; spiteful; hateful

815
悦 ⑩

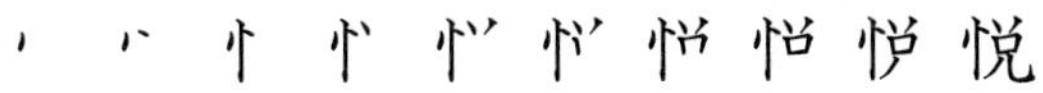

音	悦	**エツ**	rapture; joy
熟	悦楽	**エツラク**	joy; happiness; delight —***vi***. be full of joy; be happy/delighted
訓	悦ばす	よろこばす	***vt***. please; gladden; make happy
	悦ぶ	よろこぶ	***vi***. be happy/glad/delighted

816
悟 ⑩

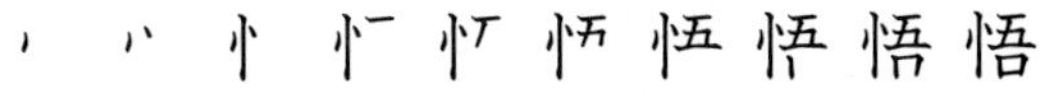

音	悟	**ゴ**	realize; perceive
訓	悟る	さとる	***vt***. realize; perceive; be enlightened
	悟り	さとり	enlightenment; perception

817

悩 ⑩

音	悩	ノウ	worry
熟	悩殺	ノウサツ	fascination; enchantment —*v*. fascinate; enchant; bewitch; captivate; charm
訓	悩ます	なやます	***vt***. afflict; torment; harass; torture
	悩み	なやみ	worry; anguish
	悩む	なやむ	***vi***. be troubled/worried/distressed

818

惨 ⑪

音	惨	サン ザン	piteous; wretched; miserable
熟	惨劇	サンゲキ	tragedy; disaster
	惨事	サンジ	disaster; tragic incident; terrible accident
	惨状	サンジョウ	terrible sight; horrible spectacle
	惨敗	ザンパイ	crushing/humiliating defeat —***vi***. suffer a crushing/humiliating defeat
訓	惨め	みじめ	miserable; wretched; pitiable; pathetic

819

情 ⑪

音	情	ジョウ	feeling; sentiment; emotions; heart; affection; love
		(セイ)	
熟	情愛	ジョウアイ	affection; love; compassion
	情感	ジョウカン	emotion
	情景	ジョウケイ	scene
	情交	ジョウコウ	sexual intercourse
	情死	ジョウシ	lover's suicide —***vi***. carry out a suicide pact
	情事	ジョウジ	love affair
	情実	ジョウジツ	private considerations; favoritism
	情趣	ジョウシュ	artistic; tasteful; elegant; charming
	情状	ジョウジョウ	circumstances; allowances
	情状酌量	ジョウジョウシャクリョウ	consideration of the extenuating circumstances

	情勢	ジョウセイ	situation; state of affairs; conditions
	情操	ジョウソウ	sentiments
	情緒	ジョウチョ	emotion; sentiment
	情熱	ジョウネツ	passion; ardor; enthusiasm
	情熱的	ジョウネツテキ	passionate; ardent; enthusiastic
	情報	ジョウホウ	information; news; data; report
	情報機関	ジョウホウキカン	secret service
	情報処理	ジョウホウショリ	data processing
	情欲	ジョウヨク	sexual desire; lust
	情理	ジョウリ	reason and sentiment
訓	情け	なさけ	sympathy; pity; compassion; charity; love
	情けない	なさけない	deplorable; shameful; heartless; miserable; disgraceful

820

惜 ⑪ 丶 丶丶 忄 忄一 忄十 忄卄 忄廾 惜 惜 惜 惜

音	惜	セキ	regrettable; precious; wasteful
熟	惜敗	セキハイ	narrow defeat —*vi*. be narrowly defeated
	惜別	セキベツ	reluctant parting —*v*. part reluctantly
訓	惜しい	おしい	regretful
	惜しむ	おしむ	*vt*. regret; value; be reluctant to part with

821

悼 ⑪ 丶 丶丶 忄 忄' 忄⺊ 忄⺊ 忄卢 忄卢 悼 悼 悼

音	悼	トウ	grieve
訓	悼む	いたむ	*vi*. moan; grieve; lament

822

慌 ⑫ 丶 丶丶 忄 忄一 忄十 忄卄 忄卄 忄芒 忄芒 忄荒 慌 慌

音	慌	コウ	busy; hurry; confused
訓	慌ただしい	あわただしい	busy; bustling; hurried; restless
	慌てる	あわてる	*vi*. be confused; hurry; be flurried/disconcerted

823
惰 ⑫

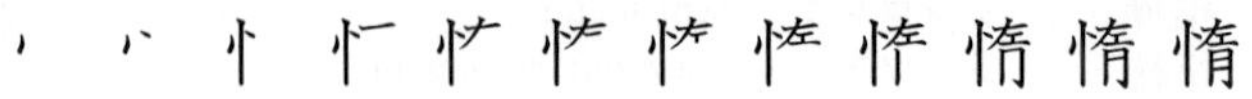

音	惰	ダ	neglect; laziness
熟	惰性	ダセイ	inertia
	惰力	ダリョク	inertia; momentum

824
愉 ⑫

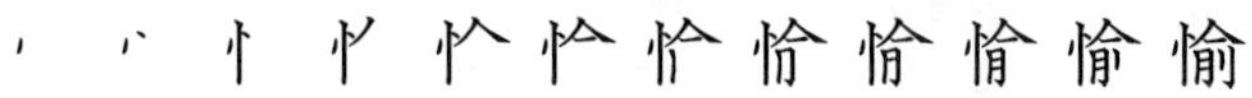

音	愉	ユ	joy; pleasure
	愉快	ユカイ	pleasant; merry; cheerful
	愉楽	ユラク	pleasure; joy
訓	※愉しい	たのしい	pleasant; delightful; fun

825
慨 ⑬

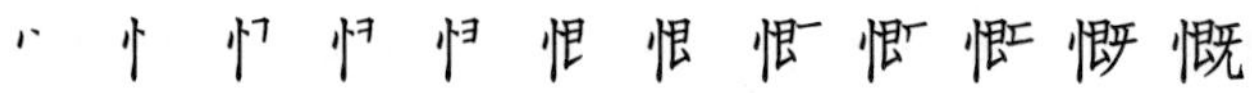

音	慨	ガイ	lament; deplore
熟	慨嘆	ガイタン	deploring; lamentation; regret —*v*. deplore; lament; regret
訓	※慨く	なげく	*v*. grieve; moan; lament

826
慎 ⑬

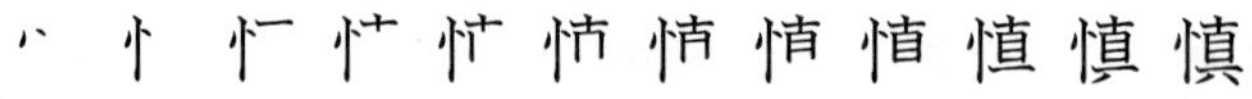

音	慎	シン	prudent
熟	慎重	シンチョウ	careful; prudent; cautious; discreet
訓	慎む	つつしむ	***vt***. be careful/discreet; refrain; abstain
	慎み	つつしみ	prudence; discretion; modesty
	慎ましい	つつましい	prudent; discreet; modest

827
慣 ⑭

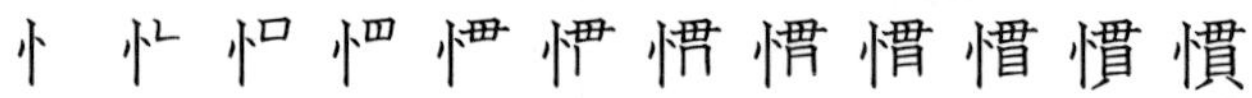

音	慣	カン	custom; get used to

熟	慣習	カンシュウ	rules and conventions
	慣性	カンセイ	inertia
	慣用	カンヨウ	usage; common use
	慣例	カンレイ	custom; usage; convention
訓	慣れる	なれる	***vi***. get used to; grow accustomed to
	慣らす	ならす	***vt***. tame; domesticate; accustom; familiarize

828

憎 ⑭

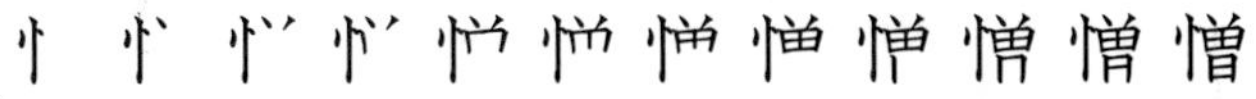

音	憎	ゾウ	hate
熟	憎悪	ゾウオ	hatred; abhorrence
訓	憎い	にくい	hateful; horrible; repulsive
	憎む	にくむ	***vt***. hate
	憎しみ	にくしみ	hatred; animasity
	憎らしい	にくらしい	hateful; horrible; repulsive

829

慢 ⑭

音	慢	マン	lazy; scorn; deride; prolonged; chronic; boasting
熟	慢心	マンシン	self-conceit —***v***. be conceited
	慢性	マンセイ	chronic

830

憤 ⑮

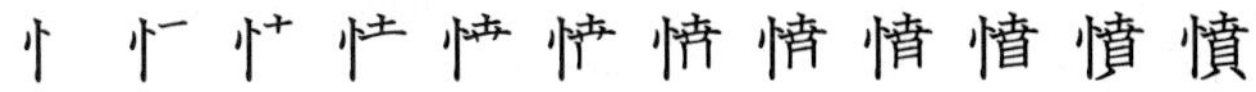

音	憤	フン	resent; be indignant/enraged
熟	憤慨	フンガイ	indignation; resentment —***v***. be indignant; resent
	憤激	フンゲキ	anger; wrath; indignation —***vi***. become enraged/indignant
	憤死	フンシ	dying in a fit of anger —***vi***. die in a fit of anger —***bas***. be put out (with men on base)
	憤然	フンゼン	indignantly
	憤怒	フンヌ (フンド)	anger; wrath; indignation —***vi***. be angry/indignant
訓	憤る	いきどおる	get angry; resent; be indignant/enraged

831

憶 ⑯

音	憶	オク	remember; think; guess
熟	憶説	オクセツ	hypothesis
	憶測	オクソク	conjecture; surmise; guess —*v*. conjecture; surmise; guess
	憶病	オクビョウ	timid; cowardly
訓	※憶える	おぼえる	***vi***. remember; learn; feel
	※憶う	おもう	***vt***. think; guess; conjecture

832

懐 ⑯

音	懐	カイ	long for; recollect
熟	懐疑	カイギ	doubt; skepticism; disbelief —***v***. doubt; be skeptical; disbelieve
	懐古	カイコ	nostalgia; yearning for the past —***vi***. remember the past; recollect the old days
	懐柔	カイジュウ	appeasememt; conciliation; pacification —***v***. appease; conciliate; pacify
	懐石料理	カイセキリョウリ	light meal served before a tea ceremony; *kaiseki* cuisine
	懐中	カイチュウ	pocket (watch, flashlight, etc.); wallet
	懐妊	カイニン	conception; pregnancy —***vi***. conceive; become pregnant
	懐炉	カイロ	body heater
訓	懐かしい	なつかしい	dear; beloved; longed/yearned for
	懐かしむ	なつかしむ	***vt***. yearn/long for; miss; think fondly of
	懐く	なつく	***vi***. become attached to; become familiar with
	懐ける	なつける	***vt***. win someone's heart; make someone fall in love with you
	懐	ふところ	bosom; breast; pocket; purse

833

憾 ⑯

音	憾	カン	regret
訓	※憾み	うらみ	regret
	※憾む	うらむ	***vt***. be sorry for; regret

4 小 したごころ bottom heart

834

⑩ 一 十 艹 土 共 共 恭 恭 恭 恭

音	恭	**キョウ**	respectful; reverent
熟	恭賀	**キョウガ**	respectful congratulations
	恭賀新年	**キョウガシンネン**	Happy New Year
	恭順	**キョウジュン**	submission; obedience
訓	恭しい	**うやうや**しい	respectful; reverent

835
慕 ⑭ 艹 艹 节 节 苜 荁 莫 莫 菓 慕 慕 慕

音	慕	**ボ**	yearn for; desire; love dearly; idolize
熟	慕情	**ボジョウ**	affection; love; longing
訓	慕う	**した**う	***vt***. yearn for; desire; love dearly; idolize; admire
	慕わしい	**した**わしい	dear; beloved

4 戈 ほこがまえ tasseled spear

836
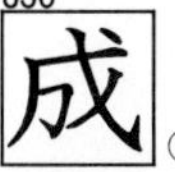
⑥ ノ 厂 万 成 成 成

音	成	**セイ** (**ジョウ**)	be completed; achieve; accomplish
熟	成就	**ジョウジュ**	accomplishment; attainment —***v***. accomplish; attain
	成仏	**ジョウブツ**	death; Buddhahood —***vi***. enter Nirvana; die; pass away
	成育	**セイイク**	growth; development —***v***. grow; develop; raise
	成因	**セイイン**	origin; cause
	成果	**セイカ**	result; fruits; achievement
	成句	**セイク**	set phrase; idiomatic expression; common saying; proverb

	成形	セイケイ	molding —***v***. mold
	成型	セイケイ	casting —***v***. cast
	成功	セイコウ	success; achievement —***vi***. succeed; be successful; pass; achieve
	成熟	セイジュク	maturity; ripeness —***vi***. ripen; mature
	成熟期	セイジュクキ	adolescence; puberty; period of maturity
	成人	セイジン	adult; grown-up —***vi***. grow-up; attain adulthood
	成人教育	セイジン キョウイク	adult education
	成人式	セイジンシキ	*seijinshiki* (coming-of-age ceremony)
	成績	セイセキ	result; record; grade; mark; performance; showings
	成層圏	セイソウケン	stratosphere
	成虫	セイチュウ	imago
	成長	セイチョウ	growth; development —***vi***. grow; grow up; develop
	成長率	セイチョウリツ	growth rate
	成年	セイネン	adult age; majority
	成敗	セイハイ	success and failure
	成敗	セイバイ	judgment; punishment —***v***. judge; punish
	成否	セイヒ	success or failure; result
	成分	セイブン	ingredient; component; constituent
	成立	セイリツ	formation —***vi***. come into existence/being; be organized/concluded
訓	成す	なす	***vt***. accomplish; achieve; take shape; form
	成る	なる	***vi***. become; be completed; consist; be made up; be promoted
	成り上がり者	なりあがりもの	upstart
	成金	なりキン	upstart; newly rich
	成り立ち	なりたち	history; the origin; structure; formation
	成り行き	なりゆき	course of events; developments
¥	成り行き(注文)	なりゆき(チュウモン)	market order; at the market

837

⑦

音	我	ガ	self; selfish; ego; obstinacy
熟	我意	ガイ	self-will; obstinacy
	我田引水	ガデンインスイ	drawing water for one's own field ***fig***. promoting one's own interests

	我慢	ガマン	patience; tolerance; perseverance; endurance —*v*. be patient/tolerant; persevere; endure
	我流	ガリュウ	self-taught method; one's own way (of doing something)
訓	我	わ	I
	我輩	わがハイ	***clas***. I; myself; me
	我	われ	I; one's side
	我等	われら	we; our; us
	我々	われわれ	we; our; us

838

戒 ⑦ 一 二 チ 开 戒 戒 戒

音	戒	カイ	admonition; remonstrance
熟	戒厳令	カイゲンレイ	martial law
	戒告	カイコク	admonition; reprimand; warning —*v*. admonish; reprimand; warn
	戒名	カイミョウ	posthumous Buddhist name
	戒律	カイリツ	Buddhist precepts
訓	戒め	いましめ	warning; admonition
	戒める	いましめる	***vt***. warn; prohibit

839

戦 ⑬ 丶 丷 ⺍ 㐬 当 肖 肙 単 単 戦 戦 戦

音	戦	セン	war; battle
熟	戦域	センイキ	war zone; theater of war
	戦火	センカ	(the flames of) war
	戦艦	センカン	battleship
	戦記物	センキもの	account of a war
	戦況	センキョウ	war situation
	戦局	センキョク	war situation
	戦後	センゴ	after the war; post war (in particular, World War Ⅱ)
	戦国	センゴク	country torn apart by civil war
	戦国時代	センゴクジダイ	***hist***. era of civil wars (1467-1568)
	戦災	センサイ	war devastation
	戦士	センシ	warrior; soldier
	戦死	センシ	death in battle; killed in action —***vi***. be killed/die in action

	戦時	センジ	wartime; war period
	戦車	センシャ	tank
	戦術	センジュツ	tactics
	戦場	センジョウ	battlefield; front
	戦線	センセン	battle line; front
	戦前	センゼン	before the war; prewar (in particular, World War Ⅱ)
	戦争	センソウ	war —***vi***. fight; go to war
	戦隊	センタイ	corps; squadron
	戦地	センチ	battlefield; front
	戦中	センチュウ	during the war
	戦闘	セントウ	action; combat; battle; fighting —***vi***. go into action/combat; battle; fight
	戦犯	センパン	war crime/criminal
	戦没者	センボツシャ	fallen soldier
	戦友	センユウ	comrade-in-arms
	戦乱	センラン	upheavals of war
	戦慄	センリツ	shivering; trembling with fear —***vi***. shiver; tremble with fear
	戦利品	センリヒン	war spoils; booty
	戦略	センリャク	strategy
	戦力	センリョク	war fighting capacity
	戦歴	センレキ	war experience; combat record
訓	戦う	たたかう	***vt***. fight; wage war
	戦	いくさ	war
	※戦く	おののく	***vi***. shudder; tremble; shiver
	※戦ぐ	そよぐ	***vi***. rustle; stir; sway; tremble; quiver

840

⑮

音	戯	ギ	play; joke
熟	戯画	ギガ	caricature; cartoon
	戯曲	ギキョク	drama; play
訓	戯れる	たわむれる	***vi***. play; tease; joke; flirt
	戯れ	たわむれ	play; joke; fun; flirtation

4 戸 と door

841

戸 ④ 一 ㇆ ㇋ 戸

音	戸	コ	door; house; (counter for houses and buildings)
熟	戸外	コガイ	outdoors; out of doors; open air
	戸籍	コセキ	census; registration; person's family register
	戸籍抄本	コセキショウホン	abstract of one's family register
	戸籍謄本	コセキトウホン	copy of one's family register
	戸別	コベツ	from door to door; each house
訓	戸	と	door
	戸締り	とじまり	locking up —*vi*. lock up
	戸棚	とだな	cabinet; cupboard; sideboard; closet
	戸惑う	とまどう	*vi*. be puzzled; be at a loss

842

戻 ⑦ 一 ㇆ ㇋ 戸 戸 戸 戻

音	戻	レイ	go back; come back; return
訓	戻す	もどす	*vt*. return; go back; come back; throw up; vomit
	戻る	もどる	*vi*. return; give back; send back; restore

843

所 ⑧ 一 ㇆ ㇋ 戸 戸 所 所 所

音	所	ショ	place
熟	所轄	ショカツ	jurisdiction
	所管	ショカン	jurisdiction
	所感	ショカン	impressions; thoughts; feelings
	所見	ショケン	one's view/opinion
	所在	ショザイ	site; one's whereabouts; location
	所産	ショサン	product; fruit of one's efforts
	所持	ショジ	possession —*v*. possess; have; store/put away one's possessions
	所信	ショシン	one's beliefs/opinions/views

	所詮	ショセン	after all; any way
	所蔵	ショゾウ	possession —*v*. possess; own; store/put away one's possessions
	所属	ショゾク	one's position —*vi*. belong to; be with; be attached to
	所帯	ショタイ	property; household
	所長	ショチョウ	the head
	所定	ショテイ	fixed; appointed
	所望	ショモウ	desire; wish; request —*v*. wish; desire; ask for; request
	所有	ショユウ	ownership; possession —*vt*. own; possess
	所有権	ショユウケン	ownership; title
	所用	ショヨウ	business
訓	所	ところ	place; spot; locality
¥	所持人	ショジニン	bearer; holder
	所得	ショトク	income; earnings
	所得税	ショトクゼイ	income tax
	所有	ショユウ	possession —*v*. own; possess

844

房 ⑧

一 ㇇ ヨ 戸 戸 戸 房 房

音	房	ボウ	chamber; room; tassel
熟	房中	ボウチュウ	in the room/bedroom
訓	房	ふさ	tassel; tuft; cluster; bunch (of grapes)
	房々	ふさふさ	tufty/bushy/profuse (hair)

845

扇 ⑩

一 ㇇ ヨ 戸 戸 戸 戸 扇 扇 扇

音	扇	セン	folding fan
熟	扇形	センケイ	fan shape; sector; segment
	扇状地	センジョウチ	alluvial fan; delta
	扇子	センス	fan
	扇動	センドウ	instigation; incitement; agitation —*v*. instigate; incite; agitate
	扇風機	センプウキ	electric fan
訓	扇	おうぎ	fan

846

扉 ⑫

一 ㇀ ㇁ 戸 戸 戸 戸 戸 戸 扉 扉 扉

音	扉	ヒ	door
訓	扉	とびら	door; title page (of a book); frontispiece

4 手 て hand 扌 (p.389)

847

手 ④

一 二 三 手

音	手	シュ	hand
熟	手記	シュキ	note; memorandum; private papers
	手芸	シュゲイ	handicrafts
	手工業	シュコウギョウ	handicraft/manual industry
	手術	シュジュツ	***med***. operation; surgery —***v***. operate; perform an operation
	手段	シュダン	means; step; measure
	手動	シュドウ	manual operation
	手法	シュホウ	technique; technical skill
	手練	シュレン	skill; dexterity
	手腕	シュワン	ability; capability
訓	手	て	hand; handle; trouble; means
	手足	てあし	hands and feet; arms and legs; limbs
	手当たり次第	てあたりシダイ	at random
	手当	てあて	medical treatment/care; salary; allowance; cover; provision —***v***. treat (a burn, etc.)
	手薄	てうす	short of hands
	手書き	てがき	handwriting —***v***. write; draft
	手数	てかず (てスウ)	trouble
	手堅い	てがたい	steady; sound; safe; trustworthy; reliable
	手紙	てがみ	letter; note
	手柄	てがら	exploit; great deed; feat
	手軽	てがる	light; simple
	手際	てぎわ	skill
	手口	てぐち	method; way; trick; *modus operandi*
	手首	てくび	wrist

手心（を加える）	てごころ（をくわえる）	consideration; allowance —***v.*** consider; allow for
手応え	てごたえ	effect; resistance; response
手頃	てごろ	proper; handy; suitable; reasonable; moderate
手強い	てごわい	strong; tough; formidable
手細工	てザイク	handiwork; handicraft
手先	てさき	fingertips
手探り	てさぐり	groping
手提げ	てさげ	handbag; bag
手下	てした	underling; henchmen
手品	てじな	magic; conjuring trick; sleight of hand
手品師	てじなシ	magician; conjurer
手順	てジュン	order; plan; arrangements; process; procedure
手錠	てジョウ	handcuffs
手製	てセイ	handmade; homemade
手相	てソウ	palmistry
手出し	てだし	interference —***vi.*** meddle; interfere; make advances; dabble
手立て	てだて	means; process; order
手近	てぢか	close at hand; within reach
手違い	てちがい	mistake; blunder; accident
手帳	てチョウ	notebook; pocket diary
手作り	てづくり	homemade; handmade
手伝う	てつだう	***vt.*** help; assist; aid
手続き	てつづき	procedure; formalities
手並み	てなみ	skill; dexterity
手習い	てならい	practice; learning
手慣れる	てなれる	***vi.*** get used (to); get skillful (in)
手荷物	てにモツ	baggage
手拭い	てぬぐい	towel
手配	てハイ	arrangements; preparations; search —***v.*** arrange; prepare
手放す	てばなす	***vt.*** dispose; do away with; part; sell
手引き	てびき	guidance; guide; introduction; manual
手袋	てぶくろ	gloves; mittens
手解き	てほどき	initiation
手本	てホン	copy; model; copy book
手前	てまえ	before; near; in front
手間取る	てまどる	***vi.*** take time; be delayed; be kept long
手回し	てまわし	preparation; arrangements
手短か	てみじか	brief; short
手持ち	てもち	on a hand; in stock; holdings

	手元	てもと	at hand
	手料理	てリョウリ	home cooking
¥	手当	てあて	allowance; cover; procurement; purchase
	手形	てがた	handprint; document; bill; draft; note
	手形割引	てがたわりびき	discount of bills
	手仕舞	てジまい	evening up
	手数料	てスウリョウ	fee; change; commission
	手付金	てつけキン	earnest; deposit; bargain deposit; bargain-money deposit paid on contracts; security money; hand money
	手取り	てどり	net profit/income/receipts; one's salary after tax/deduction; clear gain
	手直し	てなおし	later adjustment; readjustment
	手控え	てびかえ	holding off
	手引書	てびきショ	introduction; manual; handbook

848

⑧

音	承	ショウ	consent; agree; accept
熟	承諾	ショウダク	consent; agreement; acceptance; assent —*v*. consent; agree; give one's consent
	承知	ショウチ	consent; agreement; assent —*v*. know; understand; be aware; consent; agree; permit; allow
	承認	ショウニン	approval; consent; assent —*v*. approve; consent; acknowledge
	承服	ショウフク	submission —*v*. yield to; accept; consent
訓	承る	うけたまわる	***vt***. hear; understand; comply; consent

849

⑩

音	挙	キョ	raise; lift; enumerate; list; happen; occur; move; shake
熟	挙行	キョコウ	performance; celebration —*v*. perform (a ceremony); hold (a reception); celebrate (a marriage)
	挙国一致	キョコクイッチ	the whole country; nationwide
	挙式	キョシキ	(bridal) ceremony; celebration —***vi***. hold a ceremony; celebrate
	挙手	キョシュ	raising one's hand; show of hands —***vi***. raise one's hand; give a show of hands

心 忄 小 戈 戸 手 扌 支 攵 文 斗 斤 方 日 曰 月 肉 月 木 欠 止 歹 殳 母 毋 比 毛 氏 气 水 氺 氵 火 灬 爫 父 片 牛 犬 犭 王 ネ 耂

	挙動	キョドウ	behavior; conduct; demeanor
	挙兵	キョヘイ	raising an army; taking up arms —*vi*. raise an army; take up arms
訓	挙がる	あがる	*vi*. raise; be lifted/elevated
	挙げる	あげる	*vt*. raise; lift; elevate

850

掌 ⑫

音	掌	ショウ	palm; administer
熟	掌握	ショウアク	control; command; power —*v*. control; command; come into power
	掌中	ショウチュウ	in (his/her) hands

851

撃 ⑮

音	撃	ゲキ	strike; attack
熟	撃退	ゲキタイ	repulsion; rejection; refusal —*v*. drive back; repulse; reject; refuse
	撃沈	ゲキチン	sinking a ship —*v*. sink a ship; send a ship to the bottom
	撃墜	ゲキツイ	shooting down a plane —*v*. shoot down a plane
	撃破	ゲキハ	defeat; destruction —*v*. defeat; beat; destroy
	撃滅	ゲキメツ	destruction; extermination —*v*. destruct; exterminate
訓	撃つ	うつ	*vt*. fire; shoot

852

摩 ⑮

音	摩	マ	rub; scrape
熟	摩擦	マサツ	friction —*v*. create/feel/apply friction
	摩天楼	マテンロウ	skyscraper
	摩滅	マメツ	abrasion; wear —*v*. wear out
訓	※摩る	さする	*vt*. pat; stroke; rub

3 扌 てへん hand at left

853
才 一 十 才 ③

音	才	サイ	wit; talent; ability
熟	才覚	サイカク	wit; resources; contrivance; device
	才気	サイキ	quick-witted; gifted; brilliant
	才女	サイジョ	talented woman
	才能	サイノウ	talent; ability; gift

854
打 一 十 扌 扌 打 ⑤

音	打	ダ	beat; bat; strike; hit; shoot
熟	打開	ダカイ	breakthrough; development; solution —*v*. breakthrough; effect a development
	打楽器	ダガッキ	percussion instrument
	打球	ダキュウ	***bas***. batting
	打撃	ダゲキ	blow; hit; knock; shock
	打算的	ダサンテキ	calculating; selfish; self-centered; mercenary
	打者	ダシャ	***bas***. batter
	打順	ダジュン	***bas***. batting order
	打診	ダシン	inquire; percussion —***med***. tapping —***v***. inquire; sound out —***med***. tap
	打席	ダセキ	***bas***. at bat
	打線	ダセン	***bas***. the batting line-up
	打倒	ダトウ	overthrow —***v***. overthrow; defeat; knock down; topple
	打破	ダハ	breaking; destruction; defeat; conquest; overthrow —***v***. break down; overthrow; conquer; destroy; defeat
	打撲	ダボク	blow; strike; hit —***v***. blow; strike; hit
	打撲傷	ダボクショウ	bruise; contusion
	打率	ダリツ	***bas***. batting average
訓	打つ	うつ	***vt***. hit; strike; shoot; make noodles; send a telegram; gamble
	打ち勝つ	うちかつ	***vi***. overcome; get over; conquer
	打ち切る	うちきる	***vt***. stop doing something; call off
	打ち込む	うちこむ	***vt***. devote oneself (to); drive in; shoot into

心 忄 小 戈 戸 手 • 扌 支 攵 文 斗 斤 方 日 曰 月 肉 月 木 欠 止 歹 殳 母 毋 比 毛 氏 气 水 氺 氵 火 灬 爫 父 片 牛 犬 犭 王 ネ 耂

855

払 ⑤

一 † 才 扎 払

音	払	フツ	pay; sweep/drive away
熟	払拭	フッショク	sweeping away; wiping out —*v*. sweep away; wipe out
訓	払う	はらう	*vt*. pay; sweep/drive away; sell; dispose; pay; pay (attention)
	払い	はらい	payment; defrayment; discharge; quittance; acquittance; settlement; clearance; liquidation; repayment
¥	払い込み	はらいこみ	payment; installment
	払い下げる	はらいさげる	*vt*. sell; dispose of
	払い済み	はらいずみ	paid up; settled
	払い出し	はらいだし	payment
	払出銀行	はらいだしギンコウ	paying bank
	払い戻し	はらいもどし	refund; repayment

856

扱 ⑥

一 † 才 扌 扨 扱

音	扱	(ソウ)	manage; handle; deal
訓	扱う	あつかう	*vt*. manage; handle; deal; arbitrate; treat
	※扱く	しごく	*vt*. squeeze through one's hands; draw through one's hands; put a person through hard training

857

技 ⑦

一 † 才 扌 扌 抆 技

音	技	ギ	skill; art; craft
熟	技巧	ギコウ	craftmanship; workmanship; technical skill
	技師	ギシ	engineer; technician
	技術	ギジュツ	technique; technology; technical skill
	技能	ギノウ	technical skill; ability
	技法	ギホウ	technique
	技量	ギリョウ	skill; ability; talent; capability
訓	技	わざ	art; trick; skill

858

抗 ⑦

一 丁 扌 扌 扩 扩 抗

音	抗	コウ	resist; protest; oppose
熟	抗議	コウギ	protest; objection; complaint —*vi*. protest; object; complain
	抗生物質	コウセイブッシツ	***med***. antibiotics
	抗争	コウソウ	contention; dispute —*vi*. contend; struggle against; resist
	抗体	コウタイ	***med***. antibody

859

抄 ⑦

一 丁 扌 扌 扌 扌 抄

音	抄	ショウ	extract
熟	抄本	ショウホン	abridgment; abridged version of one's family register
	抄録	ショウロク	extract; summary —*v*. extract; summarize

860

折 ⑦

一 丁 扌 扌 扩 扩 折

音	折	セツ	break; divide; be folded
熟	折角	セッカク	kindly; with much effort; go to the trouble of
	折衷	セッチュウ	compromise; cross; blending —*v*. compromise; cross; blend
	折半	セッパン	halving —*v*. halve; divide into two
訓	折る	おる	*v*. fold; break; bend
	折れる	おれる	*vi*. break; be folded; bend; turn; yield
	折	おり	occasion; opportunity
	折り合う	おりあう	*vi*. agree; come to terms
	折り返す	おりかえす	*v*. make a turn; turn back
¥	折衝	セッショウ	negotiation —*vi*. negotiate

861

択 ⑦

一 丁 扌 扌 扌 扌 択

音	択	タク	choose; select

熟	択一的	タクイツテキ	alternative

862

投 ⑦

一 十 扌 扌 扌 扮 投

音	投	トウ	throw; fling; cast
熟	投影	トウエイ	casting a shadow; projection —*v*. project; reflect; cast a refection
	投下	トウカ	dropping; throwing down —*v*. drop; throw down
	投函	トウカン	mailing; posting —*v*. mail; post
	投球	トウキュウ	***bas***. pitching —*v*. ***bas***. throw; pitch
	投降	トウコウ	surrender —***vi***. surrender; lay down one's arms
	投稿	トウコウ	magazine/newspaper contribution —***vi***. contribute/write for (a magazine, newspaper, etc.)
	投合	トウゴウ	agreement; coincidence —***vi***. agree/coincide with
	投獄	トウゴク	imprisonment; confinement —*v*. imprison; confine
	投資	トウシ	investment —***vi***. invest; make investments
	投宿	トウシュク	registering/staying at a hotel —***vi***. register/stay at a hotel
	投書	トウショ	contribution; reader's letter; letter to the editor —***vi***. write a letter to the editor; contribute to (a magazine, newspaper, etc.)
	投身	トウシン	suicide by drowning —***vi***. commit suicide by drowning
	投石	トウセキ	stone throwing —***vi***. throw stones
	投入	トウニュウ	investment; capital injection; commitment —*v*. invest in; commit to
	投票	トウヒョウ	vote; suffrage; poll; ballot; voting; election —***vi***. ballot; cast a vote; elect; vote
	投薬	トウヤク	prescription —*v*. prescribe medicine; medicate
訓	投げる	なげる	***vt***. throw; fling; cast; abandon; give up
	※投網	とあみ	cast net
¥	投機	トウキ	speculation; venture
	投資家	トウシカ	investor
	投資顧問業	トウシコモンギョウ	investment advisor
	投資信託（投信）	トウシシンタク（トウシン）	investment trust
	投資有価証券	トウシユウカショウケン	investments in securities
	投げ	なげ	sacrifice; shaking out

863

把 ⑦ 一 十 扌 扌 扣 扣 把

音 把 ハ grasp

熟 把握 ハアク grasp; hold; grip —*v*. grasp; get hold of; grip; seize

864

抜 ⑦ 一 十 扌 扌 扐 抜 抜

音 抜 バツ pull out

熟 抜群 バツグン preeminent; conspicuous; distinguished; outstanding

抜糸 バッシ removal of stitches —***vi***. remove stitches

抜歯 バッシ tooth extraction —***vi***. extract a tooth

抜粋 バッスイ extraction; excerpt; selection —***v***. extract; excerpt; select

抜擢 バッテキ choice; selection —***v***. choose; select

訓 抜かす ぬかす ***vt***. omit; leave out; look over; skip

抜かる ぬかる ***vi***. commit a blunder; make a slip

抜く ぬく ***v***. draw/pull out; extract; remove; omit

抜け道 ぬけみち byway; secret passage; excuse

抜け目 ぬけめ something missing/lacking; incomplete

抜ける ぬける ***vi***. come/fall out; be left out/omitted

865

批 ⑦ 一 十 扌 扌 扎 批 批

音 批 ヒ criticize

熟 批准 ヒジュン ratification (of a treaty); sanction —***v***. ratify (a treaty); sanction

批判 ヒハン criticism; comment; critique —***v***. criticize; comment

批評 ヒヒョウ criticism; critique; critical essay —***v***. criticize; comment

批評家 ヒヒョウカ critic; reviewer

批評眼 ヒヒョウガン critical eye

4 心 忄 小 戈 戸 手 扌● 支 攵 文 斗 斤 方 日 曰 月 肉 月 木 欠 止 歹 殳 母 毋 比 毛 氏 气 水 氺 氵 火 灬 爫 父 片 牛 犬 犭 王 礻 耂

心 忄 小 戈 戸 手 • 扌 支 攵 文 斗 斤 方 日 曰 月 肉 月 木 欠 止 歹 殳 毋 母 比 毛 氏 气 水 氺 氵 火 灬 爫 父 片 牛 犬 犭 王 ネ 耂

866

扶 ⑦

一 十 扌 扌 扌 扌 扶

音	扶	フ	help
熟	扶助	フジョ	help; aid; assistance —*v.* help; aid; assist
	扶養	フヨウ	support; maintenance —*v.* support; maintain; keep up
訓	※扶ける	たすける	help; assist; aid
¥	扶養控除	フヨウコウジョ	allowance/tax exemption for dependents
	扶養家族	フヨウカゾク	dependent family member; dependent

867

抑 ⑦

一 十 扌 扌 扌 扌 抑

音	抑	ヨク	hold; down; control; suppress
熟	抑圧	ヨクアツ	suppression; restraint —*v.* suppress; restrain
	抑制	ヨクセイ	restraint; control; suppression —*v.* restrain; control; suppress
	抑揚	ヨクヨウ	intonation; modulation
	抑留	ヨクリュウ	detention; internment —*v.* detain; intern
訓	抑える	おさえる	***vt.*** hold down; control; suppress
	抑え難い	おさえがたい	irrepressible; uncontrollable
	抑え付ける	おさえつける	***vt.*** hold down; curb; control

868

押 ⑧

一 十 扌 扌 扌 扌 扌 押

音	押	オウ	press; push
熟	押印	オウイン	sealing —***vi.*** seal; affix a seal to
	押韻	オウイン	rhyme; rhyming —*v.* rhyme; make a rhyme
	押収	オウシュウ	seizure; confiscation —*v.* seize; impound; confiscate
	押捺	オウナツ	fingerprinting —*v.* fingerprint
訓	押す	おす	***vt.*** push; press
	押さえる	おさえる	***vt.*** press down; keep down; suppress; restrain; control
	押し	おし	push; pushing
	押入れ	おしいれ	closet; cupboard
	押し花	おしばな	pressed flowers

	押し問答	おしモンドウ	repeated questioning and answering; argument —*vi*. bandy words with; wrangle with
¥	押し上げる	おしあげる	*vt*. push up
	押し売り	おしうり	high-pressure selling
	押し切る	おしきる	*vt*. push through; have one's own way
	押目	おしめ	dip; reaction

869

拐 ⑧

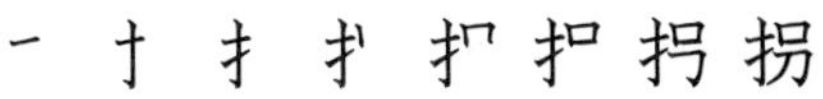

音	拐	カイ	kidnap

870

拡 ⑧

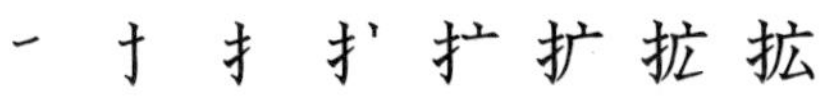

音	拡	カク	expand; spread
熟	拡散	カクサン	proliferation; diffusion —*v*. spread; proliferate
	拡充	カクジュウ	expansion; amplification —*v*. expand; amplify
	拡声器	カクセイキ	loudspeaker
	拡大	カクダイ	enlargement; magnification —*v*. magnify; expand
	拡張	カクチョウ	extension; expansion; enlargement —*v*. extend; expand; enlarge; increase
訓	拡げる	ひろげる	*vt*. spread; widen; expand
¥	拡散指数	カクサンシスウ	diffusion index
	拡大基調	カクダイキチョウ	expansive keynote
	拡大再生産	カクダイサイセイサン	reproduction on an expanded scale; expanded reproduction

871

拒 ⑧

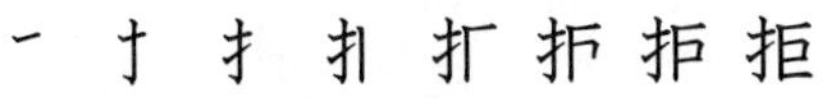

音	拒	キョ	refuse; reject; decline; turn down
熟	拒絶	キョゼツ	refusal; rejection; denial; repudiation —*v*. refuse; reject; deny
	拒否	キョヒ	denial; veto; disapproval —*v*. deny; veto; disapprove
訓	拒む	こばむ	*vt*. refuse; reject; decline; turn down
¥	拒否権	キョヒケン	veto right

872

拠 ⑧

一 十 扌 扌 扌 扨 拠 拠

音	拠	キョ コ	reliable; depend; base
熟	拠点	キョテン	position; strong point base; foothold
¥	拠出金	キョシュツキン	contribution
	拠出制国民年金	キョシュツセイコクミンネンキン	national annuity through premium payment

873

拘 ⑧

一 十 扌 扌 扚 扚 拘 拘

音	拘	コウ	arrest; detain; custody
熟	拘束	コウソク	restriction; restraint; constraint —***v***. restrict; restrain; constrain; bind; be binding
	拘置	コウチ	detention; confinement —***v***. detain; confine; keep a person in custody
	拘泥	コウデイ	adherence —***vi***. adhere/stick to
	拘留	コウリュウ	detention; custody; confinement —***v***. detain; keep a person in custody; lock a person up

874

招 ⑧

一 十 扌 扌ワ 扨 扨 招 招

音	招	ショウ	invite
熟	招集	ショウシュウ	call/invitation to a group of people —***v***. call/invite a group of people
	招待	ショウタイ	invitation —***v***. invite; get an invitation
	招待状	ショウタイジョウ	(letter of) invitation
	招聘	ショウヘイ	invitation/offer (of employment) —***v***. invite/offer (someone) a job
訓	招く	まねく	***vt***. call; beckon; invite

875

拙 ⑧

一 十 扌 扎 扎 扎 拙 拙

音	拙	セツ	clumsy; unskilled

熟	拙者	セッシャ	***hum***. I
	拙宅	セッタク	***hum***. my house
	拙文	セツブン	***hum***. my writings; poor writings

876

拓 ⑧

一 十 扌 扌 扩 扩 拓 拓

音	拓	タク	cultivate; print
熟	拓殖	タクショク	colonization; exploitation —***vi***. colonize; exploit; settle
	拓本	タクホン	rubbed copy; rubbing

877

担 ⑧

一 十 扌 扌 扣 扣 担 担

音	担	タン	shoulder; carry; bear
熟	担架	タンカ	stretcher; lifter
	担当	タントウ	charge; duty; person in charge —***v***. take charge; assume responsibility
	担任	タンニン	charge; duty; homeroom teacher —***v***. take charge; be in charge; be in charge of a homeroom class; be a class teacher
訓	担ぐ	かつぐ	***vt***. carry on one's shoulder; shoulder; bear
	担う	になう	***vt***. carry on one's shoulder; bear; shoulder responsibility
¥	担保	タンポ	collateral; mortgage; security; warranty
	担保権	タンポケン	security interest/right
	担保付社債	タンポつきシャサイ	secured debenture; collateral trust bonds

878

抽 ⑧

一 十 扌 扌 扣 抽 抽 抽

音	抽	チュウ	extract; abstract
熟	抽出	チュウシュツ	abstraction; extraction —***v***. abstract; extract
	抽象	チュウショウ	abstraction —***v***. abstract
	抽象画	チュウショウガ	abstract painting
	抽象的	チュウショウテキ	abstract; non-objective; metaphysical
	抽選	チュウセン	drawing lots; ballot; lottery; raffle —***vi***. draw lots; ballot

879

抵 ⑧

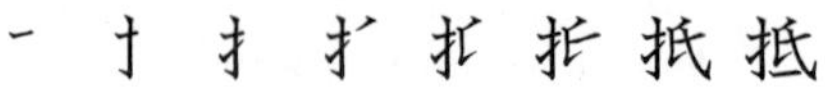

音	抵	テイ	resist
熟	抵抗	テイコウ	resistance; opposition; defiance; struggle; drag —*v*. resist; offer resistance; put up a struggle; defy
	抵抗器	テイコウキ	resistor
	抵抗力	テイコウリョク	resistance; resistivity; resistibility
	抵触	テイショク	infringement; contradiction; conflict; collision —*v*. conflict; contradict; be incompatible/inconsistent
¥	抵抗線	テイコウセン	resistence level
	抵当	テイトウ	mortgage
	抵当権	テイトウケン	mortgage; hypothec
	抵当証券	テイトウショウケン	mortgage certificate
	抵当流れ	テイトウながれ	mortgage forfeit; foreclosure

880

拝 ⑧

音	拝	ハイ	worship; pray; bow; look; witness; (prefix to make an expression humble)
熟	拝する	ハイする	***vt***. worship —***hon***. receive; see
	拝謁	ハイエツ	***hum***. audience (with a superior) —***v***. ***hum***. be granted an audience
	拝観	ハイカン	***hum***. inspection; visit to a temple, etc. —***v***. ***hum***. see; inspect; look at; view
	拝顔	ハイガン	***hum***. seeing/meeting (someone) —***v***. ***hum***. see/meet (someone)
	拝啓	ハイケイ	(opening phrase in a letter)
	拝見	ハイケン	***hum***. looking; inspection —***v***. ***hum***. have the honor of seeing; see; inspect
	拝察	ハイサツ	***hum***. guess
	拝借	ハイシャク	***hum***. borrowing; loan —***v***. ***hum***. have a loan; borrow
	拝受	ハイジュ	***hum***. acceptance —***v***. ***hum***. receive; accept
	拝聴	ハイチョウ	***hum***. listening; hearing —***v***. ***hum***. listen; hear
	拝殿	ハイデン	front shrine; hall of worship
	拝読	ハイドク	***hum***. reading —***v***. ***hum***. read; note
	拝復	ハイフク	***hum***. in reply to your letter

	拝礼	ハイレイ	worship —*v*. worship
訓	拝む	おがむ	***vt*. *hum*.** look; view; witness; worship; pray; bow; implore
	拝み倒す	おがみたおす	***vt*.** entreat (a person) into consent; win over by persuasive entreaty

881

拍 ⑧

音	拍	ハク	clap one's hands
		(ヒョウ)	beat
熟	拍車	ハクシャ	spur
	拍手	ハクシュ	hand clapping; applause —***vi*.** clap one's hands; applaud
	拍子	ヒョウシ	rhythm; chance; moment; time (in music)
	拍子抜け	ヒョウシぬけ	disappointment —***vi*.** be disappointed

882

披 ⑧

音	披	ヒ	open
熟	披露	ヒロウ	announcement; introduction; advertisement —***v*.** announce; introduce; advertise
	披露宴	ヒロウエン	wedding reception/dinner

883

抱 ⑧

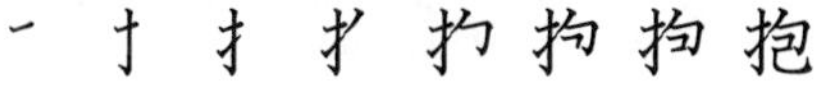

音	抱	ホウ	embrace; hug; hold in one's arms
熟	抱懐	ホウカイ	cherishing; entertaining/harboring (an idea in one's heart) —***v*.** cherish; entertain/harbor (an idea in one's heart)
	抱負	ホウフ	ambition; aspiration
	抱擁	ホウヨウ	embrace; hug —***vt*.** embrace; hug
訓	抱く	だく	***vt*.** embrace; hug; hold in one's arms
	抱く	いだく	***vt*.** embrace; hold; have; harbor (feelings)
	抱える	かかえる	***vt*.** carry in one's arms; hire; have (children)
	お抱え	おかかえ	employing
	抱え込む	かかえこむ	***vt*.** hold/carry in one's arms; take in; take upon oneself

抱き合う	だきあう	*vt*. embrace/hold each other; cuddle
抱き込む	だきこむ	*vt*. win (someone) to your side; embrace; enfold
抱き締める	だきしめる	*vt*. embrace closely; cuddle; hug

884

抹 ⑧ 一 十 扌 扌 扌 扌 抹 抹

音	抹	マツ	erase; expurge; rub; paint
熟	抹殺	マッサツ	denial; expurgement —*v*. deny; expurge; ignore
	抹消	マッショウ	erasing; crossing out —*v*. erase; cross out
	抹茶	マッチャ	powdered tea

885

括 ⑨ 一 十 扌 扌 扌 扌 扌 括 括

音	括	カツ	tie
熟	括弧	カッコ	brackets; parentheses
訓	※括り	くくり	tying; fastening; knot; conclusion
	※括る	くくる	*vt*. tie; fasten; bundle

886

挟 ⑨ 一 十 扌 扌 扌 扌 扌 挟 挟

音	挟	キョウ	get between; be caught in; be sandwiched; put between; insert; jam
訓	挟まる	はさまる	*vi*. get between; be caught in; be sandwiched between
	挟む	はさむ	*vt*. put between; pinch; insert; put in

887

拷 ⑨ 一 十 扌 扌 扌 扌 扌 拷 拷

音	拷	ゴウ	torture
熟	拷問	ゴウモン	torture; the rack —*v*. torture

888

指 ⑨ 一 扌 扌 扌 扌 扌 指 指 指

音	指	シ	finger; point; indicate
熟	指圧	シアツ	*shiatsu* (form of massage) —***v***. give *shiatsu*
	指揮	シキ	command; direction —***v***. command; direct; lead; conduct an orchestra
	指揮者	シキシャ	conductor
	指示	シジ	instructions; indications; directions —***v***. indicate; instruct; direct
	指針	シシン	guide; indicator; pointer; compass needle
	指数	シスウ	***math***. index; exponent
	指定	シテイ	appointment; specification; designation —***v***. appoint; specify; designate; reserve
	指定席	シテイセキ	reserved seat
	指摘	シテキ	indication; pointing out —***v***. indicate; point out
	指導	シドウ	guidance; leadership; coaching —***v***. lead; guide; coach
	指導者	シドウシャ	leader; guide
	指導力	シドウリョク	leadership
	指南	シナン	instruction; teaching —***v***. teach; instruct; coach
	指標	シヒョウ	index
	指名	シメイ	nomination; designation —***v***. nominate; designate
	指紋	シモン	fingerprint
	指令	シレイ	order —***v***. order; instruct; give instructions
訓	指す	さす	***vt***. point to; indicate
	指図	さしズ	direction; directions
	指	ゆび	finger; toe
	指折り	ゆびおり	leading; prominent
	指先	ゆびさき	fingertip
	指差す	ゆびさす	***vt***. point
	指輪	ゆびわ	ring

889

⑨ 一 扌 扌 扌 扌 扌 持 持 持

音	持	ジ	have; hold
熟	持する	ジする	have; hold
	持久	ジキュウ	endurance; perserverance; tenacity —***vi***. endure; perservere

	持久戦	ジキュウセン	protracted war
	持久力	ジキュウリョク	tenacity; stamina; staying power
	持参	ジサン	bringing; taking —***v***. bring; take
	持参金	ジサンキン	dowry
	持説	ジセツ	one's cherished opinion
	持続	ジゾク	continuing; lasting —***v***. continue; last
	持続性	ジゾクセイ	durability
	持続的	ジゾクテキ	continuous; lasting
	持病	ジビョウ	chronic disease
	持論	ジロン	pet theory
訓	持つ	もつ	***v***. have; hold; take; carry; own; possess
	持ち	もち	durability; wear
	持ち上げる	もちあげる	***vt***. lift; raise; flatter
	持ち味	もちあじ	characteristic; peculiar flavor
	持ち合わせる	もちあわせる	***vt***. carry with oneself
	持ち込む	もちこむ	***vt***. bring in
	持ち主	もちぬし	owner; proprietor
¥	持ち株会社	もちかぶガイシャ	holding company
	持ち分法	もちブンホウ	equity method

890

拾 ⑨

一 十 扌 扌 扌 扴 拾 拾 拾

音	拾	シュウ	pick up
熟	拾得	シュウトク	picking up from the ground; finding something that has been dropped —***v***. find/pick up something that has been dropped
	拾得物	シュウトクブツ	thing found (on the road); found article; find; windfall
訓	拾う	ひろう	***vt***. pick up; gather; find
	拾い読み	ひろいよみ	scanning —***vt***. scan; read here and there

891

挑 ⑨

一 十 扌 扌 扌 扌 挑 挑 挑

音	挑	チョウ	challenge
熟	挑戦	チョウセン	challenge; defiance; offer of combat —***vi***. challenge; defy; offer combat

	挑発	チョウハツ	provocation; excitement; incitement —*v*. provoke; excite; stir up; arouse
訓	挑む	いどむ	***vi***. challenge; provoke

892

振 ⑩

音	振	シン	swing
熟	振興	シンコウ	promotion; advancement —*v*. promote; advance
	振動	シンドウ	vibration —*v*. vibrate; swing; oscillate
	振幅	シンプク	amplitude
訓	振る	ふる	*v*. shake; wave; swing; sprinkle; abandon; desert
	振るう	ふるう	*v*. exercise; show off; demonstrate; display; sieve
	振替	ふりかえ	change; transfer
	振り返る	ふりかえる	***vt***. turn round; look back
	振り込む	ふりこむ	***vt***. transfer/pay into another's bank account
	振袖	ふりそで	long-sleeved kimono
	振り向く	ふりむく	***vi***. turn one's face; turn/look around
	振る舞い	ふるまい	behavior; conduct; entertainment; treat

893

捜 ⑩

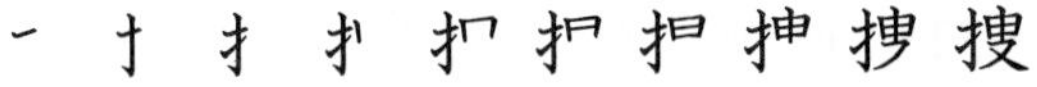

音	捜	ソウ	search; look for
熟	捜査	ソウサ	investigation —*v*. investigate
	捜索	ソウサク	search —*v*. search
	捜索隊	ソウサクタイ	search party
訓	捜す	さがす	***vt***. search; look for

894

挿 ⑩

音	挿	ソウ	insert
熟	挿図	ソウズ	figure; illustration
	挿入	ソウニュウ	insertion —*v*. insert
	挿話	ソウワ	episode; anecdote
訓	挿す	さす	***vt***. insert; put in

	挿し絵	さしえ	illustration

心 忄 小 戈 戸 手 • 扌 支 攵 文 斗 斤 方 日 曰 月 肉 月 木 欠 止 歹 殳 母 毋 比 毛 氏 气 水 氺 氵 火 灬 爫 父 片 牛 犬 犭 王 礻 耂

895

捕 ⑩

一 十 扌 扌 扩 扩 护 捎 捕 捕

音	捕	ホ	catch
熟	捕獲	ホカク	capture; seizure —*v*. catch; seize
	捕鯨	ホゲイ	whaling
	捕鯨船	ホゲイセン	whaling ship
	捕手	ホシュ	***bas***. catcher
	捕虫網	ホチュウあみ	insect net
	捕縛	ホバク	arrest; capture —*v*. arrest; capture
	捕虜	ホリョ	captive; prisoner of war
訓	捕まえる	つかまえる	***vt***. catch; capture; arrest; grab hold of; grasp
	捕まる	つかまる	***vi***. be caught/captured/arrested
	捕る	とる	***vt***. catch; capture; seize; grasp
	捕らえる	とらえる	***vt***. catch; capture; seize; grasp
	捕らわれる	とらわれる	***vi***. be caught/captured; be unable to think freely
	捕物	とりもの	capture; arrest

896

掛 ⑪

一 十 扌 扌 扌 扌 挂 挂 挂 掛 掛

音	掛	カイ	hang; suspend; multipy
訓	掛かる	かかる	***vi***. hang; set
	掛り	かかり	charge; duty; business; expenses; charges; tax; dependance; scale; bite; hold; relation; attack; anchorage
	掛かり合う	かかりあう	have relations with; be involved in
	掛ける	かける	***vt***. hang; multiply
	掛け算	かけザン	***math***. multiplication
	掛け軸	かけジク	hanging scroll; *kakemono*
¥	掛け値	かけね	overcharge; fancy price; two prices

897

掘 ⑪

一 十 扌 扌 扌 护 护 掘 掘 掘 掘

音	掘	クツ	dig; digging

熟 掘削 クッサク digging; excavation

訓 掘る ほる *vt*. dig

掘り下げる ほりさげる *vt*. dig down; investigate; delve

898

掲 ⑪

音 掲 ケイ put up; display

熟 掲載 ケイサイ publishing; carrying/running an article —*v*. publish; carry/run an article

掲示 ケイジ notice —*v*. put up; post

掲示板 ケイジバン bulletin board

掲揚 ケイヨウ hoisting/putting up a flag —*v*. hoist/put up a flag

訓 掲げる かかげる *vt*. put up; hoist; display

899

控 ⑪

音 控 コウ note; write down; refrain; moderate; wait; deduct

熟 控訴 コウソ intermediate appeal —*vi*. bring an intermediate appeal to court

訓 控え ひかえ note; memo; duplicate; copy; waiting; reserve

控える ひかえる *vt*. hold back; refrain; desist; be moderate; note; write down; wait

控え室 ひかえシツ anteroom; waiting room

控え目 ひかえめ moderate; conservative

¥ 控除 コウジョ deduction; subtraction —*v*. deduct; subtract; take away; cut off

900

採 ⑪

音 採 サイ choose; take

熟 採掘 サイクツ mining; digging —*v*. mine; dig

採決 サイケツ vote; parlimentary decision —*v*. vote; take a vote

採血 サイケツ ***med***. blood sample/collection —***vi***. collect blood; take a blood sample

心 忄 小 戈 戸 手 • 扌 支 攵 文 斗 斤 方 日 曰 月 肉 月 木 欠 止 歹 殳 母 毋 比 毛 氏 气 水 氺 氵 火 灬 爫 父 片 牛 犬 犭 王 礻 耂

	採光	サイコウ	lighting
	採鉱	サイコウ	mining —*vi.* work a mine; mine
	採取	サイシュ	collecting; extracting; collection; extract —*v.* gather; pick; collect; extract
	採集	サイシュウ	collecting; gathering; hunting —*v.* collect; hunt; gather
	採択	サイタク	adoption; selection —*v.* adopt; select; choose
	採炭	サイタン	coal mining —*vi.* mine coal
	採点	サイテン	marking papers; grading assignments —*v.* give marks; grade exams or papers
	採否	サイヒ	adoption or rejection; employment and rejection; result; decision
	採用	サイヨウ	adoption; employment; usage —*v.* adopt; employ; use; choose
訓	採る	とる	*vt.* adopt; employ; select; choose; prefer
¥	採算	サイサン	commercial profit
	採算買い	サイサンがい	buying on yield basis
	採算価格	サイサンカカク	break-even price
	採算分岐点	サイサンブンキテン	break-even point
	採算割れ	サイサンわれ	below (prime) cost
	採用条件	サイヨウジョウケン	employment conditions
	採用通知	サイヨウツウチ	notification of employment

901

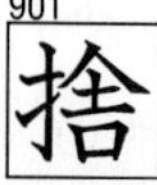

⑪ 一 十 扌 扌 扌 扌 扌 拎 拎 捨 捨

音	捨	シャ	throw away
訓	捨てる	すてる	*vt.* throw away; dump; abandon; desert
	捨て金	すてがね	wasted money
	捨て子	すてご	abandoned child; foundling
	捨て値	すてね	dirt-cheap; giveaway price
	捨て身	すてみ	wholeheartedly

902

⑪ 一 十 扌 扌 扌 扌 扌 扌 扌 授 授

音	授	ジュ	grant; give; teach
熟	授業	ジュギョウ	lesson; lecture —*vi.* teach/give a lecture
	授産所	ジュサンジョ	work center; labor exchange; place for the unemployed to find work

	授賞	ジュショウ	prize-giving —***vi***. give/award a prize
	授乳	ジュニュウ	nursing (a baby); breast-feeding —***vi***. nurse (a baby); breastfeed
	授与	ジュヨ	awarding; conferring —***v***. award; confer
訓	授かる	さずかる	***vi***. be given/granted/taught
	授ける	さずける	***vt***. give; grant; teach; instruct

903

推 ⑪

音	推	スイ	propel; recommend
熟	推移	スイイ	transition; change; progress —***vi***. change; undergo a change; shift; progress
	推挙	スイキョ	proposal; recommendation —***v***. propose; recommend
	推計	スイケイ	estimation —***v***. estimate
	推敲	スイコウ	polish; elaboration —***v***. polish; elaborate; file; improve
	推考	スイコウ	speculation —***v***. speculate
	推察	スイサツ	conjecture; guess; inference; surmise —***v***. guess; conjecture; infer; surmise
	推奨	スイショウ	recommendation; commendation —***v***. recommend; commend
	推進	スイシン	propulsion; drive —***v***. propel; drive forward; promote; further
	推進力	スイシンリョク	thrust; impulse; driving force
	推薦	スイセン	recommendation; proposal —***v***. recommend; propose
	推測	スイソク	conjecture; surmise; supposition —***v***. conjecture; surmise; suppose
	推定	スイテイ	presumption; assumption; inference —***v***. presume; assume; infer
	推理	スイリ	reasoning; deduction; detection —***v***. reason; deduct; detect
	推理小説	スイリショウセツ	detective story; mystery; thriller
	推量	スイリョウ	guess; conjecture —***v***. guess; conjecture
	推論	スイロン	reasoning; inference; induction; deduction —***v***. reason; infer; induce; deduce
訓	推す	おす	***vt***. infer; deduce; conclude; recommend; propose; nominate
	推し量る（推し測る）	おしはかる	***vt***. guess; conjecture

904

据 ⑪ 一 十 扌 扌 护 护 护 护 据 据 据

音	据	キョ	set; lay; fix; place
訓	据える	すえる	***vt***. set; lay; fix; place
	据え膳	すえゼン	meal set before one
	据え付ける	すえつける	***vt***. install; set; fit; mount
	据わる	すわる	***vi***. sit; take a seat; set; be set

905

接 ⑪ 一 十 扌 扌 扩 扩 扩 拉 接 接 接

音	接	セツ	contact; join; near; touch
熟	接する	セッする	***v***. make contact; touch
	接角	セッカク	***math***. adjacent angles
	接近	セッキン	approaching; drawing near —***v***. approach; draw near
	接合	セツゴウ	joining; union —***v***. join; put together; unite
	接骨医	セッコツイ	bone setter; bonesetting —***v***. set bones
	接写	セッシャ	close-up photo —***v***. take close-up pictures
	接種	セッシュ	inoculation; vaccination —***v***. inoculate; vaccinate
	接収	セッシュウ	requisition; take over —***v***. requisite; take over
	接触	セッショク	contact; touch —***v***. make contact; touch
	接戦	セッセン	close combat/contest
	接線	セッセン	***math***. tangent
	接続	セツゾク	connection; joining —***v***. connect; join
	接続詞	セツゾクシ	***gram***. conjunction
	接待	セッタイ	reception; welcome; serving; offering —***v***. give a reception; welcome; serve; offer
	接着	セッチャク	adhesion —***v***. be adhesive; adhere to; stick
	接点	セッテン	point of tangency; contact
	接頭語	セットウゴ	***gram***. prefix
	接尾語	セツビゴ	***gram***. suffix
	接吻	セップン	kiss —***vi***. kiss
訓	接ぐ	つぐ	***vt***. join; piece
	接ぎめ	つぎめ	joint; seam

906

措 ⑪

音	措	ソ	put aside; leave as is; desist from; except
熟	措置	ソチ	measure; steps —*v*. take measures/steps
訓	措く	おく	*v*. put aside; desist from

907

掃 ⑪

音	掃	ソウ	sweep
熟	掃除	ソウジ	sweeping; cleaning —*v*. sweep; clean
	掃除機	ソウジキ	vacuum cleaner
訓	掃く	はく	***vt***. sweep

908

探 ⑪

音	探	タン	search; inquire; investigate; explore
熟	探究	タンキュウ	research; investigation; inquiry; study —*v*. investigate; inquire into; explore; research into
	探求	タンキュウ	quest; search; pursuit —*v*. search for; pursue
	探検	タンケン	exploration; expedition; —*v*. explore; make an exploration; go on an expedition
	探索	タンサク	search —*v*. search/look for
	探知	タンチ	detection —*v*. detect; spy; trace
	探偵	タンテイ	detective work; espionage; detective; spy
	探訪	タンボウ	inquiry —*v*. make inquiries into; inquire into
訓	探す	さがす	***vt***. search/look for; trace; locate
	探る	さぐる	***vt***. search; look for; explore; spy
	探り	さぐり	spy; probe

909

排 ⑪

音	排	ハイ	drive away

熟	排する	ハイする	***vt***. drive/push/keep away/aside; refuse; arrange; put in order
	排外思想	ハイガイシソウ	chauvinism; xenophobia
	排気	ハイキ	exhaust; exhalation —***vi***. exhaust; exhale
	排気ガス	ハイキガス	exhaust fumes (from a car, etc.)
	排撃	ハイゲキ	rejection; denunciation —***v***. reject; denounce; show strong dissapproval of
	排出	ハイシュツ	discharge; exhaust; excretion —***v***. discharge; exhaust; transpire
	排除	ハイジョ	exclusion; removal; elimination —***v***. exclude; remove; eliminate
	排水	ハイスイ	drainage; draining; displacement —***vi***. drain; pump; bail; displace
	排斥	ハイセキ	expulsion; rejection; exclusion —***v***. keep out; drive out; reject; eject
	排泄	ハイセツ	excretion; discharge; evacuation; dejection —***v***. excrete; purge; evacuate; discharge
	排泄物	ハイセツブツ	***med***. excreta
	排日	ハイニチ	anti-Japanese
	排列	ハイレツ	arrangement; grouping; configuration —***v***. arrange/group together

910

描 ⑪

音	描	ビョウ	draw
熟	描写	ビョウシャ	description; portrayal; depiction —***v***. describe; portray; depict
訓	描く	えがく	***vt***. draw; paint; sketch; describe; depict; imagine

911

握 ⑫

音	握	アク	hold; grasp; seize; refuse to release
熟	握手	アクシュ	handshake —***vi***. shake hands
	握力	アクリョク	grip; grasping power
訓	握る	にぎる	***vt***. clasp; hold; grasp; grip; clutch; seize
	握り締める	にぎりしめる	***vt***. hold tight in one's hand; clasp; clench
	握り飯	にぎりめし	rice ball

912
援 ⑫

音	援	エン	aid; help; raise; pull out
熟	援軍	エングン	reinforcements
	援護	エンゴ	support; relief; protection —*v.* back up; support; protect
	援助	エンジョ	help; assistance; aid; support —*v.* help; assist; aid; support
	援用	エンヨウ	quotation —*v.* quote; invoke; claim

913
換 ⑫

音	換	カン	change
熟	換気	カンキ	ventilation —*v.* ventilate
	換言	カンゲン	in other words —*v.* say in other words; rephrase
訓	換える	かえる	***vt***. change; exchange
	換わる	かわる	***vi***. relieve; change
¥	換金	カンキン	realization (of securities/property); liquidation (of goods); cash —*v.* realize (one's securities, property); convert (goods) into money
	換金売り	カンキンうり	realization sales
	換算	カンサン	conversion from one unit into another —*v.* convert; change

914
揮 ⑫

音	揮	キ	wield; command
熟	揮発	キハツ	volatilization —***vi***. volatize
	揮発油	キハツユ	gasoline; benzine

915
提 ⑫

音	提	テイ	present

熟 提案 テイアン proposal; offer; suggestion; overture —*v*. propose; suggest; make a proposal
提起 テイキ institution; lodging —*v*. institute; lodge
提議 テイギ proposal; proposition; suggestion —*v*. propose; make a proposition; suggest; recommend
提供 テイキョウ offer; proffer; tender —*v*. offer; make an offer; produce evidence
提携 テイケイ cooperation; coalition; concert —*v*. cooperate; act in concert
提示 テイジ presentation —*v*. exhibit; present
提出 テイシュツ presentation; introduction; exhibition; production —*v*. present; introduce; submit
提唱 テイショウ advocacy; proposal —*v*. advocate; put forward; advance; lecture
提訴 テイソ indictment —*v*. bring a case to court
提督 テイトク admiral; commodore
提要 テイヨウ summary; compendium

訓 提げる さげる ***vt***. carry in one's hand

¥ 提携 テイケイ affiliation; cooperation; tie-up
提携会社 テイケイガイシャ affiliated company

916
搭 ⑫
一 十 扌 扌 扩 拦 拶 搭 搭 搭 搭 搭

音 搭 トウ board

熟 搭載 トウサイ loading; embarkation —*v*. load; embark
搭乗 トウジョウ boarding an airplane or ship —***vi***. get on/board an airplane

917
揚 ⑫
一 十 扌 扌 扣 押 担 担 担 揚 揚 揚

音 揚 ヨウ raise; elevate; praise

熟 揚言 ヨウゲン profess; declare; assert; speak in a loud voice
揚々 ヨウヨウ in high spirits
揚力 ヨウリョク dynamic lift

訓 揚がる あがる ***vi***. rise; be fried; fly high
揚げる あげる ***v***. raise; fry; fly (a kite)
揚げ物 あげもの deep-fried food

918
揺 ⑫

音	揺	ヨウ	shake; sway; vibrate
熟	揺籃期	ヨウランキ	infancy
訓	揺れる	ゆれる	***vi***. shake; sway; vibrate
	揺らぐ	ゆらぐ	***vi***. shake
	揺るぐ	ゆるぐ	***vi***. shake; sway; vibrate
	揺さぶる	ゆさぶる	***vt***. shake; rock
	揺すぶる	ゆすぶる	***vt***. shake; rock
	揺する	ゆする	***vt***. shake

919
携 ⑬

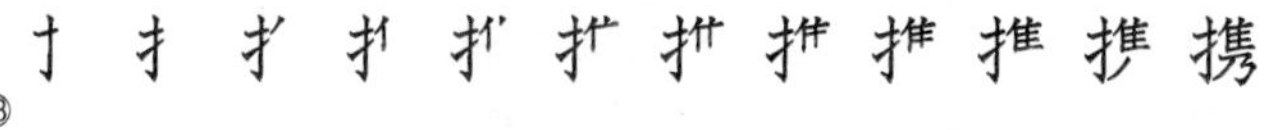

音	携	ケイ	carry; bring; accompany
熟	携行	ケイコウ	carrying; bringing —***v***. carry; bring
	携帯	ケイタイ	carrying; bringing —***v***. carry; bring
	携帯用	ケイタイヨウ	portable
訓	携える	たずさえる	***vt***. carry; accompany
	携わる	たずさわる	***vi***. participate; be involved in

920
搾 ⑬

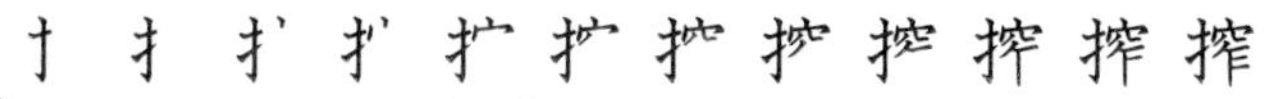

音	搾	サク	squeeze; press
熟	搾取	サクシュ	exploitation —***v***. exploit
訓	搾る	しぼる	***vt***. squeeze; press; wring; limit; strain

921
摂 ⑬

音	摂	セツ	adopt; act in place of; take
熟	摂氏	セッシ	Celsius; centigrade
	摂取	セッシュ	intake, adoption —***v***. ingest; take in
	摂政	セッショウ	regency; regent

	摂生	セッセイ	care of health —*vi*. take care of someone's health
	摂理	セツリ	providence

922

損 ⑬

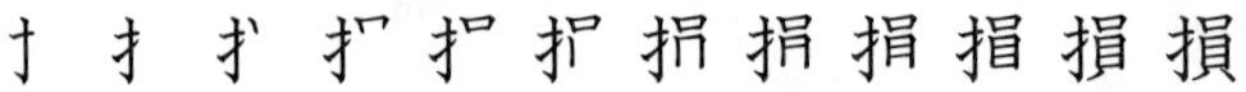

音	損	ソン	loss; damage; disadvantage
熟	損壊	ソンカイ	destruction —*v*. destroy
	損害	ソンガイ	damage; loss; injury —*v*. damage; loss; injure
	損失	ソンシツ	loss —*v*. lose
	損傷	ソンショウ	damage; injury —*v*. damage; injure
	損得	ソントク	loss and gain; advantages and disadvantages
訓	損なう	そこなう	*vt*. harm; spoil; hurt
	損ねる	そこねる	*vt*. injure; hurt; harm
¥	損益	ソンエキ	profit and loss
	損害	ソンガイ	damage; loss
	損害保険会社	ソンガイホケンガイシャ	non-life insurance company
	損失補塡	ソンシツホテン	making up for a client's loss

923

搬 ⑬

音	搬	ハン	convey
熟	搬出	ハンシュツ	taking; bringing —*v*. take/bring out
	搬入	ハンニュウ	carrying; bringing; sending; taking —*v*. carry in; bring/send/take in

924

摘 ⑭

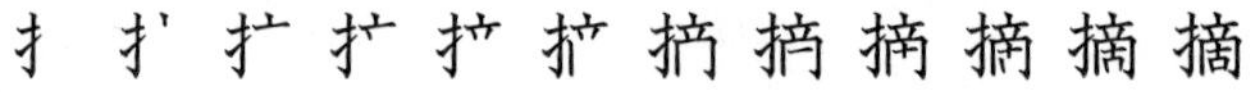

音	摘	テキ	pick; extract
熟	摘出	テキシュツ	extraction; exposure —*v*. pick/take out; extract; expose
	摘発	テキハツ	exposure; disclosure —*v*. expose; disclose; unmask
	摘要	テキヨウ	summary; synopsis
訓	摘む	つむ	*vt*. pick; pluck

摘み草	つみくさ	gathering young herbs

925

撮 ⑮

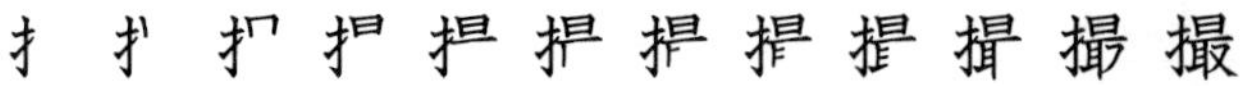

音	撮	サツ	photograph
熟	撮影	サツエイ	photography —*v.* photograph; take a picture
	撮影所	サツエイジョ	photographic studio
訓	撮る	とる	*vt.* take (a picture/photograph)

926

撤 ⑮

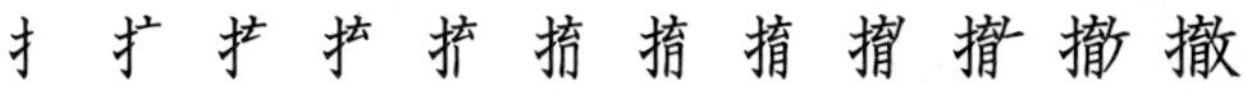

音	撤	テツ	remove
熟	撤回	テッカイ	withdrawal; revocation; recantation; relinquishment —*v.* withdraw; revoke; take away; relinquish
	撤去	テッキョ	removal; withdrawal; evacuation —*v.* remove; withdraw; evacuate
	撤収	テッシュウ	withdrawal; removal —*v.* withdraw; remove
	撤退	テッタイ	evacuation; withdrawal; pull-out; retreat —*vi.* withdraw; evacuate; pull out; retreat
	撤廃	テッパイ	abolition; removal —*v.* abolish; remove; do away with; repeal
	撤兵	テッペイ	withdrawal of troops; military withdrawal; disengagement —*vi.* withdraw/pull out troops

927

撲 ⑮

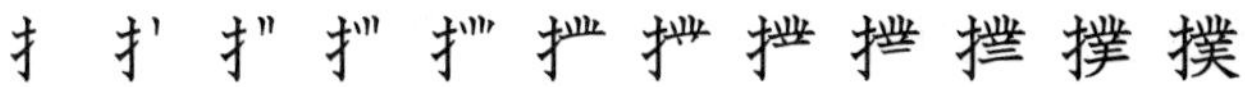

音	撲	ボク	hit; strike
熟	撲殺	ボクサツ	clubbing to death; punching to death —*v.* club to death; punch to death
	撲滅	ボクメツ	extermination; eradication —*v.* exterminate; eradicate
訓	撲る	なぐる	*vt.* hit; punch; club
	※撲つ	うつ	*vt.* hit; strike

928

操 ⑯

音	操	ソウ	manipulate; operate
熟	操業	ソウギョウ	operation; work
	操行	ソウコウ	conduct; department
	操作	ソウサ	operation; handing; control —*v*. operate; handle; control
	操車	ソウシャ	operation (of trains)
	操縦	ソウジュウ	handling; manipulation; control —*v*. handle; manipulate; control; operate
	操練	ソウレン	military exercises; drill
訓	操る	あやつる	***vt***. manipulate; operate
	操	みさお	chastity; virginity; constancy; fidelity; honor

929

擁 ⑯

音	擁	ヨウ	embrace
熟	擁護	ヨウゴ	defense; protection —*v*. defend; protect
	擁護者	ヨウゴシャ	defender; supporter; advocate
	擁立	ヨウリツ	supporting/backing —*v*. support/back (one's lord, leader, etc.)

930

擬 ⑰

音	擬	ギ	imitate
熟	擬音	ギオン	imitation sound
	擬人法	ギジンホウ	personification; impersonation
	擬声	ギセイ	onomatopoeia
	擬声語	ギセイゴ	***gram***. onomatopoeic word
	擬態	ギタイ	mimesis; simulation
	擬態語	ギタイゴ	***gram***. mimesis; mimetic word
訓	※擬える	なぞらえる	***vt***. liken; compare; imitate

931

擦 ⑰

音	擦	サツ	rub; graze; friction
熟	擦過傷	サッカショウ	***med.*** abrasion; graze
訓	擦る	する	***vt.*** rub; chafe; strike
	擦れる	すれる	***vi.*** rustle; wear out; rub; be chafed; become shrewd

4 支 じゅうまた／しにょう／えだにょう branch

932

支 ④

音	支	シ	branch; separate; pay; support; prop up
熟	支援	シエン	support —***v.*** support; help; back up
	支給	シキュウ	supply —***v.*** provide; issue; supply
	支局	シキョク	branch office
	支持	シジ	support; backing —***v.*** support; back; stand by
	支社	シシャ	branch office (of a company)
	支障	シショウ	hindrance; trouble
	支度	シタク	preparations; arrangements —***v.*** prepare; arrange
	支柱	シチュウ	support; prop; mainstay
	支店	シテン	branch store/office
	支点	シテン	fulcrum
	支配	シハイ	rule; control; direction; management —***v.*** rule; control; direct; manage
	支配人	シハイニン	manager (of hotels, restaurants, etc.)
	支払う	シはらう	***vt.*** pay; make payments
	支部	シブ	branch/local office; chapter (of an organization)
	支離滅裂	シリメツレツ	inconsistent
	支流	シリュウ	branch (of a river or family); tributary; faction; splinter group
訓	支える	ささえる	***vt.*** support; prop up; hold
¥	支出	シシュツ	expenditure; disbursements; expenses —***v.*** pay out; spend; expend
	支払承諾	シはらいショウダク	acceptance and guarantee; bank's liabilities in account of guarantees

支払手形	シはらいてがた	notes payable-trade
支払利息割引料	シはらいリソクわりびきリョウ	interest and discount expenses

---

4 攵 のぶん *no* (katakana); literature

933

改 ⑦

ㄱ コ 己 己' 己⺊ 改 改

音	改	カイ	improve; change; reform
熟	改悪	カイアク	change for the worse; deterioration —*v*. get worse; deteriorate
	改革	カイカク	reform; reformation —*v*. reform; reorganize
	改行	カイギョウ	new line/paragraph —*vi*. start a new line/paragraph
	改元	カイゲン	change of an imperial era —*v*. change an imperial era
	改作	カイサク	adaptation; recomposition —*v*. adapt; recompose; remodel
	改札	カイサツ	ticket inspection —*v*. inspect tickets
	改札口	カイサツぐち	ticket gate; wicket
	改宗	カイシュウ	conversion; proselytism —*vi*. be converted; change one's religion
	改修	カイシュウ	repair; improvement —*v*. repair; fix; improve
	改心	カイシン	reform; mending one's ways —*vi*. reform; mend one's ways
	改新	カイシン	renovation; reformation —*v*. renovate; reform
	改正	カイセイ	revision; amendment —*v*. revise; amend
	改選	カイセン	reelection —*v*. reelect
	改善	カイゼン	improvement —*v*. improve; make better
	改装	カイソウ	remodeling; refurbishing; modification —*v*. remodel; refurbish; modify
	改造	カイゾウ	reconstruction; reorganization —*v*. reconstruct; reorganize
	改築	カイチク	rebuilding; reconstruction —*v*. rebuild; reconstruct
	改定	カイテイ	reform; revision —*v*. reform; revise
	改訂	カイテイ	revision of (manuscript, etc.) —*v*. revise
	改名	カイメイ	name change —*vi*. change one's name
	改良	カイリョウ	improvement; reformation —*v*. improve; reform
訓	改まる	あらたまる	*vi*. be renewed
	改める	あらためる	*vt*. renew; improve; change

934

攻 ⑦

音	攻	**コウ**	attack; assault; assail
熟	攻撃	**コウゲキ**	attack; charge; assault; raid; drive —*v*. attack; assail; assault; charge; storm
	攻守	**コウシュ**	offense and defense
	攻勢	**コウセイ**	the offensive; aggression
	攻防	**コウボウ**	offense and defense
訓	攻める	せめる	***vt***. attack; assault; assail

935

放 ⑧

音	放	**ホウ**	let go; release; fire (a gun); emit
熟	放歌	**ホウカ**	loud singing —***vi***. sing loudly
	放火	**ホウカ**	arson —***vi***. deliberately set on fire
	放火狂	**ホウカキョウ**	pyromania; pyromaniac
	放火犯	**ホウカハン**	arson; arsonist
	放課後	**ホウカゴ**	after school
	放棄	**ホウキ**	abandonment; renouncement; waiver; forfeit —***v***. abandon; renounce; waive; forfeit
	放言	**ホウゲン**	unreserved talk; speaking without thinking —***v***. talk without reservations; speak without thinking
	放校	**ホウコウ**	expulsion from school —***v***. expel from school
	放散	**ホウサン**	radiation; diffusion; evaporation —***vi***. radiate; diffuse; evaporate
	放射	**ホウシャ**	radiation; emission; discharge —***v***. radiate; emit; discharge
	放射線	**ホウシャセン**	radiation
	放射線科	**ホウシャセンカ**	***med***. radiology
	放射能	**ホウシャノウ**	radioactivity; radiation
	放出	**ホウシュツ**	emittance; release; discharge —***v***. emit; release; discharge
	放心	**ホウシン**	absent-mindedness; uncertain psychological state —***vi***. be absent-minded; have one's mind on other things; relax; feel reassured
	放水	**ホウスイ**	drainage; pour water on a fire with a hose —***vi***. drain; be drained; put a fire out with a hose
	放送	**ホウソウ**	broadcasting; broadcast —***v***. broadcast

	放送局	ホウソウキョク	broadcasting station
	放題	ホウダイ	(verb suffix) all you can (eat, drink, sing, etc.)
	放談	ホウダン	unreserved talk —*vi*. talk without any reservations
	放置	ホウチ	leaving something as it is —*v*. leave as is; leave to chance; let alone
	放逐	ホウチク	expulsion; banishment; exile —*v*. expel; banish; exile
	放電	ホウデン	electric discharge —*vi*. discharge electricity
	放蕩	ホウトウ	dissipation; fast living —*vi*. live fast
	放尿	ホウニョウ	urination —*vi*. urinate
	放任	ホウニン	nonintervention; indifference —*v*. do not intervene; be indifferent
	放熱	ホウネツ	radiant heat —*vi*. radiate heat
	放熱器	ホウネツキ	radiator
	放念	ホウネン	relaxed mind —*vi*. feel at ease; relax; have no worries
	放屁	ホウヒ	farting; breaking wind —*vi*. fart; break wind
	放物線	ホウブツセン	***math***. parabola
	放牧	ホウボク	grazing —*v*. let graze; put out to pasture
	放牧地	ホウボクチ	grazing land; pasture
	放漫	ホウマン	loose; lax; reckless
	放免	ホウメン	release; acquittal —*v*. release; acquit
	放流	ホウリュウ	stocking (rivers with fish); draining (a river)
	放る	ホウる	*vt*. throw; leave as is
	放浪	ホウロウ	wandering; roving —*v*. wander; rove
	放浪者	ホウロウシャ	wanderer; vagabond; tramp; vagrant
	放ったらかす	ホッたらかす	*vt*. neglect; lay aside; leave undone
訓	放す	はなす	*vt*. set free; release; let go
	放つ	はなつ	*vt*. set free; release; fire (a gun); emit; set fire to; chase away
	放れる	はなれる	get free; be released/fired (arrow/bullet, etc.)

936

⑨ 一 十 𠂇 古 古 古 古 故 故

音	故	コ	intentional; deliberate; willful; knowingly; (prefix) late; deceased
熟	故意	コイ	intentional; deliberate; wilful; knowingly
	故郷	コキョウ	one's hometown
	故国	ココク	one's homeland/native country

	故事	コジ	historical fact; tradition; folklore
	故実	コジツ	ancient practices/customs
	故障	コショウ	hindrance; obstacle; trouble; breakdown; failure; damage —*v*. break down; fail; be out of order
	故人	コジン	the deceased/departed
訓	故	ゆえ	reason; cause; meaning
	※故郷	ふるさと	one's hometown; the town where one was born

937
政 ⑨

音	政	セイ	govern
		(ショウ)	government
熟	政界	セイカイ	political world/circles; politics
	政教分離	セイキョウブンリ	religion and politics; Church and State
	政局	セイキョク	political situation
	政経	セイケイ	politics and economics
	政見	セイケン	political views
	政権	セイケン	political power; government; administration
	政綱	セイコウ	political program/platform
	政策	セイサク	policy
	政治	セイジ	government; politics
	政治家	セイジカ	statesman; politician; strategist
	政情	セイジョウ	political situation
	政党	セイトウ	political party
	政府	セイフ	government; administration
	政変	セイヘン	political change; change in government; cabinet reshuffle
	政務	セイム	State affairs; affairs of State
	政略	セイリャク	political tactics/maneuvers
	政令	セイレイ	government ordinance
訓	政	まつりごと	administration; government; politics
¥	政策	セイサク	policy
	政策運営	セイサクウンエイ	policy manoeuvre
	政策目標	セイサクモクヒョウ	aim; goal; target; focus objective; purpose
	政府保証債	セイフホショウサイ	government-guaranteed bond
	政府補助金	セイフホジョキン	government subsidy

938
敏 ⑩

音	敏	ビン	quick; agile; alart
熟	敏感	ビンカン	sensitivity; sensibility; susceptibility
	敏捷	ビンショウ	agile; nimble; quick; alert
	敏捷性	ビンショウセイ	agility; nimbleness; quickness
	敏速	ビンソク	prompt; quick; brisk
	敏腕	ビンワン	able; capable

939
救 ⑪

音	救	キュウ	assistance; help; aid
熟	救援	キュウエン	relief; rescue; deliverance
	救急	キュウキュウ	first aid
	救護	キュウゴ	relief; aid —*v.* relieve; help; aid
	救済	キュウサイ	relief; help; aid; redemption —*v.* relieve; help; aid; redeem
	救出	キュウシュツ	rescue; saving; relief —*v.* rescue; save; relieve
	救助	キュウジョ	rescue; relief —*v.* rescue; relieve
	救世主	キュウセイシュ	savior; Jesus Christ
	救命	キュウメイ	lifesaving
訓	救う	すくう	***vt.*** rescue
¥	救済事業	キュウサイジギョウ	relief work
	救済資金	キュウサイシキン	relief funds

940

⑪

音	教	キョウ	teach; instruction
熟	教育	キョウイク	education —*v.* educate
	教員	キョウイン	teacher; member of the teaching staff
	教化	キョウカ	culture; enlightenment; edification —*v.* culture; enlighten; edificate
	教科	キョウカ	subject; course of study; curriculum
	教科書	キョウカショ	textbook; school book
	教会	キョウカイ	Christian church

	教官	キョウカン	teacher; instructor; faculty; teaching staff
	教義	キョウギ	doctrine; dogma; tenet; creed
	教訓	キョウクン	teachings; lesson; injunction
	教材	キョウザイ	teaching materials
	教師	キョウシ	schoolteacher; schoolmaster; schoolmistress
	教示	キョウジ	instruction; teaching —*v*. instruct; teach
	教室	キョウシツ	classroom
	教授	キョウジュ	teachings; instruction; professor —*v*. teach; instruct
	教習所	キョウシュウジョ	training school/institute
	教書	キョウショ	message
	教職	キョウショク	teaching profession
	教祖	キョウソ	founder of a religion
	教徒	キョウト	believer in a religion; convert
	教養	キョウヨウ	culuture; education
	教理	キョウリ	principles; teachings; doctrine (of a religion)
訓	教える	おしえる	***vt***. teach; instruct; inform
	教え子	おしえご	one's pupil
	教わる	おそわる	***vt***. be taught/informed

941

敗 ⑪

丨 冂 冃 目 目 貝 貝 貝 貯 敗 敗

音	敗	ハイ	be defeated
熟	敗因	ハイイン	cause of defeat
	敗軍	ハイグン	defeated army
	敗者	ハイシャ	defeated person; the vanquished; loser
	敗色	ハイショク	signs of defeat
	敗戦	ハイセン	defeat; lost battle/war —***vi***. be defeated; lose the war
	敗走	ハイソウ	flight; rout; debacle —***vi***. take to flight; be routed; flee
	敗退	ハイタイ	defeat; setback —***vi***. retreat; be defeated
	敗北	ハイボク	defeat; loss; setback —***vi***. be defeated/beaten; suffer a setback
訓	敗れる	やぶれる	***vi***. be beaten/defeated; lose

942

敢 ⑫

一 丅 工 干 干 干 吾 耳 耳 耳 敢 敢

音	敢	カン	dare

4

心忄⺌戈戸手扌支攵文斗斤方日曰月肉月木欠止歹殳母毋比毛氏气水氺氵火灬爫父片牛犬犭王礻耂

熟	敢行	カンコウ	daring/resolute action —*v*. take decisive action; carry out; execute
	敢然	カンゼン	boldly; resolutely; bravely; fearlessly
	敢闘	カントウ	courageous fight —*vi*. fight courageously
訓	※敢えて	あえて	boldly; resolutely; daringly

943

敬 ⑫

一 十 廾 艹 芍 芍 苟 苟 苟 苟 苟 敬

音	敬	ケイ	respect
熟	敬愛	ケイアイ	love and respect —*v*. love and respect
	敬意	ケイイ	respect; reverence; tribute
	敬遠	ケイエン	at a distance —*v*. keep at a distance
	敬具	ケイグ	Truly yours; Yours respectfully/faithfully (closing phrase of a letter)
	敬虔	ケイケン	piety; reverance
	敬語	ケイゴ	***gram***. honorific expression; term of respect
	敬称	ケイショウ	title of honor; courtesy title
	敬服	ケイフク	admiration; regard —*vi*. admire; have great regard for
	敬礼	ケイレイ	salute; bow —*vi*. salute; bow; greet
	敬老	ケイロウ	respect for the aged —*vi*. respect the aged
訓	敬う	うやまう	*vt*. respect; hold in high esteem; look up to

944

散 ⑫

一 十 廾 卄 艹 昔 昔 昔 昔 昔 散 散

音	散	サン	scatter; spread; messy; powder
熟	散逸	サンイツ	scattered and lost —*vi*. be scattered and lost
	散会	サンカイ	adjournment —*vi*. adjourn; break up
	散開	サンカイ	deployment —*vi*. spread out; deploy
	散在	サンザイ	scattered; spread about —*vi*. be scattered; be spread about
	散財	サンザイ	squandering; waste of money —*vi*. squander; waste money
	散策	サンサク	walk —*vi*. take a walk
	散々	サンザン	severely; utterly; thoroughly
	散水	サンスイ	watering —*vi*. water; spray/sprinkle water
	散水機	サンスイキ	water sprinkler
	散発	サンパツ	scattering; occasional happenings —*v*. scatter; occur sporadically; happen occasionally

	散髪	サンパツ	haircut —***vi***. have one's haircut
	散布	サンプ	scattering; sprinkling; spraying —***v***. scatter; sprinkle; spray
	散文	サンブン	prose
	散歩	サンポ	walk; stroll —***vi***. take a walk; have a stroll; stroll
	散漫	サンマン	vague; loose; careless
	散乱	サンラン	scattered; littered —***vi***. be scattered about; diffuse; be littered
訓	散る	ちる	***vi***. fall; scatter; disperse; spread
	散らす	ちらす	***vt***. scatter; shower; distract
	散らかす	ちらかす	***vt***. scatter about; leave in disorder
	散らかる	ちらかる	***vi***. be scattered; be all over the place; be in a mess

945

数 ⑬

音	数	スウ	number; count
		(ス)	number; count
熟	数回	スウカイ	several times
	数学	スウガク	mathematics
	数奇	スウキ	adverse fortune; hapless fate
	数日	スウジツ	several days
	数値	スウチ	numerical value; result
	数量	スウリョウ	quantity; volume
訓	数	かず	number; figure
	数々	かずかず	numerous; many; varied
	数える	かぞえる	***vt***. count

946

敵 ⑮

音	敵	テキ	enemy; foe; opponent; adversary; rival; competitor
熟	敵する	テキする	***vi***. turn/fight against; antagonize
	敵意	テキイ	enmity; hostility; animosity
	敵愾心	テキガイシン	hostility; enmity; animosity
	敵視	テキシ	enmity; hostility —***v***. be hostile; regard somone as an enemy
	敵情	テキジョウ	enemy movements

	敵陣	テキジン	enemy camp
	敵対	テキタイ	hostility; contention; antagonism —***v***. be hostile to; turn against
	敵地	テキチ	enemy country
訓	敵	かたき	enemy; foe; opponent
	敵討ち	かたきうち	revenge; vendetta

947

敷 ⑮

音	敷	フ	spread; lay; put down
熟	敷衍	フエン	amplification; extention; development —***v***. amplify; extend; develop
	敷設	フセツ	laying (railway tracks, etc.) building; construction —***v***. lay; build; construct
訓	敷く	しく	***v***. spread; lay; put down
	敷居	しきい	threshold
	敷石	しきいし	paving stone
	敷地	しきチ	site
	敷布	しきフ	sheet
	敷布団	しきブトン	floor mattress
	敷物	しきもの	carpet; rug
¥	敷金	しきキン	deposit

948

整 ⑯

音	整	セイ	arrange
熟	整形	セイケイ	***med***. orthopedics; orthopedic surgery; plastic/cosmetic surgery —***v***. have plastic surgery
	整形外科	セイケイゲカ	***med***. orthopedic surgery
	整形手術	セイケイシュジュツ	***med***. plastic/cosmetic surgery —***v***. undergo cosmetic surgery
	整数	セイスウ	***math***. integral number
	整然	セイゼン	orderly; regular; systematic
	整地	セイチ	ground leveling; soil preparation —***vi***. prepare the land for construction of a house
	整頓	セイトン	order —***v***. put in order; straighten up
	整備	セイビ	full equipment —***v***. be fully equipped; maintain; equip

	整理	セイリ	arrangement; adjustment; reorganization —***v***. arrange; adjust; reorganize
	整列	セイレツ	array; line up —***vi***. array; stand in a line; line up
訓	整う	ととのう	***vi***. be put in order/arranged/prepared
	整える	ととのえる	***vt***. put in order; arrange; prepare

4 文 ぶん literature

949

文 ⑨ 丶 亠 ナ 文

音	文	ブン	writing; composition; sentence; text; style; literature
		モン	character; word; design; *mon* (former unit of currency); *mon* (unit of measurement, approx. 2.4㎝)
熟	文案	ブンアン	draft; rough copy
	文意	ブンイ	meaning of (a passage/sentence)
	文化	ブンカ	culture
	文化遺産	ブンカイサン	cultural heritage
	文化勲章	ブンカクンショウ	Order of Cultural Merit
	文化圏	ブンカケン	cultural sphere
	文化交流	ブンカコウリュウ	cultural exchange
	文化祭	ブンカサイ	cultural/school festival
	文化財	ブンカザイ	cultural assets/properties
	文化施設	ブンカシセツ	cultural facilities
	文化人	ブンカジン	cultivated person; man of culture
	文化人類学	ブンカジンルイガク	cultural anthoropology
	文化水準	ブンカスイジュン	cultural level; level/standard of culture
	文化生活	ブンカセイカツ	civilized life
	文化的	ブンカテキ	cultural
	文科	ブンカ	liberal arts
	文学	ブンガク	literature
	文官	ブンカン	civil servant; public official; civil service
	文教	ブンキョウ	education
	文具	ブング	stationery
	文型	ブンケイ	***gram***. sentence pattern
	文芸	ブンゲイ	literature and the arts; liberal arts; literature
	文芸映画	ブンゲイエイガ	film based on a literary classic

文芸家　ブンゲイカ　literary man; man of letters
文芸学　ブンゲイガク　study of literature
文芸批評　ブンゲイヒヒョウ　literary criticism
文献　ブンケン　literature; documents
文庫　ブンコ　library; collection of books; pocket-sized book
文庫本　ブンコボン　pocket-sized book
文語　ブンゴ　written/literary/classic language
文語体　ブンゴタイ　literary style (classical, etc.)
文豪　ブンゴウ　great/distinguished writer
文才　ブンサイ　literary talent; talent for writing
文士　ブンシ　writer; man of letters
文集　ブンシュウ　anthology; collection of works
文書　ブンショ　document; record; archives
文章　ブンショウ　sentence; writing; composition
文人　ブンジン　literary man; man of letters
文節　ブンセツ　***gram***. minimum division in a Japanese sentence
文選　ブンセン　typesetting —***v***. typeset
文体　ブンタイ　(writing) style
文題　ブンダイ　theme; subject (of an essay)
文壇　ブンダン　literary world/circles
文鎮　ブンチン　paperweight
文通　ブンツウ　correspondence —***vi***. write/exchange letters
文頭　ブントウ　beginning of a sentence; opening passage
文筆　ブンピツ　literary pursuits/career; writing
文武　ブンブ　civil and military affairs; the pen and the sword
文武両道　ブンブリョウドウ　literary and military arts
文法　ブンポウ　grammar
文房具　ブンボウグ　stationery; writing materials
文末　ブンマツ　end of a sentence; closing sentence
文脈　ブンミャク　context
文明　ブンメイ　civilization
文明国　ブンメイコク　civilized country/nation
文明社会　ブンメイシャカイ　civilized society
文面　ブンメン　contents of a letter
文楽　ブンラク　Bunraku (puppet show/performance)
文理　ブンリ　literature and science
文例　ブンレイ　model sentence; example sentence
文字　モジ　letter; writing; character
文句　モンク　words; expression; phrase; complaint; objection
文殊　モンジュ　Monju (Buddhist saint of wisdom)
文無し　モンなし　broke; penniless

	文盲	モンモウ	illiteracy
訓	文	ふみ	letter; note
	※文	あや	design; figure of speech; plan; plot
¥	文部省	モンブショウ	Ministry of Education
	文部大臣（文相）	モンブダイジン（ブンショウ）	minister of education

4 斗 とます dots and cross

950

斗 ④ 　丶 ⺀ 𠂤 斗

音	斗	ト	*to* (unit of capacity, approx. 18ℓ); ladle; dipper; cluster of stars
熟	斗酒	トシュ	kegs of saké

951

料 ⑩ 　丶 丷 䒑 半 米 米 米 米 米- 料

音	料	リョウ	material; charge; fee
熟	料金	リョウキン	charge; fee; fare
	料簡	リョウケン	idea; forgive
	料亭	リョウテイ	Japanese restaurant
	料理	リョウリ	cooking; cuisine; dish; food —*v.* cook
	料理屋	リョウリや	restaurant

952

斜 ⑪ 　丿 人 亼 今 全 余 余 余 余 余- 斜

音	斜	シャ	slant
熟	斜視	シャシ	squint; cross-eyed
	斜線	シャセン	oblique/slanted line
	斜塔	シャトウ	leaning tower
	斜辺	シャヘン	***math.*** hypotenuse; oblique side
	斜面	シャメン	slope
	斜陽	シャヨウ	setting sun; declining
訓	斜め	ななめ	slant; lean; slope; diagonal

心 忄 小 戈 戸 手 扌 支 攵 文 斗 斤 方 日 曰 月 肉 月 木 欠 止 歹 殳 母 毋 比 毛 氏 气 水 氺 氵 火 灬 爫 父 片 牛 犬 犭 王 礻 耂

4 斤 おのづくり ax

953
斤 ④ 丿 厂 斤 斤

音	斤	キン	*kin* (unit of mass, approx. 600g)

954
斥 ⑤ 丿 厂 斤 斤 斥

音	斥	セキ	reject; repel; repulse; scout
熟	斥候	セッコウ	scout; patrol; spy
訓	斥ける	しりぞける	***vt***. repel; repulse; reject

955
断 ⑪ 丶 丷 亠 半 米 米 迷 迷 断 断 断

音	断	ダン	decision; judgment; resolution; sever; refuse
熟	断じる	ダンじる	***vt***. decide; judge; resolve
	断崖	ダンガイ	precipice; cliff; bluff
	断言	ダンゲン	assertion; affirmation; declaration —***vi***. assert; affirm; declare
	断固	ダンコ	firm; decisive; resolute
	断交	ダンコウ	break in relations; rupture —***vi***. break off relations
	断行	ダンコウ	decisive action; resolute enforcement —***v***. carry out; execute; effect; enforce
	断食	ダンジキ	fast; fasting —***vi***. fast
	断じて	ダンじて	definitely
	断水	ダンスイ	suspension of water supply —***vi***. cut off the water supply
	断絶	ダンゼツ	extinction; discontinuation; severance; rupture —***v***. become extinct; cease to exist; sever; cut off
	断然	ダンゼン	positively; resolutely; absolutely; without hesitation
	断層	ダンソウ	geological fault; throw; dislocation; shift; jump
	断続	ダンゾク	intermittence —***vi***. be intermittent
	断腸	ダンチョウ	heartbreak; broken heart

	断定	ダンテイ	conclusion; decision —*v.* conclude; decide; come to a conclusion
	断念	ダンネン	abandonment; relinquishment; despair —*v.* give up; abandon; forgo; relinquish
	断片	ダンペン	piece; fragment; shred; scrap
	断片的	ダンペンテキ	fragmentary; scrappy; piecemeal
	断末魔	ダンマツマ	hour of death
	断面	ダンメン	section; phase; profile
訓	断る	ことわる	***vt.*** decline; ask to be excused; apologize; dismiss; prohibit
	断つ	たつ	***vt.*** sever; cut; chop/break off; abstain; exterminate

956

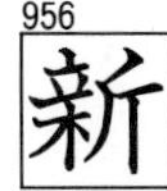
⑬

音	新	シン	new; novel; (prefix) neo-
熟	新案	シンアン	new device/design/idea
	新入り	シンいり	newcomer
	新鋭	シンエイ	new and powerful
	新開地	シンカイチ	newly developed land
	新型	シンガタ	new/latest style; new model
	新館	シンカン	new building/wing
	新刊	シンカン	new publication/book
	新奇	シンキ	novel; latest
	新規	シンキ	new; anew
	新機軸	シンキジク	innovation; new departure/direction
	新旧	シンキュウ	old and new
	新居	シンキョ	new house/home
	新教	シンキョウ	Protestantism
	新劇	シンゲキ	*shingeki* (Western plays put on by Japanese players)
	新月	シンゲツ	new moon
	新香	シンコ	pickles
	新語	シンゴ	new word; newly coined word
	新興	シンコウ	newly risen; rising; burgeoning
	新興国	シンコウコク	rising nation
	新興宗教	シンコウシュウキョウ	new religion
	新興都市	シンコウトシ	new town
	新婚	シンコン	newlyweds; newly married
	新婚旅行	シンコンリョコウ	honeymoon

新作	シンサク	new work/composition
新参	シンザン	newcomer; new hand
新式	シンシキ	new type/style/method
新春	シンシュン	New Year
新進	シンシン	new face; up-and-coming
新進気鋭	シンシンキエイ	young and spirited
新人	シンジン	new member/figure/face
新人作家	シンジンサッカ	budding writer
新制	シンセイ	new system
新星	シンセイ	nova
新生	シンセイ	new birth; rebirth
新生児	シンセイジ	newborn infant
新設	シンセツ	newly established; new —***v***. found; establish; set up; organize
新説	シンセツ	new theory/view
新鮮	シンセン	freshness; fresh; new
新装	シンソウ	redecoration; refurbishment —***v***. redecorate; refurbish
新卒	シンソツ	new graduate
新大陸	シンタイリク	the New World
新築	シンチク	new house; newly built
新茶	シンチャ	first tea of the season
新着	シンチャク	new arrivals; newly imported
新調	シンチョウ	newly made; brand-new —***v***. make new (clothes, etc.)
新陳代謝	シンチンタイシャ	metabolism
新訂	シンテイ	new revision
新天地	シンテンチ	new world; new field of activity
新任	シンニン	newly appointed —***v***, appoint a new person
新年	シンネン	new year
新派	シンパ	new school
新品	シンピン	new article; brand-new; new
新婦	シンプ	bride
新風	シンプウ	new life; fresh current
新聞	シンブン	newspaper; the press
新聞記者	シンブンキシャ	newspaper reporter
新聞社	シンブンシャ	newspaper company
新聞発表	シンブンハッピョウ	press release —***v***. send out a press release
新米	シンマイ	new rice; first rice of the season ***fig***. newcomer; beginner
新味	シンミ	novelty; fresh; novel; original
新芽	シンメ	sprout; shoot; bud

	新緑	シンリョク	fresh verdure; new green leaves
	新暦	シンレキ	solar/Western calendar
	新郎	シンロウ	bridegroom; groom
訓	新しい	あたらしい	new; novel; fresh; modern
	新た	あらた	new; renewed
	新手	あらて	new member/player; innovation
	新	にい	(prefix) new-
	新妻	にいづま	newly married woman
¥	新株引受権証書	シンかぶひきうけケンショウショ	warrant
	新興工業経済群	シンコウコウギョウケイザイグン	Newly Industrializing Economies
	新興工業国	シンコウコウギョウコク	newly industrializing countries

4 方 ほう／ほうへん direction; side

957

方 ④

丶 亠 方 方

音	方	ホウ	direction; side; square
熟	方位	ホウイ	direction; bearing (based on the four points of the compass)
	方円	ホウエン	round and/or square
	方角	ホウガク	direction; bearing
	方眼紙	ホウガンシ	graph paper
	方形	ホウケイ	square; regular quadrilateral
	方言	ホウゲン	dialect
	方向	ホウコウ	direction; destination —***fig***. one's aim
	方策	ホウサク	plan
	方式	ホウシキ	formula; method; system
	方丈	ホウジョウ	1 square *jo* (unit of area, approx. 3㎡) ***Bud***. chief priest; chief priest's quarters
	方針	ホウシン	compass needle; course; policy
	方陣	ホウジン	square formation (of soldiers); phalanx; magic square (square of integers arranged so that the sum of each row, column or diagonal is always the same)
	方図	ホウズ	end; limit

	方寸	ホウスン	1 square *sun* (unit of area, approx. 3㎠); very small area; heart; mind; intention
	方程式	ホウテイシキ	***math***. equation
	方途	ホウト	way; means; method
	方便	ホウベン	expedient; means; instrument
	方法	ホウホウ	method; way; means
	方法論	ホウホウロン	methodology
	方々	ホウボウ	all directions; all over the place; everywhere
	方面	ホウメン	general direction; district; standpoint
訓	方	かた	***hon***. person; direction; way; means; (mother's/father's) side of a family
	～方	～がた	***hon***. plural suffix to denote people

958
施 ⑨

音	施	シ	install; do; perform
		セ	give; donate; provide
熟	施行	シコウ (セコウ)	enforcement —***v***. enforce; carry out
	施策	シサク	policy; measure
	施政	シセイ	administration
	施設	シセツ	facilities; institution; establishment
	施主	セシュ	donor to temple or priest; chief mourner
	施肥	セヒ	fertilization —***vi***. fertilize; manure
訓	施す	ほどこす	***vt***. do; perform; provide; give
	施し	ほどこし	almsgiving; charity
¥	施工	セコウ (シコウ)	construction —***v***. construct; carry out a construction project; put into operation; enforce

959
旅 ⑩

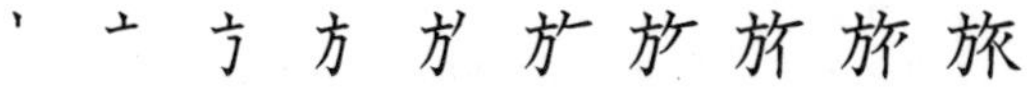

音	旅	リョ	travel; trip journey
熟	旅客	リョカク リョキャク	traveler
	旅館	リョカン	hotel; inn
	旅券	リョケン	passport
	旅行	リョコウ	journey; trip; travel —***vi***. make a trip; journey; travel
	旅行案内	リョコウアンナイ	travel/tour guide

	旅行記	リョコウキ	travel journal
	旅愁	リョシュウ	loneliness on a journey
	旅情	リョジョウ	one's mood while traveling
	旅装	リョソウ	traveling clothes
	旅程	リョテイ	itinerary; distance to be covered
	旅費	リョヒ	traveling expenses
訓	旅	たび	travel; trip; journey
	旅芸人	たびゲイニン	itinerant performer
	旅心	たびごころ	one's mood while traveling
	旅先	たびさき	destination
	旅路	たびジ	journey
	旅立つ	たびだつ	***vi.*** start on a journey
	旅人	たびびと	traveler; wayfarer; pilgrim

960

旋 ⑪

丶 亠 亠 方 方 方 方 扩 扩 旋 旋

音	旋	セン	rotate; revolve
熟	旋回	センカイ	revolution; turning —***vi.*** revolve; turn; circle
	旋盤	センバン	lathe
	旋風	センプウ	whirlwind; tornado
	旋律	センリツ	melody

961

族 ⑪

丶 亠 亠 方 方 方 方 扩 扩 族 族

音	族	ゾク	family; tribe

962

旗 ⑭

亠 亠 方 方 方 扩 扩 旂 旂 旂 旗 旗

音	旗	キ	flag
熟	旗手	キシュ	standard bearer; ensign
訓	旗	はた	flag
	旗揚げ	はたあげ	opening —***vi.*** start an enterprise/business
	旗印	はたじるし	flag mark
	旗日	はたび	national holiday

4 日 ひ／ひへん sun

963
日 ④ 丨 冂 日 日

音	日	ニチ	sun; day; Japan
		ジツ	sun; day
熟	日伊	ニチイ	Italian-Japanese
	日印	ニチイン	Indo-Japanese
	日英	ニチエイ	Anglo-Japanese
	日豪	ニチゴウ	Japanese-Australian
	日時	ニチジ	date and time
	日常	ニチジョウ	usually; daily; everyday
	日常生活	ニチジョウセイカツ	everyday/daily life
	日舞 (日本舞踊)	ニチブ (ニホンブヨウ)	Japanese dancing
	日米	ニチベイ	Japanese-American
	日没	ニチボツ	sunset; sundown
	日夜	ニチヤ	day and night; constantly; around the clock
	日曜日	ニチヨウび	Sunday
	日用品	ニチヨウヒン	daily necessities
	日蓮宗	ニチレンシュウ	Nichiren sect of Buddhism
	日露	ニチロ	Russo-Japanese
	日課	ニッカ	daily work/schedule
	日刊	ニッカン	daily publication
	日韓	ニッカン	Japanese-Korean
	日記	ニッキ	diary; journal
	日給	ニッキュウ	daily wages
	日系	ニッケイ	Japanese (-related)
	日光	ニッコウ	sunlight
	日光浴	ニッコウヨク	sunbathing —***vi***. sunbathe
	日誌	ニッシ	diary; journal
	日射病	ニッシャビョウ	sunstroke
	日照	ニッショウ	sunshine
	日章旗	ニッショウキ	national flag of Japan; the Rising Sun
	日食	ニッショク	solar eclipse
	日進月歩	ニッシンゲッポ	ever-progressing; constantly advancing
	日赤 (日本赤十字社)	ニッセキ (ニホンセキジュウジシャ)	Red Cross (Society)

	日中	ニッチュウ	in the daytime; China and Japan; Sino-Japanese
	日直	ニッチョク	day duty
	日程	ニッテイ	day's program/schedule; agenda for the day
	日当	ニットウ	daily wages/allowance
	日本画	ニホンガ	Japanese painting
	日本語	ニホンゴ	the Japanese language
	日本	ニホン（ニッポン）	Japan
訓	日	か	day
	日	ひ	sun; sunshine; day; date
	日帰り	ひがえり	day trip; excursion
	日付	ひづけ	date; dating
	日の出	ひので	sunrise
	日焼け	ひやけ	sunburn; suntan —***vi.*** tan
	日和	ひより	weather; fine weather; perfect day
¥	日銀（日本銀行）	ニチギン（ニホンギンコウ）	Bank of Japan
	日経連（日本経営者団体連盟）	ニッケイレン（ニホンケイエイシャダンタイレンメイ）	Japan Federation of Employer's Association; Nikkeiren

964

旧 ⑤

丨 丨丨 丨冂 丨日 旧

音	旧	キュウ	old; previous; former; classic; old calendar
熟	旧家	キュウカ	old family
	旧教	キュウキョウ	Roman Catholicism; Roman Catholic Church
	旧式	キュウシキ	old type; old-fashioned; classic
	旧姓	キュウセイ	maiden name
	旧制度	キュウセイド	old/former system; ancient regime
	旧跡	キュウセキ	historic site; place of historic interest
	旧石器時代	キュウセッキジダイ	Stone Age; Paleolithic Period
	旧知	キュウチ	old friend/acquaintance
	旧道	キュウドウ	old road
	旧年	キュウネン	the old year; last year
	旧約聖書	キュウヤクセイショ	Old Testament
	旧友	キュウユウ	old friend
	旧暦	キュウレキ	old (lunar) calendar

965

旬 ⑥

丿 勹 勺 旬 旬 旬

音	旬	ジュン	period of ten days; one-third of a month
熟	旬刊	ジュンカン	published every ten days
	旬日	ジュンジツ	period of ten days

966

早 ⑥

丨 冂 日 日 旦 早

音	早	ソウ （サッ）	swift; early; fast
熟	早期	ソウキ	early stage/phase
	早急	ソウキュウ	urgently; without delay
	早計	ソウケイ	premature; hasty; rash (plan or idea)
	早産	ソウザン	premature birth
	早熟	ソウジュク	precocious; maturing early
	早春	ソウシュン	early spring
	早々	ソウソウ	quickly; early; immediately
	早退	ソウタイ	leaving early —***vi***. leave earlier than usual
	早朝	ソウチョウ	early morning
	早晩	ソウバン	sooner or later
	※早速	サッソク	immediately; at once
訓	早い	はやい	quick; early; fast
	早合点	はやガテン （はやガッテン）	jumping to a conclusion —***vi***. jump to a conclusion
	早口	はやくち	speaking fast
	早瀬	はやせ	swift current; rapids
	早まる	はやまる	***vi***. be hasty/in a hurry
	早道	はやみち	shortcut
	早見表	はやみヒョウ	chart; table
	早耳	はやみみ	quick-eared; in the know
	早目	はやめ	a little early
	早める	はやめる	***vt***. hasten; accelerate
¥	早耳	はやみみ	tip

967

易 ⑧

音	易	イ	easy; simple
		エキ	trade; divination
熟	易々	イイ	easy; easily
	易者	エキシャ	fortuneteller
訓	易しい	やさしい	easy; simple; soft

968

昆 ⑧

音	昆	コン	insect
熟	昆虫	コンチュウ	insect; bug
	昆布	コンブ	kelp

969

昇 ⑧

音	昇	ショウ	rise; advance
熟	昇華	ショウカ	sublimation —***vi***. sublimate; sublime
	昇格	ショウカク	promotion —***vi***. be promoted
	昇級	ショウキュウ	promotion —***vi***. be promoted
	昇給	ショウキュウ	raise in salary; rise —***vi***. have one's salary raised; get a raise
	昇降	ショウコウ	elevating —***vi***. go up and down; rise and fall
	昇進	ショウシン	promotion —***vi***. be promoted
	昇天	ショウテン	ascension; death —***vi***. die; pass away
訓	昇る	のぼる	***vi***. rise; climb; ascend; go up; advance

970

昔 ⑧

音	昔	セキ （シャク）	old times
熟	昔日	セキジツ	old times; formerly; in the past
訓	昔	むかし	long ago; formerly; in the past

昔話　むかしばなし　fairy/folk tale

971
春 ⑨
一 = 三 孝 夫 夫 春 春 春

音	春	シュン	spring
熟	春夏秋冬	シュンカシュウトウ	the four seasons; all year around
	春季	シュンキ	springtime; spring
	春期	シュンキ	spring
	春秋	シュンジュウ	spring and fall; year; years; age
	春風	シュンプウ	spring breeze
	春分	シュンブン	vernal/spring equinox
	春眠	シュンミン	sleeping on a spring night
訓	春	はる	spring; springtime of life; prime; puberty
	春先	はるさき	early spring
	春雨	はるさめ	spring rain; sticks of bean jelly
	春巻き	はるまき	spring roll
	春めく	はるめく	***vi***. become spring/springlike
Y	春闘（春期闘争）	シュントウ（シュンキトウソウ）	the spring labor offensive

972
是 ⑨
丨 冂 日 日 旦 早 早 昰 是

音	是	ゼ	right; approve
熟	是正	ゼセイ	correction —***v***. correct; rectify
	是々非々	ゼゼヒヒ	free and unbiased; free and just
	是認	ゼニン	approval; approbation; admission —***v***. approve of; approbate; warrant; endorse
	是非	ゼヒ	right or wrong; by all means; without fail

973
星 ⑨
丨 冂 日 日 月 旦 早 星 星

音	星	セイ（ショウ）	star
熟	星雲	セイウン	nebula
	星座	セイザ	constellation

心 忄 小 戈 戸 手 扌 支 攵 文 斗 斤 方 ● 日 曰 月 肉 月 木 欠 止 歹 殳 母 毋 比 毛 氏 气 水 氺 氵 火 灬 爫 父 片 牛 犬 犭 王 礻 耂

	星団	セイダン	star cluster
訓	星	ほし	star; spot; mark; asterisk; aim
	星占い	ほしうらない	astrology
	星影	ほしかげ	starlight
	星空	ほしぞら	starry sky

974

昼 ⑨

音	昼	チュウ	daytime; noon; lunch
熟	昼食	チュウショク	lunch; luncheon
	昼夜	チュウヤ	day and night
	昼夜兼行	チュウヤケンコウ	around the clock
訓	昼	ひる	daytime; noon
	昼下がり	ひるさがり	early afternoon
	昼過ぎ	ひるすぎ	early afternoon
	昼寝	ひるね	afternoon nap; siesta —***vi***. take an afternoon nap
	昼間	ひるま	day; daytime
	昼飯	ひるめし	lunch
	昼休み	ひるやすみ	lunchbreak

975

景 ⑫

音	景	ケイ	scenery; appearance; looks
熟	景観	ケイカン	scenery
	景勝	ケイショウ	picturesque scenery; scenic beauty
	景品	ケイヒン	gift; premium
訓	※景色	けしき	scenery; landscape
¥	景気	ケイキ	business conditions

976

暑 ⑫

音	暑	ショ	hot; summer
熟	暑中	ショチュウ	hot season; height of summer
	暑中見舞	ショチュウみまい	summer greeting card

訓 暑い　あつい　hot; warm

977
晶 ⑫

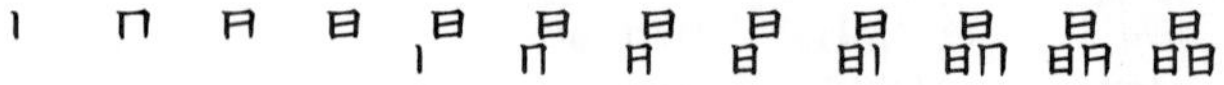

音 晶　ショウ　crystal

978
普 ⑫

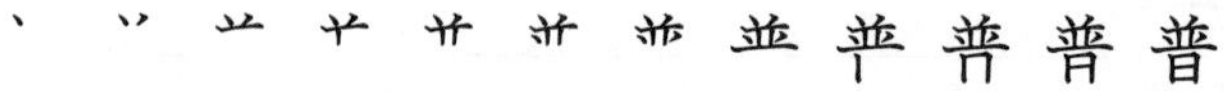

音 普　フ　general; common

熟 普及　フキュウ　diffusion; wide use; popularization —*v.* spread; diffuse; propagate; become widespread; popularize

普請　フシン　building; construction —*v.* build; construct

普段　フダン　usual; ordinary; constant

普通　フツウ　common; usual; ordinary

普遍　フヘン　universal; general

¥ 普通銀行　フツウギンコウ　ordinary bank

普通預金　フツウヨキン　ordinary deposit

979
暮 ⑭

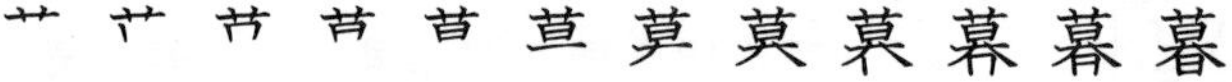

音 暮　ボ　get dark; come to an end

熟 暮秋　ボシュウ　late fall/autumn

暮春　ボシュン　late spring

暮色　ボショク　evening twilight

暮夜　ボヤ　evening; night

訓 暮れ　くれ　nightfall; year-end; end of a season

暮れる　くれる　***vi.*** get dark; become night; come to the end of (a day, year)

暮らす　くらす　***vi.*** live; dwell

暮らし　くらし　(daily) living

暮らし向き　くらしむき　(financial) circumstances; livelihood

980

暦 ⑭

音	暦	レキ	calendar
熟	暦年	レキネン	calendar year; time
	暦法	レキホウ	calendar making
訓	暦	こよみ	calendar

981

暫 ⑮

音	暫	ザン	short time
熟	暫時	ザンジ	short while/time
	暫定的	ザンテイテキ	temporary; provisional; tentative; interim
訓	※暫く	しばらく	short while; a few minutes; for the time being
¥	暫定予算	ザンテイヨサン	provisional budget

982

暴 ⑮

音	暴	ボウ	violence; sudden
		(バク)	expose; reveal
熟	暴露	バクロ	exposure —*v*. expose; be exposed; bring to light
	暴飲	ボウイン	heavy excessive drinking —***vi***. drink to excess
	暴漢	ボウカン	ruffian; goon; thug
	暴挙	ボウキョ	violence; recklessness; riot
	暴君	ボウクン	tyrant; despot
	暴言	ボウゲン	violent/abusive language
	暴行	ボウコウ	violence; rape; assault —***vi***. use violence/force; rape; assault
	暴食	ボウショク	gluttony; gorging oneself —***vi***. be gluttonous; gorge oneself; eat too much
	暴政	ボウセイ	tyranny; oppressive rule
	暴走	ボウソウ	wild; (running) out of control; joyride —***vi***. run wild/out of control; take a car for a joyride
	暴走族	ボウソウゾク	motorbike gang; bikers
	暴徒	ボウト	mob; rioters

	暴動	ボウドウ	riot; disturbance; uprising
	暴発	ボウハツ	sudden/spontaneous occurrence; accidental firing of a gun —*vi*. occur suddenly/spontaneously; go off accidentally (pistols, guns, etc.)
	暴風	ボウフウ	wind storm; high winds
	暴風雨	ボウフウウ	rainstorm
	暴風圏	ボウフウケン	storm zone/area
	暴利	ボウリ	profiteering; excessive profits; illegal profit
	暴力	ボウリョク	violence; force
	暴力団	ボウリョクダン	gangster organization
	暴論	ボウロン	irrational/wild argument
訓	暴く	あばく	***vt***. disclose; expose; bring to light; dig up
	暴れる	あばれる	***vi***. act violently; rage; rampage
¥	暴騰	ボウトウ	sudden rise (in prices); sharp rise; skyrocketing; abnormal rise —***vi***. rise suddenly (prices)
	暴落	ボウラク	break; crash; heavy fall

983

⑯

音	曇	ドン	cloudy
熟	曇天	ドンテン	cloudy/overcast sky
訓	曇り	くもり	cloudiness; cloudy weather; shadow; cloud; dimness; dullness
	曇る	くもる	***vi***. become cloudy/dim

984

⑧

音	明	ミョウ	light; next; following
		メイ	light
		(ミン)	Ming dynasty
熟	明春	ミョウシュン	next spring
	明星	ミョウジョウ	the morning star; the planet Venus
	明神	ミョウジン	gracious god
	明朝	ミョウチョウ	tomorrow morning
	明日	ミョウニチ	tomorrow; next/following day
	明年	ミョウネン	next year
	明晩	ミョウバン	tomorrow evening

	明暗	メイアン	light and dark; shading; happiness and sadness
	明快	メイカイ	clear; lucid
	明解	メイカイ	clear
	明確	メイカク	clear; distinct; well-defined
	明記	メイキ	clearly written/stated —*v*. stipulate; specify (in writing)
	明君	メイクン	wise ruler
	明月	メイゲツ	bright/full moon
	明言	メイゲン	declaration; assertation —*v*. declare; assert
	明細	メイサイ	details; particulars
	明示	メイジ	clear statement/indication —*v*. state/indicate clearly
	明治	メイジ	***hist***. Meiji (period/emperor 1868-1912)
	明度	メイド	brightness; luminosity
	明答	メイトウ	definite answer
	明白	メイハク	clear; unmistakable
	明敏	メイビン	intelligent; discerning
	明朗	メイロウ	cheerful; clear; open
訓	明かす	あかす	***vt***. pass; spend the night; confide; divulge
	明らむ	あからむ	***vi***. become light
	明かり	あかり	light; clearness
	明るい	あかるい	bright; cheerful; knowledgeable
	明るむ	あかるむ	***vi***. become light
	明らか	あきらか	clear; definite
	明く	あく	***vi***. be open; be visible
	明くる	あくる	next; following
	明ける	あける	***vi***. dawn; (a new year) begin; expire (a term of office) ***vt***. open (up)
	※明日	あす	tomorrow; next/following day

985

映 ⑨

丨 冂 日 日 日' 日冖 日冂 映 映

音	映	エイ	project; reflect
熟	映画	エイガ	motion picture; movie; film
	映画館	エイガカン	movie theater; cinema
	映画俳優	エイガハイユウ	movie actor
	映写	エイシャ	projection —*v*. project an image onto a screen
	映像	エイゾウ	reflection; image; video
訓	映す	うつす	***vt***. reflect
	映る	うつる	***vi***. reflect; match; harmonize

	映える	はえる	***vi.*** shine; gleam

986 昨 ⑨

音	昨	サク	yesterday
熟	昨日	サクジツ	yesterday
	昨年	サクネン	last year
	昨晩	サクバン	last night
	昨夜	サクヤ	last night
	昨今	サッコン	these days; lately; recently
訓	※昨日	きのう	yesterday

987 昭 ⑨

音	昭	ショウ	clear
熟	昭和	ショウワ	Showa (period/emperor 1925-1988)

988 時 ⑩

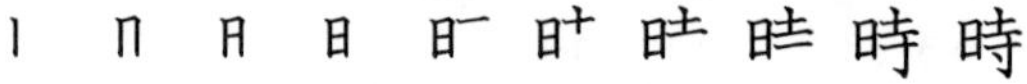

音	時	ジ	time; hour; opportunity
熟	時間	ジカン	time; hour
	時期	ジキ	time; timing; season
	時機	ジキ	opportunity; chance
	時給	ジキュウ	payment by the hour
	時局	ジキョク	situation; current state of affairs
	時限	ジゲン	closing time; time limit; deadline
	時効	ジコウ	prescription (in the legal sense); statute of limitations
	時候	ジコウ	seasonal weather
	時刻	ジコク	time; the hour; appointed time
	時差	ジサ	time difference
	時事	ジジ	current events
	時々刻々	ジジコクコク	every moment; hour to hour; moment to moment
	時制	ジセイ	***gram.*** tense
	時勢	ジセイ	trend of the times; the times

	時世	ジセイ	the times; the day; the age
	時節	ジセツ	the season; the times; the occasion; the moment; good opportunity
	時速	ジソク	speed per hour
	時代	ジダイ	the times; era; age; antiquity
	時代遅れ	ジダイおくれ	old-fashioned
	時代錯誤	ジダイサクゴ	anachronism
	時分	ジブン	time; season; opportunity
	時報	ジホウ	time signal; current news
訓	時	とき	time; hour; case; opportunity; then; the times; the season
	時折	ときおり	sometimes; occasionally
	時々	ときどき	sometimes
	時めく	ときめく	***vi***. prosper; flourish
	時計	とケイ	watch; clock
¥	時価	ジカ	current price; market value; today's price
	時価総額	ジカソウガク	aggregate market value
	時価発行	ジカハッコウ	public offering of new shares at market prices; issue at market price
	時系列	ジケイレツ	time series
	時差出勤	ジサシュッキン	staggered office hours
	時差相関	ジサソウカン	timing relationship; leadlag correlation

989

暁 ⑫ 丨 ⺆ 月 日 日一 日十 日土 日圭 日垚 日垚 日垚 暁

音	暁	ギョウ	dawn; daybreak; understand
熟	暁天	ギョウテン	dawn
訓	暁	あかつき	dawn; daybreak

990

晴 ⑫ 丨 ⺆ 月 日 日一 日十 日丰 日丰 日青 晴 晴 晴

音	晴	セイ	clear
熟	晴雨	セイウ	rain or shine; weather
	晴耕雨読	セイコウウドク	plowing on fine days and reading on wet days; free life-style
	晴天	セイテン	fine weather; blue sky
訓	晴れる	はれる	***vi***. clear; be dispelled

4 心 忄 小 戈 戸 手 扌 支 攵 文 斗 斤 方 日 ● 曰 月 肉 月 木 欠 止 歹 殳 母 毋 比 毛 氏 气 水 氺 氵 火 灬 爫 父 片 牛 犬 犭 王 礻 耂

晴れ	はれ	sunny/fine weather; clear skies
晴れ着	はれぎ	one's best clothes; one's Sunday best
晴れやか	はれやか	radiant; beaming; cheerful
晴らす	はらす	***vt.*** clear oneself; avenge oneself; dispel; remove (doubts, etc.)

991

晩 ⑫

音	晩	バン	evening; late
熟	晩夏	バンカ	late summer; latter part of summer
	晩学	バンガク	learning late in life; late education
	晩婚	バンコン	marrying late in life
	晩餐	バンサン	dinner; supper
	晩酌	バンシャク	drinking with one's evening meal —***vi.*** have a drink at dinner
	晩秋	バンシュウ	late autumn; latter part of autumn
	晩春	バンシュン	late spring; latter part of spring
	晩冬	バントウ	late winter; latter part of winter
	晩年	バンネン	one's closing years; last part of one's life

992

暗 ⑬

音	暗	アン	dark; dull; secret; hidden; learn by heart; foolish
熟	暗雲	アンウン	dark clouds
	暗影	アンエイ	shadow; gloom; penumbra
	暗記	アンキ	memorizing; learning by heart —***v.*** memorize; learn by heart
	暗号	アンゴウ	code; cipher; cryptograph; passsword
	暗黒	アンコク	darkness; blackness
	暗殺	アンサツ	assassination —***v.*** assassinate
	暗算	アンザン	***math.*** mental arithmetic —***v.*** do sums in one's head
	暗示	アンジ	hint; suggestion; reminder —***v.*** hint; suggest; remind
	暗唱	アンショウ	recital; recitation —***v.*** recite
	暗礁	アンショウ	reef; rock; deadlock
	暗然	アンゼン	tearful; doleful; gloomy
	暗中模索	アンチュウモサク	groping in the dark —***vi.*** grope in the dark
	暗幕	アンマク	blackout curtain

	暗黙	アンモク	tacit
	暗躍	アンヤク	secret maneuvers; furtive activities —*vi*. be active behind the scenes
訓	暗い	くらい	dark; black
	暗闇	くらやみ	darkness; blackness

993

暇 ⑬

丨 冂 日 日 日 日 日 日 日 日 日 暇

音	暇	カ	spare time
訓	暇	ひま	spare time; leisure
	暇	いとま	leave-taking; leave of absence; dismissal

994

暖 ⑬

丨 冂 日 日 日 日 日 日 日 日 日 暖

音	暖	ダン	warmth; heat
熟	暖冬	ダントウ	mild winter
	暖房	ダンボウ	heating
	暖流	ダンリュウ	warm sea current
	暖炉	ダンロ	fireplace
訓	暖か	あたたか	warmly; kindly
	暖かい	あたたかい	warm; mild; kind; friendly
	暖まる	あたたまる	***vi***. warm oneself; get warm
	暖める	あたためる	***vt***. warm; heat; heat up

995

曜 ⑱

冂 日 日 日 日 日 日 日 日 日 日 曜

音	曜	ヨウ	day of the week
熟	曜日	ヨウび	day of the week

4 曰 いわく／ひらび flat sun

996
曲 ⑥

音	曲	キョク	bend; wrong; detail; unusual; song; play
熟	曲芸	キョクゲイ	acrobatics; trick; stunt
	曲折	キョクセツ	winding; meandering; bending —***vi***. wind; meander; bend
	曲線	キョクセン	curved line; curve
	曲目	キョクモク	musical program; one's repertoire; musical number
	曲解	キョッカイ	perversion; distortion —***v***. pervert; distort
訓	曲がる	まがる	***vi***. bend; twist; turn; wind
	曲げる	まげる	***vt***. bend; twist; turn; wind
	※曲者	くせもの	scoundrel; rascal

997
更 ⑦

音	更	コウ	change; revise; reform; alter
熟	更衣	コウイ	changing one's clothes —***v***. change one's clothes
	更衣室	コウイシツ	dressing/locker/changing room
	更改	コウカイ	rennovation; renewal; change; alteration —***v***. rennovate; renew; change; alter
	更新	コウシン	renewal; replacement; rennovation —***v***. renew; replace; rennovate
	更生	コウセイ	regeneration; rebirth; revival —***v***. be born again; revive; ressurect
	更正	コウセイ	correction; revision; rectification —***v***. correct; revise; rectify
	更訂	コウテイ	revision; ammendment —***v***. revise; ammend; edit
	更迭	コウテツ	change in job; switch of position; reshuffle; shake-up —***v***. change someone's position; make a switch; reshuffle
訓	更	さら	new; fresh; again; furthermore; moreover; further; more
	更かす	ふかす	***vt***. stay up till late
	更ける	ふける	***vi***. grow late; be late

998

⑩

音	書	ショ	write; letter; book
熟	書架	ショカ	bookshelf
	書画	ショガ	paintings and calligraphic works
	書簡	ショカン	letter; correspondence; note
	書記	ショキ	clerk; secretary
	書記長	ショキチョウ	secretary-general (of the UN, Japanese Communist Party, etc.)
	書庫	ショコ	library
	書斎	ショサイ	study; private library
	書式	ショシキ	set way of writing or filling out (forms, etc.)
	書写	ショシャ	transcription
	書状	ショジョウ	letter
	書生	ショセイ	student; houseboy
	書籍	ショセキ	book
	書体	ショタイ	style of handwriting/type
	書店	ショテン	bookstore; bookshop; publisher
	書道	ショドウ	calligraphy
	書評	ショヒョウ	book review
	書風	ショフウ	style of calligraphy
	書名	ショメイ	title of a book
	書面	ショメン	letter; writing; document
	書物	ショモツ	book
	書類	ショルイ	documents; papers
訓	書く	かく	***vt***. write; spell; compose
	書き入れる	かきいれる	***vt***. enter; fill out (a form)
	書き置き	かきおき	note left behind; memo; message
	書き初め	かきぞめ	first calligraphy of the New Year (Japanese custom)
	書留	かきとめ	registered mail
¥	書き換え	かきかえ	rewriting; renewal; transfer

999

⑪

音	曹	ソウ	friend; comrade; officer
熟	曹長	ソウチョウ	sergeant major; master sergeant

1000

音	最	サイ	utmost; the most
熟	最愛	サイアイ	one's dearest/closest
	最悪	サイアク	worst
	最下位	サイカイ	lowest rank; last place; bottom
	最強	サイキョウ	strongest
	最近	サイキン	lately; recently
	最敬礼	サイケイレイ	most respectful bow —*vi*. bow most respectfully
	最古	サイコ	oldest
	最後	サイゴ	last; end; final; in conclusion
	最後通牒	サイゴツウチョウ	ultimatum
	最期	サイゴ	one's death/last moment
	最高	サイコウ	highest; best; maximum
	最高裁判所	サイコウサイバンショ	Supreme Court
	最高潮	サイコウチョウ	climax; peak; the height
	最高峰	サイコウホウ	highest peak; most prominent; greatest authority
	最終	サイシュウ	last; final
	最終駅	サイシュウエキ	terminal station; last station
	最初	サイショ	first; beginning; start; initial
	最小	サイショウ	smallest; minimum
	最少	サイショウ	least; smallest; lowest
	最上	サイジョウ	best; finest; highest
	最新	サイシン	latest; newest; most up to date
	最盛期	サイセイキ	golden age; heyday
	最前	サイゼン	foremost; forefront
	最善	サイゼン	best; ideal
	最多	サイタ	most
	最大	サイダイ	maximum; largest; biggest
	最短	サイタン	shortest
	最中	サイチュウ	in the middle; while
	最長	サイチョウ	longest
	最低	サイテイ	lowest; minimum
	最適	サイテキ	best; most suitable; perfect; optimum
	最年少	サイネンショウ	youngest
	最年長	サイネンチョウ	oldest
	最良	サイリョウ	best; ideal
訓	最も	もっとも	most

※最寄り	もより	nearest; nearby

1001

替 ⑫ 一 二 ナ 夫 夫一 夫二 夫ナ 夫夫 夫夫 替 替 替

音	替	タイ	be replaced
訓	替える	かえる	***vt***. change; alter; reverse; shift; convert
	替わり	かわり	substitute; change
	替わる	かわる	***vi***. take the place of; relieve; be substituted

4 月 つき／つきへん moon 月 (にくづき) ⇨p.458

1002

月 ④ ノ 刀 月 月

音	月	ゲツ	month; moon
		ガツ	month; moon
熟	月刊	ゲッカン	monthly issue
	月光	ゲッコウ	moonlight; moonshine
	月謝	ゲッシャ	monthly tuition/fee
	月食	ゲッショク	lunar eclipse
	月曜日	ゲツヨウび	Monday
	月例	ゲツレイ	monthly
訓	月	つき	moon; month
	月並み	つきなみ	conventional; commonplace; hackneyed
	月日	つきひ	time; days; years
¥	月額	ゲツガク	monthly sum
	月給	ゲッキュウ	salary
	月産	ゲッサン	monthly output
	月収	ゲッシュウ	monthly income
	月賦	ゲップ	monthly payment

1003

有 ⑥ ノ ナ 𠂇 冇 有 有

音	有	ユウ	possession
		ウ	existence; being

熟	有する	ユウする	***vt***. have; possess; own
	有象無象	ウゾウムゾウ	rabble; riff-raff
	有頂天	ウチョウテン	exaltation; rapture; ecstacy
	有無	ウム	existence; presence; yes or no
	有為	ユウイ	promising; capable; efficient
	有意義	ユウイギ	significant
	有益	ユウエキ	beneficial; profitable; instructive; edifying
	有害	ユウガイ	harmful; noxious; destructive
	有閑	ユウカン	leisure
	有機	ユウキ	organic
	有給	ユウキュウ	salaried
	有形	ユウケイ	concrete; material; visible
	有限	ユウゲン	limited; finite
	有権者	ユウケンシャ	qualified person; electorate
	有効	ユウコウ	validity; efficiency; effectiveness
	有罪	ユウザイ	guilt; criminality
	有志	ユウシ	volunteer; interest; sympathy
	有史以来	ユウシイライ	since the dawn of history
	有識者	ユウシキシャ	intellectual person
	有刺鉄線	ユウシテッセン	barbed wire
	有終	ユウシュウ	perfection; fine conclusion
	有色人種	ユウショク ジンシュ	colored race
	有数	ユウスウ	leading; prominent; distinguished
	有線	ユウセン	cable; wire
	有段者	ユウダンシャ	grade holder (of Japanese go, shōgi or martial arts)
	有毒	ユウドク	poisonous; toxic
	有能	ユウノウ	able; capable; efficient
	有望	ユウボウ	promising; good prospects
	有名	ユウメイ	famous; well-known; notorious; proverbial
	有名無実	ユウメイムジツ	nominal; titular
	有用	ユウヨウ	useful; available; serviceable
	有利	ユウリ	profitable; advantageous
	有料	ユウリョウ	charge; toll
	有力	ユウリョク	influential; powerful
訓	有る	ある	***vi***. be; have; exist; occur; be located; consist of
	有り様	ありさま	situation; circumstances; sight; the naked truth
¥	有価証券	ユウカショウケン	negotiable/marketable securities
	有給休暇	ユウキュウ キュウカ	paid vacation/holiday
	有形 固定資産	ユウケイ コテイシサン	tangible/fixed assets

有形財産	ユウケイザイサン	tangible property/assets
有限会社	ユウゲンガイシャ	limited company
有効求人倍数	ユウコウキュウジンバイスウ	ratio of effective labor demand to effective supply

1004

服 ⑧ 丿 刀 月 月 月' 肥 服 服

音	服	フク	clothes; dress; dose; obey; serve; admit to
熟	服する	フクする	*v*. obey; submit; serve; drink; wear; put on
	服役	フクエキ	penal servitude; military service —***vi***. serve a prison sentence; do military service
	服地	フクジ	cloth; fabric; material
	服従	フクジュウ	obedience; submission —***vi***. obey; submit to
	服飾	フクショク	clothing and accessories; attire
	服装	フクソウ	dress; attire
	服毒	フクドク	taking poison —***vi***. take poison
	服務	フクム	service; duties —***vi***. serve; be on duty
	服喪	フクモ	mourning —***vi***. mourn
	服薬	フクヤク	taking medicine —***vi***. take medicine
	服用	フクヨウ	taking (medicine) —***vi***. take (medicine)

1005

朕 ⑩ 丿 刀 月 月 月' 月" 月丷 月䒑 朕 朕

音	朕	チン	I (used now only by the emperor)

1006

朗 ⑩ ' ㇇ ㇉ ㇋ 自 良 良 朗 朗 朗

音	朗	ロウ	clear; bright; cheerful
熟	朗詠	ロウエイ	recitation —***v***. recite
	朗読	ロウドク	recitation —***v***. read aloud
	朗報	ロウホウ	good news; glad tidings
	朗々	ロウロウ	clear; sonorous
訓	朗らか	ほがらか	clear; bright; cheerful

1007

⑪ 丶 亠 七 七 切 切 切 切 望 望 望

音	望	ボウ モウ	hope; desire; look into the distance; full moon
熟	望遠鏡	ボウエンキョウ	telescope
	望外	ボウガイ	unexpected; not even dreamed of
	望郷	ボウキョウ	nostalgia; homesickness
	望見	ボウケン	watching from afar —*v.* watch from afar
	望楼	ボウロウ	watchtower
訓	望む	のぞむ	***vt.*** desire; hope for; look into the distance; look up; long for
	望み通り	のぞみどおり	as desired

1008
期 ⑫ 一 十 廾 甘 甘 甘 其 其 期 期 期 期

音	期	キ	time; period
		（ゴ）	time; period
熟	期間	キカン	period; time
	期限	キゲン	time limit; term; deadline
	期日	キジツ	fixed date
	期待	キタイ	expectation —*v.* expect; hope
	期末	キマツ	end of a term
¥	期日指定定期	キジツシテイテイキ	maturity-designated time deposit
	期首	キシュ	beginning of a period/term

1009
朝 ⑫ 一 十 十 市 古 古 直 卓 朝 朝 朝 朝

音	朝	チョウ	morning; court; dynasty; reign; regime; period; era
熟	朝会	チョウカイ	morning assembly
	朝刊	チョウカン	morning edition/newspaper
	朝食	チョウショク	breakfast
	朝夕	チョウセキ	morning and evening; day and night; always; usually
	朝廷	チョウテイ	imperial court

朝礼	チョウレイ	morning assembly/gathering; morning meetings (at school or a company)
訓 朝	あさ	morning
朝露	あさつゆ	morning dew
朝寝	あさね	getting up late —*vi*. get up late; sleep late into the morning
朝寝坊	あさねボウ	person who sleeps late —*vi*. oversleep
朝晩	あさバン	morning and evening
朝日	あさひ	morning sun
朝風呂	あさブロ	morning bath

6 肉 にく meat 月 (p.458)

1010

肉 ⑥ 丨 冂 内 内 肉 肉

音 肉	ニク	flesh; muscles; meat
熟 肉眼	ニクガン	naked eye
肉食	ニクショク	meat diet; meat-eating; flesh-eating —*vi*. eat meat; live on a meat diet
肉親	ニクシン	blood relation; flesh and blood
肉声	ニクセイ	natural/human voice
肉体	ニクタイ	body; flesh
肉団子	ニクダンご	meat dumpling/ball
肉薄	ニクハク	bitter/hand-to-hand fighting —*vi*. press hard; close in
肉筆	ニクヒツ	autograph; one's own handwriting
肉太	ニクぶと	full-faced; bold-faced; thick type
肉片	ニクヘン	piece of meat
肉欲	ニクヨク	lust; animal passions; carnal desire; sexual appetite

1011

⑭ 亠 广 广 广 庁 府 府 府 腐 腐 腐 腐

音 腐	フ	rot; decay
熟 腐食	フショク	corrosion —*v*. corrode; erode; eat away
腐心	フシン	great pains/trouble/worry —*vi*. worry; take pains; be intent
腐肉	フニク	tainted meat; carrion; gangrene

	腐敗	フハイ	decomposition; corruption —*vi*. decay; rot; perish; decompose; grow corrupt
	腐乱	フラン	decomposition; decay —*vi*. decompose; decay
訓	腐る	くさる	*vi*. rot; decay
	腐らす	くさらす	*vt*. let rot/spoil; corrode
	腐れる	くされる	*vi*. rot; decay
	腐れ縁	くされえん	unfortunate but inescapable relationship; fatal bond

4 月 にくづき meat; body

月（つきへん）⇨P.453

1012

⑦

音	肖	ショウ	resemble
熟	肖像	ショウゾウ	portrait

1013

⑧

音	育	イク	bring up; grow up; breed; train
熟	育英	イクエイ	cultivation of young talent; education and scholarship
	育児	イクジ	child/baby care; infant rearing
	育成	イクセイ	rearing; upbringing —*v*. bring up; rear; raise; foster
訓	育つ	そだつ	*vi*. grow up; be brought up; be bred
	育てる	そだてる	*vt*. bring up; rear; raise; nurture
	育む	はぐくむ	*vt*. bring up; nurse; foster; cultivate

1014

⑧

音	肩	ケン	shoulder
熟	肩章	ケンショウ	epaulet
訓	肩	かた	shoulder
	肩書	かたがき	title; honor; degree

肩掛け	かたかけ	shawl
肩身	かたみ	face; attitude towards other people
¥ 肩書	かたがき	title
肩代わり	かたがわり	*v*. take over a business; substitute

1015
肯 ⑧ 丨 ⺊ 止 止 屮 肯 肯 肯

音 肯	コウ	agree; affirm
熟 肯定	コウテイ	affirmation; affirmative —*v*. affirm; acknowledge

1016
胃 ⑨ 丨 冂 冂 田 田 甲 胃 胃 胃

音 胃	イ	stomach
熟 胃液	イエキ	***med***. gastric juice
胃潰瘍	イカイヨウ	***med***. stomach ulcer
胃癌	イガン	***med***. stomach cancer
胃散	イサン	stomach powder
胃腸	イチョウ	***med***. stomach and intestines; gastrointestinal tract; digestive organs
胃腸科	イチョウカ	gastrointestinal medicine; hospital department for diseases of the gastrointestinal tract
胃袋	イぶくろ	stomach

1017
背 ⑨ 丨 ⺊ 丬 北 北 北 背 背 背

音 背	ハイ	back; height; rebel
熟 背泳	ハイエイ	backstroke
背教	ハイキョウ	renegation; apostacy
背景	ハイケイ	background; scenery; setting
背後	ハイゴ	back; rear
背信	ハイシン	betrayal; infidelity —*v*. betray a person's confidence
背水の陣	ハイスイのジン	with one's back to the wall
背徳	ハイトク	immorality; corruption
背任	ハイニン	breach of trust; malpractice
背反	ハイハン	rebellion; revolt —***vi***. rebel; revolt

	背面	ハイメン	rear; back
	背理	ハイリ	irrationality; absurdity; preposterous
訓	背	せ	back; stature; height; ridge
	背	せい	stature; height
	背負う	せおう	***vt***. carry (a burden) on one's back; shoulder (a burden)
	背泳ぎ	せおよぎ	backstroke
	背筋	せすじ	line of the backbone; seam of the back
	背丈	せたけ	height; stature
	背伸び	せのび	straightening one's back —***vi***. straighten one's back
	背広	せびろ	gentleman's suit
	背骨	せぼね	backbone; spine; spinal column
	背く	そむく	***v***. go against; be contrary; disobey; violate; rebel; revolt
	背ける	そむける	***vt***. turn one's face away; look away

1018

能 ⑩

音	能	ノウ	talent; faculty; ability; Noh drama
熟	能楽	ノウガク	Noh drama
	能動	ノウドウ	activity
	能動的	ノウドウテキ	active
	能筆	ノウヒツ	good writing/writer
	能弁	ノウベン	eloquence; oratory
	能面	ノウメン	Noh mask
	能率	ノウリツ	efficiency
	能力	ノウリョク	ability; capacity; capability

1019

脅 ⑩

音	脅	キョウ	threaten; menance
熟	脅威	キョウイ	menance; threat; danger to
	脅喝	キョウカツ	threat; menace; blackmail; intimidation —***vt***. threaten; intimidate; blackmail
	脅迫	キョウハク	threat; menance —***v***. intimidate
訓	脅かす	おどかす	***vt***. threaten; menance; frighten; scare
	脅す	おどす	***vt***. threaten; menance; intimidate

脅かす　おびやかす　*vt*. threaten; menance; intimidate

1020
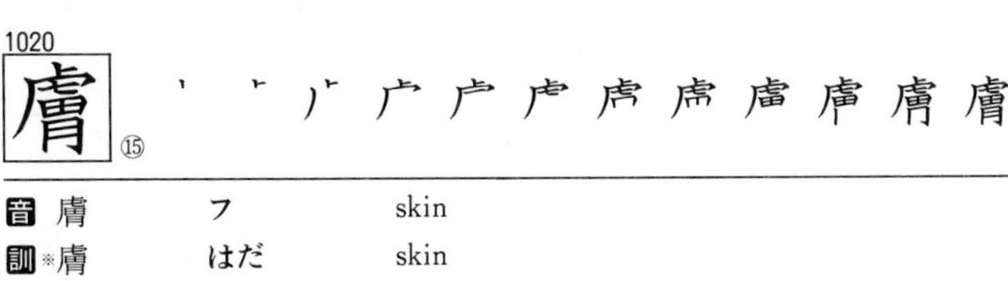

膚 ⑮

音 膚　フ　skin
訓 ※膚　はだ　skin

1021

肌 ⑥　丿 几 月 月 肌 肌

音 肌　キ　skin
訓 肌　はだ　skin; body; grain; character; nature; surface
肌合い　はだあい　disposition
肌色　はだいろ　skin/flesh color
肌着　はだぎ　underwear
肌寒い　はだざむい　chilly
肌身　はだみ　body

1022

肝 ⑦　丿 几 月 月 月 肝 肝

音 肝　カン　liver; heart
熟 肝心　カンジン　essential; main; important
肝腎　カンジン　important
肝臓　カンゾウ　***med***. liver
肝胆　カンタン　one's true heart
肝油　カンユ　cod-liver oil
肝要　カンヨウ　vital; important
訓 肝　きも　liver; heart

1023

肢 ⑧　丿 几 月 月 月 肚 肢 肢

音 肢　シ　limbs
熟 肢体　シタイ　body and limbs; arms and legs

1024

肥 ⑧

音	肥	ヒ	grow fat/fertile
熟	肥育	ヒイク	fattening —*v*. fatten
	肥大	ヒダイ	fleshiness; corpulence ***med***. hypertrophy —***vi***. get fat; become corpulent/fleshy; swell
	肥満	ヒマン	fatness; corpulence; obesity —***vi***. grow corpulent/stout; become fat
	肥沃	ヒヨク	fertility/richness (of soil)
	肥料	ヒリョウ	fertilizer; manure
訓	肥	こえ	manure; night soil
	肥える	こえる	***vi***. grow fat/fertile; gain experience
	肥やし	こやし	manure; fertilizer
	肥やす	こやす	***vt***. fertilize; fatten (livestock); enrich
	肥る	ふとる	***vi***. get fat

1025

肪 ⑧

音	肪	ボウ	(animal) fat

1026

胎 ⑨

音	胎	タイ	womb; embryo; conception
熟	胎教	タイキョウ	prenatal care
	胎児	タイジ	***med***. embryo
	胎動	タイドウ	fetal movement; signs; indications —***vi***. quicken in the womb
	胎内	タイナイ	inside the womb

1027

胆 ⑨

音	胆	タン	gallbladder; liver; spirit; courage; pluck; grit; nerves
熟	胆汁	タンジュウ	***med***. bile; gall

	胆石	タンセキ	***med***. gallstone
	胆嚢	タンノウ	***med***. gall; gallbladder; cholecyst
訓	胆	きも	liver

1028

肺 ⑨

丿 刀 月 月 月' 肝 肝 肺 肺

音	肺	ハイ	lung
熟	肺炎	ハイエン	***med***. pneumonia; inflammation of the lung
	肺活量	ハイカツリョウ	***med***. breathing/lung capacity
	肺結核	ハイケッカク	***med***. tuberculosis
	肺臓	ハイゾウ	***med***. lungs
	肺病	ハイビョウ	***med***. lung disease

1029

胞 ⑨

丿 刀 月 月 月' 肑 肑 胞 胞

音	胞	ホウ	sac; sheath; placenta; afterbirth
熟	胞子	ホウシ	spore

1030

胸 ⑩

丿 刀 月 月 月' 肑 肑 胸 胸 胸

音	胸	キョウ	chest; bosom; heart
熟	胸囲	キョウイ	chest measurement; girth of the chest
	胸像	キョウゾウ	bust
	胸中	キョウチュウ	feelings; thoughts; intent
訓	胸	むね	chest; bosom; heart
	胸	むな	(prefix) chest; bosom; heart; feelings
	胸騒ぎ	むなさわぎ	uneasiness; vague apprehension; presentiment
	胸算用	むなザンヨウ	mental arithmetic; expectation; anticipation
	胸元	むなもと	pit of the stomach; bosom; breast

1031

脂 ⑩

丿 刀 月 月 月' 肚 肸 脂 脂 脂

音	脂	シ	fat; resin

熟 脂肪　シボウ　fat; grease; lard; blubber
訓 脂　あぶら　fat

1032
胴 ⑩
丿 冂 月 月 刖 肌 肕 胴 胴 胴

音 胴　ドウ　trunk
熟 胴体　ドウタイ　trunk; body; torso

1033
脈 ⑩
丿 冂 月 月 肞 肞 肞 脈 脈 脈

音 脈　ミャク　blood vessel; pulse; vein
熟 脈打つ　ミャクうつ　***vi***. pulsate; beat
脈管　ミャクカン　***med***. blood vessel; duct
脈動　ミャクドウ　***med***. pulsation —***vi***. pulsate; beat
脈搏　ミャクハク　***med***. pulse (rate)
脈拍　ミャクハク　***med***. pulse (rate)
脈々　ミャクミャク　continuous; unbroken
脈絡　ミャクラク　logical connection; coherence

1034
脚 ⑪
丿 冂 月 月 肀 肘 肚 肚 胠 脚 脚

音 脚　キャク（キャ）　leg; walking; base; position
熟 脚色　キャクショク　dramatization —***v***. dramatize
脚線美　キャクセンビ　beauty of leg lines; leggy
脚注　キャクチュウ　footnote
脚本　キャクホン　play; drama; script; scenario
脚力　キャクリョク　strength of one's legs
脚立　キャたつ　stepladder
脚光　キャッコウ　footlights
※脚気　カッケ　***med***. beriberi
訓 脚　あし　leg; legs

1035

脱 ⑪

ノ 刀 月 月 月' 月' 月'' 月'' 胪 脖 脱

音	脱	ダツ	take off; remove; withdraw; escape
熟	脱する	ダッする	*v.* withdraw; leave
	脱衣	ダツイ	divestiture; divestment; undressing —*vi.* undress; take off one's clothes
	脱会	ダッカイ	withdrawal from a group; leaving an organization —*vi.* withdraw; give up; break away; leave (a group)
	脱却	ダッキャク	break away —*v.* get rid of; free oneself of; emerge from
	脱臼	ダッキュウ	***med.*** dislocation of a joint —*vi.* dislocate; put out of joint
	脱穀	ダッコク	threshing; thrashing —*vi.* thresh; thrash
	脱獄	ダツゴク	prison break; escaping from jail —*vi.* escape from prison; break jail
	脱字	ダツジ	omission; missing letter
	脱脂綿	ダッシメン	absorbent cotton; cotton wool
	脱臭	ダッシュウ	deodorization —*vi.* deodorize
	脱出	ダッシュツ	escape; prolapse —*vi.* escape; extricate; fall down; prolapse
	脱水	ダッスイ	dehydration; desiccation; evaporation —*vi.* dehydrate; dessicate; dry; evaporate
	脱線	ダッセン	derailment; deviation; digression —*v.* be derailed; derail; deviate; digress
	脱走	ダッソウ	flight; escape; breakout; desertion —*v.* flee; escape; abscond; break away
	脱退	ダッタイ	withdrawal; secession —*v.* withdraw; secede
	脱皮	ダッピ	ecdysis; casting off; self-renewal —*v.* cast off a skin; shed; emerge
	脱帽	ダツボウ	taking off one's hat (to) —*v.* take off one's hat (to)
	脱落	ダツラク	omission; being unable to keep up —*v.* omit; be unable to keep up
訓	脱ぐ	ぬぐ	*vt.* take off; strip; remove; undress
	脱げる	ぬげる	*vi.* come off; slip off/down
¥	脱税	ダツゼイ	tax evasion —*vi.* evade/dodge taxes

1036

脳 ⑪

ノ 刀 月 月 月' 月' 月'' 月'' 脳 脳 脳

音	脳	ノウ	brain

熟	脳外科	ノウゲカ	***med.*** brain surgery
	脳出血	ノウシュッケツ	***med.*** cerebral hemorrhage
	脳髄	ノウズイ	brain; brains
	脳天	ノウテン	pate; crown
	脳貧血	ノウヒンケツ	***med.*** cerebral anemia
	脳味噌	ノウミソ	brain; brains
	脳裏	ノウリ	one's mind/memory

1037

脹 ⑫ 丿 刀 月 月 月' 肝 肝 肝 肝 脹 脹 脹

音	脹	チョウ	expand
訓	脹れる	ふくれる	***vi.*** swell; bulge; expand

1038

腕 ⑫ 丿 刀 月 月 月' 月' 肸 肸 脝 脝 腕 腕

音	腕	ワン	arm; skill
熟	腕章	ワンショウ	armband
	腕白	ワンパク	naughty; mischievous
	腕力	ワンリョク	physical strength; strength in one's arms
訓	腕	うで	arm; ability; skill
	腕利き	うできき	skilled; able
	腕前	うでまえ	ability; skill
	腕輪	うでわ	bracelet
	※腕	かいな	arm
¥	腕力相場	ワンリョクソウば	forced market

1039

腸 ⑬ 丿 刀 月 月 月冂 月冂 月日 月日 胆 腸 腸 腸

音	腸	チョウ	intestines; entrails; gut
熟	腸捻転	チョウネンテン	***med.*** volvulus; twist in the intestines
訓	腸	はらわた	bowels; intestines; entrails; gut

1040

腹 ⑬

音	腹	フク	belly; stomach; heart; mind
熟	腹案	フクアン	(secret) plan; forethought
	腹式呼吸	フクシキコキュウ	abdominal breathing
	腹心	フクシン	confidant; trusted associate
	腹痛	フクツウ	***med.*** stomachache; abdominal pain
	腹部	フクブ	***med.*** abdomen; belly
	腹膜	フクマク	***med.*** peritoneum
	腹話術	フクワジュツ	ventriloquism
	腹筋	フッキン	***med.*** abdominal muscles
訓	腹	はら	belly; stomach; heart; mind
	腹切	はらきり	suicide by disembowlment; hara-kiri
	腹立つ	はらだつ	***vi.*** get angry
	腹八分	はらハチブ	moderate eating
	腹巻	はらまき	stomack wrapper

1041

腰 ⑬

音	腰	ヨウ	waist; pelvic region; loins; hips; small of the back
熟	腰部	ヨウブ	waist; hips; loins
訓	腰	こし	waist; loins; hips; small of the back
	腰掛ける	こしかける	sit down (on a chair)
	腰元	こしもと	***clas.*** lady's maid

1042

膜 ⑭

音	膜	マク	membrane; film

1043

膨 ⑯

音	膨	ボウ	expand; swell

心 忄 小 戈 戸 手 扌 支 攵 文 斗 斤 方 日 曰 月 肉 ●月 ●木 欠 止 歹 殳 母 毋 比 毛 氏 气 水 氺 氵 火 灬 爫 父 片 牛 犬 犭 王 礻 耂

熟	膨大	ボウダイ	swelling; large; enormous
	膨張	ボウチョウ	expansion; swelling —***vi***. swell; expand
訓	膨らむ	ふくらむ	***vi***. swell; expand
	膨れる	ふくれる	***vi***. swell; expand; sulk

1044

臓 ⑲ 月 月 月艹 月艹 月芦 月芦 月芹 月荊 月藏 臓 臓 臓

音	臓	ゾウ	entrails; internal organs
熟	臓器	ゾウキ	***med***. internal organs; viscera
	臓器移植	ゾウキイショク	***med***. organ transplant
	臓腑	ゾウフ	***med***. entrails; viscera
	臓物	ゾウモツ	entrails; giblets

4 木 き／きへん tree

1045

木 ④ 一 十 才 木

音	木	ボク	tree; wood
		モク	tree; wood
熟	木刀	ボクトウ	wooden sword
	木訥	ボクトツ	simple; straightforward; honest
	木魚	モクギョ	wooden temple drum
	木材	モクザイ	wood; lumber
	木質	モクシツ	ligneous
	木製	モクセイ	wooden; made of wood
	木星	モクセイ	the planet Jupiter
	木造	モクゾウ	wooden; made of wood
	木像	モクゾウ	wooden image
	木炭	モクタン	charcoal
	木彫	モクチョウ	wood carving
	木馬	モクバ	wooden/rocking/carousel/vaulting horse
	木版	モクハン	woodblock printing/print
	木片	モクヘン	block/chip/splinter of wood
	木目	モクめ	wood grain
	木曜日	モクヨウび	Thursday
	木琴	モッキン	xylophone

	木工	モッコウ	carpenter; woodworker; carpentry; woodworking
	木綿	モメン	cotton (cloth)
訓	木	き	tree; wood
	木屑	きくず	wood shavings/chips
	木戸	きど	gate; wicket; entrance; castle gate
	木	こ	(prefix) wood; tree
	木立	こだち	grove; thicket
	木霊	こだま	spirit of a tree; echo

1046

本 ⑤ 一 十 才 木 本

音	本	ホン	book; this; main; origin; (counter for long objects)
熟	本意	ホンイ	one's real intention
	本院	ホンイン	main institution; this institution
	本営	ホンエイ	(military) headquarters
	本懐	ホンカイ	long-cherished desire
	本格的	ホンカクテキ	full-scale; genuine; in earnest
	本官	ホンカン	one's permanent/principal function; I (used by officials); the present official
	本気	ホンキ	serious; in earnest
	本義	ホンギ	true meaning; basic principle
	本決まり	ホンぎまり	final decision
	本給	ホンキュウ	basic/regular salary
	本拠	ホンキョ	military headquarters; base
	本業	ホンギョウ	one's main occupation
	本家	ホンケ	main family; originator
	本校	ホンコウ	this school
	本国	ホンゴク	one's own country
	本腰	ホンごし	earnest effort
	本山	ホンザン	head temple; this temple
	本紙	ホンシ	this newspaper
	本誌	ホンシ	this magazine
	本旨	ホンシ	main purpose
	本式	ホンシキ	regular; orthodox
	本質	ホンシツ	essence
	本日	ホンジツ	today
	本社	ホンシャ	head office; main shrine; this shrine
	本州	ホンシュウ	Honshu

本性	ホンショウ	true nature/character
本職	ホンショク	one's regular occupation; expert
本心	ホンシン	one's right mind/senses; real intention/motive; conscience
本陣	ホンジン	troop headquarters; daimyo's inn; stronghold
本筋	ホンすじ	plot (of a story)
本姓	ホンセイ	real/original surname
本籍	ホンセキ	one's legal domicile
本線	ホンセン	main (railway) line
本尊	ホンゾン	***Bud***. main image (of worship); idol
本体	ホンタイ	true form
本隊	ホンタイ	main body (of troops)
本題	ホンダイ	main (this) issue/subject/problem
本宅	ホンタク	principal residence
本棚	ホンだな	bookshelf
本調子	ホンチョウシ	proper key (of an instrument); regular form
本邸	ホンテイ	principal residence
本店	ホンテン	head office; main store; this store
本殿	ホンデン	main/inner Shinto shrine
本土	ホンド	mainland
本当	ホントウ	true; real
本島	ホントウ	main island; this island
本堂	ホンドウ	main temple building
本人	ホンニン	the person himself; the said person; the principal figure
本音	ホンね	real intention; underlying motive
本年	ホンネン	this year
本能	ホンノウ	instinct
本場	ホンば	the best place for (a product); the place where something is produced (food, etc.)
本箱	ホンばこ	bookcase
本番	ホンバン	actual performance (not a rehearsal)
本文	ホンブン	main text; body of a letter
本分	ホンブン	duty (as a student, soldier, etc.)
本俸	ホンポウ	basic/regular salary
本末転倒	ホンマツテントウ	getting things backward
本丸	ホンまる	castle proper; donjon; keep
本名	ホンミョウ	one's real name
本務	ホンム	duty (as a student, soldier, etc.)
本命	ホンメイ	probable winner; favorite (to win)
本望	ホンモウ	satisfaction; long cherished desire
本物	ホンもの	real thing; genuine article
本屋	ホンや	bookstore; bookshop

	本来	ホンライ	in essence; naturally; originally; primarily
	本流	ホンリュウ	mainstream
	本領	ホンリョウ	characteristic; nature; true ability
	本塁	ホンルイ	base; stronghold ***bas***. homeplate
	本塁打	ホンルイダ	***bas***. home run
	本論	ホンロン	main subject/discussion; this subject
訓	本	もと	the origin; former
¥	本部	ホンブ	head office; headquarters

1047

末 ⑤ 一 二 キ 才 末

音	末	マツ バツ	end; powder
熟	末裔	マツエイ	descendant
	末期	マッキ	last/closing years; last stage
	末期	マツゴ	one's last dying moments
	末座	マツザ	lowest-ranking seats
	末日	マツジツ	last day
	末子	マッシ (バッシ)	youngest child
	末世	マッセ	future ages —***Bud***. last days of the world
	末席	マッセキ	lowest-ranking seats
	末代	マツダイ	all ages to come; eternity; the next world; future ages
	末端	マッタン	tip; end; terminal
	末尾	マツビ	end; last; final
	末筆	マッピツ	closing written remarks
	末葉	マツヨウ	close; end of an era
	末流	マツリュウ	descendants; lower reaches of a river
	末路	マツロ	last days; end; end of one's life; old age
訓	末	すえ	end; future; descendant; youngest child; trivialities
	末恐ろしい	すえおそろしい	potential to do something terrible in the future
	末っ子	すえっこ	youngest child

1048

未 ⑤ 一 二 キ 未 未

音	未	ミ	not yet; (prefix) un-
熟	未開	ミカイ	uncivilized; barbarous; undeveloped

未開拓	ミカイタク	undeveloped
未開発	ミカイハツ	undeveloped
未解決	ミカイケツ	unsolved; unsettled
未刊	ミカン	unpublished
未完	ミカン	incomplete; unfinished
未完成	ミカンセイ	incomplete; unfinished
未決	ミケツ	undecided; pending; unsettled
未見	ミケン	unacquainted; unknown
未婚	ミコン	single; unmarried
未済	ミサイ	unpaid; unsettled; outstanding
未熟	ミジュク	unripe; inexperienced; premature; immature
未遂	ミスイ	attempt
未成年	ミセイネン	underage; minority; minor
未然	ミゼン	before it happens; beforehand
未知	ミチ	unknown; strange
未知数	ミチスウ	unknown quantity
未定	ミテイ	undecided; pending
未到	ミトウ	untrodden; unexplored
未踏	ミトウ	untrodden; unexplored; as yet unachieved (record, etc.)
未納	ミノウ	nonpayment; default; arrears
未亡人	ミボウジン	widow
未満	ミマン	less than; below
未明	ミメイ	early dawn before sunrise
未聞	ミモン	unheard of; unknown
未来	ミライ	future ***gram***. future tense
未了	ミリョウ	unfinished
未練	ミレン	regret; lingering affection
訓 ※未だ	まだ	still; not yet
※未だ	いまだ	still; as yet; to this day; ever
※未	ひつじ	the sheep (eighth sign of the Chinese zodiac)
¥ 未完成工事	ミカンセイコウジ	long-term construction in progress
未決	ミケツ	pending
未実現損益	ミジツゲンソンエキ	unrealized profit and loss
未収収益	ミシュウシュウエキ	accrued revenue (income)
未収入金	ミシュウニュウキン	uncollected balance
未払い金	ミばらいキン	account payable
未払い費用	ミばらいヒヨウ	accrued expenses

1049

朱 ⑥

ノ ⺈ 二 牛 牛 朱

音	朱	シュ	vermilion
熟	朱肉	シュニク	vermilion inkpad
	朱筆	シュヒツ	correcting a manuscript

1050

条 ⑦

ノ ク 夂 夂 夅 夅 条

音	条	ジョウ	branch; reason
熟	条件	ジョウケン	condition; prerequisite; terms; requirement
	条項	ジョウコウ	article; clause; provision
	条文	ジョウブン	provision; the text; notes
	条約国	ジョウヤクコク	treaty power/nation
	条理	ジョウリ	reason
	条例	ジョウレイ	ordinance; rules; regulation
訓	※条	えだ	branch
¥	条約	ジョウヤク	convention; pact; treaty

1051

束 ⑦

一 丆 冖 𠁣 申 束 束

音	束	ソク	bundle; sheaf; ream
熟	束縛	ソクバク	restraint; constraint; shackles
	束髪	ソクハツ	bun hairdo
訓	束	たば	bundle; bunch; sheaf
	束ねる	たばねる	***vt.*** bundle; govern; manage; control
	束	つか	handbreadth; span; brief time; thickness
	束ねる	つかねる	***vt.*** tie in bundles; fold (one's arms)

1052

果 ⑧

丨 冂 日 日 旦 甲 果 果

音	果	カ	fruit; effect; complete
熟	果敢	カカン	daring; boldness

	果実	カジツ	fruit
	果樹	カジュ	fruit tree
	果汁	カジュウ	fruit juice
	果然	カゼン	as expected; sure enough
	果報	カホウ	good fortune; luck; reward
訓	果たして	はたして	as expected; sure enough
	果たす	はたす	***vt***. carry out; accomplish; finish; complete; effect
	果て	はて	limits; end; outcome
	果てる	はてる	***vi***. terminate; end; die
	※果物	くだもの	fruit

1053

⑧

音	東	トウ	east
熟	東亜	トウア	eastern Asia
	東欧	トウオウ	Eastern Europe
	東海道	トウカイドウ	Tokaido (route between Kyoto and Tokyo)
	東京	トウキョウ	Tokyo
	東宮	トウグウ	crown prince
	東経	トウケイ	east longitude
	東国	トウゴク	eastern country; Kanto provinces
	東奔西走	トウホンセイソウ	on the move —***vi***. be on the move; move around busily
	東洋	トウヨウ	Orient
訓	東	ひがし	east
	※東	あずま	east

1054

⑨

音	栄	エイ	prosper; thrive; glory
熟	栄華	エイガ	prosperity; glory; splendor; luxury
	栄冠	エイカン	honor; the crown
	栄枯	エイコ	prosperity and decline; rise and fall
	栄光	エイコウ	glory; honor
	栄転	エイテン	promotion; transference —***vi***. be promoted; be transferred to another post
	栄誉	エイヨ	honor; glory

	栄養	エイヨウ	nutrition
	栄養価	エイヨウカ	nutritive value
訓	栄える	さかえる	***vi***. prosper; be prosperous; flourish
	栄え	はえ	glory
	栄える	はえる	***vi***. shine; be brilliant

1055

架 ⑨

音	架	カ	frame; lay
熟	架橋	カキョウ	bridge construction —***vi***. build bridges
	架空	カクウ	aerial; overhead; imaginary; fanciful
	架設	カセツ	erection; installation —***v***. erect; put up; install
	架線	カセン	wiring; aerial line
訓	架かる	かかる	***vi***. be built/constructed/laid
	架ける	かける	***vt***. construct; build; lay; install; span

1056

査 ⑨

音	査	サ	investigation; inquiry
熟	査察	ササツ	inspection —***v***. inspect
	査察官	ササツカン	inspector
	査証	サショウ	visa —***v***. grant a visa
	査定	サテイ	assessment —***v***. assess; make an assessment
	査問	サモン	inquiry —***v***. inquire
訓	※査べる	しらべる	***vt***. investigate; inspect; inquire
¥	査定価格	サテイカカク	assessed price
	査定額	サテイガク	assessed value
	査定機関	サテイキカン	assessing agency

1057

柔 ⑨

音	柔	ジュウ	soft; gentle; soften
		ニュウ	tender; weak
熟	柔順	ジュウジュン	gentleness; obedience; submission
	柔道	ジュウドウ	judo

	柔軟	**ジュウナン**	soft; supple; flexible; pliant; pliable
	柔弱	**ニュウジャク**	weakness
	柔和	**ニュウワ**	gentle; mild; tender; sweet
訓	柔らかい	**やわらかい**	soft; gentle; mild; tender
	柔らげる	**やわらげる**	***vt***. soften; moderate; ease; lessen; relieve; appease; pacify

1058

染 ⑨

丶 冫 氵 氿 汍 汣 染 染 染

音	染	**セン**	dye; color
熟	染色	**センショク**	dyeing; staining —***v***. dye; stain
	染料	**センリョウ**	dyestuff
訓	染み	**しみ**	stain; blot; smudge
	染みる	**しみる**	***vi***. be influenced/infected; hurt
	染まる	**そまる**	***vi***. be dyed/imbued with
	染める	**そめる**	***vt***. dye; color

1059

某 ⑨

一 十 廾 廿 甘 甘 草 某 某

音	某	**ボウ**	certain; one
熟	某氏	**ボウシ**	somebody; certain person
	某所	**ボウショ**	somewhere; certain place
	某地	**ボウチ**	certain place
訓	※某	**それがし**	certain person; I
	※某	**なにがし**	certain person/amount/place/thing

1060

案 ⑩

丶 丶 宀 宀 安 安 安 案 案 案

音	案	**アン**	desk; investigate; idea; plan; proposal; draft
熟	案じる	**アンじる**	***vt***. worry over; be anxious; be concerned; devise; consider
	案	**アン**	plan; draft; idea
	案外	**アンガイ**	contrary to expectations; unexpectedly; unforeseen
	案内	**アンナイ**	guidance; conduct; lead; information —***v***. guide; conduct; lead; notify; inform

	案内状	アンナイジョウ	letter of invitation; advice note
¥	案件	アンケン	matter; item on the agenda

1061

栽 ⑩

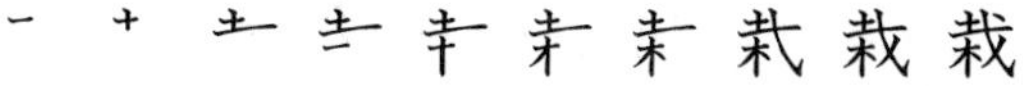

音	栽	サイ	plant; grow; cultivate
熟	栽培	サイバイ	cultivation; culture —*v.* cultivate; grow; raise
訓	※栽える	うえる	***vt.*** plant; grow

1062

桑 ⑩

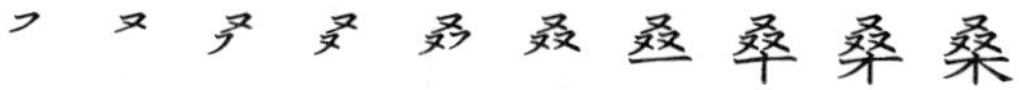

音	桑	ソウ	mulberry
熟	桑田	ソウデン	mulberry field
訓	桑	くわ	mulberry

1063

森 ⑫

音	森	シン	forest
熟	森閑	シンカン	stillness; quiet; silence
	森林	シンリン	forest
訓	森	もり	wood; forest

1064

楽 ⑬

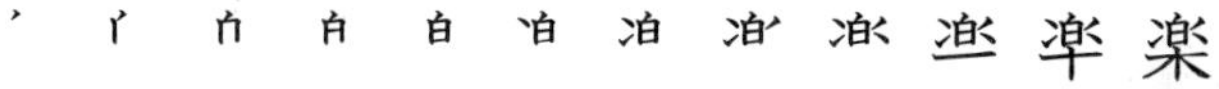

音	楽	ガク	music
		ラク	pleasure; ease; comfort; relief
熟	楽聖	ガクセイ	celebrated musician
	楽隊	ガクタイ	band; orchestra
	楽団	ガクダン	band; orchestra
	楽壇	ガクダン	musical circles
	楽典	ガクテン	rules of musical composition
	楽譜	ガクフ	musical notation/score; sheet music

	楽屋	ガクや	dressing room; backstage; behind the scenes; secret
	楽器	ガッキ	musical instrument
	楽園	ラクエン	paradise
	楽勝	ラクショウ	easy victory —***vi***. win an easy victory
	楽天	ラクテン	optimism
	楽天家	ラクテンカ	optimist
	楽天的	ラクテンテキ	optimistic; cheerful
	楽々	ラクラク	comfortably; with great ease
	楽観	ラッカン	optimism —***v***. be optimistic; look on the bright side
	楽観的	ラッカンテキ	optimistic; hopeful
訓	楽しい	たのしい	fun; enjoyable; pleasant
	楽しむ	たのしむ	***vt***. enjoy
	楽しみ	たのしみ	pleasure; enjoyment; delight; happiness

1065 棄 ⑬

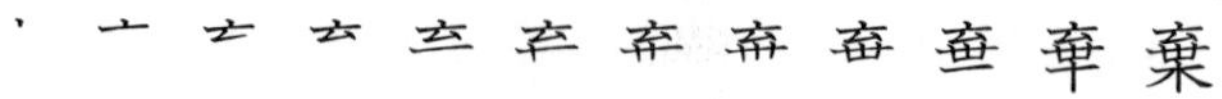

音	棄	キ	abandon; cast away
熟	棄却	キキャク	dismissal; abandon; rejection —***v***. dismiss; abandon; reject
	棄権	キケン	abstention from voting —***v***. abstain from voting
訓	※棄てる	すてる	***vt***. abandon; reject

1066 業 ⑬

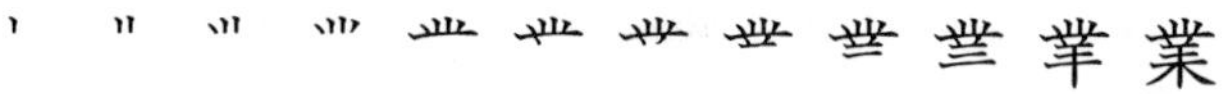

音	業	ギョウ ゴウ	work; duty; enterprise; achievement; karma
訓	業	わざ	work; deed; act
¥	業界	ギョウカイ	business world; industry; trade
	業況	ギョウキョウ	business activity/conditions
	業況調査	ギョウキョウチョウサ	business research/survey
	業者	ギョウシャ	traders; makers
	業種	ギョウシュ	type of business/industry; industrial branch/sector
	業種別分類	ギョウシュベツブンルイ	classification by industry; industry-by-industry breakdown
	業績	ギョウセキ	business results; achievements

業績報告	ギョウセキホウコク	business report
業態	ギョウタイ	business conditions
業務	ギョウム	business; service
業務管理	ギョウムカンリ	business management

1067
札 ⑤ 一 十 才 木 札

音	札	サツ	card; ticket; bill; bank note
訓	札	ふだ	card; ticket
	札所	ふだショ	***Bud***. temple from which amulets may be obtained
	札付き	ふだつき	price label/ticket; (person with) bad reputation

1068
机 ⑥ 一 十 才 木 朷 机

音	机	キ	desk
熟	机上	キジョウ	on the desk; on top of a desk
	机上の空論	キジョウのクウロン	unrealistic/impractical idea
訓	机	つくえ	desk; table

1069
朽 ⑥ 一 十 才 木 朩 朽

音	朽	キュウ	rot; decay; cumble
熟	朽木	キュウボク	***vi***. decayed/rotted wood
訓	朽ちる	くちる	rot; decay; molder; crumble
	朽木	くちき	decayed tree; rotted wood
	朽葉	くちば	dead leaves

1070
朴 ⑥ 一 十 才 木 朩 朴

音	朴	ボク	simple; plain

1071

材 ⑦ 一 十 才 木 木一 村 材

音	材	ザイ	material; talent
熟	材木	ザイモク	lumber; wood; timber
	材料	ザイリョウ	materials; raw materials; data; factor; ingredients

1072

杉 ⑦ 一 十 才 木 木ノ 杉 杉

音	杉	サン	cedar (tree)
訓	杉	すぎ	cedar (tree)

1073

村 ⑦ 一 十 才 木 木一 村 村

音	村	ムラ	village
熟	村議会	ソンギカイ	village assembly
	村長	ソンチョウ	village mayor
	村民	ソンミン	villagers
	村落	ソンラク	village; hamlet
	村立	ソンリツ	established by the village
訓	村	むら	village
	村雨	むらさめ	passing shower
	村八分	むらハチブ	social ostracism
	村人	むらびと	villager

1074

枝 ⑧ 一 十 才 木 木一 木十 枝 枝

音	枝	シ	branch
熟	枝葉	シヨウ（えだは）	branches and leaves ***fig***. minor details
	枝葉末節	シヨウマッセツ	trivia; minor details
訓	枝	えだ	branch
	枝豆	えだまめ	green soybeans

1075

松 ⑧

一 十 才 木 木' 朩ハ 松 松

音	松	ショウ	pine
熟	松竹梅	ショウチクバイ	pine, bamboo, and plum
訓	松	まつ	pine tree
	松飾り	まつかざり	New Year pine decorations
	松葉杖	まつばづえ	crutches
	※松明	たいまつ	torch

1076

枢 ⑧

一 十 才 木 朩一 朩フ 枢 枢

音	枢	スウ	pivot
熟	枢機	スウキ	cardinal; most important
	枢要	スウヨウ	important; principal; cardinal; responsible
¥	枢密院	スウミツイン	Privy Council

1077

析 ⑧

一 十 才 木 木' 朩厂 析 析

音	析	セキ	analyze
熟	析出	セキシュツ	eduction; extract —*v.* educe; extract

1078

杯 ⑧

一 十 才 木 朩一 朩フ 杯 杯

音	杯	ハイ	winecup; (counter for cups)
訓	杯	さかずき	saké cup

1079

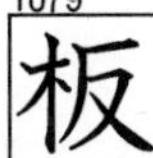

板 ⑧

一 十 才 木 朩一 朩厂 板 板

音	板	バン	board
		ハン	

熟	板金	バンキン	sheet metal
	板書	バンショ	writing on a blackboard —*v.* write on the blackboard
訓	板	いた	board; plank; plate; the stage
	板塀	いたベイ	fence; wooden wall
	板前	いたまえ	cook/chef (who prepares Japanese food)
	板目	いため	wood grain of a plank

1080

枚 ⑧

一 十 才 木 木' 朩 杓 枚

音	枚	マイ	sheet; (counter for flat, thin objects)
熟	枚挙	マイキョ	enumeration; list —*v.* enumerate; list; count
	枚数	マイスウ	number of sheets

1081

林 ⑧

一 十 才 木 木一 村 林 林

音	林	リン	forest; wood
熟	林間学校	リンカンガッコウ	camp; outdoor school
	林業	リンギョウ	forestry
	林産物	リンサンブツ	forest products
	林道	リンドウ	forest road/trail
	林野	リンヤ	forests and fields; woodlands
	林立	リンリツ	standing close together —*vi.* stand close together
訓	林	はやし	wood; forest
¥	林野庁	リンヤチョウ	Forestry Agency

1082

枠 ⑧

一 十 才 木 木' 朳 枠 枠

訓	枠	わく	frame; restriction; framework; limit
	枠外	わくガイ	beyond the limits
	枠組み	わくぐみ	frame; framework; framing; scope
	枠内	わくナイ	within the limits

1083

枯 ⑨

一 十 才 木 木 朩 村 枯 枯

音	枯	コ	wither; die
熟	枯渇	コカツ	exhausted; drained —*v.* dry up; run dry; be exhausted/drained
	枯死	コシ	withering; blight —*v.* wither and die; be blighted
	枯淡	コタン	simple but refined
訓	枯らす	からす	***vt***. let die; blight; season (wood)
	枯れる	かれる	***vi***. die; wither; season; mature
	枯れ木	かれき	dead/bare tree
	枯れ野	かれの	desolate field

1084

柱 ⑨

一 十 才 木 木 朩 村 柱 柱

音	柱	チュウ	pillar; cylinder
熟	柱石	チュウセキ	mainstay; pillar; prop; support
訓	柱	はしら	pillar; support

1085

柄 ⑨

一 十 才 木 木 朩 柄 柄 柄

音	柄	ヘイ	handle; grip; hilt
訓	柄	え	handle; grip; hilt
	柄	がら	pattern; design; build; physique; character; nature
	※柄	つか	handle; grip; hilt
	※柄杓	ひシャク	ladle; dipper; scoop

1086

柳 ⑨

一 十 才 木 木 朩 柳 柳 柳

音	柳	リュウ	willow tree
熟	柳眉	リュウビ	beautiful eyebrows
訓	柳	やなぎ	willow tree

	柳腰	やなぎごし	slender graceful hips

1087

桜 ⑩

音	桜	オウ	cherry tree; cherry
熟	桜花	オウカ	cherry blossoms
	桜桃	オウトウ	cherry
訓	桜	さくら	cherry tree
	桜色	さくらいろ	pink; cerise
	桜肉	さくらニク	horsemeat

1088

格 ⑩

音	格	カク (コウ)	character; syntactic case; rank
熟	格言	カクゲン	maxim; proverb; adage; saying
	格式	カクシキ	formality; social status
	格段	カクダン	special; marked difference
	格調	カクチョウ	style and tone of poetry
	格闘	カクトウ	hand-to-hand fighting —***vi***. fight hand-to-hand; grapple
	格納庫	カクノウコ	aircraft hangar
	格好	カッコウ	shape; form; appearance; dress; style
	格子	コウシ	lattice; latticework
¥	格上げ	カクあげ	raise the status; upgrade
	格差	カクサ	gap; differential; difference in quality
	格付け	カクづけ	ranking; rating; grading; classification
	格付け機関	カクづけキカン	bond-rating agency; rating agency
	格安	カクやす	inexpensive; moderate in price

1089

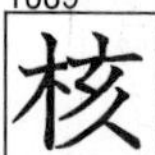 ⑩

音	核	カク	nucleus; fruit stone
熟	核心	カクシン	core; kernel
	核爆発	カクバクハツ	nuclear explosion

	核分裂	カクブンレツ	(nuclear) fission; nuclear division —*vi*. fission; undergo fission
	核兵器	カクヘイキ	nuclear weapons
訓	※核	さね	stone; kernel; core

1090

株 ⑩

音	株	(シュ)	stump; root; share; stocks
¥	株	かぶ	stump; root; share; stocks
	株価	かぶカ	stock prices
	株券	かぶケン	stock certificate
	株式	かぶシキ	stocks; shares
	株式会社	かぶシキガイシャ	corporation; joint-stock company
	株式償却	かぶシキショウキャク	retirement of shares; cancellation of shares
	株式配当	かぶシキハイトウ	stock dividend
	株式分割	かぶシキブンカツ	stock split; split-ups
	株式分布	かぶシキブンプ	distribution of stocks
	株主	かぶぬし	stockholder
	株主総会	かぶぬしソウカイ	stockholders meeting

1091

校 10 91

音	校	コウ	school; correct; compare
熟	校医	コウイ	school doctor
	校閲	コウエツ	revision; supervision —*v*. revise; supervise
	校旗	コウキ	school banner/flag
	校訓	コウクン	school precepts/motto
	校舎	コウシャ	school house/building
	校正	コウセイ	proofreading —*v*. proofread; correct
	校則	コウソク	school regulations/rules
	校長	コウチョウ	principal; headmaster
	校庭	コウテイ	school grounds; schoolyard; campus
	校風	コウフウ	school spirit/tradition
	校友	コウユウ	schoolmate
訓	※校倉作り	あぜくらづくり	style of architecture in which the sides of the building are made by placing triangularly cut logs across each other

1092

根 ⑩

一 十 才 木 朩ㄱ 朩ヨ 朩ヨ 根 根 根

音	根	コン	root; foundation; basis
熟	根幹	コンカン	basis; root; nucleus
	根気	コンキ	patience; perseverance; endurance; stamina
	根拠	コンキョ	ground; basis; foundation
	根拠地	コンキョチ	headquarters; stronghold
	根源	コンゲン	origin; root; source
	根治	コンジ（コンチ）	radical/permanent cure —*v.* cure permanently/radically
	根性	コンジョウ	nature; disposition; spirit; mind; willpower
	根絶	コンゼツ	extermination; eradication —*v.* exterminate; eradicate
	根底	コンテイ	root; bottom; foundation
	根本	コンポン	root; source; origin; foundation; basis
	根本的	コンポンテキ	fundamental; cardinal; basic
	根負け	コンまけ	losing stamina/patience —*vi.* have one's patience exhausted
訓	根	ね	root; origin; nature
	根深い	ねぶかい	deep-rooted; ingrained; incurable
	根掘り葉掘り	ねほりはほり	inquisitively
	根元	ねもと	root; base

1093

桟 ⑩

一 十 才 木 朩 朩 朩 栈 桟 桟

音	桟	サン	temporary bridge; plank bridge; plank
熟	桟道	サンドウ	bridge between two cliffs; road along a mountainside
	桟橋	サンばし	pier; jetty
	※桟敷	サじき	box; the stands; dress circle
訓	※桟	かけはし	temporary/makeshift bridge

1094

栓 ⑩

一 十 才 木 朩 朩 朩 朩 栓 栓

音	栓	セン	cork

1095

桃 ⑩

一 十 才 木 杉 杉 杉 朷 朷 桃

音	桃	トウ	peach
熟	桃源郷	トウゲンキョウ	Shangri-La; earthly paradise
訓	桃	もも	peach
	桃色	ももいろ	pink; rosy; sexual affair
	桃尻	ももじり	poor at riding horses
	桃太郎	ももタロウ	Momotarō (Japanese fairy tale character)
	桃の節句	もものセック	girl's day; Doll's Festival

1096

梅 ⑩

一 十 才 木 朾 杧 梅 梅 梅 梅

音	梅	バイ	plum tree
熟	梅雨	バイウ	rain in the wet/rainy season
	梅毒	バイドク	***med***. syphillis
訓	梅	うめ	plum; plum tree
	梅酒	うめシュ	plum wine
	梅干し	うめぼし	pickled plum
	※梅雨	つゆ	rainy/wet season

1097

械 ⑪

一 十 才 木 杧 杧 杧 栎 械 械 械

音	械	カイ	device; apparatus
訓	械	かせ	shackles; handcuffs

1098

棺 ⑫

一 十 才 木 朩 朩 柠 柠 棺 棺 棺 棺

音	棺	カン	coffin; casket
熟	棺桶	カンおけ	coffin; casket
訓	※棺	ひつぎ	coffin; casket

1099
棋 ⑫

音	棋	キ	game of go or shōgi
熟	棋士	キシ	professional go player

1100
極 ⑫

音	極	キョク	go to extremes; the end; the poles; magnetic/electrical poles
		ゴク	
熟	極言	キョクゲン	so far as to say —*v*. go so far as to say; go to the length of saying
	極限	キョクゲン	utmost limits; bounds
	極端	キョクタン	extreme; extremity
	極致	キョクチ	culmination; acme; height
	極地	キョクチ	polar region; wilderness
	極度	キョクド	highest degree; utmost
	極東	キョクトウ	far east
	極力	キョクリョク	to the utmost; to the best of one's ability
	極論	キョクロン	carrying logic to extremes —*v*. carry logic to extremes
	極悪	ゴクアク	atrocity; brutality; villainy
	極意	ゴクイ	the secret; the mystery; the essence
	極彩色	ゴクサイシキ	rich coloring; full color
	極上	ゴクジョウ	first rate; premier quality
	極道	ゴクドウ	wicked; dissipated
	極秘	ゴクヒ	top secret
	極楽	ゴクラク	paradise; heaven
訓	極まる	きわまる	***vi***. end; terminate; be at an end; reach an extreme
	極める	きわめる	***vt***. go to the end; go to the extremes
	極み	きわみ	height; apex; end; limit

1101
検 ⑫

音	検	ケン	investigate; examine; test; inspect

熟 検疫　ケンエキ　quarantine —*v*. quarantine; inspect
検閲　ケンエツ　censorship; inspection —*v*. inspect; examine; censor
検眼　ケンガン　eye test —*vi*. examine a person's eyes
検挙　ケンキョ　arresting —*v*. arrest
検挙者　ケンキョシャ　person in custody/under arrest
検査　ケンサ　test; inspection; examination; audit —*v*. inspect; examine; check; test; audit
検索　ケンサク　reference; retrieval —*v*. look up; refer to
検察　ケンサツ　investigation; examination; prosecution
検察側　ケンサツがわ　the prosecution
検察庁　ケンサツチョウ　Public Prosecutor's Office
検算　ケンザン　verification of accounts —*v*. check/verify the accounts
検事　ケンジ　public prosecutor; the prosecution
検出　ケンシュツ　detection —*v*. detect; find
検証　ケンショウ　verification; inspection —*v*. verify; inspect
検診　ケンシン　medical examination —*v*. examine (a person's) body
検針　ケンシン　meter inspection —*v*. read a meter
検定　ケンテイ　official approval —*v*. give official approval; sanction; authorize
検討　ケントウ　examination; investigation; consideration —*v*. examine; investigate; consider; discuss
検分　ケンブン　survey; inspection; examination —*v*. inspect; examine
検便　ケンベン　stool test —*vi*. examine a stool sample
検問　ケンモン　check; inspection —*v*. check; inspect; examine

1102
植 ⑫
一 十 才 木 木一 木十 木𠂉 杧 枯 植 植 植

音 植　ショク　plant; cultivate; set type

熟 植字　ショクジ　typesetting —*vi*. set type
植樹　ショクジュ　tree planting —*vi*. plant a tree
植物　ショクブツ　plant; vegetation
植物園　ショクブツエン　botanical garden
植物学　ショクブツガク　botany
植民　ショクミン　colonization; settler; colonial —*vi*. colonize
植民地　ショクミンチ　colony
植林　ショクリン　afforestation —*vi*. plant trees

訓 植える　うえる　*vt*. plant; grow
植わる　うわる　*vi*. be planted

	植木	うえき	garden plant

1103
棚 ⑫ 一 十 才 木 朾 杁 朷 枂 栶 棚 棚 棚

音	棚	ホウ	shelf
訓	棚	たな	shelf
	棚上げ	たなあげ	sheltering; pigeonhole —*v.* shelve; put something into pigeonhole
	棚卸し	たなおろし	stocktaking; inventory —*v.* take an inventory

1104
棟 ⑫ 一 十 才 木 杧 杧 枦 枦 枱 柙 棟 棟

音	棟	トウ	ridge of a roof
熟	棟梁	トウリョウ	pillar/chief support/master carpenter/builder (of a country, family, etc.)
訓	棟	むな	(prefix) roof; ridge
	棟	むね	ridge of a roof
	棟上げ式	むねあげしき	framework raising ceremony

1105
棒 ⑫ 一 十 才 木 杧 杧 枆 栐 栜 桲 棒 棒

音	棒	ボウ	stick; pole
熟	棒暗記	ボウアンキ	indiscriminate memorization; memorization without understanding —*v.* memorize indiscriminately; memorize without understanding
	棒組	ボウぐみ	typesetting
	棒縞	ボウじま	wide stripes
	棒状	ボウジョウ	cylindrical; stick
	棒高跳び	ボウたかとび	pole vault
	棒立ち	ボウだち	frozen in an upright position with shock
	棒読み	ボウよみ	monotone reading
¥	棒上げ	ボウあげ	straight climb
	棒下げ	ボウさげ	straight fall
	棒引き	ボウびき	cancellation of a debt; writing off (a debt); drawing a line

1106
楼 ⑬

音	楼	ロウ	tower; turret; lookout
熟	楼閣	ロウカク	tower; castle
	楼門	ロウモン	two-story gate

1107
概 ⑭

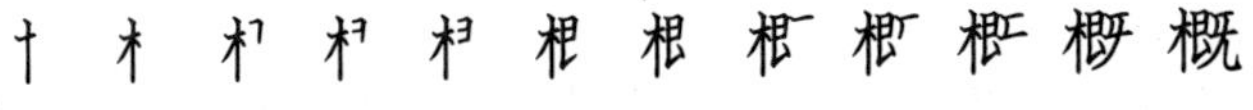

音	概	ガイ	rough; general
熟	概括	ガイカツ	summary; generalization —*v*. summarize; sum up; generalize
	概観	ガイカン	general view; overview; summary
	概況	ガイキョウ	general condition/situation
	概算	ガイサン	rough estimate —*v*. make a rough estimate
	概数	ガイスウ	round figures; approximation
	概説	ガイセツ	general statement —*v*. give an outline/overview
	概念	ガイネン	concept; general idea; notion
	概要	ガイヨウ	outline; summary; synopsis
	概して	ガイして	generally; in general; on the whole
訓	※概ね	おおむね	generally speaking; in general; for the most part

1108
構 ⑭

音	構	コウ	structure; attitude; concern
熟	構外	コウガイ	outside the premises
	構図	コウズ	composition; plot
	構成	コウセイ	composition; organization; construction —*v*. make; compose; organize; construct
	構想	コウソウ	plan; plot; conception; idea —*v*. plan; plot; conceive an idea
	構造	コウゾウ	structure; construction; framework; organization
	構築	コウチク	construction; structure —*v*. build; construct; erect
	構内	コウナイ	premises; precincts; grounds
訓	構う	かまう	*vi*. mind; care about; be concerned; meddle; interfere; entertain

心 忄 小 戈 戸 手 扌 支 攵 文 斗 斤 方 日 曰 月 肉 月 木● 欠 止 歹 殳 母 毋 比 毛 氏 气 水 氺 氵 火 灬 爫 父 片 牛 犬 犭 王 礻 耂

	構える	かまえる	***vt***. keep; set up; build; pose; feign; pretend
	構え	かまえ	structure; construction; posture; position; attitude

1109

模 ⑭

十 木 木一 木十 木廿 木廿 柑 栉 栉 梼 模 模

音	模	ボ	model; copy; imitation
		モ	model; copy; imitation
熟	模する	モする	***vt***. model; copy; imitate
	模擬	モギ	imitation; mock; dry-run
	模型	モケイ	model; mold
	模索	モサク	fumbling; grope —***v***. fumble; grope
	模写	モシャ	copy; replica —***v***. copy; make a replica
	模造	モゾウ	imitation —***v***. imitate; copy
	模範	モハン	model; exemplar
	模倣	モホウ	imitation; copy —***v***. imitate; copy
	模様	モヨウ	pattern; design; appearance; situation
¥	模様	モヨウ	pattern; sign; looks; condition; state of affairs
	模様眺め	モヨウながめ	wait and see; watch and wait

1110

様 ⑭

十 木 木' 木" 栏 栏 栏 样 样 様 様 様

音	様	ヨウ	way; manner; similar; like; condition
熟	様式	ヨウシキ	mode; form; style
	様子	ヨウス	situation; appearance; aspect
	様相	ヨウソウ	phase; aspect; condition
	様態	ヨウタイ	situation; condition
訓	様	さま	appearance
	様々	さまざま	various; varied

1111

横 ⑮

十 木 木一 木十 木廿 栱 栱 栱 構 横 横 横

音	横	オウ	side; direction; dishonesty
熟	横臥	オウガ	lying down on one's side —***vi***. lie down on one's side
	横隔膜	オウカクマク	***med***. diaphragm; midriff

横行	オウコウ	swaggering; walking sideways —***vi***. overrun; swagger; walk sideways
横隊	オウタイ	rank; line
横断	オウダン	crossing; intersection —***v***. cross; intersect
横断歩道	オウダンホドウ	pedestrian/zebra crossing
横着	オウチャク	cunning; wayward; dishonest —***vi***. be cunning/wayward/dishonest
横転	オウテン	turning sideways; rolling —***vi***. turn sideways; roll
横暴	オウボウ	oppression; tyranny; violence
横領	オウリョウ	usurpation; embezzlement; misappropriation —***v***. usurp; embezzle; misappropriate
訓 横	よこ	width; side; wicked; dishonest
横顔	よこがお	face in profile; profile
横書き	よこがき	horizontal writing
横切る	よこぎる	***vi***. go across; cross
横滑り	よこすべり	sideslip —***v***. slip sideways
横たえる	よこたえる	***vt***. lay
横たわる	よこたわる	***vi***. lie
横町	よこチョウ	alleyway; alley
横綱	よこづな	*yokozuna* (grand champion sumo wrestler)
横取り	よこどり	snatching; stealing —***v***. take away
横腹	よこばら	side; flank
横笛	よこぶえ	flute
横道	よこみち	byroad; sidetrack
横文字	よこモジ	Western language/alphabet
¥ 横這い	よこばい	leveling-out; leveling-off —***vi***. hold level; remain flat; change little

1112

権 ⑮

† 木 木 木 桁 桁 桁 桁 桁 椎 権 権

音 権	ケン	authority
	ゴン	secondary
熟 権威	ケンイ	authority
権威主義	ケンイシュギ	authoritarianism
権限	ケンゲン	authority; power
権謀術数	ケンボウジュッスウ	trickery; scheming; Machiavellianism
権利	ケンリ	right; rights; claim
権力	ケンリョク	power; authority
権化	ゴンゲ	incarnation; embodiment; personification
¥ 権利落ち	ケンリおち	ex rights; ex warrants

1113

槽 ⑮

音	槽	ソウ	trough

1114

標 ⑮

音	標	ヒョウ	mark; sign
熟	標記	ヒョウキ	mark; heading —***vt***. mark
	標語	ヒョウゴ	slogan; motto
	標高	ヒョウコウ	above sea level
	標識	ヒョウシキ	mark; sign; beacon
	標準	ヒョウジュン	standard; criterion; level; average; normal
	標準語	ヒョウジュンゴ	standard language
	標準時	ヒョウジュンジ	standard time
	標的	ヒョウテキ	target
	標榜	ヒョウボウ	advocation; self-profession —***v***. profess (oneself to be); advocate; stand for
	標本	ヒョウホン	sample; specimen

1115

機 ⑯

音	機	キ	mechanism; loom; machine; chance
熟	機運	キウン	fortune; opportunity; chance
	機会	キカイ	opportunity; chance
	機械	キカイ	machine; machinery
	機械化	キカイカ	mechanization —***v***. mechanize; introduce machinery
	機械的	キカイテキ	mechanical
	機関	キカン	engine; organ; agency; institution
	機器	キキ	machinery; tools; apparatus
	機嫌	キゲン	mood; temper; disposition
	機構	キコウ	mechanism; system; organization; structure
	機首	キシュ	nose of a plane
	機種	キシュ	type of airplane
	機上	キジョウ	aboard an aircraft; in flight
	機知	キチ	wit

	機長	キチョウ	captain; chief pilot
	機転	キテン	wit; tact
	機能	キノウ	function; faculty —*v.* function; work; operate
	機敏	キビン	smart; keen; astute
	機密	キミツ	secret; secrecy
訓	機	はた	loom
¥	機関	キカン	organization; institution; agency
	機関投資家	キカントウシカ	institutional investor
	機動性	キドウセイ	mobility

1116

橋 ⑯

音	橋	キョウ	bridge
熟	橋脚	キョウキャク	pier
訓	橋	はし	bridge
	橋渡し	はしわたし	mediation; good offices —*v.* mediate (between); act as intermediary

1117

樹 ⑯

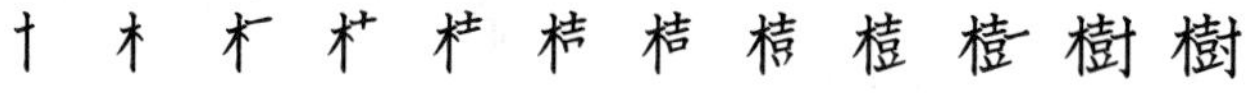

音	樹	ジュ	tree; establish
熟	樹海	ジュカイ	sea of trees; broad expanse of dense woodland
	樹脂	ジュシ	resin
	樹氷	ジュヒョウ	rime on trees; coat of ice of tree branches
	樹木	ジュモク	trees
	樹立	ジュリツ	establishment; founding —*v.* establish; found
	樹齢	ジュレイ	age of a tree

1118

欄 ⑳

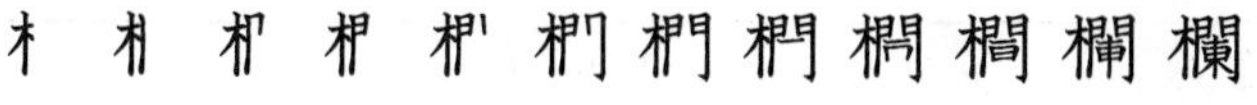

音	欄	ラン	newspaper column; blank; space; railing
熟	欄外	ランガイ	margin
	欄干	ランカン	railing; banister

4 欠 かける／あくび yawning

1119

欠 ④ ノ ㇰ ケ 欠

音	欠	ケツ	lack
熟	欠員	ケツイン	vacancy
	欠陥	ケッカン	defect; flaw; deficiency
	欠勤	ケッキン	absence —***vi***. be absent from work
	欠航	ケッコウ	flight/ship cancellation —***vi***. cancel a sailing/a flight
	欠如	ケツジョ	lack; want; shortage —***vi***. want; lack; be wanting
	欠場	ケツジョウ	failure to make an appearance —***vi***. fail to appear; cancel an appearance
	欠席	ケッセキ	absence —***vi***. be absent
	欠損	ケッソン	loss; deficit —***vi***. lose
	欠点	ケッテン	defect; fault; shortcoming; drawback
	欠番	ケツバン	missing number
	欠乏	ケツボウ	want; shortage —***vi***. want; lack; be wanting; run short of
	欠落	ケツラク	lack —***v***. lack
訓	欠く	かく	***vt***. break; chip; lack; be wanting in; fail to carry out
	欠ける	かける	***vi***. break/chip off; wane; lack; miss; be short
	欠け	かけ	fragment; broken piece
	欠かす	かかす	lack; be deficient

1120

次 ⑥ 丶 冫 冫 ケ 次 次

音	次	ジ	next; order
		シ	order
熟	次回	ジカイ	next time
	次官	ジカン	vice-minister; undersecretary
	次期	ジキ	next period/term/session
	次元	ジゲン	dimension; sphere
	次席	ジセキ	second position/place; deputy of a bureau/department

	次第	シダイ	order; process; reason; circumstances
	次第に	シダイに	gradually
	次点	ジテン	second-best mark
	次男	ジナン	second son
訓	次	つぎ	next; following; adjoining
	次ぐ	つぐ	***vi***. rank next to; follow
	次々	つぎつぎ	one after another; in rapid succession

1121

⑧

音	欧	オウ	Europe
熟	欧亜	オウア	Europe and Asia
	欧州	オウシュウ	Europe
	欧文	オウブン	European writing
¥	欧州共同体	オウシュウキョウドウタイ	the European Community (EC)
	欧米	オウベイ	Europe and America; the West

1122

欲 ⑪

音	欲	ヨク	desire
熟	欲情	ヨクジョウ	passions; desires
	欲得	ヨクトク	selfishness; self-interest
	欲念	ヨクネン	desires; wishes; passions
	欲張り	ヨクばり	greed; covetousness
	欲望	ヨクボウ	desire; craving
	欲目	ヨクめ	favorable view; partiality; favoritism
	欲求	ヨッキュウ	desires; wants —***v***. desire; want
	欲求不満	ヨッキュウフマン	frustration
訓	欲しい	ほしい	want
	欲する	ほっする	***vt***. want

1123

款 ⑫

音	款	カン	sincere

熟	款待	カンタイ	hospitality; warm reception —*v*. be hospitable; give a warm reception
訓	※款	まこと	sincerity; honesty; devotion

1124

欺 ⑫

一 十 廾 廾 甘 甘 其 其 其 欺 欺 欺

音	欺	ギ	deceive
訓	欺く	あざむく	***vt***. deceive; cheat

1125

歌 ⑭

一 Ｔ 可 可 可 哥 哥 哥 哥 歌 歌 歌

音	歌	カ	song; sing; poem
熟	歌曲	カキョク	song
	歌劇	カゲキ	opera
	歌詞	カシ	lyrics
	歌手	カシュ	singer
	歌集	カシュウ	collection of *tanka* poems; collection of odes
	歌人	カジン	*tanka* poet
	歌道	カドウ	the art of *waka* poetry; poetry
	歌風	カフウ	poetical style
	歌舞伎	カブキ	Kabuki (classical Japanese drama)
	歌謡	カヨウ	song; ballad
	歌謡曲	カヨウキョク	Japanese popular song
訓	歌	うた	*tanka* poem; song
	歌う	うたう	***vt***. sing
	歌声	うたごえ	singing voice

1126

歓 ⑮

ノ 乍 乍 乍 乍 乍 乍 隹 隺 雚 歓 歓

音	歓	カン	joy; delight
熟	歓喜	カンキ	delight; joy; gladness —***vi***. rejoice; be glad/delighted
	歓迎	カンゲイ	welcome —*v*. welcome
	歓呼	カンコ	ovation; cheer —***vi***. cheer; applaud
	歓声	カンセイ	shout of joy
	歓送	カンソウ	send-off —*v*. give a send-off

	歓待	カンタイ	warm reception; hospitality; entertainment —*v*. entertain; welcome; be hospitable
	歓談	カンダン	pleasant talk —*vi*. have a pleasant chat
	歓楽街	カンラクガイ	pleasure haunt; amusement quarter
訓	※歓ぶ	よろこぶ	*vi*. rejoice; be pleased

4 止 とめる stop

1127
止 ④ 丨 ⺊ 屮 止

音	止	シ	stop
熟	止血	シケツ	***med***. hemostasis —***v***. stop the bleeding
訓	止まる	とまる	***vi***. stop; come to an end
	止める	とめる	***vt***. stop; put an end to; check

1128
正 ⑤ 一 丅 下 𤴓 正

音	正	ショウ	right; just
		セイ	just; correct; formal
熟	正気	ショウキ	sanity; soberness; consciousness
	正午	ショウゴ	noon; noontime; midday
	正直	ショウジキ	honest; upright; square
	正真正銘	ショウシン ショウメイ	real; true; genuine; authentic
	正体	ショウタイ	true character/form; consciousness
	正札	ショウフダ	price mark/tag
	正味	ショウミ	net; clear; the actual amount
	正面	ショウメン	front; facade
	正課	セイカ	regular subject/curriculum; compulsory subject
	正解	セイカイ	right answer; correct interpretation —***v***. interpret correctly; give a right answer
	正確	セイカク	accuracy; precision; exactness; correctness
	正規	セイキ	regularity; formality; rule
	正義	セイギ	justice; right; righteousness; correct meaning
	正誤	セイゴ	correction
	正攻法	セイコウホウ	frontal attack

	正座	セイザ	*seiza* (formal kneeling position) —***vi***. sit upright; sit square; sit in the correct manner; kneel in the Japanese manner
	正視	セイシ	looking straight at —***v***. look in the face; face up to
	正式	セイシキ	formal; proper; regular; official
	正常	セイジョウ	normal; regular
	正数	セイスウ	***math***. positive number
	正々堂々	セイセイドウドウ	fair and square; open and above board
	正装	セイソウ	full/formal dress —***vi***. dress up; be in full uniform
	正当	セイトウ	just; justifiable; warrantable; right; rightful
	正当防衛	セイトウボウエイ	legal defense; legitimate self-defense
	正統	セイトウ	legitimacy; orthodoxy; direct line; lineal descent
	正道	セイドウ	right track; path of righteousness
	正反対	セイハンタイ	exact opposite/reverse
	正否	セイヒ	right or wrong
	正比例	セイヒレイ	direct proportion —***vi***. be in direct proportion
	正方形	セイホウケイ	square; four-square; quadrate
	正論	セイロン	just argument
訓	正しい	ただしい	right; just; correct; formal
	正す	ただす	***vt***. correct; rectify; put right; redress
	正	まさ	right; exact; true
	正に	まさに	just; exactly; precisely; surely; certainly
	正夢	まさゆめ	dream that comes true; prophetic dream

1129

⑧

音	武	ブ ム	military
熟	武器	ブキ	arms; weapon
	武家	ブケ	samurai
	武芸	ブゲイ	martial arts
	武骨	ブコツ	boorish; uncouth; rude
	武士	ブシ	samurai; warrior
	武士道	ブシドウ	samurai code of chivalry
	武術	ブジュツ	martial arts
	武将	ブショウ	military commander
	武装	ブソウ	arming for war —***vi***. arm oneself; militarize
	武道	ブドウ	martial arts
	武門	ブモン	military family; samurai family

	武勇	ブユウ	valor; bravery
	武力	ブリョク	military force
	武者	ムシャ	warrior; samurai

1130

歩 ⑧

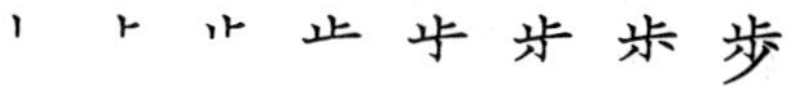

音	歩	ホ	walk; step; pace
		ブ	rate; one percent; *bu* (unit of area, approx. 3.3㎡)
		(フ)	pawn (in shogi)
熟	歩行	ホコウ	walking; ambulatory —***vi***. walk
	歩行者	ホコウシャ	pedestrian
	歩測	ホソク	measurement by paces —***v***. measure off a distance by pacing
	歩調	ホチョウ	pace; step
	歩道	ホドウ	sidewalk; footpath; pavement
	歩道橋	ホドウキョウ	pedestrian overpass
	歩幅	ホはば	length of a pace/step/stride
	歩兵	ホヘイ	infantry; foot soldier
訓	歩く	あるく	***vi***. walk
	歩む	あゆむ	***vi***. walk; progress step-by-step; tread
	歩み	あゆみ	step; pace; walking; progress
	歩み寄る	あゆみよる	***vi***. walk towards; converge on; compromise
¥	歩合	ブあい	rate; percentage; commission
	歩引き	ブびき	discount
	歩割り	ブわり	proportion; commission

1131

歳 ⑬

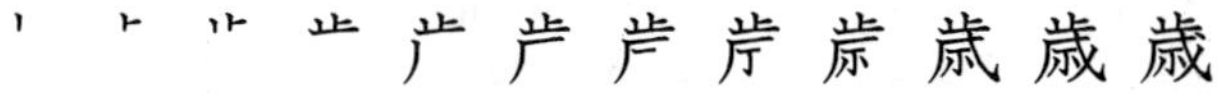

音	歳	サイ	time; age
		(セイ)	year
熟	歳月	サイゲツ	time; years
	歳末	サイマツ	year-end
	お歳暮	おセイボ	year-end gift
¥	歳出	サイシュツ	annual expenditure
	歳入	サイニュウ	revenue; annual income
	歳費	サイヒ	annual expenditure/salary

4 心忄小戈戸手扌支攵文斗斤方日曰月肉月木欠•止•歹殳母毋比毛氏气水氺氵火灬爫父片牛犬犭王礻耂

1132

歴 ⑭

一 厂 厂 厈 厈 厤 厤 厤 厤 歷 歷 歴

音	歴	レキ	continuation; passage of time; successive; clear
熟	歴史	レキシ	history
	歴然	レキゼン	clear; unmistakable
	歴代	レキダイ	successive generations
	歴任	レキニン	successively holding various posts —*v*. hold various post in succession
	歴訪	レキホウ	round of calls/visits —*v*. make a round of calls/visits

4 歹 いちたへん／かばねへん death

1133

死 ⑥

一 ア 万 歹 歹 死

音	死	シ	die; death; inactivity
熟	死因	シイン	cause of death
	死骸	シガイ	corpse; dead body; carcass
	死角	シカク	blind spot; dark corner
	死火山	シカザン	extinct/dead volcano
	死活問題	シカツモンダイ	matter of life and death
	死期	シキ	hour/time of death
	死球	シキュウ	***bas***. dead ball
	死去	シキョ	death —***vi***. die
	死刑	シケイ	death penalty; capital punishment
	死後	シゴ	after one's death; posthumously
	死語	シゴ	dead language
	死罪	シザイ	capital punishment/crime
	死産	シザン	***med***. stillbirth —***vi***. give birth to a stillborn baby
	死屍	シシ	dead body; corpse
	死者	シシャ	dead person; the dead; the deceased
	死守	シシュ	defense to the death/last —*v*. defend to the death/last
	死傷	シショウ	casualities
	死相	シソウ	look like a dead person; shadow of death; face of a dead person

死蔵	シゾウ	shutting/locking up; storing away —*v*. shut/lock up; store away
死体	シタイ	dead body; corpse; cadaver
死地	シチ	jaws of death; death trap; place to die
死闘	シトウ	desperate struggle; fight —*vi*. put up a desperate struggle; fight
死人	シニン	dead person
死病	シビョウ	fatal disease
死別	シベツ	bereavement —*vi*. be bereaved; lose someone close
死亡	シボウ	death —*vi*. die
死亡率	シボウリツ	death rate
死滅	シメツ	extinction —*vi*. become extinct; perish; die out
死力	シリョク	desperate efforts
訓 死ぬ	しぬ	***vi***. die; pass away; be lifeless; be unusable
死なす	しなす	***vt***. let die; kill
死に顔	しにがお	face of a dead person
死に絶える	しにたえる	***vi***. die out; become extinct
死に目	しにめ	the moment a person dies
死に物狂い	しにものぐるい	desperately; madly; very hard

1134

残 ⑩

一 ア 歹 歹 歹 歹 歹 残 残 残

音 残	ザン	remain; survive; cruel; brutal
熟 残骸	ザンガイ	wreck; dead body; remains; ruins
残額	ザンガク	account balance
残虐	ザンギャク	cruelty; atrocity
残業	ザンギョウ	overtime work —*vi*. work overtime
残酷	ザンコク	cruelty; brutality
残暑	ザンショ	lingering summer heat
残雪	ザンセツ	remaining/unmelted snow
残像	ザンゾウ	afterimage; lingering impression
残存	ザンゾン	survival —*vi*. survive; remain; be extant
残忍	ザンニン	brutality; cruelty
残念	ザンネン	regrettable; disappointing; vexing; pity
残飯	ザンパン	leftover rice; leftover food; leftovers
残部	ザンブ	remainder; the rest
残余	ザンヨ	the rest; residue
残留	ザンリュウ	remaining; stay behind —*vi*. remain; stay behind

心 忄 小 戈 戸 手 扌 支 攵 文 斗 斤 方 日 曰 月 肉 月 木 欠 止 • 歹 殳 母 毋 比 毛 氏 气 水 氺 氵 火 灬 爫 父 片 牛 犬 犭 王 礻 耂

訓	残る	のこる	*vi*. be left; remain; stay; remain; survive
	残す	のこす	*vt*. leave; save
	残り	のこり	remainder; the rest
	残り物	のこりもの	leftovers
¥	残金	ザンキン	balance; remainder
	残高	ザンだか	balance
	残高表	ザンだかヒョウ	balance sheet
	残品	ザンピン	remaining stock
	残余額	ザンヨガク	balance

1135

殊 ⑩

一 ア 歹 歹 歹 歺 歼 歽 殊 殊

音	殊	シュ	unusually
熟	殊勲	シュクン	distinguished services
	殊勝	シュショウ	praiseworthy; admirable; commendable
訓	殊	こと	in particular; especially; moreover
	殊更	ことさら	especially; on purpose; deliberately

1136

殉 ⑩

一 ア 歹 歹 歹 歹 殉 殉 殉 殉

音	殉	ジュン	follow one's lord to the grave
熟	殉教	ジュンキョウ	martyrdom —*vi*. become a martyr
	殉死	ジュンシ	following one's lord to the grave —*vi*. follow one's lord to the grave
	殉職	ジュンショク	dying at one's post of duty —*vi*. die at one's post of duty

1137

殖 ⑫

一 ア 歹 歹 歹 歹 歼 殖 殖 殖 殖 殖

音	殖	ショク	increase
熟	殖財	ショクザイ	moneymaking
	殖産	ショクサン	promotion of industry
訓	殖える	ふえる	*vi*. increase; multiply
	殖やす	ふやす	*vt*. increase; add to; enlarge

4 殳 るまた windy again

1138

殴 ⑧

音	殴	**オウ**	beating; battering
熟	殴殺	**オウサツ**	beating to death —***v***. beat to death
	殴打	**オウダ**	assault; blow; thrashing —***v***. beat; strike; hit; batter
訓	殴る	**なぐる**	***vt***. beat; hit; knock
	殴り合い	**なぐりあい**	fight
	殴り込む	**なぐりこむ**	***vt***. attack; raid

1139

段 ⑨

音	段	**ダン**	steps; stairs; column; grade; degree; extent
熟	段階	**ダンカイ**	steps; grade; rank
	段丘	**ダンキュウ**	natural terrace/bench
	段々	**ダンダン**	gradually; increasingly; growingly; more and more
	段々畑	**ダンダンばたけ**	terraced farm/fields; field in terraces
	段取り	**ダンどり**	program; plan; arrangements
	段落	**ダンラク**	end of a paragraph; conclusion; ending
¥	段階的移行	**ダンカイテキイコウ**	step-by-step transition; gradual transition
	段階的引下げ	**ダンカイテキひきさげ**	step-by-step reduction; gradual reduction; reduction by degrees

1140

殺 ⑩

音	殺	**サツ**	kill; get rid of
		(サイ)	lessen
		(セツ)	
熟	殺意	**サツイ**	murderous intent; urge to kill
	殺気	**サッキ**	thirst for blood; stormy atmosphere

	殺菌	サッキン	sterilization; pasteurization —*v.* sterilize; pasteurize
	殺傷	サッショウ	killing and wounding; blood shedding —*v.* kill and wound; shed blood
	殺人	サツジン	murder; manslaughter; homicide
	殺人罪	サツジンザイ	murder; homicide
	殺人的	サツジンテキ	deadly
	殺人犯人	サツジンハンニン	murderer
	殺虫剤	サッチュウザイ	insecticide; pesticide
	殺到	サットウ	rush; flood —***vi***. rush in; throng; flood; pour into
	殺伐	サツバツ	bloody; savage; fierce; brutal
	殺風景	サップウケイ	desolate; bleak; dreary; drab; prosaic; matter-of-fact; unimaginative
	殺生	セッショウ	slaughter; cruelty —*v.* kill; take life
訓	殺す	ころす	***vt***. kill; murder; surpress; restrain
	殺し文句	ころしモンク	clincher; killing expression

1141

殻 ⑪

一 十 士 壱 声 壳 壳 壳 壳 殻 殻

音	殻	カク	shell
訓	殻	から	shell; slough; husk; corpse

1142

殿 ⑬

㇕ コ 尸 尸 尸 屏 屏 屏 展 殿 殿 殿

音	殿	デン テン	hall; palace
熟	殿下	デンカ	Your (Imperial) Highness; His/Her (Imperial) Highness
	殿堂	デンドウ	palace; hall; shrine
訓	殿	との	lord; mansion; palace
	殿	どの	Mr./Ms. (used in official documents, etc.)
	殿方	とのがた	gentlemen
	殿御	とのゴ	man; gentleman; husband
	殿様	とのさま	lord; prince; feudal lord

1143

⑤

音	母	ボ	mother
熟	母音	ボイン	vowel
	母系	ボケイ	maternal line (of a family)
	母系制度	ボケイセイド	matriarchal system
	母校	ボコウ	*alma mater*
	母国	ボコク	mother/native country
	母国語	ボコクゴ	mother/native tongue
	母子	ボシ	mother
	母性	ボセイ	motherhood; maternity
	母船	ボセン	mother ship
	母胎	ボタイ	***med***. womb; uterus
	母体	ボタイ	mother's body; parent organization
	母堂	ボドウ	***hon***. mother
	母乳	ボニュウ	mother's milk
訓	母	はは	one's mother
	母上	ははうえ	***hon***. mother
	母親	ははおや	mother
	母君	ははぎみ	***hon***. mother
	母屋(母家)	おもや	main building/house
	※お母さん	おかあさん	mom ***hon***. mother

1144

毎 ⑥

音	毎	マイ	every; each
熟	毎回	マイカイ	every time
	毎号	マイゴウ	every issue
	毎時	マイジ	per hour; every hour
	毎週	マイシュウ	every week; weekly
	毎食	マイショク	each meal; at mealtime
	毎月	マイつき	every month; monthly
	毎度	マイド	each time; frequently; always
	毎日	マイニチ	every day; daily

心 忄 小 戈 戸 手 扌 支 攵 文 斗 斤 方 日 曰 月 肉 月 木 欠 止 歹 殳 母 • 毋 • 比 毛 氏 气 水 氺 氵 火 灬 爫 父 片 牛 犬 犭 王 礻 耂

毎年	マイネン （マイとし）	every year; annually
毎秒	マイビョウ	every second

1145

毒 ⑧

一 十 丰 主 圭 责 毒 毒

音	毒	ドク	poison; toxicant; virus; germ; harm
熟	毒する	ドクする	***vt***. poison; corrupt; contaminate
	毒気	ドクケ	poisonous character; virulence; malice; spite
	毒殺	ドクサツ	death by poisoning —***v***. poison; kill by poison
	毒舌	ドクゼツ	spiteful/malicious tongue
	毒素	ドクソ	toxin; poisonous matter
	毒々しい	ドクドクしい	poisonous-looking
	毒物	ドクブツ	poisonous substance; poison; toxicant
	毒味(毒見)	ドクミ（ドクみ）	tasting for poison
	毒虫	ドクむし	poisonous insect
	毒矢	ドクや	poison arrow/dart
	毒薬	ドクヤク	poisonous drug; poison

4 比 くらべる／ならびひ comparing

1146

比 ④

一 ヒ 比 比

音	比	ヒ	compare; ratio; the Philippines
熟	比する	ヒする	***vt***. compare
	比較	ヒカク	comparison —***v***. compare
	比較的	ヒカクテキ	comparatively; relatively
	比肩	ヒケン	comparable —***vi***. be comparable to; rank with
	比重	ヒジュウ	***phy***. specific gravity
	比熱	ヒネツ	***phy***. specific heat
	比喩	ヒユ	simile; metaphor; allegory
	比率	ヒリツ	percentage; rate; ratio
	比類	ヒルイ	parallel; equal
	比例	ヒレイ	proportion; ratio —***vi***. be proportioned/proportionate
訓	比べる	くらべる	***vt***. compare

4 毛 け hair; fur

1147

毛 ④ 丿 二 三 毛

音	毛	モウ	hair; tiny amount; 1/10,000 yen
熟	毛細血管	モウサイケッカン	capillary
	毛頭ない	モウトウない	by no means; not at all
	毛髪	モウハツ	hair (on the head)
	毛布	モウフ	blanket
訓	毛	け	hair; fur; wool
	毛孔	けあな	pores
	毛糸	けいと	woolen yarn; worsted
	毛色	けいろ	color of hair; nature; type; kind
	毛織物	けおりもの	woolen goods
	毛皮	けがわ	fur; skin; pelt
	毛嫌い	けぎらい	prejudice; dislike; antipathy —*v.* be prejudiced; dislike; have an antipathy
	毛並み	けなみ	lie of the hair ***fig.*** social standing/status of a family; birth; stock
	毛虫	けむし	caterpillar

4 氏 うじ clan

1148

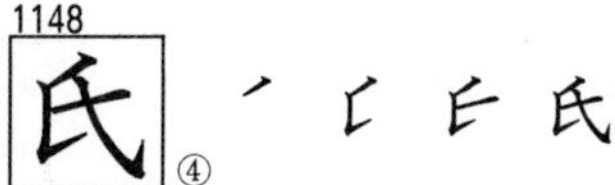

音	氏	シ	clan; family; Mr.
熟	氏族	シゾク	family; clan
	氏族制度	シゾクセイド	family system
	氏名	シメイ	one's full name
訓	氏	うじ	family name; birth; lineage
	氏神	うじがみ	tutelary deity; patron god
	氏子	うじこ	local residents under the protection of the same guardian deity

1149

民 ⑤

一 コ 尸 戸 民

音	民	ミン	the people
熟	民家	ミンカ	private house
	民間	ミンカン	private (not public)
	民芸	ミンゲイ	folk art/craft
	民権	ミンケン	civil rights
	民事	ミンジ	civil affairs; civil
	民主	ミンシュ	democratic
	民主主義	ミンシュシュギ	democracy
	民主的	ミンシュテキ	democratic
	民衆	ミンシュウ	the people; populace; the masses
	民宿	ミンシュク	lodging house
	民心	ミンシン	popular sentiment; the people's feelings
	民生委員	ミンセイイイン	district welfare officer
	民俗	ミンゾク	folk customs; ethnic
	民俗学	ミンゾクガク	folklore
	民族	ミンゾク	race; a people
	民兵	ミンペイ	militia
	民法	ミンポウ	the civil law/code
	民有	ミンユウ	privately owned
	民謡	ミンヨウ	folk song
	民力	ミンリョク	national strength
	民話	ミンワ	folk tale; folklore
訓	民	たみ	the people
	民草	たみぐさ	the people; the populace
¥	民営	ミンエイ	private management
	民営化	ミンエイカ	privatization —*v.* privatize
	民活 (民間活力)	ミンカツ (ミンカンカツリョク)	vitality of private industry
	民間	ミンカン	private; nongovernmental
	民間外資	ミンカンガイシ	private foreign capital
	民間企業	ミンカンキギョウ	private enterprise
	民間消費	ミンカンショウヒ	private consumption
	民社党	ミンシャトウ	the Japan Democratic Social Party (DSP)
	民主党	ミンシュトウ	(US) Democratic Party

4 气 きがまえ steam

1150

気 ⑥

丿 𠂉 ⺈ 气 気 気

音	気	キ	air; weather; feeling
		ケ	sign; appearance
熟	気圧	キアツ	atmospheric pressure
	気圧配置	キアツハイチ	distribution of atmospheric pressure
	気運	キウン	tendency
	気鋭	キエイ	spiritedness
	気後れ	キおくれ	diffidence; self-distrust; timidity —***vi***. be timid/diffident
	気温	キオン	temperature
	気化	キカ	evaporation; vaporization —***vi***. evaporate; vaporize
	気概	キガイ	mettle; backbone; pluck
	気兼ね	キがね	constraint; scruples —***vi***. feel constraint; have scruples
	気構え	キがまえ	expectation; preparedness
	気軽	キがる	lighthearted; cheerful
	気管	キカン	***med***. trachea; windpipe
	気管支	キカンシ	***med***. bronchial tubes
	気球	キキュウ	balloon
	気苦労	キグロウ	worries; care; anxiety
	気候	キコウ	climate
	気質	キシツ	temperament; disposition
	気性	キショウ	temper; nature; disposition
	気象	キショウ	atmospheric phenomena; meteorology
	気色	キショク	countenance; feeling
	気勢	キセイ	spirit; ardor
	気絶	キゼツ	fainting —***vi***. faint; pass out; black out
	気体	キタイ	gas; vapor
	気違い	キちがい	***derog***. madness; insanity; mania; madman; fan; crazy
	気疲れ	キづかれ	mental fatigue; worry; boredom —***vi***. be mentally tired; worry; be bored
	気付	キつけ	encouragement; resurrection
	気の毒	キのドク	pitiable; regrettable; feeling sorry for
	気乗り	キのり	interest; inclination —***vi***. be interested in; feel inclined

	気迫	キハク	spirit; vigor
	気晴らし	キばらし	diversion; recreation
	気品	キヒン	nobility; dignity; grace
	気風	キフウ	character; disposition; temper
	気分	キブン	feeling; mood; atmosphere
	気前	キまえ	generosity; liberality
	気味	キミ	feeling; sensation; touch of; tinge
	気短か	キみじか	short-tempered; rash; impatient
	気持ち	キもち	feeling; sensation; mood
	気休め	キやすめ	relieving one's conscience
	気楽	キラク	feeling at ease; carefree; easygoing
	気流	キリュウ	air current/steam
	気力	キリョク	spirit; guts; vitality
	気色	ケシキ	appearance; countenance
	気配	ケハイ	sign; indication
¥	気配	キハイ	quotes; quotation; tone of the market

4 水 みず water

氺 (p.515) 氵 (p.516)

1151

水 ④

音	水	スイ	water; river; Wednesday
熟	水圧	スイアツ	water/hydraulic pressure
	水位	スイイ	water level
	水域	スイイキ	water area
	水運	スイウン	water transport; transportation by water
	水泳	スイエイ	swimming; bathing —***vi***. swim; bathe; have a swim
	水煙	スイエン	(clouds) of spray
	水温	スイオン	water temperature
	水化	スイカ	hydration —***v***. hydrate
	水化物	スイカブツ	hydrate
	水害	スイガイ	flood disaster/damage
	水銀	スイギン	***chem***. mercury; quicksilver
	水源	スイゲン	riverhead; fountain head; source of water supply; reservoir
	水郷	スイゴウ	riverside/lakeside district
	水彩画	スイサイガ	watercolor (painting)

水産	スイサン	fishing
水死	スイシ	drowning
水質	スイシツ	water quality
水車	スイシャ	water mill/wheel
水準	スイジュン	level; standard; water level
水準器	スイジュンキ	level
水晶	スイショウ	crystal; crystallized quartz
水蒸気	スイジョウキ	steam; water vapor
水深	スイシン	depth of water
水星	スイセイ	the planet Mercury
水勢	スイセイ	force of water; current
水生動物	スイセイドウブツ	aquatic animal
水洗	スイセン	flushing; washing; rinsing
水素	スイソ	***chem***. hydrogen
水族館	スイゾクカン	aquarium
水中	スイチュウ	in the water; underwater
水滴	スイテキ	water drop; drop of water
水田	スイデン	rice paddy
水筒	スイトウ	canteen; flask; water bottle
水道	スイドウ	water works/supply/way
水難	スイナン	drowning; disaster at sea; shipwreck
水爆	スイバク	hydrogen/fusion bomb
水盤	スイバン	basin
水分	スイブン	water; moisture; humidity; juice; sap
水兵	スイヘイ	seaman; sailor
水平	スイヘイ	horizontally
水平線	スイヘイセン	horizon; horizontal line
水泡	スイホウ	bubble; foam
水防	スイボウ	flood control/prevention
水墨画	スイボクガ	India ink painting; black-and-white drawing
水面	スイメン	water surface
水門	スイモン	floodgate; sluice gate
水薬	スイヤク	liquid medicine
水溶液	スイヨウエキ	***chem***. solution
水曜日	スイヨウび	Wednesday
水浴	スイヨク	bathing —***vi***. bathe
水利	スイリ	water facility/supply; irrigation; navigability
水量	スイリョウ	water volume; quantity of water
水量計	スイリョウケイ	water gauge
水力	スイリョク	water/hydraulic power
水力学	スイリョクガク	hydraulics; hydrodynamics
水路	スイロ	waterway; water course/conduit

訓	水	みず	water; flood; innundation
	水足	みずあし	speed of flowing water
	水鏡	みずかがみ	reflective surface of water
	水瓶座	みずがめザ	Aquarius, the water carrier
	水着	みずぎ	swimsuit; bathing costume
	水煙	みずけむり	(clouds) of spray
	水先案内	みずさきアンナイ	pilot; pilotage; piloting
	水商売	みずショウバイ	night-time entertainment business such as bars, clubs

1152

永 ⑤ 丶 亅 刁 永 永

音	永	エイ	long; eternal; forever
熟	永遠	エイエン	eternity; perpetuity; infinity; permanence; immortality
	永久	エイキュウ	permanence; eternity; perpetuity
	永久歯	エイキュウシ	permanent/second teeth
	永住	エイジュウ	domiciliation; permanent residence —***vi***. settle down; take up permanent residence
	永世中立	エイセイチュウリツ	permanent neutrality
	永続	エイゾク	permanence; perpetuity; perpetuation —***vi***. last long; endure; remain; perpetuate
	永年	エイネン	many years; eternity; a long time
	永眠	エイミン	passing away; eternal sleep; death —***vi***. pass away; die
訓	永い	ながい	long; lengthy

1153

⑤ 亅 亅 刁 氵 氷

音	氷	ヒョウ (ヒ)	ice
熟	氷河	ヒョウガ	glacier
	氷河時代	ヒョウガジダイ	ice age
	氷海	ヒョウカイ	frozen sea
	氷塊	ヒョウカイ	block of ice; ice floe
	氷解	ヒョウカイ	cleared away; dispelled —***vi***. be cleared (of suspision, etc.); be dispelled
	氷結	ヒョウケツ	frozen over; icebound —***vi***. freeze
	氷原	ヒョウゲン	ice field

氷山　ヒョウザン　iceberg
氷室　ヒョウシツ　icehouse; ice room
氷雪　ヒョウセツ　ice and snow
氷柱　ヒョウチュウ　icicle; ice pillar placed in a room in summer
氷点　ヒョウテン　***chem***. freezing point

訓 氷　こおり　ice
※氷る　こおる　***vi***. freeze (up)

1154
泉 ⑨
丶 ㇒ 冖 白 白 白 宇 臬 泉 泉

音 泉　セン　spring

熟 泉下　センカ　underworld
泉水　センスイ　ornamental pond; pond of spring water

訓 泉　いずみ　spring

---

5 氺 したみず water at bottom

1155
求 ⑦
一 寸 寸 才 求 求 求

音 求　キュウ　request; search; want; desire; demand

熟 求刑　キュウケイ　sentence desired by the prosecution
求婚　キュウコン　marriage proposal; courtship; wooing —***vi***. propose marriage (to a girl)
求心力　キュウシンリョク　centripetal force

訓 求める　もとめる　***vt***. want; wish for; desire; request; demand; pursue

¥ 求償　キュウショウ　barter
求償貿易　キュウショウボウエキ　barter trade
求職　キュウショク　job hunting; looking for a job —***vi***. hunt/look for a job
求職者　キュウショクシャ　job appliant; people seeking work
求人　キュウジン　situation vacant; job offer
求人市場　キュウジンシジョウ　job market

1156

泰 ⑩

一 二 三 丰 夫 夫 夫 泰 泰 泰

音	泰	タイ	tranquil; peace; large; very
熟	泰然	タイゼン	composed; collected; calm; cool
	泰平	タイヘイ	peace; tranquillity; quiet

---

3 氵 さんずい water at left

1157

汁 ⑤

丶 冫 氵 汁 汁

音	汁	ジュウ	juice
訓	汁	しる	soup; sap
	汁粉	しるこ	*shiruko* (sweet red-bean soup with rice cake)

1158

汚 ⑥

丶 冫 氵 汀 汚 汚

音	汚	オ	dirty; stain; defile; pollute; wrong; not right
熟	汚辱	オジョク	disgrace; dishonor; slander —***v***. disgrace; dishonor
	汚水	オスイ	dirty/foul water; sewage
	汚染	オセン	pollution; contamination —***v***. pollute; contaminate
	汚損	オソン	stain; corruption —***v***. stain; soil; spoil
	汚濁	オダク	corruption; decadence —***vi***. be corrupt/decadent
	汚点	オテン	stain; dirty spot; blot
	汚物	オブツ	filth; dirt; muck; impurities; feces
	汚名	オメイ	disgrace; bad name; slur
訓	汚い	きたない	dirty; mean; base
	汚す	けがす	***vt***. stain; soil; pollute; contaminate; disgrace
	汚らわしい	けがらわしい	dirty; odious; foul; nasty; disgusting
	汚れる	けがれる	***vi***. get dirty; become soiled; be polluted/contaminated
	汚す	よごす	***vt***. soil; stain; defile; foul; slur
	汚れ	よごれ	dirt; soil; spot; stain

	汚れる	よごれる	***vi***. become dirty; be stained/blemished
¥	汚職	オショク	official corruption; bribery

1159

汗 ⑥

音	汗	**カン**	sweat
熟	汗腺	**カンセン**	***med***. sweat glands
訓	汗	**あせ**	sweat

1160

江 ⑥

音	江	**コウ**	inlet; large river; creek
熟	江河	**コウガ**	Yangtze and Yellow rivers; big rivers
訓	江	**え**	inlet
	江戸	**えど**	Edo (the former name of Tokyo)
	江戸時代	**えどジダイ**	***hist***. Edo period (1603-1867)

1161

池 ⑥

音	池	**チ**	pond; lake
熟	池畔	**チハン**	pondside
訓	池	**いけ**	pond; lake

1162

汽 ⑦

音	汽	**キ**	steam; vapor
熟	汽車	**キシャ**	(steam) train
	汽船	**キセン**	steam ship
	汽笛	**キテキ**	steam whistle

1163

決 ⑦ 丶 冫 氵 氵 氵 沪 決

音	決	ケツ	fix; settle; decide, collapse
熟	決する	ケッする	fix; settle; decide
	決壊	ケッカイ	collapse —***v***. collapse; break down
	決起	ケッキ	going into action —***vi***. rise and go into action
	決行	ケッコウ	execution —***v***. carry out; go ahead
	決裁	ケッサイ	sanction; approval —***v***. sanction; approve
	決死	ケッシ	desperate; ready to die
	決勝	ケッショウ	finals (of a competition)
	決心	ケッシン	determination; resolution —***vi***. determine; be determined; make up one's mind; resolve
	決戦	ケッセン	decisive battle
	決然	ケツゼン	determinedly; decisively; resolutely
	決断	ケツダン	decision; determination —***vi***. decide; make a decision
	決着	ケッチャク	conclusion; the end; settlement —***vi***. conclude; end; settle
	決定	ケッテイ	decision; conclusion; determination —***v***. decide; determine; set; fix
	決闘	ケットウ	duel —***vi***. fight a duel
	決裂	ケツレツ	break down; rupture —***vi***. breakdown; come to a rupture
訓	決まる	きまる	***vi***. be decided/settled
	決める	きめる	***vt***. decide; fix; settle; determine
Y	決意	ケツイ	resolution; determination —***vi***. determine; make up one's mind
	決議	ケツギ	resolution; vote; decision —***v***. pass a resolution; resolve
	決済	ケッサイ	settlement; payment —***v***. settle an account; pay up
	決算	ケッサン	settlement of accounts —***v***. settle/balance an account
	決算期	ケッサンキ	settlement term; accounting period

1164

⑦ 丶 冫 氵 氵 氵 沪 沢

音	沢	タク	swamp; marsh; bog
熟	沢庵	タクアン	*takuan* (type of pickled radish)
	沢山	タクサン	many; much; a lot of

訓 沢　さわ　swamp; marsh; bog; pond

1165
沖 ⑦
丶 冫 氵 氵 汩 汩 沖

音 沖　チュウ　offing; open sea; rise to heaven
熟 沖天　チュウテン　ascendant; rising skyward
訓 沖　おき　offing; open sea

1166
沈 ⑦
丶 冫 氵 氵 氵 沙 沈

音 沈　チン　sink
熟 沈下　チンカ　subsidence; sinking; settlement —*vi*. subside; sink; settle
沈思　チンシ　meditation; contemplation; deep thought —*vi*. meditate; contemplate
沈静　チンセイ　stillness; quietness; tranquillity —*vi*. be still/quiet/tranquil
沈滞　チンタイ　dullness; slackness; stagnation; inactivity —*vi*. stagnate; become inactive
沈着　チンチャク　composure; self-possession; presence of mind
沈痛　チンツウ　grave; serious; pathetic; sad
沈澱　チンデン　precipitation; sedimentation; subsidence —*vi*. settle; be precipitated/deposited
沈没　チンボツ　sinking; submersion; foundering —*vi*. sink; go down; be submerged; founder
沈黙　チンモク　silence; taciturnity; reticence —*vi*. become/fall silent
訓 沈む　しずむ　*vi*. sink; be submerged; go down; mope; be downcast
沈める　しずめる　*vt*. sink; send to the bottom; submerge

1167
没 ⑦
丶 冫 氵 氵 氵 沙 没

音 没　ボツ　sink; lose; die
熟 没する　ボッする　*v*. sink; go down; hide; disappear; die
没却　ボッキャク　ignoring; forgetting —*v*. ignore; forget
没後　ボツゴ　after one's death; posthumous
没収　ボッシュウ　confiscation —*v*. confiscate

没頭	ボットウ	absorption; engrossment —*vi*. be absorbed/engrossed
没入	ボツニュウ	absorption; immersion —*vi*. be absorbed/immersed in
没年	ボツネン	one's age at death; year of death
没落	ボツラク	downfall; ruin; bankruptcy —*vi*. be ruined/bankrupt

1168

泳 ⑧

丶 冫 氵 氵 氵 汀 汸 泳 泳

音	泳	エイ	swimming
熟	泳者	エイシャ	swimmer
訓	泳ぎ	およぎ	swimming; swim
	泳ぐ	およぐ	*vi*. swim

1169

沿 ⑧

丶 冫 氵 氵 氵 沁 沿 沿

音	沿	エン	lie along; go along; run parallel
熟	沿海	エンカイ	coast
	沿革	エンカク	history; chronicle; development; changes
	沿岸	エンガン	coast; shore
	沿線	エンセン	along a railroad
	沿道	エンドウ	roadside; route; course
訓	沿う	そう	*vi*. go/lie along; run parallel

1170

河 ⑧

丶 冫 氵 氵 汀 沂 沪 河

音	河	カ	river; Yellow River
熟	河岸	カガン	riverbank
	河口	カコウ	mouth of a river; river mouth
	河川	カセン	rivers
	河川敷	カセンしき	riverside
訓	河	かわ	river
	河原	かわら	dry riverbed; river beach
	※河岸	かし（かわぎし）	riverside

1171

泣 ⑧

音	泣	キュウ	crying; weeping
熟	泣訴	キュウソ	tearful supplication/appeal —*v*. implore/supplicate/appeal with tears in one's eyes
訓	泣く	なく	***vi***. cry; weep
	泣き声	なきごえ	tearful voice; whine
	泣き言	なきごと	complaint; grieviance; whimper
	泣き上戸	なきジョウゴ	sentimental drinker; crying drunk
	泣きっ面	なきっつら	tearstained face
	泣き虫	なきむし	crybaby

1172

況 ⑧

音	況	キョウ	condition; state of things

1173

沼 ⑧

音	沼	ショウ	marsh
熟	沼沢	ショウタク	marsh
訓	沼	ぬま	marsh; swamp; bog
	沼地	ぬまチ	marshland; swampland

1174

治 ⑧

音	治	チ ジ	govern; rule; cure; heal; remedy; recover
熟	治安	チアン	public peace and order
	治外法権	チガイホウケン	extraterritoriality; extraterritorial rights
	治水	チスイ	flood control; river improvement —***vi***. carry out flood control work
	治癒	チユ	healing; curing; recovery —***vi***. cure; heal; recover; be cured

	治療	チリョウ	medical treatment; remedy —*v*. treat; doctor; cure; remedy
訓	治まる	おさまる	***vi***. be at peace; be tranquil; calm down
	治める	おさめる	***vt***. rule; govern; administer; manage; put down; suppress
	治す	なおす	***vt***. mend; repair; put in order; reform; correct; cure; heal; remedy
	治る	なおる	***vi***. get well/better; recover; be cured

1175

注 ⑧

音	注	チュウ	annotation; notes; comments; flow into; pour
熟	注意	チュウイ	attention; observation; note; notice; care; caution —***vi***. pay attention; give heed; observe; take note; be cautious
	注意人物	チュウイジンブツ	dangerous person; suspicious character
	注意力	チュウイリョク	attentiveness
	注記	チュウキ	note; entry —*v*. note; make entries; write down
	注視	チュウシ	gaze; close observation; scrutiny —*v*. watch carefully; contemplate; scrutinize
	注射	チュウシャ	injection; shot; inoculation —*v*. inject; syringe; inoculate
	注射器	チュウシャキ	injector; syringe
	注釈	チュウシャク	commentary; notes; comments —*v*. annotate; comment; expound
	注水	チュウスイ	watering; pouring water —***vi***. pour water; water
	注入	チュウニュウ	injection; infusion; infiltration —*v*. pour into; inject; impregnate; infuse; implant
	注目	チュウモク	attention; observation; notice; remark —*v*. pay attention; observe; remark; notice
	注文	チュウモン	order; commission; request; demand; wish; desire —*v*. order; request; demand; desire; wish
	注油	チュウユ	oiling; lubrication —*v*. oil; lubricate
訓	注ぐ	そそぐ	*v*. pour into; irrigate; flow into; drain

1176

⑧

音	泥	デイ	mud
熟	泥水	デイスイ	muddy water
	泥酔	デイスイ	extreme drunkeness —***vi***. get dead drunk

	泥炭	デイタン	peat; turf
訓	泥	どろ	mud; mire; dirt
	泥仕合	どろジあい	mud slinging
	泥縄	どろなわ	thief; robber
	泥沼	どろぬま	bog; swamp
	泥棒	どろボウ	thief; crook; robber —*v*. steal; rob

1177
波 ⑧
丶 冫 氵 氵 汇 沪 波 波

音	波	ハ	wave
熟	波及	ハキュウ	influence —*vi*. extend/spread to; influence; affect
	波状	ハジョウ	wave; undulation
	波長	ハチョウ	wavelength
	波動	ハドウ	undulation; fluctuation —*vi*. undulate; fluctuate; wave
	波紋	ハモン	ripple; water ring
	波乱	ハラン	trouble; disturbance; commotion; storm
	波浪	ハロウ	waves; billow; surge
	※波止場	ハとば	pier; wharf; quay; jetty
訓	波	なみ	wave; sea; billow; surge
	波風	なみかぜ	wind and waves; trouble; discord; quarrel
	波立つ	なみだつ	*vi*. be choppy; run high; billow

1178
泊 ⑧
丶 冫 氵 氵 氵 泊 泊 泊

音	泊	ハク	berth
訓	泊まる	とまる	*vi*. stop; lodge; stay; lie at anchor
	泊める	とめる	*vt*. lodge; shelter; accommodate

1179
泌 ⑧
丶 冫 氵 氵 沙 泌 泌 泌

音	泌	ヒ	secrete; flow
		ヒツ	secrete; flow
熟	泌尿器	ヒニョウキ	*med*. urinary organs
	泌尿器科	ヒニョウキカ	*med*. urology department (in a hospital)

1180

沸 ⑧

丶 冫 氵 氵⁻ 氵ᄀ 沪 沸 沸

音	沸	フツ	boil
熟	沸点	フッテン	boiling point
	沸騰	フットウ	boiling; excitement; agitation —***vi***. boil up; be excited/agitated
訓	沸かす	わかす	***vt***. boil; heat up
	沸く	わく	***vi***. boil; seethe
	沸き返る	わきかえる	***vi***. boil hard; seethe; be in an uproar; be furious
	沸き立つ	わきたつ	***vi***. come to a boil; seethe; be in an uproar

1181

法 ⑧

丶 冫 氵 氵⁻ 汁 汢 法 法

音	法	ホウ (ホ) (ハ)	law; method; religion
熟	法度	ハット	ban; law; prohibition
	法衣	ホウイ	***Bud***. vestments; priestly robes
	法医学	ホウイガク	forensic medicine
	法王	ホウオウ	Pope
	法皇	ホウオウ	ex-emperor who has become a monk
	法貨	ホウカ	legal tender
	法外	ホウガイ	unreasonable; preposterous
	法学	ホウガク	law; jurisprudence
	法官	ホウカン	judicial officer; judge
	法規	ホウキ	laws and regulations
	法権	ホウケン	legal right
	法号	ホウゴウ	(priest's or posthumous) Buddhist name
	法師	ホウシ	***Bud***. priest
	法事	ホウジ	***Bud***. memorial service
	法式	ホウシキ	regulation; rite; rule
	法制	ホウセイ	legislation; laws
	法曹	ホウソウ	legal profession
	法則	ホウソク	law; rule
	法治国	ホウチコク	constitutional state
	法廷	ホウテイ	(law) court; courtroom
	法定	ホウテイ	legal; prescribed by law

	法典	**ホウテン**	law code
	法名	**ホウミョウ**	(priest's or posthumous) Buddhist name
	法要	**ホウヨウ**	***Bud***. memorial service
	法力	**ホウリキ**	merits/powers of Buddhism
	法律	**ホウリツ**	law
	法律上	**ホウリツジョウ**	legally
	法令	**ホウレイ**	laws and (cabinet or ministerial) orders
	法華経	**ホケキョウ**	Lotus Sutra
¥	法案	**ホウアン**	(legislative) bill/measure
	法人	**ホウジン**	corporation; juridical person; legal entity
	法人株主	**ホウジンかぶぬし**	institutional stockholder
	法人税	**ホウジンゼイ**	corporate (income) tax
	法定準備金	**ホウテイジュンビキン**	legal reserve
	法務省	**ホウムショウ**	Ministry of Justice

1182

泡 ⑧

丶 冫 氵 氵 汋 泃 泃 泡

音	泡	**ホウ**	foam; bubble; froth; suds
訓	泡	**あわ**	foam; bubble; froth; suds
	泡立つ	**あわだつ**	***vi***. froth; lather
	泡立てる	**あわだてる**	***vt***. beat; whip

1183

油 ⑧

丶 冫 氵 氵 汩 汩 油 油

音	油	**ユ**	oil
熟	油煙	**ユエン**	soot
	油脂	**ユシ**	oils and fats; fats
	油井	**ユセイ**	oil well
	油断	**ユダン**	carelessness; inattentiveness
	油田	**ユデン**	oil field
訓	油	**あぶら**	oil
	油絵	**あぶらエ**	oil painting
	油ぎる	**あぶらぎる**	***vi***. be oily/fatty; glisten with oil
	油っこい	**あぶらっこい**	oily; fatty

1184

海 ⑨

音	海	カイ	sea
熟	海王星	カイオウセイ	the planet Neptune
	海外	カイガイ	abroad; overseas; foreign countries
	海岸	カイガン	seaside
	海峡	カイキョウ	strait; channel
	海軍	カイグン	the navy
	海国	カイコク	maritime country/power
	海産物	カイサンブツ	marine products
	海図	カイズ	nautical chart
	海水	カイスイ	sea water
	海水浴	カイスイヨク	swimming at the beach
	海藻	カイソウ	seaweed
	海賊	カイゾク	pirate
	海抜	カイバツ	above sea level
	海浜	カイヒン	beach; seaside
	海風	カイフウ	sea wind/breeze
	海綿	カイメン	sponge
	海洋	カイヨウ	ocean
	海里	カイリ	nautical mile; knot
	海流	カイリュウ	ocean current
	海路	カイロ	sea route
訓	海	うみ	sea; lake; well of an inkstone
¥	海運	カイウン	marine transportation; shipping
	海上保険	カイジョウホケン	marine insurance

1185

活 ⑨

音	活	カツ	vivid; live; life
熟	活火山	カッカザン	active/live volcano
	活気	カッキ	vigor; liveliness; activity
	活況	カッキョウ	activity; animated appearance; briskness
	活字	カツジ	printing type
	活字体	カツジタイ	typeface
	活動	カツドウ	activity; action —*vi*. be active; lead an active life; play an active part

	活発	カッパツ	lively; brisk; active
	活版	カッパン	typography; letterpress
	活躍	カツヤク	activity; action —*vi*. be active; take an active part in
	活用	カツヨウ	practical use; application —*v*. apply; utilize; put to practical use
	活力	カツリョク	vitality; vigor
	活路	カツロ	means of escape; way out
訓	活き	いき	freshness
	活きる	いきる	*vi*. live; be alive
	活ける	いける	*vt*. arrange flowers
¥	活性化	カッセイカ	activation

1186

洪 ⑨

音	洪	コウ	flood
熟	洪水	コウズイ	flood; deluge

1187

浄 ⑨

音	浄	ジョウ	pure
熟	浄化	ジョウカ	purification; purge; clean-up —*v*. purify; purge; clean up
	浄化設備	ジョウカセツビ	sanitation facilities
	浄財	ジョウザイ	offertory; donation
	浄水	ジョウスイ	clean water
	浄水場	ジョウスイジョウ	water purification plant
	浄水池	ジョウスイチ	pure-water reservoir
	浄土	ジョウド	promised land; Pure Land
	浄土宗	ジョウドシュウ	Jōdo sect of Buddhism; Pure Land Buddhism

1188

津 ⑨

音	津	シン	harbor; port; ferry
熟	津々	シンシン	absorbing; deep; profound

訓	津	つ	harbor; port; ferry
	津々浦々	つつうらうら	all over the country
	津波	つなみ	tsunami; tidal wave

1189

洗 ⑨

丶 氵 氵 氵 汁 汢 洗 洗 洗

音	洗	セン	wash
熟	洗眼	センガン	eyewashing
	洗顔	センガン	washing one's face —*vi*. wash one's face
	洗剤	センザイ	detergent
	洗車	センシャ	car wash —*vi*. wash the car
	洗浄	センジョウ	washing; rinsing; cleansing —*v*. wash; rinse; clean
	洗濯	センタク	washing; laundering —*v*. wash; launder
	洗濯機	センタクキ	washing machine
	洗濯物	センタクもの	the wash; laundry
	洗脳	センノウ	brainwashing —*v*. brainwash
	洗面	センメン	washing one's face —*vi*. wash one's face
	洗面台	センメンダイ	wash basin
	洗礼	センレイ	baptism
	洗練	センレン	refinement; polishing —*v*. refine; polish
訓	洗う	あらう	*vt*. wash; probe

1190

浅 ⑨

丶 氵 氵 氵 汇 浐 浅 浅 浅

音	浅	セン	shallow
熟	浅学	センガク	shallow learning; superficial knowledge
	浅薄	センパク	shallow/superficial (knowledge, beliefs); flimsy
訓	浅い	あさい	shallow
	浅瀬	あさせ	shoal; shallows; ford
	浅ましい	あさましい	shameful; mean

1191

洞 ⑨

丶 氵 氵 氵 汈 洞 洞 洞 洞

音	洞	ドウ	cave

熟	洞窟	ドウクツ	cave
	洞察	ドウサツ	discernment; penetration; insight —*v.* discern; penetrate; see through
訓	洞	ほら	cave
	洞穴	ほらあな	cave

1192

派 ⑨

音	派	ハ	group; school; sect; denomination
熟	派遣	ハケン	dispatch; detachment —*v.* dispatch; detach; send; detail
	派出	ハシュツ	dispatch —*v.* send out; dispatch; detach
	派出所	ハシュツジョ	branch office; police office/box
	派生	ハセイ	derivation —***vi.*** derive; be derived from; originate
	派手	ハで	showy; gaudy; flashy; vain
	派閥	ハバツ	clique; faction; coterie
	派兵	ハヘイ	dispatch of troops —***vi.*** dispatch troops

1193

洋 ⑨

音	洋	ヨウ	ocean; foreign; western
熟	洋画	ヨウガ	Western picture/movie
	洋学	ヨウガク	Western learning
	洋楽	ヨウガク	Western music
	洋菓子	ヨウガシ	Western cakes
	洋館	ヨウカン	Western-style building
	洋行	ヨウコウ	travels to the US or Europe —***vi.*** go to the US or Europe
	洋裁	ヨウサイ	Western-style dressmaking
	洋式	ヨウシキ	Western-style
	洋室	ヨウシツ	Western-style room; non-*tatami* room
	洋酒	ヨウシュ	Western liquors
	洋書	ヨウショ	foreign/Western book
	洋上	ヨウジョウ	on the sea; seagoing
	洋食	ヨウショク	Western food
	洋装	ヨウソウ	Western dress —*v.* wear Western dress
	洋品店	ヨウヒンテン	haberdashery; hosier
	洋風	ヨウフウ	Western-style

洋服　ヨウフク　(Western-type) clothes
洋間　ヨウま　Western-style room
洋々たる　ようようたる　wide; broad; vast

1194
消 ⑩
丶 冫 氵 氵' 氵'' 氵'' 氵'' 消 消 消

音 消　ショウ　vanish; extinguish; consume

熟 消火　ショウカ　fire extinguisher —*vi*. extinguish a fire
消化　ショウカ　digestion; consumption; absorption —*v*. digest; consume; absorb
消却　ショウキャク　spending; consumption —*v*. spend; consume; use up
消極的　ショウキョクテキ　negative; passive; half-hearted
消失　ショウシツ　disappearance; vanishing —*vi*. disappear; vanish
消息　ショウソク　news; information
消灯　ショウトウ　lights off —*vi*. put out/turn off the lights
消毒　ショウドク　disinfection; sterilization; fumigation —*v*. disinfect; sterilize; fumigate
消費　ショウヒ　consumption; expenditure —*v*. consume; use up
消防　ショウボウ　fire fighting —*v*. fight a fire
消耗　ショウモウ　waste; consumption; exhaustion —*v*. waste; consume; exhaust; wear out

訓 消える　きえる　*vi*. go out; die; disappear; go/fade away
消す　けす　*vt*. put out; extinguish; switch/turn off; erase; liquidate
消印　けしイン　postmark
消しゴム　けしゴム　pencil eraser
消し止める　けしとめる　*vt*. put out; extinguish

¥ 消費財　ショウヒザイ　consumption goods
消費者　ショウヒシャ　consumer
消費税　ショウヒゼイ　consumption tax

1195
浸 ⑩
丶 冫 氵 氵 氵 氵 氵 浔 浔 浸

音 浸　シン　soak

熟 浸食　シンショク　erosion; corrosion —*v*. erode; corrode
浸水　シンスイ　inundation; flooding —*v*. be flooded/inundated
浸透　シントウ　infiltration; penetration; permeation —*v*. penetrate; infiltrate; permeate

	浸入	シンニュウ	permeation; penetration; infiltration —*v*. permeate; penetrate; infitrate
訓	浸す	ひたす	***vt***. soak; moisten
	浸る	ひたる	***vi***. be flooded/immersed/soaked; wallow in

1196

浜 ⑩

丶 ⺀ 氵 氵 氵 沪 浐 浜 浜 浜

音	浜	ヒン	beach; seashore
訓	浜	はま	beach; seashore
	浜辺	はまべ	beach; sands; shore

1197

浮 ⑩

丶 ⺀ 氵 氵 氵 氵 沪 浮 浮 浮

音	浮	フ	float
熟	浮説	フセツ	rumor
	浮沈	フチン	ups and downs; rise and fall; ebb and flow
	浮動	フドウ	wafting; floating —***vi***. waft; float
	浮薄	フハク	fickle; frivolous; insincere; shallow
	浮標	フヒョウ	buoy; float (for a fishing net, etc.)
	浮遊	フユウ	floating; wafting; suspension —***vi***. float; waft; be suspended
	浮力	フリョク	buoyancy; lift
	浮浪児	フロウジ	juvenile vagrant
	浮浪者	フロウシャ	street bum; tramp; hobo
訓	浮く	うく	***vi***. float; rise to the surface; feel buoyant/lighthearted
	浮かぶ	うかぶ	***vi***. float; rise to the surface; think of; be revealed; appear
	浮かべる	うかべる	***vt***. set afloat; show; reveal
	浮かれる	うかれる	***vi***. be in high spirits; be excited
	浮いた	ういた	cheerful; buoyant; frivolous
	浮き	うき	float
	浮き立つ	うきたつ	***vi***. be enlivened/exhilarated/buoyant
	浮名	うきな	rumor; gossip; gossip about a love affair
	浮世	うきよ	this transitory world
	浮世絵	うきよエ	ukiyoe woodblock print
	※浮つく	うわつく	***vi***. be fickle/flippant/restless
	※浮気	うわキ	marital infidelity; love affair

¥ 浮動株　フドウかぶ　floating stock

1198

浦 ⑩

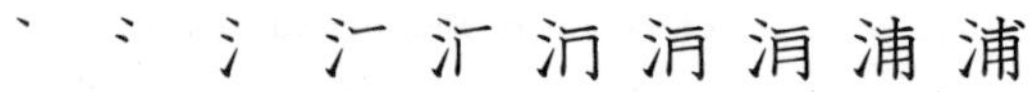

音	浦	ホ	inlet; shore; bay
訓	浦	うら	inlet; shore; bay

1199

浴 ⑩

音	浴	ヨク	bathe; bath
熟	浴室	ヨクシツ	bathroom
	浴場	ヨクジョウ	bathroom; bath house
	浴槽	ヨクソウ	bathtub
	※浴衣	ゆかた	*yukata* (light cotton kimono)
訓	浴びる	あびる	***vt.*** pour over oneself; bathe in
	浴びせる	あびせる	***vt.*** pour on; shower upon

1200

流 ⑩

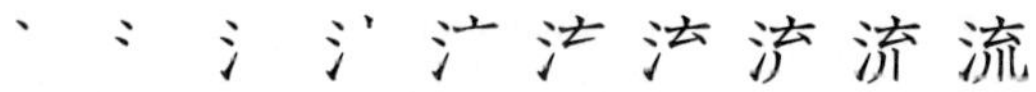

音	流	リュウ (ル)	flow; wander; style; school; rank; class
熟	流域	リュウイキ	river basin/valley
	流会	リュウカイ	adjournment —***vi.*** be adjourned/called off
	流感	リュウカン	influenza; flu
	流儀	リュウギ	style; system; method
	流刑	リュウケイ	deportation, exile; banishment
	流血	リュウケツ	bloodshed
	流言	リュウゲン	false rumor
	流行	リュウコウ	fashionable; popular; prevalent —***vi.*** be in fashion; be popular/prevalent/epidemic
	流行性感冒	リュウコウセイカンボウ	influenza
	流行病	リュウコウビョウ	epidemic
	流産	リュウザン	miscarriage —***v.*** suffer a miscarriage
	流失	リュウシツ	washed away —***vi.*** be washed away
	流出	リュウシュツ	outflow —***vi.*** outflow; flow out

	流星	リュウセイ	shooting star; meteor
	流線型	リュウセンケイ	streamline
	流体	リュウタイ	***phy.*** fluid
	流暢	リュウチョウ	fluent
	流通	リュウツウ	circulation; distribution —***vi.*** circulate; distribute
	流動	リュウドウ	flowing; liquid (assets); current —***vi.*** flow; be liquid/current
	流動体	リュウドウタイ	fluid
	流入	リュウニュウ	influx —***vi.*** flow in
	流派	リュウハ	school (of thought/art)
	流氷	リュウヒョウ	drift ice; ice floe
	流木	リュウボク	driftwood
	流用	リュウヨウ	multipurpose —***v.*** use for other purposes
	流罪	ルザイ	banishment; exile
	流転	ルテン	constant change; wandering; vagrancy; reincarnation —***vi.*** change constantly; wander
	流布	ルフ	circulation; dissemination —***vi.*** circulate; spread; disseminate
	流浪	ルロウ	wandering; roaming —***vi.*** wander about; roam
訓	流す	ながす	***vt.*** let flow
	流し	ながし	sink
	流れる	ながれる	***vi.*** flow
	流れ	ながれ	stream
¥	流通機構	リュウツウキコウ	distribution/marketing system
	流通市場	リュウツウシジョウ	secondary/trading market
	流動資産	リュウドウシサン	current/liquid assets
	流動負債	リュウドウフサイ	current/liquid liabilities

1201

⑩

音	涙	ルイ	tear; sympathy
熟	涙腺	ルイセン	***med.*** lachrymal/tear glands
訓	涙	なみだ	tear; sympathy
	涙顔	なみだがお	tearful face
	涙金	なみだキン	consolation money
	涙声	なみだごえ	tearful voice
	涙もろい	なみだもろい	given to weeping

心 忄 小 戈 戸 手 扌 支 攵 文 斗 斤 方 日 曰 月 肉 月 木 欠 止 歹 殳 母 毋 比 毛 氏 气 水 氺 • 氵 火 灬 爫 父 片 牛 犬 犭 王 礻 耂

1202
浪 ⑩

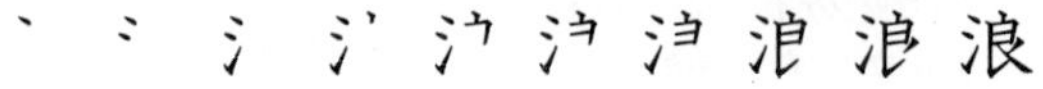

音	浪	**ロウ**	waves; wander
熟	浪人	**ロウニン**	masterless samurai; student who has failed the university entrance examinations and will resit them the following year —*v.* be forced to resit university examinations
	浪費	**ロウヒ**	waste; squander —*v.* waste; squander
	浪漫主義	**ロウマンシュギ**	romanticism

1203
液 ⑪

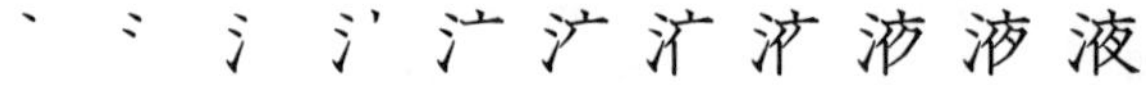

音	液	**エキ**	liquid; fluid; juice; sap
熟	液化	**エキカ**	liquefaction —*v.* be liquefied
	液剤	**エキザイ**	liquid medicine
	液状	**エキジョウ**	liquid form
	液体	**エキタイ**	liquid substance; fluid

1204
涯 ⑪

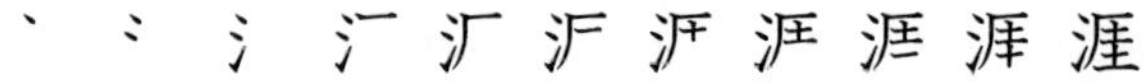

音	涯	**ガイ**	horizon; shore; end

1205
渇 ⑪

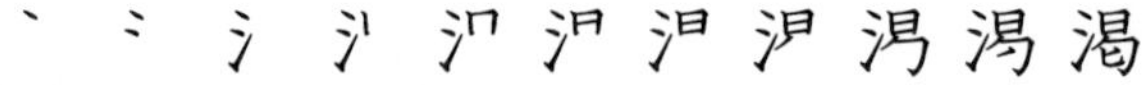

音	渇	**カツ**	thirsty; yearn for
熟	渇する	**カッする**	***vi.*** be/feel thirsty
	渇水	**カッスイ**	shortage of water; drought
	渇望	**カツボウ**	craving; earnest desire —*v.* crave/yearn for; be thirsty for
訓	渇く	**かわく**	***vi.*** dry up; feel thirsty

1206

渓 ⑪

丶 冫 氵 氵 氵 氵 氵 浮 浮 渓 渓

音	渓	ケイ	valley; canyon; gorge; ravine; river valley
熟	渓谷	ケイコク	gorge; ravine
	渓流	ケイリュウ	mountain torrent/stream
訓	※渓	たに	valley; ravine; gorge

1207

混 ⑪

丶 冫 氵 氵 氵 氵 氵 浔 浔 混 混

音	混	コン	mix
熟	混血児	コンケツジ	half-breed; child of mixed blood
	混合	コンゴウ	mixture —*v*. mix; mingle; blend; compound
	混雑	コンザツ	congestion; confusion; disorder —***vi***. be congested/confused; be in disorder
	混戦	コンセン	confused/free fight —***vi***. fight in confusion
	混線	コンセン	cross; contact; entanglement —***vi***. be crossed; be mixed up; be entangled
	混同	コンドウ	mixing; confusion; merger —***v***. confuse; confound; mix-up
	混沌	コントン	chaos; nebulosity; confusion
	混入	コンニュウ	mixing; mixture; blending —***v***. mix; mingle; blend
	混紡	コンボウ	mixed spinning
	混用	コンヨウ	composite —***v***. mingle; use together
	混乱	コンラン	confusion; disorder; chaos —***vi***. be confused/chaotic; be mixed up
訓	混ざる	まざる	***vi***. be mixed/blended
	混じる	まじる	***vi***. mix; mingle; blend
	混ぜる	まぜる	***vt***. blend; mix

1208

済 ⑪

丶 冫 氵 氵 氵 氵 氵 済 済 済 済

音	済	サイ	relieve; help; end; finish; repay
熟	済度	サイド	***Bud***. salvation; redemption —***v***. ***Bud***. save; redeem
訓	済ます	すます	***vt***. finish; repay; payback; make do; manage; settle; solve

	済む	すむ	***vi***. be over; finish; be paid; settle; complete; manage
	済みません	すみません	excuse me; pardon; sorry; thank you

1209 **渋** ⑪

音	渋	ジュウ	astringent; hesitate
熟	渋滞	ジュウタイ	delay; congestion; traffic jam —***vi***. be delayed/held up/congested
	渋面	ジュウメン	frown; grimace
訓	渋	しぶ	persimmon tannin
	渋い	しぶい	astringent; quiet; tasteful; glum; sullen
	渋る	しぶる	***v***. hesitate; be reluctant; stick; be constipated
	渋々	しぶしぶ	unwillingly; reluctantly
	渋味	しぶミ	astringency

1210 **淑** ⑪

音	淑	シュク	graceful
熟	淑女	シュクジョ	lady

1211 **渉** ⑪

音	渉	ショウ	ford; cross over
熟	渉外	ショウガイ	public relations; liason

1212 **深** ⑪

音	深	シン	deep
熟	深遠	シンエン	profound; deep
	深淵	シンエン	abyss; the depths
	深海	シンカイ	deep sea
	深紅	シンク	deep red
	深呼吸	シンコキュウ	deep breathing —***vi***. breathe deeply

	深刻	シンコク	serious; grave; critical
	深山	シンザン	deep mountains
	深謝	シンシャ	hearty thanks; sincere apology —*v*. express one's gratitude; make a sincere apology
	深窓	シンソウ	tender care; happy family circumstances
	深層	シンソウ	the depths
	深長	シンチョウ	profound; deep
	深度	シンド	depth
	深部	シンブ	depth
	深夜	シンヤ	midnight; dead of night
	深緑	シンリョク	dark green
訓	深い	ふかい	deep; profound; late; serious
	深まる	ふかまる	***vi***. become deep; deepen
	深める	ふかめる	***vt***. make deep; deepen
	深入り	ふかいり	deeply involved —***vi***. be deeply involved

1213

清 ⑪

丶 冫 氵 氵一 氵十 氵丰 浐 涛 清 清 清

音	清	セイ (ショウ)	pure; clear; clean
熟	清閑	セイカン	quiet; secluded
	清教徒	セイキョウト	Puritan
	清潔	セイケツ	clean; untainted
	清算	セイサン	liquidation; settlement; clearance —*v*. settle; clear; liquidate
	清酒	セイシュ	refined saké
	清純	セイジュン	purity; innocence
	清書	セイショ	fair/clean copy —*v*. write a clean copy
	清浄	セイジョウ	purity; innocence
	清々	セイセイ	relief —***vi***. feel relieved
	清楚	セイソ	neat and clear
	清掃	セイソウ	cleaning —*v*. clean
	清掃車	セイソウシャ	garbage truck; dustcart
	清聴	セイチョウ	paying attention; listening quietly
	清貧	セイヒン	honest poverty
	清流	セイリュウ	limpid/clear stream
	清涼	セイリョウ	cool; refreshing
	清涼飲料水	セイリョウインリョウスイ	cooling/refreshing/soft drinks
	清廉	セイレン	integrity; upright; honest

訓	清い	きよい	clean; clear; pure
	清まる	きよまる	***vi***. become clean; be purified
	清める	きよめる	***vt***. cleanse; make clean; purify; purge
	※清水	しみず	clean/pure water; springwater

1214
淡 ⑪

音	淡	タン	light; plain; simple
熟	淡水	タンスイ	fresh water
	淡々	タンタン	indifference; being unconcerned; plainness; lightness
	淡泊(淡白)	タンパク	lightness; plainness; simplicity; candidness; frankness; indifference
訓	淡い	あわい	light; faint; pale
	淡雪	あわゆき	light snow

1215
添 ⑪

音	添	テン	add
熟	添加	テンカ	annexing; addition —***v***. annex; append; affix; add
	添加物	テンカブツ	annex; appendix; addition; additive
	添削	テンサク	correction; editing —***v***. correct; look over; touch up
	添付	テンプ	appending; annexing —***v***. append; annex; attach
訓	添う	そう	***vi***. accompany; go with; marry; be married to
	添える	そえる	***vt***. add/attach to; affix; append; annex
	添え書き	そえがき	legend; postscript
	添状	そえジョウ	accompanying letter
	添え物	そえもの	addition; premium; giveaway; supplement

1216
涼 ⑪

音	涼	リョウ	cool
熟	涼気	リョウキ	cool air
	涼風	リョウフウ	cool breeze

	涼味	リョウミ	the cool; coolness
訓	涼しい	すずしい	cool; refreshing
	涼む	すずむ	***vi***. cool off

1217

温 ⑫

音	温	オン	warmth; temperature; gentle
熟	温厚	オンコウ	gentle; courteous
	温室	オンシツ	hothouse; greenhouse
	温室効果	オンシツコウカ	greenhouse effect
	温順	オンジュン	obedient; gentle; submissive; docile
	温床	オンショウ	hotbed; bed of soil enclosed in glass used for raising seedlings —***fig***. environment that favors rapid growth or development
	温情	オンジョウ	warm; cordial; kind
	温泉	オンセン	hot spring; spa
	温存	オンゾン	preservation; maintainence —***v***. preserve; retain; keep
	温帯	オンタイ	temperate zone
	温暖	オンダン	mild; warm; temperate
	温度	オンド	temperature
	温良	オンリョウ	gentle; amiable
	温和	オンワ	pleasantly mild; gentle hearted
訓	温かい	あたたかい	warm; mild; genial; kind
	温か	あたたか	warm; mild
	温かみ	あたたかみ	warmth
	温まる	あたたまる	***vi***. get warm
	温める	あたためる	***vt***. warm; heat; keep

1218

渦 ⑫

音	渦	カ	whirlpool
熟	渦中	カチュウ	eddy; whirlpool; vortex
	渦紋	カモン	scroll; scroll pattern
訓	渦	うず	eddy; whirlpool; vortex
	渦潮	うずしお	swirling sea water
	渦巻き	うずまき	eddy; whirlpool; vortex

1219 減 ⑫

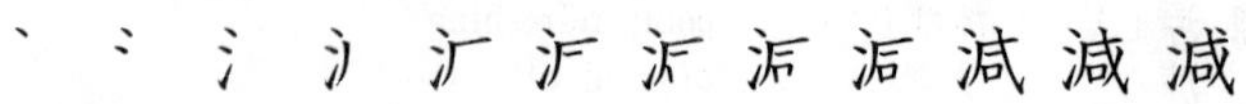

音	減	ゲン	decrease; reduce
熟	減額	ゲンガク	reduction; cut —*v*. reduce; cut
	減収	ゲンシュウ	decrease in income; drop in revenue
	減少	ゲンショウ	decrease; diminution —*v*. fall off; go down; drop; diminish; be decreased/reduced
	減食	ゲンショク	diet —*vi*. eat less; cut down; diet
	減水	ゲンスイ	fall in water level —*v*. drop; fall; reduce
	減速	ゲンソク	speed reduction; deceleration —*v*. reduce speed; decelerate; slow down
	減退	ゲンタイ	decline —*vi*. decline; fall off; weaken; fail
	減点	ゲンテン	demerit marks; deducted points
	減量	ゲンリョウ	weight loss; losing weight —*v*. lose weight
訓	減る	へる	*vi*. decrease; diminish; run short; dwindle; drop; lose
	減らす	へらす	*vt*. reduce; decrease; cut down; take away
¥	減益	ゲンエキ	decrease of profit
	減産	ゲンサン	reduction/decrease in production/output; decreased production —*v*. decrease/reduce output/production
	減資	ゲンシ	capital reduction
	減税	ゲンゼイ	tax reduction/cut —*v*. reduce/cut/lower taxes
	減俸	ゲンポウ	salary reduction —*v*. reduce salaries

1220 湖 ⑫

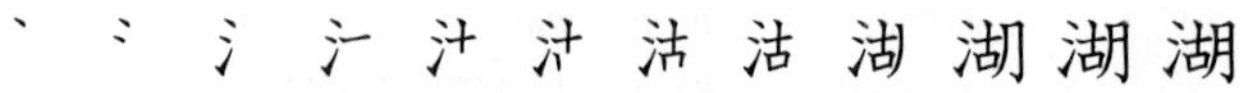

音	湖	コ	lake
熟	湖水	コスイ	lake
	湖畔	コハン	lakeside
訓	湖	みずうみ	lake

1221 港 ⑫

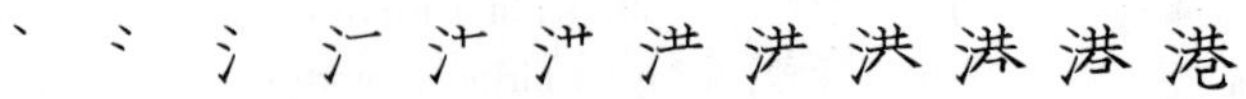

音	港	コウ	port; harbor
熟	港口	コウコウ	harbor entrance

港湾　コウワン　harbor

訓 港　みなと　port; harbor

1222

滋 ⑫

音	滋	ジ	rich; luxurious
熟	滋味	ジミ	savoriness; tastiness; delicious; delicacy; rich food
	滋養	ジヨウ	nourishment; nutrition

1223

湿 ⑫

音	湿	シツ	moisten; damp; humid
熟	湿気	シッケ	moisture; humidity; damp
	湿原	シツゲン	damp plain
	湿潤	シツジュン	wet; damp; moist; humid
	湿疹	シッシン	eczema
	湿地	シッチ	damp ground
	湿度	シツド	humidity
	湿布	シップ	compress —*v.* compress
訓	湿る	しめる	***vi***. become damp; moist
	湿す	しめす	***vt***. moisten; wet; make wet

1224

測 ⑫

音	測	ソク	measure
熟	測地	ソクチ	land surveying; geodetic
	測定	ソクテイ	measurement —*v.* measure
	測度	ソクド	measurement; gauging
	測量	ソクリョウ	survey; measurement —*v.* survey; measure
	測距儀	ソッキョギ	range finder
	測候所	ソッコウジョ	weather station
訓	測る	はかる	***vt***. measure; estimate

1225
渡 ⑫

丶 冫 氵 氵 汁 汸 浐 浐 浐 浐 渡 渡

音	渡	ト	cross
熟	渡航	トコウ	voyage; passage; sailing; crossing —*vi*. make a passage; set sail for
	渡米	トベイ	going to America; visit to America —*vi*. go/visit/America; emigrate to America
	渡来	トライ	visit; introduction; importation; influx —*vi*. come over the sea; make an overseas visit; be introduced/brought over
訓	渡す	わたす	*vt*. pass over; carry across; hand over; transfer
	渡し	わたし	ferry crossing; delivery
	渡し船	わたしぶね	ferryboat; ferry *fig*. help
	渡る	わたる	*vi*. go over; cross; traverse; be imported; migrate
	渡り	わたり	passage; transit; negotiations
	渡り歩く	わたりあるく	*vi*. wander; go from one place to another

1226
湯 ⑫

丶 冫 氵 氵 沪 沪 浔 浔 浔 湯 湯 湯

音	湯	トウ	hot water
熟	湯治	トウジ	hot-spring cure; taking the baths —*v*. take the baths/waters
訓	湯	ゆ	hot water/bath; public bath
	湯気	ゆゲ	steam; vapor
	湯呑み	ゆのみ	teacup; cup; mug
	湯元	ゆもと	source of a hot spring

1227
満 ⑫

丶 冫 氵 汁 汁 汫 汫 汫 湍 湍 満 満

音	満	マン	full; abundant; Manchuria
熟	満員	マンイン	no vacancy; full
	満悦	マンエツ	great delight; rapture; satisfaction
	満開	マンカイ	in full bloom
	満期	マンキ	expiration
	満喫	マンキツ	enough; full —*v*. have enough; have one's fill of; enjoy to the full

	満月	マンゲツ	full moon
	満座	マンザ	the whole company; everyone present
	満載	マンサイ	full load —***v***. be fully loaded
	満州	マンシュウ	Manchuria
	満場	マンジョウ	the whole company/hall
	満場一致	マンジョウイッチ	unanimous
	満身	マンシン	the whole body
	満水	マンスイ	filled to the brim with water —***vi***. be filled to the brim with water
	満足	マンゾク	satisfaction; contentment —***vi***. be satisfied/contented with
	満潮	マンチョウ	high tide
	満天	マンテン	the whole sky
	満点	マンテン	full marks; perfect score
	満腹	マンプク	full stomach/belly
	満々	マンマン	full of; brimming with
	満面	マンメン	the whole face
	満了	マンリョウ	expiration
	満塁	マンルイ	***bas***. full base
訓	満たす	みたす	***vt***. fill; satisfy; fulfill
	満ちる	みちる	***vi***. be full; (tide) come in; expire; be fulfilled
	満ち潮	みちしお	high tide
¥	満期	マンキ	maturity
	満期日	マンキび	due date; date of maturity

1228

湾 ⑫

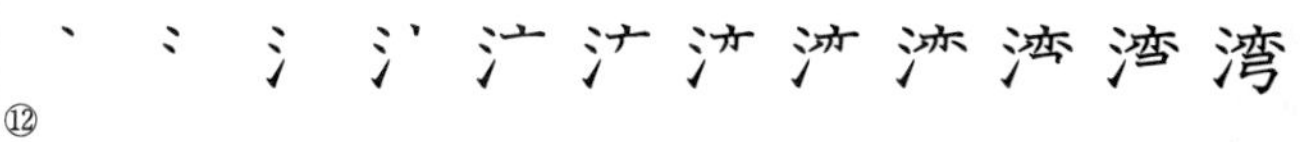

音	湾	ワン	bay; gulf
熟	湾岸	ワンガン	the Persian Gulf area; bay area
	湾岸戦争	ワンガンセンソウ	***hist***. Gulf War (1991)
	湾曲	ワンキョク	curve; curvature; bend —***vi***. curve; bend; be curved/bent
	湾内	ワンナイ	inside the bay
	湾流	ワンリュウ	Gulf Stream

1229

滑 ⑬

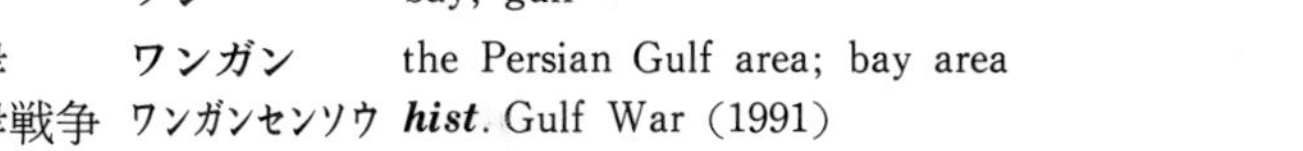

音	滑	カツ	slide; smooth

熟	滑車	カッシャ	pulley
	滑走	カッソウ	gliding —***vi***. glide; plane; taxi
	滑稽	コッケイ	comic; amusing
訓	滑る	すべる	***vi***. slide; slip
	滑らか	なめらか	smooth

1230
漢 ⑬

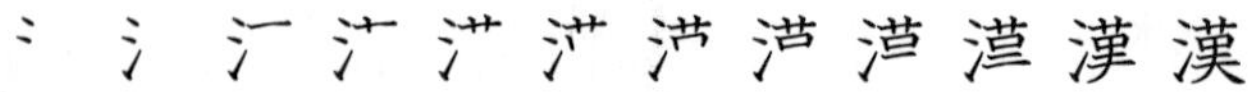

音	漢	カン	Han dynasty; fellow
熟	漢学	カンガク	study of Chinese classics
	漢語	カンゴ	Chinese word
	漢詩	カンシ	Chinese poetry
	漢字	カンジ	*kanji* (Chinese character)
	漢数字	カンスウジ	Chinese numerals
	漢文	カンブン	Chinese classics
	漢方薬	カンポウヤク	medicinal herb
	漢民族	カンミンゾク	the Han race; the Chinese
	漢和辞典	カンワジテン	Chinese-character dictionary with Japanese definitions; *kanji* dictionary

1231
源 ⑬

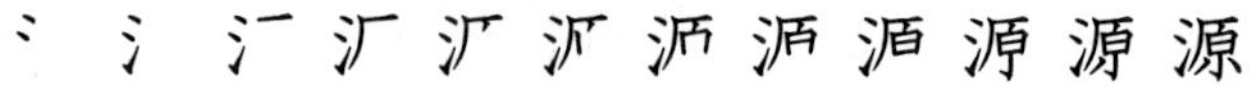

音	源	ゲン	source
熟	源泉	ゲンセン	source; origin
	源流	ゲンリュウ	source; origin
訓	源	みなもと	source; origin
¥	源泉徴収	ゲンセンチョウシュウ	taxation at source

1232
溝 ⑬

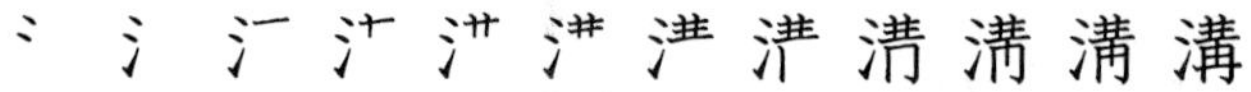

音	溝	コウ	ditch
訓	溝	みぞ	ditch; gutter; drain; groove; gap

1233
準 ⑬

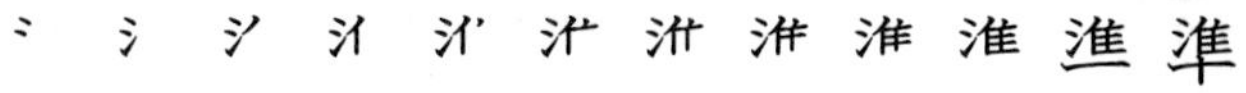

音 準　ジュン　rule; standard; measure

熟 準じる　ジュンじる　*vi*. follow; conform
準急　ジュンキュウ　local express
準拠　ジュンキョ　based on; following —*vi*. be based on; follow
準決勝　ジュンケッショウ　semi-final
準備　ジュンビ　preparations —*v*. prepare; make preparations; get ready

¥ 準備金　ジュンビキン　reserve fund

1234
滞 ⑬

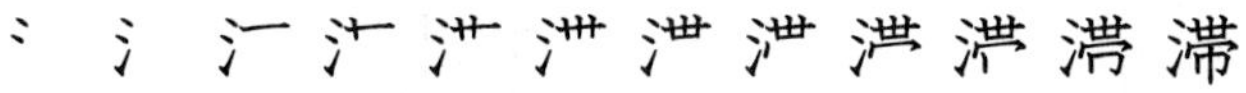

音 滞　タイ　stagnate; stay

熟 滞貨　タイカ　freight congestion; backlog; stockpiles
滞空　タイクウ　staying in the air; flying —*vi*. stay airborne; fly
滞在　タイザイ　stay; stop; sojourn —*vi*. stay; stop; sojourn
滞日　タイニチ　staying in Japan —*vi*. stay in Japan
滞納　タイノウ　nonpayment; default; failure to pay —*v*. default on payments; fail to keep up payments

訓 滞る　とどこおる　*vi*. stagnate; be stagnant; be left undone; fall into arrears

1235
滝 ⑬

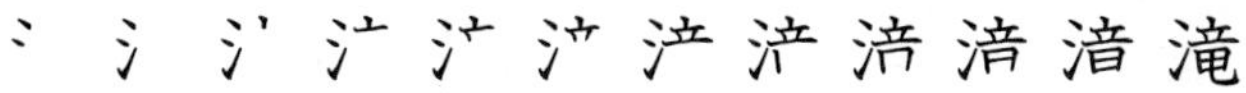

訓 滝　たき　waterfall
滝壷　たきつぼ　basin of a waterfall

1236
漠 ⑬

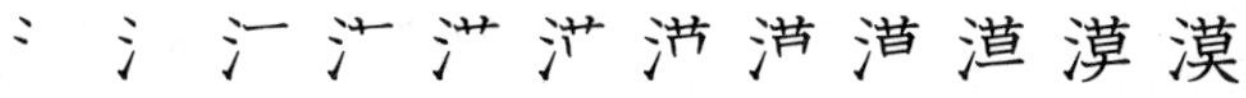

音 漠　バク　vast; boundless; vague; obscure

熟 漠然　バクゼン　vague; obscure; ambiguous

1237
滅 ⑬

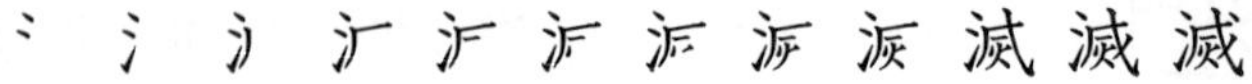

音	滅	メツ	ruin; perish; die out
熟	滅茶苦茶	メチャクチャ	incoherent; preposterous; mess; wreck; ruin
	滅却	メッキャク	destruction —*v*. extinguish; destroy
	滅多	メッタ	seldom; rarely
	滅亡	メツボウ	destruction —*vi*. be destroyed/wasted/exhausted
	滅裂	メツレツ	in chaos; incoherent
	※滅入る	メいる	*vi*. discouraged; shattered; let down
訓	滅びる	ほろびる	*vi*. perish; fall into ruin; die out
	滅ぼす	ほろぼす	*vt*. ruin; destroy; overthrow; annihilate

1238
溶 ⑬

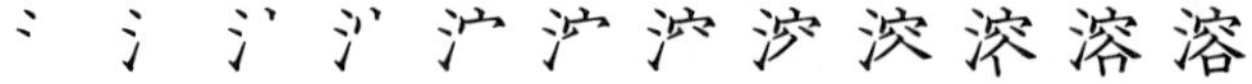

音	溶	ヨウ	dissolve; melt
熟	溶液	ヨウエキ	solution
	溶解	ヨウカイ	solution; melting —*v*. melt; dissolve
	溶岩	ヨウガン	lava
	溶鉱炉	ヨウコウロ	blast furnace
	溶剤	ヨウザイ	solvent
	溶性	ヨウセイ	soluble
	溶接	ヨウセツ	welding —*v*. weld
	溶媒	ヨウバイ	solvent
	溶融	ヨウユウ	molten —*vi*. fuse; melt
訓	溶かす	とかす	*vt*. melt; dissolve
	溶く	とく	*vt*. dissolve; melt
	溶ける	とける	*vi*. dissolve; thaw; melt

1239
演 ⑭

音	演	エン	state; act; apply
熟	演じる	エンじる	perform; play act; act
	演技	エンギ	acting; performance —*vi*. act; perform
	演芸	エンゲイ	performance; dramatic art

演劇	**エンゲキ**	play; drama
演算	**エンザン**	***math***. operation —***v***. operate; calculate; cipher; figure out
演習	**エンシュウ**	seminar; practice; exercise —***vi***. practice; carry out exercises
演出	**エンシュツ**	production —***v***. produce; stage; present
演説	**エンゼツ**	public speech; oration; address —***v***. make a speech; address
演奏	**エンソウ**	musical performance —***v***. give a musical performance
演壇	**エンダン**	platform; rostrum

1240

漁 ⑭

氵 氵 氵 氵 氵 氵 氵 漁 漁 漁 漁 漁

音	漁	**ギョ** **リョウ**	fishing; angling
熟	漁獲	**ギョカク**	fishery; fishing; haul; catch
	漁業	**ギョギョウ**	fishery; the fishing industry
	漁具	**ギョグ**	fishing tackle
	漁港	**ギョコウ**	fishing harbor
	漁場	**ギョジョウ**	fishing ground
	漁村	**ギョソン**	fishing village/community
	漁夫	**ギョフ**	fisherman; fisher
	漁民	**ギョミン**	fishermen; fishing people
	漁師	**リョウシ**	fishermen
訓	※漁火	**いさりび**	fisherman's fire

1241

漆 ⑭

氵 氵 汁 汁 汁 汁 沬 漆 漆 漆 漆 漆

音	漆	**シツ**	Japanese lacquer
熟	漆器	**シッキ**	lacquerware
	漆黒	**シッコク**	jet-black
訓	漆	**うるし**	lacquer

1242

漸 ⑭

氵 氵 氵 氵 氵 氵 氵 漸 漸 漸 漸 漸

音	漸	**ゼン**	gradually

4 心忄小戈戸手扌支攵文斗斤方日曰月肉月木欠止歹殳母毋比毛氏气水氺氵火灬爫父片牛犬犭王礻耂

熟	漸減	ゼンゲン	diminution; gradual decrease —*v*. diminish; decrease gradually
	漸次	ゼンジ	gradually
	漸進	ゼンシン	gradual procession —*vi*. proceed gradually
	漸増	ゼンゾウ	gradual increase —*v*. increase gradually

1243

漬 ⑭

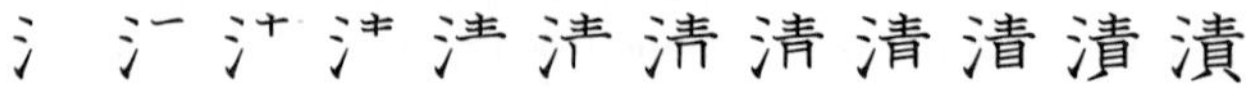

音	漬	（シ）	soak; pickle
訓	漬ける	つける	***vt***. soak; salt; pickle; preserve
	漬物	つけもの	*tsukemono* (Japanese pickles)
	漬かる	つかる	***vi***. soak; be soaked in/seasoned

1244

滴 ⑭

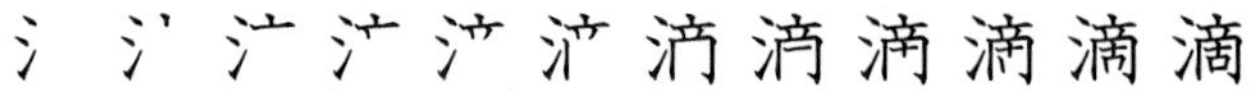

音	滴	テキ	drop
訓	滴	しずく	drop
	滴る	したたる	***vi***. drip; drop; dribble
	滴り	したたり	dripping; drop; trickle; dribble

1245

漂 ⑭

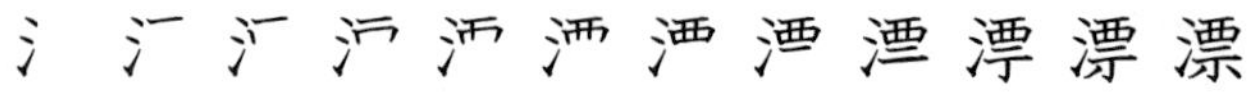

音	漂	ヒョウ	drift; float
熟	漂着	ヒョウチャク	drifting ashore —***vi***. drift ashore; be washed/cast ashore
	漂白	ヒョウハク	bleach —***v***. bleach
	漂泊	ヒョウハク	wandering; roaming; drifting —***vi***. wander; roam; drift
	漂流	ヒョウリュウ	drifting —***vi***. drift
訓	漂う	ただよう	drift; float

1246

漫 ⑭

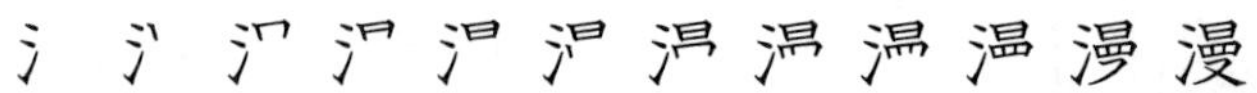

音	漫	マン	rambling; aimless; involuntarily

熟	漫画	マンガ	cartoon; comic book/strip
	漫才	マンザイ	comic dialog
	漫然	マンゼン	random; rambling; careless
	漫談	マンダン	idle chat —***vi***. chat idlely
	漫歩	マンポ	stroll; walk; rambling —***vi***. stroll; walk; ramble
	漫遊	マンユウ	tour; trip; travel —***vi***. make a tour/trip; travel
訓	※漫ろ	そぞろ	involuntarily; in spite of oneself; somehow

1247

漏 ⑭

音	漏	ロウ	leak; be disclosed
熟	漏洩	ロウエイ	leakage; disclosure —***v***. leak out; be let out/revealed
	漏出	ロウシュツ	leaking out; escape —***v***. leak out; escape
	漏水	ロウスイ	water leakage —***vi***. leak
	漏電	ロウデン	short circuit —***vi***. short circuit
	漏斗	ロウト	funnel
訓	漏らす	もらす	***vt***. reveal; divulge
	漏る	もる	***vi***. leak; be disclosed
	漏れる	もれる	***vi***. leak; be disclosed

1248

潟 ⑮

音	潟	セキ	lagoon; inlet; beach
訓	潟	かた	lagoon; inlet; beach

1249

潔 ⑮

音	潔	ケツ	pure
熟	潔白	ケッパク	innocence; purity
	潔癖	ケッペキ	clean; fastidious; punctilious
訓	潔い	いさぎよい	manly; frank; honorable; brave

1250

潤 ⑮

音	潤	ジュン	be moistened
熟	潤滑	ジュンカツ	lubrication
	潤滑油	ジュンカツユ	lubricating oil
	潤色	ジュンショク	embellishment —*v*. embellish; color
	潤沢	ジュンタク	abundance
訓	潤う	うるおう	***vi***. be moistened; benefit; enrich; help
	潤す	うるおす	***vt***. wet; water; moisten; benefit (someone); enrich (someone)
	潤む	うるむ	***vi***. be wet/emotional
	潤い	うるおい	moisture

1251

潜 ⑮

音	潜	セン	dive; hide
熟	潜行	センコウ	undercover activity; incognito —***vi***. travel incognito; go underground
	潜航	センコウ	submarine voyage —***vi***. cruise underwater; be submerged
	潜在	センザイ	latent; hidden; potential —***vi***. be latent/hidden; have potential
	潜水	センスイ	diving; submerging —***vi***. dive; submerge
	潜水艦	センスイカン	submarine
	潜水服	センスイフク	diving suit
	潜入	センニュウ	infiltration —***vi***. infiltrate
	潜伏	センプク	latency; dormancy —***vi***. hide; be hidden/dormant/latent
	潜望鏡	センボウキョウ	periscope
訓	潜む	ひそむ	***v***. lurk; lie hidden
	潜める	ひそめる	***vt***. conceal; hide
	潜る	もぐる	***vi***. dive; crawl into; crawl under; intiltrate

1252

潮 ⑮

音	潮	チョウ	tide; salt water

熟	潮流	チョウリュウ	tide; current; trend; tendency
訓	潮	しお	tide; current; sea water; brine; opportunity; chance
	潮風	しおかぜ	sea breeze
	潮騒	しおさい	sound of the waves/sea
	潮時	しおどき	tidal hour; opportunity; chance
	潮干狩り	しおひがり	gathering sea shells (at low tide)

1253

澄 ⑮

氵 氵 氵 氵 氵 氵 氵 氵 浐 浐 澄 澄

音	澄	チョウ	clear
訓	澄ます	すます	***vt.*** clear; make clear; clarify; look demure/prim
	澄む	すむ	***vi.*** become clear; clear; clarify

1254

激 ⑯

氵 氵 氵 氵 氵 氵 氵 氵 氵 氵 激 激

音	激	ゲキ	violent; acute; sharp; sudden; excite; encourage
熟	激する	ゲキする	***v.*** get excited; be agitated
	激化	ゲキカ	intensification —***vi.*** become intense; intensify
	激減	ゲキゲン	sharp/marked decrease —***vi.*** fall sharply; drop sharply
	激震	ゲキシン	severe earthquake
	激戦	ゲキセン	fierce battle
	激増	ゲキゾウ	sharp increase; sudden rise —***vi.*** increase sharply; show a sudden increase
	激痛	ゲキツウ	acute/sharp pain
	激怒	ゲキド	wrath; rage; fury —***vi.*** be enraged by; be infuriated at; fly into a rage
	激動	ゲキドウ	violent shaking/shock; excitement; turbulence —***vi.*** shake violently; be excited/turbulent
	激突	ゲキトツ	crash —***vi.*** crash; smash into
	激変	ゲキヘン	violent/sudden change —***vi.*** undergo a violent/sudden/rapid change
	激務	ゲキム	hard work; demanding job; pressing duties
	激流	ゲキリュウ	rapids; torrent; swift current
	激励	ゲキレイ	encouragement —***v.*** encourage; cheer up
	激烈	ゲキレツ	violence
	激論	ゲキロン	hot argument; heated discussion

訓 激しい はげしい violent; extreme; severe; intense

1255

濁 ⑯

音 濁 ダク become muddy

熟 濁音 ダクオン sonant; voiced sound

濁点 ダクテン symbol used to indicate a voiced sound in written Japanese (〃)

濁流 ダクリュウ muddy stream

訓 濁す にごす *vt.* make muddy/cloudy; speak ambiguously

濁る にごる *vi.* become muddy; have a voiced sound; be vague

濁り にごり muddiness; turbidity; voiced sound

1256

濃 ⑯

音 濃 ノウ thick

熟 濃厚 ノウコウ thickness; density; deepening

濃縮 ノウシュク concentration; enrichment; graduation —*v.* concentrate; enrich; graduate

濃淡 ノウタン light and shade

濃度 ノウド density; thickness; concentration

濃霧 ノウム dense fog

訓 濃い こい dark; deep; thick; heavy; strong (coffee, etc.); close; intimate

1257

濯 ⑰

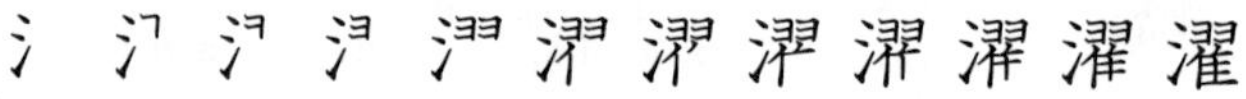

音 濯 タク wash

1258

濫 ⑱

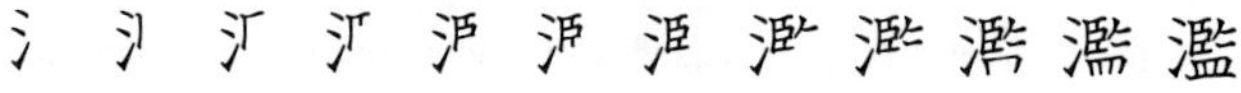

音 濫 ラン overflow; excessive; indiscriminate

熟 濫造 ランゾウ overproduction; careless manufacture —*v.* overproduce; manufacture carelessly

濫読	ランドク	indiscriminate/random reading —*v.* read indiscriminately/randomly
濫費	ランピ	waste; extravagance —*v.* waste; dissipate; lavish; squander
濫用	ランヨウ	abuse; misuse; misappropriation —*v.* abuse; misuse; missappropriate

1259

瀬 ⑲ 氵 氵 汸 沪 沸 涑 涑 涑 洓 漸 瀬 瀬

訓	瀬	せ	rapids; torrent; current; shallows; shoal
	瀬戸際	せとぎわ	critical moment; crisis
	瀬戸物	せともの	porcelain; china; earthenware; crockery

4 火 ひ／ひへん fire 灬 (p.558)

1260

火 ④ 丶 丷 火 火

音	火	カ	fire; flame; light
熟	火炎	カエン	flames; blaze
	火気	カキ	fire; heat of fire
	火器	カキ	firearms
	火口	カコウ	(volcano) crater; muzzle (of a gun)
	火災	カサイ	fire; conflagration; large disastrous fire
	火山	カザン	volcano
	火事	カジ	fire; conflagration; disastrous fire
	火星	カセイ	the planet Mars
	火勢	カセイ	force of the flames
	火葬	カソウ	cremation —*v.* cremate
	火薬	カヤク	gunpowder; explosives
	火曜日	カヨウび	Tuesday
	火力	カリョク	heat; calorific force; thermal power
訓	火	ひ	fire; flame; light
	火加減	ひカゲン	how well/poorly a fire is burning
	火箸	ひばし	tongs
	火柱	ひばしら	pillar of fire
	火鉢	ひばち	charcoal brazier
	火花	ひばな	sparks; hot glowing particles heated by friction

	火蓋	ひぶた	cover (of a gun barrel)
	火元	ひもと	origin of a fire
	火	ほ	fire
	※火傷	やけど	burn; injury resulting from exposure to fire/heat —*vi*. be/get burnt; have/suffer a burn

1261

灰 ⑥

音	灰	カイ	ash
熟	灰塵	カイジン	ashes
訓	灰	はい	ash
	灰色	はいいろ	gray ***fig***. hopelessness; uncertain attitude
	灰皿	はいざら	ashtray

1262

灯 ⑥

音	灯	トウ	light
熟	灯火	トウカ	light/lamplight
	灯台	トウダイ	lighthouse/light/beacon
	灯油	トウユ	lamp oil; kerosene
	灯篭	トウロウ	garden/hanging lantern
訓	灯	ひ	light

1263

災 ⑦

音	災	サイ	calamity; disaster; misforturne
熟	災禍	サイカ	disaster; calamity
	災害	サイガイ	disaster; calamity
	災難	サイナン	misfortune; disaster; accident
	災厄	サイヤク	disaster; misfortune; catastrophe
訓	災い	わざわい	disaster; misfortune; calamity

1264

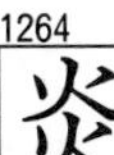

炎 ⑧

音	炎	エン	flame; hot; heat; inflammation
熟	炎々	エンエン	flaming; blazing
	炎暑	エンショ	intense heat
	炎症	エンショウ	***med.*** inflammation
	炎上	エンジョウ	in flames; destruction by fire —***vi.*** be destroyed by fire; be burnt down
訓	炎	ほのお	flame

1265

炊 ⑧

音	炊	スイ	boil
熟	炊事	スイジ	cooking; kitchen work —***vi.*** cook; do the cooking
	炊事場	スイジば	kitchen; cookery; cookhouse
	炊飯	スイハン	cooking rice
	炊飯器	スイハンキ	rice cooker
訓	炊く	たく	***vt.*** boil; cook

1266

炉 ⑧

音	炉	ロ	hearth; furnace
熟	炉だな	ロだな	mantelpiece
	炉端	ロばた	fireside; hearth
	炉辺	ロヘン	fireside; hearth

1267

炭 ⑨

音	炭	タン	charcoal; coal
熟	炭坑	タンコウ	coal mine
	炭鉱	タンコウ	coal mine
	炭酸	タンサン	***chem.*** carbonic acid

	炭酸水	タンサンスイ	***chem***. carbonated water
	炭素	タンソ	carbon
	炭田	タンデン	coal field
訓	炭	すみ	charcoal

1268

焼 ⑫

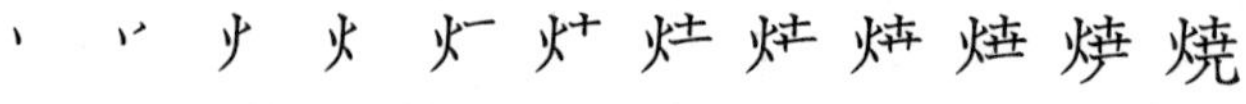

音	焼	ショウ	burn
熟	焼却	ショウキャク	burning; incineration —***v***. burn up; incinerate
	焼却炉	ショウキャクロ	incinerator
	焼香	ショウコウ	incense offering —***vi***. burn insense
	焼死	ショウシ	death by fire —***vi***. be burned to death
	焼失	ショウシツ	destruction by fire —***vi***. be burned down; be destroyed by fire
	焼酎	ショウチュウ	*shōchū* (white distilled liquor)
訓	焼く	やく	***v***. burn; heat; bake; grill; boil; roast
	焼ける	やける	***vi***. be burned/grilled/sun-tanned
	焼き餅	やきもち	toasted rice cake ***fig***. jealousy
	焼き物	やきもの	ceramic ware; pottery; porcelain; china

1269

煙 ⑬

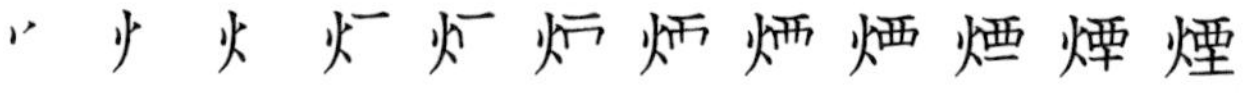

音	煙	エン	smoke; smoking
熟	煙雨	エンウ	drizzling rain; drizzle
	煙害	エンガイ	smoke pollution
	煙突	エントツ	chimney; smokestack
	煙幕	エンマク	smoke screen
訓	煙	けむり	smoke; fumes
	煙る	けむる	***vi***. smoke; smoulder
	煙い	けむい	smoky
	煙たい	けむたい	smoky; feeling awkward
	煙たがる	けむたがる	***vi***. be sensitive to smoke; feel awkward; keep away from (a person)
	※煙管	きせる	long-stemmed pipe
	※煙草	たばこ	tobacco; cigarette

1270

煩 ⑬

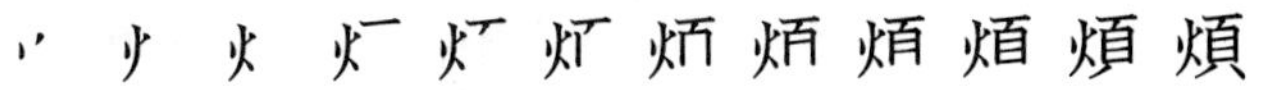

音	煩	ハン （ボン）	troublesome
熟	煩雑	ハンザツ	trouble; agony; worry
	煩悶	ハンモン	agony; anguish; worry; qualm —*vi*. be in agony; fret; worry; be troubled
	煩悩	ボンノウ	evil/worldly passions; lust; carnal desire
訓	煩う	わずらう	*v*. be ill/sick; suffer from; be afflicted with
	煩わしい	わずらわしい	troublesome; onerous; annoying; cumbersome
	煩わす	わずらわす	*vt*. trouble; bother; keep busy; annoy; plague; pester

1271

燃 ⑯

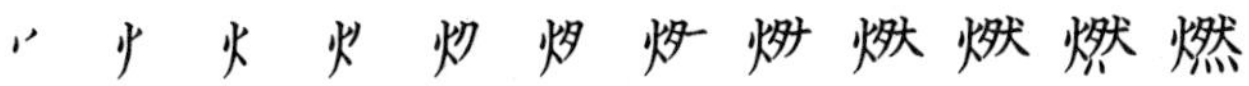

音	燃	ネン	burn
熟	燃焼	ネンショウ	combustion; burning; ignition —*vi*. combust; burn; ignite
	燃料	ネンリョウ	fuel
訓	燃える	もえる	*vi*. burn; blaze; be in flames
	燃す	もす	*vt*. burn; light; kindle; ignite
	燃やす	もやす	*vt*. burn; kindle; ignite

1272

燥 ⑰

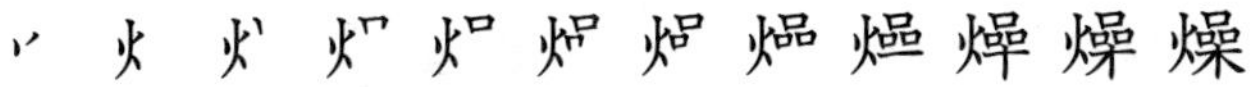

音	燥	ソウ	dry

1273

爆 ⑲

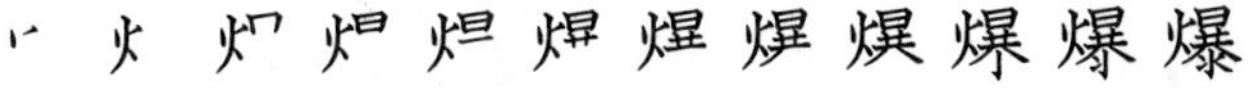

音	爆	バク	explode; bomb
熟	爆音	バクオン	roaring; explosion; detonation
	爆撃	バクゲキ	bombing; bombardment from the air —*v*. bomb; drop bombs; make a bombing raid

爆死	バクシ	death from bombing —***vi***. bomb to death; be killed by bombing
爆笑	バクショウ	burst/roar of laughter —***vi***. burst out laughing
爆弾	バクダン	bomb
爆沈	バクチン	sinking by explosion; blowing up and sinking —***v***. blow up and sink
爆破	バクハ	blasting; blowing up; explosion —***v***. blast; blow up; explode
爆発	バクハツ	explosion; detonation; blowing up —***vi***. explode; detonate; blow up
爆風	バクフウ	bombshell blast; blast from an explosion
爆薬	バクヤク	explosive compound; detonator; blasting powder

---

4 灬 よつてん／れっか fire in a row; four dots

1274

⑨

音	為	イ	do; for
熟	為政者	イセイシャ	ruler; governor; statesman; administrator
訓	為	ため	benefit; interests; sake; advantage; profit
	為す	なす	***vt***. do; perform; commit; practice; carry out
¥	※為替	かわせ	money order; exchange; transfer
	※為替裁定	かわせサイテイ	arbitration of exchange
	※為替差益	かわせサエキ	(foreign) exchange profit/gain
	※為替差損	かわせサソン	(foreign) exchange loss; loss from currency fluctuation
	※為替相場	かわせソウば	foreign exchange rate
	※為替手形	かわせてがた	bill of exchange
	※為替取組	かわせとりくみ	negotiation of export bills
	※為替予約	かわせヨヤク	exchange contract

1275

⑨

音	点	テン	dot; spot; mark; grades; points; score; fault; defect; item; piece
熟	点火	テンカ	ignition; lighting —***vi***. ignite; light; kindle; set off; fire

	点眼	テンガン	dropping eyedrops in the eyes —***v***. apply eyewash; drop eyedrops in the eyes
	点検	テンケン	inspection; examination; checking; muster —***v***. inspect; examine; scrutinize; check
	点呼	テンコ	roll call; calling of the roll —***v***. call the roll
	点在	テンザイ	scattered —***vi***. be dotted with; be scattered
	点字	テンジ	braille type; braille; raised letters
	点数	テンスウ	marks; points; score; number of articles
	点線	テンセン	dotted/perforated line
	点滴	テンテキ	falling drop of water; raindrops; intravenous drip
	点々	テンテン	here and there; sporadically; in drops
	点灯	テントウ	lighting —***vi***. light; light up; turn on a light
	点描	テンビョウ	sketch
	点滅	テンメツ	on/off —***v***. switch on and off
訓	点ける	つける	***vt***. light; put a match to; turn/switch on

1276

烈 ⑩

一 ア 歹 歹 歹 列 列 列 烈 烈

音	烈	レツ	violent; intense
熟	烈火	レッカ	raging fire
	烈日	レツジツ	blazing sun
	烈震	レッシン	violent earthquake
	烈風	レップウ	gale
	烈々	レツレツ	ardent; fierce; fervent
訓	※烈しい	はげしい	violent; intense

1277

煮 ⑫

一 十 土 耂 耂 者 者 者 煮 煮 煮 煮

音	煮	シャ	boil
熟	煮沸	シャフツ	boiling —***v***. boil
訓	煮る	にる	***vt***. boil; simmer; stew
	煮える	にえる	***vi***. be cooked; cook
	煮込む	にこむ	***vt***. boil well; cook together
	煮立つ	にたつ	***vi***. boil briskly
	煮物	にもの	cooking
	煮やす	にやす	***v***. be cooked; cook

1278
焦 ⑫

音	焦	ショウ	scorch; burn; impatience
熟	焦燥	ショウソウ	fretfulness; impatience
	焦点	ショウテン	focus; center; crucial point
	焦土	ショウド	scorched land
	焦慮	ショウリョ	impatience; worry; anguish —*vi*. be impatient; worry; feel anxious
訓	焦る	あせる	***vi***. be in a hurry; be impatient/anxious
	焦がす	こがす	***vt***. burn; scorch
	焦げる	こげる	***vi***. be burned/charred/scorched
	焦がれる	こがれる	***vi***. crave; yearn; be ardently in love

1279
然 ⑫

音	然	ゼン	yes
		ネン	nature

1280
無 ⑫

音	無	ム ブ	nothing; without; (prefix) -less, -free, un-
熟	無愛想	ブアイソウ	unsociable; curt
	無遠慮	ブエンリョ	unreserved; forward; impertinent
	無気味	ブキミ	ominous; eerie; uncanny
	無器用	ブキヨウ	unskillful; clumsy
	無骨	ブコツ	boorish; uncouth
	無細工	ブサイク	clumsy; plain; ugly
	無作法	ブサホウ	bad manners; rudeness
	無事	ブジ	safe and sound
	無精	ブショウ	idle; lazy
	無勢	ブゼイ	numerical inferiority
	無難	ブナン	safe; not dangerous; acceptable
	無用心	ブヨウジン	carelessness
	無礼	ブレイ	rudeness; discourtesy

無意義	ムイギ	meaningless; not significant
無意識	ムイシキ	unconscious; involuntary
無意味	ムイミ	meaningless; pointless
無医村	ムイソン	doctorless village
無一物	ムイチモツ	penniless; possessionless
無一文	ムイチモン	penniless
無益	ムエキ	useless; futile
無縁	ムエン	unrelated; with no surviving relatives
無価	ムカ	priceless
無我	ムガ	selflessness; self-forgetfulness
無我夢中	ムガムチュウ	total absorption; being totally involved in; forgetting oneself
無害	ムガイ	harmless
無学	ムガク	uneducated; ignorant
無学文盲	ムガクモンモウ	uneducated and illiterate
無価値	ムカチ	worthless
無関心	ムカンシン	indifference; unconcern; apathy
無期	ムキ	indefinite (period of time)
無機	ムキ	inorganic
無傷	ムきず	undamaged; unblemished; unhurt
無軌道	ムキドウ	trackless; erratic; aberrant
無記名	ムキメイ	unregistered
無休	ムキュウ	no holidays; always open
無給	ムキュウ	unpaid; non-salaried
無気力	ムキリョク	spiritless; flabby; gutless
無口	ムくち	reticent; taciturn; laconic
無下	ムゲ	(refuse) flatly/roundly
無形	ムケイ	intangible
無形文化財	ムケイブンカザイ	intangible cultural assets (the skills of art, music and drama)
無欠	ムケツ	flawless; faultless
無限	ムゲン	infinite
無効	ムコウ	invalid; null; void; ineffective
無根	ムコン	groundless; unfounded
無言	ムゴン	silent; mute
無罪	ムザイ	innocent; not guilty
無差別	ムサベツ	indiscriminate
無産	ムサン	without property
無産者	ムサンシャ	proletariat
無残	ムザン	cruel; ruthless; pitiful
無私	ムシ	unselfish; disinterested
無視	ムシ	disregard —***v.*** ignore; disregard

無地	ムジ	solid color; patternless
無実	ムジツ	false; unfounded; innocent
無慈悲	ムジヒ	merciless; ruthless
無邪気	ムジャキ	innocent; ingenuous
無償	ムショウ	free of charge; gratuitous
無上	ムジョウ	supreme; greatest; highest
無情	ムジョウ	unfeeling; callous; cruel
無常	ムジョウ	transitory; mutable; uncertain
無条件	ムジョウケン	unconditional
無色	ムショク	colorless; achromatic
無職	ムショク	no occupation; unemployed
無所属	ムショゾク	independent; unaffiliated
無心	ムシン	not thinking of anything
無神経	ムシンケイ	dull; insensitive; unfeeling
無尽蔵	ムジンゾウ	inexhaustible supply
無人地帯	ムジンチタイ	no man's land
無人島	ムジントウ	uninhabited island
無数	ムスウ	innumerable; countless
無声	ムセイ	silent; mute; voiceless; noiseless
無税	ムゼイ	duty-free; tax-free
無制限	ムセイゲン	unlimited; unrestricted
無生物	ムセイブツ	inanimate object
無責任	ムセキニン	irresponsibility
無線	ムセン	wireless; radio
無銭	ムセン	without money; penniless
無造作	ムゾウサ	with ease; simple; artless
無駄	ムダ	futile; useless; wasteful
無断	ムダン	unannounced; unauthorized
無知	ムチ	ignorance
無恥	ムチ	shameless; brazen
無茶	ムチャ	absurd; rash; excessive
無茶苦茶	ムチャクチャ	mixed up; confused; nonsensical; reckless
無賃	ムチン	free of charge
無敵	ムテキ	invincible; unrivaled
無鉄砲	ムテッポウ	reckless; rash
無二	ムニ	peerless; unequaled
無念	ムネン	regret; resentment; vexation
無能	ムノウ	incompetent; ineffective
無比	ムヒ	matchless; incomparable; unrivaled
無病	ムビョウ	well; healthy
無風	ムフウ	windless; dead calm
無分別	ムフンベツ	indiscrete; imprudent; thoughtless; rash

	無法	ムホウ	outrageous; unlawful; unjust
	無謀	ムボウ	reckless; incautious
	無味乾燥	ムミカンソウ	dry as dust; uninteresting
	無名	ムメイ	nameless; unknown; anonymous
	無用	ムヨウ	unnecessary; useless; prohibited
	無欲	ムヨク	unselfish; free from avarice
	無理	ムリ	unreasonable; impossible; beyond one's power; too difficult; by force; against one's will
	無理解	ムリカイ	lack of understanding
	無理算段	ムリサンダン	scraping together —*v.* scrape together
	無理難題	ムリナンダイ	unreasonable demand
	無理矢理	ムリやり	forcibly; under compulsion
	無料	ムリョウ	free of charge; free
	無量	ムリョウ	beyond measure; immense
	無力	ムリョク	powerless; ineffectual; feeble; incompetent
	無類	ムルイ	finest; choicest
	無論	ムロン	of course; naturally
訓	無い	ない	not; no
	無くす	なくす	***vt.*** lose; get rid of
	無くなる	なくなる	***vi.*** be gone/lost; run out of; die; pass away
¥	無形固定資産	ムケイコテイシサン	intangible fixed assets
	無形財産	ムケイザイサン	intangible property
	無償交付	ムショウコウフ	free share distribution

1281

照 ⑬

丨 ㄇ 日 日ㇷ 日ㇷ 旳 昭 昭 昭 照 照 照

音	照	ショウ	shine; check
熟	照応	ショウオウ	correspondence; agreement; accordance —*vi.* correspond; agree; accord
	照会	ショウカイ	inquiry; reference —*v.* refer; inquire; make inquiries
	照会状	ショウカイジョウ	letter of inquiry
	照合	ショウゴウ	check; collation —*v.* check; collate
	照準	ショウジュン	aim; aiming
	照度	ショウド	illumination
	照明	ショウメイ	illumination; lighting —*v.* illuminate; light up
訓	照らす	てらす	***vt.*** shine; light up; flash; consult; refer
	照らし合わせる	てらしあわせる	***vt.*** check; confirm

照る	てる	***vi***. shine; illuminate
照れる	てれる	***vi***. feel self-conscious/shy; be embarrassed
照れ屋	てれや	bashful person; person who blushes easily
照り	てり	sunshine; glaze; glare
照り焼き	てりやき	teriyaki (broiling meat/fish that has been soaked in soy sauce)

1282

熟 ⑮

亠 亡 亩 亨 享 享 享 𠅘 孰 孰 孰 熟

音	熟	ジュク	ripen; mature; thorough
熟	熟する	ジュクする	***vi***. ripen; mature
	熟語	ジュクゴ	phrase; idiom; compound
	熟視	ジュクシ	intense stare
	熟睡	ジュクスイ	sound sleep —***vi***. sleep soundly/well
	熟成	ジュクセイ	ripe; mature —***vi***. ripen; mature; age
	熟達	ジュクタツ	mastering —***vi***. master; become proficient in
	熟知	ジュクチ	well-known; well-informed; familiar —***v***. know well; be familiar with; be well informed
	熟読	ジュクドク	careful reading —***v***. read carefully
	熟年	ジュクネン	middle-aged
	熟練	ジュクレン	skill; mastery —***vi***. be skilled/expert in
	熟考	ジュッコウ	consideration; deliberation —***v***. consider; deliberate
訓	熟れる	うれる	***vi***. ripen

1283

熱 ⑮

一 十 土 圭 坴 坴 坴 埶 埶 埶 埶 熱

音	熱	ネツ	hot; heat; zeal; ardor; enthusiasm
熟	熱する	ネッする	***vt***. heat up ***vi***. become hot/excited
	熱愛	ネツアイ	passionate love; devotion —***v***. love passionately/fervently; be madly in love
	熱意	ネツイ	zeal; ardor; enthusiasm
	熱演	ネツエン	ardent/impassioned performance —***v***. give an impassioned performance
	熱気	ネッキ	heat; ardor; hot air; heated atmosphere; feverishness
	熱狂	ネッキョウ	frenzy; fanaticism; mania; excitement —***vi***. be wildly excited/mad/frantic
	熱狂的	ネッキョウテキ	enthusiastic; wild; mad; frantic; manic
	熱血	ネッケツ	zeal; hot blood; enthusiasm; ardor

	熱源	ネツゲン	heat source
	熱情	ネツジョウ	fervor; ardor; passion; warmth; ardent love
	熱心	ネッシン	enthusiasm; zeal; fervor; ardor; earnestness
	熱誠	ネッセイ	feverish; earnest; devoted; sincere; enthusiastic
	熱戦	ネッセン	hot contest; hard fight
	熱帯	ネッタイ	torrid zone; tropics
	熱中	ネッチュウ	absorption; enthusiasm; zeal —***vi***. become enthusiastic; have a mania for
	熱伝導	ネツデンドウ	***phy***. thermal conduction
	熱湯	ネットウ	boiling water
	熱病	ネツビョウ	fever
	熱風	ネップウ	hot wind; blast of hot air; hot blast
	熱弁	ネツベン	fervent speech
	熱望	ネツボウ	ardent wish; eager desire —***v***. desire earnestly; be anxious for
	熱量	ネツリョウ	***phy***. heat capacity; calorific value
	熱烈	ネツレツ	ardent; passionate; fervent; fiery
訓	熱い	あつい	hot; heated; be madly in love
	熱さ	あつさ	heat; warmth

1284

⑮

音	勲	クン	award; medal
熟	勲功	クンコウ	distinguished services; merits
	勲章	クンショウ	decoration; order; medal
	勲等	クントウ	medals for merit

4 爫 つめ／つめかんむり nail

1285

爵 ⑰

音	爵	シャク	peerage; Baron
熟	爵位	シャクイ	peerage

4 父 ちち father

1286
父 ④ ノ ハ グ 父

音	父	フ	father
熟	父兄	フケイ	father and elder brother; guardians or parents of children
	父母	フボ	father and mother; parents
訓	父	ちち	one's father
	父親	ちちおや	father
	※お父さん	おとうさん	father

4 片 かたへん right side

1287
片 ④ ノ ル 片 片

音	片	ヘン	one half of a whole; one side; fragment; piece; pence (unit of British currency)
熟	片影	ヘンエイ	shadow; sign; glimpse; partial view of a figure
	片々	ヘンペン	in pieces; in small fragments
	片鱗	ヘンリン	very tiny fragment; indication; partial glimpse
訓	片	かた	one (of two); one side; single
	片足	かたあし	one leg/foot
	片意地	かたイジ	stubborn; bigoted
	片一方	かたイッポウ	one side/party; other side/party
	片田舎	かたいなか	remote village in the country
	片腕	かたうで	one arm; righthand man
	片思い	かたおもい	unrequited love
	片親	かたおや	one parent
	片仮名	かたかな	*katakana* (the non-cursive syllabary)
	片側	かたがわ	one side
	片側通行	かたがわツウコウ	One Way (traffic)
	片言	かたこと	baby talk; broken (English); few words
	片隅	かたすみ	corner; nook; cranny
	片便り	かただより	one-way correspondence

片付く	かたづく	***vi***. be tidied up; be put away; be settled; be disposed of; be married off
片付ける	かたづける	***vt***. tidy up; put away; settle; dispose of; marry off
片手間	かたてま	in one's spare time; on the side
片時	かたとき	a moment; instant
片刃	かたは	single-edge blade
片端	かたはし	edge; end; side
片腹痛い	かたはらいたい	ridiculous; absurd; laughable
片方	かたホウ	one side/party; other side/party
片身	かたみ	one side of the body
片道	かたみち	one-way (trip/ticket)
片目	かため	one eye; one-eyed
片寄る	かたよる	***vi***. lean to one side; be unfair
片割れ	かたわれ	fragment; member of a group/gang (of criminals)

1288

版 ⑧

音	版	ハン	plate
熟	版画	ハンガ	print
	版権	ハンケン	copyright

4 牛 うし／うしへん cow

1289

牛 ④

音	牛	ギュウ	cow; ox; beef; dairy
熟	牛飲馬食	ギュウインバショク	heavy eating and drinking; immoderation in eating and drinking —***vi***. eat and drink heavily
	牛舎	ギュウシャ	cattle stall; cow barn
	牛耳る	ギュウジる	***vt***. take the lead; control
	牛肉	ギュウニク	beef
	牛乳	ギュウニュウ	cow's milk
訓	牛	うし	cow; ox; bull

1290

物 ⑧

ノ ⺈ 牛 牛 牜 牞 物 物

音	物	ブツ	thing; object
		モツ	thing; object
熟	物議	ブツギ	public criticism/discussion
	物件	ブッケン	thing; article; object
	物故	ブッコ	death —*vi*. die; pass away
	物故者	ブッコシャ	the deceased
	物産	ブッサン	product; produce; commodity
	物資	ブッシ	goods; resources
	物質	ブッシツ	matter; substance
	物質的	ブッシツテキ	material; physical
	物色	ブッショク	ransacking; rummaging; looking for —*v*. ransack; rummage; look/search for; select
	物騒	ブッソウ	unsettled; troubled; dangerous
	物体	ブッタイ	body; object; substance
	物的	ブッテキ	material; physical
	物品	ブッピン	goods; article; commodity
	物欲	ブツヨク	worldly desires/ambition
	物理	ブツリ	law of nature; physics
	物理学	ブツリガク	physics
	物理療法	ブツリリョウホウ	physiotherapy
訓	物	もの	thing; object
	物入り	ものいり	expenses
	物語	ものがたり	story; narrative
	物乞い	ものごい	begging; begger
	物心	ものごころ	discretion; judgment
	物腰	ものごし	manner; demeanor
	物事	ものごと	things; matters
	物好き	ものずき	curious; whimsical; eccentric
	物足りない	ものたりない	unsatisfying; something missing
	物干し	ものほし	(frame for) drying clothes
	物見	ものみ	sightseeing; watchtower; scout; patrol
	物見遊山	ものみユサン	pleasure trip; sightseeing tour
	物々しい	ものものしい	showy; imposing; elaborate; overdone; excessive
	物分かり	ものわかり	understanding
	物忘れ	ものわすれ	forgetfulness
¥	物価	ブッカ	prices (of commodities)

物価指数	ブッカシスウ	price index
物色買い	ブッショクがい	selective buying
物々交換	ブツブツコウカン	barter —*vi.* do business by barter
物流	ブツリュウ	distribution of goods
物別れ	ものわかれ	reaching no agreement; being broken off

1291

牧 ⑧

ノ ᅳ 牛 牛 牜 牜 牧 牧

音	牧	ボク	pasture
熟	牧牛	ボクギュウ	grazing/pasturing cattle
	牧師	ボクシ	pastor; minister
	牧舎	ボクシャ	cattleshed
	牧場	ボクジョウ	ranch; (cattle/sheep) farm
	牧神	ボクシン	Pan
	牧草	ボクソウ	grass; pasturage; meadow
	牧畜	ボクチク	livestock raising
	牧畜業	ボクチクギョウ	stock farming; ranching
	牧童	ボクドウ	cowboy; shepherd boy
訓	牧	まき	ranch; (cattle/sheep) farm
	牧場	まきば	ranch; (cattle/sheep) farm

1292

牲 ⑨

ノ ᅳ 牛 牛 牜 牜 牪 牪 牲

音	牲	セイ	sacrifice

1293

特 ⑩

ノ ᅳ 牛 牛 牜 牜 牯 牯 特 特

音	特	トク	special; specific; particular
熟	特異	トクイ	unique; singular
	特技	トクギ	specialty; special talent/ability
	特産	トクサン	special product; specialty
	特使	トクシ	special envoy/express messenger
	特質	トクシツ	characteristic; property; special quality
	特赦	トクシャ	amnesty
	特殊	トクシュ	special; specific; particular; peculiar; distinct; typical

特需	トクジュ	special/emergency demand
特集	トクシュウ	special edition (of a newspaper, magazine, etc.) —*v.* bring out a special edition
特賞	トクショウ	special prize
特色	トクショク	character; feature; distinguishing mark; idiosyncrasy
特性	トクセイ	special quality; characteristic; distinguishing mark
特製	トクセイ	special make/manufacture
特設	トクセツ	special establishment/installment/accomodation
特選	トクセン	special selection/approval; recognition
特大	トクダイ	outsize
特種	トクだね	scoop; exclusive news
特長	トクチョウ	merit; forte; strong point
特徴	トクチョウ	feature; characteristic; distinctive feature
特定	トクテイ	specific —*v.* specify
特典	トクテン	privilege; special favor; benefit
特電	トクデン	special telegram
特等	トクトウ	special/top grade
特派	トクハ	special dispatch —*v.* send a special dispatch; send; detail
特売	トクバイ	bargain/special sale; sale at a special price —*v.* sell at a special/reduced prices
特筆	トクヒツ	special mention —*v.* make a special mention/feature of
特別	トクベツ	special; extraordinary
特報	トクホウ	news flash —*v.* give a news flash
特約	トクヤク	special contract/agreement —*v.* make/come to a special agreement
特有	トクユウ	peculiar; characteristic; special
特例	トクレイ	special case/treatment; exception
特価	トッカ	special/bargain price
特急	トッキュウ	limited/super express
特許	トッキョ	patent; charter; license; special permission
特権	トッケン	privilege; special right; charter; option
特効薬	トッコウヤク	specific remedy
¥ 特定金銭信託	トクテイキンセンシンタク	designated money in trust
特定引当金	トクテイひきあてキン	specific reserve
特定銘柄	トクテイメイがら	specified stock
特別積立金	トクベツつみたてキン	special retained earnings
特約店	トクヤクテン	specified agent
特約取引	トクヤクとりひき	seller's option

特許	トッキョ	patent
特許庁	トッキョチョウ	Patent Office
特許品	トッキョヒン	patented article; patent

1294

犠 ⑰ 　牛 牜 … 犠 犠 犠

音	犠	ギ	sacrifice; victim
熟	犠牲	ギセイ	sacrifice
訓	※犠	いけにえ	sacrifice; scapegoat

4 犬 いぬ dog; animal 　犭 (p.572)

1295

④ 　一 ナ 大 犬

音	犬	ケン	dog
熟	犬猿の仲	ケンエンのなか	dog and monkey ***fig***. bitter enmity; on bad terms
	犬歯	ケンシ	canine teeth
訓	犬	いぬ	dog
	犬死に	いぬじに	unrewarded death —***vi***. die for nothing

1296

⑦ 　… 状 状

音	状	ジョウ	condition; letter
熟	状況	ジョウキョウ	conditions; situation; state of affairs; circumstances
	状勢	ジョウセイ	situation; state of affairs; conditions
	状態	ジョウタイ	state; condition

1297

献 ⑬ 　一 十 … 献 献

音	献	ケン	give; present; offer; contribute; dedicate

心 忄 小 戈 戸 手 扌 支 攵 文 斗 斤 方 日 曰 月 肉 月 木 欠 止 歹 殳 母 毋 比 毛 氏 气 水 氺 氵 火 灬 爫 父 片 牛 ●犬 ●犭 王 礻 耂

	献	(コン)	fine dishes; good food
熟	献じる	ケンじる	***vt***. present; make a present of; offer; dedicate
	献金	ケンキン	contribution; donation; collection —***v***. contribute; donate
	献血	ケンケツ	blood donation —***vi***. donate/give blood
	献上	ケンジョウ	presentation —***v***. present; offer
	献身	ケンシン	devotion; unselfish aid —***vi***. devote oneself to helping others
	献身的	ケンシンテキ	devotedly; unselfishly
	献呈	ケンテイ	dedication —***v***. dedicate
	献立	コンだて	menu; bill of fare

1298

獣 ⑯

音	獣	ジュウ	beast
熟	獣医	ジュウイ	veterinary surgeon; vet
訓	獣	けもの	animal; beast

3 犭 けものへん animal

1299

犯 ⑤

音	犯	ハン	offense
熟	犯行	ハンコウ	crime; offense; criminal act
	犯罪	ハンザイ	crime; offense
	犯人	ハンニン	criminal; offender
訓	犯す	おかす	***vt***. commit an offense; violate; attack; assault; rape

1300

狂 ⑦

音	狂	キョウ	mad; insane
熟	狂気	キョウキ	insanity; madness
	狂喜	キョウキ	ecstasy; rapture —***vi***. be in ecstasy; go into raptures

	狂言	キョウゲン	*Kyogen* (Japanese comic play)
	狂人	キョウジン	lunatic; madman
	狂暴	キョウボウ	range; frenzy; fury
訓	狂う	くるう	***vi***. go mad; get out of order; go wrong; be upset
	狂おしい	くるおしい	mad/crazy (with grief, etc.)

1301

狭 ⑨

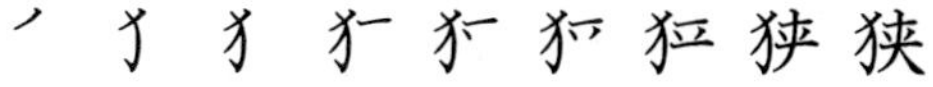

音	狭	キョウ	narrow; tight
熟	狭義	キョウギ	narrow sense/meaning
	狭量	キョウリョウ	narrow mindedness; intolerence
訓	狭まる	せばまる	***vi***. become narrow; contract
	狭める	せばめる	***vt***. narrow; contract; reduce (the width)
	狭い	せまい	narrow; tight

1302

狩 ⑨

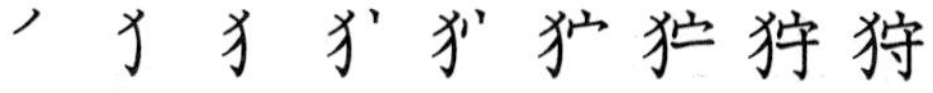

音	狩	シュ	hunting
熟	狩猟	シュリョウ	hunting; shooting
訓	狩り	かり	hunting
	狩人	かりうど (かりゅうど)	huntsman; hunter
	狩る	かる	***vt***. hunt

1303

独 ⑨

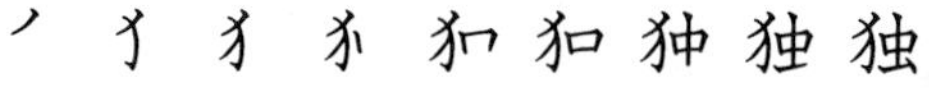

音	独	ドク	alone; by oneself; Germany
熟	独逸	ドイツ	Germany
	独演	ドクエン	recital; single; solo performance —***v***. give a solo performance/recital
	独学	ドクガク	self-education; self-instruction —***v***. teach/educate oneself
	独語	ドクゴ	the German language
	独裁	ドクサイ	dictatorship; despotism; autocracy —***vi***. dictate; hold a country under despotic rule
	独裁者	ドクサイシャ	dictator

心 忄 小 戈 戸 手 扌 支 攵 文 斗 斤 方 日 曰 月 肉 月 木 欠 止 歹 殳 母 毋 比 毛 氏 气 水 氺 氵 火 灬 爫 父 片 牛 犬 犭● 王 ネ 耂

心 忄 小 戈 戸 手 扌 支 攵 文 斗 斤 方 日 曰 月 肉 月 木 欠 止 歹 殳 母 毋 比 毛 氏 气 水 氺 氵 火 灬 爫 父 片 牛 犬 • 犭 王 ネ 耂

	独裁主義	ドクサイシュギ	dictatorship
	独裁的	ドクサイテキ	dictatorial; despotic; autocratic
	独自	ドクジ	original; peculiar; individual; oneself
	独習	ドクシュウ	self-teaching; self-study —*v*. teach oneself; study without a teacher
	独唱	ドクショウ	vocal solo; recital —*v*. sing a solo
	独身	ドクシン	single life; single; celibacy; bachelorhood
	独占	ドクセン	monopoly; exclusive possession —*v*. monopolize; keep a thing to oneself
	独善	ドクゼン	self-righteousness
	独走	ドクソウ	running alone; runaway; walkover —*vi*. run away; walkover
	独奏	ドクソウ	solo; recital —*v*. play a solo/alone
	独創	ドクソウ	originality
	独断	ドクダン	arbitrary decision; dogmatism
	独特	ドクトク	unique; peculiar; special; original
	独房	ドクボウ	cell; prison cell
	独立	ドクリツ	independence; self-help; self-reliance; freedom; self-support —*vi*. become independent/free/isolated
	独立心	ドクリツシン	independent spirit
	独立独歩	ドクリツドッポ	independence; self-reliance; self-help
	独力	ドクリョク	one's own efforts; single-handed
訓	独り	ひとり	alone; by oneself
	独り言	ひとりごと	monolog; soliloquy
¥	独占禁止法（独禁法）	ドクセンキンシホウ（ドクキンホウ）	Antimonopoly (Antitrust) Law

1304

猫 ⑪

音	猫	ビョウ	cat
訓	猫	ねこ	cat
	猫舌	ねこじた	tongue that is sensitive to heat
	猫背	ねこぜ	stoop; round shoulders
	猫ばば	ねこばば	embezzlement; misappropriation

1305

猛 ⑪

音	猛	モウ	fierce; strong; intense

熟	猛威	モウイ	ferocity; vehemence
	猛火	モウカ	raging flames; conflagration
	猛犬	モウケン	fierce/vicious dog
	猛攻	モウコウ	heavy blow/attack —*v*. mount a heavy attack
	猛獣	モウジュウ	ferocious animal
	猛進	モウシン	rushing/plunging ahead —***vi***. rush forward; plunge ahead
	猛然	モウゼン	violently; fiercely; resolutely
	猛打	モウダ	heavy hit/blow (sports)
	猛毒	モウドク	deadly/virulent poison
	猛烈	モウレツ	violent; fierce; intense
	※猛者	モサ	stalwart; veteran; man of courage
訓	※猛る	たける	***vi***. rush; rage; rave
	※猛々しい	たけだけしい	fierce; ferocious; audacious

1306

猟 ⑪

音	猟	リョウ	hunting
熟	猟期	リョウキ	hunting season
	猟犬	リョウケン	hound; hunting dog
	猟師	リョウシ	hunter
	猟銃	リョウジュウ	hunting gun; shotgun
	猟場	リョウば	game preserve; hunting ground

1307

猶 ⑫

音	猶	ユウ	delay; still; still more
熟	猶予	ユウヨ	postponement; deferment; hesitation —***vi***. reprieve; postpone; defer; hesitate
¥	猶予期間	ユウヨキカン	grace period

1308

猿 ⑬

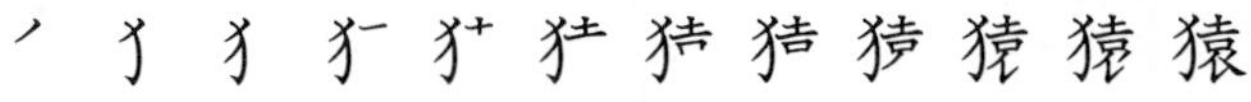

音	猿	エン	monkey; ape
訓	猿	さる	monkey
	猿芝居	さるしばい	monkey show; shallow-minded trick

猿真似　さるまね　blind imitation
猿回し　さるまわし　monkey showman

1309
獄 ⑭
ノ 犭 犭 犭 犭 犭 犭 犭 犭 犭 獄 獄

音 獄　ゴク　prison; punishment; judgment; hell

1310
獲 ⑯
ノ 犭 犭 犭 犭 犭 犭 犭 犭 犭 獲 獲

音 獲　カク　catch; gain
熟 獲得　カクトク　gain; acquisition —*v.* get; acquire; obtain
訓 獲る　える　*vt.* capture
獲物　えもの　wild game

4 王 see ⇨p.578

4 ネ see ⇨p.623

4 耂 see ⇨p.684

5 玄 げん dark

1311

玄 ⑤

音	玄	ゲン	black; dark; deep
熟	玄関	ゲンカン	entrance; hallway
	玄米	ゲンマイ	*genmai* (unpolished/brown rice)
訓	※玄人	くろうと	professional

1312

率 ⑪

音	率	ソツ	lead; all; light; easy
		リツ	proportion; percentage; rate
熟	率先	ソッセン	taking the lead —***vi***. take the lead; be the first
	率然	ソツゼン	suddenly; unexpectedly
	率直	ソッチョク	frank; straightforward
訓	率いる	ひきいる	***vt***. lead; be in command of

5 玉 たま jewel 王 (p.578)

1313

玉 ⑤

音	玉	ギョク	jewel; pearl; jewel like
熟	玉石混交	ギョクセキコンコウ	good and bad
訓	玉	たま	jewel; gem

1314

⑲

音	璽	ジ	Privy Seal; imperial seal

4 王 おう／たまへん／おうへん king

1315

王 ④ 一 丅 干 王

音	王	オウ	king; prince; lord
熟	王位	オウイ	the throne; the crown
	王冠	オウカン	crown; bottle top
	王宮	オウキュウ	king's palace; royal palace
	王侯	オウコウ	king and his feudal lords
	王国	オウコク	kingdom
	王座	オウザ	the throne
	王様	オウさま	king
	王子	オウジ	prince
	王室	オウシツ	royal family
	王者	オウシャ（オウジャ）	king; monarch; ruler
	王女	オウジョ	princess
	王政	オウセイ	imperial rule
	王政復古	オウセイフッコ	***hist***. restoration of imperial rule (1867)
	王族	オウゾク	royal family
	王朝	オウチョウ	dynasty
	王手	オウて	checkmate; *ote* (shogi)
	王妃	オウヒ	queen; empress

1316

⑨

音	珍	チン	curious; strange; odd; rare; remarkable
熟	珍奇	チンキ	rarity; novelty; curiosity
	珍客	チンキャク	rare visitor; welcome guest
	珍事	チンジ	rare event; unexpected occurrence
	珍重	チンチョウ	something that one values —***v***. treasure; value; esteem; prize
	珍品	チンピン	rarity; curio; curiosity
	珍味	チンミ	delicacy; unusual taste
	珍妙	チンミョウ	queer; odd
訓	珍しい	めずらしい	rare; odd; queer; remarkable

1317
珠 ⑩

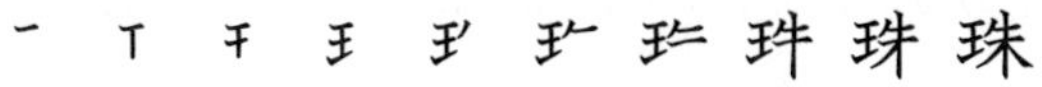

音	珠	シュ	pearl; bead
熟	珠玉	シュギョク	pearls and jewels; precious object; literary gem
	珠算	シュザン	calculation on the abacus
訓	※珠	たま	bead; jewel; gem

1318
班 ⑩

音	班	ハン	group
熟	班長	ハンチョウ	squad/section/group leader

1319
球 ⑪

音	球	キュウ	ball; sphere; spherical; baseball
熟	球技	キュウギ	ball game
	球根	キュウコン	bulb
	球状	キュウジョウ	spherical shape; globe
	球場	キュウジョウ	baseball ground; ballpark
	球審	キュウシン	***bas***. plate/chief umpire
	球速	キュウソク	***bas***. (pitcher's) pace; speed of a pitcher's ball
訓	球	たま	ball

1320
現 ⑪

音	現	ゲン	appear; now; current; present
熟	現役	ゲンエキ	active service/duty
	現金	ゲンキン	cash; ready money ***adj***. mercenary; calculating; selfish
	現行	ゲンコウ	current; present; existing
	現行犯	ゲンコウハン	flagrant offense; red-handed
	現在	ゲンザイ	now; the present; existing; current —***v***. exist; be current

	現実	ゲンジツ	reality; actuality; hard fact
	現実化	ゲンジツカ	realization —*v*. realize; be realized; put into effect
	現実主義	ゲンジツシュギ	realism
	現住所	ゲンジュウショ	present address
	現出	ゲンシュツ	appearance; emergence; revelation —*v*. appear; emerge; come out; reveal
	現象	ゲンショウ	phenomenon; happening; phase; aspect
	現状	ゲンジョウ	present state; actual situation; status quo
	現職	ゲンショク	one's present post/office
	現世	ゲンセ	this world/life; worldly; earthy; temporal; secular
	現像	ゲンゾウ	film development —*v*. develop (a film)
	現存	ゲンゾン	existence —*vi*. exist; be extant
	現代	ゲンダイ	today; modern; the present age; contempory
	現地	ゲンチ	on the spot; locality; the field; the actual place
	現地時間	ゲンチジカン	local time
	現場	ゲンば	the spot; the field; the actual place
	現品	ゲンピン	goods; the actual article
訓	現す	あらわす	***vt***. express; show; reveal
	現れる	あらわれる	***vi***. come out; appear; emerge
¥	現先取引	ゲンさきとりひき	repurchase agreement (transaction)
	現地法人	ゲンチホウジン	local affiliated firm (overseas)
	現物	ゲンブツ	spot goods; actuals
	現渡し	ゲンわたし	actual delivery of stock sold

1321

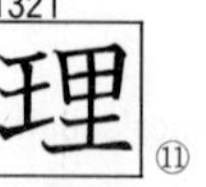

⑪

音	理	リ	reason; justice; truth; principle
熟	理科	リカ	science
	理解	リカイ	understanding; comprehension —*v*. understand; comprehend
	理化学	リカガク	physics and chemistry
	理屈	リクツ	reason; logic; theory; argument; pretext
	理事	リジ	director; trustee
	理性	リセイ	reason; reasoning power
	理想	リソウ	ideal
	理想郷	リソウキョウ	utopia; ideal land; Shangri-La
	理想的	リソウテキ	ideal
	理知	リチ	intellect; intelligence
	理念	リネン	idea; doctrine; ideology

理髪	リハツ	haircutting
理髪師	リハツシ	barber; hairdresser
理非	リヒ	rights and wrongs; relative merits
理由	リユウ	reason; cause
理容	リヨウ	hairdressing
理路整然	リロセイゼン	logical; well-argued; cogent
理論	リロン	theory

1322

琴 ⑫

音	琴	キン	harp; zither
熟	琴線	キンセン	heartstrings; one's innermost feelings
訓	琴	こと	*koto* (Japanese zither)

1323

環 ⑰

音	環	カン	ring; enclose
熟	環境	カンキョウ	environment
	環礁	カンショウ	atoll
	環状線	カンジョウセン	loop line
訓	※環	わ	ring; circle; loop

5 瓦 かわら tile

1324

瓶 ⑪

音	瓶	ビン	bottle; jar
熟	瓶詰	ビンづめ	bottled (beer, etc.)

5 甘 あまい sweet

1325

甘 ⑤ 一 十 廾 廿 甘

音	甘	カン	sweet
熟	甘言	カンゲン	flattery
	甘受	カンジュ	submission; resignation —*v*. submit (tamely) to; be resigned to (one's fate)
	甘味料	カンミリョウ	sweetening
訓	甘い	あまい	sweet; sugary; flattering; indulgent
	甘える	あまえる	***vi***. behave like a spoiled child; be indulgent; take advantage of
	甘やかす	あまやかす	***vt***. indulge; pamper; overindulge; spoil
	甘口	あまくち	light; sweet
	甘酒	あまざけ	sweet alcoholic drink made from saké
	甘党	あまトウ	person with a sweet tooth

1326

甚 ⑨ 一 十 廾 廿 甘 其 甚 甚 甚

音	甚	ジン	greatly
熟	甚大	ジンダイ	serious; great; enormous
訓	甚だ	はなはだ	very; much; greatly
	甚だしい	はなはだしい	extreme; enormous; blatant; outrageous

5 生 うまれる life; birth

1327

生 ⑤ ノ ㇀ 十 牛 生

音	生	ショウ	live; life
		セイ	life; living; birth; produce; grow
熟	生じる	ショウじる	***v***. develop; accrue; come about; engender
	生姜	ショウが	ginger
	生涯	ショウガイ	life; career; working life

生国	ショウゴク（ショウコク）	country/province of one's birth
生育	セイイク	growth; development —*v*. grow; raise; be born and bred; vegetate
生家	セイカ	one's parents' house; house one was born in
生花	セイカ	real flower; flower arrangement
生活	セイカツ	life; existence; livelihood —*vi*. live; exist; make a living
生活水準	セイカツスイジュン	standard of living
生活費	セイカツヒ	living expenses
生還	セイカン	surviving —*vi*. come back alive; survive
生気	セイキ	vitality; life; animation; vigor; spirit
生計	セイケイ	living; livelihood
生彩	セイサイ	vividness; luster; brilliance; live
生産	セイサン	production —*v*. produce; make; turn/put out
生産高	セイサンだか	output; yield
生産地	セイサンチ	producing center
生死	セイシ	life or death; safety; fate
生殖	セイショク	generation; reproduction; procreation
生殖器	セイショクキ	*med*. sexual/reproductive organs; genitals
生成	セイセイ	creation; formulation; generation —*vi*. be created/formed
生鮮	セイセン	fresh; perishable
生前	セイゼン	while alive; during one's lifetime; before one's death
生息	セイソク	inhabited —*vi*. inhabit; live
生存	セイゾン	existence; being; life —*vi*. exist; live; survive; outlive
生存競争	セイゾンキョウソウ	struggle for existence
生存者	セイゾンシャ	survivor
生態	セイタイ	mode of life; ecology
生態学	セイタイガク	ecology
生誕	セイタン	birth; nativity —*vi*. be born
生地	セイチ	birthplace/home
生年	セイネン	year of birth; age
生年月日	セイネンガッぴ	date of birth
生物	セイブツ	living thing; organism; creature; life
生物学	セイブツガク	biology
生別	セイベツ	eternal/lifelong separation —*v*. never meet again
生命	セイメイ	life; the soul
生来	セイライ	by nature; naturally; by birth
生理	セイリ	physiology; menstruation
訓 生きる	いきる	*vi*. live; exist; survive
生かす	いかす	*vi*. revive; resuscitate; bring to life; give life to

生ける	いける	***vt***. arrange flowers
生まれる	うまれる	***vi***. be born
生む	うむ	***vt***. bear; give birth to; produce
生う	おう	***v***. grow; come out
生える	はえる	***vi***. grow; come out
生やす	はやす	***vt***. grow; cultivate
生	き	pure; raw
生一本	きイッポン	pure; neat; straight; straightforward; honest
生糸	きいと	raw silk
生地	きジ	cloth
生真面目	きまじめ	honest; earnest; sincere
生	なま	raw; uncooked; rare; draft
生意気	なまイキ	conceit; self-conceit; selfishness
生演奏	なまエンソウ	live performance
生傷	なまきず	fresh wound
生々しい	なまなましい	fresh; green; vivid; graphic
生返事	なまヘンジ	vague answer; noncommittal reply
生放送	なまホウソウ	live broadcast
¥ 生産財	セイサンザイ	production goods
生産性	セイサンセイ	productivity
生産費	セイサンヒ	costs of production; production costs
生産目標	セイサンモクヒョウ	production target
生産力	セイサンリョク	production capacity
生命保険	セイメイホケン	life insurance

1328

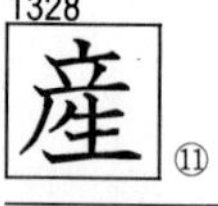

⑪ 、 亠 亠 亣 立 产 产 产 産 産 産

音	産	サン	give birth to; produce; output
熟	産院	サンイン	maternity hospital
	産科	サンカ	***med***. obstetrics; the obstetrical department
	産気	サンケ	feeling that a baby is about to be born
	産児制限	サンジセイゲン	birth control —***vi***. practice birth control
	産地	サンチ	producing area/center
	産婦人科	サンフジンカ	***med***. gynecology
	産物	サンブツ	products; produce
	産卵	サンラン	laying eggs; spawning —***vi***. lay eggs; spawn
訓	産む	うむ	***vt***. have a baby; bear; give birth to; produce
	産まれる	うまれる	***vi***. be born; be established; be started
	産	うぶ	naive; innocent; unsophisticated

	産毛	うぶげ	downy hair
¥	産休	サンキュウ	maternity leave
	産業	サンギョウ	industry
	産業化	サンギョウカ	industrialization —*v.* industrialize
	産業革命	サンギョウカクメイ	industrial revolution
	産業資本	サンギョウシホン	industrial capital
	産出	サンシュツ	production —*v.* produce; yield; output
	産油国	サンユコク	oil producing nation

5 用 もちいる using

1329

用 ⑤

丿 冂 月 月 用

音	用	ヨウ	business; errand; use
熟	用意	ヨウイ	preparations; arrangements
	用意周到	ヨウイシュウトウ	thoroughly prepared; well arranged
	用器	ヨウキ	instrument; tool
	用具	ヨウグ	equipment; kit
	用件	ヨウケン	business; things to be done
	用語	ヨウゴ	term; terminology
	用材	ヨウザイ	lumber; materials
	用紙	ヨウシ	(application) form; stationery
	用字	ヨウジ	use of characters
	用事	ヨウジ	business; errand; things to be done
	用心	ヨウジン	caution; care —***vi.*** take care of; pay attention to
	用心棒	ヨウジンボウ	bodyguard
	用水	ヨウスイ	city/irrigation water
	用談	ヨウダン	business talk —***vi.*** have an important business talk
	用地	ヨウチ	lot; site; land for some use
	用途	ヨウト	use; purpose
	用品	ヨウヒン	supplies
	用便	ヨウベン	going to the toilet —*v.* go to the toilet
	用法	ヨウホウ	how to use; directions
	用務	ヨウム	business
	用務員	ヨウムイン	janitor; custodian
	用命	ヨウメイ	command; order

	用例	ヨウレイ	example; illustration
訓	用いる	もちいる	***vt***. use

---

5 田 た／たへん rice field

1330

田 ⑤

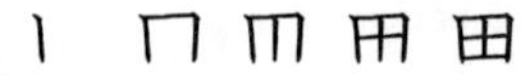

音	田	デン	field
熟	田園	デンエン	fields and gardens; the country; rural districts
	田園生活	デンエンセイカツ	country life; life in the country
	田園都市	デンエントシ	rural city
	田楽	デンガク	*dengaku* (ritual music and dancing performed in Shinto shrines)
	田畑	デンぱた	cultivated fields
	田野	デンヤ	cultivated fields
訓	田	た	rice field
	田植え	たうえ	rice planting
	田畑	たはた	rice field; farmland; fields
	田圃	たんボ	rice field
	※田舎	いなか	the country; countryside

1331

甲 ⑤

音	甲	コウ	grade A; the first in a series; crust; shell; carapace
		カン	
熟	甲斐	カイ	use; effect; result ***hist***. former name of Yamanashi prefecture (until the Meiji period)
	甲高い	カンだかい	high-pitched; shrill
	甲板	カンパン	ship's deck
	甲乙	コウオツ	A and B; difference (between A and B)
	甲殻	コウカク	crust; shell; carapace
	甲殻類	コウカクルイ	crustacea
	甲虫	コウチュウ	beetle
	甲羅	コウラ	shell; carapace

1332

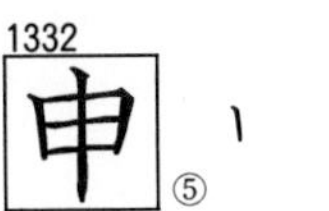

⑤

音	申	シン	state; say; report; declare
熟	申告	シンコク	report; return; declaration —*v*. report; declare
	申告書	シンコクショ	report; declaration
	申請	シンセイ	application; petition —*v*. apply; make an application
	申請書	シンセイショ	application form
訓	申す	もうす	***hum. vt.*** say; speak; mention
	申し上げる	もうしあげる	***hum. vt.*** tell; inform
	申し込む	もうしこむ	***vt.*** propose; request; apply; reserve; subscript
	申し訳ない	もうしわけない	sorry; excuse me; thank you
	※申	さる	the monkey (ninth sign of the Chinese zodiac)

1333

由

⑤

音	由	ユ ユウ (ユイ)	reason; cause; significance; means; way
熟	由緒	ユイショ	history; lineage; origin
	由々しい	ユユしい	grave; serious
	由来	ユライ	origin; derivation; originally; by nature —***vi***. date back to; originate
訓	由	よし	reason; cause; significance; means; way

1334

男

⑦

音	男	ダン ナン	man; male; baron man
熟	男子	ダンシ	male; man; boy; son
	男児	ダンジ	boy
	男女	ダンジョ	man and woman; couple
	男性	ダンセイ	male sex; man; masculinity; manliness
	男性的	ダンセイテキ	manly; masculine
	男尊女卑	ダンソンジョヒ	predominance of men over women; male supremacy

訓	男	おとこ	man; boy

1335

町 ⑦

音	町	チョウ	town; street; block
熟	町会	チョウカイ	town block association; town assembly
	町村	チョウソン	towns and villages; municipalities
	町長	チョウチョウ	town headman/manager
	町内	チョウナイ	town; streets; neighborhood
訓	町	まち	town; city; street
	町中	まちなか	the streets; the middle of the town
	町並み	まちなみ	row of stores and houses on a street
	町外れ	まちはずれ	outskirts of a town

1336

界 ⑨

音	界	カイ	border; circles; scope
熟	界隈	カイワイ	neighborhood; vicinity
訓	界	さかい	border; limit

1337

畑 ⑨

訓	畑	はた	plowed field; farm; plantation
	畑	はたけ	plowed field; farm; plantation ***fig***. specialty; one's field

1338

畝 ⑩

訓	畝	うね	ridge; furrow; groove
	畝	せ	*se* (unit of area, approx. 0.991 a)

1339

⑩

音	畜	チク	breed; raise; beast; cattle
熟	畜産	チクサン	stock raising/breeding
	畜生	チクショウ	beast ***col.*** Damn it!; Shit!

1340

⑩

音	畔	ハン	side
訓	※畔	あぜ	ridge between rice fields

1341
留
⑩

音	留	リュウ (ル)	stop; hold; fast; detain; keep
熟	留意	リュウイ	attention; mindful —***vi***. pay attention to; give head to; be mindful of
	留任	リュウニン	remaining in office —***vi***. remain in office
	留学	リュウガク	studying abroad —***vi***. study abroad
	留置	リュウチ	detention; custody —***v***. detain; lockup; hold in custody
	留保	リュウホ	reservation; withholding —***v***. reserve; withhold
	留守	ルス	absence; being away from home; neglecting
	留守番	ルスバン	looking after the house (while the owner is away); someone who looks after a house (while the owner in away)
	留守番電話	ルスバンデンワ	answering machine
訓	留まる	とまる	***vi***. stop; be fixed in one position
	留める	とめる	***vt***. stop; detain; fix in one position
	留め立て	とめだて	dissuasion

1342

⑪

音	異	イ	different; unusual; curious; peculiar; uncommon

熟	異義	イギ	different/another meaning
	異議	イギ	objection; complaint
	異郷	イキョウ	strange/foreign land
	異境	イキョウ	foreign country/land
	異口同音	イクドウオン	with one voice/accord; unanimously
	異国	イコク	foreign land/country
	異彩	イサイ	striking/conspicuous color
	異質	イシツ	heterogeneity
	異種	イシュ	different species/kind; variety
	異状	イジョウ	something wrong; accident; change; disorder
	異常	イジョウ	unusual; abnormal; extraordinary
	異色	イショク	different color
	異人	イジン	foreigner; stranger; alien
	異性	イセイ	the opposite sex
	異説	イセツ	different view/theory; conflicting views
	異存	イゾン	objection
	異端	イタン	heresy; heterodoxy
	異同	イドウ	difference
	異動	イドウ	change; reshuffle
	異物	イブツ	foreign matter
	異変	イヘン	accident; mishap
	異邦人	イホウジン	foreigner; alien; outsider
	異名	イミョウ	nickname; another name; alias
	異様	イヨウ	strange; outlandish; fantastic; grotesque
	異例	イレイ	exception; singular case
	異論	イロン	different opinion; objection; controversial opinion
訓	異なる	ことなる	***vi.*** differ; be different/dissimilar/unlike

1343

略 ⑪

音	略	リャク	omission; abridgement; abbreviation
熟	略する	リャクする	***vt.*** omit; abbreviate; abridge; shorten
	略画	リャクガ	rough sketch
	略語	リャクゴ	abbreviation
	略字	リャクジ	simplified Chinese character
	略式	リャクシキ	informal; summary
	略述	リャクジュツ	brief account; outline —***v.*** give a brief account; outline
	略称	リャクショウ	abbreviation —***v.*** abbreviate
	略図	リャクズ	rough sketch; outline map

	略装	リャクソウ	everyday clothes; informal wear
	略奪	リャクダツ	plunder; pillage; looting —*v*. plunder; pillage; loot
	略歴	リャクレキ	brief personal history; résumé
	略記	リャッキ	brief account; outline —*v*. give a brief account; outline

1344

畳 ⑫

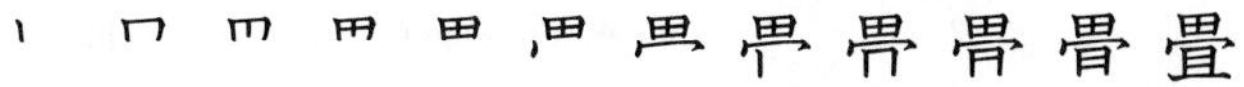

音	畳	ジョウ	fold; *jō* (counter for *tatami* mats)
熟	畳語	ジョウゴ	reduplication; repetitive use of the same word or root
訓	畳	たたみ	*tatami* (straw mat layed on the floors of Japanese homes)
	畳む	たたむ	***vt***. fold up; close/shut down

1345

番 ⑫

音	番	バン	watch; vigil; guard; turn; number
熟	番外	バンガイ	extra; outsize
	番傘	バンがさ	coarse oil-paper umbrella
	番組	バンぐみ	program billing (of performers)
	番狂わせ	バンくるわせ	upsetting of arrangements
	番犬	バンケン	watchdog; housedog
	番号	バンゴウ	number
	番台	バンダイ	watch stand; raised platform for a ticket seller, etc.
	番地	バンチ	lot/house number; address
	番茶	バンチャ	*bancha* (coarse green tea)
	番付	バンづけ	program; list; ranking list
	番頭	バントウ	clerk; secretary
	番人	バンニン	guard; watchman
	番兵	バンペイ	sentry; guard

5 疋 ひき animal counter

1346

⑫

音	疎	ソ	sparse; estrangement; shun; neglect
熟	疎遠	ソエン	estrangement; long separation
	疎開	ソカイ	evacuation; removal; dispersal —*vi*. evacuate; remove; dispense
	疎外	ソガイ	alienation; estrangement —*v*. shun; alienate; estrange
	疎忽	ソコツ	carelessness; heedlessness; thoughtlessness; rashness
	疎食	ソショク	coarse food; plain/simple diet; poor meal
	疎水	ソスイ	drainage; canal
	疎通	ソツウ	mutual understanding —*vi*. understand one another
	疎略	ソリャク	coarse; crude
訓	疎い	うとい	little known; unfamiliar; distant; estranged
	疎む	うとむ	***vt***. neglect; shun; estrange
	※疎ましい	うとましい	negligent; remiss
	※疎か	おろそか	disagreeable

1347

⑭

音	疑	ギ	doubt
熟	疑獄	ギゴク	scandal; criminal case; graft case
	疑似	ギジ	looking very alike
	疑点	ギテン	doubtful point; doubt
	疑念	ギネン	doubt; suspicion
	疑問	ギモン	question; problem; doubt
	疑惑	ギワク	distrust; doubt; suspicion
訓	疑い	うたがい	doubt; suspicion
	疑う	うたがう	***vt***. doubt; suspect; distrust
	疑わしい	うたがわしい	doubtful; questionable

1348
疫 ⑨ 丶 亠 广 疒 疒 疒 疒 疫 疫

音	疫	エキ	epidemic
		(ヤク)	plague
熟	疫病	エキビョウ	***med***. epidemic
	疫痢	エキリ	***med***. infant dysentery

1349
疾 ⑩ 丶 亠 广 疒 疒 疒 疒 疒 疾 疾

音	疾	シツ	disease; speedy
熟	疾患	シッカン	disease; ailment
	疾走	シッソウ	speed —***vi***. run at full speed; make a dash
	疾風	シップウ	gale; strong wind
	疾病	シッペイ	disease; illness

1350
症 ⑩ 丶 亠 广 疒 疒 疒 疒 疒 疒 症

音	症	ショウ	condition of an illness
熟	症状	ショウジョウ	***med***. symptom; condition

1351
疲 ⑩ 丶 亠 广 疒 疒 疒 疒 疒 疲 疲

音	疲	ヒ	get tired
熟	疲弊	ヒヘイ	impoverishment; ruin; exhaustion —***vi***. become impoverished; fall into ruin; exhaust oneself
	疲労	ヒロウ	fatigue; weariness; exhaustion —***vi***. tire; exhaust oneself
訓	疲れる	つかれる	***vi***. get tired
	疲れ果てる	つかれはてる	***vi***. get tired out; be exhausted

1352

病 ⑩

丶 亠 广 广 疒 疒 疒 疔 病 病 病

音	病	ビョウ （ヘイ）	disease; illness; sickness
熟	病院	ビョウイン	hospital; clinic; infirmary; doctor's office/surgery
	病臥	ビョウガ	bedridden —***vi***. be bedridden/ill in bed
	病気	ビョウキ	disease; illness; sickness ***fig***. failing; weakness —***vi***. be ill/sick
	病苦	ビョウク	pain/suffering caused by illness
	病欠	ビョウケツ	sick leave —***vi***. be absent because of sickness
	病原菌	ビョウゲンキン	***med***. pathogenic bacteria/fungi; bacillus
	病後	ビョウゴ	convalescence; after-care
	病根	ビョウコン	cause of a disease; root of an evil
	病死	ビョウシ	death from disease —***vi***. die from a disease
	病室	ビョウシツ	sickroom; sick bay; infirmary
	病弱	ビョウジャク	weak; sickly; weak constitution
	病床	ビョウショウ	sickbed; bedridden; laid up
	病状	ビョウジョウ	condition of a disease; (patient's) condition
	病身	ビョウシン	ill/poor health; sickly; susceptible to illness
	病中	ビョウチュウ	during illness/sickness
	病的	ビョウテキ	morbid; abnormal
	病毒	ビョウドク	***med***. disease-causing virus; pathogen
	病人	ビョウニン	sick person; invalid; patient; the sick
	病没	ビョウボツ	death from disease —***vi***. die from disease/illness
	病魔	ビョウマ	disease
	病理学	ビョウリガク	pathology
訓	病	やまい	sickness; illness; disease; bad habit; weakness
	病む	やむ	be ill; get sick; suffer from
	病み上がり	やみあがり	convalescence
	病み付き	やみつき	addicted to; hooked on; unable to give up

1353

痛 ⑫

丶 亠 广 广 疒 疒 疒 疗 痏 痏 痏 痛

音	痛	ツウ	ache
熟	痛快	ツウカイ	keen pleasure; thrill
	痛感	ツウカン	strong/intense feeling; intuition —***v***. feel strongly; take to heart; fully realize

	痛撃	ツウゲキ	severe blow/attack —*v*. attack severely
	痛切	ツウセツ	keen; poignant; acute
	痛風	ツウフウ	***med***. gout
	痛烈	ツウレツ	severe; fierce; sharp; bitter; biting
訓	痛い	いたい	painful; sore; ache
	痛む	いたむ	***vi***. feel/suffer pain; be wounded/injured
	痛める	いためる	***vt***. hurt; injure; ache
	痛手	いたで	serious wound; heavy blow

1354

痘 ⑫

丶 亠 广 广 疒 疒 疒 疒 疒 疒 痘 痘

音	痘	トウ	smallpox
熟	痘苗	トウビョウ	vaccine

1355

痢 ⑫

丶 亠 广 广 疒 疒 疒 疒 疒 疒 痢 痢

音	痢	リ	diarrhea

1356

痴 ⑬

丶 亠 广 广 疒 疒 疒 疒 疾 痴 痴 痴

音	痴	チ	fool
熟	痴漢	チカン	molester of women; pervert —***vi***. molest; be a pervert
	痴人	チジン	simpleton; idiot; fool
	痴呆	チホウ	imbecility; dementia

1357

療 ⑰

广 疒 疒 疒 疒 疒 疒 疒 疒 疒 療 療

音	療	リョウ	cure; heal
熟	療治	リョウジ	medical treatment; remedy —*v*. treat an illness
	療法	リョウホウ	remedy; therapy; medical treatment
	療養	リョウヨウ	medical treatment/care —***vi***. receive medical treatment/care
	療養所	リョウヨウジョ	sanitarium

1358 **癖** ⑱

音	癖	ヘキ	(bad) habit; fault
訓	癖	くせ	(bad) habit; fault; bad point; cowlick

1359 **癒** ⑱

音	癒	ユ	heal; cure; satisfy; soothe
熟	癒合	ユゴウ	***med***. agglutination; adhesion —***vi***. agglutinate; adhere
	癒着	ユチャク	adhesion; healing up —***vi***. adhere; heal up
訓	※癒える	いえる	***vi***. be healed; recover
	※癒す	いやす	***vt***. heal; cure; satisfy; soothe

5  はつがしら departing head

1360 **発** ⑨

音	発	ハツ	discharge; break out; disclose; start
		ホツ	occur
熟	発する	ハッする	***vi***. discharge; fire; issue; publish; cry out; start off; leave
	発案	ハツアン	proposition; suggestion; motion —***v***. propose; suggest; move
	発育	ハツイク	growth; development —***vi***. grow; develop
	発音	ハツオン	pronunciation; articulation —***v***. pronounce; articulate
	発芽	ハツガ	germination; sprouting; budding —***vi***. germinate; sprout; bud
	発会	ハッカイ	first club meeting —***vi***. have the first club meeting
	発覚	ハッカク	revelation; detection; discovery; disclosure; exposure —***vi***. be revealed/detected/discovered/exposed
	発刊	ハッカン	publication; issue —***v***. publish; issue; bring out; start; launch

発汗	ハッカン	sweating; perspiration —***vi***. sweat; perspire
発揮	ハッキ	manifestation; exhibition; demonstration; display —***v***. make manifest; exhibit; demonstrate; display; show
発狂	ハッキョウ	madness; craziness; insanity —***vi***. go mad/crazy/out of one's mind
発禁	ハッキン	prohibition of sale or publication
発掘	ハックツ	excavation; exhumation; digs; find —***v***. excavate; exhume; dig up; unearth
発見	ハッケン	discovery; revelation; detection —***v***. discover; detect; spot
発言	ハツゲン	utterance; speaking; speech; opinion —***vi***. speak; utter; open one's mouth; give an opinion
発光	ハッコウ	radiation; luminescence —***vi***. radiate; emit light; luminate
発行	ハッコウ	issue; publication; flotation —***v***. issue; publish; float
発効	ハッコウ	effectuation; coming in to effect —***v***. become effective; come/put into effect
発酵	ハッコウ	fermentation —***v***. ferment
発散	ハッサン	exhalation; radiation; diffusion; evaporation; divergence —***v***. exhale; emit; radiate; evaporate
発車	ハッシャ	departure (of a train, car, etc.) —***vi***. start; leave; depart
発射	ハッシャ	firing; shooting; lift-off —***v***. discharge firearms; fire; shoot
発祥	ハッショウ	beginning —***vi***. begin; start off; originate
発信	ハッシン	dispatch of a letter, telegram, etc. —***vi***. send/dispatch a letter; telegraph; cable
発進	ハッシン	start; departure; take-off; launch —***vi***. start; depart; take-off; launch
発疹	ハッシン (ホッシン)	eruption; rash —***vi***. break out into a rash
発生	ハッセイ	occurrence; outbreak; appearance; birth; creation —***v***. occur; happen; come into existence
発声	ハッセイ	utterance —***vi***. utter; speak out; exclaim
発送	ハッソウ	sending; forwarding; shipping; dispatch —***v***. send out; forward; ship; dispatch
発想	ハッソウ	expression; conception; idea —***v***. conceive/come up with an idea
発達	ハッタツ	development; growth; progress —***vi***. develop; grow; make progress
発着	ハッチャク	departure and arrival —***vi***. depart and arrive
発注	ハッチュウ	ordering —***v***. order; give an order
発展	ハッテン	expansion; extension; progress; prosperity; dissipation —***vi***. expand; extend; develop; grow
発電	ハツデン	electricity generation; sending a telegram —***vi***. generate electricity; send a telegram; wire

	発電所	ハツデンショ	power station/plant
	発動	ハツドウ	motion; activity; exercise —***v***. move; put in motion; exercise
	発熱	ハツネツ	fever; generation of heat ***phy***. calorification —***vi***. break out into a fever ***phy***. generate heat
	発表	ハッピョウ	announcement; publication; statement —***v***. announce; publish; make public
	発病	ハツビョウ	outbreak of a disease —***vi***. contract a disease; fall sick
	発布	ハップ	promulgation; proclamation; issue —***v***. promulgate; proclaim; issue
	発奮	ハップン	inspiration; stimulation —***vi***. be inspired/stimulated
	発砲	ハッポウ	gunfire —***vi***. fire; open fire; discharge firearms
	発明	ハツメイ	invention; contrivance; cleverness; brightness —***v***. invent; devise; contrive
	発令	ハツレイ	official announcement; proclamation —***v***. announce; proclaim
	発露	ハツロ	manifestation; expression; exhibition —***vi***. manifest; express; exhibit
	発起	ホッキ	proposal; suggestion —***v***. project; propose; suggest
	発句	ホック	haiku poetry; first line of a *renga*
	発作	ホッサ	spasm; fit
	発作的	ホッサテキ	spasmodic; fitful
	発足	ホッソク	starting; inauguration —***vi***. start; make a start; be inaugrated
	発端	ホッタン	origin; genesis; beginning
¥	発券	ハッケン	issue of banknotes/securities; note issuing —***vt***. issue banknotes/securities
	発行者利回り	ハッコウシャりまわり	issuer's cost
	発展途上国	ハッテントジョウコク	developing countries
	発売	ハツバイ	sale —***v***. sell; put on the market
	発売中	ハツバイチュウ	now on sale

1361

⑫

音	登	ト トウ	climb; attendance
熟	登記	トウキ	registration; registry —***v***. register; get on the register
	登校	トウコウ	school attendance; attending school

			—*vi*. go to/attend school
	登場	トウジョウ	entry; advent —*vi*. make an entrance; enter upon the stage; appear; show up
	登頂	トウチョウ	reaching the summit —*vi*. reach/climb to the summit
	登板	トウバン	***bas***. going up to the mound —*vi*. ***bas***. take the plate; go to the mound
	登用	トウヨウ	appointment; assignment; elevation; promotion; advancement —*v*. appoint; assign; designate; promote
	登竜門	トウリュウモン	gateway to success
	登録	トウロク	registration; record; entry —*v*. register; enter on a register; enroll
	登山	トザン	mountaineering; mountain climbing —*vi*. go up/climb/scale a mountain
訓	登る	のぼる	*vi*. climb; scale; go up; ascend; rise
¥	登録商標	トウロクショウヒョウ	registered trademark

5 白 しろい white

1362

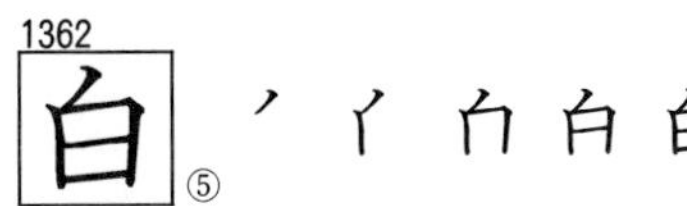

音	白	ハク	white; clean; clear
		ビャク	white
熟	白衣	ハクイ	white robe
	白眼視	ハクガンシ	cold/indifferent look; frown —*v*. look coldly; frown upon; look with indifference
	白銀	ハクギン	silver
	白紙	ハクシ	blank paper; clean sheet of paper
	白日	ハクジツ	daytime; broad daylight; bright day
	白書	ハクショ	white paper; economic white paper
	白状	ハクジョウ	confession; avowal —*v*. confess; avow; own up to; admit to
	白色人種	ハクショクジンシュ	white race
	白人	ハクジン	white person
	白痴	ハクチ	***derog***. idiot
	白昼	ハクチュウ	daytime; broad daylight
	白昼夢	ハクチュウム	day dream
	白鳥	ハクチョウ	swan
	白銅	ハクドウ	nickel

	白熱	ハクネツ	climax; white heat; incandescence —***vi***. grow excited; climax; become white hot; be incandescent
	白髪	ハクハツ	white/gray hair
	白票	ハクヒョウ	white/blank vote
	白米	ハクマイ	polished/cleaned rice
	白金	ハッキン	platinum
	白血病	ハッケツビョウ	***med***. leukemia
	白夜	ビャクヤ	nights with the midnight sun
訓	白	しろ	white
	白い	しろい	white; fair; blank; spotless; immaculate; clean
	白身	しろみ	white meat/fish; white of an egg; albumen
	白	（しら）	white
	白髪	しらが	gray/white hair
	白樺	しらかば	white birch
	白壁	しらかべ	whitewashed wall
	白木	しらき	plain/unpainted wood
	白ける	しらける	***vi***. become chilled/spoiled
	白々しい	しらじらしい	tense; awkward
	白む	しらむ	***vi***. grow light

1363

 ⑥

音	百	ヒャク	hundred; numerous; many
熟	百害	ヒャクガイ	many evils; much harm
	百獣	ヒャクジュウ	all beasts; all kinds of animals
	百姓	ヒャクショウ	farmer; farm laborer
	百戦錬磨	ヒャクセンレンマ	veteran; old-timer
	百点	ヒャクテン	perfect score; full marks
	百人一首	ヒャクニン イッシュ	*hyakuninisshu* (Hundred Poems by One Hundred Poets)
	百年	ヒャクネン	one hundred years; century
	百聞	ヒャクブン	hearing many things
	百分	ヒャクブン	one hundred parts —***v***. divide into one hundred parts
	百分率	ヒャクブンリツ	percentage
	百万	ヒャクマン	million
	百万長者	ヒャクマン チョウジャ	millionnaire
	百面相	ヒャクメンソウ	all kinds of comic faces; many facial expressions

	百科事典	ヒャッカジテン	encyclopedia
	百貨店	ヒャッカテン	department store
	百発百中	ヒャッパツヒャクチュウ	never fail to hit the mark; all correct; right on target
訓	※百合	ゆり	lily

1364
的 ⑧

音	的	テキ	target; exact
熟	的確	テキカク	exact; precise; accurate
	的中	テキチュウ	hit —*vi*. hit the bull's eye
訓	的	まと	target

1365
皆 ⑨

音	皆	カイ	all
熟	皆既食	カイキショク	total eclipse
	皆勤	カイキン	perfect attendance; nonabsence —*vi*. attend regularly
	皆無	カイム	nothing
訓	皆	みな	everybody; all

1366
皇 ⑨

音	皇	オウ	emperor; imperial
		コウ	emperor; lord; imperial
熟	皇子	オウジ	prince
	皇女	オウジョ	princess
	皇位	コウイ	the throne
	皇居	コウキョ	imperial palace
	皇后	コウゴウ	empress; queen; empress/queen consort
	皇室	コウシツ	imperial household; royal family
	皇族	コウゾク	imperial/royal family
	皇太后	コウタイゴウ	queen
	皇太子	コウタイシ	crown prince

皇帝　**コウテイ**　emperor

5 皮 ひのかわ／けがわ leather; skin

1367 皮 ⑤ 丿 厂 广 皮 皮

音	皮	**ヒ**	skin; hide; leather; bark
熟	皮下	**ヒカ**	under the skin; subcutaneous
	皮下注射	**ヒカチュウシャ**	***med***. hypodermic injection
	皮革	**ヒカク**	hide; skin; leather
	皮相	**ヒソウ**	superficial; outward
	皮肉	**ヒにく**	irony; sarcasm
	皮膚	**ヒフ**	skin
	皮膚科	**ヒフカ**	***med***. dermatology
	皮膚病	**ヒフビョウ**	***med***. skin disease
	皮膜	**ヒマク**	***med***. membrane
訓	皮	**かわ**	skin
	皮切り	**かわきり**	beginning; start
	皮算用	**かわザンヨウ**	count one's chickens before they are hatched

5 皿 さら dish; plate

1368 皿 ⑤ 丶 冂 冖 皿 皿

訓	皿	**さら**	dish; plate

1369 盆 ⑨ ノ 八 今 分 分 盆 盆 盆 盆

音	盆	**ボン**	the Bon/Lantern Festival; Festival of the Dead; tray
熟	盆栽	**ボンサイ**	bonsai; potted dwarf tree
	盆石	**ボンセキ**	miniature landscape arranged on a tray

盆地	ボンチ	basin; round valley

1370

益 ⑩

音	益	エキ	profit; gain; use; benefit
		（ヤク）	use; benefit
熟	益する	エキする	***vt***. be beneficial/useful
	益虫	エキチュウ	useful/beneficial insect
	益鳥	エキチョウ	useful/beneficial bird
	益金	エッキン	profit; gain
訓	益す	ます	increase; multiply; augment
	益々	ますます	increasingly; more and more

1371

盛 ⑪

音	盛	セイ	prosperous
		（ジョウ）	
熟	盛夏	セイカ	midsummer; height of summer
	盛会	セイカイ	successful meeting
	盛況	セイキョウ	prosperity; flourishing
	盛業	セイギョウ	thriving business; success in business
	盛衰	セイスイ	rise and fall; ups and downs; vicissitudes
	盛大	セイダイ	grand; magnificent; lavish
訓	盛る	さかる	***vi***. thrive; prosper; flourish; be popular
	盛ん	さかん	prospering; flourishing; popular; enthusiastic
	盛る	もる	***vt***. heap; pile up; serve; fill; poison
	盛り上がる	もりあがる	***vi***. swell; rise; arise; surge
	盛り沢山	もりダクサン	various; colorful; full

1372

盗 ⑪

音	盗	トウ	steal
熟	盗作	トウサク	plagiarism; literary/artistic theft —***vi***. plagiarize
	盗賊	トウゾク	thief; robber; burglar

玄 玉 王 瓦 甘 生 用 田 疋 疒 癶 白 皮 皿 ● 目 矛 矢 石 示 礻 禾 穴 立 罒 旡 母 氺 衤

5

玄玉王瓦甘生用田疋疒癶白皮皿目矛矢石示ネ禾穴立罒旡母氺ネ

	盗聴	トウチョウ	wiretapping; wire tap —*v*. wiretap; listen in; eavesdrop
	盗難	トウナン	robbery; theft; burglary
	盗品	トウヒン	stolen article/goods; loot; hot goods
	盗品売買	トウヒンバイバイ	dealing in stolen goods; fencing
	盗癖	トウヘキ	kleptomania
	盗用	トウヨウ	appropriation; embezzlement; plagiarism —*v*. appropriate; embezzle
	盗塁	トウルイ	***bas***. stealing a base —***vi.bas***. steal a base
訓	盗み	ぬすみ	theft; stealing; larceny
	盗む	ぬすむ	***vt***. steal; rob; pilfer
	盗人	ぬすびと	robber; thief; burglar

1373

盟 ⑬

丨 冂 日 日 日) 明 明 明 明 盟 盟 盟

音	盟	メイ	pledge; oath; alliance
熟	盟邦	メイホウ	allied nation
	盟約	メイヤク	pledge; pact; alliance
	盟友	メイユウ	comrade; sworn friend; staunch ally

1374

監 ⑮

丨 𠂆 𠂆 𠂆 臣 臣 臣 臣 臣 臣 監 監

音	監	カン	watch; lookout
熟	監禁	カンキン	confinement; imprisonment; detention in custody —*v*. imprison; confine
	監獄	カンゴク	prison
	監査	カンサ	inspection; superintendence —*v*. inspect; superintend
	監視	カンシ	watch; surveillance —*v*. watch; keep watch; be on the lookout
	監修	カンシュウ	editorial supervision —*v*. supervise the editing (of an anthology, dictionary, etc.)
	監督	カントク	supervisor; superintendent; director —*v*. supervise; direct
¥	監査	カンサ	audit
	監査法人	カンサホウジン	audit corporation
	監査役	カンサヤク	auditor

1375

盤 ⑮ ′ ′ 丿 舟 … 般 盤 盤 盤

音	盤	バン	plate; board; disk
熟	盤石	バンジャク	huge rock; firmness

5 目 め／めへん eye

1376

目 ⑤ 丨 冂 冃 月 目

音	目	モク （ボク）	eye; classification; order
熟	目撃	モクゲキ	witnessing; observation —***v***. witness; observe
	目撃者	モクゲキシャ	witness
	目算	モクサン	expectation; estimate; plan —***v***. expect; estimate; plan
	目次	モクジ	table of contents
	目前	モクゼン	before one's eyes
	目測	モクソク	measuring by eye —***v***. measure by eye
	目的	モクテキ	purpose; object; aim
	目標	モクヒョウ	aim; target; goal; objective
	目礼	モクレイ	eye greeting —***v***. greet by eye
	目録	モクロク	contents; catalog; list; inventory
	目下	モッカ	at present; now
訓	目	め （ま）	eye; look; judgment; pip; grain
	目当て	めあて	guide; aim
	目上	めうえ	one's superior/senior
	目移り	めうつり	waivering —***vi***. waiver/be at a loss what to choose
	目方	めかた	weight
	目先	めさき	before one's eyes; the near future; foresight
	目指す	めざす	***vt***. aim at/for
	目覚し時計	めざましどケイ	alarm clock
	目覚める	めざめる	***vi***. wake up; awaken
	目下	めした	one's inferior/subordinate/junior
	目印	めじるし	mark; sign

	目立つ	めだつ	***vi***. be conspicuous; stand out
	目玉	めだま	eyeball
	目付き	めつき	look; expression
	目鼻	めはな	eyes and nose
	目分量	めブンリョウ	by eye measure; by sight
	目星	めぼし	aim; object
	目盛り	めもり	graduation; scale
	目安	めやす	standard; yardstick
¥	目先	めさき	near future
	目先筋	めさきすじ	day-to-day trader
	目玉	めだま	eyeball; striking point
	目玉商品	めだまショウヒン	leader; loss leader
	目論見書	モクロみショ	prospectus

1377

⑧

音	直	ジキ	direct; at once; soon
		チョク	straight; directly; upright; frank
熟	直々	ジキジキ	personal; direct
	直筆	ジキヒツ	one's own handwriting; autograph
	直営	チョクエイ	direct management/control/operation —***v***. manage/control directly
	直撃	チョクゲキ	direct hit —***v***. score a direct hit
	直言	チョクゲン	plain speaking; straight talking —***v***. speak plainly; speak without reserve; speak one's mind
	直後	チョクゴ	just/soon after
	直視	チョクシ	looking in the face —***v***. look a person directly in the face
	直射	チョクシャ	direct rays/fire —***v***. fire point-blank/directly
	直進	チョクシン	straight on —***vi***. go straight on; make straight for
	直接	チョクセツ	directly
	直線	チョクセン	straight line
	直前	チョクゼン	just before
	直送	チョクソウ	direct delivery —***v***. send directly
	直属	チョクゾク	under the direct control of —***v***. be under the direct control of
	直腸	チョクチョウ	***med***. rectum
	直通	チョクツウ	direct service/communication —***vi***. be in direct communication
	直配	チョクハイ	direct distribution —***v***. distribute directly

直売	チョクバイ	direct sales —***v***. sell directly
直面	チョクメン	confrontation —***vi***. confront; face; be up against
直訳	チョクヤク	literal translation —***v***. translate/render literally
直喩	チョクユ	simile
直輸入	チョクユニュウ	direct import —***v***. import directly
直立	チョクリツ	erectness —***vi***. stand erect; rise perpendicularly
直立不動	チョクリツフドウ	standing at attention
直流	チョクリュウ	direct current (DC)
直下	チョッカ	directly/right under —***vi***. fall perpendicularly/down
直角	チョッカク	***math***. right angle
直轄	チョッカツ	direct control; immediate supervision —***v***. have the direct control of
直感	チョッカン	intuition; hunch —***v***. know by intuition; have a hunch
直観	チョッカン	intuition —***v***. know by intuition
直系	チョッケイ	direct line of family descent
直径	チョッケイ	***math***. diameter
直結	チョッケツ	direct connection —***v***. connect/link directly
直行	チョッコウ	going straight; uprightness —***vi***. go straight/direct
訓 直す	なおす	***vt***. mend; repair; do over again
直る	なおる	***vi***. be mended; get better; recover; be corrected
直ちに	ただちに	at once; directly; immediately
¥ 直物市場	ジキものシジョウ	spot market
直接税	チョクセツゼイ	direct tax
直接投資	チョクセツトウシ	direct investment

1378

盲 ⑧

音 盲	モウ	blind
熟 盲学校	モウガッコウ	school for the blind
盲従	モウジュウ	blind obedience —***vi***. be very obedient
盲信	モウシン	blind acceptance; credulity —***v***. accept blindly
盲人	モウジン	blind person
盲腸	モウチョウ	***med***. appendix
盲点	モウテン	blind spot
盲導犬	モウドウケン	guide dog
盲目	モウモク	blindness
盲目的	モウモクテキ	blind; reckless

1379

看 ⑨

一 二 三 手 手 看 看 看 看

音	看	カン	care; watch
熟	看過	カンカ	connivance (at wrong doing) —*v*. overlook an error
	看護	カンゴ	caring; nursing —*v*. nurse; care for the sick
	看護婦	カンゴフ	nurse
	看守	カンシュ	guard; warder; jailer
	看取	カンシュ	discernment; perception —*v*. discern; perceive; notice; detect
	看破	カンパ	penetration —*v*. penetrate; see through
	看板	カンバン	signboard; sign
	看病	カンビョウ	nursing the sick —*v*. nurse; tend; care for a sick person
訓	※看る	みる	***vt***. see

1380

県 ⑨

丨 冂 冃 月 目 且 県 県 県

音	県	ケン	prefecture
熟	県議会	ケンギカイ	prefectural assembly
	県政	ケンセイ	prefectural government
	県庁	ケンチョウ	prefectural office
	県道	ケンドウ	prefectural road
	県立	ケンリツ	prefectural (school, hospital, etc.)

1381

盾 ⑨

一 厂 斤 斤 斤 盾 盾 盾 盾

音	盾	ジュン	shield
訓	盾	たて	shield
	盾突く	たてつく	***vi***. oppose; rebel against

1382
 ⑨

音	省	ショウ	omit
		セイ	review; consider
熟	省略	ショウリャク	omission; abbreviation —*v*. omit; abbreviate
訓	省みる	かえりみる	***vt***. consider; think of; reflect on; worry about
	省く	はぶく	***vt***. omit; leave out; cut down; save

1383
相 ⑨

音	相	ソウ	each other; reciprocal; aspect; phase; physiognomy
		ショウ	minister
熟	相伴	ショウバン	accompaniment —***vi***. accompany
	相違	ソウイ	difference; discrepancy —***vi***. be different; have a discrepancy
	相応	ソウオウ	suitable; fitting —***vi***. be suitable/fitting
	相関	ソウカン	correlation —***vi***. correlate
	相関関係	ソウカンカンケイ	correlation; relation; relationship
	相関的	ソウカンテキ	interrelated
	相互	ソウゴ	mutual; reciprocal
	相殺	ソウサイ	offset; counteraction; compensation —***v***. offset; countervail
	相似	ソウジ	similarity; resemblance; analogy —***vi***. be similar/analogous; resemble
	相続	ソウゾク	inheritance; succession —***v***. inherit; succeed
	相続人	ソウゾクニン	heir; heiress; successor
	相対	ソウタイ	relativity
	相対的	ソウタイテキ	relative
	相談	ソウダン	consultation; discussion —***v***. consult; confer; discuss
	相当	ソウトウ	fit; suitable; appropriate; equivalent —***vi***. be equivalent/correspond to
	相等	ソウトウ	equality; equivalence
訓	相	あい	together; fellow; each other
	相変わらず	あいかわらず	as usual
	相性	あいショウ	affinity; compatibility
	相対する	あいタイする	***vi***. facing each other directly
	相次ぐ	あいつぐ	***vi***. follow in succession

5

	相手	あいて	the other party; partner; opponent
	※相撲	すもう	sumo wrestling
¥	相対取引（売買）	あいタイとりひき（バイバイ）	negotiated transaction
	相関係数	ソウカンケイスウ	coefficient of correlation
	相互援助	ソウゴエンジョ	mutual aid
	相互銀行（相銀）	ソウゴギンコウ（ソウギン）	mutual savings and loan bank
	相続財産	ソウゾクザイサン	inheritance; inherited property
	相続税	ソウゾクゼイ	inheritance (sucession) tax
	相場	ソウば	current/market price; speculation; estimation; the market

1384

冒 ⑨

丨 冂 冃 冃 冃 冐 冐 冐 冒

音	冒	ボウ	brave; risk; defy; dare
熟	冒険	ボウケン	adventure —*vi.* have an adventure
	冒頭	ボウトウ	opening; beginning; start
	冒瀆	ボウトク	blasphemy; sacrilege; desecration —*v.* blaspheme; desecrate
訓	冒す	おかす	*vt.* risk; brave; defy; dare; challenge; (a disease) attack

1385

真 ⑩

一 十 广 冇 冇 育 直 直 真 真

音	真	シン	truth; genuine; real
熟	真意	シンイ	one's real mind; real intention; true meaning
	真因	シンイン	true cause/motive
	真打ち	シンうち	star performer; headliner
	真価	シンカ	real value; true worth
	真偽	シンギ	true or false; authenticity
	真紅	シンク	crimson
	真空	シンクウ	vacuum; evacuated
	真空包装	シンクウホウソウ	vacuum packing
	真剣	シンケン	sword; true; honest
	真摯	シンシ	sincere
	真実	シンジツ	truth; true; real; truly; really
	真珠	シンジュ	pearl

	真珠湾	シンジュワン	Pearl Harbor
	真情	シンジョウ	true feelings
	真髄	シンズイ	essence; quintessence; soul
	真性	シンセイ	genuine
	真正	シンセイ	genuine; true
	真善美	シンゼンビ	truth, good, and beauty
	真相	シンソウ	the truth; fact
	真否	シンピ	truth or falsehood; the truth
	真理	シンリ	truth
訓	真	ま	truth; sincerity
	真新しい	まあたらしい	brand-new
	真顔	まがお	serious look/face
	真心	まごころ	sincerity
	真四角	まシカク	perfect square
	真面目	まじめ	serious; earnest; honest; reliable
	真っ赤	まっか	deep red
	真っ青	まっさお	azure; deep blue; white as a sheet; pale
	真っ盛り	まっさかり	at their best
	真っ白	まっしろ	pure white; snow-white
	真っ直ぐ	まっすぐ	straight; in a straight line; in a beeline
	真夏	まなつ	midsummer
	真似	まね	imitation; mimicry; aping; copying; action; behavior —*v*. imitate; mimic; copy
	真似る	まねる	***vt***. imitate; mimic; copy; follow
	真昼	まひる	midday; high noon
	真冬	まふゆ	midwinter
	真水	まみず	fresh water
	真夜中	まよなか	middle of the night; at midnight
	※真	まこと	true; real

5

玄玉王瓦甘生用田疋疒癶白皮皿目●矛矢石示ネ禾穴立罒旡母氺ネ

1386

眠 ⑩

丨 冂 月 月 目 目 目 目 眀 眠

音	眠	ミン	sleep
訓	眠い	ねむい	sleepy; drowsy; tired
	眠る	ねむる	***vi***. sleep
	眠たい	ねむたい	sleepy; drowsy; tired
	眠り薬	ねむりぐすり	sleeping pills
	眠気	ねむケ	sleepiness; drowsiness

1387
眼 ⑪

音	眼	ガン (ゲン)	eye; point
熟	眼下	ガンカ	under one's eyes
	眼科	ガンカ	***med***. ophthalmology
	眼球	ガンキュウ	eyeball
	眼光	ガンコウ	glitter of one's eyes; discernment; insight
	眼中	ガンチュウ	in one's eyes; consideration
	眼目	ガンモク	main point; gist; essence
	眼力	ガンリキ	insight; penetration; perception
訓	眼	まなこ	eye; eyeball
	※眼	め	eye; optics
	※眼鏡	めがね	glasses; spectacles

1388
眺 ⑪

音	眺	チョウ	look
熟	眺望	チョウボウ	view; prospect; lookout —***v***. view; look out
訓	眺め	ながめ	view; scene; outlook; prospect
	眺める	ながめる	***vt***. look; stare; gaze

1389
睡 ⑬

音	睡	スイ	sleep
熟	睡魔	スイマ	Morpheus (god of sleep)
	睡眠	スイミン	sleep; slumber —***vi***. sleep; slumber
訓	※睡る	ねむる	***vi***. sleep

1390
督 ⑬

音	督	トク	control

熟	督促	トクソク	urge; demand; pressing —*v*. urge; press
	督励	トクレイ	encouragement —*v*. encourage; urge

1391
瞬 ⑱ 冂 月 目 𥃩 𥃩 𥄇 𥆩 瞬 瞬 瞬 瞬 瞬

音	瞬	シュン	moment
熟	瞬間	シュンカン	moment
	瞬時	シュンジ	moment; instant
訓	瞬く	またたく	*vi*. wink; blink
	瞬き	またたき	blink; twinkle

5 矛 ほこ spear

1392
矛 ⑤ マ マ 予 予 矛

音	矛	ム	halberd; spear; lance
熟	矛盾	ムジュン	contradiction —*vi*. be contradictory
訓	矛	ほこ	halberd
	矛先	ほこさき	spearhead; point of a spear

5 矢 や／やへん arrow

1393
矢 ⑤ ノ 𠂉 ⺈ 午 矢

音	矢	シ	arrow
訓	矢	や	arrow
	矢先	やさき	arrowhead; moment; point; in time
	矢印	やじるし	arrow-shaped mark
	矢玉	やだま	arrows and bullets

玄 玉 王 瓦 甘 生 用 田 疋 疒 癶 白 皮 皿 目 矛 • 矢 石 示 ネ 禾 穴 立 罒 旡 母 氺 衤

1394

知 ⑧

ノ ⺈ ⺈ 㐅 矢 矢 知 知

音	知	チ	knowledge; wisdom; intellect; acquaintance
熟	知恵	チエ	wisdom; sense; wits; brains
	知覚	チカク	perception; sensation; feeling —*v.* perceive; sense; feel
	知己	チキ	acquaintance; intimate friend
	知事	チジ	governor (of a prefecture)
	知識	チシキ	knowledge; information; know-how; learning; understanding
	知識階級	チシキカイキュウ	intelligentsia
	知人	チジン	acquaintance; friend
	知性	チセイ	intellect; intelligence
	知的	チテキ	intellectual; mental
	知能	チノウ	intellect; intelligence; mental faculties
	知名	チメイ	noted; distinguished; famous; well-known
訓	知る	しる	***vt.*** know; be aware of; learn; understand; recognize; realize; feel
	知らせ	しらせ	information; notice; report; news
	知らせる	しらせる	***vt.*** inform; advise; notify; report
	知らん顔	しらんかお	feigned ignorance; indifference; nonchalance
	知り合い	しりあい	friend; acquaintance
¥	知的所有権	チテキショユウケン	intellectual property

1395

短 ⑫

ノ ⺈ ⺈ 㐅 矢 矢 矢 知 知 短 短 短

音	短	タン	short; brief; close
熟	短歌	タンカ	*tanka* (31-syllable Japanese poem)
	短気	タンキ	quick/short temper
	短期	タンキ	short term
	短縮	タンシュク	shortening; contraction; curtailment —*v.* shorten; contract; curtail
	短所	タンショ	defect; fault; demerit; failing; shortcoming
	短針	タンシン	the short hand (of a clock)
	短調	タンチョウ	minor key (in music)
	短波	タンパ	shortwave
	短編	タンペン	short piece/story; sketch

	短命	タンメイ	short life
訓	短い	みじかい	short; brief; abbreviated
¥	短期借入金	タンキ かりいれキン	short-term loans repayable

1396

矯 ⑰

音	矯	キョウ	rectify; correct; train
熟	矯正	キョウセイ	reform; rectification; correction —*v.* reform; rectify; correct
訓	矯める	ためる	***vt***. reform; correct; rectify

5 石 いし／いしへん stone

1397

 ⑤

音	石	セキ	stone; jewel
		（コク）	*koku* (unit of volume, approx. 0.18 *ml*)
		（シャク）	
熟	石像	セキゾウ	stone image; statue
	石炭	セキタン	coal
	石碑	セキヒ	stone monument; tombstone
	石仏	セキブツ	stone image of Buddha
	石墨	セキボク	graphite
	石油	セキユ	oil; petroleum; kerosene
	石灰	セッカイ	lime
	石器	セッキ	prehistoric/Stone Age tools
	石器時代	セッキジダイ	Stone Age
	石鹼	セッケン	soap
訓	石	いし	stone
	石頭	いしあたま	bigot
	石畳	いしだたみ	stone pavement
	石橋	いしばし	stone bridge
¥	石油	セキユ	oil; petroleum
	石油化学	セキユカガク	petrochemistry

1398

研 ⑨

音	研	ケン	polish; research
熟	研究	ケンキュウ	research; study; investigation; inquiry —*v*. study; make a study of; do research in; investigate
	研究員	ケンキュウイン	research worker
	研究科	ケンキュウカ	post-graduate course
	研究開発	ケンキュウカイハツ	R & D; (Research and Development)
	研修	ケンシュウ	study and training —*v*. study; be trained
	研磨	ケンマ	polishing; grinding —*v*. polish; grind
	研磨機	ケンマキ	grinder; abrader; polishing machine
	研磨材	ケンマザイ	abradant; abrasive
	研磨紙	ケンマシ	sandpaper; emery cloth; glass paper
訓	研ぐ	とぐ	***vt***. grind; sharpen; whet

1399

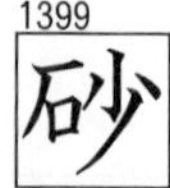

砂 ⑨

音	砂	サ	sand
		シャ	sand
熟	砂丘	サキュウ	sand hill; dune
	砂金	サキン	gold dust
	砂鉄	サテツ	iron sand
	砂糖	サトウ	sugar
	砂漠	サバク	desert
	砂利	ジャリ	gravel
訓	砂	すな	sand; dune
	砂時計	すなどケイ	hourglass
	砂場	すなば	sand pit
	砂浜	すなはま	sandy beach; sands

1400

砕 ⑨

音	砕	サイ	crush; break; smash

熟	砕石	サイセキ	rubble; smashed rock; macadam —*vi*. macadamize
訓	砕く	くだく	***vt***. break; smash; crush
	砕ける	くだける	***vi***. break; be broken; be simple; be informal

1401

破 ⑩

音	破	ハ	destroy; break; demolish
熟	破戒	ハカイ	apostasy; breaking a Buddhist commandment
	破壊	ハカイ	destruction; demolition; breakdown —***v***. destroy; break; ruin; wreck; demolish
	破格	ハカク	exception
	破棄	ハキ	destruction; annulment; cancellation —***v***. destroy; annul; cancel
	破局	ハキョク	catastrophe; collapse
	破傷風	ハショウフウ	***med***. tetanus; lockjaw
	破損	ハソン	damage; injury; breakdown; dilapidation —***v***. be damaged; breakdown; be dilapidated/destroyed
	破綻	ハタン	failure; rupture; breaking —***vi***. fail; rupture; break
	破談	ハダン	cancellation; rupture; breaking off; rejection
	破天荒	ハテンコウ	unprecedented
	破片	ハヘン	fragment; splinter; broken piece
	破滅	ハメツ	destruction; wreck; ruin; collapse —***vi***. destroy; wreck; ruin; collapse
	破門	ハモン	expulsion; excommunication —***v***. expel; excommunicate
	破約	ハヤク	breach of promise/contract —***v***. break a promise; breach a contract
	破裂	ハレツ	burst; rupture; explosion; eruption —***v***. burst; be ruptured; explode; erupt
	破廉恥	ハレンチ	shamelessness; infamy; ignominy
	ご破算	ごハサン	new calculation
訓	破る	やぶる	***v***. tear; rip; break; destroy; violate; infringe
	破れる	やぶれる	***vi***. be torn/ripped/broken/destroyed
	破れ	やぶれ	rupture; breach; failure; ruin; breakdown; collapse
¥	破産	ハサン	bankruptcy; insolvency; financial failure —***v***. go bankrupt; fail; be ruined

1402

砲 ⑩

一 ㇇ 丆 石 石 石' 石㇆ 砂 砲 砲

音	砲	ホウ	cannon; gun
熟	砲煙	ホウエン	cannon smoke; gunsmoke
	砲火	ホウカ	gunfire; shellfire
	砲艦	ホウカン	gunboat
	砲丸	ホウガン	cannonball; shot (as in shot put)
	砲丸投げ	ホウガンなげ	shot put
	砲撃	ホウゲキ	bombardment; shelling —*v*. bombard; shell
	砲口	ホウコウ	muzzle (of a gun); caliber
	砲手	ホウシュ	gunner; artilleryman
	砲術	ホウジュツ	gunnery
	砲身	ホウシン	gun barrel
	砲声	ホウセイ	sound of firing/shelling
	砲戦	ホウセン	artillery engagement
	砲台	ホウダイ	gun battery
	砲弾	ホウダン	shell; cannonball
	砲塔	ホウトウ	gun (turret)
	砲兵	ホウヘイ	artillerist; artilleryman; gunner
	砲門	ホウモン	muzzle (of a gun); gunport
訓	砲	つつ	gun

1403

硬 ⑫

一 ㇇ 丆 石 石 石一 石⼀ 砢 砢 硬 硬 硬

音	硬	コウ	hard; stiff; firm; strong
熟	硬化	コウカ	hardening; vulcanization; stiffening; development —*vi*. stiffen; harden; metallize; ossify
	硬質	コウシツ	hard
	硬水	コウスイ	hard water
	硬直	コウチョク	stiffness; rigidity —*vi*. stiffen; become rigid
	硬度	コウド	hardness; solidity
訓	硬い	かたい	hard; stiff; firm
¥	硬貨	コウカ	hard currency; coin

1404
硝 ⑫

音	硝	ショウ	saltpeter
熟	硝煙	ショウエン	powder smoke
	硝石	ショウセキ	***chem***. saltpeter
	※硝子	がらす	glass

1405
硫 ⑫

音	硫	リュウ	sulfur
熟	硫安	リュウアン	***chem***. ammonium sulfate
	硫酸	リュウサン	***chem***. sulfuric acid
	硫酸紙	リュウサンシ	parchment paper
	※硫黄	いおう	***chem***. sulfur

1406
碁 ⑬

音	碁	ゴ	the game of go
熟	碁石	ゴいし	black and white stones for go
	碁盤	ゴバン	go board

1407
磁 ⑭

音	磁	ジ	magnet; pottery; ceramics
熟	磁気	ジキ	magnetism
	磁器	ジキ	porcelain; china; chinaware
	磁極	ジキョク	magnetic pole
	磁石	ジシャク	magnet; magnetite; compass
	磁針	ジシン	magnetic/compass needle
	磁力	ジリョク	magnetic force

1408

碑 ⑭ 一 厂 石 石 石′ 矿 砷 砷 砷 砷 碑 碑

音	碑	ヒ	stone monument; tombstone
熟	碑文	ヒブン	inscription (on a stone monument); epitaph
	碑銘	ヒメイ	epitaph
訓	碑	いしぶみ	(inscribed) stone monument

1409

確 ⑮ 一 厂 石 石 石′ 矿 矿 矿 碎 碎 確 確

音	確	カク	certainty; steady; sure
熟	確実	カクジツ	certainty; reliability
	確証	カクショウ	corroboration; confirmation; positive proof
	確信	カクシン	conviction; firm belief; confidence —*v*. convince oneself; believe firmly; be confident
	確定	カクテイ	final settlement; decision —*v*. decide; settle; fix; confirm
	確認	カクニン	confirmation; validation —*v*. confirm; acertain; validate
	確保	カクホ	guarantee; security —*v*. guarantee; secure
	確約	カクヤク	definite promise —*v*. give one's word; commit oneself to
	確立	カクリツ	establishment —*v*. establish; build up
	確率	カクリツ	probability
	確固	カッコ	firm; steady
訓	確か	たしか	sound; right; perhaps; firm; certain; probable
	確かめる	たしかめる	***vt***. ascertain
¥	確定申告	カクテイシンコク	final tax return
	確定利付き証券	カクテイリづきショウケン	fixed interest-bearing securities

1410

磨 ⑯ 一 广 广 庁 床 床 麻 麻 麻 摩 磨 磨

音	磨	マ	polish; brush
熟	磨耗	マモウ	wear and tear; abrasion
訓	磨く	みがく	***vt***. polish/brush (one's teeth); shine (shoes, etc.)

※磨る	する	*vt*. rub; chafe; file

1411

礁 ⑰ 一 ア 石 石 矿 矿 矿 矿 碓 碓 礁 礁

音 礁	ショウ	reef

1412

礎 ⑱ 一 ア 石 石 矿 矿 矿 礎 礎 礎 礎 礎

音 礎	ソ	foundation; stone; cornerstone
熟 礎材	ソザイ	foundation materials
礎石	ソセキ	footstone; foundation stone
訓 礎	いしずえ	foundation stone; cornerstone

5 示 しめす show 礻 (p.623)

1413

示 ⑤ 一 二 亍 亓 示

音 示	シ ジ	show; display; express; teaching
熟 示威	ジイ	demonstration —*v*. demonstrate
示唆	シサ	suggestion; hint —*v*. suggest
示談	ジダン	private settlement; settlement out of court —*v*. settle out of court
訓 示す	しめす	*vt*. show; display; reveal; indicate; prove
示し	しめし	display; revelation; example; indication; proof
示し合わせる	しめしあわせる	*vt*. prearrange; conspire

1414

祭 ⑪ ノ ク タ タ タ⁷ 夕又 夕又 祭 祭 祭 祭

音 祭	サイ	festival; feast; deify; worship

熟	祭日	サイジツ	national holiday; festival day
	祭壇	サイダン	altar
	祭典	サイテン	festival
	祭礼	サイレイ	festival
訓	祭り	まつり	feast; festival
	祭る	まつる	***vt***. deify; worship

1415

票 ⑪

音	票	ヒョウ	slip of paper; ballot; vote
熟	票決	ヒョウケツ	voting; vote —***v***. vote

1416

禁 ⑬

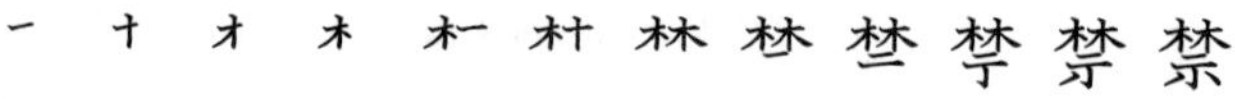

音	禁	キン	forbid; prohibit
熟	禁じる	キンじる	***vt***. forbid; prohibit
	禁煙	キンエン	no smoking —***vi***. forbid/prohibit smoking
	禁忌	キンキ	taboo
	禁固	キンコ	imprisonment; incarceration; confinement
	禁止	キンシ	prohibition; embargo; ban —***v***. forbid; prohibit; embargo; ban
	禁酒	キンシュ	temperance —***vi***. be temperant; prohibit/forbid alcohol
	禁制	キンセイ	prohibition; taboo; embargo; ban
	禁断	キンダン	prohibition; withdrawal
	禁物	キンモツ	taboo; prohibited object
	禁猟	キンリョウ	closed season
	禁漁	キンリョウ	no fishing
	禁令	キンレイ	prohibitory decree; prohibition; ban
¥	禁輸	キンユ	ban (no export or import); embargo
	禁輸商品	キンユショウヒン	embargo goods
	禁輸品	キンユヒン	article under the embargo; contraband

1417

礼 ⑤ 丶 ラ ネ ネ 礼

音 礼 レイ courtesy; politeness; salutation; bow
ライ

熟 礼讃 ライサン ***Bud***. adore; worship; glorify
礼拝 ライハイ Buddhist worship/services —*v*. worhship Buddha
礼儀 レイギ manners; courtesy; politeness
礼金 レイキン honorarium; fee
礼式 レイシキ etiquette
礼状 レイジョウ letter of thanks
礼節 レイセツ decorum; propriety; politeness
礼装 レイソウ formal/ceremonial dress; full dress
礼典 レイテン ceremony; ritual; rites
礼拝 レイハイ Christian worship/services —*v*. worship God
礼服 レイフク formal dress

1418

社 ⑦ 丶 ラ ネ ネ ネ一 ネ十 社

音 社 シャ shrine; company; society

熟 社会 シャカイ society; community; class; world
社会運動 シャカイウンドウ social movement
社会科 シャカイカ social studies
社会学 シャカイガク sociology
社会主義 シャカイシュギ socialism
社会人 シャカイジン public person; working adult
社会的 シャカイテキ social
社会奉仕 シャカイホウシ social service
社会面 シャカイメン general news page of a newspaper
社会問題 シャカイモンダイ social problem
社訓 シャクン company motto
社交 シャコウ social intercourse/contact; society
社交家 シャコウカ sociable person
社交界 シャコウカイ the fashionable world; high society
社交性 シャコウセイ sociability; outgoing; extrovert

玄 玉 王 瓦 甘 生 用 田 疋 疒 癶 白 皮 皿 目 矛 矢 石 示 • 礻 禾 穴 立 罒 旡 母 氺 衤

	社主	シャシュ	company owner
	社説	シャセツ	editorial; leading article
	社宅	シャタク	company house/housing
	社団	シャダン	association; corporation
	社長	シャチョウ	company president
	社殿	シャデン	main hall of a shrine
	社務所	シャムショ	shrine office
訓	社	やしろ	Shinto shrine
¥	社会党	シャカイトウ	the Socialist Party
	社会福祉	シャカイフクシ	social welfare
	社会保障	シャカイホショウ	social security
	社債	シャサイ	corporate bond; debenture; (company) bond; debenture
	社債券	シャサイケン	debenture bond
	社費	シャヒ	company expenses
	社有	シャユウ	company owned
	社用	シャヨウ	company business

1419

祈 ⑧

丶 ラ ネ ネ ネ 祈 祈 祈

音	祈	キ	pray
熟	祈願	キガン	prayer —*v.* pray
	祈禱	キトウ	prayer —*v.* pray
	祈念	キネン	prayer —*v.* pray
訓	祈る	いのる	***vt***. pray; say a prayer

1420

祉 ⑧

丶 ラ ネ ネ 礼 补 祉 祉

音	祉	シ	welfare

1421

祝 ⑨

丶 ラ ネ ネ ネ 祀 祀 祝 祝

音	祝	シュク (シュウ)	celebrate
熟	祝する	シュクする	***vt***. congratulate; celebrate

	祝儀	シュウギ	celebration; ceremony; tip; gratuity
	祝宴	シュクエン	banquet; feast
	祝賀	シュクガ	celebration; congratulations
	祝祭日	シュクサイジツ	public/national holiday
	祝辞	シュクジ	congratulatory address/speeches
	祝日	シュクジツ	public/national holday
	祝典	シュクテン	festival; celebration; jubilee
	祝電	シュクデン	congratulatory telegram
	祝杯	シュクハイ	toast
	祝福	シュクフク	blessing —*v.* bless
	祝砲	シュクホウ	salute of guns
訓	祝う	いわう	***vt.*** congratulate; celebrate; observe an anniversary, etc.
	※祝詞	のりと	Shinto prayer

1422

⑨

音	神	シン	god
		ジン	god
熟	神学	シンガク	theology
	神格化	シンカクカ	deification —*v.* deify
	神官	シンカン	Shinto priest
	神宮	ジングウ	major Shinto shrine
	神経	シンケイ	nerve; nervous; nerves
	神経科	シンケイカ	neurology; department of neurology
	神経質	シンケイシツ	nervous temperament; nervousness
	神経症	シンケイショウ	***med.*** neurosis
	神権	シンケン	divine right
	神社	ジンジャ	Shinto shrine
	神出鬼没	シンシュツキボツ	elusiveness; be everywhere at once; appearing and disappearing
	神聖	シンセイ	holiness; sacredness; sanctity
	神代	ジンダイ	mythological age; age of the gods
	神通力	ジンツウリキ	magical power
	神殿	シンデン	shrine
	神道	シントウ	Shintoism; Shinto
	神秘	シンピ	mystery
	神秘主義	シンピシュギ	mysticism
	神秘的	シンピテキ	mystic; mysterious
	神父	シンプ	Roman Catholic priest; Father

	神仏	シンブツ	gods and Buddhas; Shintoism and Buddhism
	神妙	シンミョウ	docile; meek; gentle; unresisting
	神話	シンワ	myth; mythology
訓	神	かみ	god; deity
	神風	かみかぜ	kamikaze
	神棚	かみだな	household Shinto altar
	神業	かみわざ	act of God; divine work; miracle
	神	(かん)	(prefix) Shinto
	神主	かんぬし	Shinto priest
	神	(こう)	divine; sublime
	神々しい	こうごうしい	divine; sublime
	※お神酒	おみき	sacred saké; libation
	※神楽	かぐら	*kagura* (sacred mucic and dancing)

1423

祖 ⑨

丶 ラ ネ ネ 礻 礻 礽 祖 祖

音	祖	ソ	ancestor
熟	祖国	ソコク	homeland; fatherland
	祖先	ソセン	ancestor; forefathers
	祖父	ソフ	grandfather
	祖父母	ソフボ	grandparents
	祖母	ソボ	grandmother

1424

祥 ⑩

丶 ラ ネ ネ 礻 礻 祥 祥 祥 祥

音	祥	ショウ	good omen/sign

1425

禍 ⑬

丶 ラ ネ ネ 礻 礻 礻 礻 礻 禍 禍 禍 禍

音	禍	カ	misfortune; disaster; trouble
熟	禍根	カコン	the root of evil; the source of trouble
	禍福	カフク	fortune and misfortune
訓	禍	わざわい	trouble; evil; disaster —***vi***. bring trouble on; inflict evil

1426

禅 ⑬ 丶 ラ ネ ネ ネ' ネ" ネ" 衤" 衤艹 衤畄 禅 禅

音 禅 ゼン silent meditation; Zen

熟 禅師 ゼンシ ***Bud***. the Reverend
禅宗 ゼンシュウ Zen sect of Buddhism

1427

福 ⑬ 丶 ラ ネ ネ ネ一 ネ一 ネ冖 ネ戸 ネ畐 福 福 福

音 福 フク fortune; happiness; welfare; wealth

熟 福音 フクイン the gospel; good news
福運 フクウン happiness and good fortune
福祉 フクシ welfare
福利 フクリ welfare; well-being
福利厚生 フクリコウセイ welfare program

---

5 禾 のぎへん *no* (katakana)＋tree

1428

私 ⑦ 一 二 千 禾 禾 私 私

音 私 シ I; private

熟 私案 シアン one's private plan
私意 シイ personal opinion; selfish motive
私益 シエキ personal interest/gain
私怨 シエン personal enmity; grudge; grievance
私学 シガク private school/college/university
私企業 シキギョウ private enterprise; privately owned company
私見 シケン personal view/opinion
私語 シゴ whisper; whispering
私恨 シコン personal grudge
私財 シザイ private property
私事 シジ personal affairs; private matter
私室 シシツ private room
私書 シショ private document; personal letter

	私書箱	シショばこ	post office box
	私情	シジョウ	personal feelings
	私小説	シショウセツ	"I" novel; novel based on the author's own life
	私心	シシン	selfishness; one's own idea
	私信	シシン	private letter/message
	私生活	シセイカツ	one's private life
	私生児	シセイジ	illegitimate child; love child
	私設	シセツ	private establishment
	私蔵	シゾウ	private ownership —*v*. own privately
	私鉄	シテツ	privately owned railway
	私道	シドウ	private road; driveway; drive
	私費	シヒ	one's own expense
	私服	シフク	plain clothes; civillian clothes
	私腹	シフク	one's own pockets; one's own profit or estate
	私物	シブツ	private property; personal effects
	私有	シユウ	private ownership; —*v*. own privately
	私用	シヨウ	private use/business
	私欲	シヨク	self-interest; selfish desire
	私利	シリ	self-interest; one's own interest
	私立	シリツ	private; non-governmental
訓	私	わたし	I; me
	私	わたくし	I; me; private
	私事	わたくしごと	private matters
¥	私営	シエイ	private management/enterprise
	私法人	シホウジン	private corporation
	私募債	シボサイ	bonds offered through private placement

1429

⑦

音	秀	シュウ	eminent
熟	秀逸	シュウイツ	excellence; superb
	秀才	シュウサイ	talented man; brilliant person
	秀作	シュウサク	excellent work
	秀麗	シュウレイ	graceful; beautiful
訓	秀でる	ひいでる	***vi***. be superior/prominent; excel

1430
科 ⑨

音	科	カ	course of study; offense
熟	科学	カガク	science; natural science
	科目	カモク	academic subject; curriculum; items
	科料	カリョウ	minor fine
訓	※科	しな	items
	※科	とが	fault; blame; offense

1431

⑨

音	秋	シュウ	fall; autumn
熟	秋季	シュウキ	fall; autumn
	秋期	シュウキ	fall season; autumn
	秋分	シュウブン	autumnal equinox
訓	秋	あき	fall; autumn
	秋風	あきかぜ	autumn breeze
	秋晴れ	あきばれ	fine autumn day
	秋雨	あきさめ	autumn rain
	※秋刀魚	さんま	saury

1432

⑨

音	秒	ビョウ	second (of time/arc)
熟	秒針	ビョウシン	second hand (of a watch/clock)
	秒速	ビョウソク	velocity per second
	秒読み	ビョウよみ	countdown —*vi.* count down

1433
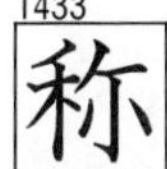
⑩

音	称	ショウ	name; praise
熟	称する	ショウする	*vt.* call; name; claim; pretend; feign

称号 ショウゴウ title; degree
称賛 ショウサン praise; admiration; applause —*v.* praise; admire; applaud

1434
租 ⑩
丿 二 千 禾 禾 利 和 和 租 租

音 租 ソ tribute; crop tax
¥ 租界 ソカイ (foreign) settlement; concession
租借 ソシャク leasing a foreign territory —*v.* hold a foreign territory by lease
租借権 ソシャクケン lease; leasehold
租税 ソゼイ taxes

1435
秩 ⑩
丿 二 千 禾 禾 禾 秆 秆 秩 秩

音 秩 チツ order; discipline; stipend
熟 秩序 チツジョ order; discipline; system; method

1436
秘 ⑩
丿 二 千 禾 禾 禾 利 秘 秘 秘

音 秘 ヒ secret
熟 秘する ヒする *vt.* keep secret; conceal
秘境 ヒキョウ unexplored territory; land of mystery
秘訣 ヒケツ the secret/key to
秘策 ヒサク secret plot/plan/measures
秘史 ヒシ hidden history; historical secrets; unknown historical facts
秘事 ヒジ secret; mystery
秘術 ヒジュツ secret art; secrets/mysteries of
秘書 ヒショ (private) secretary
秘書課 ヒショカ secretariat; secretarial section
秘書官 ヒショカン minister's secretary
秘蔵 ヒゾウ treasuring —*v.* treasure; prize; cherish; keep (a thing) under lock and key
秘伝 ヒデン secret/esoteric mysteries; the secret/mystery of
秘匿 ヒトク concealment —*v.* conceal; keep secret
秘宝 ヒホウ hidden treasure

秘法 ヒホウ secret method/formula
秘本 ヒホン treasured book; secret/hidden/forbidden book
秘密 ヒミツ secret; confidential; private
秘薬 ヒヤク secret medicine/remedy
秘録 ヒロク confidential notes; private papers
秘話 ヒワ secret story
秘か ひそか secret
秘める ひめる ***vt***. conceal; keep secret

1437
移 ⑪

移 イ move; shift; change
移行 イコウ uniform motion of a body in a straight line —***vi***. move; transfer; shift; switch
移住 イジュウ migration; emigration; transmigration —***vi***. migrate; emigrate; transmigrate; settle
移出 イシュツ export; shipment; clearance —***v***. export; ship out
移植 イショク transplantation; implantation; naturalization —***v***. transplant; implant; naturalize
移転 イテン moving; removal; transfer —***v***. move house; transfer
移動 イドウ movement; motion; locomotion; transfer —***v***. move; get around; be mobile
移入 イニュウ import; shipping in; introduction —***v***. import; ship in; introduce
移民 イミン emigration; immigration; settlement —***vi***. emigrate; immigrate; settle
移す うつす ***vt***. move; transfer; change; divert; turn; direct
移り気 うつりギ wandering mind; inability to concentrate
移る うつる ***vi***. move; remove; change; swift; be infected; spread

1438
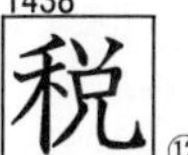
税 ⑫

税 ゼイ tax
税額控除 ゼイガクコウジョ tax credit; tax exemption; tax reduction
税関 ゼイカン customhouse; customs
税金 ゼイキン tax
税込み ゼイこみ including tax

税収	ゼイシュウ	tax revenues/yields
税制	ゼイセイ	tax system
税引き	ゼイびき	after tax
税引き前当期利益	ゼイびきまえトウキリエキ	net profit before tax
税法	ゼイホウ	tax law; method of taxation
税務署	ゼイムショ	tax office
税吏	ゼイリ	customs officer
税率	ゼイリツ	tax rates

1439

程 ⑫

音	程	テイ	degree
熟	程度	テイド	degree; extent; measure; proportion
訓	程	ほど	extent; limit; time; distance
	程々	ほどほど	moderate; within bounds

1440

稚 ⑬

音	稚	チ	infant
熟	稚魚	チギョ	fry
	稚児	チゴ	infant; boy; child in a Buddhist procession
	稚拙	チセツ	crudeness; artlessness

1441

穀 ⑭

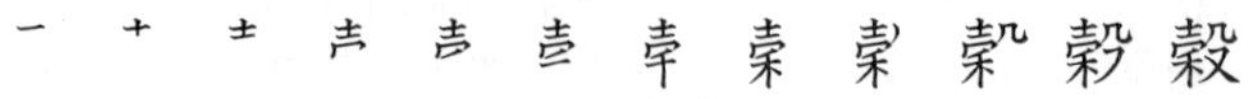

音	穀	コク	grain
熟	穀倉	コクソウ	granary
	穀物	コクモツ	grain; cereal; corn

1442

種 ⑭

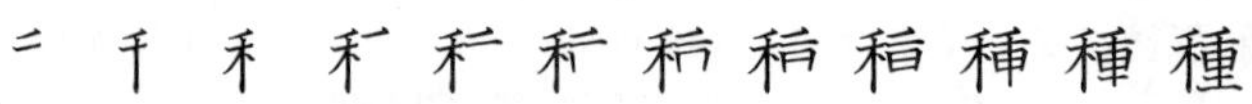

音	種	シュ	seed; kind; type; variety

熟	種子	シュシ	seed; stone; pip
	種々	シュジュ	various; variety; all kinds
	種族	シュゾク	race; tribe
	種痘	シュトウ	***med***. vaccination
	種別	シュベツ	classification; class; kind —***v***. classify
	種目	シュモク	item; event
	種類	シュルイ	kind; sort; species
訓	種	たね	seed; stone; kernel; breed; stock; topic
	種明かし	たねあかし	revealing the secret (of magic, etc.)
	種油	たねあぶら	seed/rape oil
	種馬	たねうま	stud horse; stallion
	種切れ	たねぎれ	short of topics
	種本	たねホン	source of a written work, etc.
	種蒔	たねまき	sowing; seeding —***vi***. sow; seed

1443

稲 ⑭

音	稲	トウ	rice plant
訓	稲	いな	(prefix) rice plant; lightning
	稲作	いなさく	rice crop
	稲妻	いなづま	flash of lightning
	稲光	いなびかり	lightning; flash of lightning
	稲荷	いなり	*inari* (god of harvests, fox deity)
	稲	いね	rice plant; paddy

1444

稼 ⑮

音	稼	カ	earn
熟	稼業	カギョウ	occupation; work; trade; business
	稼働	カドウ	work; operation —***v***. work; operate
訓	稼ぐ	かせぐ	***vi***. work; earn a living; earn money

1445

稿 ⑮

音	稿	コウ	manuscript; straw; straw-paper

熟	稿料	コウリョウ	copy money; manuscript fee
訓	※稿	わら	straw; straw-paper

1446

穂 ⑮

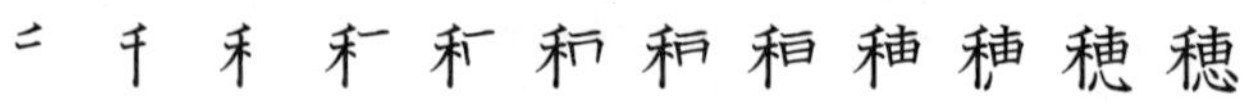

音	穂	スイ	head
訓	穂	ほ	ear; spearhead
	穂先	ほさき	tip of an ear; head; spearhead
	穂波	ほなみ	waving heads

1447

穏 ⑯

音	穏	オン	gentle; calm; mild
熟	穏健	オンケン	moderate
	穏当	オントウ	proper; just; right
	穏便	オンビン	gentle; quiet; amicable
	穏和	オンワ	moderate
訓	穏やか	おだやか	calm; mild; tranquil; gentle

1448

積 ⑯

音	積	セキ	accumulate; product; size; area; volume
熟	積載	セキサイ	loading —*v.* load
	積載量	セキサイリョウ	carrying capacity; load
	積雪	セキセツ	fallen snow
	積極的	セッキョクテキ	positive; active
訓	積む	つむ	***vt.*** heap; load
	積もる	つもる	***vi.*** accumulate; pile up; estimate
	積み上げる	つみあげる	***vt.*** pile/heap up
	積み立てる	つみたてる	***vt.*** save; lay aside; put by
¥	積金	つみキン	installment; installment savings
	積立金	つみたてキン	surplus reserve; reserve fund
	積荷保険	つみにホケン	cargo insurance

1449 穫 ⑱

音	穫	カク	harvest

5 穴 あな／あなかんむり hole

1450

⑤

音	穴	ケツ	hole
熟	穴居	ケッキョ	cave dwelling —*vi*. live in a cave
訓	穴	あな	hole
	穴場	あなば	excellent but little known place
¥	穴埋め	あなうめ	fill a blank; cover (a deficit); make up (a loss)

1451

⑦

音	究	キュウ	go to the end of; investigate thoroughly; end; terminate; reach an extreme
熟	究極	キュウキョク	extreme; ultimate
	究明	キュウメイ	study; investigation; inquiry —*v*. study; investigate; inquire into
訓	究める	きわめる	*vt*. go to the end of; master; go to extremes

1452

⑧

音	空	クウ	empty; useless; the sky; the heavens; aircraft
熟	空間	クウカン	space; the infinite
	空気	クウキ	air; atmosphere
	空虚	クウキョ	emptiness; void; vacuum
	空軍	クウグン	air force
	空港	クウコウ	airport

	空車	クウシャ	empty car; For Hire; taxi for hire
	空襲	クウシュウ	air raid/attack —*v*. launch an air raid/attack
	空席	クウセキ	empty/vacant seat
	空前	クウゼン	unprecedented; unheard of
	空前絶後	クウゼンゼツゴ	the first and probably the last
	空想	クウソウ	daydream; fantasy —*v*. daydream; fantasize
	空中	クウチュウ	air; sky; space; midair
	空洞	クウドウ	cave; cavern; cavity
	空白	クウハク	blank; space; vacuum; void
	空費	クウヒ	waste —*v*. waste
	空腹	クウフク	empty stomach
	空輸	クウユ	air/aerial transport —*v*. transport by air
	空路	クウロ	air route/way
	空論	クウロン	empty theory
訓	空く	あく	***vi***. open; be opened
	空ける	あける	***vt***. open (something)
	空	から	empty
	空回り	からまわり	skidding; racing; ineffective business activity; fruitless effort —***vi***. skid; race; prove/turn out ineffective
	空	そら	sky

1453

⑧

音	突	トツ	thrust
熟	突貫	トッカン	charge; rush
	突起	トッキ	projection; prominence; protuberance —***vi***. project; protrude; rise
	突撃	トツゲキ	charge; rush; onrush; dash; assault —***vi***. charge; rush; make a dash; assault
	突出	トッシュツ	projection; protrusion; prominence —***vi***. project; protrude; jut/stick out
	突如	トツジョ	suddenly
	突進	トッシン	rush; onrush; dash; charge —***vi***. rush; dash; push ahead
	突然	トツゼン	suddenly; abruptly; all at once
	突端	トッタン	tip; point
	突入	トツニュウ	inrush; thrust —***vi***. rush; dash; charge; crush
	突破	トッパ	breakthrough; breaking through; breakout —***v***. break/smash through; breach
	突発	トッパツ	outbreak; sudden occurrence —***vi***. occur suddenly

突風　トップウ　gust; strong blast

訓 突く　つく　*vt*. thrust; pierce; transfix; push; strike; attack; rush

突き刺す　つきさす　*vt*. stick; stab; thrust

1454

窃 ⑨

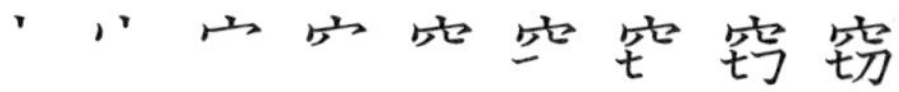

音 窃　セツ　steal

熟 窃取　セッシュ　intake; adoption; theft —*v*. take in; adopt; steal

窃盗　セットウ　theft —*v*. steal; commit theft

1455

窓 ⑪

音 窓　ソウ　window

熟 窓外　ソウガイ　outside the window

訓 窓　まど　window

窓際　まどぎわ　windowside; by the window

窓口　まどぐち　(ticket) window

¥ 窓口販売　まどぐちハンバイ　over-the-counter sale/selling

1456

窒 ⑪

音 窒　チツ　suffocation; nitrogen

熟 窒素　チッソ　***chem***. nitrogen

窒息　チッソク　suffocation; asphyxiation —*v*. be suffocated/choked/asphyxiated

1457

窮 ⑮

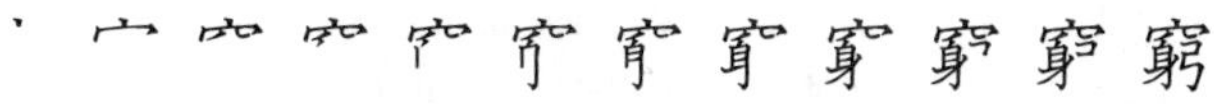

音 窮　キュウ　investigate thoroughly; reach an extreme; reach its limits

熟 窮する　キュウする　*vi*. be in need; be destitute; be in a dilemma

窮極　キュウキョク　the extreme/ultimate

	窮屈	キュウクツ	narrowness; tightness
	窮状	キュウジョウ	distress; sorry plight
	窮地	キュウチ	predicament; difficult situation
	窮乏	キュウボウ	want; destitution; poverty
訓	窮まる	きわまる	*vi*. reach an extreme; come to an end
	窮める	きわめる	*vt*. carry to extremes; bring to an end

1458

窯 ⑮

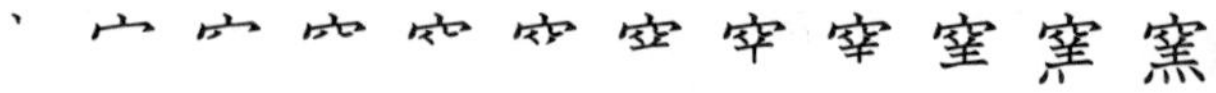

音	窯	ヨウ	kiln
熟	窯業	ヨウギョウ	ceramics
訓	窯	かま	kiln

5 立 たつ standing

1459

立 ⑤

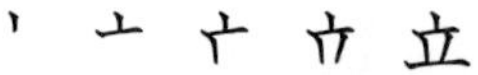

音	立	リツ (リュウ)	stand; rise
熟	立案	リツアン	plan; devise; draft —*v*. make/form a plan; devise; design
	立夏	リッカ	first day of summer
	立脚	リッキャク	based on —*vi*. be based on
	立憲	リッケン	adopting a constitution
	立憲政治	リッケンセイジ	constitutional government
	立候補	リッコウホ	candidacy; running for office —*vi*. stand/run for office
	立国	リッコク	founding of a state
	立志伝	リッシデン	success story
	立秋	リッシュウ	first day of autumn
	立春	リッシュン	first day of spring
	立証	リッショウ	proof —*v*. prove; establish
	立身出世	リッシンシュッセ	success in life —*v*. succeed in life
	立像	リツゾウ	statue of someone standing
	立体	リッタイ	solid; three-dimensional
	立体感	リッタイカン	sense of depth

立体交差　リッタイコウサ　grade separation
立体的　リッタイテキ　three-dimensional
立地　リッチ　location; siting
立地条件　リッチジョウケン　geographical conditions
立冬　リットウ　first day of winter
立派　リッパ　splendid; fine; magnificient
立腹　リップク　anger; offense —***vi***. get angry; lose one's temper
立方　リッポウ　cubic; cube
立方体　リッポウタイ　cube
立法　リッポウ　legislation; law making
立論　リツロン　argument —***vi***. put forth an argument

訓 立つ　たつ　***vi***. erect; rise; stand
立ち会う　たちあう　***vi***. attend; witness
立ち上がる　たちあがる　***vi***. stand up
立ち入る　たちいる　***vi***. enter; interfere; go into (an issue)
立ち往生　たちオウジョウ　***vi***. standing death —***vi***. come to a standstill; be in a dilenma
立ち退く　たちのく　***vi***. leave
立場　たちば　standpoint; viewpoint; position
立ち回る　たちまわる　***vi***. act
立ち向かう　たちむかう　***vi***. confront; fight; stand against
立てる　たてる　***vt***. erect; set up; raise
立て替える　たてかえる　***vt***. pay in advance; pay (for another)
立行司　たてギョウジ　head sumo refree
立札　たてふだ　signboard

¥ 立会い　たちあい　session

1460

⑪ 丶 亠 亣 立 产 音 章

音 章　ショウ　chapter; passage; writing

熟 章句　ショウク　passage of writing
章節　ショウセツ　chapters and sections (of a thesis, etc.)

1461
童 ⑫ 丶 亠 亣 立 产 音 童

音 童　ドウ　child

熟	童顔	ドウガン	child's face; childlike face
	童心	ドウシン	child's mind; childlike heart
	童貞	ドウテイ	virginity; chastity
	童謡	ドウヨウ	nursery song/rhyme
	童話	ドウワ	nursery tale; children's story
訓	童	わらべ	child

1462

端 ⑭

音	端	タン	end; tip; edge; margin; beginning
熟	端午	タンゴ	Boys' Festival
	端子	タンシ	terminal
	端緒	タンショ	clue; beginning; start
	端正	タンセイ	correct; right; just
	端的	タンテキ	plain; direct; pointblank
	端麗	タンレイ	grace; elegance; beauty
訓	端	は	edge; margin
	端	はし	end; tip; edge; margin; beginning
	端数	はスウ	***math***. fraction; odd sum; fragment; scrap
	端	はた	edge; bank; side
¥	端株	はかぶ	odd-lot (broken-lot) stocks

1463

競 ⑳

音	競	キョウ ケイ	rival; compete; dispute; quarrel
熟	競泳	キョウエイ	swimming race/competition —***v***. compete in a swimming race
	競演	キョウエン	contest —***v***. contest; enter a competition
	競技	キョウギ	match; contest; competition —***v***. contest; compete
	競争	キョウソウ	competition; contest; rivalry —***vi***. compete; contest; be rivals
	競走	キョウソウ	race; running race —***vi***. run in a race
	競馬	ケイバ	horse race
	競輪	ケイリン	bicycle race
訓	競う	きそう	***vi***. compete; rival
	競る	せる	***vt***. compete with

¥	競合	**キョウゴウ**	competition; rivalry
	競争市場	**キョウソウシジョウ**	competitive market place
	競争品	**キョウソウヒン**	competitor
	競争力	**キョウソウリョク**	competitiveness
	競売	**キョウバイ（ケイバイ）**	(public) auction; auction sale —***v***. auction; sell by auction

---

5 罒 あみがしら net

1464

罪 ⑬

音	罪	**ザイ**	crime; sin
熟	罪悪	**ザイアク**	vice; crime
	罪人	**ザイニン**	criminal; offender; convict
	罪名	**ザイメイ**	offence; charge
訓	罪	**つみ**	sin; crime; act of wrong doing

1465

署 ⑬

音	署	**ショ**	divide; office
熟	署長	**ショチョウ**	chief of police
	署名	**ショメイ**	signature —***vi***. sign

1466

置 ⑬

音	置	**チ**	put; place; positon
訓	置き換える	**おきかえる**	***vt***. replace; substitute; transpose
	置き去りにする	**おきざりにする**	***vt***. leave (a person) in the lurch
	置場	**おきば**	yard; garage; shed; storage space
	置物	**おきもの**	ornament
	置き忘れる	**おきわすれる**	***vt***. mislay; misplace
	置く	**おく**	***vt***. put; place; position; leave; allow; let; keep; hold

玄 玉 王 瓦 甘 生 用 田 疋 疒 癶 白 皮 皿 目 矛 矢 石 示 ネ 禾 穴 立 ● 罒 ● 旡 母 氺 衤

1467

罰 ⑭

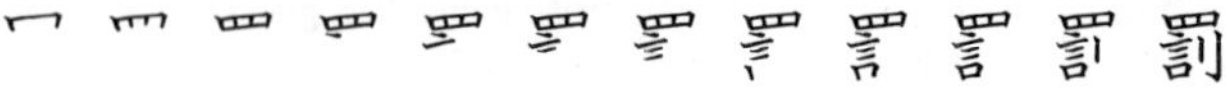

音	罰	バチ	punishment
		バツ	punishment
熟	罰金	バッキン	fine
	罰則	バッソク	penal regulations

1468

罷 ⑮

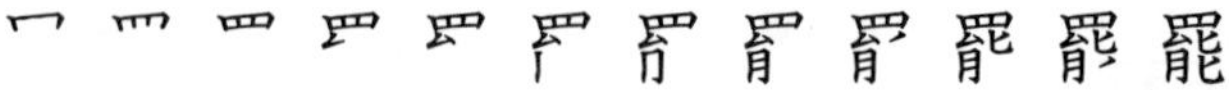

音	罷	ヒ	stop; end; discontinue
訓	※罷り通る	まかりとおる	***vi***. pass; go unchallenged
	※罷る	まかる	***vt***. leave; withdraw
	※罷む	やむ	***vi***. end; discontinue; stop
	※罷める	やめる	***vt***. end; discontinue; stop
¥	罷業	ヒギョウ	strike; walkout
	罷免	ヒメン	dismissal; discharge (from a job) —***v***. dismiss; discharge; relieve (a person) of his post; fire (someone)

1469

羅 ⑲

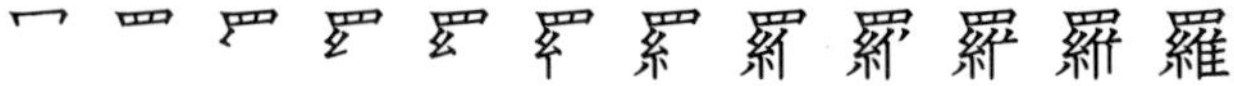

音	羅	ラ	net; silk gauze; thin silk
熟	羅漢	ラカン	arhat (person who attains Nirvana)
	羅針盤	ラシンバン	(magnetic) compass
	羅列	ラレツ	list; enumeration —***v***. list; enumerate

5 旡 むにょう crooked heaven

1470

既 ⑩

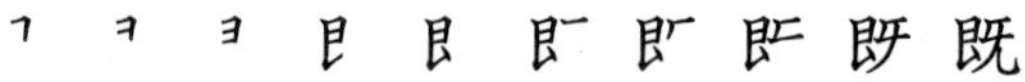

音	既	キ	already
熟	既往症	キオウショウ	medical history; anamnesis

既刊	**キカン**	previous publication; backlist book
既婚	**キコン**	married
既製	**キセイ**	ready-made; ready to wear
既成	**キセイ**	completed; accomplished; established
既知	**キチ**	known; established
既定	**キテイ**	fixed; predetermined; established
訓 既に	すでに	already; previously; before
¥ 既発債	**キハッサイ**	outstanding bond

5 母 see ⇨p.507

5 氺 see ⇨p.515

5 衤 see ⇨p.708

6 竹 たけ／たけかんむり bamboo

1471

竹 ⑥

ノ 𠂉 𠂊 ⺮ ⺮ 竹

音	竹	チク	bamboo
熟	竹馬の友	チクバのとも	childhood friend
	竹林	チクリン	bamboo forest
訓	竹	たけ	bamboo
	竹の子	たけのこ	bamboo shoot
	竹藪	たけやぶ	bamboo grove
	※竹刀	しない	*shinai* (bamboo sword for kendo practice)

1472

笑 ⑩

音	笑	ショウ	laugh
訓	笑う	わらう	***v.*** laugh; smile; chuckle; giggle
	笑い	わらい	laugh; smile
	笑話	わらいばなし	humorous/amusing story
	笑む	えむ	***vi.*** come out; open; bloom; smile
	※笑顔	えがお	smiling face; smile

1473

第 ⑪

音	第	ダイ	(ordinal prefix)
熟	第一	ダイイチ	first; number one; foremost; primary
	第一印象	ダイイチインショウ	first impressions
	第一人者	ダイイチニンシャ	first man; most talented person (in a group etc.)
	第一線	ダイイッセン	first line; front line; front
	第三者	ダイサンシャ	third party
	第六感	ダイロクカン	sixth sense
¥	第一次産業	ダイイチジサンギョウ	primary industry

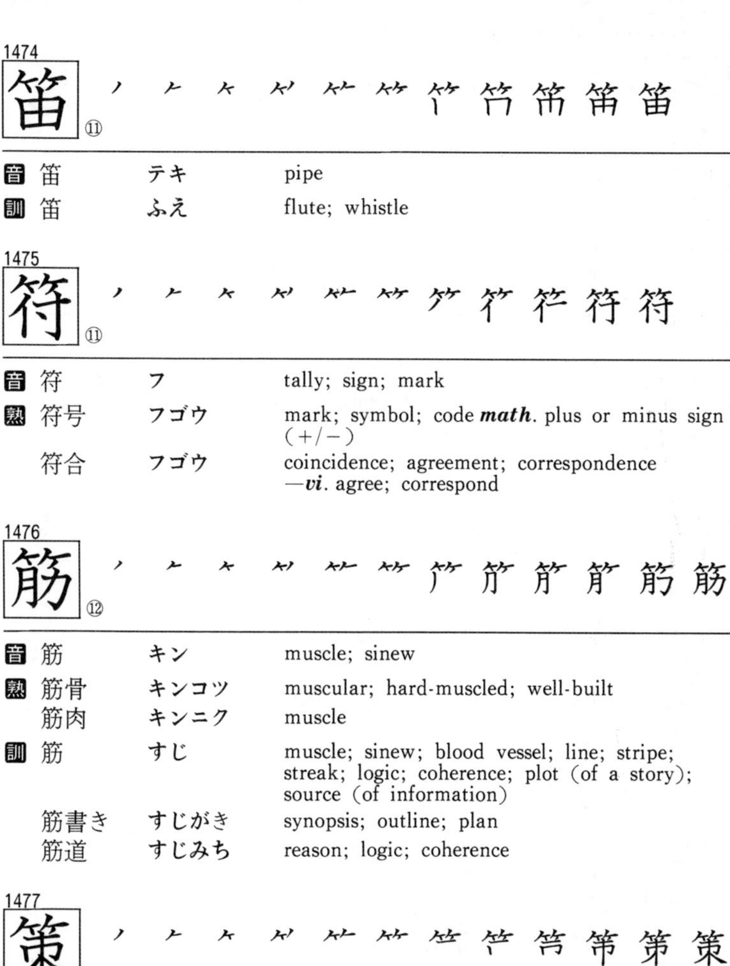

1474
笛 ⑪

音	笛	テキ	pipe
訓	笛	ふえ	flute; whistle

1475
符 ⑪

音	符	フ	tally; sign; mark
熟	符号	フゴウ	mark; symbol; code ***math***. plus or minus sign (＋/－)
	符合	フゴウ	coincidence; agreement; correspondence —***vi***. agree; correspond

1476
筋 ⑫

音	筋	キン	muscle; sinew
熟	筋骨	キンコツ	muscular; hard-muscled; well-built
	筋肉	キンニク	muscle
訓	筋	すじ	muscle; sinew; blood vessel; line; stripe; streak; logic; coherence; plot (of a story); source (of information)
	筋書き	すじがき	synopsis; outline; plan
	筋道	すじみち	reason; logic; coherence

1477
策 ⑫

音	策	サク	plan; plot; whip stick
熟	策する	サクする	***vt***. plan; plot; scheme
	策謀	サクボウ	plot; scheme; intrigue —***v***. plot; scheme
	策略	サクリャク	plot; strategem; trick

1478

答 ⑫

ノ ⺈ ⺮ 𥫗 ... 答 答

音	答	トウ	answer
熟	答案	トウアン	written answers; examination paper
	答辞	トウジ	formal reply
	答申	トウシン	report; reply (to one's superior) —*v*. report; submit a report (to a superior)
	答弁	トウベン	reply; answer; account; explanation —*v*. reply; answer; say something in self-defense
	答礼	トウレイ	return salute
訓	答え	こたえ	answer; reply; response
	答える	こたえる	***vt***. answer; reply; respond

1479

等 ⑫

ノ ⺈ ⺮ 𥫗 ... 等 等

音	等	トウ	equal
熟	等圧	トウアツ	uniform pressure
	等圧線	トウアツセン	isobar
	等価	トウカ	equivalence; parity
	等外	トウガイ	failure; also-ran
	等級	トウキュウ	grade; class; order; rank
	等号	トウゴウ	equal sign (=)
	等式	トウシキ	***math***. equality
	等時性	トウジセイ	***phy***. isochronism
	等質	トウシツ	homogeneity
	等身	トウシン	life size
	等分	トウブン	division into equal parts —*v*. divide into equal parts
訓	等しい	ひとしい	equal; similar; like

1480

筒 ⑫

ノ ⺈ ⺮ 𥫗 ... 筒 筒

音	筒	トウ	tube
訓	筒	つつ	pipe; tube; case; cylinder; gun; canon
	筒抜け	つつぬけ	leaving out entirely

1481

⑫ ノ ト ⺮ 竹 ... 筆

音	筆	ヒツ	writing brush
熟	筆記	ヒッキ	note-taking; notes —*v*. take notes
	筆記体	ヒッキタイ	longhand (writing)
	筆耕	ヒッコウ	copying; copyist —*v*. copy
	筆算	ヒッサン	calculations on paper —*v*. do sums on a piece of paper
	筆写	ヒッシャ	copying; transcription —*v*. copy; transcribe
	筆者	ヒッシャ	author; writer
	筆順	ヒツジュン	stroke order (of Chinese characters)
	筆跡	ヒッセキ	penmanship; handwriting; written letters
	筆舌し難い	ヒツゼツしがたい	beyond description
	筆談	ヒツダン	written communication —*vi*. communicate in writing
	筆頭	ヒットウ	tip of a writing brush; first on the list
	筆頭者	ヒットウシャ	head of a family (as recorded in a family register)
	筆答	ヒットウ	written answer —*vi*. answer in writing
	筆法	ヒッポウ	manner of using a writing brush ***fig***. method; way of thinking
	筆名	ヒツメイ	pen name; pseudonym
	筆力	ヒツリョク	power of the brush stroke/pen; powerful writing
訓	筆	ふで	writing brush
	筆入れ	ふでいれ	pencil case
	筆箱	ふでばこ	pencil box
	筆無精(筆不精)	ふでブショウ	poor correspondent
	筆まめ	ふでまめ	ready pen; (someone who) likes writing letters, etc.

1482

⑬ ノ ト ⺮ 竹 ... 節

音	節	セツ	season; occasion; section; paragraph; verse; joint; knot
		(セチ)	
熟	節句	セック	annual festivals
	節減	セツゲン	curtailment —*v*. curtail

	節制	セッセイ	moderation; temperance —*v.* moderate one's lifestyle
	節操	セッソウ	constancy; fidelity; integrity; chastity
	節度	セツド	moderation; rule; standard
	節分	セツブン	last day of winter
	節約	セツヤク	economy; saving; thrift —*v.* economize; save
訓	節	ふし	knot; joint; tune; point; item

1483
箇 ⑭

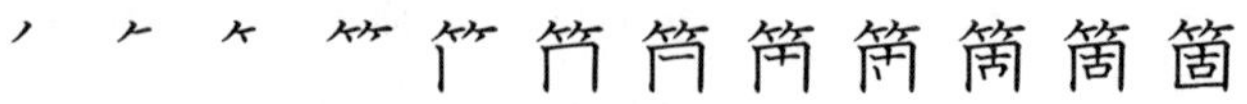

音	箇	カ	piece
熟	箇所	カショ	place; part; point
	箇条	カジョウ	article; provision; clause
	箇条書き	カジョウがき	itemization

1484
管 ⑭

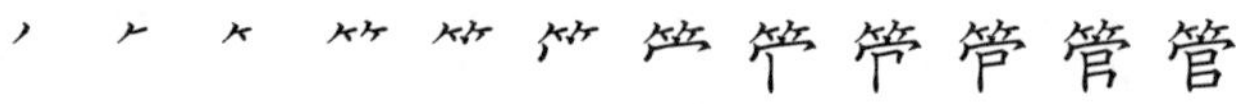

音	管	カン	pipe; administer
熟	管轄	カンカツ	jurisdiction; control —*vt.* have jurisdiction/control over
	管楽器	カンガッキ	wind instrument
	管弦楽	カンゲンガク	orchestra
	管内	カンナイ	within the jurisdiction
	管理	カンリ	control; administration; supervision —*v.* control; administrate; supervise
訓	管	くだ	tube; pipe
¥	管理職	カンリショク	administrator; management
	管理費	カンリヒ	administrative expenses; maintenance fee

1485
算 ⑭

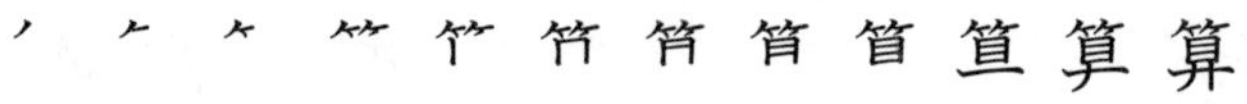

音	算	サン	count; calculation; reckoning; counting sticks
熟	算出	サンシュツ	calculation; computation —*v.* calculate; compute
	算数	サンスウ	arithmetic; calculation
	算段	サンダン	contrivance; thinking —*v.* contrive/think of a good way

	算定	サンテイ	computation; calculation; estimate; estimation —*v*. calculate; estimate; appraise
	算入	サンニュウ	item in an calculation —*v*. include in a calculation
	算用数字	サンヨウスウジ	Arabic figures/numerals
訓	※算盤	そろばん	abacus

1486
箱 ⑮

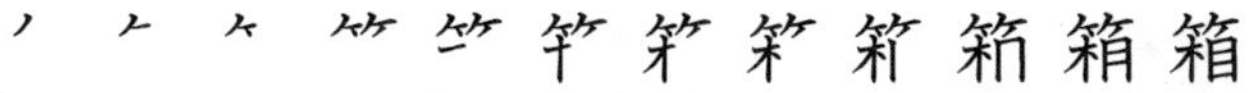

訓	箱	はこ	box; case; casket
	箱入り娘	はこいりむすめ	innocent/over-protected girl
	箱庭	はこにわ	miniature garden

1487
範 ⑮

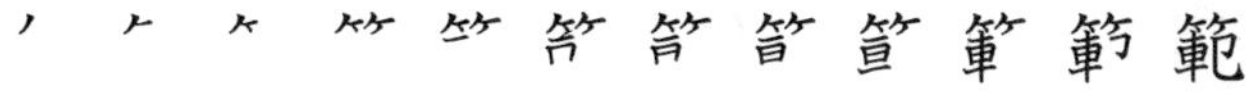

音	範	ハン	model
熟	範囲	ハンイ	extent; scope; sphere; range; limits

1488
築 ⑯

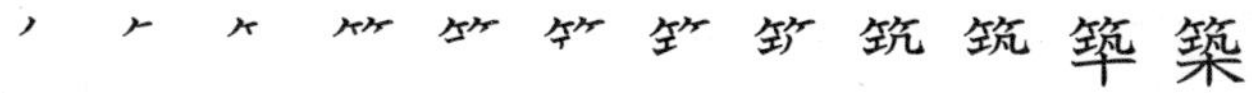

音	築	チク	construct; build
熟	築城	チクジョウ	construction of a castle; fortification —*vi*. fortify; build a castle
訓	築く	きずく	*vt*. build; make; construct; erect

1489
篤 ⑯

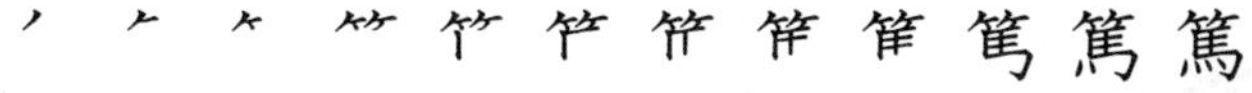

音	篤	トク	hospitable
熟	篤学	トクガク	love of learning; devotion to one's studies
	篤志	トクシ	benevolence; charity
	篤志家	トクシカ	volunteer; supporter
	篤実	トクジツ	sincerity; faithfulness

1490
簡 ⑱ 𠂉 𠂉 ⺮ 𥫗 𥫗 𥫗 𥫗 𥫗 𥫗 𥫗 𥫗 簡

音	簡	カン	letter; brevity
熟	簡易	カンイ	simplicity; ease; easiness
	簡潔	カンケツ	brevity; conciseness
	簡素	カンソ	simplicity
	簡単	カンタン	simplicity; simple; ease; easy
	簡便	カンベン	handiness; expediency; convenience; simplicity
	簡明	カンメイ	conciseness; brevity
	簡略	カンリャク	simplicity; conciseness

1491
簿 ⑲ 𠂉 𠂉 ⺮ 𥫗 𥫗 𥫗 𥫗 𥫗 𥫗 𥫗 簿 簿

音	簿	ボ	record book; ledger; register; list
¥	簿価	ボカ	book value
	簿記	ボキ	bookkeeping

1492
籍 ⑳ 𠂉 𠂉 ⺮ 𥫗 𥫗 𥫗 𥫗 𥫗 𥫗 籍 籍 籍

音	籍	セキ	writing; membership; books; record

6 米 こめ／こめへん rice

1493
米 ⑥ 丶 丷 䒑 半 米 米

音	米	ベイ	rice; eighty-eight years of age; America; meter (unit of measurement)
		マイ	rice
熟	米国	ベイコク	the United States
	米穀	ベイコク	rice; grain
	米作	ベイサク	rice cultivation/crop
	米寿	ベイジュ	one's eighty-eighth birthday

	米収	ベイシュウ	rice crop/harvest
	米食	ベイショク	diet with rice as the staple
	米人	ベイジン	American person
	米兵	ベイヘイ	US soldier/sailor
訓	米	こめ	(uncooked) rice
	米所	こめどころ	rice-producing area
	米問屋	こめどんや	rice wholesaler
	米屋	こめや	rice dealer
	※米	メートル	meter (unit of measurement)
	※米	よね	rice; eighty-eighth birthday
¥	米価	ベイカ	price of rice (set by the govermnent)

1494

粋 ⑩

音	粋	スイ	pure; smart
熟	粋狂	スイキョウ	whimsical; freakish; capricious; eccentric
	粋人	スイジン	man of refined tastes/the world
訓	※粋	いき	smart; stylish

1495

粉 ⑩

音	粉	フン	flour; powder
熟	粉骨	フンコツ	assidousness —***vi***. be assidious
	粉骨砕身	フンコツサイシン	one's best/utmost —***vi***. do one's best/utmost
	粉砕	フンサイ	crushed; pulverized —***v***. crush; pulverize; smash/break into pieces
	粉飾	フンショク	embellishment; window dressing —***v***. embellish; window-dress
	粉炭	フンタン	powdered coal
	粉本	フンポン	copy (for a painting/writing); rough sketch
	粉末	フンマツ	powder
訓	粉	こ	powder
	粉	こな	flour; powder
	粉薬	こなぐすり	powdered medicine
	粉々	こなごな	pieces; dust
	粉状	こなジョウ	powder form; powdered
	粉微塵	こなミジン	tiny fragments; pieces; smithereens

6 ¥ 粉飾決算 フンショクケッサン window-dressing settlement

1496

粗 ⑪

丶 丷 䒑 半 米 米 米 粈 粈 粗 粗

音	粗	ソ	coarse; rough
熟	粗悪	ソアク	coarse; crude; inferior
	粗雑	ソザツ	coarse; crude
	粗品	ソしな	small gift
	粗食	ソショク	coarse food; plain diet
	粗製	ソセイ	crudely made; inferior make
	粗相	ソソウ	carelessness; blunder —***vi***. be careless; blunder
	粗大	ソダイ	big and coarse; large and rough
	粗茶	ソチャ	(coarse) tea
	粗暴	ソボウ	wild; rough; violent
	粗末	ソマツ	coarse; plain; crude; rough; rude
	粗野	ソヤ	rude; rustic; loutish; vulgar
訓	粗い	あらい	coarse; rough

1497

粘 ⑪

丶 丷 䒑 半 米 米 米 粘 粘 粘 粘

音	粘	ネン	stick
熟	粘液	ネンエキ	***med***. mucus; phlegm
	粘性	ネンセイ	viscosity
	粘着	ネンチャク	adhesion; viscosity —***vi***. stick/adhere to
	粘土	ネンド	clay; plasticene
	粘膜	ネンマク	***med***. mucosa membrane
訓	粘る	ねばる	***vi***. be sticky/glutinous/adhesive
	粘り気	ねばりケ	sticky
	粘り強い	ねばりづよい	perservering; tenacious

1498

粒 ⑪

丶 丷 䒑 半 米 米 米 粒 粒 粒 粒

音	粒	リュウ	grain; drop(let)
熟	粒子	リュウシ	(atomic) particle; grain
	粒状	リュウジョウ	granular; granulated

訓	粒	つぶ	grain; drop(let)
	粒揃い	つぶぞろい	uniformly excellent
	粒々	つぶつぶ	lumps; grains
	粒選り	つぶより	the best; picked; choice

1499

粧 ⑫

音	粧	ショウ	dress

1500

精 ⑭

音	精	セイ （ショウ）	spirit; energy; vitality; semen; precise
熟	精進	ショウジン	devotion; diligence; purification —***vi***. abstain from meat or fish
	精進料理	ショウジン リョウリ	vegetarian cooking/cuisine
	精霊	ショウリョウ	spirit of a dead person
	精一杯	セイイッパイ	with all one's strength; as hard as possible
	精鋭	セイエイ	elite; crack; the best
	精液	セイエキ	semen
	精確	セイカク	accurate; precise; exact
	精巧	セイコウ	exquisite; detailed; delicate
	精根	セイコン	energy; vitality
	精魂	セイコン	spirit; energy; vitality
	精彩	セイサイ	luster; vitality
	精算	セイサン	exact calculation; settling of accounts —***v***. settle accounts
	精子	セイシ	sperm
	精神	セイシン	mind; spirit
	精神科	セイシンカ	psychiatry
	精神病	セイシンビョウ	mental disorder
	精製	セイセイ	refining; careful manufacture —***v***. refine
	精選	セイセン	careful/choice selection —***v***. choose/select carefully
	精通	セイツウ	well-informed; familiarity —***vi***. be familiar/well versed in
	精度	セイド	precision; accuracy
	精読	セイドク	careful reading —***v***. read carefully

	精分	セイブン	nourishment; vitality
	精米	セイマイ	polished rice —*v*. polish rice
	精密	セイミツ	precision
	精力	セイリョク	energy; vigor; vitality
	精励	セイレイ	diligence —*vi*. be diligent; work hard
	精霊	セイレイ	spirit; soul
	精錬	セイレン	refining; smelting —*v*. refine; smelt
¥	精密機械	セイミツキカイ	precision machine

1501

糖 ⑯

音	糖	トウ	sugar; sweetened carbohydrate
熟	糖尿病	トウニョウビョウ	***med***. diabetes
	糖分	トウブン	sugar (content)
	糖類	トウルイ	saccharide

1502

糧 ⑱

音	糧	リョウ (ロウ)	food; provisions
熟	糧食	リョウショク	food; provisions
	糧道	リョウドウ	road for supplying; provisions to troops
訓	糧	かて	food; provisions

6 糸 いと／いとへん thread

1503

糸 ⑥

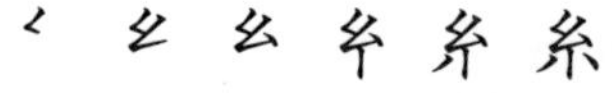

音	糸	シ	thread
訓	糸	いと	thread; string; line
	糸口	いとぐち	end of a thread ***fig***. first step; beginning; lead; clue

1504
 ⑦

音	系	ケイ	system; descent
熟	系図	ケイズ	genealogy; lineage
	系統	ケイトウ	system; lineage; genealogy; school; party
	系統的	ケイトウテキ	systematically; methodically
	系譜	ケイフ	genealogy; lineage
	系列	ケイレツ	order; series
訓	系ぐ	つなぐ	***vt.*** connect; join
¥	系列会社	ケイレツガイシャ	affiliated company

1505
 ⑩

音	索	サク	seek; cord
熟	索引	サクイン	index

1506
素 ⑩

音	素	ス	naked; uncovered; simple
		ソ	element; beginning
熟	素足	スあし	barefoot
	素顔	スがお	unpainted face; face without makeup
	素性	スジョウ	birth; lineage; identity
	素手	スで	bare hands
	素敵	ステキ	splendid; marvelous; great; beautiful; nice
	素直	スなお	frank; gentle; meek; docile; honest
	素肌	スはだ	bare skin
	素晴らしい	スばらしい	splendid; magnificent
	素因	ソイン	contributing factor; cause
	素行	ソコウ	behavior; conduct
	素材	ソザイ	material; subject matter
	素地	ソジ	groundwork; the makings of
	素質	ソシツ	quality; nature; makeup
	素数	ソスウ	***math.*** prime number

	素読	ソドク	reading aloud without making any effort to understand what is written —*v*. read aloud without making any effort to understand what is written
	素描	ソビョウ	rough sketch —*v*. make a rough sketch
	素振り	ソぶり	manner; behavior; attitude; air; look
	素朴	ソボク	simple; artless; ingenuous
	素養	ソヨウ	culture; one's knowledge; attainments
訓	※素	もと	beginning; base
	※素人	しろうと	amateur; layman

1507

紫 ⑫

音	紫	シ	purple
熟	紫外線	シガイセン	ultraviolet rays
	紫紺	シコン	purple blue
訓	紫	むらさき	purple; gromwell

1508

累 ⑪

音	累	ルイ	accumulate; pile up; encumber; incessantly
熟	累加	ルイカ	acceleration; progressive increase —*v*. accelerate; increase progressively
	累計	ルイケイ	total; sum
	累減	ルイゲン	regression; progressive decrease —*v*. regress; decrease progressively
	累次	ルイジ	successive; repeated
	累進	ルイシン	successive promotions; progressive; graduated —***vi***. be successively promoted; progress; graduate
	累積	ルイセキ	accumulation —*v*. accumulate
	累々	ルイルイ	in heaps; piled up

1509

緊 ⑮

音	緊	キン	strict; tight; severe

熟	緊急	キンキュウ	emergency; urgency
	緊縮	キンシュク	shrinkage; contraction —*v*. shrink; contract
	緊張	キンチョウ	strain; tension —***vi***. be strained/tense
	緊迫	キンパク	tension; strain; under pressure —***vi***. be tense/under pressure
	緊密	キンミツ	close; tight; tightly knit

1510

繁 ⑯

音	繁	ハン	prosper
熟	繁栄	ハンエイ	prosperity —***vi***. prosper; thrive; flourish
	繁華街	ハンカガイ	shopping mall/parade; busy street
	繁雑	ハンザツ	complicated; complex; intricate; troublesome
	繁盛	ハンジョウ	prosperity; success —***vi***. prosper; flourish; thrive; be successful
	繁殖	ハンショク	breeding; reproduction; propagation; multiplication —***vi***. breed; reproduce; propagate; multiply
	繁茂	ハンモ	luxuriant growth; rankness —***vi***. grow thick; exuberate; flourish

1511

繭 ⑱

音	繭	ケン	cocoon
熟	繭	まゆ	cocoon

1512

⑨

音	紀	キ	account; writing; era; year
熟	紀元	キゲン	era; epoch
	紀行	キコウ	travelogue

1513

⑨

音	級	キュウ	class; grade; position; symbol; group

6

竹 米 ● 糸 缶 羊 羽 老 耂 而 耒 耳 肉 自 至 舌 舟 色 虍 虫 血 行 衣 衤 西 艮

熟	級数	キュウスウ	***math.*** series; progression
	級長	キュウチョウ	president of a class; homeroom president
	級友	キュウユウ	classmate

1514

糾 ⑨

音	糾	キュウ	twist; intertwine; collect together; tangle; entangle; correct; rectify
熟	糾合	キュウゴウ	rally; muster ***—v.*** rally; muster
	糾弾	キュウダン	impeachment ***—v.*** impeach
	糾明	キュウメイ	searching examination ***—v.*** examine (a matter) closely

1515

紅 ⑨

音	紅	コウ (ク)	crimson; rouge; red
熟	紅一点	コウイッテン	only woman in a group
	紅顔	コウガン	rosy face; ruddy cheeks
	紅茶	コウチャ	tea
	紅潮	コウチョウ	blush; flush ***—vi.*** blush; flush; turn red/rosy
	紅白	コウハク	red and white
	紅葉	コウヨウ	autumnal leaves ***—vi.*** turn red/yellow
訓	紅	くれない	deep red; crimson
	紅	べに	rouge; deep red; crimson
	※紅葉	もみじ	maple tree

1516

⑨

音	約	ヤク	promise; appproximately; curtail
熟	約する	ヤクする	***vt.*** promise; reduce; abbreviate
	約言	ヤクゲン	contraction; summary
	約定	ヤクジョウ	promise; agreement; contract ***—vi.*** promise; make a contract; agree
	約数	ヤクスウ	***math.*** divisor; factor
	約束	ヤクソク	promise; appointment ***—v.*** make a promise/appointment

約諾	ヤクダク	promise; commitment —***vt***. promise; commit
約分	ヤクブン	***math***. reduction of a factor to its lowest terms —***v***. ***math***. reduce a fraction to its lowest terms
約款	ヤッカン	agreement; stipulation
¥ 約束手形	ヤクソクてがた	promissory note

1517

紙 ⑩

く 幺 幺 糸 糸 糸 紅 紅 紙 紙

音 紙	シ	paper; newspaper
熟 紙型	シケイ	paper mold/mat (used to make a printing plate)
紙質	シシツ	paper quality
紙上	シジョウ	in the press; in the papers; on paper
紙幣	シヘイ	paper money; bill; note
紙片	シヘン	piece/strip/slip of paper
紙面	シメン	the papers; the press
訓 紙	かみ	paper
紙切れ	かみきれ	piece of paper
紙屑	かみくず	wastepaper
紙一重	かみひとえ	very fine line

1518

純 ⑩

く 幺 幺 糸 糸 糸 紅 紅 紅 純

音 純	ジュン	pure; naive; genuine; authentic
熟 純愛	ジュンアイ	pure/true love
純化	ジュンカ	purification —***v***. purify
純金	ジュンキン	pure gold
純銀	ジュンギン	pure silver
純潔	ジュンケツ	purity; chastity
純血	ジュンケツ	pure-blooded; thoroughbred
純情	ジュンジョウ	pure heart; naivety; innocence
純真	ジュンシン	pure heart; purity; naiveté
純粋	ジュンスイ	purity
純正	ジュンセイ	pure; genuine
純然	ジュンゼン	pure; sheer; utter; absolute
純度	ジュンド	purity
純白	ジュンパク	snow-white
純文学	ジュンブンガク	serious literature

	純朴	ジュンボク	simple; naive
	純綿	ジュンメン	pure cotton
	純毛	ジュンモウ	pure wool
	純良	ジュンリョウ	pure and good; grade A
¥	純益	ジュンエキ	net profit
	純資産	ジュンシサン	net assets (worth)
	純増	ジュンゾウ	net increase
	純投資	ジュントウシ	portfolio investment
	純利益	ジュンリエキ	net profit/income

1519

納 ⑩

く 幺 幺 糸 糸 糸 糹 糹冂 納 納

音	納	ノウ	offer; accept
		(トウ)	
		(ナッ)	
		(ナン)	put away
熟	納得	ナットク	understanding; consent; assent; compliance —*v*. understand; assent; give consent; agree
	納屋	ナや	barn
	納戸	ナンど	closet; wardrobe; storeroom
	納会	ノウカイ	last meeting of the year
	納期	ノウキ	time of delivery; payment date
	納骨	ノウコツ	laying a person's ashes to rest —*vi*. lay a person's ashes to rest
	納税	ノウゼイ	payment of taxes —*vi*. pay one's taxes
	納税者	ノウゼイシャ	taxpayer
	納入	ノウニュウ	delivery; payment —*v*. deliver; pay; supply
	納品	ノウヒン	delivery of goods —*v*. deliver; supply
	納品書	ノウヒンショ	statement of delivery
	納付	ノウフ	delivery; payment —*v*. deliver; supply; pay
	納涼	ノウリョウ	enjoying the cool of the evening —*vi*. enjoy the cool of the evening
訓	納まる	おさまる	*vi*. stay; be contented; be paid; settle down
	納める	おさめる	*vt*. obtain; gain; acquire; deliver; supply
¥	納税準備預金	ノウゼイジュンビヨキン	deposit for tax; deposit earmarked for tax payment

1520
紛 ⑩

音	紛	フン	be mistaken for; be hardly distinguishable; get mixed
熟	紛議	フンギ	controversy; dissension —*vi*. be controversial
	紛糾	フンキュウ	complication; entanglement —*vi*. be complicated/entangled
	紛失	フンシツ	loss —*v*. lose
	紛然	フンゼン	confused; in a jumble
	紛争	フンソウ	trouble; dispute; strife; disturbance —*vi*. cause trouble/strife; dispute
	紛々	フンプン	divided; mixed; in confusion; conflicting
訓	紛れる	まぎれる	*vi*. be mistaken for; get mixed up; disappear (in the midst of); be diverted/distracted
	紛らす	まぎらす	*vt*. divert; distract; conceal; evade
	紛らわしい	まぎらわしい	ambiguous; misleading; confusing
	紛らわす	まぎらわす	*vt*. divert; distract; conceal; evade
	紛れ込む	まぎれこむ	*vi*. be lost/disappear among
	紛れもない	まぎれもない	unmistakable; obvious
	※紛う	まがう	*vi*. be mistaken for; be confused with; be mixed together; be mixed up

1521
紡 ⑩

音	紡	ボウ	spin; make yarn
熟	紡糸	ボウシ	spinning; yarn
	紡織	ボウショク	spinning and weaving
	紡錘	ボウスイ	spindle
	紡績	ボウセキ	spinning
	紡績工	ボウセキコウ	spinner
訓	紡ぐ	つむぐ	*vt*. spin; make yarn

1522
紋 ⑩

音	紋	モン	family crest; textile pattern
熟	紋切り型	モンきりがた	crest pattern; conventional; stereotyped

	紋章	モンショウ	crest; coat of arms
	紋所	モンどころ	family crest

1523

経 ⑪

音	経	ケイ	elapse; pass; go through; normal; usual
		キョウ	sutra; mantra
熟	経文	キョウモン	sutra; text of a sutra
	経緯	ケイイ	longitude and latitude; warp and woof; details
	経営	ケイエイ	management —*v*. manage; run; operate
	経過	ケイカ	progress; development; passage —***vi***. pass; elapse
	経験	ケイケン	experience —*v*. experience; go through; undergo
	経済	ケイザイ	economy; husbandry; the economy; finances
	経済的	ケイザイテキ	economical; frugal; thrifty
	経線	ケイセン	meridian
	経典	ケイテン	Scriptures; classics; literary works by the sages
	経度	ケイド	longitude
	経由	ケイユ	via; by way of; through —***vi***. go via/by way of/through
	経歴	ケイレキ	personal history; background; career
	経路	ケイロ	course; route; process
訓	経る	へる	***vi***. pass; elapse; go/pass through; experience
¥	経営難	ケイエイナン	financial difficulty
	経済活動	ケイザイカツドウ	economic activity
	経済企画庁	ケイザイキカクチョウ	Economic Planning Agency
	経済成長	ケイザイセイチョウ	economic growth
	経常収支	ケイジョウシュウシ	current account balance
	経常費	ケイジョウヒ	working expenses; operating costs
	経常利益	ケイジョウリエキ	recurring profit
	経費	ケイヒ	expenses(s); cost(s); expenditure
	経理	ケイリ	accounting
	経理士	ケイリシ	public accountant

1524

紺 ⑪

音	紺	コン	dark blue

熟	紺色	コンいろ	dark/navy blue
	紺青	コンジョウ	deep/Prussian blue
	紺碧	コンペキ	dark/deep blue
	紺屋	コンや (コウや)	dyer; dyer's shop

1525

細 ⑪

音	細	サイ	narrow; thin; fine; minute; detail
熟	細菌	サイキン	germ; microbe; bacteria
	細工	サイク	workmanship; handiwork; trick —*v.* use tricks; play tricks
	細事	サイジ	trifle
	細心	サイシン	very careful; scrupulous; meticulous
	細則	サイソク	bylaws
	細大	サイダイ	minutest detail; detailed; full
	細部	サイブ	details; particulars
	細分	サイブン	subdivision; segmentation —*v.* subdivide; segment
	細別	サイベツ	subdivision —*v.* subdivide
	細胞	サイボウ	cell
	細密	サイミツ	fine; close; minute
	細目	サイモク	details; particulars; specifications
訓	細かい	こまかい	small; fine; close; minute; delicate; subtle
	細か	こまか	small; fine; delicate; subtle
	細々	こまごま	in detail; minutely
	細る	ほそる	***vi.*** become thin; slim down
	細い	ほそい	fine; thin; narrow; slender
	細面	ほそおもて	slender face
	細長い	ほそながい	slender; long and narrow
	細道	ほそみち	narrow lane

1526

終 ⑪

音	終	シュウ	finish; last; complete
熟	終える	おえる	***vt.*** finish; complete; go through with
	終わる	おわる	***vi.*** end; be over; finish; be finished; come to an end
	終演	シュウエン	end of a performance

終業	シュウギョウ	close of work/school —***vi***. close; break-up
終曲	シュウキョク	finale; last song of a musical
終極	シュウキョク	ultimate
終局	シュウキョク	end; close
終結	シュウケツ	conclusion; end —***vi***. end; be concluded
終始	シュウシ	throughout; unchanged from beginning to end —***vi***. remain unchanged throughout
終始一貫	シュウシイッカン	consistency
終止	シュウシ	end; stop; termination —***vi***. stop; terminate; end; come to end
終止符	シュウシフ	period; full stop
終日	シュウジツ	all day long; from morning to night; throughout the day
終身刑	シュウシンケイ	life imprisonment
終生	シュウセイ	all one's life; life-long
終戦	シュウセン	end of a war
終着駅	シュウチャクエキ	terminal train station; terminus
終点	シュウテン	terminal train station; end of the line; last stop
終電	シュウデン	last train
終幕	シュウマク	final scene; end of the performance
終末	シュウマツ	end; conclusion
終夜	シュウヤ	all night
終夜営業	シュウヤエイギョウ	stay open all night
終了	シュウリョウ	close; end —***v***. come to an end; be completed; finish
¥ 終業時間	シュウギョウジカン	closing time
終身雇用	シュウシンコヨウ	lifetime employment

1527

紹 ⑪

音 紹	ショウ	introduce
熟 紹介	ショウカイ	introduction; presentation —***v***. introduce; present; report; review

1528

紳 ⑪

音 紳	シン	gentleman
熟 紳士	シンシ	gentleman

1529
組 ⑪

音	組	ソ	set; association; group; class; company
熟	組閣	ソカク	Cabinet formation —*vi*. form a Cabinet
	組織	ソシキ	organization; setup —*v*. organize; set up
	組織的	ソシキテキ	systematic
	組成	ソセイ	composition; makeup —*v*. compose; constitute; make up
訓	組	くみ	class; set; group; company
	組む	くむ	*v*. put together; assemble; cross one's legs; form; group
¥	組合	くみあい	(trade) union association; (labor) union; society
	組み合わせる	くみあわせる	*vt*. combine; assemble; match
	組み立てる	くみたてる	*vt*. fabricate; assemble

1530
絵 ⑫

音	絵	エ	picture
		カイ	picture
熟	絵図	エズ	graphic drawing; scale sketch
	絵の具	エのグ	water colors
	絵葉書	エはがき	picture postcard
	絵筆	エふで	paintbrush; drawing pen
	絵本	エホン	picture/illustrated book
	絵巻物	エまきもの	picture scroll
	絵文字	エモジ	pictorial symbol
	絵画	カイガ	pictures and paintings collectively

1531
給 ⑫

音	給	キュウ	give; allowance; salary; be enough/sufficent; serve; provide
熟	給仕	キュウジ	waiter; waitress; steward —*vi*. wait on; serve

	給食	キュウショク	provision of meals (at schools, etc.) —*vi*. provide/serve meals
	給水	キュウスイ	water supply/service —*vi*. supply water
	給付	キュウフ	presentation; delivery; benefit —*v*. make a presentation; deliver; pay
	給付金	キュウフキン	benefit
	給油	キュウユ	oil supply —*vi*. lubricate; refuel
	給与	キュウヨ	allowance; grant; supplies —*v*. grant; supply
	給料	キュウリョウ	wages; salary
¥	給与水準	キュウヨスイジュン	pay level
	給与体系	キュウヨタイケイ	pay structure
	給料日	キュウリョウび	payday

1532

結 ⑫

く 幺 幺 糸 糸 糸 糸 紅 紅 結 結 結

音	結	ケツ (ケッ)	tie; join; union; conclusion
熟	結果	ケッカ	result; effect; outcome; consequence
	結核	ケッカク	***med***. tuberculosis (T.B.)
	結局	ケッキョク	after all; finally; ultimately; eventually
	結構	ケッコウ	fine; enough; sufficient
	結合	ケツゴウ	union; combination —*v*. unite; combine
	結婚	ケッコン	marriage —*vi*. marry; get married
	結実	ケツジツ	fruition —*vi*. bear fruit; realize
	結晶	ケッショウ	crystal; crystallization —*vi*. crystalize
	結成	ケッセイ	formation; organization —*v*. form; organize
	結束	ケッソク	unity; union —*v*. unite; stand together
	結託	ケッタク	collusion; conspiracy —*vi*. conspire with
	結末	ケツマツ	the end; conclusion; outcome
	結論	ケツロン	conclusion —*vi*. come to/reach a conclusion
訓	結ぶ	むすぶ	*v*. tie; join; connect; link; conclude; bear (fruit)
	結び	むすび	bow; end; conclusion
	結び目	むすびめ	knot
	結う	ゆう	*vt*. tie an *obi*; dress; put one's hair up in a traditional Japanese hairstyle
	結納	ゆいノウ	betrothal gifts
	結わえる	ゆわえる	*vt*. bind; fasten; tie

1533

絞 ⑫

音	絞	コウ	strangle; press; squeeze; wring
熟	絞殺	コウサツ	strangulation; hanging —*v*. strangle; hang; suffocate
	絞首刑	コウシュケイ	execution by hanging
訓	絞る	しぼる	***vt***. wring; squeeze; press; extort; exploit
	絞まる	しまる	***vi***. tighten; become tight
	絞める	しめる	***vt***. tie up; tighten bind; strangle; press; squeeze

1534

絶 ⑫

音	絶	ゼツ ゼッ	die out; end; fail
熟	絶する	ゼッする	*v*. die out; end; fail
	絶縁体	ゼツエンタイ	insulator; non-conductor
	絶海	ゼッカイ	distant seas
	絶叫	ゼッキョウ	scream —***vi***. scream; cry out; shout
	絶景	ゼッケイ	splendid view
	絶交	ゼッコウ	severance of relations; rupture —***vi***. sever one's relationship with
	絶好	ゼッコウ	splendid; first rate
	絶賛	ゼッサン	great admiration/praise —*v*. admire/praise greatly
	絶食	ゼッショク	fasting; —***vi***. fast
	絶世	ゼッセイ	peerless; unequaled
	絶対	ゼッタイ	absolute; definite
	絶体絶命	ゼッタイゼツメイ	desperate situation
	絶大	ゼツダイ	immense; great
	絶頂	ゼッチョウ	summit; peak; climax
	絶版	ゼッパン	out-of-print —*v*. cease publication
	絶筆	ゼッピツ	last piece of writing (before giving up, dying, etc.)
	絶品	ゼッピン	superb article; masterpiece
	絶壁	ゼッペキ	precipice; cliff
	絶望	ゼツボウ	despair —***vi***. despair; be full of despair
	絶命	ゼツメイ	death —***vi***. die
	絶滅	ゼツメツ	extermination; extinction —*v*. exterminate; eradicate; become extinct

訓	絶える	たえる	*vi*. cease; die out
	絶つ	たつ	*vt*. cut off
	絶やす	たやす	*vt*. exterminate

1535

統 ⑫

音	統	トウ	control
熟	統一	トウイツ	unity; unification; uniformity; consolidation —*v*. unify; standardize; coordinate
	統括	トウカツ	generalization —*v*. generalize
	統御	トウギョ	control; rule; management —*v*. rule; govern; control; manage
	統計	トウケイ	statistics; figures; numerical statement —*v*. show statistically/numerically
	統合	トウゴウ	integration; unification; combination; consolidation —*v*. integrate; unify; combine; consolidate
	統制	トウセイ	control; regulation —*v*. control; regulate; govern
	統率	トウソツ	command; generalship; leadership —*v*. command; take the lead; lead; direct
	統率力	トウソツリョク	leadership
	統治	トウチ	rule; reign; government; administration —*v*. rule; govern; administer
訓	統べる	すべる	*vt*. generalize

1536

絡 ⑫

音	絡	ラク	get entangled
訓	絡む	からむ	*vi*. twine around; complicate matters on purpose
	絡める	からめる	*vt*. entwine; twine around
	絡ます	からます	*vt*. entwine; twine around
	絡まる	からまる	*vi*. twine around
	絡み付く	からみつく	*vi*. coil around; cling to

1537

継 ⑬

音	継	ケイ	inherit; heir; succeed; continue

熟	継承	ケイショウ	succession —*v*. succeed to; inherit
	継続	ケイゾク	continuation —*v*. continue; go on; keep on; renew
	継父	ケイフ（ままちち）	stepfather
	継母	ケイボ（ままはは）	stepmother
訓	継ぐ	つぐ	***vt***. follow; continue; succeed
	継ぎ	つぎ	patch

1538

絹 ⑬

音	絹	ケン	silk
訓	絹	きぬ	silk
	絹糸	きぬいと	silk thread

1539

続 ⑬

音	続	ゾク	continue
熟	続出	ゾクシュツ	successive appearances —*v*. occur in succession; appear one after another
	続々	ゾクゾク	successively; one after another
	続発	ゾクハツ	successive occurences —*v*. occur in succession/one after another
	続編	ゾクヘン	sequel
	続行	ゾッコウ	continuation —*v*. continue
訓	続く	つづく	***vi***. continue
	続ける	つづける	***vt***. continue

1540

維 ⑭

音	維	イ	cord; maintenance; hold
熟	維持	イジ	maintenance; upkeep; preservation; support; conservation —*v*. maintain; keep; preserve; support; sustain
	維新	イシン	***hist***. Meiji Imperial Restoration (1867); revolution

1541

綱 ⑭

音	綱	コウ	hawser; rope; outline; summary
熟	綱目	コウモク	main points; gist; outline
	綱要	コウヨウ	elements; essentials; outline; summary
	綱領	コウリョウ	general plan/principles; outline; epitome
訓	綱	つな	rope; hawser; cord; string

1542

緒 ⑭

音	緒	ショ	beginning
		(チョ)	beginning
熟	緒戦	ショセン	first fighting; beginning of war
訓	緒	お	cord; string; rope

1543

総 ⑭

音	総	ソウ	general; overall
熟	総意	ソウイ	consensus
	総員	ソウイン	all hands; in full force
	総会	ソウカイ	general meeting; plenary session
	総画	ソウカク	the total stroke-count (of a Chinese character)
	総括	ソウカツ	summarization —*v*. summarize; generalize
	総監	ソウカン	superintendent-general
	総計	ソウケイ	total
	総合	ソウゴウ	synthesis; comprehensive —*v*. synthesize; integrate; put together
	総攻撃	ソウコウゲキ	general/all-out offensive —*v*. launch an all-out offensive; attack the enemy in full force
	総裁	ソウサイ	president; governor
	総菜	ソウザイ	everyday food; side dish
	総辞職	ソウジショク	mass resignation
	総称	ソウショウ	general/generic term —*v*. give a general name; name generically
	総数	ソウスウ	total number
	総勢	ソウゼイ	the whole army/group

	総選挙	ソウセンキョ	general election
	総体	ソウタイ	on the whole
	総代	ソウダイ	representative; delegate
	総出	ソウで	in full force; all together
	総動員	ソウドウイン	general mobilization
	総本山	ソウホンザン	head temple
	総本店	ソウホンテン	head office
	総務	ソウム	manager; general affairs
	総理	ソウリ	prime minister
	総量	ソウリョウ	gross weight
	総領	ソウリョウ	heir; eldest child
	総領事	ソウリョウジ	consul general
	総力	ソウリョク	the whole strength; all one's might
	総和	ソウワ	(sum) total
¥	総会	ソウカイ	general meeting
	総額	ソウガク	sum total; total/gross amount
	総決算	ソウケッサン	complete financial statement
	総合課税	ソウゴウカゼイ	taxation of an aggregate income
	総合銀行	ソウゴウギンコウ	universal bank
	総合口座	ソウゴウコウザ	general account
	総資産	ソウシサン	total assets
	総資本	ソウシホン	total liabilities and net worth; gross capital
	総理大臣	ソウリダイジン	prime minister

1544

綿 ⑭

音	綿	メン	cotton
熟	綿織物	メンおりもの	cotton fabrics
	綿花	メンカ	raw cotton
	綿糸	メンシ	cotton yarn/thread
	綿製品	メンセイヒン	cotton goods
	綿布	メンプ	cotton (cloth)
	綿密	メンミツ	minute; meticulous; detailed
	綿々	メンメン	continuous; endless; unabating
	綿羊	メンヨウ	sheep
訓	綿	わた	cotton

1545

網 ⑭

く 幺 糸 糸 糸 糹 糹 糹 網 網 網 網

音	網	モウ	net
熟	網膜	モウマク	***med***. retina
	網羅	モウラ	inclusion —***v***. include; comprise; be comprehensive
訓	網	あみ	net
	網戸	あみど	wire door
	網元	あみもと	head of a fishing crew

1546

緑 ⑭

く 幺 糸 糸 糸 糸 糸 緑 緑 緑 緑 緑

音	緑	リョク	green
		(ロク)	green
熟	緑陰	リョクイン	shade of trees
	緑化	リョクカ	tree planting —***v***. plant trees
	緑樹	リョクジュ	greenery; lush, green tree
	緑地	リョクチ	green track of land
	緑地帯	リョクチタイ	green belt
	緑茶	リョクチャ	green tea
	緑青	ロクショウ	verdigris; green/copper rust
訓	緑	みどり	green

1547

練 ⑭

く 幺 糸 糸 糸 糸 糸 糸 糸 練 練 練

音	練	レン	train
熟	練習	レンシュウ	practice; exercise —***v***. practice; exercise
	練達	レンタツ	skill; dexterity
	練乳	レンニュウ	condensed milk
	練磨	レンマ	training; practice —***v***. train; practice; drill
訓	練る	ねる	***v***. knead; train; polish
	練れる	ねれる	***vi***. be mellowed; be matured (of a personality, character)
	練り物	ねりもの	paste; procession; parade float

1548

縁 ⑮

音	縁	エン	edge; relation; veranda
熟	縁側	エンがわ	veranda; porch; balcony
	縁起	エンギ	story; origin (of a temple or shrine); omen
	縁組	エンぐみ	marriage; adoption
	縁故	エンコ	relation; connection; relative
	縁者	エンジャ	blood relative
	縁台	エンダイ	bench
	縁談	エンダン	marriage talk/proposal
	縁日	エンニチ	fête day of a local deity
訓	縁	ふち	edge; brim
¥	縁故募集	エンコボシュウ	private subscription

1549

緩 ⑮

音	緩	カン	loose
熟	緩急	カンキュウ	fast and slow; urgency; emergency
	緩行	カンコウ	going/moving slowly —***vi***. go/move slowly
	緩衝	カンショウ	buffer
	緩慢	カンマン	slackness; slowness; dullness; inactivity
	緩和	カンワ	relief; easing; relaxation —***v***. relieve; ease; relax
訓	緩い	ゆるい	loose; generous; lenient
	緩む	ゆるむ	***vi***. become slack; be careless
	緩める	ゆるめる	***vt***. loosen; relax
	緩やか	ゆるやか	gentle; easy; slack

1550

縄 ⑮

音	縄	ジョウ	rope
熟	縄文時代	ジョウモンジダイ	***hist***. Jōmon period (10,000BC-300BC)
訓	縄	なわ	rope; cord
	縄飛び	なわとび	skipping
	縄張り	なわばり	roped-off; territory; sphere of influence

	縄目	なわめ	knot

1551
線 ⑮

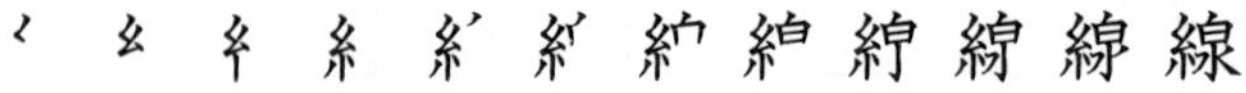

音	線	セン	line
熟	線画	センガ	line drawing
	線香	センコウ	joss/incense stick
	線路	センロ	railway track

1552
締 ⑮

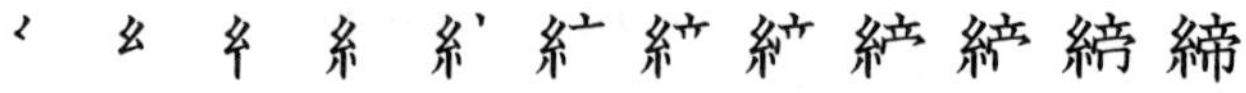

音	締	テイ	settle
熟	締結	テイケツ	conclusion —*v*. conclude; contract
訓	締まる	しまる	***vi***. be shut/closed/locked/tightened; become sober; be frugal
	締まり	しまり	tightness; firmness; steadiness
	締まり屋	しまりや	thrifty person
	締める	しめる	***vt***. tie up; tighten; strangle; shut; close; add; sum up; economize
	締め	しめ	bundle
	締切り	しめきり	deadline; closing down

1553
編 ⑮

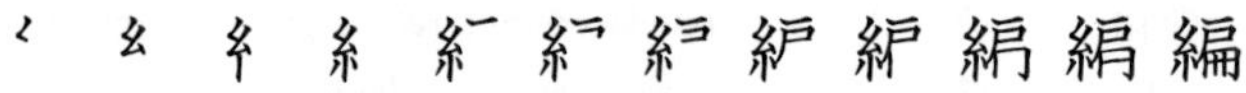

音	編	ヘン	knit; compile; edit
熟	編曲	ヘンキョク	(musical) arrangement —*v*. arrange (a piece of music)
	編纂	ヘンサン	compilation; editing —*v*. compile; edit
	編者	ヘンシャ (ヘンジャ)	editor; compiler
	編修	ヘンシュウ	compilation/editing (of books) —*v*. compile; edit
	編集	ヘンシュウ	compilation; editing —*v*. compile; edit
	編集者	ヘンシュウシャ	editor
	編集長	ヘンシュウチョウ	editor-in-chief

	編成	ヘンセイ	organization; putting into a systematic/logical form —*v*. organize
	編隊	ヘンタイ	formation flying
	編入	ヘンニュウ	entry; incorporation; transfer —*v*. enter; incorporate; transfer (to a new school, university department)
訓	編む	あむ	***vt***. knit; braid; compile; edit
	編み上げ	あみあげ	laceup (shoes, boots, etc.)
	編み出す	あみだす	***vt***. work out; think up; devise
	編み戸	あみど	(bamboo/wood) braided door
	編み針	あみばり	knitting needle; crochet hook
	編み棒	あみボウ	knitting needle/pin
	編み物	あみもの	knitting

1554
緯 ⑯

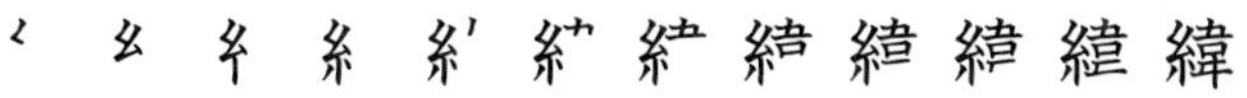

音	緯	イ	woof; latitude
熟	緯線	イセン	parallel of latitude
	緯度	イド	degree of latitude

1555
縛 ⑯

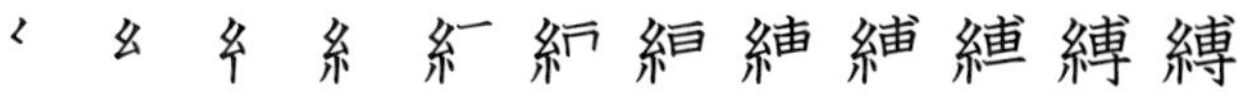

音	縛	バク	tie
訓	縛る	しばる	***vt***. bind; tie; fasten; restrict; restrain; chain

1556
縦 ⑯

音	縦	ジュウ	length
熟	縦横無尽	ジュウオウムジン	free; without opposition; in all directions
	縦線	ジュウセン	vertical line
	縦断	ジュウダン	cutting vertically; running through
	縦列	ジュウレツ	column; file
訓	縦	たて	length; height; vertical; perpendicular
	縦書き	たてがき	vertical writing
	縦横	たてよこ	length and breadth; lengthwise and crosswise

1557

縫 ⑯

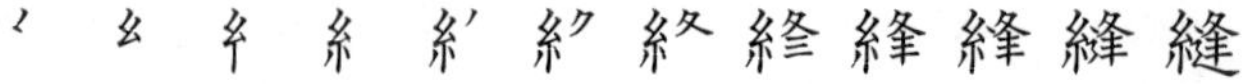

音	縫	ホウ	sew
熟	縫製	ホウセイ	sewing
	縫製品	ホウセイヒン	machine-sewn/hand-sewn goods
訓	縫う	ぬう	***vt***. sew
	縫い上げる	ぬいあげる	***vt***. tuck a child's kimono (so that it can be let out later)
	縫糸	ぬいいと	sewing thread
	縫い代	ぬいしろ	margin left for the seam; seam allowance
	縫い取り	ぬいとり	embroidery
	縫い箔	ぬいハク	embroidery; silver and gold embroidery
	縫針	ぬいばり	sewing needle
	縫い目	ぬいめ	seam; stitch
	縫物	ぬいもの	sewing; needlework

1558

縮 ⑰

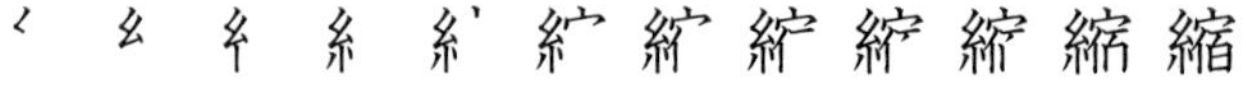

音	縮	シュク	shrink; shorten; contract; reduce
熟	縮減	シュクゲン	reduction; cut back —***v***. reduce; cut back
	縮写	シュクシャ	reduced/miniature copy —***v***. make a reduced copy
	縮尺	シュクシャク	reduced scale —***v***. reduce the scale of; make smaller
	縮小	シュクショウ	reduction; curtailment —***v***. reduce; curtail; cut back
	縮図	シュクズ	reduced drawing; miniature copy
訓	縮む	ちぢむ	***vi***. shrink; contract; crinkle
	縮まる	ちぢまる	***vi***. shrink; contract
	縮み	ちぢみ	shrinkage
	縮める	ちぢめる	***vt***. shorten; cut down; reduce; condense
	縮れる	ちぢれる	***vi***. crinkle; be frizzled/curly

1559

績 ⑰

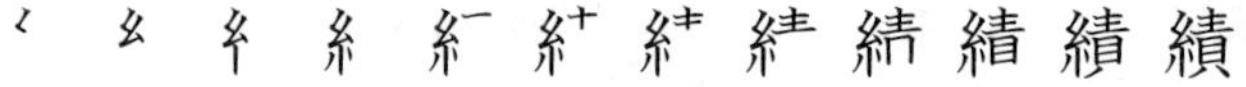

音	績	セキ	spin; achievements

1560

纖 ⑰

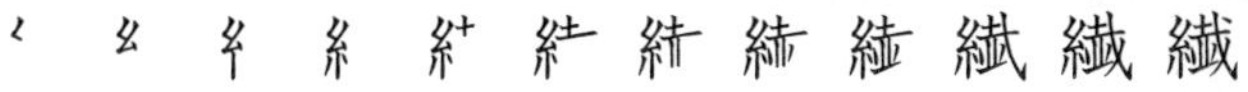

音	纖	セン	fine; fiber
熟	纖維	センイ	fiber
	纖細	センサイ	delicacy

1561

織 ⑱

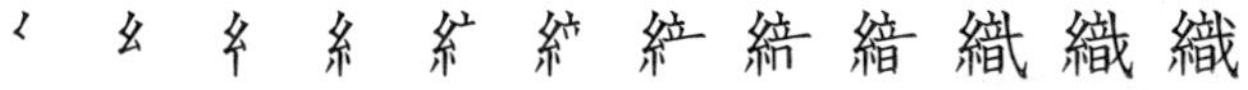

音	織	シキ	organize
		ショク	weave; textiles
熟	織機	ショッキ	weaving machine; loom
訓	織る	おる	*vt*. weave; work at the loom
	織り地	おりジ	texture of woven fabric
	織物	おりもの	textiles; fabrics; woven cloth
	織物業	おりものギョウ	textile trade/business

1562

繕 ⑱

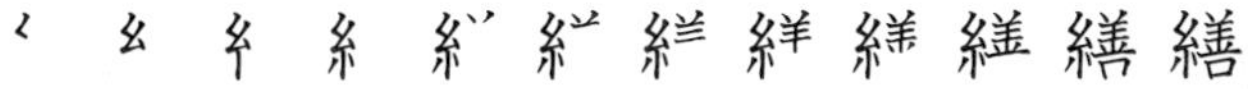

音	繕	ゼン	repair
訓	繕う	つくろう	*vt*. repair; trim

1563

繰 ⑲

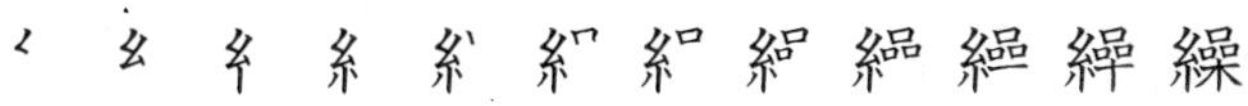

音	繰	(ソウ)	reel; gin; count
訓	繰る	くる	*vt*. reel; wind
	繰り上げる	くりあげる	*vt*. advance; move/carry up
	繰り返す	くりかえす	*vt*. repeat; reiterate; echo
	繰り下げる	くりさげる	*vt*. carry/move/take down; put off; postpone
¥	繰り上げ償還	くりあげショウカン	pre-maturity redemption
	繰延資金	ソウエンシキン	deferred assets

6 缶 ほどき jar

1564
缶 ⑥ 丿 𠂉 𠂉 午 缶 缶

音	缶	**カン**	can; boiler
熟	缶詰	**カンづめ**	canned foodstuffs

6 羊 ひつじ sheep

1565
羊 ⑥ 丶 丷 䒑 兰 兰 羊

音	羊	**ヨウ**	sheep
熟	羊皮	**ヨウヒ**	sheepskin
	羊皮紙	**ヨウヒシ**	parchment
	羊毛	**ヨウモウ**	wool
訓	羊	**ひつじ**	sheep
	羊飼い	**ひつじかい**	shepherd

1566
美 ⑨ 丶 丷 䒑 ⺶ ⺶ 𦍌 羊 美 美

音	美	**ビ**	beauty
熟	美化	**ビカ**	beautification; glorification; idealization —*v.* beautify (a city); glorify; idealize
	美学	**ビガク**	aesthetics
	美観	**ビカン**	fine view; beautiful scenery
	美技	**ビギ**	beautiful/brilliant performance; (sports) good play
	美形	**ビケイ**	beautiful; handsome
	美酒	**ビシュ**	delicious saké
	美術	**ビジュツ**	fine arts; art
	美術館	**ビジュツカン**	art gallery
	美女	**ビジョ**	beautiful/lovely woman; pretty girl
	美少年	**ビショウネン**	handsome youth; pretty boy

	美食	ビショク	delicious food —***vi***. live on/eat fancy food
	美食家	ビショクカ	gourmet; epicure
	美人	ビジン	beautiful woman
	美声	ビセイ	beautiful voice
	美談	ビダン	fine anecdote/story
	美的	ビテキ	aesthetic
	美点	ビテン	merit; virtue; good point
	美徳	ビトク	virtue; noble attribute
	美男	ビナン	handsome man
	美男子	ビナンシ	handsome man
	美風	ビフウ	fine/good custom
	美文	ビブン	flowery/elegant prose
	美文調	ビブンチョウ	ornate style
	美貌	ビボウ	beauty; beautiful face
	美味	ビミ	delicious; good; tasting
	美名	ビメイ	good/reputable name
	美容	ビヨウ	beautiful face; beautification of face or form
	美容院	ビヨウイン	beauty parlor; hairdresser
	美容外科	ビヨウゲカ	***med***. cosmetic surgery
	美容師	ビヨウシ	beautician; hairdresser
	美容整形	ビヨウセイケイ	cosmetic surgery
訓	美しい	うつくしい	beautiful
	※美味しい	おいしい	good-tasting; delicious

1567

⑫

音	着	チャク (ジャク)	put on; wear; clothe; arrive; reach
熟	着衣	チャクイ	one's clothes
	着眼	チャクガン	attention; notice; perception —***vi***. pay attention; notice; perceive
	着眼点	チャクガンテン	point of view
	着実	チャクジツ	steadiness; honesty
	着手	チャクシュ	start; commencement; outset —***vi***. start; commence; begin
	着順	チャクジュン	order of arrival
	着色	チャクショク	coloration; coloring —***vi***. color; paint
	着水	チャクスイ	alighting on the water; splashdown —***vi***. alight on the water; splashdown
	着席	チャクセキ	taking a seat; sitting down —***vi***. take a seat; sit down

	着想	チャクソウ	idea; conception
	着地	チャクチ	landing —*vi*. land
	着々	チャクチャク	steadily; step by step
	着任	チャクニン	arrival at one's post —*vi*. arrive at one's post
	着服	チャクフク	getting dressed; embezzlement; misappropriation —*v*. get dressed; misappropriate; embezzle
	着目	チャクモク	attention; notice —*vi*. pay attention to; take notice of
	着用	チャクヨウ	wearing (clothes) —*v*. wear (clothes)
	着陸	チャクリク	landing; touchdown —*vi*. land; touchdown
	着工	チャッコウ	commencement of construction work —*vi*. start construction work
訓	着る	きる	*vt*. put on; wear
	着せる	きせる	*vt*. dress someone; clothe; put on; plate; coat; cover
	着替える	きがえる	*vi*. change clothes
	着付け	きつけ	dressing; fitting
	着物	きもの	kimono
	着く	つく	*vi*. arrive at; reach; come to hand
	着ける	つける	*vt*. put on; wear

1568

⑬

音	義	ギ	justice; meaning
熟	義援金	ギエンキン	contribution; subscription; donation
	義眼	ギガン	artificial/glass eye
	義兄	ギケイ	(older) brother-in-law
	義姉	ギシ	(older) sister-in-law
	義歯	ギシ	false tooth/teeth
	義手	ギシュ	artificial arm
	義足	ギソク	artificial leg
	義弟	ギテイ	(younger) brother-in-law
	義父	ギフ	stepfather; father-in-law
	義母	ギボ	stepmother; mother-in-law
	義妹	ギマイ	(younger) sister-in-law
	義務	ギム	duty; obligation
	義務教育	ギムキョウイク	compulsory education
	義理	ギリ	obligation; justice; duty

1569

群 ⑬

音	群	グン	gather; collect; many
熟	群衆	グンシュウ	large group of people
	群集	グンシュウ	crowd; multitude; throng
	群集心理	グンシュウシンリ	group psychology
	群生	グンセイ	gregarious —*vi*. be gregarious
	群島	グントウ	group of islands
	群落	グンラク	group of villages; plant community
訓	群	(むら)	group; crowd; cluster; clump
	群がる	むらがる	*vi*. crowd (together); herd; flock; pack
	群れ	むれ	group; troop; crowd; herd; flock; pack
	群れる	むれる	*vi*. crowd (together); throng; flock together

6 羽 はね feather

1570

羽 ⑥

音	羽	ウ	feather; wing
熟	羽化	ウカ	emergence —*vi*. emerge; grow wings
	羽毛	ウモウ	feather; plume; feathering; plummage
訓	羽	はね	feather; wing
	羽	は	feather; wing; (counter for birds and rabbits)
	羽織	はおり	*haori* (Japanese overgarment)
	羽衣	はごろも	robe of feathers; winged jacket worn by angels
	羽振り	はぶり	position/status in life

1571

翁 ⑩

音	翁	オウ	old man
訓	※翁	おきな	old man

1572

習 ⑪

音	習	シュウ	study; custom
熟	習慣	シュウカン	custom; habit; practice
	習作	シュウサク	study (in art, music, etc.)
	習字	シュウジ	penmanship; calligraphy
	習熟	シュウジュク	mastering (a skill, etc.) —***vi***. master; become proficient
	習性	シュウセイ	habit; behavior; nature
	習俗	シュウゾク	manners and customs; usage; folkways; conventions
	習得	シュウトク	learning; acquiring skills —***v***. learn; acquire a skill; master
	習癖	シュウヘキ	habit
訓	習う	ならう	***vt***. learn; train; take lessons
	習わし	ならわし	practice; custom; way; tradition

1573

翌 ⑪

音	翌	ヨク	next/following
熟	翌月	ヨクゲツ	following month
	翌日	ヨクジツ	next/following day
	翌朝	ヨクチョウ	next morning
	翌年	ヨクネン	next/following year

1574

翼 ⑰

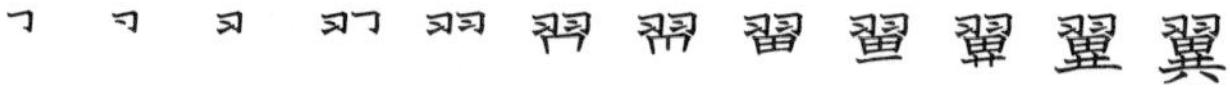

音	翼	ヨク	wing; help
熟	翼状	ヨクジョウ	wing-shaped
訓	翼	つばさ	wing (of a bird or plane)

1575

翻 ⑱

音	翻	ホン	change; turn over; flutter/swirl (in a breeze)

熟	翻案	ホンアン	adaptation —*v*. adapt (a novel, etc.)
	翻意	ホンイ	change of mind —*vi*. change one's mind
	翻刻	ホンコク	reprint —*v*. reprint
	翻然	ホンゼン	all of a sudden
	翻訳	ホンヤク	translation —*v*. translate
	翻弄	ホンロウ	trifling with —*v*. trifle/play with
訓	翻す	ひるがえす	*vt*. turn over; change suddenly (one's opinion, belief); flutter/swirl (in a breeze)
	翻る	ひるがえる	*vi*. turn over; change suddenly; flutter/swirl (in a breeze)
	※翻す	こぼす	overturn; spill

6 老 おいがしら／おいかんむり old man 耂 (p.684)

1576

老 ⑥ 一 十 土 耂 耂 老

音	老	ロウ	old age
熟	老眼	ロウガン	presbyopia
	老朽	ロウキュウ	age; decrepitude —*vi*. get old; become decrepit
	老後	ロウゴ	in one's old age
	老巧	ロウコウ	veteran; experienced
	老骨	ロウコツ	one's old bones; old person's body
	老死	ロウシ	death by old age —*vi*. die of old age
	老中	ロウジュウ	***hist***. member of the shogun's council of elders
	老熟	ロウジュク	experienced; mature —*vi*. be experienced/mature
	老女	ロウジョ	old woman
	老人	ロウジン	old man; the elderly
	老衰	ロウスイ	senility —*vi*. be senile
	老体	ロウタイ	old body; elderly person
	老大家	ロウタイカ	veteran; authority
	老若	ロウニャク	young and old; young or old
	老年	ロウネン	old age; elderly person
	老婆	ロウバ	old woman
	老婆心	ロウバシン	old-womanish solicitude
	老舗	ロウホ ※(しにせ)	long-established shop or store
	老齢	ロウレイ	old age
	老練	ロウレン	experienced; veteran
訓	老いる	おいる	*vi*. grow old

老い	おい	old age
老いらく	おいらく	old age
老ける	ふける	***vi***. grow old

4 耂 おいがしら／おいかんむり old man

1577

考 ⑥

一 十 土 耂 耂 考

音	考	**コウ**	consider; reflect; think; contemplate; test; examine
熟	考案	**コウアン**	conception; idea; plan; device; project —***v***. conceive; plan; design; devise; originate
	考古学	**コウコガク**	archaeology
	考査	**コウサ**	examination; test; consideration —***v***. test; examine; quiz; consider
	考察	**コウサツ**	contemplation; consideration; examination; study; inquiry —***v***. contemplate; consider; examine; study
	考証	**コウショウ**	historical research/investigation —***v***. carry out historical research
	考慮	**コウリョ**	consideration; deliberation; reflection; thinking —***v***. consider; think; ponder; deliberate; reflect
訓	考える	かんがえる	***vt***. think; consider; take a view; be of an opinion; regard
	考え	かんがえ	thinking; thought; ideas; conception; opinion
	考え方	かんがえかた	line of thought; point of view; solution
	考え事	かんがえごと	concern; worry

1578

者 ⑧

一 十 土 耂 耂 者 者 者

音	者	**シャ**	person
訓	者	もの	***hum***. person

6 而 しこうして rake

1579
耐 ⑨ 一 丆 丆 丙 丙 而 而 耐 耐

音	耐	タイ	endure; bear; stand; withstand; hold out
熟	耐火	タイカ	fireproof
	耐寒	タイカン	coldproof; resistance against the cold
	耐久	タイキュウ	endurance; persistance; permanence; durability
	耐震	タイシン	earthquakeproof
	耐水	タイスイ	waterproof
	耐熱	タイネツ	heat-resistant
	耐乏	タイボウ	withstanding poverty —***vi***. withstand poverty
訓	耐える	たえる	***vi***. endure; bear; support; withstand; be fit for

6 耒 すきへん plow

1580
耕 ⑩ 一 二 三 丰 耒 耒 耒 耒 耕 耕

音	耕	コウ	till; plow; cultivate
熟	耕作	コウサク	cultivation; farming; tillage —***v***. cultivate; farm; till
	耕地	コウチ	arable/cultivated/plowed land
訓	耕す	たがやす	***vt***. till; plow; cultivate

1581
耗 ⑩ 一 二 三 丰 耒 耒 耒 耒 耗 耗

音	耗	モウ (コウ)	consume; decrease

6 耳 みみ／みみへん ear

1582

耳 ⑥ 一 丅 下 FF 三 耳

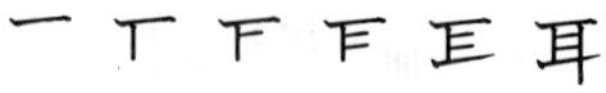

音	耳	ジ	ear
熟	耳鼻咽喉科	ジビインコウカ	***med.*** otorhinolaryngology; ear, nose, and throat department
	耳目	ジモク	seeing and hearing; eyes and ears
訓	耳	みみ	ear; hearing; (bread) crust
	耳垢	みみあか	ear wax
	耳打ち	みみうち	whispering —***vi.*** whisper
	耳掻き	みみかき	ear pick
	耳学問	みみガクモン	hearsay
	耳寄りな話	みみよりなはなし	welcome news
	耳輪	みみわ	earring

1583

聖 ⑬

音	聖	セイ	saint; holy; sacred; sage
熟	聖域	セイイキ	sacred precincts
	聖火	セイカ	sacred flame; Olympic Flame
	聖者	セイジャ	saint; holy man
	聖書	セイショ	Bible
	聖人	セイジン	sage; saint; holy man
	聖地	セイチ	sacred land; Holy Land
	聖典	セイテン	holy book; scriptures
	聖母	セイボ	Holy Mother
	聖夜	セイヤ	Christmas Eve

1584

聞 ⑭

音	聞	ブン モン	hear; listen to; heed; ask

訓 聞く きく *vt*. hear; listen to; heed; ask
聞こえる きこえる *vi*. hear; be heard/audible; be able to hear
聞き入る ききいる *vi*. listen attentively
聞き入れる ききいれる *vt*. accede to; comply with
聞き納め ききおさめ last time to hear (somebody say something)
聞き落とす ききおとす *vt*. not hear; miss
聞き覚え ききおぼえ learning by ear; heard before
聞き返す ききかえす *vt*. ask back/again
聞き書き ききがき taking notes (from a talk/lecture)
聞き苦しい ききぐるしい offensive to the ear
聞き込む ききこむ *vt*. hear about; listen; ask about; investigate (by asking)
聞き上手 ききジョウズ good listener
聞き出す ききだす *vt*. ask about; begin to listen/ask
聞き付ける ききつける *vt*. hear; learn of; be used to hearing
聞き伝え ききづたえ hearsay
聞き手 ききて listener
聞き取る ききとる *vt*. hear and understand; catch; follow
聞き流す ききながす *vt*. pay no attention to
聞き耳 ききみみ attentive ears; listening carefully
聞き漏らす ききもらす *vt*. not hear/catch
聞き役 ききヤク one who hears people's complaints
聞き分ける ききわける *vt*. distinguish between (sounds, stories, etc.); listen to reason; listen to and accept

1585
聴 ⑰

一 丅 下 耳 耳 耳 聍 聍 聴 聴 聴 聴

音 聴 チョウ listen

熟 聴覚 チョウカク *med*. auditory sense; hearing
聴講 チョウコウ attendance at a lecture —*v*. attend/listen to a lecture
聴取 チョウシュ listening; hearing; audition —*v*. listen; hear; give audience to
聴衆 チョウシュウ audience
聴診 チョウシン *med*. ausculation; stethoscopy —*vi*. examine (a patient) with a stethoscope
聴診器 チョウシンキ *med*. stethoscope
聴力 チョウリョク *med*. hearing; hearing ability

訓 聴く きく *vt*. listen; hear

1586

職 ⑱ 一 丅 F 耳 耳' 耶 聍 聕 聕 職 職 職

音	職	ショク	job; work; occupation
熟	職域	ショクイキ	one's job/occupation/area of responsibility
	職員	ショクイン	staff; personnel; member of staff
	職業	ショクギョウ	occupation; trade; profession
	職責	ショクセキ	one's work responsibility; duties
	職人	ショクニン	craftsman; workman; artisan
	職能	ショクノウ	professional ability; occupational function
	職場	ショクば	workshop; workplace; the office
	職務	ショクム	work duties
	職名	ショクメイ	official title
	職権	ショッケン	official authority
	職工	ショッコウ	worker; factory hand
¥	職種	ショクシュ	type of occupation/job; job classification
	職制	ショクセイ	office organization; managerial post; executive
	職場研修	ショクば ケンシュウ	on-the-job training
	職歴	ショクレキ	work record/experience; career record; job history

6 肉 see ⇨p. 457

6 自 みずから dotted eye

1587

自 ⑥ ′ 丨′ 冂 白 白 自

音	自	ジ	oneself
		シ	natural; nature
熟	自愛	ジアイ	self-love; self-indulgence —***vi***. take care of oneself
	自衛	ジエイ	self-defense; self-protection —***vi***. defend oneself
	自衛隊	ジエイタイ	the Self-Defense Force (SDF)
	自我	ジガ	the self/ego

自戒	ジカイ	self-discipline —***v***. exercize self-discipline
自害	ジガイ	suicide —***vi***. commit suicide
自覚	ジカク	consciousness; self-awareness —***v***. be aware/conscious
自画自賛	ジガジサン	self-praise —***vi***. sing one's own praises; praise oneself
自画像	ジガゾウ	self-portrait
自家製	ジカセイ	homemade
自家用	ジカヨウ	for private use
自活	ジカツ	self-support —***vi***. support oneself
自虐	ジギャク	masochism; self-torture
自給	ジキュウ	self-support; self-sustenance —***v***. provide for oneself
自給自足	ジキュウジソク	self-sufficiency —***vi***. be self-sufficient
自供	ジキョウ	confession —***v***. confession
自決	ジケツ	self-determination; suicide —***vi***. determine/decide for oneself; commit suicide; kill oneself
自己	ジコ	self; oneself
自己暗示	ジコアンジ	autosuggestion
自己紹介	ジコショウカイ	self-introduction —***vi***. introduce oneself
自己中心	ジコチュウシン	egocentricity
自己流	ジコリュウ	one's own way of doing something
自業自得	ジゴウジトク	natural consequence of one's evil deed; asking for it; deserving what one gets
自国	ジコク	one's own country/homeland
自国語	ジコクゴ	native language; mother tongue
自在	ジザイ	at will; freely
自作	ジサク	one's own work; made by oneself —***v***. make something by oneself
自作農	ジサクノウ	landed farmer
自殺	ジサツ	suicide —***vi***. commit suicide; kill oneself
自賛	ジサン	self-praise; narcissism —***vi***. praise oneself
自首	ジシュ	surrendering —***vi***. give oneself up; surrender
自習	ジシュウ	self-study; learning by oneself —***vi***. teach oneself; study by oneself
自粛	ジシュク	self-control; self-restraint —***vi***. exercise self-control; restrain oneself
自主的	ジシュテキ	independent; autonomous
自称	ジショウ	self-styled; self-professed —***vi***. call oneself; praise oneself
自叙伝	ジジョデン	autobiography
自身	ジシン	oneself; personally; in person
自信	ジシン	self-confidence; confidence
自炊	ジスイ	cooking one's own meals —***vi***. cook one's own meals

自制	ジセイ	self-control —*v*. control one's emotions
自省	ジセイ	reflection; self-examination —***vi***. examine oneself
自責	ジセキ	self-reproach —***vi***. reproach oneself; have a guilty conscious
自説	ジセツ	one's own view/opinion
自然	シゼン	nature; natural; spontaneous; automatic
自然界	シゼンカイ	nature; the natural world
自然科学	シゼンカガク	natural science
自然現象	シゼンゲンショウ	natural phenomenon
自然主義	シゼンシュギ	naturalism
自然林	シゼンリン	natural/virgin forest
自尊心	ジソンシン	pride; self-respect
自他	ジタ	oneself and others; other people and oneself
自体	ジタイ	itself; the thing itself; one's own body
自宅	ジタク	one's house/home
自治	ジチ	self-government; autonomy
自治会	ジチカイ	student/town council
自治体	ジチタイ	self-governing body
自治領	ジチリョウ	dominion
自重	ジチョウ	self-respect; self-love —***vi***. be prudent
自邸	ジテイ	one's private residence/home
自転	ジテン	rotation —***vi***. rotate; revolve
自転車	ジテンシャ	bicycle
自伝	ジデン	autobiography
自動	ジドウ	automatic; mechanical
自動車	ジドウシャ	car; automobile; motorcar
自動的	ジドウテキ	automatically; mechanically
自認	ジニン	acknowledgement —***v***. acknowledge
自白	ジハク	confession —***v***. confess; make a confession
自発的	ジハツテキ	voluntarily; of one's own volition
自費	ジヒ	one's own expense
自筆	ジヒツ	one's own handwriting
自負	ジフ	self-confidence —***vi***. be self-confident
自分	ジブン	oneself; myself; me; I
自分自身	ジブンジシン	oneself; I; myself
自弁	ジベン	at one's own expenses —***v***. pay one's own way
自暴自棄	ジボウジキ	despair; desperation
自慢	ジマン	boasting; bragging; pride —***v***. be proud of; brag; boast
自明	ジメイ	self-evidence; truism
自滅	ジメツ	self-destruction —***vi***. ruin oneself; destroy oneself

	自問自答	ジモンジトウ	questioning oneself; monolog —*vi*. talk to oneself
	自由	ジユウ	freedom; liberty
	自力	ジリキ	self-effort; one's own efforts
	自立	ジリツ	independence —*vi*. become independent; stand on one's feet
	自律	ジリツ	autonomy —*vi*. be autonomous
訓	自ら	みずから	oneself
¥	自己資本	ジコシホン	owned capital; net worth; equity capital
	自己資本比率	ジコシホンヒリツ	ratio of net worth to total liabilities; net worth ratio
	自主規制	ジシュキセイ	voluntary restriction
	自治省	ジチショウ	Ministry of Home Affairs
	自治大臣	ジチダイジン	minister of home affairs
	自民党（自由民主党）	ジミントウ（ジユウミンシュトウ）	Liberal Democratic Party (LDP)
	自由化	ジユウカ	liberalization —*v*. liberalize

1588

臭 ⑨

ノ 亻 白 白 自 自 自 臭 臭

音	臭	シュウ	smell
熟	臭覚	シュウカク	sense of smell
	臭気	シュウキ	bad/offensive smell; stench
訓	臭い	くさい	foul/bad smelling; stink; smell; be suspicious
	臭味	くさみ	bad smell; offensive odor; stench

6 至 いたる arriving

1589

至 ⑥

一 ㄗ 云 云 至 至

音	至	シ	arrive; reach; extend
熟	至急	シキュウ	emergency; urgent; prompt
	至近	シキン	point-blank; close range
	至芸	シゲイ	unrivaled performance
	至言	シゲン	wise saying

	至高	シコウ	supremacy; highest; tallest
	至極	シゴク	very; extremely
	至上	シジョウ	supreme; urgent
	至誠	シセイ	true sincerity; great devotion
	至難	シナン	most difficult; almost impossible
	至福	シフク	supreme bliss
	至便	シベン	most convenient
	至宝	シホウ	great treasure; valuable asset
訓	至る	いたる	***vi***. reach; arrive; come; extend; result in
	至る所	いたるところ	everywhere; all over; throughout

1590
致 ⑩

音	致	チ	do; bring about; cause
熟	致死	チシ	fatal; mortal; lethal; deadly —***v***. be fatal/mortal/lethal/deadly
	致死量	チシリョウ	lethal dose
	致命傷	チメイショウ	fatal wound; mortal injury
	致命的	チメイテキ	fatal; mortal; deadly; lethal
訓	致す	いたす	***vt. hon***. do; bring about; cause; incur; render; exert

6 舌 した tongue

1591

⑥

音	舌	ゼツ	tongue
熟	舌禍	ゼッカ	unfortunate slip of the tongue
	舌戦	ゼッセン	verbal contest; war of words; quarrel
	舌頭	ゼットウ	tip of the tongue
訓	舌	した	tongue; language
	舌打ち	したうち	clicking one's tongue —***vi***. click one's tongue
	舌先	したさき	tip of the tongue
	舌鼓	したつづみ	eating with gusto

6 舟 ふね／ふねへん ship; boat

1592
舟 ⑥

音	舟	シュウ	boat
熟	舟艇	シュウテイ	small boat
訓	舟	ふね	ship; boat
	舟	ふな	ship; boat
	舟歌	ふなうた	sailor's song; sea chantey
	舟乗り	ふなのり	seaman; sailor
	舟人	ふなびと	sailor; ferryman

1593
航 ⑩

音	航	コウ	cross; sail; navigate; fly; ship; airplane
熟	航海	コウカイ	voyage; navigation; sailing; crossing; passage —*vi*. sail; make a voyage/crossing; navigate; take a passage
	航空	コウクウ	aviation; flying; flight; air traffic
	航空機	コウクウキ	aircraft; airplane
	航空書簡	コウクウショカン	aerogram
	航空便	コウクウビン	airmail
	航空母艦	コウクウボカン	aircraft carrier
	航行	コウコウ	navigation; sailing; cruise —*vi*. navigate; sail; cruise
	航程	コウテイ	distance covered; passage; flight; lap
	航路	コウロ	course; sea route; line; service; run

1594
般 ⑩

音	般	ハン	kind
熟	般若	ハンニャ	wisdom; female demon; hag

1595

船 ⑪

音	船	セン	vessel; ship
熟	船医	センイ	ship doctor
	船員	センイン	crewman; seaman
	船客	センキャク	ship's passenger
	船号	センゴウ	ship's name
	船室	センシツ	cabin
	船主	センシュ	shipowner
	船首	センシュ	bow; prow
	船体	センタイ	hull; ship
	船団	センダン	fleet; convoy
	船長	センチョウ	captain
	船底	センテイ	bottom of a ship
	船頭	センドウ	boatman
	船舶	センパク	ship; vessel; shipping
	船尾	センビ	stern
	船腹	センプク	tonnage; counter for ships; hold; bottoms
訓	船	ふね	ship; boat
	船	ふな	ship; boat
	船歌	ふなうた	chantey; song
	船賃	ふなチン	ship fare
	船出	ふなで	sailing —***vi***. set sail; put out to sea
	船乗り	ふなのり	sailor
	船人	ふなびと	seaman
	船酔い	ふなよい	seasickness —***vi***. be seasick

1596

舶 ⑪

音	舶	ハク	large ship
熟	舶来	ハクライ	foreign/imported goods

1597

艇 ⑬

音	艇	テイ	boat

熟 艇身　テイシン　length of a boat

1598

艦 ㉑

音	艦	カン	warship
熟	艦隊	カンタイ	fleet of warships

6 色 いろ color

1599

⑥

音	色	シキ	color; looks; sexual love
		ショク	color; aspect
熟	色感	シキカン	sense of color
	色彩	シキサイ	color; coloring; hue; tint
	色紙	シキシ	square piece of fancy paper
	色弱	シキジャク	partial color blindness
	色情	シキジョウ	sexual desire
	色素	シキソ	pigment
	色調	シキチョウ	tone of color; hue
	色盲	シキモウ	color blindness
	色欲	シキヨク	lust; sexual desire
訓	色	いろ	color; complexion; expression; love affair
	色合い	いろあい	shade; hue
	色々	いろいろ	various; many kinds
	色男	いろおとこ	handsome man; ladykiller
	色紙	いろがみ	colored paper
	色気	いろケ	sex appeal; sexual passion; inclination; ambitions
	色づく	いろづく	***vi***. color; turn (red, yellow, etc.); become sexy/attractive
	色っぽい	いろっぽい	sexy; attractive
	色眼鏡	いろめがね	colored/rose-tinted spectacles
	色物	いろもの	colored clothes/fabrics; variety entertainment; variety show

6 虍 とらかんむり／とらがしら tiger

1600

虐 ⑨

音	虐	ギャク	cruel; savage; tyrannical; oppressive
熟	虐殺	ギャクサツ	slaughter; carnage; massacre; butchery —*v*. slaughter; massacre; butcher
	虐待	ギャクタイ	cruel/ill treatment; abuse —*v*. treat cruelly; abuse
訓	虐げる	しいたげる	*vt*. oppress; persecute; tyrannize over

1601

 ⑪

音	虚	キョ	emptiness; nothingness; hollow; lie; falsehood; weak; vain
		(コ)	
熟	虚栄	キョエイ	vanity; vainglory
	虚偽	キョギ	falsehood; lie; fallacy
	虚弱	キョジャク	weekness; feebleness; infirmity
	虚勢	キョセイ	bluff
	虚脱感	キョダツカン	lethargy; absentmindedness
	虚無主義	キョムシュギ	Nihilism
	虚礼	キョレイ	empty formalities; meaningless politeness
	虚空	コクウ	air; space; sky

1602

 ⑬

音	虞	グ	fear; anxiety
訓	虞	おそれ	fear; anxiety

1603

 ⑬

音	虜	リョ	captive; prisoner of war; barbarian

訓	※虜	とりこ	capture; slave; captive

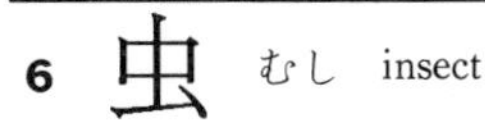

6 虫 むし insect

1604

⑥

音	虫	チュウ	insect
熟	虫害	チュウガイ	damage done by insects; blight
訓	虫	むし	insect; bug; worm; feeling
	虫食い	むしくい	vermiculation; damage by worms
	虫歯	むしば	decayed tooth
	虫眼鏡	むしめがね	magnifying glass

1605

⑩

訓	蚊	か	mosquito
	蚊取線香	かとりセンコウ	mosquito-repellent incense
	蚊屋（蚊帳）	かや	mosquito net

1606

⑩

音	蚕	サン	silkworm
熟	蚕糸	サンシ	silkwork
	蚕食	サンショク	encroachment; aggression —*v.* encroach on; make inroads; eat into
訓	蚕	かいこ	silkworm

1607

蛍 ⑪

音	蛍	ケイ	firefly

熟	蛍光	ケイコウ	fluorescence
	蛍光灯	ケイコウトウ	fluorescent lamp
	蛍光塗料	ケイコウトリョウ	fluorescent paint
訓	蛍	ほたる	firefly

1608

蛇 ⑪

丶 口 口 中 虫 虫 虫' 虫' 虫' 虻 蛇

音	蛇	ジャ	snake
		ダ	snake
熟	蛇口	ジャぐち	faucet; tap
	蛇行	ダコウ	winding; meandering —***vi***. wind; meander
	蛇足	ダソク	superfluous
訓	蛇	へび	snake; serpent

1609

蛮 ⑫

丶 亠 亣 亦 亦 亦 亦 峦 峦 蛮 蛮 蛮

音	蛮	バン	barbarian; savage
熟	蛮行	バンコウ	act of barbarity; atrocity; brutality
	蛮人	バンジン	barbarian; savage
	蛮勇	バンユウ	brute courage

1610

融 ⑯

一 丁 百 鬲 鬲 鬲 鬲 鬲 鬲 融 融 融

音	融	ユウ	dissolve; melt
熟	融解	ユウカイ	melting; dissolution; fusion —***v***. melt; dissolve; fuse
	融合	ユウゴウ	fusion; merger —***vi***. fuse; merge
	融点	ユウテン	melting point
	融和	ユウワ	harmony —***vi***. get along well with
訓	※融ける	とける	***vi***. melt; dissolve
¥	融資	ユウシ	finance; loan
	融資会社	ユウシガイシャ	financing corporation
	融通	ユウズウ	accomodation; loan; finance —***vi***. finance (an enterprise)
	融通証券	ユウズウショウケン	treasury accomodation bill

融通手形　ユウズウてがた　accomodation bill
融通手形振出人　ユウズウテガタふりだしニン　kite-flier

6 血 ち blood

1611
血 ⑥ ノ 丿 𠂉 ⺤ 血 血

音	血	ケツ	blood
熟	血圧	ケツアツ	***med***. blood pressure
	血液	ケツエキ	***med***. blood
	血液型	ケツエキがた	***med***. blood type/group
	血液銀行	ケツエキギンコウ	***med***. blood bank
	血液検査	ケツエキケンサ	blood test
	血縁	ケツエン	blood relative
	血管	ケッカン	***med***. blood vessel
	血気	ケッキ	vigor; hotbloodedness; youthfulness
	血球	ケッキュウ	***med***. blood corpuscle
	血行	ケッコウ	***med***. circulation of the blood
	血痕	ケッコン	***med***. blood stain
	血色	ケッショク	complexion
	血清	ケッセイ	***med***. serum
	血税	ケツゼイ	heavy taxes
	血相	ケッソウ	expression
	血族	ケツゾク	blood relative
	血沈	ケッチン	***med***. sedimentation of blood
	血統付	ケットウつき	pedigreed
	血尿	ケツニョウ	***med***. bloody urine
	血便	ケツベン	***med***. bloody excrement
訓	血	ち	blood
	血潮	ちしお	blood
	血筋	ちすじ	lineage; blood relationship
	血走る	ちばしる	be bloodshot
	血眼	ちまなこ	bloodshot eyes

1612

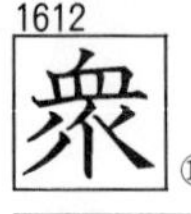

⑫

音	衆	**シュウ**	many; multitude; the people; the masses
		(シュ)	many
熟	衆議	**シュウギ**	general consultation
	衆議院	**シュウギイン**	the House of Representatives
	衆愚	**シュウグ**	vulgar masses
	衆愚政治	**シュウグセイジ**	mob rule
	衆人	**シュウジン**	the people/public
	衆人環視	**シュウジンカンシ**	public attention
	衆目	**シュウモク**	public attention
	衆生	**シュジョウ**	***Bud***. living things

6 行 ぎょうがまえ going

1613

行 ⑥

音	行	**ギョウ**	stroke; line
		コウ	go; going; do; exercise; conduct; line
		(アン)	walking tour; pilgrimage
熟	行脚	**アンギャ**	pilgrimage —***vi***. make a pilgrimage
	行間	**ギョウカン**	between the lines
	行儀	**ギョウギ**	manners; behavior; deportment
	行司	**ギョウジ**	*gyōji* (referee in sumo wrestling)
	行事	**ギョウジ**	event; function
	行書	**ギョウショ**	semicursive style of writing *kanji*
	行商	**ギョウショウ**	peddling; hawking —***v***. peddle; hawk
	行状	**ギョウジョウ**	behavior; conduct; demeanor
	行水	**ギョウズイ**	ablution —***vi***. wash oneself
	行列	**ギョウレツ**	line; queue —***vi***. line up; queue up
	行為	**コウイ**	deed; act; action; behavior; conduct
	行軍	**コウグン**	march; marching
	行使	**コウシ**	exercise; use (of one's authority, etc.) —***v***. use; make use of; employ; exercise
	行進	**コウシン**	march; parade —***vi***. march; parade; proceed
	行進曲	**コウシンキョク**	parade; musical march

	行程	コウテイ	journey; distance; itinery
	行動	コウドウ	action; act; conduct; behavior —***vi***. act; behave; conduct; move
	行楽	コウラク	pleasure trip; excursion; picnic; outing
訓	行く	いく	***vi***. go; walk; depart
	行う	おこなう	***vt***. do; perform; conduct; carry out
	行き違い	ゆきちがい	crossing; misunderstanding; disagreement
	行き詰まる	ゆきづまる	***vi***. come to a deadlock; be at a standstill
	行く	ゆく	***vi***. go; pass
	行方	ゆくえ	destination; whereabouts
	行く先	ゆくさき	whereabouts
	行く末	ゆくすえ	future; forthcoming happening
	行手	ゆくて	destination
¥	行政改革	ギョウセイカイカク	administrative reform

1614
術 ⑪

音	術	ジュツ	means; art; skill
熟	術語	ジュツゴ	technical term; terminology
	術策	ジュッサク	stratagem; trick; artifice
	術中	ジュッチュウ	trick; trap

1615
街 ⑫

音	街	ガイ	street
		(カイ)	street; highway
熟	街道	カイドウ	highway; high road
	街頭	ガイトウ	street
	街灯	ガイトウ	street lamp
	街路樹	ガイロジュ	roadside tree; trees lining a street
訓	街	まち	street; downtown

1616
衝 ⑮

音	衝	ショウ	collide; shock

6 竹米糸缶羊羽老耂而耒耳肉自至舌舟色虍虫血●行●衣衤西艮

熟	衝撃	ショウゲキ	shock; impact
	衝撃的	ショウゲキテキ	shocking
	衝動	ショウドウ	impulse; urge
	衝動買い	ショウドウがい	impulse buying —*v*. buy on impulse
	衝動的	ショウドウテキ	impulsive
	衝突	ショウトツ	collision; conflict; clash —***vi***. collide; conflict; clash

1617

衛 ⑯ 彳 彳 彳 ... 衛

音	衛	エイ	defend; guard
熟	衛視	エイシ	Diet guard
	衛生	エイセイ	hygiene; sanitation
	衛星	エイセイ	satellite
	衛星放送	エイセイホウソウ	satellite broadcasting
	衛兵	エイヘイ	sentry; guard
訓	※衛る	まもる	***vt***. protect; guard; defend

1618

衡 ⑯ 彳 彳 彳 ... 衡

音	衡	コウ	balance; equilibrium
熟	衡器	コウキ	balance; scales; weighing machine

6 衣 ころも clothes 衤 (p.708)

1619

衣 ⑥ 丶 亠 ナ 亡 衣 衣

音	衣	イ	clothes; clothing; garments; robes
熟	衣装	イショウ	costume; apparel; dress
	衣食	イショク	food and clothes
	衣食住	イショクジュウ	food, clothing, and shelter; living
	衣服	イフク	clothing; clothes
	衣料	イリョウ	clothing; clothes
	衣類	イルイ	clothes; garments

訓 衣 きぬ clothes
衣 ころも robes; garments

1620

表 ⑧

一 十 キ 主 声 耂 耒 表

音 表 ヒョウ table; chart; surface; express

熟 表する ヒョウする express/show (respect, regret, congratulations, etc.)

表意文字 ヒョウイモジ ideograph; ideogram

表音文字 ヒョウオンモジ phonetic symbol; phonogram

表記 ヒョウキ written on the face/outside —*v*. write; transcribe; show

表敬訪問 ヒョウケイホウモン courtesy call

表決 ヒョウケツ vote; voting —*v*. make a decision by; vote; vote

表現 ヒョウゲン expression; representation —*v*. express; represent

表現主義 ヒョウゲンシュギ expressionism (art, literature, etc.)

表札 ヒョウサツ nameplate (on a door, gate, etc.)

表紙 ヒョウシ cover/binding (of a book)

表示 ヒョウジ indication; sign; expression —*v*. indicate; express; show on a chart; tabulate

表出 ヒョウシュツ expression —*v*. express (one's feelings)

表彰 ヒョウショウ (official) commendation —*v*. commend; make public recognition of

表象 ヒョウショウ symbol; emblem; image; idea —*v*. symbolize

表情 ヒョウジョウ expression

表題 ヒョウダイ title (of a book, play, etc.); heading; caption

表土 ヒョウド topsoil

表皮 ヒョウヒ ***med***. cuticle; epidermis

表明 ヒョウメイ demonstration; manifestation; expression —*v*. demonstrate; show; manifest; express

表面 ヒョウメン surface; face ***fig***. superficial; appearances; pretext

表面化 ヒョウメンカ coming to the surface —***vi***. come to the surface; attract public attention

表面積 ヒョウメンセキ surface area

表裏 ヒョウリ front and back; both sides ***fig***. two faced; double-dealer

表裏一体 ヒョウリイッタイ one and indivisible

訓 表す あらわす ***vt***. express; show; reveal; manifest

表れる あらわれる ***vi***. come out; appear; come in sight; show itself; be expressed

竹米糸缶羊羽老耂而耒耳肉自至舌舟色虍虫血行 • 衣衤西艮

表	おもて	surface; right side; public; outside a house **bas**. top of an inning
表沙汰	おもてザタ	make public
表立つ	おもてだつ	***vi***. become public; be made public
表向き	おもてむき	openly; publicly; ostensibly; officially
¥ 表記価格	ヒョウキカカク	declared/insured value
表紙手形	ヒョウシてがた	consolidated bill
表面金利	ヒョウメンキンリ	nominal interest rate; coupon rate
表面預金	ヒョウメンヨキン	noainal deposit

1621

衷 ⑨

一 亠 亠 亩 亩 声 衷 衷 衷

音 衷	チュウ	in one's heart
熟 衷情	チュウジョウ	one's inmost feelings/true heart
衷心	チュウシン	one's inmost feelings/true heart

1622

衰 ⑩

丶 亠 亠 亣 亣 亩 亩 衰 衰 衰

音 衰	スイ	decline
熟 衰弱	スイジャク	weakness; prostration; breakdown; collapse —***vi***. weaken; become feeble; be worn out
衰退	スイタイ	degeneration; atrophy —***vi***. degenerate
衰微	スイビ	decline; wane; decadence —***vi***. decline; decay; wane; fall into decay
衰亡	スイボウ	decline; decay; ruin; fall; downfall —***vi***. go to ruin; be ruined; fall; decay; decline
訓 衰える	おとろえる	***vi***. become weak; lose vigor; waste away
衰え	おとろえ	weakening; emaciation; decline

1623

袋 ⑪

ノ イ 仁 代 代 代 岱 岱 袋 袋 袋

音 袋	タイ	bag
訓 袋	ふくろ	bag; sack
袋小路	ふくろコウジ	blind alley
袋物	ふくろもの	bags

1624

裁 ⑫

一 十 土 キ 圭 声 圭 表 表 裁 裁 裁

音	裁	サイ	cut; judge
熟	裁決	サイケツ	decision; verdict —*v*. decide; reach a verdict; judge
	裁断	サイダン	cutting; judgment; decision —*v*. cut; decide; judge; pass judgment
	裁判	サイバン	trial; suit —*v*. try; judge; put to the courts to decide
	裁判官	サイバンカン	judge
	裁判権	サイバンケン	jurisdiction
	裁判所	サイバンショ	court; law court
	裁縫	サイホウ	sewing; needlework —*vi*. sew; do needlework
	裁量	サイリョウ	discretion —*v*. use one's discretion
訓	裁く	さばく	*vt*. judge; sit in judgment; decide; pass verdict; punish
	裁き	さばき	judgment
	裁つ	たつ	*vt*. cut; cut out
¥	裁定取引	サイテイとりひき	arbitrage transaction

1625

装 ⑫

丨 丬 丬 丬一 丬十 壮 壮 壯 兰 奘 装 装

音	装	ソウ ショウ	wear; feigh; pretend
熟	装束	ショウゾク	dress; attire
	装具	ソウグ	equipment
	装甲	ソウコウ	armor; armor plating
	装甲車	ソウコウシャ	armored car
	装飾	ソウショク	ornament; decoration
	装身具	ソウシング	personal accessories
	装置	ソウチ	apparatus; device; equipment
	装着	ソウチャク	equipped; installed; fitted with —*v*. equip; instal; fit with
	装丁	ソウテイ	binding
	装備	ソウビ	equipment
訓	装う	よそおう	*vt*. wear; feigh; pretend

1626

裂 ⑫

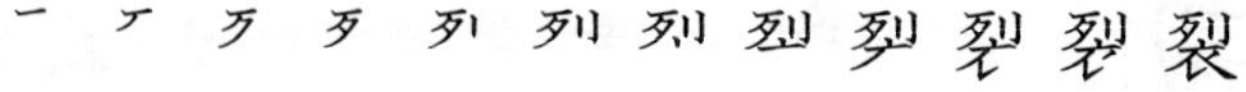

音	裂	レツ	tear; split; rip; burst
熟	裂傷	レッショウ	***med***. laceration
訓	裂く	さく	***vt***. tear; split; burst
	裂ける	さける	***vi***. tear; split; rip; burst
	裂け目	さけめ	rip; split; crack; fissure

1627

裏 ⑬

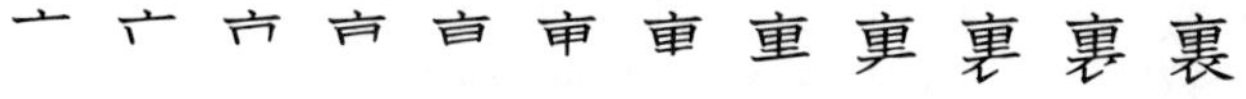

音	裏	リ	back; reverse side; opposite; rear
熟	裏面	リメン	back; reverse side; background
訓	裏	うら	back; reverse side
	裏表	うらおもて	both sides; reverse; inside out; two-faced
	裏方	うらかた	lady consort; stagehand
	裏側	うらがわ	back; reverse side; far side (of the moon)
	裏切る	うらぎる	***vt***. betray
	裏口	うらぐち	back door; rear entrance
	裏声	うらごえ	falsetto
	裏地	うらジ	lining
	裏付ける	うらづける	***vt***. support; endorse
	裏手	うらて	at the back; rear
	裏話	うらばなし	inside story
	裏腹	うらはら	reverse; opposite
	裏町	うらまち	backstreet
¥	裏書き	うらがき	endorsement
	裏書譲渡	うらがきジョウト	transfer by endorsement

1628

製 ⑭

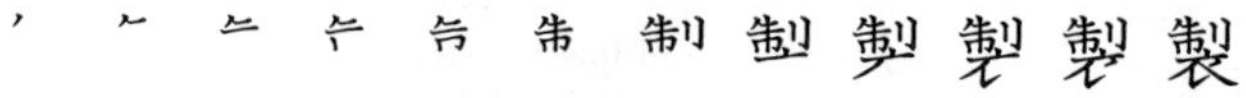

音	製	セイ	manufacture; make
熟	製する	セイする	***vt***. manufacture; make
	製材	セイザイ	lumber; sawing
	製作	セイサク	work; manufacturing; production —***v***. work; product; make

	製図	セイズ	draftsmanship; drawing; cartography —*v.* draw; draft
	製造	セイゾウ	manufacturing —*v.* manufacture
	製鉄	セイテツ	iron manufacture
	製品	セイヒン	product; manufactured goods
	製粉	セイフン	flour milling
	製法	セイホウ	manufacturing process; recipe
	製本	セイホン	bookbinding —*v.* bind books
	製薬	セイヤク	pharmacy; manufacturing drugs
	製錬	セイレン	refining; smelting —*v.* refine; smelt
¥	製造業	セイゾウギョウ	manufacturing industry

1629

⑮

音	褒	ホウ	praise
熟	褒章	ホウショウ	medal
	褒賞	ホウショウ	prize; reward; praise
	褒状	ホウジョウ	certificate of merit; commendation
	褒美	ホウビ	reward; prize
訓	褒める	ほめる	***vt.*** praise highly
	褒めちぎる	ほめちぎる	***vt.*** praise highly

1630

㉒

音	襲	シュウ	attack; succeed
熟	襲撃	シュウゲキ	surprise attack; sudden assault —*v.* raid; attack; assault
	襲名	シュウメイ	succession to another's name; assumption of one's parents' name —*v.* succeed to (a person's) stage name; inherit one's father's name
	襲来	シュウライ	raid; invasion —*v.* attack; make a raid
訓	襲う	おそう	***vt.*** attack; fall on; raid

5 衤 ころもへん clothes at the left

1631
被 16 31 ` ラ ネ ネ ネ ネ) 衤𠃌 衤𠂆 衤皮 被

音	被	ヒ	suffer; incur; receive; (prefix) -ed; -ee
熟	被害	ヒガイ	damage; harm; injury; casualties
	被害者	ヒガイシャ	victim; the injured (party)
	被疑者	ヒギシャ	suspect; person suspected of committing a crime
	被告	ヒコク	accused; defendant
	被告人	ヒコクニン	defendant
	被災	ヒサイ	suffering —***vi***. suffer from; fall victim to; be hit by (a natural disaster/fire)
	被災者	ヒサイシャ	victim (of a natural disaster/fire)
	被選挙権	ヒセンキョケン	electoral eligibility
	被選挙人	ヒセンキョニン	individual eligible for elective office
	被爆	ヒバク	being bombed (in particular, nuclear or hydrogen bomb) —***vi***. be bombed
	被爆者	ヒバクシャ	*hibakusha* (atomic bomb victim)
	被曝	ヒバク	exposure to radiation —***vi***. be exposed to radiation
	被曝者	ヒバクシャ	*hibakusha* (radiation exposure victim)
	被服	ヒフク	clothing
	被覆	ヒフク	covering —***v***. cover; coat
訓	被る	こうむる	***vt***. suffer; incur; receive
	被う	おおう	***vt***. cover
	被さる	かぶさる	***vi***. get covered; hang over
	被せる	かぶせる	***vt***. place/pour on top of; cover
	被る	かぶる	***vt***. wear/put on (one's head); take the blame
¥	被保険者	ヒホケンシャ	the insured
	被保険物	ヒホケンブツ	insured article/property

1632
補 ⑫ ` ラ ネ ネ ネ ネ一 衤𠂆 衤冂 衤冃 衤甫 補 補

音	補	ホ	assist; supplement
熟	補する	ホする	***vt***. appoint; assign
	捕角	ホカク	***math***. supplementary angle

	補完	ホカン	complement; supplement —***v***. complement; supplement
	補記	ホキ	appendage/addition (to an article) —***v***. add/append
	補給	ホキュウ	supply; replenishment —***v***. supply; replenish
	補強	ホキョウ	reinforcement —***v***. reinforce
	補欠	ホケツ	filling a vacancy; substitute; spare
	補血	ホケツ	***med***. blood replenishment —***vi***. replenish one's blood
	補語	ホゴ	***gram***. complement
	補佐	ホサ	assistant; aide; adviser; assistance; aid —***v***. assist; aid; help; advise
	補修	ホシュウ	repair —***v***. repair; fix; mend
	補習	ホシュウ	supplementary lessons; extracurricular education
	補充	ホジュウ	supplement; replacement —***v***. supplement; replace
	補助	ホジョ	aid; assistance; supplement; subsidy —***v***. help; assist; supplement; subsidize
	補色	ホショク	complementary color
	補正	ホセイ	correction; revision —***v***. correct; revise
	補則	ホソク	supplementary rules
	補足	ホソク	supplement; supply; replenishment —***v***. supplement; supply; replenish
	補聴器	ホチョウキ	hearing aid
	補塡	ホテン	filling/supplying (a deficiency); compensation —***v***. fill/supply (a deficiency); compensate
	補導	ホドウ	guidance; advice —***v***. guide; lead; advise
	補任	ホニン	appointment (to a post, vacancy) —***v***. appoint
訓	補う	おぎなう	***vt***. supply; make up/compensate for
¥	補欠選挙	ホケツセンキョ	by-election
	補償	ホショウ	compensation; indemnification —***v***. compensate; indemnify
	補償金	ホショウキン	indemnity; compensation (money)
	補助金	ホジョキン	subsidy; grant-in-aid
	補正予算	ホセイヨサン	revived budget

1633

⑫

音	裕	ユウ	rich; abundant; fruitful; fertile
熟	裕福	ユウフク	prosperity; affluence
訓	※裕	ゆたか	abundant; rich

竹米糸缶羊羽老耂而耒耳肉自至舌舟色虍虫血行衣衤西艮

1634

褐 ⑬

、 ヲ ネ ネ ネ 衵 衵 袒 袓 裼 褐 褐

音	褐	カツ	brown
熟	褐色	カッショク	brown

1635

裸 ⑬

、 ヲ ネ ネ ネ 衵 衵 袒 袒 裡 裸 裸

音	裸	ラ	nude; naked
熟	裸眼	ラガン	the naked eye
	裸身	ラシン	nakedness
	裸体	ラタイ	naked body; nudity
	裸婦	ラフ	nude woman
訓	裸	はだか	naked body; nakedness; nudity
	裸ん坊	はだかんボウ	naked person/child
	※裸足	はだし	barefoot; barefooted

1636

複 ⑭

、 ヲ ネ ネ ネ ネ 衤 衬 袙 複 複 複

音	複	フク	double; multiple; composite
熟	複眼	フクガン	compound eye (of an insect)
	複合	フクゴウ	composite; compound; complex —***v***. compound; pound together
	複合語	フクゴウゴ	***gram***. compound (word)
	複雑	フクザツ	complicated; complex
	複式	フクシキ	double-entry (bookkeeping)
	複写	フクシャ	copying; duplication; facsimile —***vi***. copy; duplicate
	複数	フクスウ	***gram***. plural
	複製	フクセイ	reproduction; duplication —***v***. reproduce; duplicate
	複線	フクセン	double track
¥	複利	フクリ	compound interest

1637

襟 ⑱

ラ ネ ネ ネ ネ 袢 袢 袢 襟 襟 襟 襟

音	襟	キン	collar; heart
訓	襟	えり	collar; neck; lapel
	襟足	えりあし	hairline above the nape
	襟元	えりもと	front of the neck

6 西 にし west

1638

西 ⑥

一 ㄏ 冂 丙 两 西

音	西	セイ	west
		サイ	
熟	西方	サイホウ	the West; Buddhist paradise
	西経	セイケイ	west longitude
	西方	セイホウ	(the) west; western
	西洋	セイヨウ	Western countries; the West; western; occidental
	西洋化	セイヨウカ	westernization; Europeanization —*v*. become westernized
	西暦	セイレキ	Christian Era; Anno Domini (AD)
訓	西	にし	west; western
	※西瓜	すいか	watermelon

1639

要 ⑨

一 ㄏ 冂 币 襾 覀 要 要 要

音	要	ヨウ	main point; principal; necessary; essential; important
熟	要する	ヨウする	require; need
	要因	ヨウイン	chief factor; principal cause
	要員	ヨウイン	essential personnel
	要求	ヨウキュウ	demand; requirement —*v*. demand; require
	要件	ヨウケン	requisite; essentials
	要港	ヨウコウ	important/strategic port

竹米糸缶羊羽老耂而耒耳肉自至舌舟色虍虫血行衣衤●西艮

	要項	ヨウコウ	essential point(s)
	要綱	ヨウコウ	summary; outline
	要塞	ヨウサイ	fortress; stronghold
	要旨	ヨウシ	gist; purport; substance
	要式	ヨウシキ	formal
	要所	ヨウショ	important/strategic place
	要職	ヨウショク	responsible position; important job
	要人	ヨウジン	leading figure; important person
	要請	ヨウセイ	request; requirement; demand —*v.* request; demand; ask; call for
	要素	ヨウソ	element; factor
	要地	ヨウチ	important strategic place
	要注意	ヨウチュウイ	requiring care/caution
	要点	ヨウテン	main point(s)
	要部	ヨウブ	principal/essential part
	要望	ヨウボウ	demand —*v.* demand
	要務	ヨウム	important business
	要目	ヨウモク	principal items
	要約	ヨウヤク	summary —*v.* summarize
	要領	ヨウリョウ	gist; purport; synopsis
訓	要る	いる	***vi***. need; cost
¥	要求払い	ヨウキュウばらい	payable on demand

1640

覆 ⑱

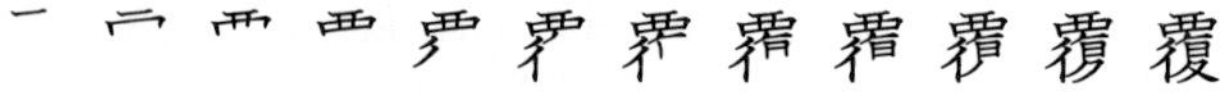

音	覆	フク	overturn; cover
熟	覆面	フクメン	(cloth) mask
訓	覆う	おおう	***vt***. cover; conceal; spread over
	覆す	くつがえす	***vt***. overturn; overthrow
	覆る	くつがえる	***vi***. be overturned/overthrown

1641

覇 ⑲

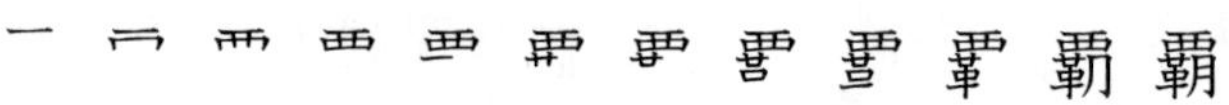

音	覇	ハ	supremacy; leadership; domination
熟	覇気	ハキ	ambition; aspiration
	覇権	ハケン	supremacy; leadership; domination
	覇者	ハシャ	supreme ruler; champion

6 艮 ねづくり／こんづくり good

1642

良 ⑦

丶 ㇉ ㇋ ヨ 㓁 㓂 良

音	良	リョウ	good
熟	良好	リョウコウ	good; favorable; satisfactory
	良妻	リョウサイ	good wife
	良識	リョウシキ	good sense
	良質	リョウシツ	superior quality
	良種	リョウシュ	good breed; thoroughbreed
	良書	リョウショ	good book
	良心	リョウシン	conscience
	良心的	リョウシンテキ	conscientious
	良知	リョウチ	intuition
	良否	リョウヒ	good or bad
	良品	リョウヒン	superior quality goods
	良民	リョウミン	good citizens
	良薬	リョウヤク	effective medicine
訓	良い	よい	good
	良し悪し	よしあし	good or evil; right or wrong; merits and demerits

7 見 みる seeing

1643

見 ⑦ 丨 冂 冃 月 目 貝 見

音	見	ケン	see; view; meet; show
熟	見解	ケンカイ	opinion; view; outlook
	見学	ケンガク	observation; tour (for educational purposes) —*v.* inspect; observe
	見学者	ケンガクシャ	visitor
	見識	ケンシキ	pride; self-respect; judgment; discernment; insight
	見地	ケンチ	standpoint; viewpoint; point of view
	見当	ケントウ	aim; direction; estimate; guess; about; approximately
	見物	ケンブツ	sightseeing —*v.* go sightseeing; see the sights
	見聞	ケンブン	information; experience; observation —*v.* go sightseeing
訓	見る	みる	***vt***. see; watch; look
	見える	みえる	***vi***. be seen; can see; seem to; visit; come; arrive
	見せる	みせる	***vt***. show; display; allow to be watched
	見合い	みあい	small party to introduce two prospective marriage candidates —***vi***. meet each other with a view to marriage
	見送る	みおくる	***vt***. see off one's guest
	見苦しい	みぐるしい	dishonorable; disgraceful; ugly; shabby
	見事	みごと	excellent; fine; splendid; superb; admirable
	見込む	みこむ	***vt***. expect; anticipate; count on; trust; estimate
	見殺し	みごろし	leaving someone to his fate
	見境	みさかい	distinction
	見世物	みせもの	show; sideshow
	見所	みどころ	promise; good points; the point; highlight
	見習う	みならう	***vt***. follow a person's example; learn
	見本	みホン	sample; specimen; example; model
	見舞い	みまい	inquiry; expression of one's sympathy; visit to a sick person
¥	見返り	みかえり	incentive goods; collateral expert goods; collateral goods
	見出し	みだし	index; contents (of a book); title; headline; heading; readline; caption
	見積り	みつもり	estimate

見積書	みつもりショ	written estimate
見通し	みとおし	outlook; forecast; prospect
見本市	みホンいち	(sample) trade fair

1644

規 ⑪

一 二 キ 夫 夫l 知 知 知 規 規 規

音	規	キ	regulation; rule
熟	規格	キカク	standard; norm
	規準	キジュン	criterion
	規正	キセイ	readjustment; correction; rectification
	規制	キセイ	regulation; control —*v*. regulate; control
	規則	キソク	rule; regulation
	規則的	キソクテキ	regular; systematic
	規定	キテイ	rule; regulations; stipulations; prescriptions —*v*. prescribe; ordain; stipulate
	規範	キハン	model; example
	規模	キボ	scale; scope
	規約	キヤク	rules; bylaws
	規律	キリツ	discipline; regulation; order; rules

1645

視 ⑪

丶 ラ ネ ネ ネl 礻口 礻日 礻目 視 視 視

音	視	シ	watch; regard
熟	視界	シカイ	field of vision; visibility; sight
	視覚	シカク	sense of sight
	視覚的	シカクテキ	visual; visually
	視察	シサツ	inspection; observation —*v*. inspection; make an inspection
	視察員	シサツイン	observer
	視線	シセン	one's gaze; one's line of vision
	視聴	シチョウ	looking and listening; attention —*v*. look and listen; be attentive
	視聴覚	シチョウカク	senses of seeing and hearing
	視聴者	シチョウシャ	audience; the viewers
	視聴率	シチョウリツ	audience rating
	視点	シテン	point of view; viewpoint
	視野	シヤ	field of vision; range of view; one's view
	視力	シリョク	sight; eyesight; vision

	視力検査	シリョクケンサ	eye test
訓	※視る	みる	***vt***. see

1646

覚 ⑫

丶 丷 ⺍ ⺍ 𰀁 ⺌ 常 … 覚

音	覚	カク	sense; feel; comprehend
熟	覚悟	カクゴ	resolution; resignation —***v***. be prepared for; be resigned to; be determined
	覚醒	カクセイ	awakening; disillusionment —***v***. awake; wake up; arouse; be awakened; be disillusioned
	覚醒剤	カクセイザイ	stimulant drug
訓	覚える	おぼえる	***vi***. feel; remember; learn
	覚ます	さます	***vt***. awake; wake up
	覚める	さめる	***vi***. wake up; become sober; be enlightened

1647

親 ⑯

亠 立 辛 亲 新 親

音	親	シン	parent; intimate
熟	親愛	シンアイ	affection; love
	親衛隊	シンエイタイ	bodyguards
	親近感	シンキンカン	sense of closeness
	親権	シンケン	parental authority
	親交	シンコウ	intimacy; friendship
	親戚	シンセキ	relative; relation
	親切	シンセツ	kind; kindhearted; good; nice
	親善	シンゼン	friendship; goodwill
	親族	シンゾク	relative; relation
	親展	シンテン	confidential; personal
	親等	シントウ	degree of kinship
	親睦	シンボク	friendship
	親身	シンミ	kind; warm; tender; blood relation
	親密	シンミツ	intimacy; close friendship
	親友	シンユウ	bosom/close/good friend
	親類	シンルイ	relative; relation
	親和	シンワ	friendship; affinity
訓	親	おや	parent
	親方	おやかた	boss; foreman; master; home; parents
	親孝行	おやコウコウ	filial devotion/piety

親心 おやごころ parental love
親父 おやじ father; old man; the boss
親潮 おやしお Kurile Current
親馬鹿 おやバカ doting/indulgent parent
親分 おやブン gang leader; boss
親元 おやもと one's parents/home
親指 おやゆび thumb; big toe
親しい したしい intimate; close; friendy; familiar
親しむ したしむ ***vi***. become familiar with; get to know; make friends with

¥ 親会社 おやガイシャ parent company

1648
覧 ⑰

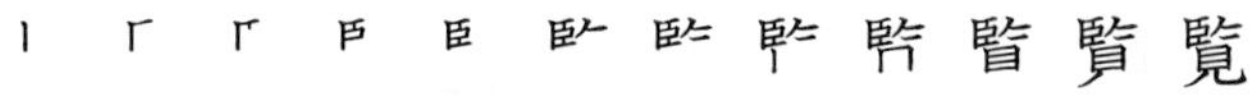

音 覧 ラン inspect; see; look at

1649
観 ⑱

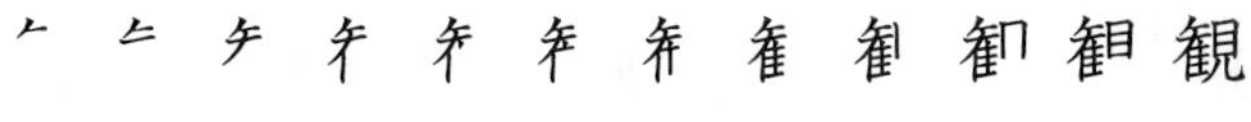

音 観 カン observe; view; see; look

熟 観客 カンキャク spectators
観劇 カンゲキ theatergoing —***v***. go to the theater; see a play
観光 カンコウ sightseeing; tourism —***v***. go sightseeing
観光客 カンコウキャク tourist
観察 カンサツ observation —***v***. observe; view; make observations
観衆 カンシュウ spectators; audience
観賞 カンショウ enjoyment; admiration —***v***. enjoy; admire
観測 カンソク observation; survey —***v***. observe; make an observation; survey
観点 カンテン standpoint; viewpoint; point of view
観念 カンネン idea; conception; notion
観念的 カンネンテキ ideal; ideological
観音 カンノン Kwannon, Avalokitesvara (Buddhist goddess of mercy)
観覧 カンラン viewing; inspection —***v***. view; inspect

訓 ※観る みる ***vt***. view; watch; observe

7 角 つの horn

1650

角 ⑦

丿 ク ク 角 角 角 角

音	角	カク	horn; angle; corner
熟	角界	カクカイ（カッカイ）	sumo wrestling world
	角材	カクザイ	square lumber
	角柱	カクチュウ	square pillar; prism
	角度	カクド	***math.*** geometric angle
	角張る	カクばる	***vi.*** be angular/square/sharp; become formal/ceremonious
訓	角	かど	corner; angle
	角	つの	animal's horn

1651

解 ⑬

ク 欠 角 角 角 角 角ᄀ 角ᄁ 角ᄁ 解 解 解

音	解	カイ	solve; untie; melt; understand; explain
		ゲ	realize; untie; melt
熟	解する	カイする	***vt.*** interpret; understand
	解決	カイケツ	solution; settlement; conclusion —***v.*** solve; settle; conclude
	解雇	カイコ	discharge; dismissal; firing —***v.*** discharge; dismiss; fire
	解散	カイサン	breakup; dispersion —***v.*** break up; disperse
	解釈	カイシャク	interpretation; explanation —***v.*** interpret; explain
	解除	カイジョ	release; cancellation; removal —***v.*** release; cancel; remove
	解消	カイショウ	dissolution; cancellation; liquidation —***v.*** dissolve; cancel; liquidate
	解説	カイセツ	commentary; explanation —***v.*** make a commentary; explain
	解答	カイトウ	solution; answer —***vi.*** solve; answer
	解読	カイドク	deciphering; decoding —***v.*** decipher; decode
	解放	カイホウ	release; emancipation; liberation —***v.*** release; emancipate; liberate
	解剖	カイボウ	dissection; autopsy; vivisection —***v.*** dissect; vivisect; cut up

	解明	カイメイ	elucidation; solution —*v*. elucidate; solve
	解せない	ゲせない	incomprehensible
	解毒剤	ゲドクザイ	***med***. antidote
	解熱剤	ゲネツザイ	***med***. antipyretic
訓	解く	とく	***vt***. untie; relieve; answer; construe
	解かす	とかす	***vt***. melt
	解ける	とける	***vi***. loose; be dispelled; be relieved; melt
	解く	ほどく	***vt***. untie; undo; unfasten; loosen
	※解る	わかる	***vi***. understand; comprehend
¥	解禁	カイキン	removal of a ban/embargo —*v*. lift a ban/embargo
	解任	カイニン	dismissal; firing —*v*. displace (a person) from (his or her) position; dismiss
	解約	カイヤク	cancellation of a contract/agreement —*v*. cancel a contract; call off (an agreement)
	解け合い	とけあい	liquidation by compromise

1652

触 ⑬

ク ク 角 角 角 角 角 角 角 角 触 触

音	触	ショク	touch; feel
熟	触手	ショクシュ	tentacle; feeler
	触媒	ショクバイ	catalyst
	触発	ショクハツ	touched off; started —*v*. touch off; start
	触角	ショッカク	antenna; feeler
	触覚	ショッカク	sense of touch
訓	触る	さわる	***vi***. touch; feel
	触れる	ふれる	***v***. touch; feel; stroke; perceive; incur

7 言 げん／ごんべん word

1653

⑦

丶 亠 亠 亠 言 言 言

音	言	ゲン	say; speak; word; language
		ゴン	word
熟	言外	ゲンガイ	implied; hinted
	言及	ゲンキュウ	mention; reference to —***vi***. mention; refer to; touch upon

	言語	ゲンゴ	language; speech
	言語学	ゲンゴガク	linguistics
	言行	ゲンコウ	words and deeds; speech and behavior
	言行一致	ゲンコウイッチ	consistency of speech and action
	言動	ゲンドウ	speech and action; p's and q's
	言明	ゲンメイ	declaration; assertion; positive statement —*v.* declare; assert; make a positive statement
	言論	ゲンロン	expression of one's opinion through speech or writing
	言論界	ゲンロンカイ	press; media
	言論機関	ゲンロンキカン	organ of public opinion
	言語道断	ゴンゴドウダン	outrageous; unspeakable; abominable; shocking
訓	言い返す	いいかえす	***vt.*** talk back; retort
	言い方	いいかた	expression; how to speak; one's words
	言い張る	いいはる	***vt.*** insist on
	言い回し	いいまわし	(mode of) expression
	言い訳	いいわけ	explanation; excuse; apology
	言う	いう	***vt.*** speak; say; mention; talk
	言	こと	word
	言伝て	ことづて	message
	言葉	ことば	word; language; speech; phrase; statement

1654

⑬

音	誉	ヨ	praise; honor
熟	誉望	ヨボウ	glory; honor; fame
訓	誉れ	ほまれ	honor; glory

1655

誓 ⑭

音	誓	セイ	oath
熟	誓約	セイヤク	vow; oath; promise —***v.*** avowal; make an oath; promise
訓	誓う	ちかう	***vt.*** swear; promise; make an oath
	誓い	ちかい	oath; promise

1656

謄 ⑰

音	謄	トウ	copy
熟	謄写	トウシャ	copy; transcription; reproduction —*v.* copy; transcribe; reproduce
	謄写版	トウシャバン	mimeographed copy
	謄本	トウホン	copy; transcript; duplicate

1657

警 ⑲

音	警	ケイ	warn; guard; vigilance; caution
熟	警戒	ケイカイ	vigilance; caution; precaution —*v.* be on one's guard; be cautious; be on guard; watch out for
	警句	ケイク	aphorism; epigram
	警護	ケイゴ	guard —*v.* guard
	警告	ケイコク	warning; caution —*v.* warn; caution; advise
	警察	ケイサツ	police
	警察官	ケイサツカン	policeman
	警察署	ケイサツショ	police station
	警察庁	ケイサツチョウ	National Police Agency
	警笛	ケイテキ	horn; alarm whistle; foghorn
	警備	ケイビ	guard; defense —*v.* guard; defend; keep guard
	警備員	ケイビイン	security guard
	警報	ケイホウ	alarm; warning
訓	※警める	いましめる	***vt.*** admonish; caution; warn

1658

計 ⑨

音	計	ケイ	count; measure; plan; estimate; gauge
熟	計画	ケイカク	plan; project; scheme —*v.* plan; project; scheme
	計画的	ケイカクテキ	planned; scheduled; premeditated
	計器	ケイキ	meter; gauge
	計算	ケイサン	calculation; computation —*v.* calculate; compute; figure out; reckon
	計算機	ケイサンキ	computer; calculator

	計上	ケイジョウ	summing/adding up; aggregate —*v*. sum/add up; appropriate
	計略	ケイリャク	stratagem; scheme; trick; plot
	計量	ケイリョウ	weighing; measuring; gauging —*v*. weigh; measure; gauge
	計量器	ケイリョウキ	gauge; scales
訓	計る	はかる	***vt***. time; measure; judge; estimate; guess
	計り	はかり	measure; weight; scales
	計らう	はからう	***vt***. take care; settle; handle

1659

訂 ⑨

音	訂	テイ	correct
熟	訂正	テイセイ	correction; rectification; revision —*v*. correct; rectify; revise

1660

記 ⑩

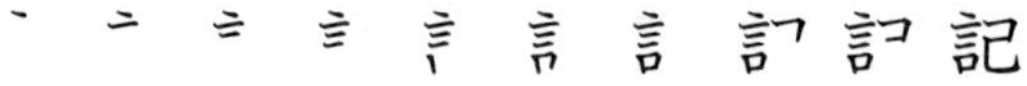

音	記	キ	write down; record; note; remember
熟	記憶	キオク	memory; recollection —*v*. remember; commit to memory; memorize
	記号	キゴウ	mark; sign; symbol
	記載	キサイ	description; statement —*v*. state; describe; mention
	記事	キジ	news story/article
	記者	キシャ	reporter; writer
	記述	キジュツ	description; account —*v*. describe; give an account of
	記入	キニュウ	recording; entering —*v*. enter; make an entry; record; fill in
	記念	キネン	commemoration; remembrance —*v*. commemorate; honor the memory of
	記念日	キネンび	anniversary
	記名	キメイ	signature —*v*. sign one's name
	記録	キロク	record; document; archives —*v*. record; register; write down
	記録的	キロクテキ	record-breaking
訓	記す	しるす	***vt***. write down; record; note

1661

訓 ⑩

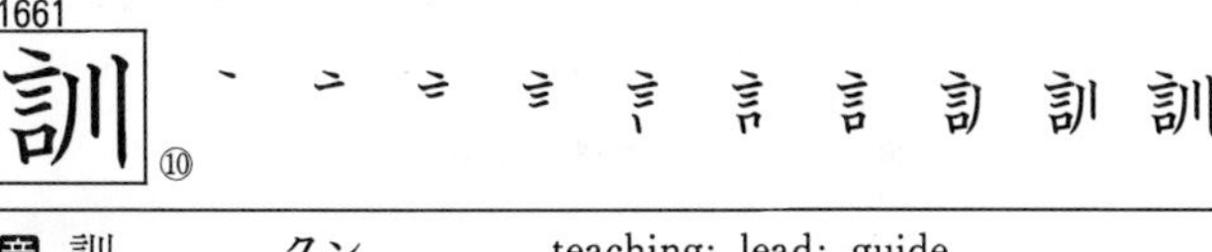

音	訓	クン	teaching; lead; guide
熟	訓戒	クンカイ	admonition; exhortation; lecture
	訓示	クンジ	instruction —***vi***. instruct
	訓辞	クンジ	admonitory speech —***v***. give an admonitory speech
	訓令	クンレイ	instructions; order; directive —***vi***. instruct; order; direct
	訓練	クンレン	training; drill; practice —***v***. train; drill; practice
	訓話	クンワ	moral discourse —***vi***. discuss morals

1662

託 ⑩

音	託	タク	entrust
熟	託する	タクする	***vt***. entrust; trust; commit
	託児所	タクジショ	day nursery; crèche
	託送	タクソウ	consignment —***v***. consign; send

1663

討 ⑩

音	討	トウ	attack
熟	討議	トウギ	discussion; debate; deliberation —***v***. discuss; deliberate; debate; hold a discussion
	討伐	トウバツ	subjugation; suppression —***v***. subjugate; suppress; subdue; put down
	討論	トウロン	debate; discussion; talk —***v***. debate; discuss; talk
	討論会	トウロンカイ	forum; discussion
訓	討つ	うつ	***vt***. strike; hit; attack; subjugate; conquer

1664

許 ⑪

音	許	キョ	forgive; permit; allow

熟	許可	キョカ	permission; license —*v.* permit; license; sanction
	許諾	キョダク	consent; assent; approval —*v.* consent; assent; approve
	許容	キョヨウ	permission; allowance; permit —*v.* permit; allow
訓	許す	ゆるす	*vt.* forgive; allow; permit; approve
¥	許可制	キョカセイ	license system; licensing
	許容限度	キョヨウゲンド	tolerance limits; allowable maximum

1665
訟 ⑪

音	訟	ショウ	sue

1666
設 ⑪

音	設	セツ	set up; establish; provide; prepare
熟	設営	セツエイ	construction; preparations —*v.* put up (a tent, etc.)
	設計	セッケイ	design; planning —*v.* design; plan
	設置	セッチ	establishment; founding; institution —*v.* establish; found
	設定	セッテイ	fixation; establishment; creation —*v.* fix; establish; create
	設備	セツビ	facilities; equipment; accommodations —*v.* facilitate; equip; accommodate
	設問	セツモン	question —*vi.* ask questions; question
	設立	セツリツ	founding; establishment —*v.* found; establish
訓	設ける	もうける	*vt.* prepare; provide; establish; set up
¥	設備	セツビ	equipment; provision
	設備投資	セツビトウシ	capital investment; investment in plant and equipment

1667
訪 ⑪

音	訪	ホウ	visit
熟	訪客	ホウキャク	visitor; guest
	訪日	ホウニチ	visiting Japan

	訪問	ホウモン	visiting; visit —*v*. visit
訓	訪れる	おとずれる	***vi***. visit
	訪ねる	たずねる	***vt***. visit

1668

訳 ⑪

音	訳	ヤク	translation
熟	訳する	ヤクする	***vt***. translate
	訳語	ヤクゴ	***gram***. translated term; equivalent
	訳者	ヤクシャ	translator
	訳文	ヤクブン	translation; translated literature
訓	訳	わけ	meaning; reason; cause; meaning; circumstances; the case
	訳無い	わけない	easy; simple

1669

詠 ⑫

音	詠	エイ	recite/compose poetry
熟	詠歌	エイカ	poetry composition
	詠嘆	エイタン	exclamation; admiration —***vi***. exclaim; admire
訓	詠む	よむ	***vt***. recite/compose poetry

1670

詐 ⑫

音	詐	サ	lie; deceive; cheat; swindle
熟	詐欺	サギ	cheat; fraud; swindling; swindle
	詐欺師	サギシ	swindler; con man; fraud
	詐取	サシュ	swindle; fraud —*v*. defraud; swindle; cheat

1671

詞 ⑫

音	詞	シ	word; writing
訓	※詞	ことば	word; writing

1672
証 ⑫

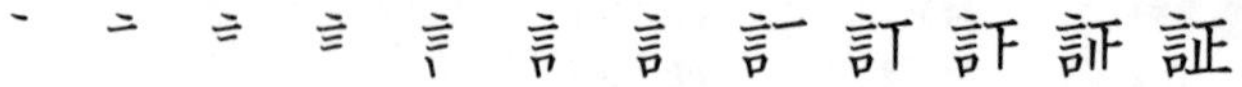

音	証	ショウ	proof
熟	証する	ショウする	***vt.*** prove; guarantee; supply evidence
	証言	ショウゲン	testimony —***v.*** testify; give evidence
	証拠	ショウコ	evidence; proof
	証書	ショウショ	bond; deed; certificate
	証人	ショウニン	witness; guarantor
	証明	ショウメイ	proof; evidence; testimony; demonstration —***v.*** prove; testity; certify; demonstrate
	証明書	ショウメイショ	certificate
	証文	ショウモン	bond; deed
¥	証券	ショウケン	(valuable) securities; bond; bill
	証券化	ショウケンカ	converting into securities
	証券会社	ショウケンガイシャ	securities company; stockbroking firm
	証券取引所	ショウケンとりひきジョ	securities/stock exchange
	証券取引法	ショウケンとりひきホウ	Securities and Exchange Law
	証書	ショウショ	certificate; bond; bill

1673
詔 ⑫

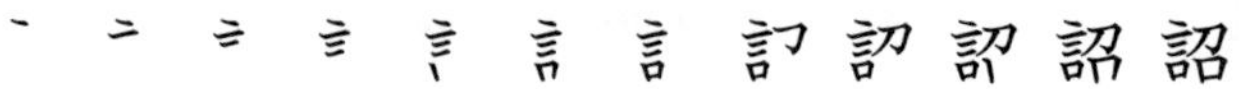

音	詔	ショウ	imperial rescript
熟	詔書	ショウショ	imperial edict
	詔勅	ショウチョク	imperial edict
訓	詔	みことのり	imperial edict

1674
診 ⑫

音	診	シン	examine
熟	診察	シンサツ	medical examination; consultation —***v.*** examine (a patient)
	診察券	シンサツケン	patient's registration card
	診察時間	シンサツジカン	consultation hours

	診察室	シンサツシツ	consultation room
	診断	シンダン	diagnosis; examination —*v*. examine (a patient); make a diagnosis
	診断書	シンダンショ	medical certificate
	診療	シンリョウ	medical examination and treatment —*v*. give medical examinations and treatment
	診療所	シンリョウジョ	clinic
訓	診る	みる	***vt***. examine

1675

訴 ⑫

丶 亠 亠 言 言 言 言 訁 訂 訢 訴 訴

音	訴	ソ	sue; complain of; appeal to
熟	訴訟	ソショウ	lawsuit; litigation —***vi***. file a lawsuit; litigate
	訴状	ソジョウ	petition; written complaint
	訴追	ソツイ	prosecution; indictment —*v*. prosecute; indict
	訴人	ソニン	suer; plaintiff
訓	訴える	うったえる	*v*. appeal; sue; complain

1676

評 ⑫

丶 亠 亠 言 言 言 言 訂 訂 評 評 評

音	評	ヒョウ	criticism; comment
熟	評する	ヒョウする	***vt***. criticize; comment on; speak of (a person) as
	評価	ヒョウカ	valuation; estimate; assessment; evaluation; appraisal —*v*. value; estimate; assess; evaluate; appraise
	評議	ヒョウギ	conference; discussion; council; meeting —*v*. hold a conference/council/meeting; discuss
	評決	ヒョウケツ	verdict (of guilty/not guilty) —*v*. pronounce a verdict; sentence
	評者	ヒョウシャ	critic; reviewer
	評釈	ヒョウシャク	annotation —*v*. annotate
	評注	ヒョウチュウ	annotation; (critical) notes —*v*. annotate
	評定	ヒョウテイ	evaluation; rating —*v*. evaluate; rate
	評点	ヒョウテン	(examination) marks/grades
	評判	ヒョウバン	(public) estimation; reputation; popularity; rumor; gossip; fame
	評論	ヒョウロン	criticism; review; comment —*v*. review; comment
	評論家	ヒョウロンカ	critic; reviewer; commentator; publicist

1677
該 ⑬

丶 亠 亖 言 言 言 訁 訁 訁 訁 該 該

音	該	ガイ	that; correspond
熟	該当	ガイトウ	relevent; applicable —*vi*. come under; be applicable

1678
詰 ⑬

丶 亠 亖 言 言 言 訁 計 訁 詁 詰 詰

音	詰	キツ	blame; rebuke; reprimand; pack; stuff
熟	詰問	キツモン	cross-examination; interrogation —*v*. cross-examine; cross-question
訓	詰まる	つまる	*vi*. be stuffed/full/packed/blocked
	詰める	つめる	*vt*. stuff; cram; pack into
	詰め込む	つめこむ	cram; load; squeeze into
	詰め物	つめもの	packing; stuffing; filling
	詰む	つむ	*vi*. be stuffed/full/packed/blocked

1679
誇 ⑬

丶 亠 亖 言 言 言 訁 訁 訁 訁 誇 誇

熟	誇示	コジ	ostentation; showing off —*v*. show off; flaunt
	誇大	コダイ	exaggeration
	誇張	コチョウ	exaggeration; overstatement —*v*. exaggerate; overstate
訓	誇る	ほこる	*vi*. boast; brag; show off
	誇り	ほこり	pride; haughtiness

1680
試 ⑬

丶 亠 亖 言 言 言 訁 訁 訁 訁 試 試

音	試	シ	try
熟	試合	シあい	match; game; tournament —*vi*. play/have a match/game; have a tournament
	試案	シアン	tentative plan; proposal
	試運転	シウンテン	test/trial run —*v*. make a test/trial run; run a trial
	試金石	シキンセキ	touchstone; test; test case

	試験	シケン	examination; test; experiment —*v*. experiment; put a thing to the test; test
	試験管	シケンカン	test tube
	試験的	シケンテキ	experimental; tentative
	試作	シサク	trial manufacture/production —*v*. make (a machine) on an experimental basis
	試作品	シサクヒン	trial product
	試写	シシャ	preview —*v*. give/hold a preview of
	試乗	シジョウ	test ride/drive —*v*. test drive a car
	試食	シショク	tasting; sampling —*v*. taste; sample; try
	試着	シチャク	trying clothes on —*v*. try on
	試着室	シチャクシツ	fitting room
	試用	シヨウ	trial —*v*. try; make a trial
	試練	シレン	ordeal; trial
訓	試みる	こころみる	***vt***. try; attempt
	試み	こころみ	trial; test; experiment; temptation (biblical sense)
	試す	ためす	***vt***. test; try

1681

詩 ⑬

丶 亠 亖 言 言 言 言 訁 計 詁 詩 詩

音	詩	シ	poetry; verse; Chinese poem
熟	詩歌	シイカ	poetry; verse
	詩吟	シギン	recitation of a Chinese poem —***vi***. recite a Chinese poem
	詩作	シサク	writing poetry —***vi***. write poetry
	詩集	シシュウ	collection of poems; poetry anthology
	詩情	シジョウ	poetic sentiment
	詩人	シジン	poet
	詩的	シテキ	poetic
訓	※詩	うた	poetry; verse; Chinese poem

1682

詳 ⑬

丶 亠 亖 言 言 言 言 訁 訁 詳 詳 詳

音	詳	ショウ	minute; fine; details
熟	詳細	ショウサイ	details; detailed; minute
	詳述	ショウジュツ	detailed explanation —*v*. make a detailed explanation; explain in detail

	詳説	ショウセツ	detailed explanation —*v*. make a detailed explanation; explain in detail
	詳報	ショウホウ	full information; detailed report
訓	詳しい	くわしい	detailed; precise; in detail; familiar

1683

誠 ⑬

音	誠	セイ	sincerity; fidelity; truth
熟	誠意	セイイ	sincerity; good faith
	誠実	セイジツ	sincere; faithful; loyal
訓	誠	まこと	sincerity; fidelity; truth

1684

話 ⑬

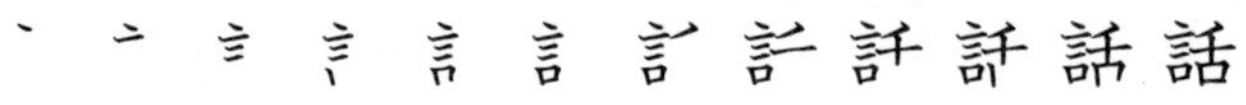

音	話	ワ	story; conversation; talk
熟	話術	ワジュツ	storytelling
	話題	ワダイ	topic; subject (of a story/discussion)
	話法	ワホウ	speech; parlance
訓	話	はなし	talk; conversation; story
	話す	はなす	***vt***. talk; speak
	話し中	はなしチュウ	while speaking; (phone is) busy/engaged
	話し手	はなして	speaker

1685

語 ⑭

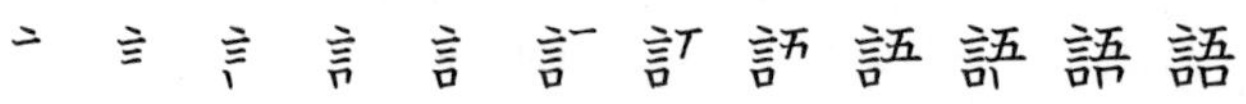

音	語	ゴ	speak; word; language
熟	語意	ゴイ	meaning of a word
	語彙	ゴイ	vocabulary
	語学	ゴガク	linguistics; language study
	語感	ゴカン	nuance; shade of meaning
	語気	ゴキ	tone of voice
	語句	ゴク	words and phrases
	語源	ゴゲン	etymology
	語順	ゴジュン	***gram***. word order

	語調	ゴチョウ	tone of voice
	語尾	ゴビ	***gram***. word ending; inflexion
	語弊	ゴヘイ	wrong word; misleading expression
	語法	ゴホウ	diction; usage; expression; wording
	語録	ゴロク	analects; collection of sayings
訓	語る	かたる	***vt***. talk; recite; narrate
	語らう	かたらう	***vt***. talk over

1686

誤 ⑭

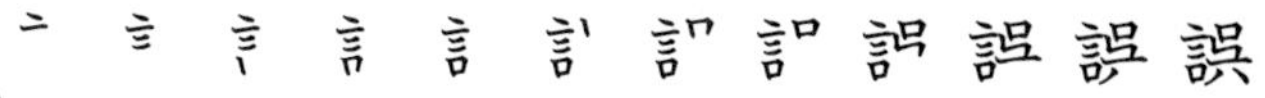

音	誤	ゴ	mistake; error
熟	誤解	ゴカイ	misunderstanding —***v***. misunderstand
	誤差	ゴサ	error; difference; margin of error; tolerance
	誤算	ゴサン	miscalculation —***vi***. miscalculate
	誤字	ゴジ	wrong letter; erratum; misprint
	誤診	ゴシン	incorrect diagnosis —***vi***. make an incorrect diagnosis; make an error in diagnosis
	誤報	ゴホウ	false report; misinformation
	誤訳	ゴヤク	mistranslation —***v***. mistranslate; make an error in translation
	誤用	ゴヨウ	misuse —***v***. misuse; use improperly
訓	誤る	あやまる	***v***. err; make a mistake
	誤り	あやまり	mistake; error

1687

誌 ⑭

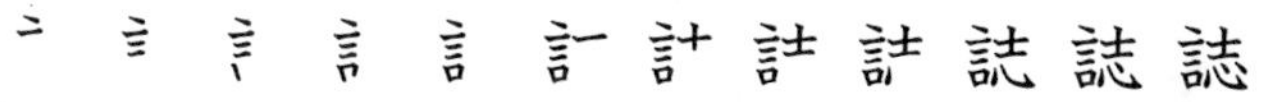

音	誌	シ	record; magazine
熟	誌上	シジョウ	in a magazine
	誌面	シメン	in a magazine

1688

説 ⑭

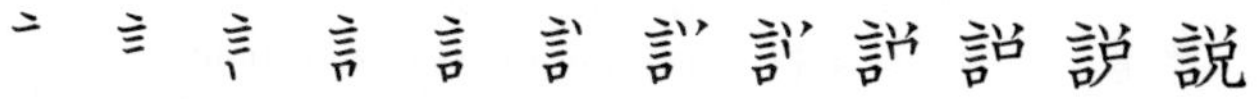

音	説	セツ	explain; view; theory; opinion
		（ゼイ）	explain; persuade
熟	説教	セッキョウ	preaching; sermon —***vi***. preach; sermonize
	説得	セットク	persuasion —***v***. persuade

	説明	セツメイ	explanation —*v*. explain
	説明文	セツメイブン	written explanation
	説話	セツワ	legend; tale; narrative
訓	説く	とく	*v*. explain; persuade

1689
読 ⑭

ニ 亖 言 言 言 訁 計 訃 訃 詰 読 読

音	読	ドク	read
		トク	read
		(トウ)	
熟	読点	トウテン	comma
	読経	ドキョウ	sutra-chanting —*vi*. chant sutras
	読者	ドクシャ	reader (of books)
	読書	ドクショ	reading —*vi*. read books
	読破	ドクハ	reading through a book —*v*. read/go through a book
	読本	トクホン	reader; reading book
訓	読む	よむ	*vt*. read; peruse; chant; recite
	読み	よみ	reading; judgment; calculation
	読み書き	よみかき	reading and writing
	読み方	よみかた	reading; pronunciation
	読み切る	よみきる	*vt*. read through; finish reading
	読み物	よみもの	reading; reading matter; literature

1690
認 ⑭

ニ 亖 言 言 言 訂 訒 訒 訒 認 認 認

音	認	ニン	recognize; approve; consent
熟	認可	ニンカ	sanction; approval; authorization; license; permission —*v*. approve; authorize; permit
	認識	ニンシキ	recognition; cognition; perception; knowledge; understanding —*v*. recognize; cognize; perceive; know; understand
	認証	ニンショウ	authentication; certification; validation; confirmation —*v*. certify; atest; authenticate; confirm
	認知	ニンチ	recognition; acknowledgment —*v*. recognize; acknowledge
	認定	ニンテイ	recognition; acknowledgment; identity —*v*. admit; recognize; find; deem

認容	ニンヨウ	admission; acknowledgment —*v*. admit; acknowledge; accept
訓 認める	みとめる	***vt***. see; witness; recognize; approve; accept; judge; conclude

1691

誘 ⑭

亠 言 言 言 言 訁 訁 訐 訐 詠 誘 誘

音 誘	ユウ	invite; induce; entice; lure
熟 誘引	ユウイン	enticement; inducement; attraction —*v*. entice; induce; attract
誘因	ユウイン	enticement; inducement —*v*. entice; induce; bring about; cause
誘拐	ユウカイ	abduction; kidnapping —*v*. abduct; kidnap
誘致	ユウチ	attraction; lure; enticement —*v*. attract; lure; entice
誘導	ユウドウ	guidance; induction; incitement —*v*. guide; induce; incite
誘発	ユウハツ	cause; inducement —*v*. cause; induce; give rise to
誘惑	ユウワク	temptation; seduction —*v*. tempt; seduce
訓 誘う	さそう	***vt***. tempt; entice; lure; invite
※誘う	いざなう	***vt***. invite; lead; entice
※誘く	おびく	***vt***. lure; entice

1692

謁 ⑮

亠 言 言 言 言 訂 訂 訂 謁 謁 謁 謁

音 謁	エツ	audience with (someone of importance)
熟 謁見	エッケン	audience with (someone in authority) —***vi***. have an audience with; be presented to

1693

課 ⑮

亠 言 言 言 言 訂 訂 訂 誀 課 課 課

音 課	カ	allot; section; impose
熟 課外	カガイ	extracurricular
課業	カギョウ	class lesson
課題	カダイ	subject; theme; problem; task; assignment
課長	カチョウ	section chief
課程	カテイ	curriculum

	課目	カモク	subject
訓	課す	かす	***vt***. impose; assign
¥	課税	カゼイ	imposition of taxes —***vi***. impose taxes
	課徴金	カチョウキン	surcharge

1694

諸 ⑮

ニ ミ 言 言 言一 計 計 訬 評 諸 諸 諸

音	諸	ショ	various
熟	諸行無常	ショギョウムジョウ	all things pass; everything is transient
	諸君	ショクン	Gentlemen!; Ladies and gentlemen!; Boys and girls!; Boys!
	諸芸	ショゲイ	accomplishments
	諸国	ショコク	various countries
	諸説	ショセツ	various views
	諸説紛々	ショセツフンプン	divided opinion on a subject
	諸島	ショトウ	archipelago; group of islands
訓	※諸々	もろもろ	various; all kinds/sorts; all

1695

請 ⑮

ニ ミ 言 言 言一 計 計 請 請 請 請 請

音	請	セイ (シン)	ask; request; invite
熟	請願	セイガン	petition; application —***v***. petition; apply
	請求	セイキュウ	claiming; demand; request —***v***. claim; demand; request
訓	請ける	うける	***vt***. receive; undertake; pay and take receipt of
	請け負い	うけおい	contracting
	請け書	うけショ	written acknowledgment
	請う	こう	***vt***. ask for
¥	請求書	セイキュウショ	bill; written claim

1696

諾 ⑮

ニ ミ 言 言 言一 計 計 訬 訬 諾 諾 諾

音	諾	ダク	consent
熟	諾否	ダクヒ	acceptance or refusal

1697

誕 ⑮

亠 言 言 言 訁 訁 訂 訃 証 証 証 誕

音	誕	タン	be born
熟	誕生	タンジョウ	birth; nativity —*vi*. be born; come into the world
	誕生日	タンジョウび	birthday

1698

談 ⑮

亠 言 言 言 言 訁 訁 訬 訬 談 談 談

音	談	ダン	talk; conversation; story; tale
熟	談じる	ダンじる	*vt*. talk
	談合	ダンゴウ	consultation; conference —*vi*. consult; confer
	談笑	ダンショウ	chat; intimate conversation —*vi*. chat
	談判	ダンパン	negotiation; bargaining —*vi*. negotiate; bargain
	談話	ダンワ	talk; conversation —*vi*. talk; chat; converse

1699

調 ⑮

亠 言 言 言 訁 訂 訂 訶 誀 調 調 調

音	調	チョウ	inspect; survey; examine; tune; tone; pitch
熟	調印	チョウイン	signing; signature; sealing —*vi*. sign; seal
	調教	チョウキョウ	horse training/breaking; train a wild animal —*v*. break in a horse; train a wild animal
	調合	チョウゴウ	compounding; mixing; preparation; concoction —*v*. compound; mix; prepare; concoct
	調査	チョウサ	examination; investigation; inquiry; survey; research —*v*. investigate; inquire; survey
	調子	チョウシ	tune; tone; key; way; manner; style; condition; order
	調子者	チョウシもの	person who is easily carried away
	調書	チョウショ	protocol; written evidence; record
	調整	チョウセイ	regulation; adjustment; correction; modulation; tuning —*v*. regulate; adjust; rectify; govern; control
	調節	チョウセツ	regulation; adjustment; control; governing —*v*. regulate; adjust; control; govern

	調達	チョウタツ	supply; procurement; provision —*v*. supply; provide; furnish; purvey; procure
	調停	チョウテイ	mediation; arbitration; intercession —*v*. mediate; arbitrate; intercede; intervene
	調度品	チョウドヒン	personal/household effects; furniture
	調髪	チョウハツ	hair dressing —*vi*. cut/style hair
	調味	チョウミ	seasoning; flavoring —*v*. season; flavor; spice
	調味料	チョウミリョウ	seasoning; flavoring
	調理	チョウリ	cooking; cookery —*v*. cook; arrange; organize
	調理師	チョウリシ	cook; chef
	調律	チョウリツ	tuning (a musical instrument) —*v*. tune (a musical instrument)
	調律師	チョウリツシ	piano tuner
	調和	チョウワ	harmony; accord; agreement —*v*. harmonize; match; agree; fit in well
訓	調べる	しらべる	***vt***. investigate; examine; survey; inspect; check
	調べ	しらべ	melody
	調う	ととのう	***vi***. be prepared/arranged/settled/concluded
	調える	ととのえる	***vt***. prepare; make ready; arrange; settle; conclude

1700

⑮

音	論	ロン	arguement; discussion; thesis
熟	論じる	ロンじる	***vt***. discuss; argue; dispute; debate
	論外	ロンガイ	out of the question; irrelevant
	論客	ロンカク (ロンキャク)	disputant; polemicist
	論議	ロンギ	discussion; argument —*v*. discuss; argue
	論及	ロンキュウ	reference —*vi*. refer to; mention
	論拠	ロンキョ	the grounds; basis (of a discussion)
	論告	ロンコク	prosecutor's summation —*v*. address (the court) for the last time
	論旨	ロンシ	point of an argument
	論述	ロンジュツ	statement; enunciation —*v*. set forth; enunciate; state
	論証	ロンショウ	proof/demonstration (by argument) —*v*. proof/demonstrate (by argument)
	論説	ロンセツ	editorial; dissertation
	論戦	ロンセン	verbal battle; war of words —*vi*. have a verbal battle; exchange views
	論争	ロンソウ	argument; dispute; controversy —*v*. argue; dispute

	論点	ロンテン	point at issue
	論破	ロンパ	refutation —*v*. refute
	論評	ロンピョウ	criticism; comment; review —*v*. criticize; comment; review
	論文	ロンブン	thesis; essay
	論弁	ロンベン	argument —*vi*. argue
	論法	ロンポウ	argument; reasoning; logic
	論理	ロンリ	logic
	論理的	ロンリテキ	logical

1701

諮 ⑯

音	諮	シ	consult
熟	諮問	シモン	inquiry; request for an inferior's opinion —*v*. consult; refer a problem to an inferior
	諮問機関	シモンキカン	advisory organ/body
訓	諮る	はかる	*vt*. consult; ask for advice

1702

謀 ⑯

音	謀	ボウ (ム)	plan; plot; devise; deceive
熟	謀議	ボウギ	conspiracy —*vi*. conspire
	謀殺	ボウサツ	premeditated murder —*v*. commit willful murder
	謀略	ボウリャク	plot; scheme
	謀反	ムホン	rebellion; insurrection
	謀反人	ムホンニン	rebel; conspirator
訓	謀る	はかる	*vt*. plan; plot; devise; deceive

1703

諭 ⑯

音	諭	ユ	admonish; remonstrate; warn; counsel
熟	諭告	ユコク	counsel; admonition —*vi*. advise; admonish
	諭旨	ユシ	admonition; instructions; explanation
訓	諭す	さとす	*vt*. admonish; remonstrate; warn; counsel; explain

1704
謡 ⑯

音	謡	ヨウ	song; Noh chanting
熟	謡曲	ヨウキョク	Noh song/chant
訓	謡	うたい	Noh chanting
	謡う	うたう	***vt.*** sing without accompaniment; chant

1705
謹 ⑰

音	謹	キン	discretion; prudence; modesty
熟	謹賀新年	キンガシンネン	Happy New Year
	謹慎	キンシン	good behavior —***v.*** conduct oneself well
	謹製	キンセイ	carefully produced
訓	謹む	つつしむ	***vt.*** be discrete/prudent/modest

1706
謙 ⑰

音	謙	ケン	modesty; humility
熟	謙虚	ケンキョ	modesty; humility
	謙譲	ケンジョウ	modesty; humility
	謙遜	ケンソン	modesty; humility —***vi.*** be modest/humble

1707
講 ⑰

音	講	コウ	lecture; speech; interpretation; training
熟	講じる	コウじる	***vt.*** lecture; give a speech; read out aloud; devise; workout
	講演	コウエン	lecture; address; discourse; talk —***vi.*** give a lecture; address; lecture
	講義	コウギ	lecture; exposition; explanation —***v.*** lecture on; give a lecture
	講師	コウシ	lecturer; speaker; reader; instructor
	講釈	コウシャク	storytelling; lecture —***v.*** lecture; explain

	講習	コウシュウ	short course; class
	講談	コウダン	storytelling; narration
	講堂	コウドウ	auditorium; lecture hall/theater
	講評	コウヒョウ	criticism; commentary; review —*v*. criticize; comment on; review
	講和	コウワ	peace; reconciliation —***vi***. make peace; bury the hatchet
	講話	コウワ	lecture; discourse; address —***vi***. lecture; deliver a lecture; address

1708

謝 ⑰

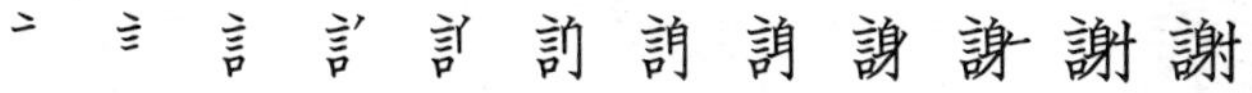

音	謝	シャ	thanks; apologize; decline; refuse
熟	謝する	しゃする	***vt***. thank a person for their help; apologize; decline; refuse
	謝意	シャイ	gratitude; thanks; apology
	謝恩	シャオン	expression of gratitude; appreciation
	謝罪	シャザイ	apology —***vi***. apologize; beg a person's forgiveness
	謝罪状	シャザイジョウ	written apology
	謝辞	シャジ	address of gratitude; a few words of thanks; apology
	謝状	シャジョウ	letter of thanks/apology
	謝絶	シャゼツ	refusal —*v*. refuse; decline
	謝礼	シャレイ	thanks; reward; renumeration
訓	謝る	あやまる	*v*. apologize

1709

識 ⑲

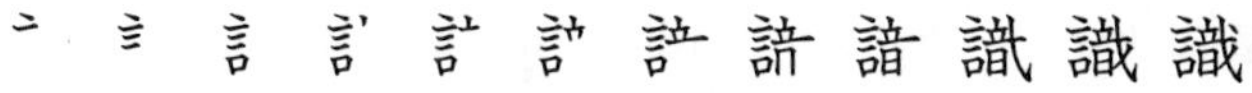

音	識	シキ	discern; sight; consciousness
熟	識見	シキケン	discernment; judgment; insight; view; opinion
	識者	シキシャ	intellectual; person of intelligence; intelligentsia
	識別	シキベツ	discrimination —*v*. discriminate; distinguish; tell apart

1710
譜 ⑲

音	譜	フ	music; note; staff; score
熟	譜代	フダイ	successive generations (of vassals)
	譜面	フメン	sheet music

1711
議 ⑳

音	議	ギ	talk over; consultation
熟	議する	ギする	***vt***. talk over; consult
	議案	ギアン	bill; measure; proposal for discussion
	議員	ギイン	elected representative; Diet member
	議院	ギイン	houses of parliament; lower and upper houses
	議会	ギカイ	assembly; national assembly; Diet
	議決	ギケツ	decision; resolution —***v***. decide; resolve; pass a vote
	議事	ギジ	proceedings; agenda
	議事堂	ギジドウ	Diet building
	議席	ギセキ	parlimentary seat
	議題	ギダイ	subject for discussion; agenda; program
	議長	ギチョウ	chairperson; president; speaker
	議論	ギロン	argument; discussion; debate; dispute —***v***. argue; discuss; debate; dispute
訓	議る	はかる	***vt***. consult; confer; deliberate
¥	議決権	ギケツケン	right to vote at a meeting; voting power (right)
	議決権信託証書	ギケツケンシンタクショウショ	voting trust certificate

1712
譲 ⑳

音	譲	ジョウ	transfer
熟	譲渡	ジョウト	conveyance; negotiation; assignment; transfer —***v***. hand over; transfer; assign
	譲歩	ジョウホ	compromise; concession —***vi***. compromise; concede; make a concession

訓	譲る	ゆずる	*vt*. hand over; transfer; sell; give; concede; save for later
	譲り	ゆずり	inheritance
	譲り合う	ゆずりあう	*vi*. make mutual concessions; compromise
	譲り受ける	ゆずりうける	*vt*. take over; obtain by transfer; inherit; buy
¥	譲渡制限	ジョウトセイゲン	restriction of transfer
	譲渡性預金	ジョウトセイヨキン	certificate of deposit (CD); negotiable deposit

1713

護 ⑳

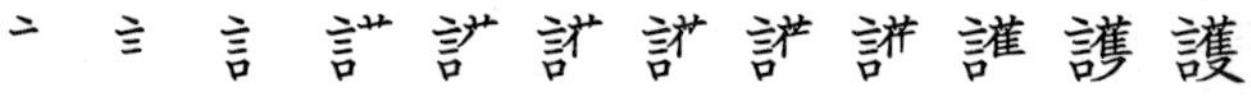

音	護	ゴ	protect; guard
熟	護衛	ゴエイ	bodyguard; escort —*v*. guard; escort
	護身	ゴシン	self-protection/-defense
	護送	ゴソウ	escort —*v*. escort; send under guard
訓	護る	まもる	*vt*. protect; guard

7 谷 たに valley

1714

谷 ⑦

音	谷	コク	valley; river valley; ravine
訓	谷	たに	valley
	谷底	たにぞこ	the bottom of ravine; valley floor
	谷間	たにま	ravine; gonge; chasm; valley

7 豆 まめ bean

1715

豆 ⑦

音	豆	ト (ズ)	bean

7

見角言谷●豆●豕貝赤走足⻊身車辛辰酉釆里臣舛

熟	豆乳	トウニュウ	soya milk
	豆腐	トウフ	tofu
訓	豆	まめ	bean; pea; soybean
	豆知識	まめチシキ	bits of knowledge/information
	豆鉄砲	まめデッポウ	popgun
	豆電球	まめデンキュウ	miniature/small bulb

1716

豊 ⑬ 丶 冂 巾 曲 曲 曲 曲 曲 曲 曹 曹 豊

音	豊	ホウ	abundant; rich
熟	豊艶	ホウエン	voluptuous; plentiful
	豊凶	ホウキョウ	rich or poor harvest; good or bad year
	豊作	ホウサク	good/abundant harvest
	豊熟	ホウジュク	ripening of crops —*vi*. (crops) ripen abundantly
	豊潤	ホウジュン	rich; abundant
	豊饒	ホウジョウ	fertile; productive
	豊年	ホウネン	fruitful/good year
	豊富	ホウフ	abundance; affluence
	豊満	ホウマン	plump; corpulent; full-figured
	豊漁	ホウリョウ	big/abundant catch (of fish)
訓	豊か	ゆたか	abundant; rich

7 豕 ぶた／いのこ pig

1717

豚 ⑪ 丿 刀 月 月 月 肝 肝 肟 肟 豚 豚

音	豚	トン	pig
熟	豚児	トンジ	*hum*. my son
訓	豚	ぶた	pig; swine

1718

象 ⑫ ノ ク ク 丹 丹 丹 争 争 旁 旁 象 象

音	象	ショウ	shape

	象	ゾウ	elephant
熟	象形	ショウケイ	hieroglyph
	象形文字	ショウケイモジ	hieroglyphic
	象徴	ショウチョウ	symbol —*v.* symbolize
	象徴的	ショウチョウテキ	symbolic
	象牙	ゾウゲ	ivory

1719

豪 ⑭

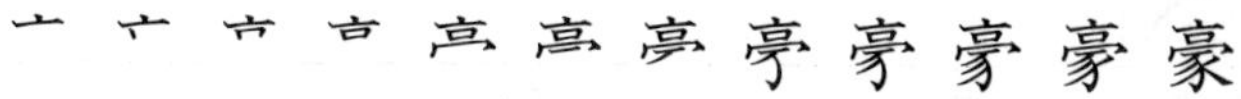

音	豪	ゴウ	mighty; splendor; grand; Australia
熟	豪雨	ゴウウ	heavy rain
	豪華	ゴウカ	gorgeousness; splendor; pomp; luxury
	豪傑	ゴウケツ	hero; great man
	豪語	ゴウゴ	boasting; big talk; bragging —*vi.* boast; talk big; brag
	豪州	ゴウシュウ	Australia
	豪勢	ゴウセイ	grand; great; magnificent
	豪壮	ゴウソウ	magnificence; splendor; grandeur
	豪遊	ゴウユウ	extravagant merry-making; orgy —*vi.* indulge in extravagant merry-making; go on a spree

7 貝 かい／かいへん shell

1720

貝 ⑦

音	貝	（バイ）	shellfish; shell
訓	貝	かい	shellfish; shell
	貝殻	かいがら	seashell
	貝細工	かいザイク	shellwork
	貝塚	かいづか	shell mound

1721

貞 ⑨

音	貞	テイ	chastity

熟	貞淑	テイシュク	chastity; female virtue
	貞女	テイジョ	chaste woman; woman of good virtue; faithful wife
	貞節	テイセツ	chastity; fidelity; faithfulness
	貞操	テイソウ	chastity; honor; virginity

1722

負 ⑨

ノ ⺈ ⺈ ⺈ ⺈ 缶 ⺈ 負 負

音	負	フ	bear; suffer; sustain; lose; be defeated
熟	負傷	フショウ	wound; injury —***vi***. be wounded; get injured
	負数	フスウ	***math***. minus/negative number
	負担	フタン	charge; responsibilty; burden; onus —***v***. bear; stand; shoulder; carry
訓	負ける	まける	***vi***. be defeated/beaten/overcome/daunted ***vt***. make something cheap
	負かす	まかす	***vt***. beat; defeat; vanquish; get the better of
	負う	おう	***vt***. bear; carry; be charged/accused of; suffer; sustain
¥	負債	フサイ	debt; liabilities; dues

1723

貢 ⑩

一 丅 工 干 于 于 盲 盲 貢 貢

音	貢	コウ （ク）	tribute; contribution; service
熟	貢献	コウケン	contribution; services —***vi***. contribute to; make a contribution to
訓	貢ぐ	みつぐ	***vt***. supply with money; finance

1724

貨 ⑪

ノ イ イ' 化 化 佇 佇 貨 貨 貨 貨

音	貨	カ	goods; coin
熟	貨客船	カキャクセン	cargo-passenger ship
	貨車	カシャ	freight car; goods wagon
¥	貨幣	カヘイ	money; coin; bill
	貨物	カモツ	goods; freight; cargo

1725

貫 ⑪

音	貫	カン	penetrate
熟	貫通	カンツウ	piercing; penetration —*v*. pierce; penetrate; pass through
	貫徹	カンテツ	accomplishment; achievement; attainment —*v*. accomplish; achieve; attain
	貫流	カンリュウ	flowing/running through —*vi*. flow/run through (a city)
	貫禄	カンロク	dignity; importance
訓	貫く	つらぬく	*vt*. pierce; penetrate; pass through; accomplish; attain
	貫	ぬき	brace

1726

⑪

音	責	セキ	condemn; censure; torture
熟	責任	セキニン	responsibility; liability
	責任感	セキニンカン	sense of responsibility
	責務	セキム	duty; obligation
訓	責める	せめる	*vt*. duty

1727

⑪

音	貧	ヒン	poverty
		ビン	poor
熟	貧窮	ヒンキュウ	poverty; poverty-stricken
	貧苦	ヒンク	poverty; hardship of poverty
	貧血	ヒンケツ	*med*. anemia —*vi*. be anemic; suffer from anemia
	貧困	ヒンコン	poverty *fig*. lack (of proper government, ideas, etc.)
	貧者	ヒンジャ	poor person; the poor
	貧弱	ヒンジャク	poverty; poor; weak; shabby; feeble; scanty; meager
	貧相	ヒンソウ	poor appearance; poor-looking
	貧富	ヒンプ	wealth and poverty; rich and poor

	貧乏	ビンボウ	poverty; poor —*vi*. be poor/badly off
	貧民	ヒンミン	the poor/needy
訓	貧しい	まずしい	poor

1728
賀 ⑫

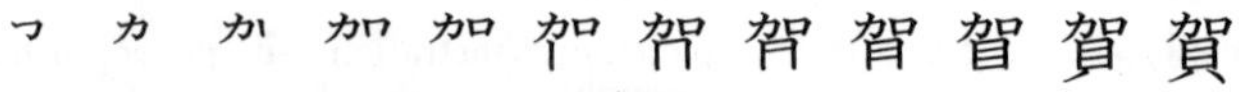

音	賀	ガ	congratulations
熟	賀春	ガシュン	spring greetings
	賀正	ガショウ	A Happy New Year!; New Year's greetings
	賀状	ガジョウ	greeting card; New Year's card

1729
貴 ⑫

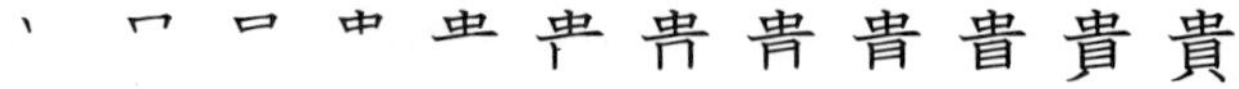

音	貴	キ	noble; precious; high
熟	貴金属	キキンゾク	precious metals
	貴族	キゾク	nobility; aristocracy
	貴重	キチョウ	valuable; precious
	貴重品	キチョウヒン	valuables
	貴賓	キヒン	honored guest
	貴婦人	キフジン	lady
訓	貴い	たっとい	noble; precious; exalted; valuable
	貴ぶ	たっとぶ	*vt*. respect; honor; value; esteem
	貴い	とうとい	noble; precious
	貴ぶ	とうとぶ	*vt*. respect; honor; value; esteem

1730
貸 ⑫

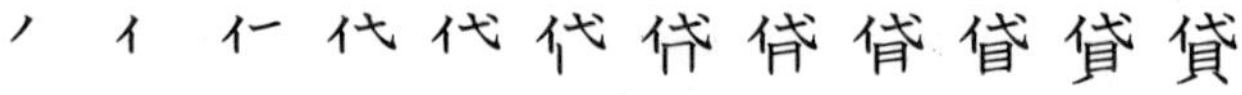

音	貸	タイ	lend
熟	貸借	タイシャク	debit and credit; lending and borrowing; loan —*v*. lend and borrow; debt and credit
	貸与	タイヨ	loan; lending —*v*. lend; lease; loan
訓	貸切	かしきり	reserved; chartered
	貸す	かす	*vt*. lend; give credit
¥	貸方勘定	かしかたカンジョウ	credit account

貸倒引当金	かしだおれ ひきあてキン	bad-debt reserve
貸出	かしだし	loan; advance
貸し付ける	かしつける	***vt***. lend
賃貸対照表	チンタイ タイショウヒョウ	balance sheet

1731

買 ⑫

音	買	バイ	buy
訓	買う	かう	***vt***. buy; purchase
	買い物	かいもの	purchases; shopping; bargain
¥	買い入れる	かいいれる	***vt***. buy (in); purchase
	買掛金	かいかけキン	accounts payable
	買い方	かいかた	buyer; purchaser; bulls; longs
	買い気配	かいキハイ (かいケハイ)	bid/bidding quotation
	買い越し	かいこし	on-balance buying
	買い支え	かいささえ	support buying/operation
	買い占める	かいしめる	***vt***. corner a market; buy up (all the goods)
	買いつなぎ	かいつなぎ	hedge-buying; hedging by buying
	買い手	かいて	buyer; purchaser; customer
	買い時	かいどき	best time to buy
	買い取り	かいとり	compulsory purchase; buy up
	買い主	かいぬし	buyer; purchaser
	買値	かいね	purchase/bid price
	買い場	かいば	buying opportunity
	買い控え	かいびかえ	hesitating; restrained purchasing
	買い戻し	かいもどし	redemption; repurchase; covering/short covering
	買価	バイカ	buying/purchase price
	買収	バイシュウ	acquisition; purchase; buying up; corruption; bribery —***v***. purchase; buy up; take over; corrupt; bribe

1732

費 ⑫

音	費	ヒ	expenses; cost
熟	費用	ヒヨウ	expenses; cost
訓	費やす	ついやす	***vt***. spend; waste; use up

	費える	ついえる	*vi.* be wasted/used up
¥	費目	ヒモク	item of expense

1733
貿 ⑫

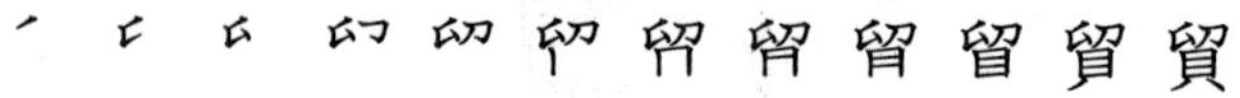

音	貿	ボウ	trade; exchange
熟	貿易風	ボウエキフウ	trade wind
¥	貿易	ボウエキ	trade; commerce —*vi.* trade; do business with
	貿易会社	ボウエキガイシャ	trading company
	貿易業	ボウエキギョウ	trading business; commerce
	貿易商	ボウエキショウ	trader
	貿易場	ボウエキジョウ	foreign market
	貿易摩擦	ボウエキマサツ	trade friction

1734
資 ⑬

音	資	シ	fund; nature; resources
熟	資格	シカク	qualification
	資源	シゲン	resources
	資材	シザイ	materials
	資質	シシツ	nature; one's nature
	資料	シリョウ	data; materials
	資力	シリョク	means; funds; money
¥	資金	シキン	funds; money
	資金運用	シキンウンヨウ	application of funds
	資金源	シキンゲン	source of funds
	資金調達	シキンチョウタツ	raising of funds
	資源	シゲン	resources
	資産	シサン	assets; property; means
	資産株	シサンかぶ	income stocks
	資産再評価	シサンサイヒョウカ	assets revaluation
	資産負債表	シサンフサイヒョウ	financial statement; statement of assets and liabilities
	資本	シホン	capital; funds; stockholder's equity
	資本家	シホンカ	capitalist
	資本回転率	シホンカイテンリツ	turnover of capital

資本金	シホンキン	capital
資本合計	シホンゴウケイ	total stockholder's equity
資本財	シホンザイ	capital goods
資本集約的産業	シホンシュウヤクテキサンギョウ	capital-intensive industry
資本主義	シホンシュギ	capitalism
資本準備金	シホンジュンビキン	legal capital surplus

1735
賃 ⑬

ノ イ 亻⁻ 仁 仟 任 任 侟 凭 凭 賃 賃

音	賃	チン	price; fare; fee; hire; wages; rent
熟	賃借	チンシャク	hire; hiring; lease —*v*. hire; lease; rent
	賃貸	チンタイ	lease; hiring out —*v*. lease; hire out
¥	賃上げ	チンあげ	wage increase —***vi***. increase/raise wages
	賃金	チンギン	wages; pay
	賃貸住宅	チンタイジュウタク	house to let; rental house
	賃貸料	チンタイリョウ	leasing charge; rent

1736
賛 ⑮

一 二 ≠ 夫 夫⁻ 夫⁼ 夫夫 夫夫 替 替 賛 賛

音	賛	サン	praise; dedication; inscription; tribute; help; support; agree
熟	賛意	サンイ	one's approval/assent
	賛歌	サンカ	song of praise; paean
	賛辞	サンジ	praise; tribute
	賛助	サンジョ	support; patronage —*v*. support; patronize
	賛成	サンセイ	approval; agreement —***vi***. approve; agree; support; favor
	賛同	サンドウ	approval; support; endorsement —***vi***. approve; support; endorse
	賛美	サンビ	praise; glorification —*v*. praise; glorify
	賛美歌	サンビカ	hymn
	賛否	サンピ	approval and disapproval; yes or no

1737
質 ⑮

音	質	シチ	pawn
		シツ	nature; disposition; temperament; matter; quality
		(チ)	
熟	質屋	シチや	pawnshop; pawnbroker
	質疑応答	シツギオウトウ	questions and answers —***vi***. have a question-and-answer session
	質実剛健	シツジツゴウケン	rough-hewn and robust
	質素	シッソ	simple; plain; modest
	質的	シツテキ	qualitative
	質点	シツテン	***phy***. particle
	質問	シツモン	question —***v***. question; ask questions
	質量	シツリョウ	mass; quality and quantity
訓	※質	たち	nature; disposition; temperament

1738

賞 ⑮

音	賞	ショウ	prize; reward
熟	賞金	ショウキン	prize money; prize; reward
	賞賛	ショウサン	praise; admiration —***v***. praise; admire; applaud
	賞状	ショウジョウ	certificate of merit; honorary certificate
	賞罰	ショウバツ	reward and punishment
	賞品	ショウヒン	prize; award
	賞味	ショウミ	relishment/enjoyment of food —***v***. relish; enjoy food
	賞与	ショウヨ	bonus; reward
訓	※賞める	ほめる	***vt***. praise; admire

1739

賓 ⑮

音	賓	ヒン	guest
熟	賓客	ヒンキャク (ヒンカク)	guest of honor; honored/distinguished guest; company

1740

賢 ⑯

音	賢	ケン	wise
熟	賢人	ケンジン	wise man; sage
	賢明	ケンメイ	wise; advisable
訓	賢い	かしこい	clever; wise; smart

1741

財 ⑩

音	財	ザイ (サイ)	property; finance; business
熟	財界人	ザイカイジン	big businessman; financier
	財布	サイフ	purse; pocketbook; wallet
	財宝	ザイホウ	treasures; riches
	財力	ザイリョク	financial power
¥	財界	ザイカイ	financial world/circles
	財形貯蓄	ザイケイチョチク	workers property accumulation savings
	財源	ザイゲン	source of revenue; financial resources
	財産	ザイサン	estate; property; fortune
	財政	ザイセイ	public finance; finances
	財団	ザイダン	foundation
	財団法人	ザイダンホウジン	foundation; nonprofit corporation
	財テク	ザイテク	financial technique/technology
	財閥	ザイバツ	*zaibatsu* (financial conglomerate)
	財務諸表	ザイムショヒョウ	financial statements

1742

 ⑪

音	販	ハン	deal
¥	販売	ハンバイ	sale; selling; marketing —*v.* sell; market; deal in; handle
	販路	ハンロ	market (for goods); outlet

1743
貯 ⑫

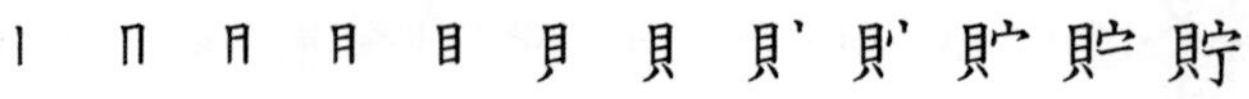

音	貯	チョ	store; stock; save; savings
熟	貯金	チョキン	savings; deposit —***vi***. save money; put money by
	貯水	チョスイ	storage of water; impoundment; reservoir water
	貯水池	チョスイチ	reservoir
	貯蔵	チョゾウ	storage; storing; preservation —***v***. store; put aside; conserve; preserve
	貯蓄	チョチク	saving; storing up; savings —***v***. save; store; put aside
訓	貯える	たくわえる	***vt***. save; store; conserve
	貯める	ためる	***vt***. save; store

1744
賊 ⑬

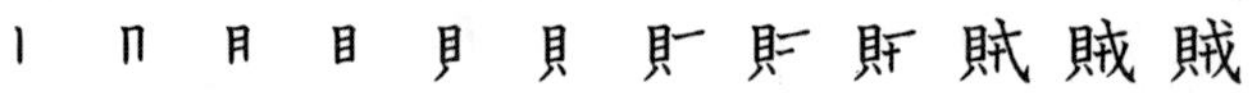

音	賊	ゾク	rebel; robber
熟	賊軍	ゾクグン	rebel army; rebels
	賊子	ゾクシ	rebel; traitor
	賊徒	ゾクト	rebels; traitors

1745
賄 ⑬

音	賄	ワイ	pay; cover
熟	賄賂	ワイロ	bribe; bribery
訓	賄う	まかなう	***vt***. obtain; provide (food); carry out (household chores)

1746
賜 ⑮

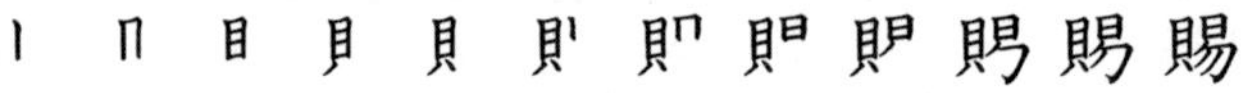

音	賜	シ	gift
熟	賜暇	シカ	leave; leave of absence
訓	賜る	たまわる	***vt***. ***hum***. receive; get
	賜物	たまもの	***hum***. gift received

1747
賠 ⑮

音	賠	バイ	indemnify
熟	賠償	バイショウ	reparation; indemnity; compensation —*v*. indemnify; compensate

1748
賦 ⑮

音	賦	フ	tribute; payment; installment
熟	賦課	フカ	levy; assessment; imposition —*v*. levy; assess; impose
	賦与	フヨ	inate; endowed; blessed —*v*. grant; give

1749
購 ⑰

音	購	コウ	purchase; buy; procure
熟	購読	コウドク	subscription —*v*. subscribe; take a newspaper, etc.
	購入	コウニュウ	purchase; buying —*v*. purchase; buy; procure
	購買	コウバイ	purchase; buying —*v*. purchase; buy; procure
訓	※購う	あがなう	***vt***. purchase; buy

1750
贈 ⑱

音	贈	ゾウ	present; give; bestow
		(ソウ)	present
熟	贈収賄	ゾウシュウワイ	bribery
	贈呈	ゾウテイ	presentation; gift —*v*. make a presentation; offer a gift
	贈答	ゾウトウ	exchange of gifts —*v*. exchange gifts
	贈与	ゾウヨ	donation; gift —*v*. donate; make a gift
	贈賄	ゾウワイ	bribery —*v*. bribe
訓	贈る	おくる	***vt***. present; give; bestow
	贈り物	おくりもの	gift; present

7 赤 あかい red

1751
赤 ⑦ 一 十 土 ナ 赤 赤 赤

音	赤	セキ （シャク）	red
熟	赤銅	シャクドウ	gold-copper alloy
	赤外線	セキガイセン	infrared rays
	赤心	セキシン	sincerity; true heart
	赤道	セキドウ	equator
	赤飯	セキハン	rice with red beans
	赤貧	セキヒン	dire poverty
	赤面	セキメン	blush —*vi*. blush; go red in the cheeks
	赤裸々	セキララ	frank; outspoken; stark naked
	赤痢	セキリ	dysentery
	赤化	セッカ	making Communist —*v*. make Communist
	赤血球	セッケッキュウ	red corpuscles
訓	赤	あか	red
	赤字	あかジ	deficit; in the red
	赤ちゃん	あかちゃん	baby
	赤帽	あかボウ	redcap; luggage porter
	赤い	あかい	red
	赤らむ	あからむ	***vi***. become red; blush
	赤らめる	あからめる	***vt***. make red
¥	赤字	あかジ	deficit; balance (figure) in the red; loss
	赤字国債	あかジコクサイ	bond issued for deficit financing; deficit bond
	赤字財政	あかジザイセイ	deficit spending (by the government); deficit finance

1752
赦 ⑪ 一 十 土 ナ 赤 赤 赤 赤 赤 赦 赦

音	赦	シャ	pardon
熟	赦免	シャメン	pardon —*v*. pardon; remit

1753

走 ⑦

一 十 土 キ 丰 未 走

音	走	ソウ	run; run away
熟	走者	ソウシャ	runner
	走破	ソウハ	running the whole distance —***vi***. run the whole distance
	走法	ソウホウ	form of running; running style
	走馬灯	ソウまトウ	revolving lantern
	走路	ソウロ	running track/course
訓	走る	はしる	***vi***. run; run away
	走り書き	はしりがき	scribbling —***v***. scribble; write hurriedly

1754

赴 ⑨

一 十 土 キ 丰 未 走 赴 赴

音	赴	フ	go
熟	赴任	フニン	one's place of appointment; one's new post —***vi***. start one's new post
訓	赴く	おもむく	***vi***. go; proceed towards; get; become

1755

起 ⑩

一 十 土 キ 丰 未 走 起 起 起

音	起	キ	get up; be stirred up; happen
熟	起因	キイン	origin; cause; attribute —***vi***. originate in; be caused by; be attributable to
	起源	キゲン	origin; beginning; source
	起工	キコウ	start of construction work —***vi***. begin construction
	起床	キショウ	rising in the morning; getting up —***vi***. rise; get up
	起訴	キソ	prosecution; indictment; litigation —***v***. prosecute; indict
	起草	キソウ	drafting —***v***. draft; draw up
	起点	キテン	starting point

	起用	キヨウ	appointment; employment —*v*. appoint; employ
	起立	キリツ	rising; standing up —*vi*. rise; stand up
訓	起きる	おきる	*vi*. get up; rise
	起こす	おこす	*vt*. raise up; awake; bring about; wake up
	起こる	おこる	*vi*. happen; come to pass
¥	起債	キサイ	issue of bonds
	起債市場	キサイシジョウ	bond issuance market

1756

越 ⑫

一 十 土 キ 丰 赱 走 走 赱 赵 越 越

音	越	エツ	cross; go to excess; pass over; exceed
熟	越境	エッキョウ	violation of a border; border jumping —*vi*. jump/violate a border
	越権	エッケン	exceeding one's authority; abuse of power
	越冬	エットウ	spending the winter —*vi*. pass the winter; winter
	越年	エツネン	seeing the old year out —*vi*. see the old year out
訓	越える	こえる	*vi*. cross; go across; pass; go over; exceed
	越す	こす	*vt*. cross; go over; exceed; pass; surpass

1757

超 ⑫

一 十 土 キ 丰 赱 走 起 起 超 超 超

音	超	チョウ	exceed; excel; (prefix) super-; ultra-
熟	超越	チョウエツ	transcendence; transcendancy —*vi*. transcend; rise above; be superior
	超音速	チョウオンソク	supersonic speed
	超音波	チョウオンパ	supersonic waves
	超過	チョウカ	excess; surplus —*v*. exceed; be over
	超自然	チョウシゼン	supernaturalness
	超人	チョウジン	superman
	超然	チョウゼン	unworldliness
	超大国	チョウタイコク	superpower
	超特急	チョウトッキュウ	super express (train)
	超満員	チョウマンイン	overflowing with people; filled beyond capacity
訓	超える	こえる	*vi*. cross; go across; exceed; pass; go over
	超す	こす	*vt*. cross; go over; pass; spend; tide over; pass; exceed; surpass

1758
趣 ⑮

一 土 キ キ 走 走 走 赶 赶 趄 趣 趣

音	趣	シュ	taste
熟	趣意	シュイ	purpose; aim; point; purport
	趣意書	シュイショ	prospectus
	趣向	シュコウ	idea; plan
	趣旨	シュシ	purpose; aim
	趣味	シュミ	taste; liking; hobby
訓	趣	おもむき	import; effect; contents; air; looks; appearances; taste; elegance

7 足 ⻊ あし／あしへん leg

1759
足 ⑦

丶 口 口 早 早 足 足

音	足	ソク	foot; leg; suffice; add
熟	足下	ソッカ	at one's foot; you
	足跡	ソクセキ（あしあと）	footprint
	足労	ソクロウ	trouble of coming
訓	足	あし	leg; foot
	足音	あしおと	sound of footsteps
	足首	あしくび	ankle
	足場	あしば	foothold; scaffold
	足元	あしもと	at one's feet
	足す	たす	***vt***. add; supply
	足りる	たりる	***vi***. be enough; suffice
	足る	たる	***vi***. be enough; suffice
	※足袋	たび	*tabi* (Japanese socks)

1760
距 ⑫

丶 口 口 早 早 足 足 趴 趴 距 距 距

音	距	キョ	distance; interval; space
熟	距離	キョリ	distance; interval; space between two places

1761

跡 ⑬

音 跡 セキ footprint

訓 跡 あと trace; ruins; remains
跡継ぎ あとつぎ inheritor; heir; successor
跡取り あととり inheritor; heir; successor

1762

践 ⑬

音 践 セン do

1763

跳 ⑬

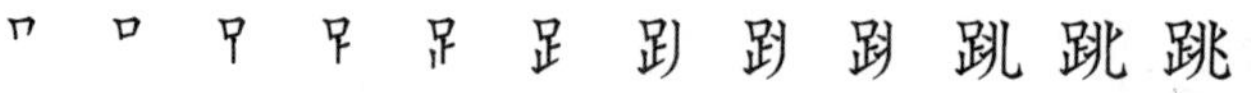

音 跳 チョウ leap

熟 跳躍 チョウヤク jump; spring; skip —***vi***. spring; jump; leap; skip; prance

訓 跳ぶ とぶ ***vi***. leap; jump; skip
跳ねる はねる ***vi***. leap; skip; jump

1764

路 ⑬

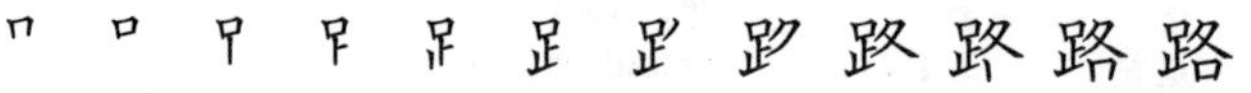

音 路 ロ road; path; way

熟 路肩 ロかた edge of a road
路地 ロジ alley; lane; path
路上 ロジョウ on the road
路頭 ロトウ road side; wayside
路傍 ロボウ roadside; wayside
路面 ロメン road surface

訓 路 じ road; path; way
※路 みち road; path; way

1765

踊 ⑭

ｍ ロ 卩 ⻊ 𧾷 ... 踊

音	踊	ヨウ	dance
訓	踊る	おどる	***vi***. dance
	踊り	おどり	dance; dancing
	踊り子	おどりこ	dancer; dancing girl
	踊り場	おどりば	dance hall/floor; landing; halfpace

1766

踏 ⑮

音	踏	トウ	step
熟	踏査	トウサ	survey; exploration; investigation —***v***. survey; explore; investigate
	踏襲	トウシュウ	following; continuing; carrying on with —***v***. follow in someone's footsteps
	踏破	トウハ	traveling on foot —***v***. traverse; travel on foot; hike; travel all over
訓	踏む	ふむ	***vt***. step; trample; tread; value; experience
	踏まえる	ふまえる	***vt***. step/stand on; be based on
	踏み絵	ふみエ	*fumie* (copper tablet with a religious image on it to be trodden on to prove oneself a non-Christian) ***fig***. loyalty test
	踏切	ふみきり	railway crossing
	踏み台	ふみダイ	step; stool; footstool
	踏み段	ふみダン	step; stair
¥	踏み	ふみ	short covering at a loss

1767

躍 ㉑

音	躍	ヤク	jump; leap; hop
熟	躍進	ヤクシン	advance by leaps and bounds —***vi***. rush; make a dash
	躍動	ヤクドウ	lively motion —***vi***. move lively/actively
	躍起	ヤッキ	excitement; enthusiasm
訓	躍る	おどる	***vi***. leap; hop

7 身 み body

1768
身 ⑦

丿 丨 亻 门 自 身 身

音	身	シン	body
熟	身上	シンジョウ	personal reasons; merit; asset
	身上書	シンジョウショ	personal information form
	身上持ち	シンショウもち	fortune; wealthy person; housekeeper; handling the household budget
	身心	シンシン	body and mind
	身体	シンタイ	body; physical; bodily
	身体検査	シンタイケンサ	physical examination; medical check-up; search; frisking —*vi*. have a check-up; be searched/frisked
	身体障害者	シンタイショウガイシャ	physically handicapped/disabled person
	身長	シンチョウ	height; stature
	身辺	シンペン	personal
訓	身	み	body; position; place; status
	身内	みうち	relative; family; fellow; all over the body
	身重	みおも	pregnant; expecting; with child
	身勝手	みがって	selfish
	身構え	みがまえ	posture; attitude
	身柄	みがら	person; one's social position
	身軽	みがる	light; agile; nimble
	身代わり	みがわり	subsitution; substitute
	身近	みぢか	near/close to oneself
	身投げ	みなげ	suicide by drowning or jumping —*vi*. drown oneself; throw oneself from a high place
	身の上	みのうえ	history; personal circumstances
	身振り	みぶり	gesture; motion
	身震い	みぶるい	shudder; shiver; trembling —*vi*. shudder; shiver; tremble
	身分	みブン	social position; rank; means; circumstances; birth
	身元	みもと	one's identity; background
	身元引受人	みもとひきうけニン	surety; guarantor; guarantee

7 車 くるま／くるまへん car

1769

車 ⑦

音	車	シャ	car; vehicle
熟	車間距離	シャカンキョリ	the distance between two cars
	車検	シャケン	car inspection; safety check on a motor vehicle
	車庫	シャコ	garage; car port; bus depot
	車軸	シャジク	wheel axle
	車種	シャシュ	type/model of car
	車掌	シャショウ	conductor (on a bus or train)
	車線	シャセン	traffic lane
	車窓	シャソウ	car/train window
	車体	シャタイ	the body of a car; bicycle frame
	車中	シャチュウ	in a train/car
	車道	シャドウ	roadway; road
	車内	シャナイ	in a car/train
	車両	シャリョウ	cars; vehicles; rolling stock; coach; car; carriage
	車輪	シャリン	wheel
訓	車	くるま	wheel; vehicle; car
	車椅子	くるまイス	wheelchair
	車座	くるまザ	sitting in a circle
	車酔い	くるまよい	carsickness

1770

軌 ⑨

音	軌	キ	track; rule; railway line; norm
熟	軌跡	キセキ	locus (in geometry)
	軌道	キドウ	orbit; railway track

1771

軍 ⑨

音	軍	グン	military; army; soldiers

熟	軍医	グンイ	military physician; army doctor; medic
	軍艦	グンカン	warship; battleship
	軍港	グンコウ	naval station
	軍国主義	グンコクシュギ	militarism
	軍事	グンジ	naval and military; military
	軍資金	グンシキン	war/campaign funds
	軍縮	グンシュク	arms reduction —*vi*. reduce arms/military expenditure
	軍人	グンジン	soldier; serviceman; service woman
	軍隊	グンタイ	troops; forces; army
	軍配	グンバイ	stratagem; tactics
	軍備	グンビ	armaments; military preparation

1772

⑩

音	軒	ケン	eaves
訓	軒	のき	eaves; edge of the roof
	軒先	のきさき	along the eaves; in front of the houses
	軒下	のきした	under the eaves

1773

転 ⑪

音	転	テン	roll; tumble; move
熟	転じる	テンじる	*v*. turn round; revolve; rotate; shift; alter; convert; remove
	転位	テンイ	transposition; dislocation; displacement
	転移	テンイ	change; transition; transfer —*v*. change; transfer
	転化	テンカ	change; transformation; inversion; conversion —*vi*. change; be transformed/inverted
	転回	テンカイ	revolution; rotation; evolution —*v*. revolve; rotate; evolve
	転換	テンカン	conversion; switch; turnabout; diversion —*v*. convert; switch to; divert; turn
	転換期	テンカンキ	turning point
	転記	テンキ	copying information into another (family) register —*v*. copy information into another (family) register
	転機	テンキ	turning point; point of change

7

見角言谷豆豕貝赤走足⻊身車●辛辰酉釆里臣舛

転居	テンキョ	moving; change of address —***vi***. move; change one's address
転業	テンギョウ	change of trade; change of occupation —***vi***. change one's employment/trade
転勤	テンキン	transferal (to another city, etc.) —***vi***. be transferred (to another city, etc.)
転向	テンコウ	conversion; turn; turning —***vi***. turn; be converted; abandon an idea
転校	テンコウ	change of schools —***vi***. change one's school
転載	テンサイ	reproduction; reprinting —***v***. reproduce; reprint
転写	テンシャ	transference; copying; transcription —***v***. transfer; copy; transcribe
転出	テンシュツ	transfer out; moving out —***vi***. be transferred out; move out
転職	テンショク	change of occupation —***vi***. change one's occupation
転身	テンシン	turnover; complete change —***vi***. change over; change completely
転成	テンセイ	transformation; transmutation —***vi***. be transformed; change into
転送	テンソウ	transmission; forwarding —***v***. transmit; forward; send on
転地	テンチ	moving away for a change of air; trying a change of climate —***vi***. go somewhere for a change of air; try a change of air
転調	テンチョウ	modulation (music); transition —***vi***. modulate
転々	テンテン	from one place to another; from hand to hand —***vi***. go from one place to another; pass from hand-to-hand
転倒	テントウ	violent fall; inversion; reversal; upset —***v***. fall down; invert; reverse; lose one's head
転入	テンニュウ	transference in; moving in —***vi***. be transfered in; move into
転任	テンニン	transferal (to another city, etc.) —***vi***. be transferred (to another city, etc.)
転変	テンペン	mutation; change
転用	テンヨウ	diversion —***v***. divert; convert
転落	テンラク	fall; degradation —***vi***. fall; have a fall; degrade
訓 転がす	ころがす	***vt***. roll; trundle
転がる	ころがる	***vi***. roll; tumble; fall; lie down
転げる	ころげる	***vi***. roll; tumble; fall
転ばす	ころばす	***vt***. roll over; knock down
転ぶ	ころぶ	***vi***. roll; tumble; fall over
¥ 転換社債	テンカンシャサイ	convertible bond (CB)
転売	テンバイ	resale —***v***. resell

1774

軟 ⑪

音	軟	ナン	soft
熟	軟化	ナンカ	soften; mollification —*v*. soften; tone down; be mollified
	軟球	ナンキュウ	soft ball
	軟膏	ナンコウ	ointment; salve
	軟骨	ナンコツ	cartilage; gristle
	軟弱	ナンジャク	weakness; effeminacy
	軟水	ナンスイ	soft water
	軟派	ナンパ	moderate party; light/erotic literature; playing around with women —*v*. play around with women
訓	軟らかい	やわらかい	soft; tender; limp; plastic
	軟らか	やわらか	soft; tender

1775

⑫

音	軽	ケイ	light; light-hearted; slight; easy; casual
熟	軽音楽	ケイオンガク	light/easy-listening music
	軽快	ケイカイ	light; cheerful; casual
	軽金属	ケイキンゾク	light metals
	軽減	ケイゲン	reduction; commutation; alleviation —*v*. reduce; commute; lighten; alleviate; relieve; ease
	軽視	ケイシ	making light of; slighting; belittling —*v*. make light of; slight; belittle
	軽傷	ケイショウ	slight injury/wound
	軽症	ケイショウ	slight illness; mild case
	軽少	ケイショウ	slight; trifling
	軽食	ケイショク	light meal; snack
	軽震	ケイシン	light earthquake; earth tremor
	軽装	ケイソウ	light/casual dress —*vi*. be lightly/casually dressed
	軽卒	ケイソツ	rashness; haste; carelessness; imprudence
	軽度	ケイド	slight
	軽薄	ケイハク	thoughtlessness; frivolity; flippancy; imprudence
	軽蔑	ケイベツ	contempt; scorn; disdain —*v*. contempt; scorn
	軽妙	ケイミョウ	smart; witty
訓	軽い	かるい	light; agile; slight; mild; easy

	軽やか	かろやか	lightly
	軽んじる	かろんじる	***vt***. look down upon; make light of
¥	軽工業	ケイコウギョウ	light industry
	軽油	ケイユ	light oil

1776

軸 ⑫

音	軸	ジク	spindle; axle; pivot; scroll; holder

1777

⑬

音	較	カク	compare
訓	※較べる	くらべる	***vt***. compare; contrast

1778

載 ⑬

音	載	サイ	load; write
訓	載せる	のせる	***vt***. put on; place; load; publish; carry (an article in a newspaper)
	載る	のる	***vi***. appear; be printed/carried (in a newspaper)

1779

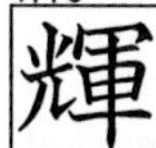

⑮

音	輝	キ	shine; glitter; brilliant
訓	輝かしい	かがやかしい	bright; brilliant; shiny
	輝かす	かがやかす	***vt***. light up; brighten; glorify
	輝き	かがやき	brilliancy; radiance; brightness; glow
	輝く	かがやく	***vi***. shine; sparkle; gleam; be brilliant

1780

輩 ⑮

音	輩	ハイ	fellow; people

見角言谷豆豕貝赤走足⻊身●車辛辰酉釆里臣舛

熟	輩出	ハイシュツ	in succession; in great numbers —***vi***. appear in succession/one after another

1781

輪 ⑮

音	輪	リン	wheel; circle; rotate; (counter for flowers/ wheels)
熟	輪禍	リンカ	traffic accident
	輪郭	リンカク	outline; facial features; contours
	輪姦	リンカン	gang rape; gangbang —***v***. gangrape; gangbang
	輪唱	リンショウ	canon (in music); round —***v***. sing a canon
	輪状	リンジョウ	circular; ring-shaped
	輪転	リンテン	rotation; revolution
	輪転機	リンテンキ	rotary press
	輪読	リンドク	reading a book in turns —***v***. take turns reading a book
	輪廻	リンネ	transmigration of souls
	輪番	リンバン	rotation; taking turns
訓	輪	わ	ring; wheel; circle; hoop; loop
	輪切り	わぎり	round slices

1782

輸 ⑯

音	輸	ユ	transport; send
熟	輸血	ユケツ	blood transfusion —***vi***. give a blood transfusion
	輸出	ユシュツ	exports —***v***. export
	輸送	ユソウ	transport —***v***. transport; convey; carry; forward
	輸入	ユニュウ	imports —***v***. import
¥	輸出入銀行	ユシュツニュウギンコウ	export-import bank

1783

轄 ⑰

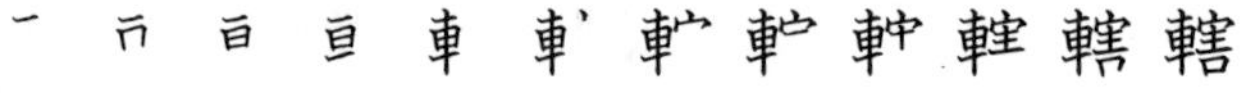

音	轄	カツ	jurisdiction
訓	轄	くさび	wedge; tie

7 辛 からい bitter

1784

辛 ⑦ 丶 亠 亡 立 立 辛 辛

音	辛	シン	pungent; bitter
熟	辛苦	シンク	hardship; trials; pains
	辛酸	シンサン	hardships; trials and tribulations
	辛勝	シンショウ	narrow victory; close margin —*vi*. win by a close margin
	辛抱	シンボウ	endurance; patience; staying power —*vi*. endure; be patient; perservere; bear; stand; hold out
	辛辣	シンラツ	biting; caustic; sharp; scathing; severe
訓	辛い	からい	hot; pungent; salty; spicy
	辛口	からくち	dry; hot
	辛子	からシ	mustard
	辛味	からミ	sharp/salty taste

1785

辞 ⑬ ノ 二 千 千 舌 舌 舌' 舌' 舌' 辞 辞 辞

音	辞	ジ	word; address; resign; give up
熟	辞する	ジする	*vi*. resign; give up (one's post)
	辞意	ジイ	intention to resign
	辞書	ジショ	dictionary; lexicon; thesaurus
	辞職	ジショク	resignation; giving up one's job —*vi*. resign one's post; hand in one's notice; give up work
	辞世	ジセイ	one's dying poem; one's death
	辞退	ジタイ	declination; refusal —*v*. refuse; decline; turn down
	辞典	ジテン	dictionary
	辞任	ジニン	resignation; notice —*v*. resign; hand in one's resignation
	辞表	ジヒョウ	one's resignation
	辞令	ジレイ	written appointment to a position
訓	辞める	やめる	*vi*. resign; retire; give up
	※辞	ことば	word; phrase

7 辰 しんのたつ small dragon

1786

⑩

音	辱	ジョク	humiliation
訓	辱める	はずかしめる	*vt.* humiliate; insult; disgrace someone; bring disrepute; violate; rape
	辱め	はずかしめ	humiliation; disgrace

1787

⑬

音	農	ノウ	cultivate; farming; agriculture
熟	農園	ノウエン	farm; plantation
	農家	ノウカ	farmhouse; farming family
	農閑期	ノウカンキ	farmer's slack season
	農機具	ノウキグ	agricultural implement
	農業	ノウギョウ	farming; agriculture
	農業国	ノウギョウコク	farming country
	農具	ノウグ	farm implements
	農耕	ノウコウ	farming; agriculture
	農作	ノウサク	cultivation of land; tillage of soil; farming
	農作物	ノウサクモツ (ノウサクブツ)	crops; farm produce
	農産物	ノウサンブツ	farm produce; agricultural products
	農場	ノウジョウ	farm
	農村	ノウソン	farm village; rural community
	農地	ノウチ	farm/agricultural land
	農地改革	ノウチカイカク	farmland/agrarian reform
	農繁期	ノウハンキ	farming season
	農夫	ノウフ	farmer
	農民	ノウミン	farmers
	農薬	ノウヤク	agricultural chemicals
	農林	ノウリン	agriculture and forestry
¥	農協 (農業協同組合)	ノウキョウ (ノウギョウキョウドウくみあい)	agricultural cooperative

農相	ノウショウ	Minister of Agriculture, Forestery, and Fisheries
農林水産省	ノウリン スイサンショウ	Ministry of Agriculture, Forestery, and Fisheries

7 酉 さけづくり／とりへん liquor; sake

1788

酌 ⑩ 一 丅 冂 丙 襾 西 酉 酉' 酌 酌

音	酌	シャク	serve saké
熟	酌量	シャクリョウ	consideration; allowance —*v.* take into consideration; make allowance for
訓	酌む	くむ	***vt.*** pour out wine

1789

酒 ⑩ 丶 ⺀ 氵 氵一 汀 沂 洒 洒 酒 酒

音	酒	シュ	saké; wine; liquor
熟	酒宴	シュエン	feast; banquet
	酒気	シュキ	smell of alcohol
	酒豪	シュゴウ	heavy drinker
	酒色	シュショク	wine and women
	酒精	シュセイ	alcohol
	酒造	シュゾウ	saké brewing; wine making; distilling
訓	酒	さけ	rice wine; saké; liquor
	酒癖	さけぐせ	one's behavior when drunk
	酒飲み	さけのみ	drinker
	酒	さか	rice wine; saké; liguor
	酒蔵	さかぐら	room for storing saké
	酒代	さかダイ	beer money; money for drinks
	酒樽	さかだる	wine casket; beer barrel
	酒場	さかば	bar; pub
	酒盛り	さかもり	drinking party
	酒屋	さかや	wine shop; liquor store

1790

配 ⑩

一 厂 冂 币 西 西 酉 酉 酉 配

音	配	ハイ	distribute
熟	配する	ハイする	***vt***. allot; arrange; match; exile; place under
	配下	ハイカ	followers; subordinates
	配給	ハイキュウ	distribution; supply; rationing —***v***. distribute; supply; deal out; ration
	配偶者	ハイグウシャ	spouse
	配合	ハイゴウ	combination; harmony; match; mixture; blending —***v***. combine; distribute; arrange; match; tone
	配車	ハイシャ	car allocation —***v***. alllocate cars
	配色	ハイショク	color scheme
	配水	ハイスイ	water supply —***vi***. supply/distribute water
	配線	ハイセン	electric wiring —***vi***. wire (a house) for electricity
	配属	ハイゾク	assignment; job allocation —***v***. assign (a person to a position)
	配達	ハイタツ	delivery —***v***. deliver
	配置	ハイチ	arrangement; disposition; posting; placement —***v***. arrange; distribute; post; station; detail
	配電	ハイデン	supply of electric power; power distribution —***vi***. supply electricity; distribute power
	配布	ハイフ	distribution —***v***. distribute
	配付	ハイフ	distribution; division; handing out —***v***. distribute; give/hand out
	配分	ハイブン	distribution; division; allotment; allocation —***v***. distribute; divide; share; allot; allocate
	配役	ハイヤク	the cast; casting
	配慮	ハイリョ	consideration; attention; care; concern; anxiety; trouble —***v***. give consideration/attention to; be concerned/troubled
	配列	ハイレツ	arrangement; disposal; grouping —***v***. arrange; dispose; put in order; array
訓	配る	くばる	***vt***. distribute; deliver; hand out
¥	配当	ハイトウ	allotment; share; cut; dividend —***v***. allocate dividends
	配当率	ハイトウリツ	dividend rate

1791
酔 ⑪

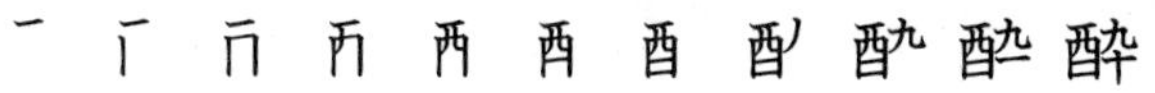

音	酔	スイ	get drunk
熟	酔客	スイカク	drunkard
	酔漢	スイカン	drunkard
	酔狂	スイキョウ	whimsical; freakish; capricious; eccentric
	酔態	スイタイ	drunkenness; intoxication; tipsiness
訓	酔う	よう	***vi***. get drunk; become intoxicated; feel sick; be poisoned
	酔っ払い	よっぱらい	drunkard; boozer
	酔っ払う	よっぱらう	***vi***. get drunk/tipsy/intoxicated

1792
酢 ⑫

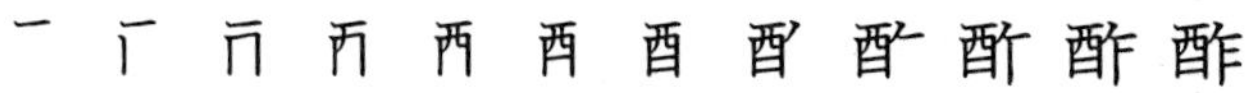

音	酢	サク	vinegar
熟	酢酸	サクサン	***chem***. acetic acid
訓	酢	す	vinegar

1793
酬 ⑬

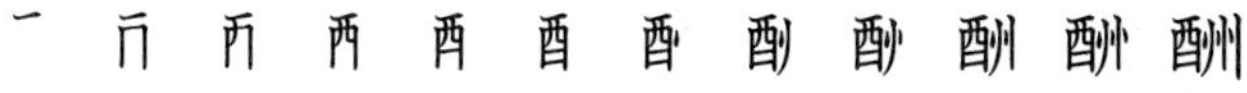

音	酬	シュウ	reward

1794
酪 ⑬

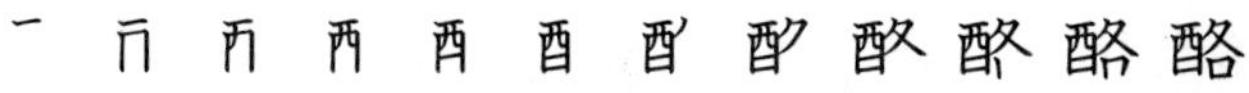

音	酪	ラク	whey
熟	酪酸	ラクサン	***chem***. butyric acid
	酪農	ラクノウ	dairy farming

1795
酵 ⑭

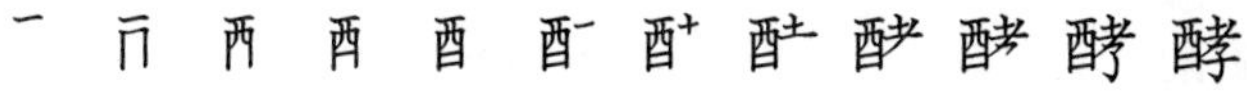

音	酵	コウ	yeast; ferment

熟	酵素	コウソ	***chem***. enzyme
	酵母	コウボ	yeast

1796

酷 ⑭ 一 丆 万 西 西 酉 酉' 酉' 酉 酉 酷 酷

音	酷	コク	harsh; bitter; intense
熟	酷使	コクシ	forced labor —***v***. work to death; make someone work hard
	酷似	コクジ	close resemblance; striking likeness —***vi***. be very much like; be similar
	酷暑	コクショ	intense heat
	酷評	コクヒョウ	severe criticism; cruel remark —***v***. speak bitterly; offer harsh criticism
	酷寒	コッカン	intense cold

1797

酸 ⑭ 一 丆 万 西 西 酉 酉 酉 酉 酉 酸 酸

音	酸	サン	sour; acid
熟	酸化	サンカ	***chem***. oxidation —***vi***. be oxidized
	酸性	サンセイ	***chem***. acidity
	酸性雨	サンセイウ	acid rain
	酸素	サンソ	***chem***. oxygen
	酸味	サンミ	sourness; sour taste; acidity
訓	酸い	すい	sour; acidic; vinegary
	酸っぱい	すっぱい	sour; acidic; vinegary

1798

醜 ⑰ 一 丆 万 西 西 酉 酉' 酉 酉 酉 醜 醜

音	醜	シュウ	ugly
熟	醜悪	シュウアク	ugly; mean
	醜行	シュウコウ	disgraceful conduct
	醜態	シュウタイ	disgraceful behavior
	醜聞	シュウブン	scandal; bad reputation
訓	醜い	みにくい	ugly; bad-looking; plain

1799

醸 ⑳

音	醸	ジョウ	brew
熟	醸成	ジョウセイ	brewing; fermenting —*v.* brew; ferment
	醸造	ジョウゾウ	brewing —*v.* brew
訓	醸す	かもす	***vt.*** brew; cause; bring out; arouse
	醸し出す	かもしだす	***vt.*** brew; cause; bring out; arouse

7 釆 のごめ topped rie

1800

釈 ⑪

音	釈	シャク	explain; Buddhism
熟	釈迦	シャカ	Shakyamuni; Gautama; Buddha
	釈然	シャクゼン	mind relieved of all doubt, anxiety, and ill feeling; clear and free mind
	釈放	シャクホウ	release —*v.* release; set a person free
	釈明	シャクメイ	explanation; vindication —*v.* explain; vindicate

7 里 さと／さとへん village

1801

里 ⑦

音	里	リ	village; *ri* (unit of length, approx. 3.9 km)
熟	里程	リテイ	distance; milage
	里程標	リテイヒョウ	milepost; milestone
訓	里	さと	village; the country; hometown
	里親	さとおや	foster parents
	里帰り	さとがえり	bride's first call at her old (parent's) house
	里子	さとご	foster child
	里心	さとごころ	homesickness; nostalgia

1802

重 ⑨

音	重	ジュウ	heavy; steady; pile up; important
		チョウ	heavy
熟	重圧	ジュウアツ	strong pressure
	重圧感	ジュウアツカン	oppressive feeling
	重刑	ジュウケイ	severe sentence
	重厚	ジュウコウ	solid; dignified
	重婚	ジュウコン	bigamy
	重罪	ジュウザイ	felony; grave offense/crime
	重視	ジュウシ	attaching greater importance —*v*. attach greater importance; take seriously
	重々	ジュウジュウ	very; well; fully
	重症	ジュウショウ	serious illness
	重傷	ジュウショウ	serious wound/injury
	重心	ジュウシン	center of gravity/mass
	重責	ジュウセキ	heavy responsibility; important mission
	重体	ジュウタイ	serious condition; critically ill
	重大	ジュウダイ	serious; grave; critical; important
	重点	ジュウテン	important point; great importance; emphasis; priority
	重罰	ジュウバツ	severe punishment
	重病	ジュウビョウ	serious illness
	重油	ジュウユ	heavy oil
	重要	ジュウヨウ	importance; essential; key; vital
	重量	ジュウリョウ	weight
	重力	ジュウリョク	gravity
	重労働	ジュウロウドウ	hard/heavy labor
	重複	チョウフク	duplication; repetition; redundancy —***vi***. duplicate; repeat; make redundant
	重宝	チョウホウ	convenient; handy; useful —*v*. be convenient/handy to use
訓	重	え	fold
	重い	おもい	heavy; important; serious
	重々しい	おもおもしい	solemn; grave; dignified
	重さ	おもさ	weight; emphasis; importance
	重たい	おもたい	heavy
	重んじる	おもんじる	***vt***. regard highly; hold in high esteem
	重荷	おもに	heavy load; burden
	重なる	かさなる	***vi***. be on top of; be piled up; come in succession

	重ねる	かさねる	***vt***. pile/stack up
	重ね重ね	かさねがさね	repeatedly; over and over again
¥	重工業	ジュウコウギョウ	heavy industry
	重商主義	ジュウショウシュギ	mercantilism
	重税	ジュウゼイ	heavy tax/taxation
	重電機（重電器）	ジュウデンキ	heavy electric apparatus/equipment
	重役	ジュウヤク	director; executive; board of directors

1803

野 ⑪

丶 口 日 日 甲 甲 里 里⁷ 里ᵛ 野 野

音	野	ヤ	field; the opposition; rustic; wild
熟	野営	ヤエイ	camp; bivouac —***vi***. camp out; make camp
	野外	ヤガイ	the open air; outdoor
	野球	ヤキュウ	baseball
	野犬	ヤケン	stray dog
	野菜	ヤサイ	vegetables
	野次	ヤジ	hooting; jeering
	野次馬	ヤジうま	curious crowd
	野趣	ヤシュ	rural beauty; rustic air
	野獣	ヤジュウ	wild animal/beast
	野心	ヤシン	ambition
	野人	ヤジン	rustic; bumpkin; uncouth person
	野性	ヤセイ	wild nature; uncouthness; wild (animal, beast, etc.)
	野戦病院	ヤセンビョウイン	field hospital
	野鳥	ヤチョウ	wild fowl/birds
	野党	ヤトウ	the Opposition; opposition party
	野蛮	ヤバン	savage; barbarous
	野卑	ヤヒ	vulgar; coarse; boorish
	野暮	ヤボ	senseless; booric
	野望	ヤボウ	ambition
	野郎	ヤロウ	***col***. fellow; guy; bastard
訓	野	の	field
	野宿	のジュク	camping out —***vi***. spend the night outdoors; sleep in the open
	野天	のテン	open air
	野中	のなか	in a field
	野原	のはら	field; plain

	野火	のび	burning off grass and weeds
	野武士	のブシ	***hist***. marauding samurai and groups of farmers who stole armor, etc., from defeated samurai
	野山	のやま	hills and fields
	野良	のら	wild; stray; outdoors

1804

量 ⑫

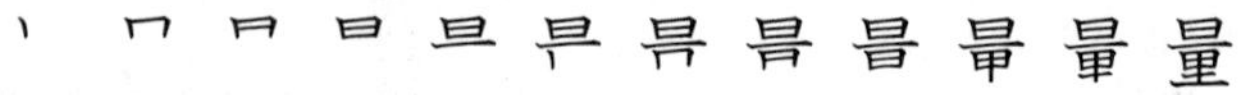

音	量	リョウ	quantity
熟	量感	リョウカン	volume; bulk; massiveness
	量産	リョウサン	mass production —*v*. produce in large quantities
	量的	リョウテキ	quantitative
	量目	リョウめ	weight
訓	量る	はかる	***vt***. weigh; measure

7 臣 しん minister

1805

臣 ⑦

音	臣	シン ジン	subject
熟	臣下	シンカ	subject; retainer
	臣民	シンミン	subject

1806

臨 ⑱

音	臨	リン	be present at; look out over; go to; copy; rule
熟	臨海	リンカイ	seaside; coastal; marine
	臨機応変	リンキオウヘン	adaptation to circumstances
	臨月	リンゲツ	the last month of pregnancy
	臨時	リンジ	extra; temporary; provisional
	臨終	リンジュウ	one's last moment
	臨床	リンショウ	clinical; attending a patient
	臨席	リンセキ	attendance; presence —***vi***. attend; be present

	臨地	リンチ	on-site
訓	臨む	のぞむ	***vt.*** face; attend; be present

7 舛 まいあし dancing legs

1807

舞 ⑮

ノ ㇒ 𠂉 ... 舞

音	舞	ブ	dance
熟	舞台	ブタイ	stage
	舞踏	ブトウ	dancing
	舞踊	ブヨウ	dance; dancing
訓	舞	まい	dance
	舞子	まいこ	(Japanese) dancing girl
	舞い込む	まいこむ	***vi.*** stray in; wander in; flutter in; be blown in (unexpectedly)
	舞う	まう	dance; twirl around; flutter

8 金 かね／かねへん metal; money

1808

 ⑧

音	金	キン	gold; currency; metal; coin
		(コン)	gold
熟	金一封	キンイップウ	gift of money (in an envelope)
	金貨	キンカ	gold coin/currency
	金科玉条	キンカギョクジョウ	golden rule
	金言	キンゲン	wise saying; watchword
	金庫	キンコ	safe
	金鉱	キンコウ	gold mine
	金策	キンサク	raising money; getting a loan —*vi*. raise money; get a loan
	金星	キンセイ	the planet Venus
	金銭	キンセン	money
	金属	キンゾク	metal; metallic
	金箔	キンパク	gold leaf; gilt
	金髪	キンパツ	blonde/fair hair
	金品	キンピン	money and other valuables
	金曜日	キンヨウび	Friday
	金利	キンリ	interest
	金色	コンジキ	gold color
訓	金	かね	metal; money
	金目	かねめ	(monetary) value
	金持ち	かねもち	rich; having a lot of money
	金	かな	(prefix) metal; money
	金具	かなグ	metal fittings; metallic parts
¥	金塊	キンカイ	gold ingot/bullion
	金額	キンガク	amount/sum of money
	金為替	キンかわせ	gold exchange
	金地金	キンジがね	gold bullion
	金銭債権	キンセンサイケン	money alarm
	金銭出納	キンセンスイトウ	receipts and expenses
	金融	キンユウ	finance
	金融機関	キンユウキカン	financial institution
	金融恐慌	キンユウキョウコウ	financial crisis

金融公庫	キンユウコウコ	financial cooperation
金融債	キンユウサイ	bank debenture
金融資産	キンユウシサン	financial asset/portfolio
金融市場	キンユウシジョウ	financial market; money and capital market
金融政策	キンユウセイサク	monetary policy
金融操作	キンユウソウサ	monetary operation
金融調節	キンユウチョウセツ	monetary and credit control
金融手形	キンユウてがた	bill; note for finance
金利	キンリ	interest
金利機構	キンリキコウ	interest rate mechanism
金利差	キンリサ	interest rate discrepancy (spread)
金利裁定取引	キンリサイテイとりひき	interest arbitrage (transaction)

1809

針 ⑩

音	針	シン	needle
熟	針小棒大	シンショウボウダイ	exaggeration; making a mountain out of a mole hill
	針葉樹	シンヨウジュ	coniferous tree
	針路	シンロ	course
訓	針	はり	needle; hook; pin
	針金	はりがね	wire
	針仕事	はりシごと	needlework

1810

釣 ⑪

音	釣	チョウ	fish; angle
熟	釣魚	チョウギョ	angling; fishing
訓	釣り	つり	angling; fishing; change (from shopping, etc.)
	釣り合い	つりあい	balance; equilibrium; poise
	釣り上げる	つりあげる	*vt.* fish/hook up; raise by manipulation
	釣り糸	つりいと	fishing line
	釣鐘	つりがね	hanging bell
	釣り竿	つりざお	fishing rod
	釣り銭	つりセン	change (from shopping, etc.)
	釣り道具	つりドウグ	fishing tackle
	釣り針	つりばり	fishing hook

釣り堀	つりぼり	fishpond
釣る	つる	***vt.*** fish; angle; decoy; allure; entice

1811

鈍 ⑫ ノ 𠆢 亼 亼 牟 伞 余 金 金 釒 釒 鈍

音	鈍	ドン	dull
熟	鈍角	ドンカク	***math.*** obtuse angle
	鈍感	ドンカン	insensible; insensitive; thick-skinned; obtuse
	鈍器	ドンキ	blunt weapon
	鈍痛	ドンツウ	dull pain
訓	鈍い	にぶい	dull; dim; thick; dense
	鈍る	にぶる	***vi.*** grow dull/dim

1812

鉛 ⑬ ノ 𠆢 亼 亼 牟 伞 余 金 金 釒 釒 鉛 鉛

音	鉛	エン	lead (metal)
熟	鉛管	エンカン	lead pipe; plumbing
	鉛直線	エンチョクセン	plumb/vertical line
	鉛筆	エンピツ	pencil
訓	鉛	なまり	lead

1813

鉱 ⑬ ノ 𠆢 亼 亼 牟 伞 余 金 金 釒 釒 鉱 鉱

音	鉱	コウ	ore; mineral; mine
熟	鉱業	コウギョウ	the mining industry; mining
	鉱山	コウザン	mine
	鉱石	コウセキ	ore; mineral; crystal
	鉱泉	コウセン	mineral spring/water; spring
	鉱夫	コウフ	miner
	鉱物	コウブツ	mineral
	鉱脈	コウミャク	vein of ore/mineral; ore/mineral deposit

1814

鉄 ⑬

音	鉄	テツ	iron; steel
熟	鉄火	テッカ	red-hot iron; gunfire; swords and guns; cuisine that uses raw tuna and *wasabi*
	鉄管	テッカン	iron pipe/tube
	鉄器	テッキ	ironware; hardware; ironmongery
	鉄橋	テッキョウ	iron bridge
	鉄筋コンクリート	テッキンコンクリート	reinforced concrete
	鉄拳	テッケン	clenched fist
	鉄工	テッコウ	ironworker; blacksmith
	鉄鉱	テッコウ	iron ore
	鉄鋼	テッコウ	steel
	鉄格子	テツゴウシ	iron-barred window
	鉄骨	テッコツ	steel frame
	鉄材	テツザイ	iron material
	鉄条網	テツジョウモウ	wire entanglements
	鉄製	テッセイ	made of steel/iron
	鉄線	テッセン	steel wire
	鉄則	テッソク	iron rule
	鉄塔	テットウ	steel tower; pylon
	鉄道	テツドウ	railroad; railway
	鉄板	テッパン	hot plate
	鉄板焼	テッパンやき	*teppanyaki* (meat and vegetables grilled on a hot plate)
	鉄瓶	テツビン	iron kettle
	鉄分	テツブン	iron content
	鉄壁	テッペキ	iron wall
	鉄砲	テッポウ	gun; firearms
	鉄砲玉	テッポウだま	bullet; gunshot; bull's-eye; lost person
	鉄面皮	テツメンピ	impudence; brazeness; shamelessness

1815

⑬

音	鉢	ハチ (ハツ)	bowl; pot; flower pot

熟 鉢植え　ハチうえ　potted/house plant
鉢巻き　ハチまき　headband; hatband; cotton cloth tied around the head

1816
鈴 ⑬

音 鈴　リン　bell
レイ　bell

訓 鈴　すず　bell
鈴虫　すずむし　bell-ring insect
鈴蘭　すずラン　lily of the valley

1817
銀 ⑭

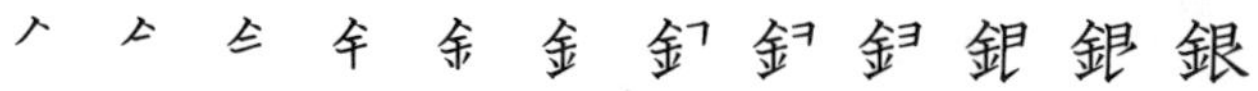

音 銀　ギン　silver; money; banking

熟 銀貨　ギンカ　silver coinage
銀河　ギンガ　Milky Way
銀行　ギンコウ　bank
銀製　ギンセイ　made from silver; silverware
銀世界　ギンセカイ　silver world; snow-covered scenery
銀幕　ギンマク　silver screen

¥ 銀行界　ギンコウカイ　banking community
銀行勘定　ギンコウカンジョウ　bank account
銀行準備金　ギンコウジュンビキン　bank reserves

1818
銃 ⑭

音 銃　ジュウ　gun

熟 銃口　ジュウコウ　muzzle of a gun
銃殺　ジュウサツ　death by shooting; execution by firing squad —*v.* shoot to death
銃声　ジュウセイ　shot; report of a gun
銃弾　ジュウダン　bullet
銃砲　ジュウホウ　firearms

1819
銭 ⑭

丿 𠂉 亼 令 余 金 釒 釒 釒 銭 銭 銭

音	銭	セン	coin
熟	銭湯	セントウ	bathhouse
訓	銭	ぜに	coin; change

1820
銑 ⑭

丿 𠂉 亼 令 余 金 釒 釒 釒 銑 銑 銑

音	銑	セン	pig iron
熟	銑鉄	センテツ	pig iron

1821
銅 ⑭

丿 𠂉 亼 令 余 金 釒 釒 釦 銅 銅 銅

音	銅	ドウ	copper
熟	銅貨	ドウカ	copper coin
	銅器	ドウキ	copper utensil; copperware
	銅山	ドウザン	copper mine
	銅像	ドウゾウ	bronze statue
	銅鐸	ドウタク	*dōtaku* (flat bell-like instrument of the Yayoi period)
	銅版	ドウバン	copperplate

1822
銘 ⑭

丿 𠂉 亼 令 余 金 釒 釒 釒 銘 銘 銘

音	銘	メイ	signature; inscription; name
熟	銘菓	メイカ	quality-brand cakes
	銘記	メイキ	bearing in mind —*v*. bear in mind
	銘々	メイメイ	each; apiece
¥	銘柄	メイがら	name; issue; brand

1823

鋭 ⑮

音	鋭	エイ	sharp
熟	鋭角	エイカク	acute angle
	鋭敏	エイビン	sharp-wits; keenness
	鋭利	エイリ	sharp-edged; keen; acute
訓	鋭い	するどい	sharp; acute; keen

1824

鋳 ⑮

音	鋳	チュウ	cast
熟	鋳造	チュウゾウ	casting; founding; minting —*v*. cast; found; mint; coin
訓	鋳る	いる	***vt***. cast; found; mint
	鋳型	いがた	mold
	鋳物	いもの	casting

1825

鋼 ⑯

音	鋼	コウ	steel
熟	鋼管	コウカン	steel tubing
	鋼材	コウザイ	steel materials; structural/rolled steel
	鋼鉄	コウテツ	steel
訓	鋼	はがね	steel

1826

錯 ⑯

音	錯	サク	error; mistake; mix; confuse
熟	錯乱	サクラン	confusion; mix-up —***vi***. be confused; be mixed-up
	錯覚	サッカク	illusion; hallucination; mistake —***vi***. have an illusion; hallucinate; make a mistake

1827
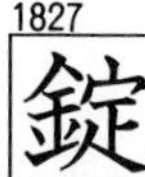
⑯

音	錠	ジョウ	lock
熟	錠剤	ジョウザイ	tablet; pill
	錠前	ジョウまえ	lock

1828

⑯

音	錘	スイ	spindle; weight
訓	錘	つむ	spindle

1829

⑯

音	錬	レン	forge; temper; refine
熟	錬金術	レンキンジュツ	alchemy
	錬成	レンセイ	training —*v.* train
	錬鉄	レンテツ	wrought iron
訓	錬る	ねる	***vi***. forge; temper; refine

1830
録
⑯

音	録	ロク	record; catalog
熟	録音	ロクオン	sound recording —*v.* make a sound recording
	録画	ロクガ	videotape recording —*v.* record on videotape
訓	※録る	とる	***vt***. record

1831
鍛
⑰

音	鍛	タン	forge; temper; train; drill
熟	鍛練	タンレン	forging; temper; training; drilling —*v.* forge; temper; train; drill

訓	鍛える	きたえる	***vt***. forge; temper; drill; train; cultivate

1832

鎖 ⑱

音	鎖	サ	chain; lock; close
熟	鎖国	サコク	national isolation; seclusion —***vi***. close up a country to the outside world
	鎖骨	サコツ	***med***. collarbone; clavicle
訓	鎖	くさり	chain

1833

鎮 ⑱

音	鎮	チン	suppress
熟	鎮圧	チンアツ	suppression; repression; subjugation —***v***. supress; repress; subjugate
	鎮火	チンカ	fire extinguishing —***v***. be put out/extinguished
	鎮座	チンザ	enshrinement —***vi***. be enshrined
	鎮静	チンセイ	calm; quiet; tranquillity —***v***. become calm; restore quiet; subside; calm
	鎮静剤	チンセイザイ	tranquilizer
	鎮痛剤	チンツウザイ	painkiller
訓	鎮まる	しずまる	***vi***. become quiet; calm down; be supressed; be enshrined
	鎮める	しずめる	***vt***. calm; quiet; still; supress; repress; quell

1834

鏡 ⑲

音	鏡	キョウ	mirror; lens; spectacles; mirrorlike
熟	鏡台	キョウダイ	dressing table; dresser
訓	鏡	かがみ	mirror; looking glass

1835

鐘 ⑳

音	鐘	ショウ	hanging bell

熟	鐘楼	ショウロウ	belfry
訓	鐘	かね	bell

1836
鑑 ㉓

音	鑑	カン	model; mirror
熟	鑑札	カンサツ	license; certificate
	鑑識	カンシキ	identification; judgment
	鑑賞	カンショウ	appreciation —*v*. appreciate; enjoy
	鑑定	カンテイ	judgment; appraisal; estimation —*v*. judge; appraise; estimate; identify
	鑑別	カンベツ	discrimination; differentiation; judgment —*v*. discriminate; distinguish; differentiate
訓	※鑑み	かんがみ	mirror; model; paragon
	※鑑みる	かんがみる	***vt***. take into consideration

8 長 ながい long

1837
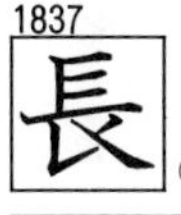
⑧

音	長	チョウ	long; far; stretch; head; chief; headman; merit; strong point
熟	長じる	チョウじる	***vi***. grow up; be older; excel; be clever
	長音	チョウオン	long vowel/sound
	長官	チョウカン	director; president; administrator; head; chief
	長期	チョウキ	long period/term
	長距離	チョウキョリ	long distance
	長子	チョウシ	oldest son
	長者	チョウジャ	millionaire
	長寿	チョウジュ	long life; longevity
	長所	チョウショ	merit; strong point; forte
	長女	チョウジョ	oldest daughter
	長身	チョウシン	tall figure; great stature
	長針	チョウシン	the long/minute hand (of a clock)
	長蛇	チョウダ	long (queue)
	長大	チョウダイ	long and stout; huge

8

金
●長
●門
隶
隹
雨
青
非
斉
飠

	長短	チョウタン	relative length; merits and demerits
	長調	チョウチョウ	major key (in music)
	長男	チョウナン	oldest son; heir
	長髪	チョウハツ	long hair
	長編	チョウヘン	long novel/movie/poem
	長方形	チョウホウケイ	***math***. rectangle; oblong
	長命	チョウメイ	longevity; long life
	長老	チョウロウ	senior; elder
訓	長い	ながい	long; lengthy; lanky
	長さ	ながさ	length
	長雨	ながあめ	long period of rain
	長居	ながい	long stay/visit —***vi***. stay too long; make a long visit
	長生き	ながいき	long life; longevity —***vi***. live long; enjoy longevity
	長椅子	ながイス	sofa; couch
	長靴	ながぐつ	boots
	長続き	ながつづき	long lasting —***vi***. last long
	長年	ながネン	long time; many years
	長引く	ながびく	***vi***. be prolonged/protracted/delayed
	長持ち	ながもち	durability; endurance —***vi***. endure; be durable; last long
¥	長期貸付金	チョウキかしつけキン	long-term loans
	長期借入金	チョウキかりいれキン	long-term loans repayable
	長期金利	チョウキキンリ	long-term rate of interest
	長期公債	チョウキコウサイ	long-term government bond
	長期信用銀行	チョウキシンヨウギンコウ	long-term credit bank
	長期未払金	チョウキみはらいキン	long-term accounts payable

8 門 もんがまえ gate

1838

門 ⑧ 丨 𠃌 ... 門

音	門	モン	gate
熟	門衛	モンエイ	guard; gatekeeper
	門下	モンカ	one's disciple/pupil

	門外漢	モンガイカン	outsider; layman
	門限	モンゲン	curfew
	門戸	モンコ	doorway
	門札	モンサツ	name plate
	門歯	モンシ	incisor; front teeth
	門人	モンジン	pupil; disciple
	門前	モンゼン	before the gate
	門柱	モンチュウ	gatepost
	門弟	モンテイ	disciple; pupil
	門灯	モントウ	gate light
	門番	モンバン	gatekeeper
	門標	モンピョウ	name plate
訓	門	かど	gate; house
	門口	かどぐち	front door; entrance
	門出	かどで	departure —*v*. depart; set out

1839

閉 ⑪

丨 ｜ 「 ｜ 「 ｢ 門 門 門 閂 閉 閉

音	閉	ヘイ	close; shut; confine; end
熟	閉会	ヘイカイ	closing/adjournment (of a meeting) —*v*. close/adjourn a meeting
	閉館	ヘイカン	closing (hall/building) —*v*. close (hall/building)
	閉口	ヘイコウ	troublesome; confoundment —***vi***. be troubled/confounded by
	閉鎖	ヘイサ	closing; closure; lockup —*v*. close; lock up
	閉塞	ヘイソク	closing/covering up; blockade —*v*. close/cover up; blockade
	閉廷	ヘイテイ	adjournment (of court) —*v*. adjourn court
	閉店	ヘイテン	closing a shop (for the day) —***vi***. close the shop
	閉幕	ヘイマク	falling of the curtain; end of a play —***vi***. curtain falls; play ends
	閉門	ヘイモン	locking up the gate; house arrest (Edo period) —***vi***. lock up the gate; be confined to one's home
訓	閉まる	しまる	***vi***. be shut/closed/locked
	閉める	しめる	***vt***. shut; close; lock
	閉ざす	とざす	***vt***. close; shut; lock
	閉じる	とじる	***vt***. close; shut; lock
	閉じ込める	とじこめる	***vt***. shut in; confine
	閉じこもる	とじこもる	***vi***. stay indoors; be confined to one's house

1840
開 ⑫

音	開	カイ	open; begin; civilize; unfold; expand; open up land; develop; reclaim
熟	開運	カイウン	improvement of one's fortune
	開演	カイエン	opening of a performance; raising of the curtain —*vi*. start a performance; raise the curtain
	開化	カイカ	Westernization; becoming civilized —*vi*. become Westernized/civilized
	開花	カイカ	fluorescence; bloom; flourishing —*vi*. flower; bloom; flourish
	開会	カイカイ	opening of a meeting —*v*. open/begin a meeting
	開口	カイコウ	opening; aperture
	開校	カイコウ	opening of a new school —*v*. open a new school
	開港	カイコウ	opening of a port to (foreign trade) —*v*. open a port (to foreign trade)
	開国	カイコク	opening of a country to the world; foundation of a country —*v*. open up a country to the world; found a nation
	開墾	カイコン	reclamation (of waste land) —*v*. reclaim waste land; bring under cultivation
	開催	カイサイ	holding (a meeting/exhibition) —*v*. hold (a meeting); open (an exhibition)
	開始	カイシ	beginning; start; commencement —*v*. begin; start; commence
	開場	カイジョウ	opening (of the doors to a hall, etc.) —*vi*. open; open the doors (to a hall, etc.)
	開設	カイセツ	opening; establishment; setting up —*v*. open; establish; set up
	開戦	カイセン	outbreak of war; commencement of hostilities —*vi*. make/wage war
	開拓	カイタク	reclamation and development; clearing; exploitation —*v*. reclaim; improve; develop; clear; exploit; pioneer
	開通	カイツウ	opening up to traffic —*v*. open up to traffic
	開発	カイハツ	development; exploitation —*v*. develop; open up; exploit
	開票	カイヒョウ	ballot counting —*v*. count votes; open ballot boxes
	開封	カイフウ	unsealing/opening a letter —*v*. unseal/open a letter
	開閉	カイヘイ	opening and shutting —*v*. open and shut
	開放	カイホウ	opening —*v*. open; throw open
	開門	カイモン	opening of a gate —*vi*. open a gate

訓	開く	あく	***vi***. open
	開ける	あける	***vt***. open; begin; bore (a hole, etc.)
	開く	ひらく	***v***. open; solve; start
	開ける	ひらける	***vi***. develop; be open; be civilized
¥	開発銀行	カイハツギンコウ	development bank

1841

間 ⑫

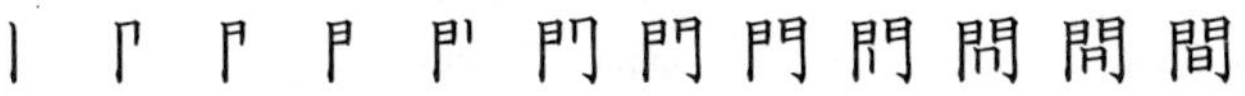

音	間	カン	interval; between; gap; opportunity
		ケン	between; middle
熟	間一髪	カンイッパツ	hair's breadth
	間隔	カンカク	interval; space; distance
	間隙	カンゲキ	gap; split; discord
	間食	カンショク	eating between meals; snack —***vi***. eat between meals
	間接	カンセツ	indirectness
	間接的	カンセツテキ	indirect
	間断	カンダン	pause; interval
訓	間	あいだ	interval; middle; gap
	間	ま	space; leisure; room; pause; interval; (counter for rooms)
	間口	まぐち	front; facade; width of a building, etc.
	間近	まぢか	nearby; close at hand
	間違う	まちがう	***v***. make a mistake
	間取り	まどり	plan of a house; room arrangement
	間引き	まびき	thinning out of plants
¥	間接税	カンセツゼイ	indirect (consumption) tax
	間接発行	カンセツハッコウ	offer for sale

1842

閑 ⑫

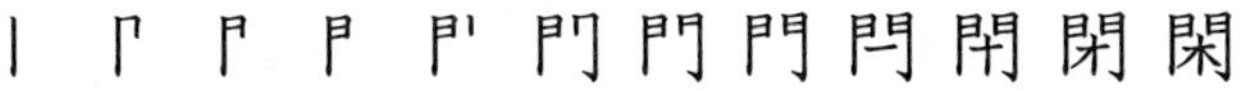

音	閑	カン	quiet; leisure
熟	閑居	カンキョ	secluded residence; quiet life —***vi***. live in seclusion/retirement
	閑散	カンサン	leisure; dullness; slackness; inactivity
	閑寂	カンジャク	quietness; tranquillity
	閑静	カンセイ	quietness; tranquillity
訓	※閑か	しずか	quiet; tranquil; peaceful; leisurely; free

1843

閣 ⑭ 丨 ｢ ｣ 門 閣

音	閣	カク	Cabinet; tower
熟	閣議	カクギ	Cabinet meeting/council
	閣下	カッカ	Your Excellency
¥	閣僚	カクリョウ	member of the Cabinet
	閣僚理事会 (閣僚理)	カクリョウリジカイ (カクリョウリ)	ministerial/Cabinet committee

1844

関 ⑭ 丨 ｢ ｣ 門 関

音	関	カン	barrier; bolt
熟	関する	カンする	***vi***. be related/connected to
	関係	カンケイ	relation; connection; relationship —***vi***. be related/connected; be involved in a relationship
	関西	カンサイ	Kansai district
	関心	カンシン	concern; interest
	関節	カンセツ	joint of the body
	関知	カンチ	concern —***vi***. be concerned with
	関東	カントウ	Kanto district
	関白	カンパク	***hist***. *Kampaku* (chancellor or chief adviser to the emperor)
	関門	カンモン	gateway; gate
	関与	カンヨ	participation —***vi***. participate
	関連	カンレン	involvement; correlation; connection; reference —***vi***. be connected/associated/correlated
訓	関	せき	checkpoint; barrier
	関所	せきショ	checkpoint; barrier
	関取	せきとり	high-ranking sumo wrestler
	※関わる	かかわる	***vi***. be related to; be connected with; have to do with
¥	関係会社	カンケイガイシャ	associated/affiliated company
	関税	カンゼイ	customs; tariff
	関税障壁	カンゼイショウヘキ	tariff barrier
	関連会社	カンレンガイシャ	affiliate company

1845

⑭

音	閥	バツ	lineage; clique

1846

⑮

音	閲	エツ	inspection; review; revision
熟	閲読	エツドク	reading; perusal —*v*. read; peruse
	閲兵	エッペイ	inspection of the troops; parade —*v*. inspect/review the troops
	閲覧	エツラン	reading; perusal —*v*. read; persue
	閲覧室	エツランシツ	reading room

1847
闘 ⑱

音	闘	トウ	fight
熟	闘牛	トウギュウ	bullfight; bullfighting
	闘鶏	トウケイ	cockfighting
	闘士	トウシ	fighter; champion
	闘志	トウシ	fight; morale; fighting spirit
	闘争	トウソウ	struggle; fight; combat —*vi*. fight; put up a struggle
	闘病	トウビョウ	fight against a disease
訓	闘う	たたかう	*vi*. fight; struggle; battle

8 隶 れいづくり servant; slave

1848
隷 ⑯

音	隷	レイ	obey; follow; servant; criminal
熟	隷従	レイジュウ	subordination (to a lord); following orders —*vi*. be subordinate (to a lord); follow orders

隷書	レイショ	angular-style of writing Chinese characters
隷属	レイゾク	subordination —*vi*. be subordinate to

8 隹 ふるとり old bird

1849

隻 ⑩

ノ イ イ' 亻' 什 仹 隹 隹 隻 隻

音	隻	セキ	single; (counter for ships)
熟	隻手	セキシュ	one arm

1850

雇 ⑫

一 ㇇ ⺕ 戸 戸 戸 戸 戸 戸 屛 雇 雇

音	雇	コ	hire; employ; employment; employee
訓	雇い	やとい	employment; hiring
	雇い人	やといニン	employee
	雇い主	やといぬし	employer
	雇う	やとう	*vt*. employ; engage; hire
¥	雇用	コヨウ	employment —*v*. employ; engage; hire; take on
	雇用者	コヨウシャ	employer

1851

集 ⑫

ノ イ イ' 亻' 什 仹 隹 隹 隹 集 集 集

音	集	シュウ	assemble; collect; gather
熟	集荷	シュウカ	cargo collection —*v*. collect cargo
	集会	シュウカイ	meeting; assembly; gathering
	集計	シュウケイ	total; sum; aggregate —*v*. total; sum; collect together
	集結	シュウケツ	collecting things in one place; gathering in one place —*v*. mass; gather; assemble
	集合	シュウゴウ	meeting; gathering; assembly ***math***. set —*v*. meet; gather; assemble
	集札	シュウサツ	ticket collection —*v*. collect tickets
	集散	シュウサン	collecting and distribution —*v*. meet and part; collect and distribute
	集積	シュウセキ	accumulation; pile —*v*. accumulate; pile up

	集大成	シュウタイセイ	collection; compilation —*v*. compile (various texts) into one book
	集団	シュウダン	group; body
	集中	シュウチュウ	concentration —*v*. center on; concentrate
	集配	シュウハイ	collection and delivery —*v*. collect and deliver
	集約	シュウヤク	putting/collecting together —*v*. put together
	集落	シュウラク	village ***bio***. colony
	集録	シュウロク	compilation of written records —*v*. compile
訓	集まり	あつまり	meeting; gathering; party; congregation; crowd; attendance
	集まる	あつまる	*v*. gather come; get together; mass; be collected/concentrated
	集める	あつめる	***vt***. gather; get together; collect; accumulate; attract; draw together
	集い	つどい	gathering; meeting; get-together
	集う	つどう	***vi***. gather; come; get together; amass
¥	集金	シュウキン	collection of money —*v*. collect money/bills
	集中投資	シュウチュウトウシ	concentrated investment

8 金長門隶隹●雨青非斉食

1852

雄 ⑫ 一 ナ 𠂇 厷 厷 𠂭 𠂭 𠂭 𠂭 雄 雄 雄

音	雄	ユウ	male; hero; great leader; superiority
熟	雄姿	ユウシ	gallant figure
	雄大	ユウダイ	magnificent; majestic; grand; sublime
	雄飛	ユウヒ	great achievement —***vi***. do something great
	雄弁	ユウベン	oratory; eloquence
訓	雄	お	male
	雄	おす	male
	雄花	おばな	male flower

1853

雅 ⑬ 一 ㇀ 工 牙 牙 牙 牙 牙 牙 牙 牙 雅

音	雅	ガ	elegance
熟	雅楽	ガガク	*gagaku* (Japanese ceremonial court music)
	雅号	ガゴウ	pen name; pseudonym
	雅趣	ガシュ	elegance; tastefulness
訓	※雅やか	みやびやか	elegant; graceful; refined

1854

雌 ⑭

丨 ⺊ 屮 止 止 此 此 此 此 此 此 雌

音	雌	シ	female
熟	雌伏	シフク	inactivity; dormancy —*vi*. remain inactive; lie dormant
	雌雄	シユウ	male and female; superior or inferior
訓	雌	め	female
	雌	めす	female
	雌花	めばな	female flower

1855

雜 ⑭

丿 九 九 卆 卆 杂 杂 杂 杂 杂 杂 雜

音	雜	ザツ	miscellaneous; sloppy; slipshod; messy
		ゾウ	miscellany; various
熟	雑役	ザツエキ	odd jobs; chores
	雑音	ザツオン	noise; static; interference (on radio, etc.)
	雑貨	ザッカ	sundry/miscellaneous goods; general merchandise; sundries
	雑貨屋	ザッカや	general store
	雑学	ザツガク	general knowledge
	雑感	ザッカン	miscellaneous thoughts; casual impressions
	雑記帳	ザッキチョウ	notebook
	雑穀	ザッコク	miscellaneous cereals (excluding rice and wheat)
	雑誌	ザッシ	magazine; journal; periodical
	雑事	ザツジ	household chores; routine work
	雑種	ザッシュ	cross; hybrid; mongrel
	雑食性	ザッショクセイ	omnivorous
	雑然	ザツゼン	untidy; messy; in disorder
	雑草	ザッソウ	weeds
	雑多	ザッタ	miscellaneous
	雑談	ザツダン	chitchat; chat; light conversation; small talk —*vi*. chitchat; chat
	雑踏	ザットウ	congestion; crowd; throng
	雑念	ザツネン	idle thoughts
	雑務	ザツム	odd duties; routine; trivial tasks
	雑用	ザツヨウ	odd business; various chores
	雑木林	ゾウきばやし	growth of trees; copse; coppice

雑巾	ゾウキン	duster; dust/floor cloth
雑炊	ゾウスイ	*zōsui* (porridge of rice and vegetables)
雑煮	ゾウに	*zōni* (soup containing rice cakes)

1856

難 ⑱

一 艹 廿 丗 芔 苩 莒 莫 菓 蔓 歎 難

音	難	ナン	difficult
熟	難易	ナンイ	hardness; difficulty
	難解	ナンカイ	difficult to understand; unintelligible
	難関	ナンカン	barrier; obstacle; hurdle; difficult situation
	難儀	ナンギ	hardship; difficulty; distress; misery; affliction; trial —***vi***. be in difficulties; have trouble; come to grief
	難行苦行	ナンギョウクギョウ	penance; ascetism; religious austerities
	難局	ナンキョク	difficult situation; crisis; deadlock
	難癖	ナンクセ	fault; blemish; faultfinding
	難航	ナンコウ	stormy voyage; rough passage —***vi***. have a difficult sailing/rough passage
	難産	ナンザン	hard labor; complicated birth —***vi***. have a difficult/complicated delivery
	難事	ナンジ	difficult matter; hard task; tough job
	難渋	ナンジュウ	hardship; suffering; distress; misery; sorrow —***vi***. suffer; be in trouble/distress
	難所	ナンショ	dangerous spot; place hard to pass
	難色	ナンショク	disapproval; reluctance; unwillingness
	難船	ナンセン	shipwreck; wreck; ship in distress —***vi***. be shipwrecked; be wrecked
	難題	ナンダイ	unreasonable terms; unfair proposal
	難聴	ナンチョウ	hard of hearing
	難点	ナンテン	crux; difficult point; weakness; fault; flaw
	難無く	ナンなく	without difficulty; with ease
	難破	ナンパ	shipwreck
	難病	ナンビョウ	serious/incurable disease
	難民	ナンミン	sufferers; refugees
	難問	ナンモン	puzzling question; question that is hard to answer
	難路	ナンロ	hard pass; rough road
訓	難い	かたい	hard; difficult
	難しい	むずかしい	hard; difficult; troublesome; problematic

1857
離 ⑱

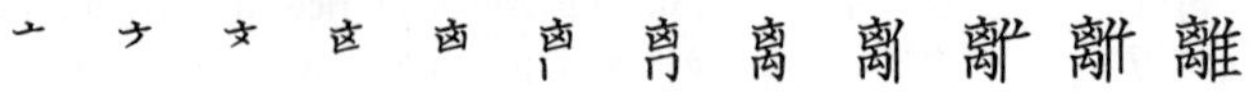

音	離	リ	separate; leave
熟	離縁	リエン	divorce; disowning —*v*. divorce; disown
	離婚	リコン	divorce —*vi*. divorce; get a divorce
	離散	リサン	dispersion; scattering —*vi*. disperse; scatter
	離職	リショク	quitting/losing one's job —*vi*. quit/lose one's job
	離島	リトウ	outlying island —*vi*. lie out
	離乳	リニュウ	weaning —*vi*. wean
	離別	リベツ	separation; divorce —*vi*. separate; divorce
	離陸	リリク	take-off (of a plane) —*vi*. take off
訓	離す	はなす	*vt*. separate; keep apart
	離れる	はなれる	*vi*. separate; leave
	離れ離れ	はなればなれ	separated; scattered; dispersed

8 雨 あめ／あめかんむり rain

1858
雨 ⑧

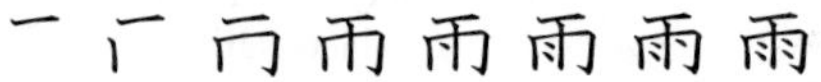

音	雨	ウ	rain
熟	雨季	ウキ	rainy season
	雨後	ウゴ	after the rain
	雨天	ウテン	rainy weather; wet day
	雨量	ウリョウ	rainfall; rain; precipitation
	雨量計	ウリョウケイ	rain gauge
訓	雨	あめ	rain
	雨上がり	あめあがり	after the rain
	雨	あま	(prefix) rain; rainy
	雨合羽	あまガッぱ	raincoat
	雨具	あまグ	rainwear
	雨靴	あまぐつ	rain shoes; galoshes
	雨雲	あまぐも	rain cloud
	雨戸	あまど	sliding door; shutter
	雨漏り	あまもり	leak (in the roof)

雨宿り　あまやどり　sheltering from the rain —*vi*. take shelter from the rain; get out of the rain

1859

雪 ⑪

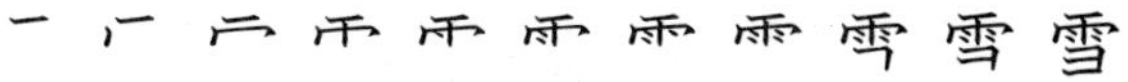

音 雪　セツ　snow

熟 雪害　セツガイ　snow damage
雪原　セツゲン　snowfield; expanse of snow
雪辱　セツジョク　revenge; vindication; clearing one's name —*vi*. have revenge; vindicate/clear one's name
雪中　セッチュウ　in/through the snow

訓 雪　ゆき　snow
雪男　ゆきおとこ　abominable snowman; yeti
雪女　ゆきおんな　snow fairy
雪合戦　ゆきガッセン　snowball fight
雪達磨　ゆきだるま　snowman
雪解け　ゆきどけ　thawing; solution of a problem —*v*. thaw; solve a problem
※雪崩　なだれ　snowslide

1860

雲 ⑫

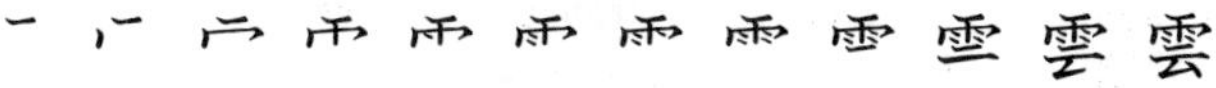

音 雲　ウン　cloud

熟 雲海　ウンカイ　sea of clouds
雲泥の差　ウンデイのサ　wide difference
雲母　ウンモ　mica
雲量　ウンリョウ　cloudiness; amount of cloud

訓 雲　くも　cloud
雲行き　くもゆき　sky; weather; circumstances; state of affairs

1861

雰 ⑫

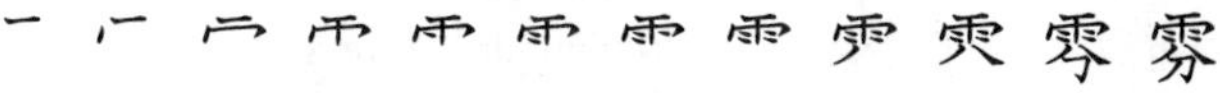

音 雰　フン　fog

熟 雰囲気　フンイキ　atmosphere; ambience

1862

⑬

音	電	デン	lightning; electricity
熟	電圧	デンアツ	voltage; tension; electric pressure
	電化	デンカ	electrification —*v*. electrify; install electricity
	電荷	デンカ	electric charge
	電界	デンカイ	electric field
	電解	デンカイ	electrolysis —*v*. electrolyze
	電気	デンキ	electricity; electric light
	電球	デンキュウ	electric light bulb
	電極	デンキョク	electrode
	電撃	デンゲキ	electric shock
	電源	デンゲン	source of electricity; power/electric source
	電工	デンコウ	electrician
	電光	デンコウ	electric light; lightning
	電子	デンシ	electron
	電子工学	デンシコウガク	electronics
	電磁気	デンジキ	electromagnetism
	電磁石	デンジシャク	electromagnet
	電磁場	デンジば	electromagnetic field
	電車	デンシャ	train
	電信	デンシン	telegraph; telegram; wire; cable
	電信柱	デンシンばしら	telegraph pole
	電線	デンセン	electric wire/cable; telegraph wire
	電送	デンソウ	electrical transmission —*v*. telegraph; wire; cable
	電池	デンチ	battery; electric cell
	電柱	デンチュウ	utility/telephone/telegraph pole
	電灯	デントウ	electric light
	電動	デンドウ	electromotion
	電動機	デンドウキ	electric motor
	電熱	デンネツ	electric heat
	電波	デンパ	electric/radio wave
	電文	デンブン	telegram
	電報	デンポウ	telegram; wire
	電離層	デンリソウ	ionosphere
	電流	デンリュウ	electric current
	電流計	デンリュウケイ	galvanometer
	電力	デンリョク	electric power; electricity

	電話	デンワ	telephone
	電話局	デンワキョク	telephone office
	電話線	デンワセン	telephone wire
	電話帳	デンワチョウ	telephone directory
	電話番号	デンワバンゴウ	telephone number
訓	※電	いなずま	flash of lightning

1863

雷 ⑬

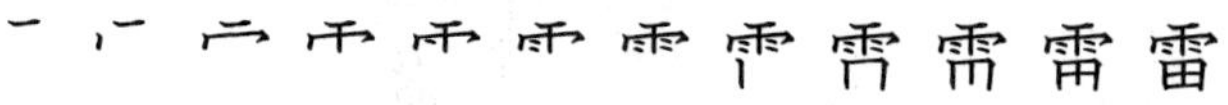

音	雷	ライ	thunder
熟	雷雨	ライウ	thunderstorm
	雷雲	ライウン	thunder cloud
	雷撃	ライゲキ	torpedo attack —*v*. torpedo (an enemy ship)
	雷同	ライドウ	agreeing blindly —***vi***. agree without thinking for oneself
	雷名	ライメイ	illustrious name
	雷鳴	ライメイ	thunder
訓	雷	かみなり	thunder

1864

零 ⑬

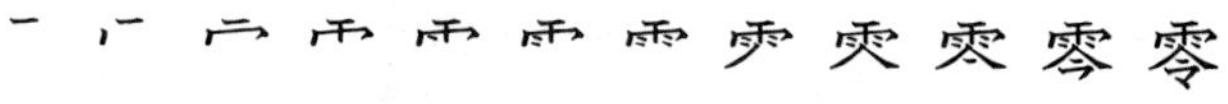

音	零	レイ	zero
熟	零下	レイカ	below zero; subzero
	零細	レイサイ	small; meager
	零時	レイジ	12 : 00 (noon or midnight)
	零落	レイラク	reduced circumstances; ruin —*v*. be ruined; fall to a low position; go down in the world
訓	※零す	こぼす	***vt***. spill
	※零れる	こぼれる	***vi***. spill; be split

1865

需 ⑭

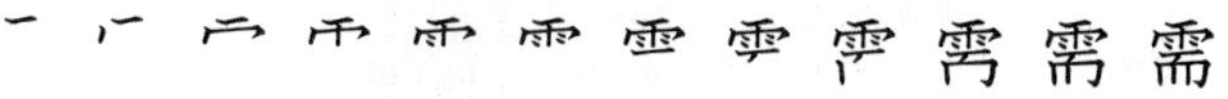

音	需	ジュ	demand
¥	需給	ジュキュウ	supply and demand
	需給関係	ジュキュウカンケイ	relation of supply and demand
	需要	ジュヨウ	demand

1866

震 ⑮

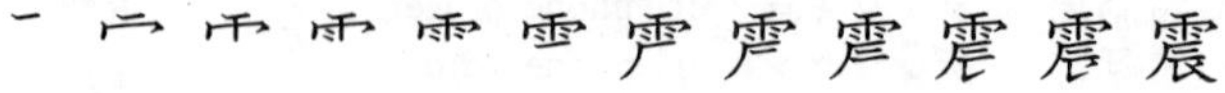

音	震	シン	quake
熟	震央	シンオウ	seismic center; epicenter
	震源地	シンゲンチ	epicenter
	震災	シンサイ	earthquake disaster
	震度	シンド	seismic; intensity
	震動	シンドウ	shock; quake —***v***. shake; quake
訓	震う	ふるう	***vi***. shiver; tremble; shake; vibrate; quiver shudder
	震える	ふるえる	***vi***. shiver; tremble; shake; vibrate; quiver; shudder

1867

霊 ⑮

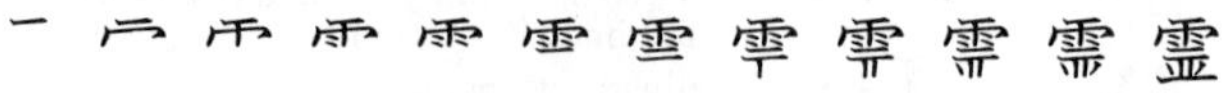

音	霊	レイ	spirit; soul
		リョウ	spirit; soul
熟	霊安室	レイアンシツ	morgue
	霊域	レイイキ	sacred ground
	霊園	レイエン	cemetery
	霊界	レイカイ	the spirit world
	霊感	レイカン	inspiration; extra-sensory perception of the supernatural
	霊柩	レイキュウ	coffin; casket
	霊柩車	レイキュウシャ	hearse
	霊験	レイゲン	miracle; wonder-working
	霊魂	レイコン	spirit; soul
	霊山	レイザン	sacred mountain
	霊場	レイジョウ	sacred place; hallowed ground
	霊前	レイゼン	before a spirit
	霊長	レイチョウ	crown of creation; mankind
	霊的	レイテキ	spiritual
	霊媒	レイバイ	spiritualist medium
	霊妙	レイミョウ	miraculous; mysterious
訓	※霊	たま	soul; spirit

1868

霜 ⑰

音	霜	ソウ	frost; years
熟	霜害	ソウガイ	frost damage
訓	霜	しも	frost
	霜柱	しもばしら	frost/ice columns
	霜焼け	しもやけ	frostbite

1869

霧 ⑲

音	霧	ム	mist; fog
熟	霧散	ムサン	dissipation; vanishing —*vi*. dissipate; vanish
	霧中	ムチュウ	in the fog
	霧笛	ムテキ	foghorn
訓	霧	きり	fog; mist
	霧雨	きりさめ	misty rain; drizzle

1870

露 ㉑

音	露	ロ	dew; exposure; Russia
		（ロウ）	open; public
熟	露営	ロエイ	camping out —*v*. camp out in the open
	露見	ロケン	exposure; disclosure —*vi*. come to light; be found out
	露光	ロコウ	exposure (in photograpy)
	露骨	ロコツ	frank; conspicuous; open
	露地	ロジ	bare ground
	露出	ロシュツ	exposure (also used for photography) —*v*. expose
	露台	ロダイ	balcony
	露呈	ロテイ	exposure; disclosure —*v*. expose; disclose
	露天	ロテン	open-air; outdoor
	露店	ロテン	street stall; vending booth
	露命	ロメイ	transitory life
訓	露	つゆ	dew

	露知らず	つゆしらず	completely ignorant
	※露	あらわ	open; public; frank

8 青 おあ／あおへん blue; green

1871

青 ⑧ 一 十 ≠ 主 丰 青 青 青

音	青	セイ （ショウ）	blue; green; young; immature
熟	青果	セイカ	fruit and vegetables; fresh produce
	青春	セイシュン	youth
	青少年	セイショウネン	young people
	青銅	セイドウ	bronze
	青年	セイネン	youth; young man
訓	青	あお	blue; azure; green
	青い	あおい	blue; azure; green; pale (face)
	青々	あおあお	deep blue; lush green; verdant
	青海原	あおうなばら	wide blue sea
	青写真	あおジャシン	blueprint
	青白い	あおじろい	pale; pallid
	青空	あおぞら	blue sky
	青空市場	あおぞらいちば	open-air market
	青二才	あおニサイ	young and inexperienced fellow
	青葉	あおば	green leaves
	青物	あおもの	greens; vegetables
	青み	あおみ	blueness; greeness
	青む	あおむ	turn blue/green
	青ざめる	あおざめる	turn pale
¥	青田買い	あおたがい	buying rice before it is reaped ***fig.*** securing a thing ahead of time; recruitment before the employee graduates from university

1872

静 ⑭ 一 十 主 丰 青 青 青 青 青 青 静 静 静 静

音	静	セイ （ジョウ）	calm; quiet; peaceful; still

熟	静脈	ジョウミャク	vein
	静観	セイカン	watching calmly —*v*. watch calmly; wait and see
	静止	セイシ	standstill; still; at rest; stationary —*vi*. come to rest/a standstill; be at rest/stationary
	静寂	セイジャク	still; silent; quiet
	静粛	セイシュク	still; silent; quiet
	静聴	セイチョウ	attention; listen quietly —*v*. pay attention
	静的	セイテキ	static
	静電気	セイデンキ	static electricity
	静物	セイブツ	still life
	静養	セイヨウ	rest; recuperation —*vi*. rest; recuperate
訓	静	しず	quiet; peaceful; still
	静か	しずか	calm; quiet; peaceful; still
	静まる	しずまる	*vi*. become quiet; subside; die down
	静める	しずめる	*vt*. calm; soothe; quell

8 非 あらず negative

1873

非 ⑧ ノ ｺ ｺ ｺ 非 非 非 非

音	非	ヒ	(prefix) non-; un-; wrong; not
熟	非運	ヒウン	misfortune; bad luck
	非金属	ヒキンゾク	nonmetallic
	非行	ヒコウ	misdeed; misconduct; delinquency
	非業	ヒゴウ	***Bud***. untimely/unnatural death
	非公開	ヒコウカイ	private/closed (meeting); closed-door (session)
	非公式	ヒコウシキ	unofficial; informal
	非公認	ヒコウニン	unauthorized
	非合法	ヒゴウホウ	illegal
	非合理	ヒゴウリ	irrational; unreasonable
	非国民	ヒコクミン	traitor; unpatriotic person
	非才	ヒサイ	lack of ability; incompetence
	非情	ヒジョウ	unfeeling; coldhearted; inanimate
	非常	ヒジョウ	emergency; extraordinary; very; exceeding; extremely
	非常勤	ヒジョウキン	part-time work
	非常口	ヒジョウぐち	emergency exit
	非常時	ヒジョウジ	emergency; crisis

	非常識	ヒジョウシキ	lack of common sense; absurd
	非常手段	ヒジョウシュダン	emergency means
	非戦論	ヒセンロン	pacificism
	非道	ヒドウ	inhuman; unjust; cruel; tyrannical
	非難	ヒナン	blame; reproach —*v*. criticize unfavorably; censure; blame; reproach
	非売品	ヒバイヒン	article not for sale; Not for Sale
	非番	ヒバン	off duty
	非武装	ヒブソウ	demilitarization; unarmed
	非凡	ヒボン	uncommon; rare
	非力	ヒリキ	incapable; powerless; useless; incompetent
	非礼	ヒレイ	impoliteness
訓	非ず	あらず	not; not so
¥	非課税	ヒカゼイ	tax-free; tax exemption

8 斉 せい alike

1874

⑧

音	斉	セイ	equal
熟	斉唱	セイショウ	unison —*v*. sing in unison

1875

斎 ⑪

音	斎	サイ	purity; purification; room
熟	斎場	サイジョウ	funeral hall

8 食 see ⇨p.817

9 面 めん face

1876
面 ⑨ 一 丆 𠂆 丙 而 而 而 面 面

音	面	メン	face; mask; surface; aspect; facet; page
熟	面影	オモかげ	face; looks; trace; vestiges
	面する	メンする	***vi***. face; front; look on
	面会	メンカイ	interview; meeting —***vi***. interview; meet and talk with
	面識	メンシキ	acquaintance
	面積	メンセキ	area
	面接	メンセツ	interview —***vi***. interview; meet and talk with
	面前	メンゼン	in the presence of; before (someone)
	面相	メンソウ	looks; face
	面談	メンダン	interview —***vi***. meet and talk with
	面倒	メンドウ	trouble; difficulty; taking care of
	面倒臭い	メンドウくさい	troublesome; bothersome
	面目	メンボク(メンモク)	honor; face; dignity
	面々	メンメン	each one; all
	面容	メンヨウ	countenance; looks
訓	面	おも	surface; face
	面影	おもかげ	face; visage; image; trace; vestige
	面白い	おもしろい	interesting; amusing
	面長	おもなが	long-faced
	面	おもて	face; surface
	面	つら	surface; face (impolite)
	面当て	つらあて	insinuating/spiteful remark; innuendo

9 革 かくのかわ／つくりのかわ shoe leather

1877

⑨ 一 十 廿 廿 廿 芇 苎 苎 革

音	革	カク	hide; leather; renew
熟	革命	カクメイ	revolution

訓	革	かわ	leather; skin
¥	革新	カクシン	reform; renovation; innovation —*v.* reform; renovate; innovate
	革新的	カクシンテキ	progressive

1878

靴 ⑬

音	靴	カ	shoes
訓	靴	くつ	shoes
	靴下	くつした	socks; stockings

---

9 音 おと noise

1879

音 ⑨

音	音	オン	sound; pronunciation; music
		(イン)	sound; tidings
熟	音韻	オンイン	phoneme
	音階	オンカイ	the whole series of recognized musical notes; musical scale; gamut
	音楽	オンガク	music
	音感	オンカン	sense of sound/pitch
	音響	オンキョウ	sound; noise
	音質	オンシツ	tonal quality; tonality
	音信	オンシン (インシン)	correspondence; communication
	音声	オンセイ	voice; audio sound
	音声学	オンセイガク	phonetics
	音節	オンセツ	syllable
	音速	オンソク	velocity of sound; sonic speed
	音痴	オンチ	tone deaf
	音程	オンテイ	musical interval; step
	音頭	オンド	leading a song
	音読	オンドク	reading aloud —*v.* read aloud
	音波	オンパ	sound waves
	音便	オンビン	euphonic change; euphony
	音符	オンプ	musical note

	音譜	オンプ	music; musical score
	音律	オンリツ	tune; rhythm; pitch
	音量	オンリョウ	sound volume; volume
訓	音	おと	sound
	音	ね	sound
	音色	ねいろ	tonal quality; tonality

1880
韻 ⑲

音	韻	イン	sound; rhyme
熟	韻文	インブン	verse
	韻律	インリツ	meter; rhythm

1881
響 ⑳

音	響	キョウ	sound; reverberate; echo
訓	響く	ひびく	***vi***. sound; resound; be echoed; affect

9 頁 おおがい big shell; page

1882
頂 ⑪

音	頂	チョウ	top of the head; top; peak; summit
熟	頂上	チョウジョウ	top; summit; crest; crown; peak
	頂戴	チョウダイ	***hon***. please —***v***. ***hon***. receive; get; have; take; eat
	頂点	チョウテン	apex; vertex; zenith; climax
訓	頂	いただき	top; summit; peak
	頂く	いただく	***vt***. wear a crown; be crowned ***hon***. receive; get; be given; eat; drink

1883

項 ⑫

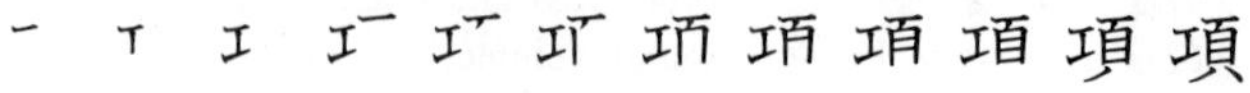

音	項	コウ	clause; term; nape
熟	項目	コウモク	item; clause; provision
訓	※項	うなじ	nape; scruff of the neck

1884

順 ⑫

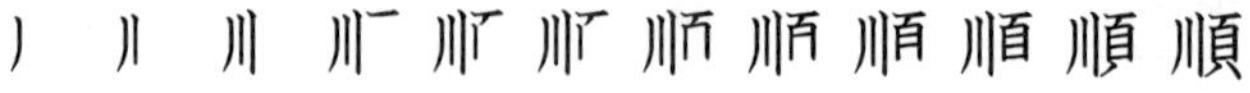

音	順	ジュン	submit; order; series
熟	順位	ジュンイ	ranking; order
	順延	ジュンエン	postponement —*v*. postpone; put off
	順繰り	ジュンぐり	by turns; in turn; one after another; one by one
	順次	ジュンジ	in order; one by one; one after another
	順々	ジュンジュン	by turns; one by one; one after another
	順序	ジュンジョ	order; procedure
	順調	ジュンチョウ	smooth; satisfactory; favorable
	順当	ジュントウ	proper; right
	順応	ジュンノウ	adaptation; adjustment —*vi*. adapt; adjust; conform
	順番	ジュンバン	order; turn; place
	順風	ジュンプウ	favorable wind
	順法	ジュンポウ	law-abiding
	順列	ジュンレツ	permutation
	順路	ジュンロ	route

1885

頑 ⑬

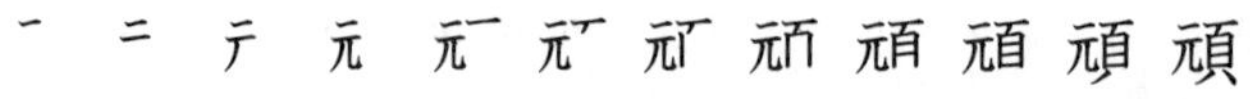

音	頑	ガン	hard; obstinate
熟	頑強	ガンキョウ	stubborn; obstinate
	頑健	ガンケン	robust health
	頑固	ガンコ	stubborn; obstinate
	頑張る	ガンばる	*vi*. try hard; not give up; persist
訓	※頑	かたくな	stubborn; obstinate

1886
頒 ⑬
ノ ハ 分 分 分 分 分 分 頒 頒 頒 頒

音	頒	ハン	distribute
熟	頒布	ハンプ	distribution; circulation —*v*. distribute; circulate
¥	頒価	ハンカ	paying in installments

1887
預 ⑬
7 マ ヌ 予 予 予 預 預 預 預 預 預

音	預	ヨ	deposit; entrust
熟	預金	ヨキン	deposit; bank account —*v*. deposit money in a bank
訓	預かる	あずかる	***vt***. receive for safekeeping
	預ける	あずける	***vt***. deposit; entrust; hand over for safe-keeping; leave in someone's care
¥	預かり金	あずかりキン	deposit
	預金証書	ヨキンショウショ	certificate of deposit
	預金通帳	ヨキンツウチョウ	bankbook; deposit passbook

1888
領 ⑭
ノ 𠆢 𠆢 今 令 令 令 領 領 領 領 領

音	領	リョウ	govern; rule; territory
熟	領域	リョウイキ	domain; territory
	領海	リョウカイ	territorial waters
	領解	リョウカイ	understanding; consent —*v*. understand; consent
	領空	リョウクウ	territorial airspace
	領事	リョウジ	consul
	領事館	リョウジカン	consulate
	領主	リョウシュ	***hist***. feudal lord (Edo period)
	領収書	リョウシュウショ	(written) receipt
	領収証	リョウシュウショウ	receipt; proof of payment
	領地	リョウチ	territory
	領土	リョウド	territory
	領分	リョウブン	territory; domain; sphere of influence
	領有	リョウユウ	possession (of land/territory) —*v*. possess (land/territory)

1889

頭 ⑯

音	頭	ズ	head
		トウ	head; beginning
		(ト)	
熟	頭蓋骨	ズガイコツ	***med.*** skull; cranium
	頭巾	ズキン	hood; skullcap; cowl
	頭上	ズジョウ	overhead; above the head
	頭痛	ズツウ	***med.*** headache
	頭脳	ズノウ	brain
	頭角	トウカク	top of the head; crown; talent
	頭取	トウどり	president; manager
	頭髪	トウハツ	hair (on the head)
	頭領	トウリョウ	boss
訓	頭	あたま	head; brains; mind; hair; chief; leader
	頭打ち	あたまうち	(highest) limit; peak; ceiling
	頭数	あたまかず	headcount; number of persons
	頭ごなし	あたまごなし	merciless
	頭割り	あたまわり	equal share
	頭	かしら	head; hair; leader
	頭文字	かしらモジ	initial; first letter
¥	頭金	あたまキン	down/initial payment

1890

頼 ⑯

音	頼	ライ	ask for; request; entrust to
訓	頼む	たのむ	***vt.*** ask for; request; entrust to
	頼み込む	たのみこむ	***vt.*** earnestly request
	頼もしい	たのもしい	reliable; dependable; promising
	頼る	たよる	***vt.*** rely; depend on
	頼り無い	たよりない	unreliable; undependable; vague

1891

頻 ⑰

音	頻	ヒン	frequent; repeated

熟	頻出	ヒンシュツ	frequent appearances —*vi*. appear/occur frequently
	頻度	ヒンド	frequency
	頻発	ヒンパツ	frequency; frequent occurence —*vi*. occur frequently
	頻繁	ヒンパン	over and over; repeatedly; frequently
	頻々	ヒンピン	frequent; repeated

1892

額 ⑱ 丶 宀 ⺂ 安 灾 客 客 客 客 額 額 額

音	額	ガク	forehead; amount; frame
熟	額縁	ガクぶち	picture frame
	額面	ガクメン	face value
訓	額	ひたい	forehead
¥	額	ガク	amount; sum; volume
	額面金額	ガクメンキンガク	face value; par price
	額面割れ	ガクメンわれ	drop below par

1893

顔 ⑱ 丶 亠 亠 立 立 产 彦 彦 彦 彦 顔 顔

音	顔	ガン	face; looks
熟	顔色	ガンショク	complexion
	顔面	ガンメン	face
訓	顔	かお	face; looks; honor
	顔色	かおいろ	expression; countenance; color of a person's face
	顔役	かおヤク	boss

1894

顕 ⑱ 丨 冂 日 日 早 昇 显 显 显 顕 顕 顕

音	顕	ケン	clear; appear; conspicuous
熟	顕著	ケンチョ	remarkable; conspicuous; striking; obvious
	顕微鏡	ケンビキョウ	microscope
訓	顕す	あらわす	*vt*. clear; appear
	顕れる	あらわれる	*vi*. come out; show itself

1895

題 ⑱

音	題	ダイ	title
熟	題する	ダイする	***vi***. entitle
	題材	ダイザイ	subject matter; theme
	題字	ダイジ	title (of a book, etc.)
	題名	ダイメイ	title (of a book, etc.)
	題目	ダイモク	prayer of the Nichiren sect; theme

1896

類 ⑱

音	類	ルイ	kind; type; genus
熟	類する	ルイする	***vi***. classify
	類型	ルイケイ	type; pattern
	類語	ルイゴ	***gram***. synonym
	類似	ルイジ	resemblance; similarity —***vi***. resemble; be similar
	類書	ルイショ	books of the same kind
	類焼	ルイショウ	spreading fire —***vi***. spread fire
	類人猿	ルイジンエン	anthropoid; ape
	類推	ルイスイ	analogy —***v***. analogize
	類同	ルイドウ	similar
	類比	ルイヒ	analogy; comparison —***v***. analogize; compare
	類別	ルイベツ	classification —***v***. classify
	類例	ルイレイ	similar example
訓	※類	たぐい	kind; sort; match; equal

1897

願 ⑲

音	願	ガン	desire; prayer
熟	願書	ガンショ	written application/request
	願望	ガンボウ	desire; wish
訓	願い	ねがい	***vt***. wish; favor; request
	願う	ねがう	pray; wish; request politely

1898
顧 ㉑

音	顧	コ	look back
熟	顧客	コキャク	customer; patron
	顧問	コモン	advisor; counsellor; consultant; teacher in charge of a club
	顧慮	コリョ	consideration —*v*. consider; regard
訓	顧みる	かえりみる	***vt***. look back; review; retrospect

9 飛 とぶ flying

1899

⑨

音	飛	ヒ	fly; jump
熟	飛行	ヒコウ	flight; flying; aviation —***vi***. fly
	飛行士	ヒコウシ	airman; aviator; flier
	飛散	ヒサン	scattering; dispersement —***vi***. scatter; disperse; fly
	飛沫	ヒマツ ※(しぶき)	splash; spray
	飛躍	ヒヤク	rapid progress; leap; activity; jump —***vi***. be active; leap; jump
	飛来	ヒライ	by air/airplane —***vi***. come flying
訓	飛ぶ	とぶ	***vi***. fly; jump; hurry; progress rapidly
	飛ばす	とばす	***vt***. fly; spatter; drive fast; skip (pages, etc.); omit
	飛び上がる	とびあがる	***vi***. fly/jump up; take off
	飛び歩く	とびあるく	***vi***. run/rush about
	飛石	とびいし	steppingstone
	飛板	とびいた	springboard; diving board
	飛び移る	とびうつる	***vi***. fly/jump from one place to other
	飛び降りる	とびおりる	***vi***. jump/leap out
	飛び込む	とびこむ	***vi***. jump/spring/plung/leap/dive/rush/dash into
	飛び出す	とびだす	***vi***. spring/bolt out; run away; protrude
	飛び出る	とびでる	***vi***. protrude; project; fly/jump out; appear suddenly; run/pop out; be exorbitant

9 食 しょく food 𩙿 (p.817)

1900

⑨ ノ 入 𠆢 今 今 今 倉 倉 食

音	食	ショク (ジキ)	eat; food; meal; appetite
熟	食塩	ショクエン	table salt
	食後	ショクゴ	after a meal
	食事	ショクジ	meal; diet —***vi***. eat; dine
	食傷	ショクショウ	sick and tired; fed up; food poisoning —***vi***. be sick and tired of; get fed up; get food poisoning
	食前	ショクゼン	before a meal
	食膳	ショクゼン	dining table
	食卓	ショクタク	table; dining table
	食中毒	ショクチュウドク	food poisoning
	食通	ショクツウ	gourmet
	食堂	ショクドウ	dining room; eating house; canteen; cafeteria
	食道	ショクドウ	***med***. gullet; esophagus
	食費	ショクヒ	food costs/expenses
	食品	ショクヒン	food
	食物	ショクモツ	food
	食用	ショクヨウ	edible
	食欲	ショクヨク	appetite
	食料	ショクリョウ	food; provisions
	食料品	ショクリョウヒン	foodstuff
	食糧	ショクリョウ	food; provision; staples
	食間	ショッカン	between meals
	食器	ショッキ	tableware; dishes, plates and bowls
訓	食う	くう	***vt***. eat (used mainly by men and in some regional dialects)
	食らう	くらう	***vt***. eat; drink
	食べる	たべる	***vt***. eat
	食べ物	たべもの	food; diet
¥	食い合い	くいあい	crossing orders
	食い止める	くいとめる	***vt***. check; curb; prevent

1901

⑮

音	養	ヨウ	foster; bring up; rear; adopt; support; cultivate; develop
熟	養育	ヨウイク	fostering; rearing —*v*. foster; bring up; near; support
	養育者	ヨウイクシャ	guardian
	養魚	ヨウギョ	fish breeding/farming
	養鶏	ヨウケイ	poultry farming
	養護	ヨウゴ	protection; care —*v*. protect
	養蚕	ヨウサン	sericulture; silkworm raising/culture
	養子	ヨウシ	adopted child
	養女	ヨウジョ	adopted daughter
	養生	ヨウジョウ	health care —*v*. take care of one's health
	養殖	ヨウショク	culture; cultivation; raising (marine products) —*v*. rear; raise; breed; cultivate
	養成	ヨウセイ	training; education; cultivation —*v*. train; educate; cultivate
	養父	ヨウフ	adoptive/foster father
	養分	ヨウブン	nourishment
	養母	ヨウボ	adoptive/foster mother
	養毛剤	ヨウモウザイ	hair tonic
	養老	ヨウロウ	provision for old age; caring for the aged
	養老金	ヨウロウキン	old-age penision
訓	養う	やしなう	***vt***. foster; bring up; rear; adopt; support; cultivate; develop

8 飠 しょくへん food

1902

⑩

音	飢	キ	hungry; hunger; famine
熟	飢餓	キガ	starvation; hunger; famine
	飢渇	キカツ	hunger and thirst
	飢饉	キキン	famine; scarcity
訓	飢える	うえる	***vi***. hunger; starve

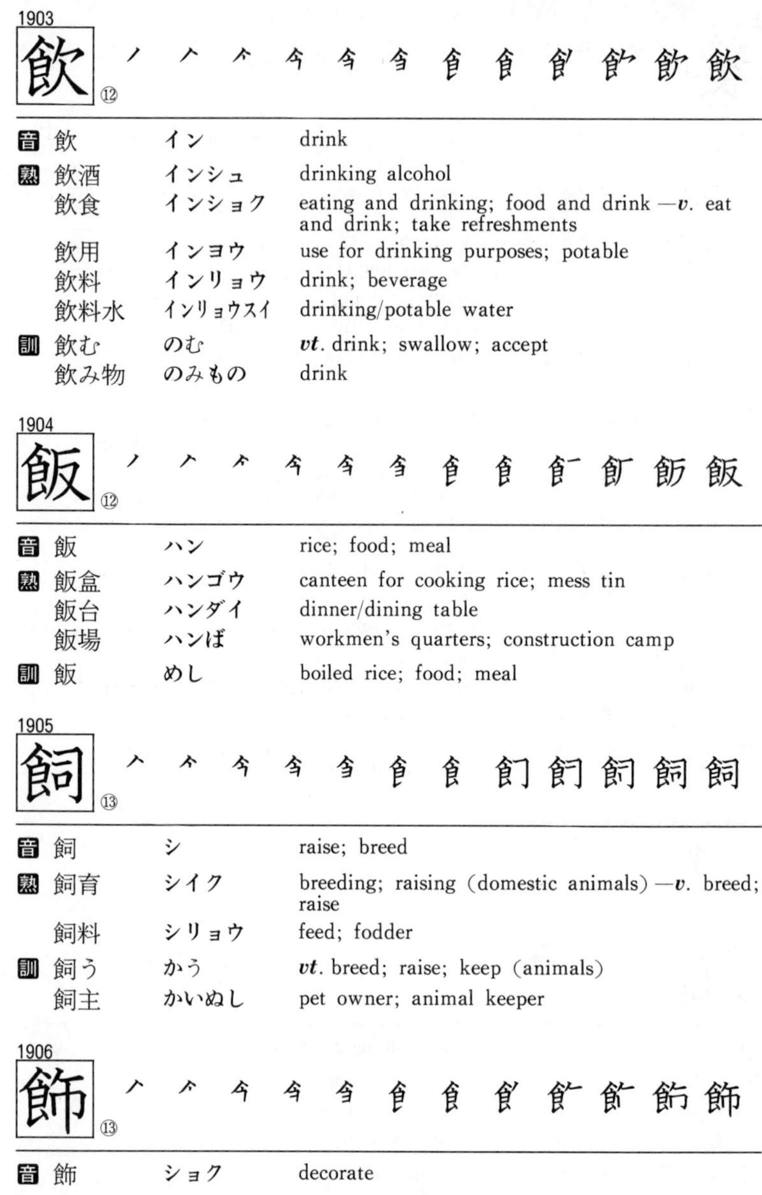

1903

飲 ⑫

音	飲	イン	drink
熟	飲酒	インシュ	drinking alcohol
	飲食	インショク	eating and drinking; food and drink —*v*. eat and drink; take refreshments
	飲用	インヨウ	use for drinking purposes; potable
	飲料	インリョウ	drink; beverage
	飲料水	インリョウスイ	drinking/potable water
訓	飲む	のむ	***vt***. drink; swallow; accept
	飲み物	のみもの	drink

1904

飯 ⑫

音	飯	ハン	rice; food; meal
熟	飯盒	ハンゴウ	canteen for cooking rice; mess tin
	飯台	ハンダイ	dinner/dining table
	飯場	ハンば	workmen's quarters; construction camp
訓	飯	めし	boiled rice; food; meal

1905

飼 ⑬

音	飼	シ	raise; breed
熟	飼育	シイク	breeding; raising (domestic animals) —*v*. breed; raise
	飼料	シリョウ	feed; fodder
訓	飼う	かう	***vt***. breed; raise; keep (animals)
	飼主	かいぬし	pet owner; animal keeper

1906

飾 ⑬

音	飾	ショク	decorate
訓	飾り	かざり	ornament; decoration

	飾り物	かざりもの	ornament; decoration
	飾る	かざる	*vt*. decorate; ornament; adorn; display

1907

飽 ⑬ 丿 𠆢 今 今 今 食 食 飠 飠 飽 飽 飽

音	飽	ホウ	have enough/grow tired of
熟	飽食	ホウショク	gluttony; engorgement; plenty of food —*vi*. be gluttonous; eat too much
	飽満	ホウマン	satiation —*vi*. be satiated; eat until one is full
	飽和	ホウワ	saturation —*vi*. be saturated
	飽和点	ホウワテン	satuaration —*vi*. be saturated
訓	飽く	あく	*vi*. grow tired/have enough of
	飽かす	あかす	*vt*. tire; bore; make (someone) fed up
	飽きる	あきる	*vi*. grow tired/have enough of; get rid of
	飽きっぽい	あきっぽい	easily bored; fickle

1908

餓 ⑮ 丿 𠆢 今 今 食 飠 飠 飠 飠 餓 餓 餓

音	餓	ガ	starve
熟	餓鬼	ガキ	hungry ghost/devil
	餓死	ガシ	starvation —*vi*. starve to death
訓	餓える	うえる	*vi*. starve; go hungry; famish

1909

館 ⑯ 丿 𠆢 今 今 食 飠 飠 飠 飠 館 館 館

音	館	カン	mansion; inn; hall
熟	館長	カンチョウ	superintendent; director; librarian; curator
	館内	カンナイ	inside the building; on the premises
訓	※館	たて	palace; mansion; fort
	※館	やかた	mansion; palace; castle

9 首 くび neck

1910

首 ⑨　丶 丷 䒑 䒑 䒒 𦣻 首 首 首

音	首	シュ	head; first; chief
熟	首位	シュイ	first place
	首相	シュショウ	premier; prime minister
	首席	シュセキ	first/top (of the class); chief
	首都	シュト	capital city; metropolis
	首脳	シュノウ	head; leader
	首班	シュハン	head; premier; prime minister
	首尾	シュビ	the result; outcome; beginning and end
	首尾一貫	シュビイッカン	consistent; throughout
	首府	シュフ	capital city
	首謀	シュボウ	ringleader; mastermind
	首領	シュリョウ	leader
訓	首	くび	neck; head
	首飾り	くびかざり	necklace
	首切り	くびきり	dismissal
	首筋	くびすじ	scruff of the neck
¥	首都圏	シュトケン	metropolitan area
	首脳	シュノウ	head; leader
	首脳会議	シュノウカイギ	summit; talks

9 香 かおり perfume

1911

⑨　一 二 千 禾 禾 秂 香 香 香

音	香	コウ (キョウ)	sweet smell; scent; fragrance
熟	香気	コウキ	fragrance; perfume; aroma
	香水	コウスイ	perfume; fragrance; scent
	香典	コウデン	monetary gift offered in place of incense to a departed soul

香料	**コウリョウ**	perfume; fragrance; sweet smell
※香港	**ホンコン**	Hong Kong
訓 香	**か**	smell; scent; odor; fragrance
香り	**かおり**	smell; scent; odor; fragrance
香る	**かおる**	***vi***. smell sweet; be fragrant

10 馬 うま／うまへん horse

1912

馬 ⑩ 丨 𠂆 𠃊 𠃊 𠃊 馬 馬 馬 馬 馬

音	馬	バ	horse
熟	馬鹿	バカ	stupid; silly; foolish ***n***. fool; idiot
	馬脚	バキャク	horse's legs ***fig***. one's true character
	馬具	バグ	harness; horse gear; trappings
	馬耳東風	バジトウフウ	utter indifference; praying to deaf ears
	馬車	バシャ	coach; carriage; omnibus
	馬術	バジュツ	horsemanship; equestrian skill
	馬上	バジョウ	horseback; mounted
	馬賊	バゾク	mounted bandits
	馬蹄	バテイ	horse's hoof
	馬場	ばば	riding ground; racecourse; race track
	馬力	バリキ	horsepower; energy
訓	馬	うま	horse
	馬面	うまづら	horseface; long face
	馬乗り	うまのり	horse riding; rider; horseman
	馬屋	うまや	stable
	馬	ま	horse
	馬子	まご	wagon driver

1913

騰 ⑳ 丿 𠂊 月 月 月 胖 胖 胖 滕 滕 騰 騰

音	騰	トウ	rise
熟	騰貴	トウキ	rise/advance/jump (in prices) —***vi***. rise; go up; jump

1914

驚 ㉒ 一 艹 芍 苟 苟 敬 敬 敬 敬 警 驚 驚

音	驚	キョウ	surprise; shock
熟	驚異	キョウイ	wonder; miracle; marvel
	驚喜	キョウキ	pleasant surprise —***vi***. be pleasantly surprised

驚嘆　キョウタン　admiration; wonder —*vi*. admire; wonder

訓 驚かす　おどろかす　*vt*. surprise

驚く　おどろく　*vi*. be surprised

1915

⑭

音 駅　エキ　post-road stage; train station

熟 駅員　エキイン　station employee

駅長　エキチョウ　station master

駅伝　エキデン　long-distance relay race

駅頭　エキトウ　at or near the train station

駅弁　エキベン　packed lunch sold at railway stations

1916

駆 ⑭

音 駆　ク　chase; pursue; follow

熟 駆使　クシ　free use —*v*. use freely/as one pleases

駆除　クジョ　extermination; destruction —*v*. exterminate; destroy

駆逐　クチク　expulsion; extermination —*v*. expel; drive away; exterminate

訓 駆ける　かける　*vi*. run; canter; gallop

駆る　かる　*vt*. drive; urge on; prompt; impel

¥ 駆け引き　かけひき　bargaining; tactics

1917

駄 ⑭

音 駄　ダ　load for a horse; petty; unimportant

熟 駄作　ダサク　poor work; shoddy craftmanship

駄目　ダめ　*col*. useless; vain; no good

1918

駐 ⑮

音 駐　チュウ　stay; resident

熟	駐在	チュウザイ	residence; stay —*v*. reside; be resident; stay
	駐在所	チュウザイショ	police substation
	駐車	チュウシャ	parking —***vi***. park
	駐車違反	チュウシャイハン	illegal parking —***vi***. be illegally parked
	駐日	チュウニチ	staying in Japan (as an ambassador, etc.)
	駐留	チュウリュウ	stationing —***vi***. stay; be stationed in
	駐留軍	チュウリュウグン	stationary troops

1919

騎 ⑱

音	騎	キ	ride (on a horse)
熟	騎士	キシ	knight
	騎手	キシュ	rider
	騎馬	キバ	horse rider; horse-riding

1920

験 ⑱

音	験	ケン	effect; test; examine
		ゲン	effect

1921

騒 ⑱

音	騒	ソウ	make a noise/fuss
熟	騒音	ソウオン	noise
	騒然	ソウゼン	noisy; tumultous
	騒々	ソウゾウ	noisy; clamorous
	騒動	ソウドウ	riot; disturbance
	騒乱	ソウラン	riot; disturbance
訓	騒ぐ	さわぐ	***vi***. clamor

10 骨 ほね／ほねへん bone

1922
骨 ⑩ 丨 冂 冂 冎 冎 冎 骨 骨 骨 骨

音	骨	コツ	bone; ashes; spirit; looks
熟	骨格	コッカク	framework; skeleton; frame; build; physique
	骨子	コッシ	gist; essential part; main part
	骨髄	コツズイ	bone marrow
	骨折	コッセツ	bone fracture —*v*. fracture a bone
	骨頂	コッチョウ	the height of; the uttermost
	骨肉	コツニク	blood relatives; flesh and blood
訓	骨	ほね	bone; frame; spirit; backbone
	骨折る	ほねおる	*vi*. make efforts; put oneself out
	骨抜き	ほねぬき	boned; filleted; spineless
	骨身	ほねみ	flesh and bones; marrow
	骨休め	ほねやすめ	rest; relaxation —*vi*. rest; relax

1923
髄 ⑲ 冂 冂 冎 冎 骨 骨 骨 骨 骨 骨 骨 髄

音	髄	ズイ	marrow; pith

10 高 たかい tall; high

1924
高 ⑩ 丶 亠 亠 亠 亠 亠 高 高 高 高

音	高	コウ	high
熟	高圧	コウアツ	high pressure/tension; coercion; oppression
	高圧的	コウアツテキ	high-handed; coercive; overbearing
	高位	コウイ	high rank; honors
	高遠	コウエン	lofty; noble; exalted
	高音	コウオン	high-pitched tone
	高温	コウオン	high temperature

10

馬
骨
• 高
髟
鬼
竜

高価	コウカ	expensive; costly; high price
高架	コウカ	overhead; high level; elevated
高額	コウガク	large sum/amount (of money)
高官	コウカン	high official
高貴	コウキ	noble; precious; valuable
高気圧	コウキアツ	high atmospheric pressure
高級	コウキュウ	high-class; seniority
高給	コウキュウ	high salary/pay
高潔	コウケツ	noble/high-mindedness; loftiness; purity
高原	コウゲン	plateau
高山	コウザン	high mountain
高所	コウショ	high ground; broad view
高尚	コウショウ	elegant; high; lofty; noble
高層	コウソウ	altostratus
高速度	コウソクド	high speed
高速道路	コウソクドウロ	expressway; highway; motorway
高低	コウテイ	high and low; uneven; rugged
高度	コウド	altitude; height; high degree
高等	コウトウ	high-grade/class
高等学校	コウトウガッコウ	senior high school
高等裁判所	コウトウサイバンショ	high court
高熱	コウネツ	high fever/temperature; intense heat
高慢	コウマン	proud; haughty; uppish
高名	コウメイ	fame; repute; renown
高率	コウリツ	high rate/interest rate
高齢	コウレイ	old/great/ripe age

訓

高	たか	amount; quantity; volume
高い	たかい	tall; high; eminent; lofty
高潮	たかしお	flood/high tide; tidal wave
高台	たかダイ	heights; high ground; high, flat area
高々	たかだか	at most; at the best; no more than
高鳴る	たかなる	***vi.*** throb; beat
高根の花	たかねのはな	unattainable object; prize beyond one's reach
高飛車	たかビシャ	high-handed; overbearing
高ぶる	たかぶる	***vi.*** be highly wrought-up; be excited; be conceited
高まる	たかまる	***vi.*** rise; be raised; increase
高める	たかめる	***vt.*** raise; lift; promote; elevate

¥

高騰	コウトウ	steep rise in prices —***vi.*** soar; skyrocket
高度成長	コウドセイチョウ	high growth
高品位テレビ	コウヒンイテレビ	high-definition television

高値	たかね	high price
高値引け	たかねびけ	closed higher

10 髟 かみかんむり／かみがしら long hair

1925

髪 ⑭ 丨 ｢ ｢ ｢ 镸 镸 長 髟 髟 髪 髪 髪

音	髪	ハツ	hair
訓	髪	かみ	hair
	髪形	かみがた	hairstyle
	髪の毛	かみのけ	hair
	髪結い	かみゆい	hairdressing

10 鬼 おに／きにょう devil; demon

1926

鬼 ⑩ ′ ′ 白 白 白 由 鬼 鬼 鬼 鬼

音	鬼	キ	demon; devil
熟	鬼才	キサイ	genius; great talent
	鬼門	キモン	unlucky quarter; weak point
訓	鬼	おに	ogre; demon; devil
	鬼瓦	おにがわら	ridge-end tile
	鬼婆	おにばば	witch; hag

1927

魂 ⑭ 一 二 テ 云 云′ 云′ 云白 云白 云由 云鬼 魂 魂

音	魂	コン	soul; heart; spirit
熟	魂胆	コンタン	intrigue; plot; soul
訓	魂	たましい	soul

1928

⑮

音	魅	ミ	charm; enchant; fascinate
熟	魅する	ミする	*vt*. charm; enchant; fascinate
	魅了	ミリョウ	charming; captivating; spellbound —*v*. charm; captivating; hold spellbound
	魅力	ミリョク	charm; appeal; fascination
	魅惑	ミワク	charm; fascination; lure —*v*. charm; fascinate; lure

1929

魔 ㉑

音	魔	マ	demon; devil; evil spirit
熟	魔王	マオウ	the devil; Satan
	魔術	マジュツ	magic; sorcery; witchcraft
	魔女	マジョ	witch; sorceress
	魔性	マショウ	diabolical
	魔法	マホウ	magic; sorcery; witchcraft
	魔法使い	マホウつかい	magician; wizard; witch
	魔法瓶	マホウビン	thermos bottle
	魔物	マもの	goblin; demon; devil
	魔力	マリョク	magical power; charm

10 竜 りゅう dragon

1930

⑩

音	竜	リュウ	dragon
訓	竜	たつ	dragon
	竜巻	たつまき	tornado; waterspout

11 魚 うお fish

1931

⑪

音	魚	ギョ	fish
熟	魚介類	ギョカイルイ	seafood; fishes and shellfish
	魚拓	ギョタク	fish print
	魚雷	ギョライ	torpedo
	魚類	ギョルイ	fishes
訓	魚	うお (さかな)	fish

1932

⑰

音	鮮	セン	clear; fresh; vivid; Korea
熟	鮮魚	センギョ	fresh fish
	鮮血	センケツ	blood
	鮮度	センド	freshness
	鮮明	センメイ	clear; distinct
訓	鮮やか	あざやか	vivid; clear; bright; colorful

1933

⑲

音	鯨	ゲイ	whale
訓	鯨	くじら	whale

11 鳥 とり bird

1934

鳥
⑪

音	鳥	チョウ	bird

11 熟 鳥瞰図 チョウカンズ bird's-eye view
鳥獣 チョウジュウ birds and beasts
鳥類 チョウルイ birds

訓 鳥 とり bird
鳥居 とりい *torii* (gateway to a Shinto Shrine)
鳥肌 とりはだ goose flesh

魚
• 鳥
• 鹿
麻
黄
黒

1935
鳴 ⑭ 丨 ㄇ 口 口′ 叫 叫 呜 呜 鳴 鳴 鳴 鳴

音 鳴 メイ cry; sing; howl

熟 鳴動 メイドウ rumbling —***vi***. rumble; move with a loud noise

訓 鳴く なく ***vi***. cry; sing; howl; chirp
鳴き声 なきごえ cry; call; chirping
鳴る なる ***vi***. sound; ring
鳴らす ならす ***vt***. sound ring

1936
鶏 ⑲ 一 ⺈ 𠫓 爫 奚 奚′ 奚 鶏 鶏 鶏 鶏 鶏

音 鶏 ケイ hen; cock; rooster

熟 鶏舎 ケイシャ henhouse
鶏卵 ケイラン chicken eggs

訓 鶏 にわとり fowl; chicken

11 鹿 しか deer

1937
麗 ⑲ 一 ㄏ 丙 丽 丽丽 麗 麗 麗 麗 麗 麗 麗

音 麗 レイ beautiful; pretty; lovely

熟 麗句 レイク beautiful phrase
麗質 レイシツ beauty; charms
麗人 レイジン beautiful woman

訓 麗しい うるわしい beautiful; pretty; lovely
※麗か うららか beautiful/bright/serene (weather, climate, etc.)

11 麻 あさ／あさかんむり hemp

1938
麻 ⑪ 丶 亠 广 广 庁 庥 床 床 府 府 麻

音	麻	マ	hemp; flax
熟	麻疹	マシン	***med***. measles
	麻酔	マスイ	***med***. anesthesia; anesthetic
	麻酔科	マスイカ	***med***. anesthesiology
	麻痺	マヒ	paralysis —***vi***. be paralysed
	麻薬	マヤク	narcotics
	※麻雀	マージャン	mahjong
訓	麻	あさ	flax; hemp
	麻布	あさぬの	hemp cloth; linen

11 黄 きいろい／き yellow

1939
黄 ⑪ 一 十 廾 廾 芈 芈 苗 带 黄 黄 黄

音	黄	コウ オウ	yellow; gold
熟	黄金	オウゴン	gold; money
	黄金時代	オウゴンジダイ	golden age; age of gods
	黄色人種	オウショクジンシュ	yellow race
	黄熱病	オウネツビョウ	***med***. yellow fever
	黄河	コウガ	Yellow River
	黄土	コウド（オウド）	loess; yellow soil
訓	黄	き	yellow
	黄色	きいろ	yellow
	黄身	きみ	yolk
	黄金色	こがねいろ	gold (color)

11 黒 くろい／くろ black

1940

黒 ⑪ 丶 ロ 㔾 曰 甲 甲 里 里 里 黒 黒

音	黒	コク	black; darkness; bad; wrong
熟	黒人	コクジン	black person
	黒点	コクテン	sunspots; black spots
	黒板	コクバン	blackboard
訓	黒	くろ	black
	黒い	くろい	black; dirty; dark
	黒船	くろふね	***hist***. 'black ships' (term used to refer to all Western ships that visited Japan from 1600 to 1868)
	黒星	くろぼし	black mark; bull's-eye
	黒幕	くろマク	wirepuller; behind-the-scenes man

1941

黙 ⑮ 丶 ロ 㔾 曰 甲 甲 里 里 野 默 默 黙

音	黙	モク	silence
熟	黙する	モクする	***vi***. be silent
	黙殺	モクサツ	ignoring —***v***. ignore; take no notice of
	黙視	モクシ	overlooking; conniving —***v***. overlook; connive at
	黙然	モクゼン (モクネン)	silent; mute; tacit
	黙想	モクソウ	meditation; contemplation —***vi***. meditate; contemplate
	黙禱	モクトウ	silent prayer/tribute —***vi***. pray silently
	黙読	モクドク	silent reading —***v***. read silently
	黙認	モクニン	tacit consent —***v***. give tacit consent
	黙秘権	モクヒケン	right to remain silent
	黙々	モクモク	silent; mute; tacit
	黙約	モクヤク	tacit agreement
	黙礼	モクレイ	non-verbal greeting —***vi***. bow silently
訓	黙る	だまる	***vi***. become silent; say nothing
	黙り	だまり	silence; reticence
	※黙す	もだす	***vi***. be silent; not say; leave as it is; ignore

12 歯 は tooth

1942 歯 ⑫

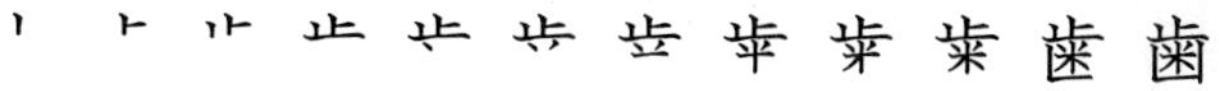

音	歯	シ	tooth; age
熟	歯科	シカ	dentistry
	歯科医	シカイ	dentist
	歯牙	シガ	teeth and tusks
	歯垢	シコウ	plaque
	歯石	シセキ	tartar; plaque
訓	歯	は	tooth; teeth
	歯医者	はイシャ	dentist
	歯車	はぐるま	gear wheel
	歯磨き	はみがき	dentifrice —*vi*. clean one's teeth
	歯向かう	はむかう	*vi*. rise/turn against

1943 齢 ⑰

音	齢	レイ	age
訓	※齢	よわい	age

13 鼓 つづみ drum

1944 鼓 ⑬

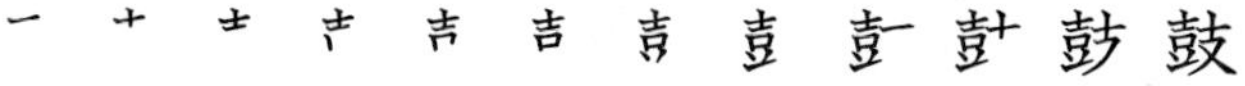

音	鼓	コ	hand drum
熟	鼓笛隊	コテキタイ	drum and fife band
	鼓動	コドウ	beating; pounding; thumping —*vi*. beat; pound; thump
	鼓舞	コブ	encouragement —*v*. encourage; inspire
	鼓膜	コマク	***med***. eardrum
訓	鼓	つづみ	hand drum

14 鼻 はな nose

1945

鼻 ⑭ 丿 亻 白 自 自 鼻 鼻 鼻 鼻 鼻 鼻 鼻

音	鼻	ビ	nose
熟	鼻炎	ビエン	***med***. nasal inflammation
	鼻音	ビオン	nasal sound
	鼻下	ビカ	under the nose; area between nose and mouth; upper lip
	鼻孔	ビコウ	nostril
訓	鼻	はな	nose
	鼻息	はないき	breathing through the nose; mood; temper
	鼻歌	はなうた	humming
	鼻毛	はなげ	nostril hairs
	鼻声	はなごえ	nasal voice
	鼻先	はなさき	tip of the nose; under one's nose
	鼻白む	はなじろむ	***vi***. look disappointed/bored
	鼻筋	はなすじ	line of the nose
	鼻高々	はなたかだか	proudly; triumphantly
	鼻血	はなぢ	nosebleed ***med***. epistasis
	鼻詰まり	はなづまり	nasal congestion
	鼻水	はなみず	nasal mucus; runny nose
	鼻持ちならない	はなもちならない	intolerable; detestable; disgusting; stinking

RADICAL INDEX

RADICAL INDEX

(by radical and kanji number)

3 STROKES

子

宀

寸

小

⺌

⺍

尢

尸

山

川

工

己

巾

帥 560
帝 561
帰 562
師 563
席 564
帯 565
常 566
帳 567
幅 568
帽 569
幕 570
幣 571

干

干 572
平 573
年 574
幸 575
幹 576

肝(月) 1022
軒(車) 1772
午(十) 241
刊(刂) 184
汗(氵) 1159

幺

幻 577
幼 578
幽 579
幾 580

玄(玄) 1311
糸(糸) 1503
郷(阝) 760

广

広 581
庁 582
序 583
床 584
底 585
店 586
府 587
度 588
庫 589
座 590
庭 591
康 592
庶 593
庸 594
廃 595
廊 596
廉 597

席(巾) 564
麻(麻) 1938
腐(肉) 1011
慶(心) 799
摩(手) 852
応(心) 768
唐(口) 292
磨(石) 1410
魔(鬼) 1929

廴

廷 598
延 599
建 600

廾

弊 601

弁(厶) 262
奔(大) 416
葬(艹) 662
算(竹) 1485
鼻(鼻) 1945

弋

式 602
弐 603

代(亻) 61
武(止) 1129

弓

弓 604
引 605
弔 606
弟 607
弦 608
弧 609
弱 610
強 611
張 612
弾 613

⺕

粛 614

君(口) 287
郡(阝) 758
書(曰) 998
雪(雨) 1859
尋(寸) 508
群(羊) 1569

彡

形 615
彩 616
彫 617
彰 618
影 619

参(厶) 263
杉(木) 1072
膨(月) 1043

彳

役 620
往 621
径 622
征 623
彼 624
後 625
待 626
律 627
従 628
徐 629
徒 630
得 631
御 632
循 633
復 634
微 635
徴 636
徳 637
徹 638

行(行) 1613
術(行) 1614
街(行) 1615
衝(行) 1616
衛(行) 1617
衡(行) 1618

艹

芋 639
芝 640
花 641
芸 642
芳 643
英 644
芽 645
苦 646
茎 647
若 648
苗 649
茂 650
荒 651
草 652
荘 653
茶 654
荷 655
華 656
菓 657
菊 658
菌 659
菜 660
著 661
葬 662
葉 663
落 664
蒸 665
蓄 666
蔵 667
薫 668
薪 669
薦 670
薄 671
薬 672
藩 673
藻 674

募(力) 225
墓(土) 361
夢(夕) 407
幕(巾) 570
慕(⺗) 835
暮(日) 979
繭(糸) 1511

⻌

込 675
辺 676
巡 677
迅 678
近 679
迎 680
返 681
述 682
迭 683
迫 684
逆 685
送 686
退 687
追 688
逃 689
迷 690
逝 691
造 692
速 693
逐 694
通 695
逓 696
途 697
透 698
連 699
逸 700
週 701
進 702

4 STROKES

拐 869
拡 870
拒 871
拠 872
拘 873
招 874
拙 875
拓 876
担 877
抽 878
抵 879
拝 880
拍 881
披 882
抱 883
抹 884
括 885
挟 886
拷 887
指 888
持 889
拾 890
挑 891
振 892
捜 893
挿 894
捕 895
掛 896
掘 897
掲 898
控 899
採 900
捨 901
授 902
推 903
据 904
接 905
措 906
掃 907
探 908
排 909
描 910
握 911
援 912
換 913
揮 914
提 915
搭 916
揚 917
揺 918
携 919
搾 920
摂 921
損 922
搬 923
摘 924
撮 925
撤 926
撲 927
操 928
擁 929
擬 930
擦 931

支

支 932

岐(山) 536
技(扌) 857
枝(木) 1074
肢(月) 1023
鼓(鼓) 1944

攵

改 933
攻 934
放 935
故 936
政 937
敏 938
救 939
教 940
敗 941
敢 942
敬 943
散 944
数 945
敵 946
敷 947
整 948

枚(木) 1080
牧(牛) 1291
致(至) 1590
倣(亻) 113
赦(赤) 1752
微(彳) 635
徴(彳) 636
徹(彳) 638
撤(扌) 926

文

文 949

対(寸) 502
斉(斉) 1874
紋(糸) 1522
蚊(虫) 1605
斎(斉) 1875

斗

斗 950
料 951
斜 952

科(禾) 1430

斤

斤 953
斥 954
断 955
新 956

匠(匚) 236
近(辶) 679
折(扌) 860
所(戸) 843
析(木) 1077
祈(ネ) 1419
漸(氵) 1242
質(貝) 1737

方

方 957
施 958
旅 959
旋 960
族 961
旗 962

防(阝) 725
放(攵) 935
肪(月) 1025
紡(糸) 1521
訪(言) 1667

日

日 963
旧 964
旬 965
早 966
易 967
昆 968
昇 969
昔 970
春 971
是 972
星 973
昼 974
景 975
暑 976
晶 977
普 978
暮 979
暦 980
暫 981
暴 982
曇 983
明 984
映 985
昨 986
昭 987
時 988
暁 989
晴 990
晩 991
暗 992
暇 993
暖 994
曜 995

旨(匕) 232
者(耂) 1578
香(香) 1911

曰

曲 996
更 997
書 998
曹 999
最 1000
替 1001

甲(田) 1331
申(田) 1332
由(田) 1333
冒(目) 1384
量(里) 1804

月

月 1002
有 1003
服 1004
朕 1005
朗 1006
望 1007
期 1008
朝 1009

青(青) 1871
前(刂) 196
宵(宀) 484
骨(骨) 1922
豚(豕) 1717
勝(力) 224
謄(言) 1656
騰(馬) 1913

肉

肉 1010
腐 1011

月

肖 1012
育 1013
肩 1014
肯 1015
胃 1016
背 1017
能 1018
脅 1019
膚 1020
肌 1021
肝 1022
肢 1023
肥 1024
肪 1025
胎 1026
胆 1027
肺 1028
胞 1029
胸 1030
脂 1031
胴 1032
脈 1033
脚 1034
脱 1035
脳 1036
脹 1037
腕 1038
腸 1039
腹 1040
腰 1041
膜 1042
膨 1043
臓 1044

骨(骨) 1922
豚(豕) 1717

木

木 1045
本 1046
末 1047
未 1048
朱 1049
条 1050
束 1051
果 1052
東 1053
栄 1054
架 1055
査 1056
柔 1057
染 1058
某 1059
案 1060
栽 1061
桑 1062
森 1063
楽 1064
棄 1065
業 1066
札 1067
机 1068
朽 1069
朴 1070
材 1071
杉 1072
村 1073
枝 1074
松 1075
枢 1076
析 1077
杯 1078
板 1079
枚 1080
林 1081
枠 1082
枯 1083
柱 1084
柄 1085
柳 1086
桜 1087
格 1088
核 1089
株 1090
校 1091
根 1092
桟 1093
栓 1094
桃 1095
梅 1096
械 1097
棺 1098
棋 1099
極 1100
検 1101
植 1102
棚 1103
棟 1104
棒 1105
楼 1106
概 1107
構 1108
模 1109
様 1110
横 1111
権 1112
槽 1113
標 1114
機 1115
橋 1116
樹 1117
欄 1118

困(口) 341
床(广) 584
相(目) 1383
麻(麻) 1938
巣(⺍) 517
集(隹) 1851
禁(示) 1416
築(竹) 1488

欠

欠 1119
次 1120
欧 1121
欲 1122
款 1123
欺 1124
歌 1125
歓 1126

吹(口) 300
炊(火) 1265
軟(車) 1774
飲(飠) 1903

止

止 1127
正 1128
武 1129
歩 1130
歳 1131
歴 1132

企(人) 48
肯(月) 1015
祉(礻) 1420
紫(糸) 1507
歯(歯) 1942
雌(隹) 1854

歹

死 1133
残 1134
殊 1135
殉 1136
殖 1137

列(刂) 186

殳

殴 1138
段 1139
殺 1140
殻 1141
殿 1142

没(氵) 1167
疫(疒) 1348
般(舟) 1594
設(言) 1666
穀(禾) 1441
役(彳) 620
投(扌) 862

母

母 1143

毋

毎 1144
毒 1145

侮(亻) 91
悔(忄) 812
海(氵) 1184
貫(貝) 1725

比

比 1146

批(扌) 865
昆(日) 968
皆(白) 1365

毛

毛 1147

尾(尸) 526
耗(耒) 1581

氏

氏 1148
民 1149

低(亻) 82
底(广) 585
邸(阝) 755
抵(扌) 879

气

気 1150

汽(氵) 1162

水

水 1151
永 1152
氷 1153

泉 1154
承（手） 848

水

求 1155
泰 1156

氵

汁 1157
汚 1158
汗 1159
江 1160
池 1161
汽 1162
決 1163
沢 1164
沖 1165
沈 1166
没 1167
泳 1168
沿 1169
河 1170
泣 1171
況 1172
沼 1173
治 1174
注 1175
泥 1176
波 1177
泊 1178
泌 1179
沸 1180
法 1181
泡 1182
油 1183
海 1184
活 1185
洪 1186
浄 1187
津 1188
洗 1189
浅 1190
洞 1191
派 1192
洋 1193
消 1194
浸 1195
浜 1196
浮 1197
浦 1198
浴 1199
流 1200
涙 1201
浪 1202
液 1203
涯 1204
渇 1205
渓 1206
混 1207
済 1208
渋 1209
淑 1210
渉 1211
深 1212
清 1213
淡 1214
添 1215
涼 1216
温 1217
渦 1218
減 1219
湖 1220
港 1221
滋 1222
湿 1223
測 1224
渡 1225
湯 1226
満 1227
湾 1228
滑 1229
漢 1230
源 1231
溝 1232
準 1233
滞 1234
滝 1235
漠 1236
滅 1237
溶 1238
演 1239
漁 1240
漆 1241
漸 1242
漬 1243
滴 1244
漂 1245
漫 1246
漏 1247
潟 1248
潔 1249
潤 1250
潜 1251
潮 1252
澄 1253
激 1254
濁 1255
濃 1256
濯 1257
濫 1258
瀬 1259

染（木） 1058
酒（酉） 1789
婆（女） 430
落（艹） 664
塗（土） 360
薄（艹） 671
藩（艹） 673

火

火 1260
灰 1261
灯 1262
災 1263
炎 1264
炊 1265
炉 1266
炭 1267
焼 1268
煙 1269
煩 1270
燃 1271
燥 1272
爆 1273

畑（田） 1337
秋（禾） 1431

灬

為 1274
点 1275
烈 1276
煮 1277
焦 1278
然 1279
無 1280
照 1281
熟 1282
熱 1283
勲 1284
馬（馬） 1912
庶（广） 593
魚（魚） 1931
鳥（鳥） 1934
黒（黒） 1940
蒸（艹） 665
窯（穴） 1458
黙（黒） 1941
薫（艹） 668

爫

爵 1285

妥（女） 425
受（又） 270
愛（心） 790

父

父 1286

交（亠） 38

片

片 1287
版 1288

牛

牛 1289
物 1290
牧 1291
牲 1292
特 1293
犠 1294

件（亻） 66

犬

犬 1295
状 1296
献 1297
獣 1298

伏（亻） 71

犭

犯 1299
狂 1300
狭 1301
狩 1302
独 1303
猫 1304
猛 1305
猟 1306
猶 1307
猿 1308
獄 1309
獲 1310

5 STROKES

玄

玄 1311
率 1312

弦（弓） 608
畜（田） 1339

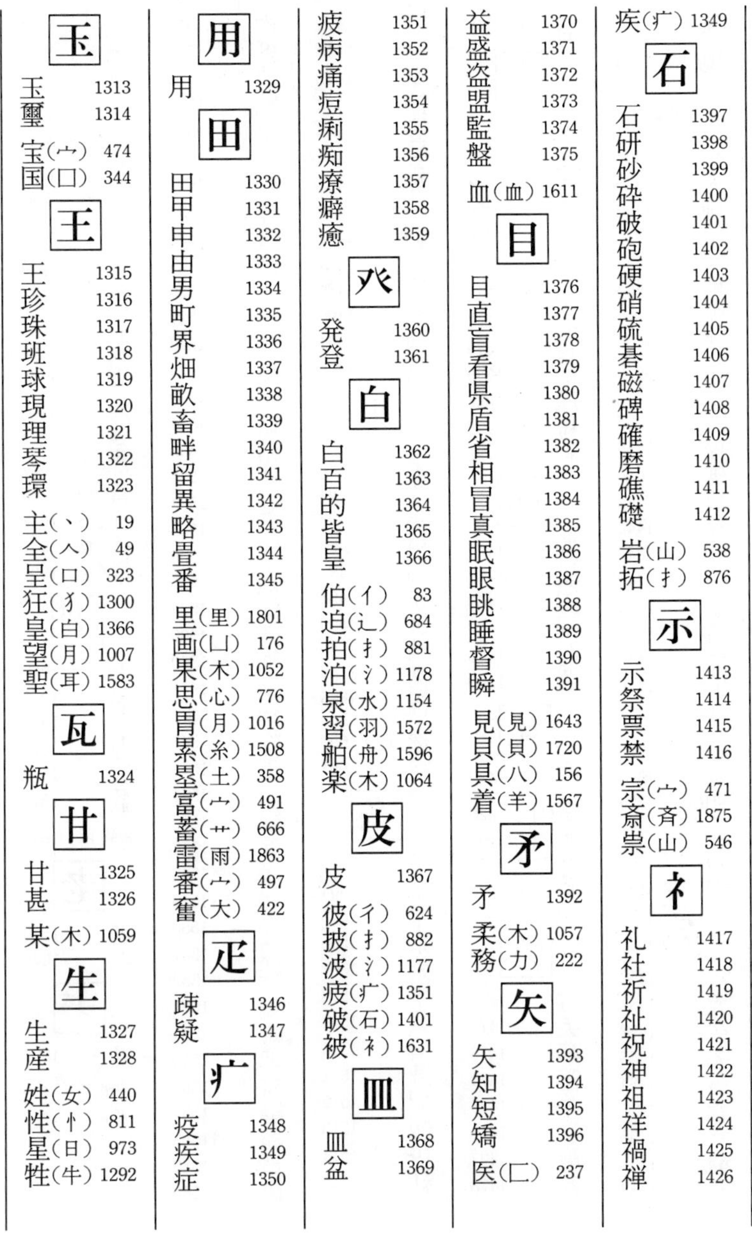

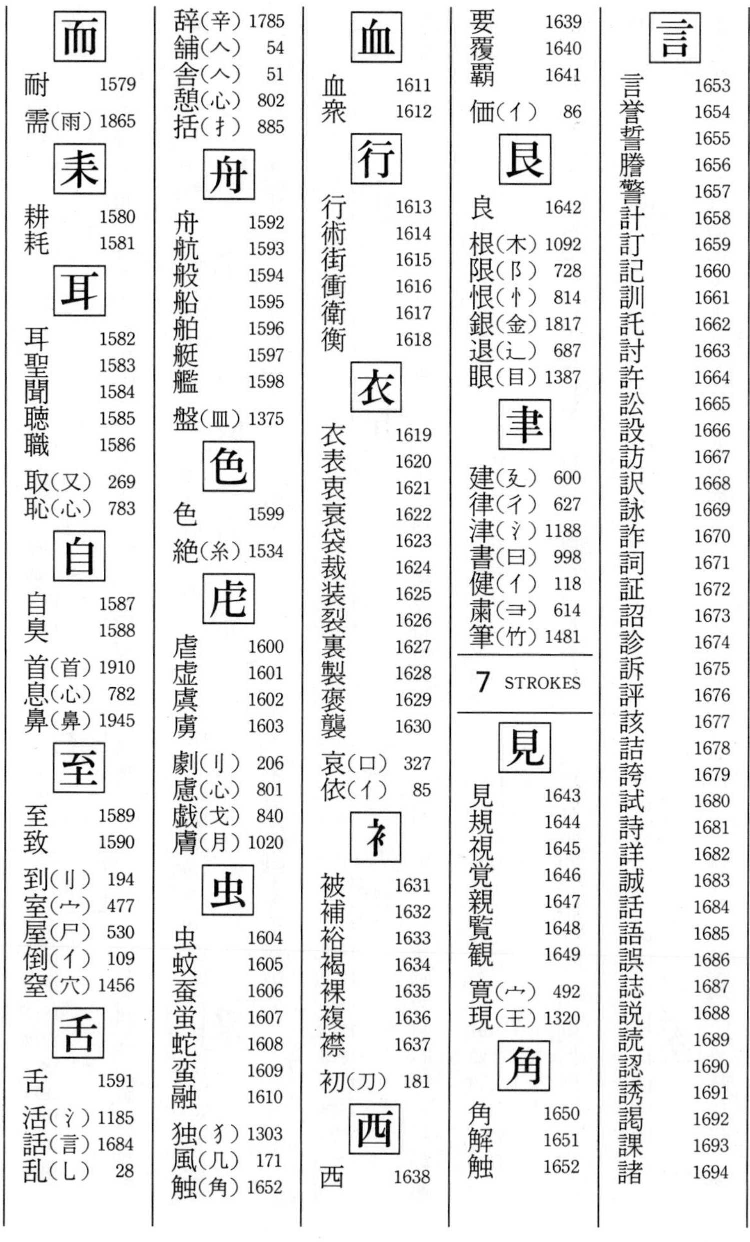

請 1695
諾 1696
誕 1697
談 1698
調 1699
論 1700
諮 1701
謀 1702
諭 1703
謡 1704
謹 1705
謙 1706
講 1707
謝 1708
識 1709
譜 1710
議 1711
譲 1712
護 1713

獄（犭） 1309

谷

谷 1714

俗（亻） 100
容（宀） 485
浴（氵） 1199
欲（欠） 1122
裕（衤） 1633

豆

豆 1715
豊 1716

頭（頁） 1889
登（癶） 1361
短（矢） 1395

豕

豚 1717
象 1718
豪 1719

家（宀） 480

逐（辶） 694
塚（土） 381
遂（辶） 707
隊（阝） 746

貝

貝 1720
貞 1721
負 1722
貢 1723
貨 1724
貫 1725
責 1726
貧 1727
賀 1728
貴 1729
貸 1730
買 1731
費 1732
貿 1733
資 1734
賃 1735
賛 1736
質 1737
賞 1738
賓 1739
賢 1740
財 1741
販 1742
貯 1743
賊 1744
賄 1745
賜 1746
賠 1747
賦 1748
購 1749
贈 1750

則（刂） 197
員（口） 329
側（亻） 119
敗（攵） 941
測（氵） 1224
頼（頁） 1890

赤

赤 1751
赦 1752

嚇（口） 313

走

走 1753
赴 1754
起 1755
越 1756
超 1757
趣 1758

足

足 1759
距 1760
跡 1761
践 1762
跳 1763
路 1764
踊 1765
踏 1766
躍 1767

促（亻） 99

身

身 1768

射（寸） 505

車

車 1769
軌 1770
軍 1771
軒 1772
転 1773
軟 1774
軽 1775
軸 1776
較 1777
載 1778
輝 1779
輩 1780
輪 1781
輸 1782
轄 1783

庫（广） 589
撃（手） 851
暫（日） 981

辛

辛 1784
辞 1785

宰（宀） 483

辰

辱 1786
農 1787

娠（女） 444
振（扌） 892
震（雨） 1866

酉

酌 1788
酒 1789
配 1790
酔 1791
酢 1792
酬 1793
酪 1794
酵 1795
酷 1796
酸 1797
醜 1798
醸 1799

釆

釈 1800

番（田） 1345

里

里 1801
重 1802
野 1803
量 1804

厘（厂） 259
埋（土） 375
理（王） 1321
黒（黒） 1940
童（立） 1461
裏（衣） 1627
墨（土） 363
黙（黒） 1941

臣

臣 1805
臨 1806

姫（女） 445
堅（土） 356
監（皿） 1374
緊（糸） 1509
賢（貝） 1740
覧（見） 1648

舛

舞 1807

8 STROKES

金

金 1808
針 1809
釣 1810
鈍 1811
鉛 1812
鉱 1813
鉄 1814
鉢 1815
鈴 1816
銀 1817

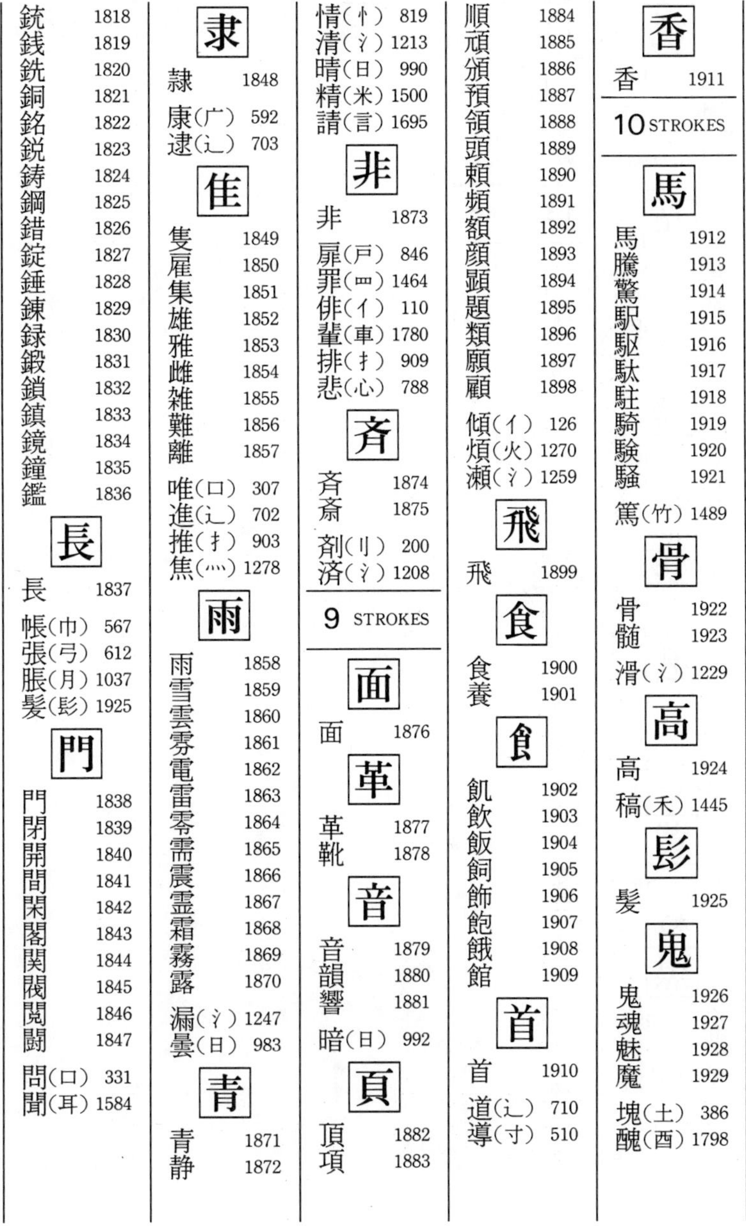

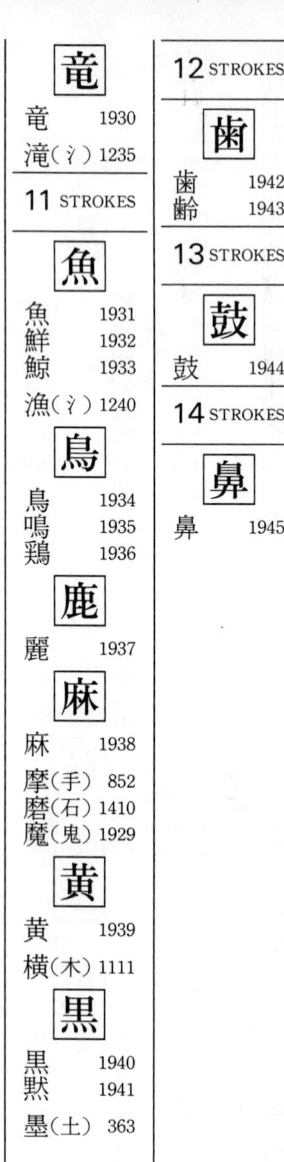

ON/KUN INDEX

ON/KUN INDEX

(by ON/KUN and kanji number)

い

う

え

お

か

き

く

け

こ

さ

し

せ

ち

つ

て

と

な

に

ぬ

ね

バツ 末 1047
罰 1467
閥 1845
はて 果 1052
はてる 果 1052
はな 花 641
華 656
鼻 1945
はなし 話 1684
はなす 放 935
話 1684
離 1857
はなつ 放 935
はなはだ 甚 1326
はなはだしい 甚 1326
はなやか 華 656
はなれる 放 935
離 1857
はね 羽 1570
はねる 跳 1763
はは 母 1143
はば 幅 568
はばむ 阻 726
はぶく 省 1382
はま 浜 1196
はやい 速 693
早 966
はやし 林 1081
はやす 生 1327
はやまる 早 966
はやめる 速 693
早 966
はら 原 260
腹 1040
はらう 払 855
はらす 晴 990
はり 針 1809
はる 張 612
はる 春 971
はれる 晴 990
ハン 伴 84
凡 170
判 187
半 243
反 267
坂 370
帆 558
藩 673
搬 923
ハン 板 1079
煩 1270
版 1288
犯 1299
班 1318
畔 1340
範 1487
繁 1510
般 1594
販 1742
頒 1886
飯 1904
バン 万 8
伴 84
判 187
晩 991
板 1079
番 1345
盤 1375
蛮 1609

ひ

ヒ 卑 248
否 289
妃 434
彼 624
避 724
悲 788
扉 846
批 865
披 882
肥 1024
比 1146
泌 1179
疲 1351
皮 1367
碑 1408
秘 1436
罷 1468
被 1631
費 1732
非 1873
飛 1899
ひ 日 963
氷 1153
火 1260
灯 1262
ビ 備 124
尾 526
微 635
美 1566
鼻 1945
ひいでる 秀 1429
ひえる 冷 166
ひかえる 控 899
ひがし 東 1053
ひかり 光 143
ひかる 光 143
ひき 匹 234
ひきいる 率 1312
ひく 引 605
弾 613
ひくい 低 82
ひくまる 低 82
ひくめる 低 82
ひける 引 605
ひさしい 久 20
ひそむ 潜 1251
ひたい 額 1892
ひたす 浸 1195
ひだり 左 552
ひたる 浸 1195
ヒツ 匹 234
必 767
泌 1179
筆 1481
ひつじ 羊 1565
ひと 一 1
人 42
ひとしい 等 1479
ひとつ 一 1
ひとり 独 1303
ひびく 響 1881
ひま 暇 993
ひめ 姫 445
ひめる 秘 1436
ひや 冷 166
ひやかす 冷 166
ヒャク 百 1363
ビャク 白 1362
ひやす 冷 166
ヒョウ 俵 112
兵 155
拍 881
標 1114
氷 1153

ま

み

STROKE INDEX

STROKE INDEX

(by stroke number and kanji number)

7

8

13

14

15

16